A Public and Political Christ

Princeton Theological Monograph Series

K. C. Hanson, Charles M. Collier, D. Christopher Spinks,
and Robin Parry, Series Editors

Recent volumes in the series:

Mitzi J. Smith
*The Literary Construction of the Other in the Acts of the Apostles:
Charismatics, the Jews, and Women*

David Rhoads
Luke-Acts and Empire: Essays in Honor of Robert L. Brawley

Julie Woods
Jeremiah 48 as Christian Scripture:

Sherri Brown
Gift Upon Gift: Covenant through Word in the Gospel of John

Donald E. Gowan
The Bible on Forgiveness

Hemchand Gossai
Power and Marginality in the Abraham Narrative—Second Edition

Christopher L. Fisher
*Human Significance in Theology and the Natural Sciences:
An Ecumenical Perspective with Reference to Pannenberg,
Rahner, and Zizioulas*

Christopher W. Skinner
*John and Thomas—Gospels in Conflict?:
Johannine Characterization and the Thomas Question*

J. Harold Ellens
Probing the Frontiers of Biblical Studies

A Public and Political Christ

*The Social-Spatial Characteristics
of Luke 18:35—19:48 and the Gospel
as a Whole in Its Ancient Context*

Bart B. Bruehler

☙PICKWICK *Publications* · Eugene, Oregon

A PUBLIC AND POLITICAL CHRIST
The Social-Spatial Characteristics of Luke 18:35—19:48 and the Gospel as a Whole in Its Ancient Context

Princeton Theological Monograph Series 157

Copyright © 2011 Bart B. Bruehler. All rights reserved. Except for brief quotations in critical publications or reviews, no part of this book may be reproduced in any manner without prior written permission from the publisher. Write: Permissions, Wipf and Stock Publishers, 199 W. 8th Ave., Suite 3, Eugene, OR 97401.

Pickwick Publications
An Imprint of Wipf and Stock Publishers
199 W. 8th Ave., Suite 3
Eugene, OR 97401

www.wipfandstock.com

ISBN 13: 978-1-60608-851-7

Cataloging-in-Publication data:

Bruehler, Bart B.

    A public and political Christ : the social-spatial characteristics of Luke 18:35—19:48 and the gospel as a whole in its ancient context / Bart B. Bruehler.

    Princeton Theological Monograph Series 157

    xii + 410 p. ; 23 cm. Includes bibliographical references and indexes.

    ISBN 13: 978-1-60608-851-7

    1. Bible. N.T. Luke XVIII, 35–XIX, 48—Criticism, interpretation, etc. I. Title. II. Series.

BR2595.2 B69 2011

Manufactured in the U.S.A.

*This book is dedicated to my wife, Anne,
who has followed Christ with me through many private
and public places.*

Contents

List of Figures / viii

List of Tables / ix

Abbreviations of Ancient Sources / x

Acknowledgments / xii

1. Introduction: Place and Politics in the Study of Luke's Gospel / 1

PART ONE: Reading Luke's Social-Spatial Context

2. From This Place: A Theoretical Framework for the Social-Spatial Analysis of Luke / 31

3. Private, Public, and Political in the Ancient Contexts of Luke's Gospel / 55

4. The Public Sphere and Local Politics in Plutarch's *Precepts* and Philostratus's *Life* / 135

PART TWO: Social-Spatial Exegesis of Luke 18:35—19:48

5. The Healing of the Blind Beggar (18:35–43): A Public Miracle Story and Its Political Implications / 165

6. Jesus Meets Zacchaeus (19:1–10): City and House as Public Settings for Conflict and Salvation / 197

7. The Story of a King and His Subjects (19:11–28): Public Pedagogy through a Political Parable / 230

8. The Procession into Jerusalem (19:28–48): The Public Culmination of Jesus' Movement and Its Political Ramifications / 256

PART THREE: Implications for Luke's Gospel and Our World

9. Luke's Emphasis on the Public Sphere and Local Politics in the Gospel as a Whole / 295

10. A Public and Political Christ: Contributions and Implications / 346

Bibliography / 365

Index of Ancient Sources / 381

Index of Authors / 401

Index of Subjects / 405

Figures

2.1	Sack's Framework / 32	
2.2	Diagram of Social-Spatial Classifications / 48	
3.1	Large View of Roman Ephesus in 104 CE / 69	
3.2	Streets and Hellenistic Agora of Ephesus in 104 CE / 70	
3.3	The Layout of Slope House 2 / 75	
3.4	Map of Pompeii / 92	
3.5	Grand-Humble/Public-Private Axes / 93	
3.6	The House of Menander / 95	
3.7	The House of Stallius Eros / 96	
3.8	The Forum of Pompeii / 97	
3.9	The House of the Moralist—Floor Plan / 98	
3.10	The House of the Moralist—Reconstructed / 99	
3.11	The House of Sallust / 100	
3.12	A *Vicus* in Reggio I.6, 7, 10 / 102	
3.13	Plan and Reconstruction of the Insula I House at Meiron, Second–Third Century CE / 118	
3.14	Plan and Reconstruction of the "Triple Courtyard House" from Capernaum, First–Second Century CE / 120	
3.15	Reconstruction of the "Peristyle House" at Aphek, Second–Third Century CE / 121	
3.16	Insula II at Capernaum / 126	
3.17	Reconstruction of Insula II / 128	
3.18	Diagram of Social-Spatial Classifications / 130	
6.1	Reconstruction of the "Peristyle House" at Aphek / 217	
6.2	The House of the Labyrinth / 219	
8.1	The Eastern Side of Jerusalem / 264	
8.2	Jerusalem in Jesus' Time / 265	
10.1	The House of Sallust / 353	

Tables

3.1	Cicero's Public and Private to Atticus / 80	
3.2	Kaiser's Categories of Vitruvius's Public Spaces / 84	
3.3	Kaiser's Categories of Vitruvius's Private Spaces / 85	
4.1	Forces in the Local Political Sphere / 145	
4.2	Forces in the Unofficial Public Sphere / 160	
5.1	Forces in the Unofficial Public and Local Political Spheres / 194	
6.1	Comparison of Luke 18:35–43 and 19:1–10 / 202	
9.1	The Synoptic Commissioning Discourses / 316	

Abbreviations of Ancient Sources

2 Tars.	Dio Chrysostom, *Second Tarsic Discourse*
Ann.	Tacitus, *Annals*
Ant.	Josephus, *Jewish Antiquities*
Apoph. lac.	Plutarch, *Spartan Sayings*
Arch.	Vitruvius, *De Architectura* (*On Architecture*)
Ars	Ovid, *The Art of Love*
Att.	Cicero, *Letters to Atticus*
b. B. Bat.	Tractate *Bava Batra* in the Babylonian Talmud
b. ʿErub.	Tractate *Eruvin* in the Babylonian Talmud
b. Ned.	Tractate *Nedarim* in the Babylonian Talmud
b. Sanh.	Tractate *Sanhedrin* in the Babylonian Talmud
b. Šabb.	Tractate *Shabbat* in the Babylonian Talmud
Bell. civ.	Appian, *Civil Wars*
Congr.	Philo, *A Meeting for the Sake of Education*
Cont.	Dio Chrysostom, *In the Public Assembly at Prusa*
Contempl.	Philo, *On the Contemplative Life*
Cor.	Demosthenes, *On the Crown*
Ctes.	Aeschines, *Ctesiphon*
Curios.	Plutarch, *On Curiosities*
Dem.	Dionysius of Halicarnassus, *On Demosthenes*
Descr.	Pausanius, *Description of Greece*
Dial.	Tacitus, *Dialogue on Orators*
Diatr.	Epictetus, *Diatribes*
Dic. Exercit.	Dio Chrysostom, *Training for Public Speaking*
Ebr.	Philo, *On Drunkenness*
Ep.	Horace, *Letters*
Ep.	Martial, *Epigrams*
Ep.	Philostratus, *Letters*
Epict. diss.	Arrian, *Discourses of Epictetus*
Fac.	Plutarch, *On the Face in the Moon*
Fam.	Cicero, *Letters to Friends*
Flac.	Cicero, *In Defense of Flaccus*
Gorg.	Plato, *Gorgias*

Abbreviations of Ancient Sources

Hist.	Livy, *History of Rome*
Ios.	Philo, *On the Life of Joseph*
J.W.	Josephus, *Jewish War*
Leg.	Plato, *Laws*
Legat.	Philo, *On the Embassy to Gaius*
Lept.	Demosthenes, *Against Leptines*
Library	Diodorus Siculus, *Library of History*
m. Šabb.	Tractate *Shabbat* in the Mishnah
Mem.	Xenophon, *Memorabilia*
Mid.	Demosthenes, *Against Meidias*
Od.	Homer, *The Odessey*
Oec.	Aristotle, *Economics*
Oed. col.	Sophocles, *Oedipus at Colonus*
Off.	Cicero, *On Duties*
Planc.	Cicero, *In Defense of Plancius*
Pol.	Aristotle, *Politics*
Praec. ger. rei publ.	Plutarch, *Precepts of Statescraft*
Prob.	Philo, *That Every Good Person Is Free*
Rec. Mag.	Dio Chrysostom, *Refusal of the Office of Archon*
Rect. rat. aud.	Plutarch, *On Listening to Lectures*
Resp.	Plato, *The Republic*
Res Gestae	Augustus, *The Deeds of Divine Augustus*
Rhes.	Euripides, *Rhesus*
Rhet.	Aristotle, *Rhetoric*
Sat.	Horace, *Satires*
Sat.	Juvenal, *Satires*
Spec.	Philo, *On the Special Laws*
t. Šabb.	Tractate *Shabbat* in the Tosefta
Theaet.	Plato, *Theaetetus*
Tib.	Suetonius, *Tiberius*
Tim.	Plato, *Timaeus*
Trach.	Sophocles, *The Women of Trachis*
Tranq.	Seneca, *On Tranquility of Mind*
Trin.	Plautus, *Trinummus*
Troj.	Dio Chrysostom, *Trojan Discourse*
y. Šabb.	Tractate *Shabbat* in the Jerusalem Talmud
Vat.	Cicero, *Against Vatinius*
Virt.	Philo, *On the Virtues*
Vit. Apoll.	Philostratus, *Life of Apollonius*
Vit. soph.	Philostratus, *Lives of the Sophists*

Acknowledgments

Though I did not know it at the time, this investigation originated in my personal and communal experience of private, public, and political spaces. My first thanks goes to Good Works, Inc., where I worked for two years as the transitional housing manager. The people and places of Good Works showed me how my home could also be a public place and how many lost in the invisible places of our world need offers of Christian hospitality to find a home once again. My second thanks goes to Clarkston, Georgia, and Cellebration Fellowship. Clarkston, situated on the eastern side of Atlanta, is the new home of many resettled refugees from around the world. It is a diverse place full of tensions and transitions. I had the privilege of living among refugees who shared their experiences of place: losing home and country, living in camps for years, and making new homes in a new political setting. They offered and received hospitality in many gracious ways. We attended church at Cellebration Fellowship, which met in a rented room at the Clarkston Community Center. While loosely tied to this public place, it became a location for worship and relationships that bound many different people together. I could not have written this study of place in Luke's Gospel without the insights that these people and places gave to me.

Many people drawn together by the spaces of Emory University also deserve my gratitude. My friends and colleagues Rob Von Thaden and Juan Hernandez offered support and constructive criticism throughout my research and writing. For two years I worked with Emory's Office of University-Community Partnerships as the program coordinator for SHINE (Students Helping in the Naturalization of Elders). The team at that office regularly demonstrated how our understanding of people and place can drive moral action and socio-political change, and SHINE enabled me to bring together my studies and experiences with refugees to create places where college students and older refugees could learn from each other. Finally, I extend my gratitude to my dissertation advisor, Vernon Robbins. I am privileged to count him as a mentor and a friend, and I consider much of what is sound in this study to come from his constant encouragement, keen acumen, and creative thinking.

I would like to thank Wipf and Stock Publishers and Chris Spinks for taking on this project and helping me to see it to completion. I am also very grateful to the scholars whose work I employed in this study, many of whom gladly allowed me to reproduce images they had created.

Finally, I would like to thank my wife, Anne, and my children, Soren, Pascal, and Eleanor. Anne lent me her loving support, a listening ear, and careful proofreading eyes throughout the process. I dedicate this book to her, and I hope that it will offer others insight and inspiration into how we might follow Christ in a variety of public and private places.

Bart B. Bruehler
Marion, Indiana
Pentecost Sunday, 2010

Introduction: Place and Politics in the Study of Luke's Gospel

Introduction

PUBLIC AND PRIVATE—THESE INTERRELATED CATEGORIES HAVE SHAPED WESTERN SOCIety since classical antiquity. They have divided and determined the locations of social life. They have identified and illuminated issues of morality. They have excluded and energized the practice of religion. Finally, they have been joined to and juxtaposed with the arena of politics and government. Often, "public" is synonymous with political in both the ancient and the contemporary world (e.g., pubic office or public service). These influential categories have come down to our contemporary world, shaping basic cultural perspectives on home and family, public places and government, churches and the practice of spirituality. They function as both popular categorizations of places and technical domains of official discourse. Because of their pervasive and powerful importance, they can also be tools for analyzing the social and spatial dynamics of communities, ethics, and religion. At the same time, and possibly because of their broad and specific manifestations, the categories and spatial domains of the public, the political, and the private are complex and contested and have been since beginnings of Western civilization. Contemporary scholars have debated the public/private dichotomy and the definition of politics, and these categories remain relevant in a variety of intellectual and practical ventures.

My wife and I live in a house, not like most houses, for we share it with college students, the formerly homeless, laboring visitors, staff, and the occasional customer. We all share the space of this transitional house, which is part of a larger ministry to the homeless.[1] *My wife and I relish our privacy as newlyweds, but we know all too well the character of the place that we inhabit. Below us is a small retail store that sells third-world fair-trade crafts, operated by people making the transition from welfare to work. Just across from there is the office with two desks, computers, and filing cabinets that part of the shelter staff calls their place of work. Down the hall from our upstairs retreat is the women's wing of the house and across from that the men's. Here, the formerly homeless share rooms and lives with committed college students who express their faith by their presence and friendship. Below them are the kitchen, dining room, and a multipurpose area. We gather here for small meals as a household, but this space*

---

1. I am referring to Good Works, Inc., a community of hope serving the poor and homeless of rural southeastern Ohio. Good Works was one of the communities that informed and inspired Pohl's study of hospitality (*Making Room*, 192).

also transforms into a hostel for groups who come to serve alongside use (even occasionally spilling over into our bedrooms upstairs). This large, complex house is a crucible that blends our private lives with friends and strangers, blends our personal choices with community standards and government regulations, and blends our home with our work. This is a place of stress and joy that unexpectedly juxtaposes a variety of people and places. We wonder where our private lives end and public encounters begin, and we relish the enriching energy that comes from the combination.

Christian faith and ministry has intersected and been impacted by the categories of the public, the political, and the private in a variety of ways. Christian voices claim the space of the public and political sphere, arguing that religion should influence public policy and cultural trends. Pastoral voices exhort change in private life, urging believers toward personal transformation and service in their homes and neighborhoods. Sometimes they are intertwined as in the transitional housing shelter described above (supported by both private and public funding), where private lives overlap with friends and strangers through hospitality and the building itself combines a variety of particular places (home, office, hotel, etc.) in an attempt to change individual lives and the local society. Contemporary debates over the place of religion in society often cite the domains of public, political, and private either to justify or delegitimize religious expression. Religious activism in politics is seen as valuable work by some and a violation of the disestablishment clause by others. Some view public worship as the core of Christian expression, while others see private discipline and devotion at the heart of the message of Jesus. How then shall we, who claim to follow Jesus and belong to the contemporary church, make sense of the public, the political, and the private both in terms of our culture and our faith? We look to many sources for guidance; one of the foremost is the Bible. In particular, the portrayal of Jesus in the Gospel of Luke presents several interesting and potentially relevant scenes that address public, political, and private people and places.

Jesus strides through the gates of Jericho surrounded by a throng of followers on the thoroughfare through the city. They are riding the crest of a wave that surged after Jesus restored a blind man's sight just outside the city. Jesus and his entourage process through the middle of the city, the street lined with rows of people trying to see him. In the midst of the bustle, Jesus stops and summons a notorious tax administrator named Zacchaeus from his perch in a tree, and together, with the crowd following, they proceed to Zacchaeus's home. Zacchaeus invites Jesus and his friends inside, but the crowd comes too, complaining about Jesus' choice of hosts. The noise and bodies overwhelm the house of Zacchaeus as the mob presses in to see what this shocking prophet will do next. Zacchaeus stands up in his overflowing house. He tells Jesus, in the hearing of the crowd, that he will donate half his possessions to the poor and restore fourfold any extortion. Jesus answers both Zacchaeus and the grumbling crowd by reinstating Zacchaeus as a son of Abraham and proclaiming the arrival of salvation at his house. Then Jesus goes on to tell a parable about a local aristocrat and his return as king to the mixed crowd of friends, opponents, and bystanders gathered in the courtyard.

The social and spatial contours of Luke's two-volume narrative have generated scholarly interest in the historical and theological nature of its geographical and political material (see details below). Many have labeled all or part of the large middle section of Luke's

Introduction: Place and Politics in the Study of Luke's Gospel

Gospel between the infancy and passion narratives as "the public ministry of Jesus."[2] Despite the prominence and potential richness of this adjective, the public nature of Jesus' ministry has remained unexplored (or at least underexplored) in the study of the Gospels, and several unanswered questions persist: How is "public" an accurate characterization of this part of Jesus' ministry? Are parts of Luke's Gospel private in nature, and how do they relate to this large section of public ministry? How are places reckoned as public or private? How does the portrayal of Jesus as a public figure fit into the possible sociocultural provenances of this Gospel? Given the strong link between public life and political action in the ancient world, what are the political ramifications of Jesus' public activity? How does the public nature of Jesus' ministry in Luke's Gospel relate to Luke's theological and ethical perspectives? The pervasiveness and power of the categories of public, political, and private, their contemporary relevance for the doctrine and practice of the Christian faith, and the ripe suitability of Luke's Gospel present a conjunction that calls for investigation. Luke was a part of and well versed in the dynamics of ancient Hellenistic-Roman culture, which both practiced and philosophized about the public, political, and private spheres. Thus, applying these categories will illuminate the impact of these cultural categories on his presentation of Jesus by explicating the often implicit social and spatial indicators that marked the domains of public, political, and private in the ancient world.

Thus, the categories of public, political, and private are pressingly relevant both to a full understanding of the portrayal of Jesus and to the contemporary expression of Christian faith. Therefore, this study will pursue a three-part investigation of Luke's portrayal of Jesus followed by a concluding reflection. The three parts focusing on Luke's Gospel will argue the following three points. First, the social-spatial spheres of the ancient world must be analyzed by more fluid and nuanced categories beyond the basic public/private dichotomy. In particular, one must make a more careful distinction between the public and political spheres. This will be demonstrated by surveying ancient literary material, exploring archaeological evidence, and comparing Luke's portrayal with other selected works. Second, an exegetical analysis of the episodes in Luke 18:35—19:48 will show that Luke places Jesus firmly in the public sphere and on the edge of local politics through a variety of social and spatial indicators in his writing. Third, this public and local political emphasis is characteristic of Luke's Gospel as a whole, and Luke's portrayal of Jesus as a public and local political figure both fits well some aspects of the ancient world and counters others. The final chapter will reflect on the relevance of Luke's portrayal of Jesus as a public and local political figure for the faith and practice of contemporary Christians in (post)modern America, paying special attention to points of contact and contrast. The rest

---

2. The following is a selection of those who have identified Jesus' ministry as "public" in Luke. Schleiermacher speaks of the "public" life or appearance of Jesus. See Schleiermacher, *Critical Essay*, 19, 40, 54. Luke 4:14–15 indicates "the first public appearance of Jesus" in Galilee for Creed, *St. Luke*, 64. Schürmann identifies all of 5:1—19:27 as "Jesu öffentliches Wirken und Lehren im Lande der Juden" in his commentary (*Das Lukasevangelium*, 1:260). The material in 4:14–44 is labeled as "die Anfänge der öffentlichen Tätigkeit Jesu" by Ernst (*Lukas*, 166). Fitzmyer calls this large section the "public ministry of Jesus" (*Luke*, 1:449–450). The sermon on the plain is "the prophet's public preaching" for Johnson (*Luke*, 105–12). Finally, Green claims, "With 4:14, then, the Lukan narrative takes a momentous step forward as it initiates the long-awaited account of Jesus' public ministry" (*Luke*, 197).

of this chapter will lay out the background and plan for this study by retelling the relevant story of scholarship and discussing the theories and text at its core.

The Story of Scholarship

An important and illuminating story of scholarship lies behind this study of the public and political character of Luke's Gospel. This story orbits around two basic questions that have been answered in various ways by previous interpreters: (Is and) how is Luke's portrayal of Jesus political, and (is and) how is Luke's portrayal of Jesus public? Many interpreters have argued that Luke's political aim was apologetic (even recent ones). However, the tide has now changed to emphasize the insider and epideictic functions of Luke's political material. Many interpreters have examined the theological and narrative significance of Luke's geographical material and assumed the public nature of Jesus' ministry. However, developments in the social and spatial analysis of NT texts have brought new perspectives and questions to the table. The story demonstrates a movement from the study of politics and geography to the study of society and space; however, this story has many chapters still to be written. NT scholarship must now explore politics as the exercise of social power within a variety of movements and hierarchies, not just within the domain of official, state government. Furthermore, NT scholarship must develop and apply a more nuanced and fluid set of categories beyond the public/private dichotomy that probes the complex relationship between places and people. Thus, this study of the social-spatial characteristics of Luke's Gospel continues this story of scholarship, building on its conclusions and offering new modes of analysis and new insights.

(Is and) How is Luke's Portrayal of Jesus Political?

The political nature of Luke-Acts stands alongside geography in the two-volume work as a topic of interest with many scholars. For hundreds of years students of Luke-Acts suggested that the named recipient, Theophilus, was probably a Roman official, and thus the two-volume work was partially written to offer a political apology.[3] This political apology cast Christianity as a sect of Judaism, and thus a *religio licita*—a religion permitted by the Roman Empire.[4] Furthermore, the exonerations of Jesus and Paul by various Roman officials (e.g., Luke 23:22 and Acts 26:31–32) show that the followers of Jesus are no threat to the Empire.[5] However, cracks in this apologetic edifice emerged in the latter half of the

---

3. This modern version of the apologetic perspective goes back at least as far as a dissertation written by C. A. Heumann in 1721. See Gasque, *History*, 21–22.

4. Easton suggests that Luke intended to portray Christianity as an αἵρεσις of Judaism, and thus a *religio licita* that should be officially recognized by Rome ("Purpose of Acts," 41–43, 46). Also see Haenchen, *Acts*, 630–31. However, Maddox notes that this section was rewritten in the seventh German edition and the phrase "*religio licita*" was removed (*Purpose of Luke-Acts*, 97 n. 2).

5. Cadbury picks up on this with some reservation and goes on to claim that Luke may have reshaped the trials of Jesus and Paul to display the innocence of Christians and indicate how the Jews had wrongly politicized a religious controversy (*Making*, 308–13). Conzelmann supports the apologetic purpose (*Theology of St. Luke*, 137–44). However, Walasky points out the contradictory nature of his evidence and his subsequent claim that Luke had no political interests ("*And So We Came to Rome*," 1–11, esp. 10).

twentieth century. Most scholars now claim that Luke was writing primarily for Christians (not Roman officials), and so his political perspective must be analyzed for how it would have functioned in a Christian community, which may have included some Roman citizens and officials. This perspective comes in two contrasting varieties: Luke writes to exhort his readers to live quiet lives that not only do not disturb the empire but also actively support it,[6] or Luke writes about a radical new social ethic inaugurated by Jesus and carried out by the disciples that threatens the oppressive political order of the Roman Empire.[7]

The variety of evidence and conclusions indicates that this complex topic requires careful nuancing. The scholarly consensus that Luke was writing to a Christian audience has led some to reevaluate the nature of Luke-Acts. While earlier interpreters interested in Luke's politics viewed his work as apologetic historiography, later studies have argued that it is more properly labeled as epideictic historiography.[8] Apologetic historiography attempts to convince *outsiders* of the honor and respectability of a group or people, epideictic historiography reinforces the identity of *insiders* by portraying their group or movement in a way that would be attractive to the broader culture. Thus, epideictic is a better label than apologetic for Luke's mode of historiography, for Luke's primary interest is to instruct believers (cf. 1:1–4) and secondarily to impress outsiders. The diversity of the political material in Luke's narrative offers a dynamic and balanced perspective on the empire. Luke unequivocally proclaims Jesus as Lord over all political and spiritual powers; however, he demonstrates that Christians can both work within a just and fair imperial government (e.g., Acts 19:35—20:1) and boldly call it to repentance when it opposes the will of God (e.g., Luke 3:19–20 or Acts 4:23–30).[9] This nuanced, epideictic perspective is the best way to proceed, for it deals with the complexity of Luke's perspective and more appropriately identifies the genre of Luke-Acts.

Despite the development of this more nuanced perspective, a recent monograph entitled *Jesus' Entry into Jerusalem*, by Brent Kinman, still espouses the apologetic perspective. Kinman's book is especially germane to this study because he examines Luke 19:28–48 in the light of its literary context in 18:35—19:27 and its ancient political context. Thus, both Kinman's choice of text and his methodology appear similar to this current study of the public and political nature of Luke, yet his approaches and conclusions vary considerably.

---

6. These scholars vary in their approaches and conclusions. Maddox contends that Luke wants his audience to cultivate a "sober, inoffensive style of life and an attitude of respect towards the government" (*Purpose of Luke-Acts*, 96). Esler contends that Luke is trying to unify a diverse community and so incorporates political themes in his work that would have legitimated the faith of those loyal to Rome (*Community and Gospel*, 201–19. Johnson (*Luke*, 8–9) affirms the apologetic nature of Luke's work but claims that its primary task was to interpret the Gospel for Christians living in a pluralistic environment, while also painting a positive picture for outsiders. Walasky has inverted the old argument and claimed that Luke is actually making an apology for the empire to the church ("*And So We Came to Rome*," 11–14).

7. Cassidy, *Jesus, Politics*, 77–79; Cassidy and Scarper, *Political*; and Yoder, *Politics of Jesus*, 21–59.

8. This direction is begun in Sterling (*Historiography*) and argued specifically by Penner, "Praise of Christian Origins," 379–86, 577–78.

9. Walton, "State They Were In," 34–35.

Kinman argues that Luke's retelling of the triumphal entry must be interpreted alongside the arrivals, entries, and triumphs of other distinguished persons in the ancient world.[10] Only then can the interpreter understand Luke's account of Jesus' triumphal entry and its impact on his audience. After setting up the thesis that Luke wants to distance Jesus from Jewish revolutionaries,[11] Kinman examines Greco-Roman and Jewish precedents to the triumphal entry and then turns to Luke's Gospel. He begins by analyzing the literary context of the entry including the story of the blind beggar, the encounter with Zacchaeus, and the parable of the nobleman. In each case, he claims to show how Luke redacts his sources and tells his stories in order to quell any suspicions about Jesus' political aims. Then he discusses the entry account proper as well as Luke's omission of the fig tree pericope, Jesus' lament over Jerusalem, and his cleansing of the temple. In each of these sections, Kinman concludes that Luke has specifically downplayed any political overtones of Jesus' entry, differentiating him from Jewish revolutionaries and portraying an "a-triumphal" entry as part of his overall political apologetic for Christianity.[12]

Kinman should be credited for the initiative and breadth of his comparative research. However, his interpretive perspective is misguided on two accounts. First, Kinman adheres to scholarship, which insists that Luke's narrative offers (among many other things) a political apology for Christianity to residents of the Roman Empire, Theophilus in particular.[13] This pillar of interpretation has nearly crumbled, and most scholars (as discussed above) now claim that Luke's main audience is Christians and his work is best viewed as epideictic historiography rather than apology. Kinman's second error is to set Jesus' entry alongside stories that deal with royal or imperial politics. The three most important comparisons discussed by Kinman are Solomon's entry into Jerusalem, Pilate's assize, and Roman triumphs in the imperial era. The first of these is more suitable, but Kinman fails to note the differences that weaken the comparison.[14] The last two, which dominate Kinman's analysis, deal with a political scale that is much larger than the scope of Jesus' ministry in Luke's Gospel. Therefore, it is inevitable that Jesus' entry would appear "a-triumphal" if the comparative materials are set on a disproportionately grandiose stage.

Thus, there are two primary faults in Kinman's study that can be redressed in this study. The first correction is to formulate a sounder and more balanced understanding of Luke's political perspective that can incorporate apologetic, prophetic, and ecclesial elements. This more balanced view should emphasize the insider perspective of Luke's

---

10. Kinman, *Jesus' Entry*, 25–27.

11. Ibid., 4.

12. Ibid., 173–78.

13. Kinman cites Conzelmann and Marshall as authoritative supporters of the apologetic perspective. He writes that "they have stated that Luke has handled the traditions of Jesus' entry in such a way to minimize a political misunderstanding on the part of his readers" (*Jesus' Entry*, 3). However, the citation of Marshall does not seem to be supported by Marshall's text.

14. The primary difference is the inverse narrative placement of Solomon's entry into Jerusalem as king and Jesus' entry as king. Solomon's entry occurs at the beginning of 1 Kings, introducing the story of his international power and renown. However, Jesus' entry as king occurs at the end of Luke's story about the life of Jesus, where it climaxes the development of Jesus' ministry. Additionally, Solomon inherits an already established kingdom, whereas Jesus seems to be in the process of inaugurating one.

Christian audience while not ignoring how outsiders may have viewed Luke's portrayal of Jesus. The second correction is that Luke's presentation of Jesus should be taken off an imperial stage and set in a local context that suits the political scale of Luke's Gospel. The politics and geography of Luke's Gospel are more local than imperial (Jesus interacts much more with Pharisees and Sadducees than any Roman officials). Therefore, one must analyze the political perspective of the Gospel on a scale that is commensurate with the Gospel itself.[15] Even with the rise of the more balanced perspective (largely overlooked by Kinman), gaps remain in our understanding of the political character of Luke-Acts. Few have paid critical attention to the role of space in the construal of Luke's political perspective.[16] To illustrate, a sensitivity to the role of space in politics raises the issue of how the setting of Zacchaeus's house (Luke 19:6ff.) affects the interpretation of Jesus' parable regarding the arrival of the kingdom of God told as a political story of a local royal figure (Luke 19:11–27). Also, political interpreters of Luke-Acts have failed to examine the internal politics of Jesus' movement itself.[17] One of Luke's ecclesiological tasks is to portray the origins and organization of the Christian community and its leaders.[18] The political issues of power, systems, ethics, ideologies, processes, and institutional organization[19] within the church should also be considered in the interpretation of Luke's political perspective as it takes shape in the Gospel.

(Is and) How Is Luke's Portrayal of Jesus Public?

This arena of interpretation begins its story with those who employed geography as a tool for interpreting Luke's Gospel (and Acts). It then shifts to more recent scholars who have addressed the topics of public space both within and beyond the Lukan material in the NT. This part of the story closes with the development of social-scientific criticism and how it uses the categories of public and private with regard to Luke-Acts. This retelling will show that while some scholars doubt that earliest Christianity had any place in the public sphere, many others identify the public nature of various elements in Luke and Acts. However, the adjective "public" is applied blithely with little reflection about the social and spatial forces that might make a character or a scene public.

---

15. Heinz Eulau demonstrates that the varying scales of political activity (from individual to the largest collective) must be considered in political analysis and that reasoning by analogy across levels is often fallacious (*Micro-Macro Political Analysis*, 1–22). The issue of scale will be discussed in greater depth in the next chapter.

16. Kohn eloquently argues for the role of space in political analysis (*Radical Space*, 3–6), stating that "a spatial heuristic can illuminate domains of political experience that have hitherto remained obscured in a culture that emphasized visual and linguistic knowledges" (4).

17. Hubert Cancik has written a suggestive article that examines Acts as "institutional history" ("History of Culture"). Cancik has not published a promised article (see ibid., 675) regarding Luke's Gospel.

18. Some scholars have done excellent work in pointing out the theological and ecclesiological importance of the twelve in Luke-Acts. See "Twelve on Israel's Thrones" (in Jervell, *Luke and the People of God*, 75–112), and Johnson, *Literary Function*, 60–69, 174–82. This study will build on their observations and explore the political nature of the movement that develops around Jesus in Luke's Gospel.

19. These categories are taken from Tansey, *Politics*, 4–6.

A PUBLIC AND POLITICAL CHRIST

Geography in the Study of Luke-Acts

Conzelman employed geography to interpret Luke's redactional and theological aims in the first part of *Die Mitte der Zeit*,[20] and on one occasion he notes that Luke's presentation of Jesus' teaching is more public than Mark's.[21] Conzelmann's study set many trajectories in Lukan studies, including an emphasis on the narrative and theological significance of geography in Luke-Acts. Scholars have examined Luke's theological map of the world,[22] the significance of the travel narrative,[23] the geographical scope of Luke-Acts,[24] and especially Luke's view of Jerusalem and the temple. Jerusalem plays a critical role in the geographical structure of Luke's two-volume work.[25] The Gospel begins and ends in the holy city, and Acts opens there as well. Parsons points out that Jerusalem is not the center of the world for Luke, but the starting point for the church's eschatological mission.[26] Chance focuses on the significance of Jerusalem and the temple as the location of two key eschatological events in Luke-Acts: the climax of Jesus' teaching to the Jewish people and the originating hub of the Gentile mission.[27] Conzelmann's emphasis on geography as a theological signifier in Luke and the central role of Jerusalem is still felt today.

Michael Bachmann carries on the tradition of Conzelmann by thoroughly investigating the "geographisch-theologischen" elements of Luke's view of the temple.[28] Bachmann discusses the centrality of Jerusalem by arguing that, for Luke, the temple is at the heart of Jerusalem, which is at the heart of Judea and the Jewish people as a whole. He claims that Jerusalem exists as the city of the temple in Luke's mind.[29] However, Bachmann relies primarily on evidence from Acts and glosses the necessarily smaller and more precise geographical comments in the Gospel. The smaller scope of Luke's first volume requires closer attention to the social-spatial development of Jesus' movement and the locales in which it occurs. In the final section of his book, Bachmann explores the heart of Luke's social and geographical world by examining the officials, institutions, and functions of the temple.[30] Bachmann demonstrates that Luke conceives of Jesus as a public (*öffentlich*)

---

20. Conzelmann, *Theology of St. Luke*, 18–94. Conzelmann first treats John (which he sees as geographically and theological separated from Jesus) and then breaks Jesus' ministry down into the spatial zones of Galilee, the Journey, and Jerusalem. This analysis of the theological significance of Luke's geography builds on his dissertation, "Die geographischen Vorstellung im Lukasevangelium."

21. Conzelmann, *Theology of St. Luke*, 224.

22. Scott, "Luke's Geographical Horizon," 483–544; and Borgen, "Philo, Luke and Geography," 273–85. On one part of that map see Bechard, "Theological Significance."

23. An annotated history of the interpretation of this section and a fresh focus on the banquet theme is offered by Moessner, *Lord of the Banquet*, 21–33, 289–324.

24. For an example and bibliography on this topic see Moore, "'To the End,'" 389–99.

25. Johnson, *Luke*, 11.

26. Parsons, "Place of Jerusalem," 167–68. Green argues that the tearing of the temple veil in Luke signals its end as the "center" of the world. See Green, "Demise of the Temple."

27. Chance, *Jerusalem*, 58–59, 112.

28. Bachmann, *Jerusalem und der Tempel*.

29. Ibid., 132–38.

30. Section 4 is divided into two parts: "Amtliche Beziehungen" and "Nichtamtliche Beziehungen," or official and unofficial connections to the temple (*Jerusalem*, 172). Later, I will use of the language of official and

teacher, for he regularly portrays Jesus teaching large crowds.[31] This is intensified in the passion narrative, where Jesus teaches *all* Israel (at least representatively) in the temple.[32] Bachmann also wrongly asserts that the Sanhedrin has no political functions for Luke since it is exclusively concerned with the religious functions of the temple.[33] Bachmann's study offers a wealth of valuable information, and he begins to notice the social dynamic of the public sphere. However, he is still views places primarily as theological markers and fails to adjust the scale of his analysis to attend to social and political significance of the houses, cities, and roads that fill Luke's Gospel.

Two other works attend to the literary and theological significance of travel in Luke's opus. First, David Moessner subtitles his classic monograph *Lord of the Banquet* by identifying it as a study of *The Literary and Theological Significance of the Lukan Travel Narrative*. Moessner argues that the travel narrative holds together around two foci: Luke's portrayal of Jesus as type of the rejected prophet like Moses of Deuteronomy, and the conflict that occurs when Jesus is received as a guest at meals. Moessner's study is rich with insight, but his focus on the literary and theological significance of this material leads him to marginalize the spatial aspects of the homes, roads, and cities that Jesus visits in this large swath of Luke's Gospel.[34] A similar emphasis appears in Baban's *On the Road Encounters in Luke-Acts*. He states that his purpose is to "understand Luke's theology of journeying in relation to his literary style."[35] He focuses specifically on three stories that occur on roads in Luke-Acts: the Emmaus encounter, Philip and the Ethiopian, and Saul's encounter with Christ near Damascus. The author mentions that one function of mimesis is the representation of the historical environment; however, Baban focuses on Luke's mimesis of journey motifs in various types of literature.[36] He pays little attention to the social and spatial dynamics of roads (even as represented spaces), but concludes that Luke manipulates time and space to design "the narrative and theological unity of these journey encounters."[37] Baban, like Moessner, proffers significant literary and theological insights, but his approach effectively eschews any information derived from Luke's use of details and cultural expectations about the spatial and social elements mentioned so frequently in

---

unofficial to subdivide the public sphere. Bachmann's usage is a partial precedent; however, he does not reflect on his choice of these labels.

31. *Jerusalem*, 265–72.

32. Bachmann, *Jerusalem*, 276–78.

33. Ibid., 217–18. The political function of the Sanhedrin will be discussed in ch. 7.

34. For example, Moessner says that "eating and drinking" is a "cipher" of the presence of God's rule (*Lord of the Banquet*, 173) and that images of the house in "parables, episodes, and illustrations" point ultimately (and therefore most importantly) to the "banquet of the 'house' of the Kingdom of God" (174). Similarly, he states that Luke is not interested in "the precise details of a journey itinerary," but that the travel narrative is held together by a "fourfold plot based on the Prophet like Moses of Deuteronomy." Moessner is right that geography does not organize this section of Luke but his conclusions wrongly push most spatial considerations aside.

35. Baban, *On the Road*, 1.

36. Ibid., 86–87 and then 119–40.

37. Ibid., 276.

his narrative. This study seeks to address this gap by exploring how Luke employs social-spatial elements in his portrayal of Jesus.

Public Space, Philosophy, and Paul

The following four pieces orbit around three related topics: Paul, philosophy, and public space. First, Stowers argues that Luke has apologetic interests in mind when he portrays Paul as a refined philosopher, distancing him from the Cynic tradition.[38] However, Stowers dismisses this as historical evidence and claims Paul lacked sufficient status to speak publicly as a politician or rhetoritician—the public arenas simply would not have been open to him as a non-elite in the Hellenistic world.[39] Leaving Acts, he turns to Paul's letters in order to reconstruct the social circumstances of his preaching. Stowers asserts that the synagogue and the private home were the most common loci of Paul's preaching.[40] Stowers concludes that Paul was socially separated from the public sphere and instead made the private home the platform of his preaching activity.[41] Stowers mounts a historical argument about Paul in this article: Where did Paul typically preach, and were those places public or private? This differs from the question asked in this dissertation about how Luke uses social and spatial material in his realistic *portrayal* of Jesus, but some aspects of Stowers's article are instructive. He describes the control of public spaces by government officials (such as the gymnasiarch) and rightly claims that adequate social status was required to access these public-political places. However, not all public space was controllable, as evidenced by Stowers's discussion of Cynic philosophers. Stowers notes that what matters is not the physical distance between places, but how social and cultural evaluations differentiate public and private locations.[42] Thus, Stowers's article is valuable for highlighting how public space was defined, controlled, and accessed in the Hellenistic world as well as how authors (like Luke) might manipulate space in the portrayal of their characters.

Not long after Stowers's article, Malherbe published an article entitled "'Not in a Corner': Early Christian Apologetic in Acts 26:26." Malherbe believes that Paul's comment in Acts 26:26 ("this was not done in a corner") bears a deep resonance with the apologists of the second century who sought to offer a social (as well as political) apology to those who accused Christianity of being a lower-class movement that lacked any philosophical sophistication.[43] Luke, through this statement and other supporting material in Acts, sought to portray Paul as an educated moral philosopher who honorably engaged in public life rather than withdrawing from it.[44] This fits quite well with the discussion of the social

---

38. Stowers, "Social Status," 61–62.

39. Ibid., 81.

40. Ibid., 68.

41. Ibid., 82. Oakes studies the home of a craftworker in depth as a social-archaeological model for understanding the audience of Paul's letter to the Romans (*Reading*, 70–73).

42. Stowers, "Social Status," 82.

43. Malherbe, "'Not in a Corner,'" 195–97.

44. Ibid., 197, 203.

role of philosophy in an essay by Engberg-Pedersen written a few years later.[45] Engberg-Pedersen picks up on Habermas's idea of the *Öffentlichkeit*, or public sphere, and applies it to the Hellenistic world to try to discern the social role of philosophy. He claims that philosophy was held in high social esteem in the Hellenistic period because it offered insight about how humans should live, and that both Stoic and Epicurean philosophers participated in public discourse.[46] This esteem helped to create "a socially supported sphere of ethico-political discourse . . . which provided the framework for the social functioning of philosophers."[47] This public sphere was indirectly (rather than directly) political and was a forum for ethical and political discussion.[48] Thus, Engberg-Pedersen claims that there was a Hellenistic *Öffentlichkeit*, a public sphere that could influence the political authorities of the ancient world. Engberg-Pedersen more fully describes this public sphere, which plays a social-apologetic role in Luke's portrayal of Paul as a reputable philosopher, according to Malherbe.

Continuing these trajectories in Malherbe and Engberg-Pedersen, Alexander has written an essay on how Jews and Christians portrayed themselves as philosophers participating in the public life of the empire.[49] Alexander states that philosophers created a "philosophy-shaped hole," which Jews and Christians could use to access the power brokers of Hellenistic society, since they were shut out of the normal channels of public space.[50] After showing how both Josephus and Philo used philosophy as a cross-cultural bridge to explain the beliefs and practices of Jews, Alexander turns to the public and private places Luke uses to portray Paul as a Christian philosopher. Alexander considers the synagogue to be public space, which Paul most often used as a platform for his preaching. She agrees with Stowers that Paul, as an outsider, would not have had access to the public-political spaces of cities.[51] Despite the fact that many public venues were closed to Paul, Alexander sees him engaging the *polis* in Acts in spaces frequented by philosophers, such as the Areopagus or the school or Tyrannus.[52] When Paul ventures outside of these, his preaching is either ineffective or dangerous. Thus, Luke does not portray the general public spaces of the cities as an appropriate arena for Christian proselytization.[53] Therefore, Paul used the synagogue as the base of his preaching activity because he had some social legitimacy there, and it offered him an audience and a base for his mission activity.[54] At

---

45. Engberg-Pedersen, "Hellenistic *Öffentlichkeit*," 15–38.

46. Ibid., 33.

47. Ibid., 33.

48. Ibid., 34.

49. Alexander, "Foolishness."

50. Ibid., 229. Alexander's description bears a strong resonance with Engberg-Pedersen's presentation of a "sphere of ethico-political discourse" filled by philoso-phers.

51. Alexander, "Foolishness," 235.

52. Alexander raises the question of how truly public such spaces are, especially since she still maintains that typically public places were controlled by the authorities (ibid., 236–38).

53. Ibid., 234–35.

54. Ibid., 235. Again, Alexander's analysis sounds very similar to Stowers's comments on Paul's lack of public status.

this point, Alexander claims that this problem of access to public space "does not arise for the Christian sect on its home ground, in Jerusalem or Galilee or Samaria; there, public space is effectively legitimate territory (until you offend the authorities)."[55] This sets a very different social-spatial stage for Luke's portrayal of Jesus in the Gospel.

These last four authors agree on many points, and each adds some insights to the understanding of the public sphere in the ancient world. It is an honorable space often populated by philosophers whose discourse influenced the ethical and political dimensions of Hellenistic society. Thus, this public-philosophical space would have been a natural entry point for Christian preaching. While these works have helped to set the stage for this dissertation, unmapped ground still exits. The primary difference lies in the fact that these studies mostly focus on Paul (and Luke's portrayal of Paul) in the context of the Greco-Roman world and its philosophical tradition. This dissertation will focus on Luke's portrayal of Jesus in his Gospel and will look beyond philosophical writings to consider history, drama, rhetoric, and Jewish sources as well. Next, whereas all of the authors discussed above have noted some connection between the public sphere and politics, this dissertation will clarify that relationship by explicating the various levels of politics and their relationship to the larger public sphere. Finally, this study will use some of the most recent work on spatial theory to help clarify the classification of spaces in the ancient world and explore how Luke uses specific places (roads, cities, homes, temples, etc.) as social cues to portray Jesus as a public and political figure.

Social-Scientific Advances

The story of the history of interpretation thus far has demonstrated four key gaps in the analysis of the public and political nature of Luke's portrayal of Jesus. First, Luke' political perspective must fit into goals as a writer of epideictic historiography. Second, Luke's political perspective must be analyzed at the appropriate scale, including lower level political actions such as Jesus' exercise of social power within his own growing movement. Third, while many scholars have examined Luke's portrayal of Paul in the public sphere, little has been done regarding Luke's portrayal of Jesus in this vein. Fourth and finally, while many scholars have fruitfully probed the literary and theological significance of places in Luke-Acts, very few have paid specific attention to the cultural aspects of these places and how this affects Luke's narrative. These gaps have been remedied in part by social-scientific interpretations of Luke-Acts and the recent inclusion of spatial analysis. Social-scientific studies of Luke-Acts have employed different approaches: sociological theory,[56] social models and reading scenarios,[57] and social history.[58] Social-scientific interpreters have explored the dynamics of human relationships in specific times and places, but tend to avoid discussions of explicit political activity, focusing on other, less official, aspects of human culture such as personality, the family, household ceremonies,

---

55. Ibid.
56. Peter Berger's theory of legitimation is at the heart of Esler, *Community and Gospel*.
57. This is the language and approach found throughout the articles found in Neyrey, ed., *Social World*.
58. Social history is the best way to categorize Corley's study, *Private Women*.

and economics.⁵⁹ Thus, the time has come for the insights of social-scientific criticism to be applied also to the study of places and politics in Luke's Gospel.

Unfortunately, the domains of public and private have not received careful analysis even in social-scientific studies of Luke. *Private Women, Public Meals* by Corley offers a promise of relevance in its title. However, she merely uses "public" to identify open-meal parties in Roman society, with little or no explanation of the meaning of this label.⁶⁰ The category of public does not enter into Esler's study on *Community and Gospel in Luke-Acts*, possibly because he is concerned with the internal dynamics of legitimation inside the Christian community. In his expansive study on the sociological significance of the economic label "lovers of money" in Luke 16:14, Moxnes concludes that this label is part of a larger set of descriptions used by Luke (and others in the ancient world) to characterize the reprehensible social behavior, like that of the Pharisees.⁶¹ Moxnes points out that the economic program expressed by Luke's Jesus actually brings some of the private standards of generalized reciprocity into a wider sphere. Thus, he hints at the relationship of the public and private sphere in Luke, but does not develop it in his study. The label "public" appears quite frequently in various essays in *The Social World of Luke-Acts*. For example, the verdict of the public is a necessary conclusion to the struggle for honor seen in the "challenge-riposte" exchange. Malina and Neyrey write, "Again, publicity and witnesses are crucial for the acquisition and bestowal of honor. Representatives of public opinion must be present, since honor is all about the court of public opinion and the reputation, which that court bestows. Literally, public praise can give life and public ridicule can kill."⁶² Despite the powerful role of the public described here, several questions are left unanswered. What exactly is publicity? How is public opinion constituted and what qualifies one to be a representative of it? What makes praise or ridicule public?⁶³ While many scholars have employed the language of public and private in the social-scientific analysis of the NT, very few have probed the spatial dimensions of this language and its impact on the social realities of the ancient world.

The Emergence of Spatial Analysis

Social-scientific analysis has recently been enriched by studies employing critical spatiality to explore and analyze the role of spaces and places in biblical literature. "Critical spatial-

---

59. This is at least true in the domain of Lukan studies, as a survey of Neyrey's *Social World* confirms.

60. Corley, in *Private Women*, has sections treating "Women in Public in the Late Republic and Early Empire" (53–65) and "Christian Women and Public Meals" (75–77). Her study appropriately focuses on the meal scene in Roman society and early Christianity. She explores the presence of women at dinner parties and the hostile social reactions to this innovation, but she fails to identify exactly what made such meals "public" and how they differed from private meals. She tantalizingly mentions women's increased involvement in the "public sphere" and "public roles" (xv), but limits herself to the assumed public nature of the meal parties at the heart of her study.

61. Moxnes, *Economy of the Kingdom*, 147.

62. Malina and Neyrey, "Honor and Shame," 36.

63. Similarly undefined uses of the label "public" can be found throughout the volume. See McVann, "Rituals," 341; Malina and Neyrey, "Conflict," 106–7; Pilch, "Sickness and Healing," 199; Neyrey, "Symbolic Universe," 273.

ity" is the label applied to recent developments in the study of space and place, which are related to but increasingly differentiated from the discipline of human or cultural geography. The growing association with critical theory and the social sciences, a dialogue with Marxism and other ideological positions, and a conscious consideration of postmodern perspectives have led to critical spatiality as a new identifiable domain of study.[64] The SBL Seminar on Constructions of Ancient Space has laudably spearheaded the application of critical spatiality to biblical and religious issues. This work began primarily with the study of the Hebrew Bible,[65] and there are now a few examples of scholars applying the insights of this discipline to NT texts.[66] We will now survey the recent work of scholars who have led the way by critically studying the role of space and place in the NT in order to set the stage for this study.

Two articles by Robbins and Neyrey in the early 1990s employ the recently published work by Robert Sack, entitled *Human Territoriality*, as a model for interpreting NT texts.[67] Robbins uses Sack's theory of territoriality to explore how the power structures of the Roman Empire and emerging Christianity (as portrayed in Luke-Acts) relate to one another. He demonstrates that while Christianity begins with territorial struggles for power in the temple (at the end of Luke and the beginning of Acts), it shifts its territorial focus to "synagogues, houses, and public areas from Galilee and Judaea to Rome."[68] Ultimately, he claims that Christianity uses a territorial strategy similar to Rome's, for it negotiates with insiders and outsiders creating a movement in the eastern half of the Mediterranean basin that many may choose to join in order to realize God's plan of salvation and peace.[69] His tangential mention of "public areas" suggests the focus of this study, which will use Ephesus as a city representative of the eastern part of the empire. An early article by Neyrey deals with the interrelation of gender, space, and rhetoric in John 4 using Sack's theory of territoriality.[70] Neyrey opens by claiming that most of the ancient world believed that the pub-

---

64. The changes in the discipline of geography and the major figures that have fueled the development of critical spatiality are outlined by Berquist, "Critical Spatiality," 1–2 and 18–21. Berquist lists identity, urbanization, interrelatedness, and constructions as some of the main considerations in critical spatiality, all of which play a role in this dissertation (24–29). This study will use the language of spatiality to reflect its explicit concern with the role of space and place; however, it embodies more of the human geography of Sack's work, which does not accept all of the philosophical stances of postmodern theorizing and tends to be oriented around moral concerns (see Sack, *Homo Geographicus*, 2–7).

65. Flanagan, "Perceptions of Space"; McNutt, "'Fathers of the Empty Spaces'"; Camp, "Storied Space." Also see the other articles on spatiality in this volume. All of these essays deal with the Hebrew Bible and most of them are based on the spatial theories of Lefebvre and Soja. The AAR/SBL Construction of Ancient Space Seminar has also generated a number of excellent papers on this topic. Again, most of them deal with the Hebrew Bible and use the theories of Lefebvre and Soja. For an example see Roland Boer, "Sanctuary and Womb."

66. See Robbins, "Luke-Acts." Also, very general considerations of space and place were applied to the Lukan passion narrative by McKeever, "Refiguring Space."

67. Both Robbins ("Mixed Population," 202) and Neyrey ("In Public," 72–73) claim this book as their theoretical basis.

68. Robbins, "Mixed Population," 214.

69. Ibid., 218–20.

70. "'What's Wrong with This Picture?'" published in 1994.

Introduction: Place and Politics in the Study of Luke's Gospel

lic sphere belonged to men while the private sphere was the territory of women. Neyrey then sets out to understand what is both wrong and right with the narrative of John 4 in light of this almost universal division of public and private territory. The key to unlocking the issue for Neyrey lies in the structure of the passage and how the rhetoric changes in the course of the story. In 4:7–15 the sexual shamelessness of the woman stands out in a conversation with Jesus that "has all the trappings of a challenge-riposte exchange," a common feature of public encounters.[71] However, the woman's ever increasing understanding reveals that Jesus is effectively recruiting her into his fictive kinship circle. The rhetoric changes in 4:16–26. Now the woman speaks with clear knowledge, and she exchanges important and revelatory information with Jesus in a friendly manner, which is characteristic of the private world.[72] Thus, in Neyrey's analysis, while the physical space remains the same, the rhetoric of the exchange alters the valence of the space from public (where the woman's challenges seem brazen) to private (where she gladly enters into Jesus' personal circle). His analysis suggests that the public-private valence of a given "territory" can be adjudicated partially on the nature of the rhetoric that occurs there.[73]

Moxnes' more recent book, *Putting Jesus in His Place*, employs spatial theory and queer theory to examine the historical Jesus.[74] Moxnes's monograph is different from the current study in that he is interested in getting behind canonical texts to discover the ways that the historical Jesus inhabited and transgressed places in ancient Palestine, but it is relevant in two respects. First, Moxnes's methodology supports the approach of this study. He discusses the theoretical reconsideration of place that has arisen since the 1960s and sees its relevance for the study of the person of Jesus.[75] At the same time, he uses queer theory to show how Jesus destabilizes traditional places, while this study claims that Luke manipulates and stretches typical concepts of place in his portrayal of Jesus.[76] On the other hand, in contrast to this study Moxnes focuses almost exclusively on the house as a place for Jesus, claiming that it is the most common place in the earliest layers of the Jesus tradition.[77] Moxnes admits that place was deployed in various ways by the different Gospel writers, showing "the importance of place for constructions of identity in the cultures of Mediterranean antiquity."[78] While being in deep agreement with Moxnes's methodology and outlook, the current study asserts that the public sphere predominates in Luke's portrayal of Jesus and seeks to understand how and perhaps why that is so.

---

71. Ibid., 84.

72. Ibid., 84–85.

73. For example, does the confrontational nature of Jesus' interaction with the Pharisees at the meal scenes in Luke's Gospel imply that these should be viewed as public scenarios?

74. Moxnes, *Putting Jesus*, 1–21.

75. Ibid., 8–10 and 12–16.

76. Ibid., 5–6.

77. Ibid., 17–18. This emphasis is revealed in each chapter for almost every one refers to the household in its title. Later, Moxnes claims that the Kingdom and the new community that inhabits it was mostly an "imagined place" in Q, while Mark (and other tridents) felt it was necessary to actually provide the new movement with a real place and naturally chose the household (114–16).

78. Ibid., 19.

A PUBLIC AND POLITICAL CHRIST

After a long silence on the topic, Neyrey published two articles dealing with public and private space in 2003. The first article treats public/private under the category of gender and focuses on the portrayal of Jesus in Matthew.[79] Neyrey states his perspective at the very beginning: "We argue that the ancient world shared a common gender stereotype, that is, a descriptive and often a proscriptive sketch of gender specific roles, tasks, tools, and places."[80] Neyrey sites three resource zones he will use to construct this ancient stereotype: ancient authors in a philosophical vein (including Aristotle, Xenophon, Philo, and others), epideictic rhetoric (and physiognomics), and the lexica associated with these categories in a variety of ancient authors.[81] He concludes that the ancients used gender to dichotomize the social world and the entire cosmos. Males were associated with outdoor activities (farming and fighting), while women were in charge of the indoor domain (crafts and care of children).[82] Men could be associated with three spatial spheres: public (politics), private (non-kin associations), and private (household), but women were restricted exclusively to the private sphere of the household.[83] Finally, Neyrey points out that the pinnacle of male existence in the public-political sphere was only available to elites in the ancient world. The huge number of peasants (over eighty percent of the population) could have no place in this sphere, which makes Jesus' public voice even more interesting.[84]

Neyrey then applies this template to the portrayal of Jesus in the Gospel of Matthew. Matthew regularly places Jesus in male-outdoor-public space and indoor-non-kin association space. However, he has no episodes with Jesus in private-indoor-kinship space. The role of kin in Jesus' life has been replaced with a fictive kin group out of obedience to his heavenly Father.[85] Neyrey then indicates several ways in which Matthew's narrative portrays Jesus as an ideal male-public-political figure.[86] Jesus' main opponents in the Gospel are the Pharisees, "influential figures in local village leadership" who were retainers of the elite.[87] Jesus generally wins in his contests with them, thus raising his honor. Jesus' authorization by God to preach the kingdom to the crowds also reinforces his public-political standing, despite his peasant background.[88] At the end of the article Neyrey makes two conclusions. First, Jesus presents an inverted hierarchy of honor, especially in his didactic conversations with his disciples, that is at "egregious variance" with the dominant male

---

79. Neyrey, "Jesus."

80. Ibid., 43.

81. In this and the next article, he explores the following pairs of terms: κοινός/ἴδιος, δημόσιος/ἴδιος, πόλις/οἶκος and *publice/privatim* ("In Public," 75–81).

82. Neyrey, "Jesus," 44–46.

83. Ibid., 47.

84. Ibid., 52–53.

85. Ibid., 54–55. This lack of care for kin women and home does make Jesus somewhat suspect in Neyrey's opinion.

86. The titles for Jesus in Matthew (e.g., Son of God) all tend toward the political or the prophetic. See ibid., 56–58.

87. Ibid., 59–60. However, exactly who the Pharisees are retainers of (Sadducees? Romans?) is not stated.

88. Ibid., 60–62.

stereotype; Jesus' code glorifies suffering, humility, service, and loss.[89] Second, Neyrey asserts that "the gender stereotype of a totally divided world is a historical fact," and while Jesus conforms to where honorable males should act, his demands on his disciples upturn the male stereotype of honor.[90]

A few unresolved issues emerge from this article. First, Neyrey asserts that the gender-division stereotype was a historical fact. A stereotype is by definition conventional, formulaic, and oversimplified. It is undeniably true that this stereotype was expressed by elite, male, philosophically oriented writers in the Greco-Roman world. However, that such a stereotype was actually "descriptive" of "historical fact" is still in question, especially in light of Neyrey's own admission that the non-elite could not participate in it. This will be explored further in the next chapter. How then should we describe the vast majority of the population whose life could not fit this neat, philosophical stereotype? David Cohen's work on law and sexuality in ancient Athens uses contemporary anthropological studies alongside ancient evidence (mostly from dramatists and historians, not philosophers)[91] to show that this stereotype was (and is) a simplification; it did (and does) not accurately describe common social practice (e.g., women commonly had non-kin associations outside of their homes and even some civic roles).[92] The stereotype did exist, but it may not have adequately depicted social realities beyond the prescriptions of the elite.[93]

Second, many of the examples cited by Neyrey to illustrate the public/private divide may also be taken to describe two fluid and interrelated domains. For example, regarding rhetoric, Aristotle says, "The deliberative kind is either hortatory or dissuasive; for both those who give advice in private [ἴδια] and those who speak in the assembly [κοινή] invariably either exhort or dissuade" (*Rhet.* 1358b). Aristotle refers to two distinct spheres, but they are similar in this case, for deliberative rhetoric has the same purposes in both. Many of the terms for public and private in these examples are linked by both/and conjunctions, indicating the connectedness of these categories rather than their stark dichotomization into exclusive domains.[94] The inside-female/outside-male division is well established as a stereotype but lacks nuance when applied to the Gospels. Matthew's mountain (5:1), Mark's wilderness (1:45), and Luke's plain (6:17) are all outdoor loca-

89. Ibid., 63–66.

90. Ibid., 65–66. The tension (or perhaps conflict) between the way Matthew's Jesus implicitly embodies cultural male norms but revolutionizes them in his explicit teaching is not discussed by Neyrey at length. It does raise the question of how these two differing trajectories are bound together in this narrative.

91. Foley notes the variations in the portrayal of women in prose and poetic texts, even within different authors in those genres. The prose writers emphasize their confinement to the private sphere, whereas the poetic writers allows them much more of a public role. See Foley, "Conceptions of Women," 128.

92. Cohen, *Law*, 130–70. Cohen's book will be discussed further in ch. 3. Neyrey opens the door to women's non-kin, non-household associations saying that women did collect water and fuel. However, he insists that women were still restricted to the private sphere because the defining element of the public sphere for Neyrey is civic life or political activity (see Neyray, "Jesus," 50).

93. Such a stereotype would have played a prescriptive role. However, Neyrey's description leads one to think that it was hegemonically applied without exception in social practice across the ancient Mediterranean world. Such implications cause his approach to be described as "positivist" in a response article later in the same volume. See du Bois, "Ancient Masculinities," 320.

94. See the examples in Neyrey, "Jesus," 46.

tions, but the functions that they serve in each of their Gospels is distinct and may not primarily reflect a gender orientation.[95] Finally, Neyrey cites Jesus' challenge-riposte encounters with the Pharisees as evidence of his public-political position. This study agrees with his assessment that these figures represented *local* leadership, but their relation to the "elite" is unclear. Their role as local religious leaders indicates an element of authority with some links to official politics, but more careful distinctions are necessary. Neyrey's work is insightful and groundbreaking, but it misrepresents the complexity of social practice, leaves crucial issues unresolved, and polarizes stark categories that do not fit NT narratives well.

Neyrey's work on public and private space culminates in an article entitled "'Teaching You in Public and from House to House' (Acts 20:20): Unpacking a Cultural Stereotype." Neyrey builds upon all of his previous historical, lexical, and theoretical work to propose the following classification of space in Luke's portrayal of Paul: public as political and civic space, private non-household space, and private household space for hospitality or kinship.[96] Neyrey shows that Luke does at times portray Paul speaking in civic centers before elites and authorities who socially define public space (e.g., Acts 13:7; 16:20; 18:12). Nevertheless, the synagogue is Paul's preferred venue in Acts, and according to Neyrey, the synagogue is a private space outside of the household for associated males to meet (e.g., Acts 13:15–50; 17:1–8; 18:5–18). Eventually, Paul finds an alternative private space for his preaching in the Hall of Tyrannus (Acts 19:9). Paul's hospitable welcome into private homes often constitutes another place for Paul to preach (e.g., Acts 16:15, 18:7, 21:8). Finally, Paul testifies in the public space of the Jerusalem temple; however, he is censured and arrested for violating the heart of Jewish sacred and public territory.[97] By applying his classification to selected scenes in Acts, Neyrey applies the territorial models to show that Luke has heightened Paul's honor by placing him in some honorable public settings and several cities of "no mean status."[98] Paul is allowed to speak freely as an honorable figure in public-political space, private–non-house space, and private-household space, and is only denied a voice in the synagogues of Acts.[99]

In this article, Neyrey has substantially advanced the classification of public and private spaces in Greco-Roman society and insightfully applied these categories to the interpretation of the portrayal of Paul in Acts. However, while cracking open the categories of public and private in a new way, Neyrey's classification is incomplete and partially flawed. First, Neyrey has more carefully analyzed and classified the private side of the public-private spectrum. Under private Neyrey has two categories, non-household and household, and under private-household there are further subcategories: private space for

---

95. Most notably, Jesus flees into the wilderness *away from* public notoriety in Mark (see 1:35–38 and 6:31–32). Most in the ancient world probably think that only a male could live in such a harsh environment, but the wilderness is still an escape from the public life of crowds and cities.

96. Neyrey, "In Public," 87–91.

97. Ibid., 91–93.

98. Ibid., 94–98.

99. Ibid., 100.

Introduction: Place and Politics in the Study of Luke's Gospel

meetings of unrelated males (hospitality), and kinship space that includes both genders.[100] Similar analytical specificity is lacking for public space, which is described almost exclusively as the arena of political activity in the ancient world.[101]

Moreover, Neyrey's own classification of private space is not fully supported by all of the evidence he cites. Neyrey relies on only a portion of his research to include social gatherings of males for business and entertainment as "private, non-political, non-household space."[102] Pieces of Neyrey's evidence, and Acts 20:20 itself, suggest that such social gatherings could be considered public in the ancient world. If we look to his climactic example taken from Lysias's speech *In Defense of Mantitheus* (16.9–12), some problems emerge with Neyrey's classification. Lysias's account begins with the presentation of Mantitheus's private life (τὰ ἴδια) in 16.10: he honorably took care of his sisters and brothers, his kinship relations. When turning to public matters (περὶ δὲ τῶν κοινῶν), Mantitheus's testimony uses three examples. In the first example, he contrasts himself with his less reputable peers: "With regard to public matters, I believe that the greatest evidence I can give of my temperance is the fact that all of the younger men who happen to spend their time playing dice or drinking or practicing similar excesses are quite different from me, as you can see" (16.11). Neyrey recognizes that this passage describes public, social relationships among males but claims that it falls between the private world of the household and the "public-political" world of the assembly and fails to consider it in his definition of public spaces.[103] Neyrey does not quote the opening of 16.12, where Mantitheus gives his second example: "And moreover Council, no one can show that I have even been charged in a disgraceful private case, or in a public offence, or in a formal accusation." This extends the public domain one more degree, where Mantitheus's private and public activity intersects with the judicial system of the state. To close his testimony about his public life, Mantitheus comments on his faithful military service to his country: "With regard to military campaigns and dangers in the face of an enemy, you can observe how I have discharged my duty to the state" (16.12).[104] It seems that Lysias has recorded a spectrum of public activity in Mantitheus's testimony: social gatherings of males, legal matters, and political-military affairs. Thus, public activity stretches from a person's social relationships to where those relationships enter the legal system of the state to a person's direct involvement in the life of the state. Spatially this public range extends from homes to forums to courts to military centers. Even though Neyrey describes these degrees of public activity in the details of Lysias's speech, they are placed under the heading of "Private = Household Space, Roles and Concerns" and play almost no role in his construction of the classifications of public space in the ancient world. Neyrey has not fully incorporated the possibility that some social, non-household

---

100. Ibid., 90.

101. Ibid., 87. Neyrey does extend public space to include the *agora* (which is still primarily a political space; 93–94) and the Jerusalem temple, which is a space of national religious identity based on purity (91–93). Yet, all of these are defined by political characters, concerns, and actions.

102. Ibid., 81. The evidence from Aristotle and Demosthenes are dominant in Neyrey's classification of this type of space.

103. Ibid., 82.

104. Neyrey cites this as well (ibid., 83).

gatherings were considered public, and that a variety of levels in the public sphere existed in the Greco-Roman world.

The status of the synagogue and Paul's activity there also brings Neyrey's classifications into question. He states, "I classify the synagogue as private, non-public space, where males gathered in association, generally out-of-doors."[105] This is despite the evidence from Lysias's speech and Neyrey's earlier claim that the outdoors is male-public space.[106] Later, Neyrey himself speaks of Paul as having a "public voice" in the synagogue, even though he understands the synagogue to be a private, non-household space.[107] Finally, he even says that Paul "enjoyed public voice" in the private homes where he was received as a guest.[108] From this, it appears that there is some fluidity in the nature of public and private space not articulated by Neyrey.

The most relevant evidence against Neyrey's classifications comes from Acts 20:20 itself, which Neyrey claims to be unpacking in the article. He concludes that the public places (δημοσιᾷ) referred to in this verse are political spaces (including the *agora*) and that the private places (house to house, κατ᾽ οἴκους) in Acts include homes, synagogues, and the hall of Tyrannus.[109] However, the immediate and broader context of this statement indicate a different classification. Luke specifies that the activity Paul undertook in these public and private settings was "proclaiming the message to you and teaching you" (ἀναγγεῖλαι ὑμῖν καὶ διδάξαι ὑμᾶς). Given the intra-ecclesial audience ("you," that is, the Ephesian elders) and the catechetical connotations of the verbs,[110] Paul's public speaking must include something more than his appearances before Sergius Paulus, the magistrates of Phillipi, the Areopagus, and the judges of his trials, which are all better characterized as extra-ecclesial and evangelistic or apologetic in nature.[111] He must have spoken didactically to members of the church *in public*.

Then in 20:21 Paul says that he testified to both Jews and Greeks in Ephesus. This statement recalls a similar description in 19:9–10 where Luke states that Paul "argued daily in the lecture hall of Tyrannus. This continued for two years, so that *all the residents of Asia, both Jews and Greeks*, heard the word of the Lord." It is difficult to believe that this province-wide and ethnically inclusive testimony occurs in what Neyrey calls private space, the hall of Tyrannus. Rather, this description strongly implies that Luke thinks of this hall as a public place accessible to a wide range of people. If this hall is public, it is quite conceivable that Luke considers Paul's synagogue preaching to be public as well, a classification confirmed given the description of Paul's departure from the synagogue in the presence of a "crowd" (ἐνώπιον τοῦ πλήθους, 19:9).[112] Thus, when Paul's religion is publicly

---

105. Ibid., 88.

106. Ibid., 84.

107. Ibid., 89.

108. Ibid., 91.

109. Ibid., 93, 100.

110. The intra-ecclesial nature of διδάσκω is apparent, but Luke also uses ἀναγγέλλω in ecclesial contexts (Acts 14:27 and 15:4).

111. These are cited as the primary public-political appearances of Paul by Neyrey ("In Public," 93–94).

112. Recall that Alexander also classifies synagogues as public ("'Foolishness,'" 235–36).

libeled in the synagogue, he moves from one public speaking venue (the synagogue) with a crowd of witnesses to a nearby alternative that is equally public, where both Jews and Greeks—indeed all of Asia—hear the word of the Lord. In light of the ancient evidence provided by Lysias, it is reasonable to classify the synagogue and the hall of Tyrannus as public spaces for social gatherings, contra Neyrey, who seems to demand that all public places be civic/political.

Neyrey's research has advanced the discussion of public and private space in the milieu of the NT and holds a numbers of critical insights. However, the critique offered above also points out some flaws and blind spots. Neyrey's work can now be a starting point for a further advance of the discussion to be taken up in this study.

From Geography and Politics to Social-Spatial Analysis

Many studies of the role of politics and geography in Luke (and Acts) emerge from the uneasy mixture of historical-critical methods and theological aims that has shaped biblical scholarship since the Enlightenment.[113] This incongruous yet enduring paradigm of historical methods and theological ends began to change in the 1960s.[114] Social-scientific approaches broke into biblical scholarship and paved the way for spatial analyses approximately thirty years later.[115] Both have brought new tools and categories for interpreting scripture. Social-scientific analysis and later spatial analysis of the Bible has been driven largely by intellectual advances outside of biblical studies. The analysis of space as a key component of human existence originated in the early works of scholars such as Foucault, Lefebvre, and Tuan,[116] and has continued in studies that rely on their work.[117] This has now been followed by a new generation of thinkers who are theorizing the role of space in human existence. Much of this recent work in what is called "critical spatiality" or "human geography" emphasizes the interrelations of space and society, especially how the two reciprocally influence one another.[118] This sociologically informed mode of spatial analysis

---

113. See the comments by Bockmuehl in *Seeing the Word*, 44–47. He discusses (needed) renewed interest in the historical study of the NT, but concludes that historical research often does not answer crucial interpretive and theological questions, though it often assumes that it is doing so. Bray also comments on the uneasy relationship of historical methods and theological perspectives (*Biblical Interpretation*, 222–24).

114. On the diversification of NT scholarship and the rise of social and cultural modes of analysis, see Robbins, *Tapestry*, 1–10; and McKenzie and Haynes, *To Each Its Own Meaning*, 6–9. The same phenomenon is detailed in part 3 of Bray's study (see *Interpretation*, 461–66), and presented as a hypothetically shocking revelation to C. H. Dodd by Bockmuehl (*Seeing the Word*, 30–39).

115. Soja cites the consideration of the spatiality of human life as one of the great intellectual and political developments of the late twentieth century (*Thirdspace*, 2). The application of spatial analysis to the Bible was spearheaded by the SBL seminar on Constructions of Ancient Space mostly with regard to the Hebrew Bible. James Flanagan has played a leading role in this development. See Flanagan, "Ancient Perceptions," 15–43; and the recent Festschrift in his honor: Gunn and McNutt, eds., *"Imagining" Biblical Worlds*.

116. See Lefebvre, *La Production*; Foucault, "Of Other Spaces," 22–27; and Tuan, *Space and Place*.

117. For example, see Laurence, *Roman Pompeii*; and Margaret Kohn, *Radical Space*.

118. Sack, *Homo Geographicus*, 2–3. Sack comments on the frequency of the rhetorical claim that space and society are "mutually constitutive," but offers his own work as a practical analysis of how this mutual influence actually operates. His framework will serve as a theoretical basis for this dissertation. Soja claims much the same in the opening of his work cited above.

is well suited for investigating the categories of public, political, and private in both the ancient and contemporary contexts. These categories present special challenges because they blend space and social norms in ways that are both culturally powerful and highly contested. However, for each challenge a corresponding opportunity for new insight also exists. As Weintraub says, "While the public/private distinction is inherently problematic and often treacherous, frequently confusing and potentially misleading, it is also a powerful instrument of social analysis and moral reflection when approached with due caution and conceptual self-awareness."[119] Weintraub's commitment to this "treacherous" distinction reflects the growing recognition of the importance of the public-private spectrum in the analysis of society, politics, morality, and law.[120] Thus the rise of social and spatial modes of analysis has brought two changes: new attention has been turned on categories like public space and social power (politics), and new tools have emerged to aid in the investigation of these realms in both the ancient and modern contexts.

This study recognizes the interrelated nature of places and society and values the tools developed by sociologists and spatial theorists. Therefore, the mode of analysis carried out is labeled "social-spatial," for "society and space are thought of as mutually constitutive, each requiring and altering the other."[121] This reflects a shift from the terminology of "geography," which viewed natural and man-made locations as reified places that somehow reflected topography and architecture but more importantly served the theological aims of biblical authors. Instead of geographical, this study is spatial, for it seeks to recognize how space intertwines with cultural constructs and social relations to create and sustain specific places in human thinking and practice.[122] "Public," "private," and "political" are important labels that identify both places (spatial) and people (social) in those places. Political elements are included under the label "social" because politics is a subset of social analysis that focuses on the issues of social organization and decision-making within and between groups of people.[123] Thus, politics too deals with the intersecting influences of space, meaning, and society with a specific focus on the flow of authority at a variety of levels.

Despite the solid contributions of characters in the story of scholarship told above, their work has certain inadequacies that demand further study of the public and political elements of Luke's Gospel. These inadequacies are thrown into sharper relief by the intellectual advances in the study of space and society, and these advances also provide new

---

119. Weintraub, "Theory and Politics," 38.

120. Two foundational studies immediately emerge: Arendt, *Human Condition*; and Habermas, *Structural Transformation of the Public Sphere*. These are followed by several more recent studies that continue to probe and apply the relevance of these categories. As a sample, see Benn and Gaus, *Public and Private in Social Life*; Swanson, *Public and the Private in Aristotle's Political Philosophy*; Elshtain, *Public Man, Private Woman*; Weintraub and Kuman, *Public and Private*; D'Entrèves and Vogel, *Public and Private*.

121. Sack, *Homo Geographicus*, 2. The earliest use of this compound adjective that I could find appears in Soja, "Socio-Spatial Dialectic." It also appeared in the title of the watershed work by Liggett and Perry, *Spatial Practices: Critical Explorations in Social/Spatial Theory*.

122. Sack, *Homo Geographicus*, 2.

123. Tansey, *Politics*, 1–4.

tools for investigating these elements.[124] There are six specific weaknesses that will be addressed in this study. First, the story of scholarship reveals an overemphasis on the apologetic nature of Luke's politics. The analysis of Luke's political perspective should emphasize insider issues and see politics as the exercise of social power rather than only the actions of official governments. Second, many (exemplified by Kinman) have misinterpreted the entry by setting it alongside disproportionate episodes in royal/imperial politics. Royal indicators appear in Luke's account, but this is the climax of Jesus' movement in the Gospel, preceded by a great deal of material on a smaller scale that leads up to it. Spatial and social factors indicate that the entry is better viewed at the level of local politics. Third, despite groundbreaking work on the public and private spheres of the ancient world (particularly by Neyrey), a wider swath of literary evidence is needed, considering drama, epic, poetry, rhetoric, and history alongside more philosophically oriented works that emerge from a very prescriptive perspective. Fourth, this literary evidence should be supplemented by an investigation of the lived spaces of Luke's milieu available to us in relevant archaeological research. Fifth, Neyrey's classification of space needs further refinement (especially in the public sphere) in order to allow it to reflect the dynamic and fluid social-spatial spheres of the ancient world. Six and finally, much of the recent work drawing on social and spatial theory has surveyed large portions of text (i.e., Luke's portrayal of Paul) rather than exegetically analyzing shorter passages. Luke-Acts presents itself as an excellent candidate for such a social-spatial analysis. Although the Gospel of Luke has many relevant passages, Luke 18:35—19:48 is perhaps one of the most appropriate texts for the consideration of these issues, as will be shown below.

The Text: Luke 18:35—19:48

It is necessary to select a sequence of text that encapsulates Luke's political and spatial perspectives in a representative way in order to carry out this investigation in a focused and effective manner. Selecting a specific unit in Luke's Gospel provides the context for both deep analysis and wide reaching conclusions.[125] While I fully accept the integrated nature of the two volumes of Luke-Acts, I have chosen to focus on the Gospel for the following reasons.[126] First, concentrating on Luke's Gospel will set reasonable limits on the scope of the dissertation. Second, I will argue that 18:35—19:48 serves as a microcosm of the preceding material in the Gospel and as a transition into the passion narrative. Thus, it is relevant to material throughout Luke's Gospel. Third, past interpretations of Luke's political and spatial perspectives have tended to focus more on Acts with some attention to Jesus' trials and a few passages from the Gospel;[127] therefore, it is appropriate to explore

---

124. These new theories and tools will be discussed in depth in ch. 2.

125. My paradigm for this is the way Todd Penner makes an argument for epideictic history as the genre of Luke-Acts based primarily on his analysis of Acts 6:1—8:1 ("In Praise of Christian Origins").

126. Many classic and contemporary studies both defend and employ the unity of Luke-Acts in powerful ways. For two excellent examples, see Cadbury, *Making*; and Tannehill, *Narrative Unity*. Recent attempts to differentiate the two volumes have not been widely accepted. For such an attempt see Parsons and Pervo, *Rethinking*.

127. This is, of course, true of Neyrey's article discussed above. Acts is also weighted more heavily in Walaskay, *"And So We Came to Rome."* The classic statement of the *religio licita* argument generally focuses on

the social and spatial contours of Luke's Gospel in order to complement these previous studies. The final factor is the integrity and importance of Luke's Gospel in his two-volume work. The third Gospel is an integral unit that must be understood in order to grasp the richness of Luke's larger literary and theological enterprise, particularly with regard to the specific topics of public space and local politics. The Gospel is a part of Luke's overall portrayal of the social and spatial development of early Christianity. It is crucial for constructing Luke's political perspective, for in it he narrates the origins and early formation of the movement and institution that grows out of Jesus' actions and leadership. The spatial and political elements of the portrayal of Jesus set narrative trajectories that are carried into the spatial and political portrayal of the early church in Acts.[128] Luke's social and spatial portrayal of Jesus' ministry in the Gospel lays the foundation for the geographical, ethnic, and organizational expansion of the church narrated in Acts.

This study will focus on Luke 18:35—19:48 because it is a representative example of Luke's emphasis on the public sphere and local politics. This section of Luke's Gospel is generally not treated as a unit in Lukan studies,[129] and so its use in this study must be explained. Several commentators cite 17:11 as a landmark in Luke's travel narrative because of the reminder of the journey to Jerusalem.[130] However, an even more important theme in Luke's narrative is sounded in 18:31-34, Jesus' passion in Jerusalem. Luke places the first two passion predictions right on top of one another in ch. 9 (vv. 21-22 and 44-45). He then proceeds with the travel narrative for nine chapters with little explicit mention of the passion.[131] When the reader comes to 18:31-34, the passion prediction stands out as

---

Acts, as in the work of Easton and Haenchen. In his section on "the political apologetic" Conzelmann devotes two pages to the Gospel and four to Acts (*Theology of St. Luke*, 139-40, 141-44). Political interpretations of Luke's Gospel have focused almost exclusively on politics as non-violent, social revolution, as in Yoder, *Politics of Jesus*; and Cassidy, *Jesus, Politics*. Some geographical studies of Luke-Acts have also had a bias toward Acts. See Bachmann, *Jerusalem*; and Scott, "Geographical Horizon."

128. For example, Luke explicitly describes the growth of the Jesus movement from 1 (4:14-15) to 4 (5:10-11) to 5 (5:28) to 12 (6:12-16) to 72 (10:1) to a "multitude" (18:37) in the Gospel and then in Acts from 120 (1:15) to 3,000 (2:41), which increases daily in the Jewish and Gentile worlds (2:47 and 14:1) up to James speaking of "myriads" of Jewish believers in Acts 21:21. Luke's preference for labeling every town in Judea a city (e.g., even Nazareth and Capernaum are called cities in 1:26 and 4:31, respectively) may be a precursor to his emphasis on major urban centers in Acts. The emphasis on the public sphere in Luke may indicate that Luke does in fact consider Paul's synagogue preaching to be public (so Alexander, contra Neyrey).

129. Kinman treats this section as the context for the triumphal entry (*Jesus' Entry*, 67-90), and Lambrecht has suggested that this section might be part of a larger unit ("Reading and Rereading," 585-87). Meynet claims to have discovered a tight chiastic structure in 18:31—19:46 strengthened by the geographical references to Jerusalem and the enumeration of six predictions in both 18:31-34 and 19:41-46 (*Selon Saint Luc*, 2:179). Many commentators make a major break at 19:28, which then begins Jesus's ministry in Jerusalem. See Ernst, *Das Evangelium*, 523; Fitzmyer, *Luke*, 2:1241; Johnson, *Luke*, 295. Green places a minor break here, but asserts (correctly in my opinion) that Jesus' ministry in Jerusalem does not begin in Luke's Gospel until 20:1 (*Luke*, 680, 696).

130. Ernst, *Das Evangelium*, 482; Marshall, *Luke*, 648 (with some reservation); Fitzmyer, *Luke*, 2:1148-49; Green, *Luke*, 615.

131. Less direct reminders of the passion appear in 12:50; 13:32-33; and 17:25.

a clear reminder of what awaits Jesus at the end of his journey. Thus, this third and final prediction probably marks the last stage of Jesus' journey, which then begins in 18:35.[132]

The last pericope of this unit, the entry into Jerusalem, is often assigned to Jesus' ministry in Jerusalem. However, some scholars have argued to include it, or part of it, with what precedes rather than with what follows. I have chosen to include all of ch. 19 for three reasons. First, the entry is tightly connected by Luke to the immediately preceding parable of the nobleman.[133] Second, even though several commentators assign 19:28-48 to Jesus' ministry in Jerusalem because Jesus is approaching the city,[134] Luke does not actually place Jesus *in* Jerusalem until he enters the temple in 19:45. Finally, it appears that Luke has set apart 20:1—21:36 with an inclusio: "Every day he was teaching in the temple... and all the people listened to him" (19:47-48 and 21:37-38). 19:47-48 concludes the unit that starts in 18:35 and flows out of the cleansing of the temple in 19:45-46. Thus, while 19:47-48 is transitional and preparatory, it is more connected to the preceding material than the following. These two verses prepare the audience for the narration of Jesus' teaching in the temple, which commences in 20:1. The role of the final passion prediction in 18:31-34 and the first half of the inclusio in 19:47-48 frames the material between these two markers, and indicates that 18:35—19:48 probably forms a unit in the Gospel narrative.

The contents of 18:35—19:48 reinforce the status of 18:35—19:48 as a unit. With the addition of Zacchaeus and the insertion of the parable of the nobleman here, this section is a distinctively Lukan creation that narrates the final stage of Jesus' journey to Jerusalem. This unit is comprised of at least four identifiable sections, each with its own history of interpretation that will be considered in the following chapters: the healing of the blind beggar (18:35-42), Jesus and Zacchaeus (19:1-10), the parable of the nobleman (19:11-28) and Jesus' entry into Jerusalem including the lament and cleansing (19:29-48). Thus, this unit has a series of representative episodes from Luke's Gospel: a healing, a house/meal scene, a parable, Jesus with his disciples, a prophetic pronouncement, and a prophetic act. The material in this unit contains thematic elements found in every major part of Luke's Gospel. 18:35—19:48 echoes themes about Jesus' Davidic ancestry, not heard since the infancy narrative. The cry at Jesus' entry picks up on the chorus of the angels in 2:14. The miracle at the beginning of the unit and Jesus' dealings with his disciples draw upon the concentration of miracles and the activity of the disciples narrated in chs. 4-10. The scene in Zacchaeus's home recalls the meal scenes found in 7:36-50; 11:37-54; and

---

132. 18:31-34 is a transitional passage that is linked to the sections that precede and follow it. Both Meynet and Lambrecht include it with the material that follows in their breakdowns. It could be included as a representative private scene between Jesus and the twelve, which sets the stage for the immediately following material. However, I have chosen not to include it for the following reasons: it belongs with the previous two pericopes in the Markan order (18:15-17 and 18-30) that Luke deviates from beginning in 18:35; it fits very nicely as a conclusion to Jesus' private discussion with Peter and the disciples in 18:28-30; it does not narrate any part of Jesus' journey as 18:35—19:48 does, but looks directly ahead to the passion narrative; the ἐγένετο δὲ ἐν + infinitive construction in 18:35 can begin a new unit in Luke (c.f. 14:1; 17:11); and finally I will include the transitional closing of this unit (19:47-48) with what precedes rather than with what follows just as I have done here.

133. Many commentators note the connection between the parable of the nobleman and the narration of Jesus' entry. See Marshall, *Luke*, 700; Johnson, "Kingship Parable"; and most recently Denaux, "King-Judge."

134. Marshall, *Luke*, 721; Ernst, *Das Evangelium*, 530-32; Fitzmyer, *Luke*, 2:1260.

14:1–25. Luke inserts the parable to continue the pedagogical aims of the travel narrative, which ends here just as the passion narrative begins. Also, the last stage of Jesus' journey described in this section is more densely saturated with geographical markers than the rest of the travel narrative.[135] Finally, the thread of kingdom language[136] and monetary ethics can be traced through several of the pericopes.[137] Consequently, both the external limits and the internal coherence of this passage commend its status as a literary unit.

In summary, Luke 18:35—19:48 is a plausible unit that exhibits the dynamics of the public, the political, and the private in the Gospel of Luke. First, this section functions as a microcosm of preceding material in the Gospel. It has a series of representative scenes, and it contains a number of themes from earlier parts of the Gospel, including some not heard since the infancy narrative (such as Jesus as the son of David; cf. 1:32–33).[138] Second, this unit concludes the travel narrative and functions as a preparation for the passion narrative. Several other elements indicate this function: the frequent markers of progress toward Jerusalem, Jesus as a royal figure (18:38; 19:38 prepares for 22:29 and 23:37–38, 42), the popular support of Jesus by the crowds (18:43 prepares for 21:38), the reference to the Son of Man (see Jesus' predictions of suffering from 9:22, 44 that connect through 19:10—23:69), an anticipation of the coming discourse on the destruction of Jerusalem (19:41–44 prepares for 21:5–36), and the switch from Pharisees to chief priests/scribes as the primary opponents of Jesus (see 19:39 and 47). Therefore, this unit serves two crucial literary functions in Luke's Gospel. It is a climactic microcosm of the material that precedes it and a preparatory transition into the final events of the passion narrative. This study will explore and defend these functions and build on them to demonstrate how this unit captures the social and spatial nature of Luke's Gospel as a whole.

Finally, this unit lends itself to social-spatial analysis. It has a substantial amount of material that should be considered political in nature: Jesus as the son of David, Jesus' interactions with a tax collector in the midst of Jericho, the parable about the kingdom, the interaction of the "nobleman-king" with his citizens and stewards, Jesus' leadership, the organization of the disciples, the public proclamation of Jesus as king, the Roman sack of Jerusalem, and Jesus' activity in the temple during the feast. The frequency of these political elements is combined with the local settings around Jerusalem that ring with public characteristics: the crowds on the road, the masses of Jericho, the invasion of the

---

135. There is a geographical marker at the beginning of every pericope in this section: 18:35; 19:1, 11, 28, 41, and 45. This was noticed but not further developed by Lambrecht ("Reading Lk 18:31—22:6," 589). This also means that careful attention to the spatial characteristics of the pericopes is in keeping with the contents of this unit.

136. Language that reflects royal or kingdom vocabulary is found explicitly in 18:38–39; 19:11, 12, 14, 15, 27, 38. Meynet organizes his analysis of 18:31—19:46 around the theme of "Jésus roi contesté" (*Selon Saint Luc*, 2:179, 187–89).

137. The blind man is a beggar. Zacchaeus donates to the poor and repays his extortions. The parable concerns ten pounds. Jesus commandeers livestock for God. Finally, Jesus drives out the "sellers" from the temple.

138. Other indicators also qualify it as a microcosm of preceding material: the significance of the healing of the blind (building on 4:18), Luke's preference for placing Jesus in cities (e.g., 4:31; 7:11), the regular role of the crowds (e.g., 5:12; 9:37), and the importance of the βασιλ-theme in Luke (e.g., 4:43; 11:20).

Introduction: Place and Politics in the Study of Luke's Gospel

public through Zacchaeus's act of hospitality, the regional rule of the nobleman, the public proclamation coming down the Mount of Olives, the timing of Passover, and the public nature of the temple. The microcosmic, preparatory, and social-spatial characteristics of this text make it an excellent selection for a focused, but simultaneously wide-ranging, examination of the public and political dimensions of Luke's Gospel.

The Plan and Contributions of This Study

This introductory chapter has set the stage for the following study on place and politics in Luke by retelling the story of scholarship on these issues in Luke-Acts and the NT in general. This has raised specific insights and gaps that this study must take into consideration. This has also led to the selection of a relevant text in Luke 18:35—19:48, which has promise both because of its rich social-spatial elements and its importance in Luke's Gospel. This chapter commented on the emergence of social analysis and spatial theory in recent years and noted the few times it has been applied to NT texts (especially in Acts). We can then move into Part 1 of this study, which will explore the social-spatial milieu of Luke's Gospel in order to prepare for the analysis that follows. Chapter 2 will explore the theoretical models that underlie this study in more detail. It will begin with an examination of Robert David Sack's book *Homo Geographicus*, which forms the primary theoretical basis and is supported by insights from Soja, Hall, and Eulau. After laying out the theoretical framework, chapter 2 will address the dismantling of the public/private dichotomy that has occurred in recent scholarship. Finally, it will present a new classification of social-spatial spheres in the ancient world that will be used throughout this study. Chapter 3 will cast a wide net, examining a variety of literary and archaeological evidence from the Roman, Jewish, and Hellenistic realms. This will substantiate and flesh out the classification of the public-private spectrum provided in chapter 2. Chapter 4 will investigate more deeply two relevant works, Plutarch's *Praecepta* and book 4 of Apollonius's *Vita Apollonii*, in order to cast more light on the local public sphere and unofficial public sphere respectively. Part 1 will both sharpen the categories of the classification and provide a sound basis for the exegesis in Part 2.

Part 2 will analyze the social-spatial characteristics of each pericope in Luke 18:35—19:48. The healing of the blind beggar (chapter 5: Luke 18:35–43) hints at the political aspects of Jesus' movement and paints a public scenario for the miracle as Jesus enters Jericho. Jesus meets Zacchaeus in 19:1–10 (chapter 6). This story initiates the increasing presence of local political officials and displays how the public sphere (crowds on the road in Jericho) can invade the private sphere (Zacchaeus's home). While in Zacchaeus's home, Jesus tells a parable filled with public and political details to a large and diverse crowd (chapter 7: Luke 19:11–27). Finally, Jesus processes to Jerusalem (chapter 8: Luke 19:28–48), where he is publicly greeted by his own disciples and opposed by the local political leaders. In each chapter, the exegesis will focus on details and hints in the text that create scenes saturated with the public sphere and local politics.

Part 3 will examine three arenas of ramifications based on the emphasis on the public sphere and local politics in Luke 18:35—19:48. Chapter 9 will build on the microcosmic and transitional functions of this passage to demonstrate that the public sphere and local politics color stories throughout the Gospel. It will also compare the social-spatial character of Luke's portrayal of Jesus to those of Mark and Matthew, highlighting how Luke redacted received traditions to achieve the public and political nature of his narrative. Chapter 10 will review the contributions of this study and draw out several implications for the history of early Christianity and for contemporary Christian theology and practice.

This study aims to make contributions on three levels, correlating to the three parts. First, it will show that social-spatial spheres in the Hellenistic-Roman world were fluid and contested. Thus, a nuanced and flexible public-private spectrum is necessary to analyze and understand the extant texts and archaeology. Second, it will offer fresh exegetical insights into the material in 18:35—19:48 from a social-spatial perspective, indicating how ancient authors used scenes and textual clues to create the social-spatial contours of their narratives. This will enrich the practice of social-scientific exegesis of the NT and exemplify how this same approach may be taken on with other texts. Third, it will claim that Luke's Gospel as a whole emphasizes the unofficial public sphere and local politics. Luke redacted these traditions to move against the increasing privatization of Roman life and the related predominance of the house church in early Christianity. He portrays Jesus achieving honor in the public sphere in order to demonstrate to the urban Christians of his day how they might live and organize themselves as a sect in growing cities where politics was becoming more and more oligarchical and privacy was becoming a commodity of the wealthy. Finally, Luke's public and political portrayal of Jesus calls Christians in our (post)modern Western context to struggle against the shrinking public sphere of our day through boundary-crossing hospitality and redemptive engagement with local politics both within and beyond the church.

PART ONE

Reading Luke's Social-Spatial Context

2

From This Place

A Theoretical Framework for the Social-Spatial Analysis of Luke

Introduction

GIVEN THE COMPLEX NATURE OF WHAT IS PUBLIC, POLITICAL, AND PRIVATE, COMBINED with the relative lack of careful attention to these social-spatial categories in NT scholarship, this study will establish a critical and contextual classification of space for Luke's Gospel. This requires three things: an informed theoretical perspective, an adequate system of classification, and broad and specific comparative material. The first third of this chapter will describe several scholars and works that contribute to the eclectic theoretical perspective of this study. However, this study does not delve into unplowed ground. Unfortunately, most previous studies of the public and private spheres in the ancient world have relied on a stark dichotomization of these two spheres. The current study will argue that this dichotomization is not supported by theoretical developments (or by much of the available evidence from the ancient world). Thus, the second third of this chapter will serve to dismantle this dichotomy. Once the theoretical ground is clear, we can then offer a new classification system that emerges from the theoretical perspective presented below. Both the theoretical perspective and the new classification system will be substantiated and exemplified by the comparative material that follows in chapters 3 and 4.

A Theoretical Perspective

Sack's Homo Geographicus

Sack's book, *Homo Geographicus*, provides the primary theoretical perspective for this dissertation. Sack, trained as a geographer, has distinguished himself as a critical philosopher of space and place in a series of important works.[1] His writings are a part of a larger trend to reassert the role of space and place in critical theory after being brushed aside by historical, philosophical, and social perspectives for many years.[2] Sack does not devote extensive discussions to the categories of public, political, or private

---

1. Sack, *Conceptions of Space* and *Human Territoriality*. These books prepared the way for his work in *Homo Geographicus*.

2. The reassertion of space in intellectual and political currents is hailed as one of the great scholarly contributions of the twentieth century by Soja, *Thirdspace*, 1–2.

PART ONE: READING LUKE'S SOCIAL-SPATIAL CONTEXT

in *Homo Geographicus*, but the model he proffers is a powerful tool for explaining the dynamics of these spheres. Sack presents a "relational framework" that draws together nature, meaning, and social relations in a way that emphasizes the importance of place, increases our awareness of diverse situational dynamics, and forms a practical frame for moral action.[3] He claims that grounding the three forces of nature, meaning, and social relations in the specificities of real geography is the most viable way to integrate them and create a well-rounded framework for moral reflection and decision making.[4] Early in the book Sack presents his relational framework through the diagram below.

Figure 2.1: Sack's Framework[5]

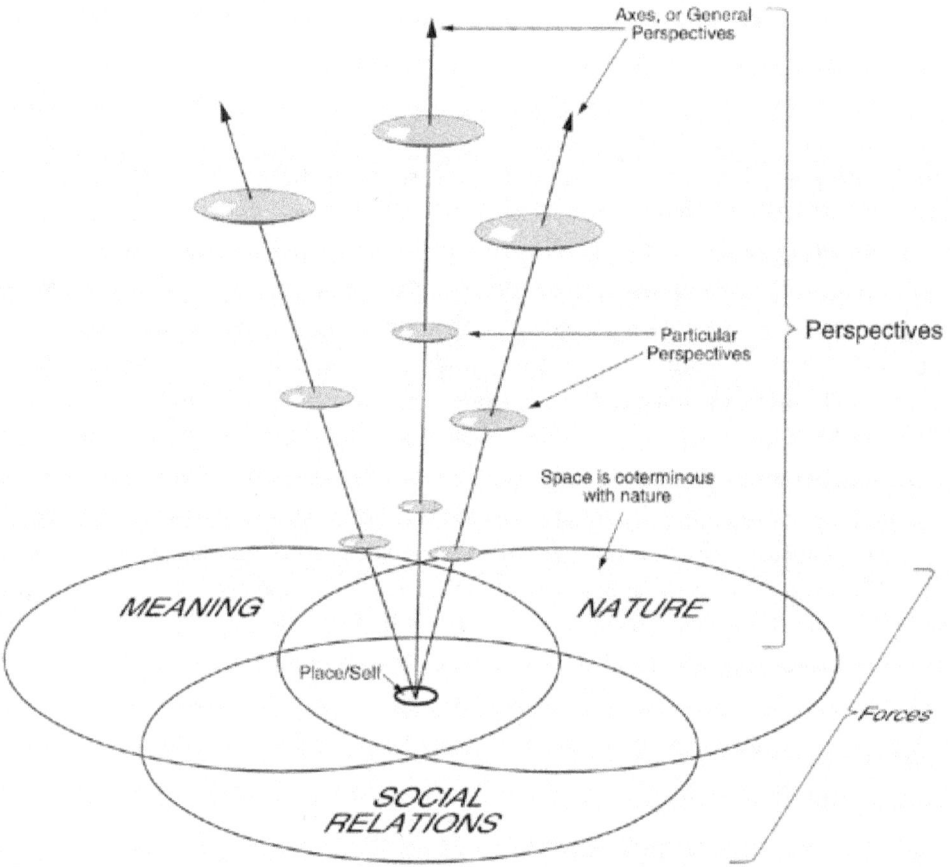

The second chapter of *Homo Geographicus* discusses the proposed framework in detail. Sack claims that all actions and all perspectives emerge from particular places be-

---

3. Sack would wholeheartedly concur with much of the work of Edward T. Hall. For instance, Hall states "it is impossible to separate the individual from the environment in which he [sic] functions" (*Beyond Culture*, 100).

4. Sack, *Homo Geographicus*, 53.

5. Ibid., 59. This illustration is used with the permission of the publisher.

cause places draw together the influences of nature and culture.⁶ Furthermore, culture is a composite of social relations and shared meanings, and so he divides these into separate and identifiable forces. The force of space is largely coterminous nature. Space simply exists and is part of the natural world that human agents encounter (the focus of the natural sciences), and it acts as a force upon human existence.⁷ Nature affects us by means of the environment that surrounds, limits, and enables our lives.⁸ Next, social relations (one part of culture and the focus of the social sciences) addresses ways that human beings interact with each other. These interactions tend to follow norms and serve both to constrain and facilitate our life together.⁹ Finally, the force of meaning draws attention to our unique role as *thinking* beings, those who can assign meaning and mentally construct the world (the focus of disciplines like philosophy and psychology). Again, these meanings tend to follow patterns and have the power to order the world.¹⁰ Sack states that these three forces both come together at and are affected by the forces of self and place. The self is a human agent that interacts with the various forces. Sack says it best in the first sentence of his book: "We humans are geographical beings transforming the earth and making it into a home, and that transformed world affects who we are."¹¹ Thus, place and self are "mutually constitutive," for both affect the other.¹² Place is culturally constructed, for human agents turn spaces into places that are delimited from other places, are guided by specific rules, and carry meanings in and of themselves.¹³ Therefore, there are five forces at work in Sack's framework: nature, social relations, meaning, place, and self. This study will focus on how the forces of nature (the physical setting), social relations (interactions among people), and meaning (cultural cues) locate particular places along the public-private spectrum. These locations are also affected by the main character of our study, Jesus, whose actions both shape and are shaped by the culturally constructed places that Luke narrates.

The forces interact to create specific placements of the self, and these interactions are viewed from perspectives. These perspectives are the axes that emerge vertically from place/self on the diagram, and "they represent our capacity increasingly to distance ourselves from the world and to reflect on our place in it."¹⁴ Perspectives are particular modes of awareness, and Sack cites three: the discursive/scientific perspective, the aesthetic perspective, and the moral perspective. Sack claims that he begins with the discursive/scientific perspective as he analytically lays out his framework, but the climax of his book deals with the moral and aesthetic axes.¹⁵ Furthermore, each axis has varying levels of abstraction. Some are lower on the axis and thus closer to experience and more partial. Others

6. Ibid., 24–25.
7. Ibid., 31.
8. Ibid., 38–39.
9. Ibid., 40.
10. Ibid., 44–45.
11. Ibid., 1.
12. Ibid., 58–59.
13. Ibid., 32.
14. Ibid., 29.
15. Ibid., 58–59.

are higher up on the axis and thus more abstract and objective.[16] Sack aims at providing tools to enable a critical awareness of perspectives by showing how various forces and places shape them. Sack convincingly argues that this framework, unified by geographical awareness, offers a thorough and balanced way to consider the interrelated structure and dynamic impact of each of the forces on human life and decision making.[17]

Sack takes a philosophical position "that strives to be rational and realistic, but takes the necessity of our differences and situatedness seriously—navigating between the arrogance of modernity and the relativizing tendencies of postmodernity."[18] Others, such as Tuan and Giddens, have labeled this position "high modernism," while Sack prefers to call it a "geographically aware position."[19] This philosophical perspective adopts a nuanced form of realism (the world actually exists apart from our perceptions of it) and values the quest for greater objectivity and impartiality, while realizing that such a quest takes place primarily through genuine dialogue with contextualized perspectives. This philosophical perspective also informs the "relational" nature of Sack's framework. Sack constantly asserts that the forces he describes, while being separated for the sake of analysis, are always interdependent and mutually constitutive.[20] This means that Sack resists the tendency for any one factor to completely explain or subsume the other forces that influence human beings. Disciplinary ethnocentrism often reduces all other aspects of human existence to subsets or effects of its special focus, and such specialization has tended to fragment knowledge and moral awareness.[21] Sack proposes the framework in *Homo Geographicus* as a solution to this, claiming that an awareness of place allows human beings to see the interdependent influence of various forces on their lives and thus become better equipped moral agents.[22] This moral orientation is shared by the present study of the public, political, and private elements of Luke's Gospel because it will close by reflecting on the significance of this analysis for contemporary Christian praxis and theology.

Granting the central position of Sack's work to this study, it is still necessary to make a few adjustments to his framework in order to fill it out and attune it to the study of Luke's Gospel. Sack identifies three overlapping forces affecting place/self: nature, social relations, and meaning. Edward Soja, another pioneer in the contemporary study of spatiality, has adduced time as a constitutive aspect of human experience, which appropriately adds a temporal force to Sack's framework.[23] Additionally, because Luke's Gospel is a theological

16. Ibid., 29.
17. Ibid., 60–87.
18. Ibid., 7.
19. Ibid.
20. Ibid., 30, 34, 91.

21. Ibid., 12, 35–36. For example, Sack points out that in the absence of geographical considerations, social science can reduce human thought and the natural world either to being effects of social forces or the inert raw material of social forces. Sack uses "sociology of knowledge" and Marxism as examples of this tendency, found in other disciplines as well, to reduce all other factors to one overriding concern (42–44).

22. Thus, Sack's approach resonates with Robbins' goal of fostering an integrative "interpretive analytics," which brings together various disciplinary specialties. See Robbins, *Tapestry*, 11–13.

23. Soja, *Thirdspace*, 30–31. Soja speaks of time as "historicality" in his "trialectics of being," which also includes "sociality" and "spatiality" (and thus omits the arena of "meaning" included by Sack). Such an addition

narrative about Jesus the Messiah, it is reasonable to include religion in the list of forces to be considered. Sack would most likely consider religion to be a part of culture, perhaps a subset of meaning, but its prominence in Luke's Gospel calls for special attention.[24] The force of religious belief and practice as well as the activity of divine beings/persons must be added to Sack's framework in order to adequately examine the nature of Luke's theological narrative. This results in the following list of interactive forces: nature, meaning, social relations, time, religion, place, and self.

As stated above, Sack does not address the public-private spectrum directly. Then, why use his theoretical framework as a heuristic lens for this study? First, his theoretical presentation claims that all of the forces come together in specific locations to shape the mutually constitutive place and self. This study assumes that Luke's use of place affects his portrayal of Jesus and that the actions of Jesus draw on and transform the places presented in the narrative. Thus, this study is in deep theoretical agreement with Sack's framework and is simply looking at the interaction of all the forces on place and self from the perspective of the public-private spectrum, which forms a new axis of consideration (one closely related to the moral perspective). Second, Sack's framework is not only theoretical but also heuristic. That is, it provides a means of analysis for Luke's narrative. One can identify the various forces at work in Luke's narrative to see how they work together to create a particular portrayal of Jesus in a particular type of place. More broadly, this heuristic lens will also guide and help to shape the presentation of the new classification system of public and private space in the Hellenistic-Roman world that will appear later in this chapter. This study will pay special attention to the forces of nature, meaning, social relations, time, religion, and especially human agency and place in order to exegetically analyze Luke 18:35—19:48. Thus, it is social-spatial exegesis, for it attends to the forces as they affect the mutually constitutive place and self that are at the heart of Sack's framework and also this study.

Scale and Political Geography

Chapter 1 argued that one of the problems inherent in Kinman's study (*Jesus' Entry*) is that he fails to attend to the issue of scale. He compares Jesus' entry into Jerusalem with much larger scale arrivals like Pilate's assize and Roman triumphs. This is not only comparing apples and oranges (two different kinds of fruit) but also comparing grapes and grapefruit (two different fruit of very different sizes). Not only is Jesus' entry not an official political event (like the assize or triumph), but it also occurs at a much smaller scale and so expectations must be adjusted accordingly. Recent work in the realm of political geography has dealt with the important, complicated, and elusive issue of scale. We now turn to their work to illuminate the idea of politics and its intersection with scale analysis.

---

is fitting to Sack's work because many of his illustrative examples also involve the factor of time. He frequently includes temporal issues in his illustration of a dinner meeting at his home in Sack, *Homo Geographicus*, 98–105. Time, along with the other forces described by Sack, will help to define the classification system presented below.

24. The addition of religion as a force in light of the special concerns of Luke's gospel is similar to the addition of "Sacred Texture" to the consideration of religious texts in Robbins, *Texture of Texts*, 120–31.

PART ONE: READING LUKE'S SOCIAL-SPATIAL CONTEXT

We begin with the work of Heinz Eulau, who began wrestling with the issues of scale and politics in the 1970s. Eulau eschews conceptual definitions of politics in favor of behavior descriptions: "What makes man's behavior political is that he rules and obeys, persuades and compromises, promises and bargains, coerces and represents, fights and fears."[25] Thus, Eulau's behaviorist definition of politics fits well into Sack's force of social relations, while focusing specifically on behavior that deals with group roles and decision making at various levels that affect how people relate to one another.[26] Eulau also agrees with Sack's argument against disciplinary reductionism, claiming that one must take an interdisciplinary approach to politics.[27] Finally, Eulau exemplifies the practical, eclectic, and corrigible approach to theory taken by this study by pointing out that theory and research are interdependent—theoretical perspectives shape fruitful research that then comes to bear on the theoretical formulations.[28] Now we turn to Eulau's comments on scale. He discusses various political strata, sets of horizontal relationships in which political behavior takes place. He points out that various social orders have different degrees of openness or mobility, and we add that the ancient Hellenistic-Roman world had limited mobility. Given the reality of these strata, he cautions that "to make inferences about integration from the larger to the smaller unit, or from the smaller to the larger, is fallacious."[29] We should explore the linkages between different strata and the impact that they have on each other, but we cannot reason by analogy across various scales.[30] Thus, when analyzing Luke's narrative, one must attend to scale in order to adduce appropriate comparative material. Eulau posits a "micro-macro continuum" (much like the public-private spectrum of this study) where one enters analysis at a particular level while always attending to its relationship to a variety of other strata.[31]

The discipline of political geography emerged in the late 1970s and early 80s and has flourished since then.[32] In the late 90s a number of scholars turned their eyes upon the uncritical use of the scale in political geography and have brought forth several helpful insights. Most political geographers now agree that scale is socially constructed rather than a "given" of political landscapes.[33] Furthermore, while scale as area and scale as level dominated previous studies in political geography, more recent and critical analysis of this concept emphasizes that scale must also be understood as a bounded yet porous network of relationships.[34] Finally, scales should not be viewed as self-contained social systems;

---

25. Eulau, *Politics*, 20.
26. Ibid., 33–34.
27. Ibid., 26.
28. Ibid., 29.
29. Ibid., 78.
30. Ibid.
31. Ibid., 90.
32. One might point to the inception of *Political Geography Quarterly* in 1982, which is now published as *Political Geography* and has eight volumes per year.
33. As examples, see Marston, "Social Construction of Scale," 219–22; and Howitt, "Scale," 138.
34. Cox, "Spaces of Dependence," 3, 21; and Howitt, "Scale," 143.

they always exist in relation to smaller and larger strata.[35] Often, scale becomes apparent as groups (or "relational networks") work to secure their interests in cooperation or conflict with other centers of social power.[36] Scale comes to be as specific cultural contexts create and perpetuate interrelated levels of relationships.[37] Scale is commonly described with labels like local, urban, regional, national, international, and global, but these labels are dependent upon the construction of scale in context. Therefore, when designing a classification system for the analysis of Luke's Gospel, one must attend to the constructions and identifications of scale within Luke's opus and the larger milieu of the Hellenistic-Roman world. To distinguish and analyze these scales one should look for the social and spatial boundaries of relational networks and how these relate to other networks, networks that are smaller and larger both in terms of space (geographical territory) and society (political power).

High and Low Context in Hall

Most of the regions and people groups of the ancient Mediterranean shared a number of unstated assumptions, perspectives, and cultural clues (especially in comparison with the modern West). Much of this shared, internalized cultural information need not and would not be stated outright in any written or spoken message. This means that Luke (and most other authors of his day) would not categorically assert that a given action was done in public or private or that it occurred at a local or imperial scale. Rather, Luke assumes that his audience naturally and correctly assesses placement of an event on the public-private spectrum (and at the appropriate scale) based on implicit clues provided in the narrative. However, as cultural outsiders, modern exegetes often cannot immediately identify these clues. This is why careful social-spatial exegesis is necessary. The interpreter must sift through the clues in Luke's Gospel in order to deduce how public or private a given scene is, and from there infer how Luke has deployed or modified ancient conceptions of place and scale in his portrayal of Jesus. Edward Hall offers a key theoretical insight to assist this task.

At the heart of *Beyond Culture*, Hall addresses the role of context in human life, thought, and behavior. He distinguishes "high-context" from "low-context" societies, quickly granting that cultures exist all over the scale in between these two extremes.[38] In high-context societies, a communicator expects that most of the information of any message is either implied by the setting or already internalized in the recipient (like the ancient Mediterranean world). Low-context societies are the opposite. Most of the information must be stated explicitly in the content of the language in order to make up for the lack of shared settings, assumptions, or perspectives (more like contemporary America). In high-context systems, a speaker will assume that the listener can and does intuit the heart of the message based on indirect clues. To provide more information than necessary or

---

35. Howitt, "Scale as Relation," 52–53.
36. Cox, "Spaces of Dependence," 15, 19.
37. Howitt, "Scale," 151.
38. Hall, *Beyond Culture*, 91.

to proclaim explicitly the main point is an insult to the listener's cultural and intellectual competence. On the other hand, in low-context systems, the speaker must assume that the listener knows little or nothing and therefore must state all pertinent details. If the speaker does not fully articulate all the relevant information, the listener might infer that she or he is ignorant, lazy or, at the very worst, deceptive. Thus, the content of a message and the understanding of that message will vary according to where a given culture falls on the low-context/high-context scale.[39] Most of the ancient Greco-Roman world consisted of low-context societies. With the increased mobility and communication capabilities that burgeoned under the Roman Empire, pluralism increased and the overall system was forced to move in a lower context direction.[40]

Because a high-context mode of expression ruled most of the communication that took place in the ancient world, authors or speakers rarely state explicitly what those shared assumptions about public and private space were. In part, this provides an even more fluid dynamic where social-spatial zones can be contested because of the lack of official delineation, but occasionally these implicit cultural codes become explicit. Dionysius of Halicarnassus provides a wonderful example of the high-context nature of public and private matters in the following quotation where he criticizes the style of a line penned by Plato:

> "These men have already received from us everything that they deserved; and having received it, they are now going their appointed way . . ." This beginning is both admirable and appropriate to the subject by employing a beautiful manner of expression with dignity and harmony. But what follows these opening words simply does not match them: ". . . escorted publicly [κοινῇ] by the state and privately [ἰδίᾳ] by their family." For when it says that those who were being buried had received everything due to them, this also *implies* [ἐνῆν] that their bodies had been escorted publicly [δημοσίᾳ] and privately [ἰδίᾳ] to the burial site, so it was unnecessary to say the same thing again . . . Therefore, Plato, it was superfluous to add anything further. (*Dem.* 24, emphasis added)[41]

Dionysius critiques Plato according to the standards of high-context communication. Readers prefer brevity of style and implicit information over unnecessary specifications. Dionysius expects that any competent reader would naturally deduce the presence of a crowd made up of both citizens and family members at any state funeral. He objects to this addition on the grounds that Plato should know that all of his readers would already know about the public and private aspects of any state funeral, and thus he should leave such details unstated unless he wishes to draw special attention to them (which he does not do here). Dionysius's comments reveal the challenges of constructing a contextual classification of the spheres and scales applicable to Luke's Gospel. Most authors in the ancient

---

39. Ibid., 91–92, 101, 113.

40. Take, for example, the parenthetical comment in Mark 7:3–4. Here, the author or editor feels compelled to explain Jewish purification rituals to the target audience. Such information would have been assumed by most ancient authors in their high-context situations, but this explanation shows how a low-context awareness was beginning to emerge.

41. Dionysius is mounting a biased attack against a little known work of Plato (the *Menexenus*) in order to later exalt the style of Demosthenes. See the introductory comments in Usher, *Dionysius*, 1:234.

world assumed that their audience intuitively understood the nature and ramifications of public and private activities. When authors state these characteristics definitively (or at all), they either must have specific intentions for doing so, or they are writing in poor taste. Thus, the interpreter is left in a double quandary. Not only does Luke not obviously state what is public and private, but it is also very rare to find an ancient writer who provides the key to decode the set of clues that identifies the public and private spheres. The same can be said about scale. Therefore, a carefully researched classification framework is necessary because no ancient insider from Luke's high-context milieu has provided it for us. The following chapters will employ a broad survey of ancient literary materials, archaeological remains, and a close examination of two works comparable to Luke's Gospel to help substantiate and flesh out this framework.

Conclusion

The theoretical perspective of this study brings together a cluster of mutually supporting and illuminating theories and methods. Sack's framework provides the foundation of this study's perspective. Sack articulates the various forces and perspectives at work in our understanding of place and self that will guide this study. Sack's theoretical insights will be buttressed by the work of political geographers on scale. Eulau and others help us to see that we must perceive on what level of scale we are focusing our attention, recognize the cultural construction of scale, and address the interrelatedness of various identifiable scales. Finally, Hall's anthropological analysis helps us to wrestle with the implicit evidence on the public-private spectrum that we find in the high-context world of Luke's Gospel. We must be prepared to use the tools provided by this theoretical framework to understand the social-spatial realities that affected and are expressed in Luke's Gospel.

Dismantling the Public/Private Dichotomy

The categories of public and private are often constructed and applied as polar opposites. Yet, the previous material has hinted that such a dichotomy is neither theoretically sound nor a useful heuristic for exploring the ancient world. Neyrey's studies (while groundbreaking and insightful) exemplify the use of the public/private dichotomy. He makes clear statements that divulge his methodological orientation. First, he says, "The ancient world shared a common gender stereotype, that is, a descriptive and often proscriptive sketch of gender-specific roles, tasks, tools, and places."[42] Second, and perhaps more to the point he also says, "We saw above that the classification of space tends to be expressed in terms of binary opposites, which is an endemic mode of thought in the ancient world."[43] Thus, it appears from Neyrey's methodological perspective that the social-spatial world of antiquity (from the fifth century BCE to the second century CE) shared one enduring, consistent, and rigid dichotomy that defined places, genders, and social interactions. This section will dismantle that dichotomy, drawing on the work of anthropologists, sociologist, feminists, ancient historians, and the scholars discussed above. They will offer war-

42. Neyrey, "Jesus," 43.
43. Neyrey, "In Public," 75.

rants for moving to the methodological use of a public-private *spectrum* rather than the public/private *dichotomy*.

Lloyd and the Critique of Anthropologists and Sociologists

Neyrey cites two works to support his claim that binary opposites were endemic in the ancient world. The first is *Polarity and Analogy* by G. E. R. Lloyd.[44] This study focuses on *early* Greek thought: from the earliest Greek philosophers up to Aristotle.[45] Also, Lloyd is clear that most of these oppositional forms of thought were derived from and applied to speculative cosmology, then to the natural world, and finally to physiological matters as well.[46] Such opposites in gender physiology could lead to social prescriptions, but Lloyd's study focuses on the speculative rather than the social use of these polarities. Lloyd tips his hat to the dualistic structural anthropology of Lévi-Strauss (as well as Durkheim and others), claiming that many societies structure reality according to binary opposites, possibly on the basis of a fundamental division between the sacred and the profane.[47]

There are three significant problems with Neyrey's citation of Lloyd's work as a justification for a public/private *dichotomy*. The first is the date. This study is focused on the earliest of Greek philosophy (sixth–fourth centuries BCE) with little correlation to later times, especially after the influx of Roman influence. The second is the deductive and speculative nature of the sources for these categories. Lloyd, and Neyrey in turn, relies primarily on writers with a philosophical bent with some citations from rhetoricians.[48] Neyrey, however, is making claims about the social world, not speculations about the cosmos. The final, and perhaps most weighty, issue is the dependence on dualistic modes of analysis indebted to the tradition of structural anthropology, which is commonly attributed to Lévi-Strauss.[49] Several ethnographers and theoreticians in sociology and anthropology have argued that the structural analysis of culture and myth according to abstract binary polarities (based largely on Saussure's theory of language) has contributed important knowledge of the human condition but carries inherent methodological flaws that must be diagnosed and corrected.[50]

Many authors have criticized the dualistic paradigm. First, structuralism often leads to the loss of history because of the built-in tendency to prioritize all-encompassing,

---

44. Lloyd, *Polarity and Analogy*.

45. Foley notes transformations in the nature/culture and public/private dichotomies that occurred after the golden age of classical ("Conceptions of Women," 145, 149).

46. Lloyd, *Polarity*, 7, 12.

47. Ibid., 19–41.

48. For example, Neyrey primarily relies on authors like Aristotle, Xenophon, Philo, Plato, Aeschines, and Lysias in key sections of his articles.

49. While Neyrey does not specifically cite or directly borrow from any structural anthropologists, the dualistic structures that are common in his work (honor:shame, male:female, public:private) do bear strong resemblances to this intellectual tradition.

50. There is no doubt that the tradition and practice of structural anthropology is still alive and well in works like Maybury-Lewis and Almagor, *Attraction of Opposites*; and Hénaff, *Claude Lévi-Strauss*. The main point here is to show that there has been significant scholarly criticism of this paradigm that merits a fresh look at the evidence.

unconscious structures and relegate actual events to mere enactments of that system or inconsequential accidents of history. Marshall Sahlins begins his study of the Sandwich Islands by saying, "Structural anthropology was founded in a binary opposition . . . a radical opposition to history."[51] He maintains that structuralism was brought into anthropology with all of its theoretical limitations intact.[52] Sahlins argues for a much more reciprocal relationship between structure and human practice in his study, claiming that culture does set the conditions for historical practice, but that such practice can reformulate and even dissolve those precedent structures.[53] Marvin Harris lodges a similar, but much more scathing, critique from a materialist perspective.[54] Harris directly attacks Lévi-Strauss's lack of attention to material detail and his willingness to dismiss or methodologically override historical evidence. Most of his critiques are enmeshed in complicated anthropological analysis. For example, he debates Lévi-Strauss on the meaning of certain clam appendages in similar myths told by the indigenous peoples of British Columbia. While Lévi-Strauss claims the alterations are due to certain binary structural transformations, Harris convincingly shows that the changes are based rather on the environmental location of the people groups and their use of particular animal parts.[55] Structuralism appears to be prone to losing historical detail in its oppositional analysis, a flaw that must be corrected in our analysis of Luke's Gospel and its milieu.

In addition to these concrete critiques, various theoreticians (who are also prominent ethnographers) have taken issue with the use of structural dichotomies in social analysis. Pierre Bourdieu asserts that anthropologists as outsiders have habitually reduced culture to a repertoire of rules that are followed with only the occasional, anomalous exception.[56] He observes that this dangerously oversimplifies the art of cultural practices in which strategies are deployed in various contexts within systems to achieve certain ends, sometimes successfully and sometimes unsuccessfully.[57] Unfortunately, such rules have generally led to models, which are often reified into inviolable culture codes.[58] For example, in the case of honor/shame systems in the Mediterranean, human practices enter the murky domain of timing, misconstrual, contextual exigencies, and dramatic variability. Thus, Bourdieu says it is better to speak of a *sense* of honor rather than a *code* of honor in these societies.[59] Ultimately, anthropologists need analytical tools to explicate the relationship of structure and practices (not just the structure as an abstract constant).[60] Such tools would reveal the potentialities of structure, the variegation of application in practice, and the enculturated dispositions that help agents improvise appropriate practices in an infinite variety of

---

51. Sahlins, *Historical Metaphors*, 3.
52. Ibid., 6.
53. Ibid., 8.
54. Harris, *Cultural Materialism*, 165–215.
55. See ibid., 202–15.
56. Bourdieu, *Outline*, 2.
57. Ibid., 6–8.
58. Ibid., 10.
59. Ibid., 15.
60. Ibid., 21.

particular contexts.⁶¹ This is Bourdieu's theory of practice, and the classification presented in this study seeks to embrace this kind of dynamic analysis. Anthony Giddens has also called for methodological corrections to the structuralist paradigm from the perspective of sociology. He too points out that structuralism privileges the generalized collective in the abstraction of polarities, viewing most human events as idiosyncratic and radically contingent.⁶² Such structures are real and should be considered, but overemphasizing them can erase real human agents and the dynamics of power relationships. Similar to Bourdieu, Giddens calls for sociologists to return to a genuine consideration of reflexive, capable human agents in their study of culture and society.⁶³ Binary polarities do exist and do serve as useful heuristic tools to a degree, but it is necessary to move beyond the methodological limitations they bear to a more nuanced and comprehensive mode of social analysis.

Cohen and the Critique of Feminists and Herzfeld

Neyrey's other citation supporting the endemic nature of binary opposites in the ancient world draws on David Cohen's *Law, Sexuality, and Society*. Neyrey claims that the widespread division of males and females in the Mediterranean world undergirds his analysis.⁶⁴ Oddly, Cohen's work itself (along with several other studies) actually challenges the polarization of male and female, public and private. Cohen *begins* with the dichotomy of public and private in his study of sexual comportment in classical Athens, claiming that "we find the antithesis of private (*idios*) and public (*demosios*) everywhere in classical Greek literature from Homer onwards."⁶⁵ However, he very quickly qualifies this position when commenting on his very first example on the following page: "A passage in Demosthenes' attack on his enemy, Medias, shows the manipulability of these labels which individuals attached to roles that could be assumed and discarded, determining the interests which came into play."⁶⁶ Cohen takes the public/private dichotomy as his starting point but proceeds to explain that these categories are fluid and malleable. Cohen argues that the categories of public and private were not abstract absolutes consistently applied to all cultural roles, tasks, and places in classical Athens. On the contrary, "it is the relational quality of the public/private dichotomy which accounts for the fluidity and makes it so easy for a speaker to manipulate these categories for his particular rhetorical purposes."⁶⁷

---

61. Ibid., 76–83.

62. Giddens, *Central Problems*, 24. He points out that Lévi-Strauss recognizes the existence of historical events and human agents, but often explicitly brackets them out in search of the structures at work (21).

63. Ibid., 39–40, 253. He posits three levels of analysis in his theoretical perspective: Structure—organized rules of social systems (emphasized by structuralism and in Neyrey's studies); System—repeated relations between groups or individuals that become regular social practices; and Structuration—conditions that govern the continuity and transformation of structures and systems (ibid., 65–73).

64. Neyrey, "In Public," 83–84.

65. Cohen, *Law*, 70.

66. Ibid., 71. This is buttressed by a citation of Bourdieu's own similar analysis of the labels of public and private among the people of Kabyle in the Mediterranean (see further on p. 78).

67. Ibid., 77.

Similarly, in agreement with this study's expansion of the public/private classification, he says, "The public sphere is larger than politics and the private sphere is more extensive than households."[68] Cohen also relies strongly on the work of Bourdieu and Giddens in the presentation of his methodology where he examines anthropological work on contemporary Mediterranean societies to show how agents manipulate binary social norms to their own ends in particular contexts. In his methodological section he states, "While speaking of a public-private dichotomy may prove useful, it should not lead to formulaic rigidity and overgeneralization."[69] Cohen prefers the language of "complementary opposition," which helps to express the interconnected and intersecting nature of these categories.[70] To cite Cohen as a supporter of endemic binary oppositions misrepresents the main thrust of his work, which is to explicate the fluid, manipulatable, and spectral nature of these categories.

Neyrey also relies heavily on the binary opposition of male and female in antiquity, a theme that is pertinent to Cohen's study of sexuality and adultery as well.[71] Here again, their perspectives differ. Neyrey maintains the absolute gender division of roles, tasks, tools, and places in the articles discussed above, using the language of "stereotype." Variations from these codes are viewed as cultural aberrations introduced in early Christianity (as with the woman in John 4). While Cohen admits that the analogous opposition of male/female and public/private is a fair generalization, he also asserts that "one cannot base the opposition of the female domestic sphere to the male public sphere on any absolute spatial, economic, or social criteria."[72] On the contrary, modern and ancient evidence presents women in alternative outdoor public spaces in local neighborhoods where their behavior could be observed,[73] and the general separation of genders does not necessarily entail the seclusion of women who often participate in a wide variety of extra-domestic activities.[74]

Feminist anthropologists and historians are also moving away from the dichotomization of public and private. Neyrey also cites the work of Helene Foley, who, like Lloyd, makes use of dichotomies drawn from the work of Lévi-Strauss, even while regularly noting their limitations in the course of her analysis.[75] Foley's very corrigible dichotomies make her interpretation of women in Greek drama more convincing, but she is still open to some of the critiques of structuralism discussed above. Others echo Cohen by insisting that the dichotomization of male/female and public/private must be qualified and cor-

68. Ibid., 78.

69. Ibid., 41.

70. Ibid., 41–42.

71. Neyrey, "Jesus," 44–45, 49–53; and Neyrey, "In Public," 83–85. Neyrey later cites other articles that examine other binary opposites that were applied to males and females. See Ortner, "Is Female to Male"; and Foley, "Conceptions of Women."

72. Cohen, *Law*, 45.

73. Ibid., 47–48.

74. Ibid., 149–54.

75. Foley, "Conceptions of Women," 139–46. She emphasizes the limitations of the nature/culture dichotomy but sees more promise in the public/private opposition. However, she notes that most women protagonists in Athenian dramas invert the dichotomy, revealing that the polarity does not fully hold at the level of practice or of ideal (152–54).

rected. Lamphere (who edited the book containing an essay by Ortner, which is also cited by Neyrey) says in a later essay, "Many of us have tired of the domestic-public dichotomy. We feel it is a constraining 'trap,' while new approaches try to get away from dichotomous thinking."[76] Several recent studies of women in Latin America have argued that the public/private dichotomy is often referred to by anthropologists and cultural insiders but fails to capture the diversity and complexity of actual social and spatial practice.[77] Feminist scholars admit the provisional usefulness of these binary opposites; however, such a framework also has critical flaws that must be transcended by new methodological approaches. The classification offered below seeks to recognize the dichotomy of public and private while simultaneously moving beyond it.

Finally, a specialist in Mediterranean anthropology, Michael Herzfeld, also relativizes the dichotomization of public and private. More broadly, Herzfeld has critiqued anthropological studies that make claims about homogenous cultural patterns across the Mediterranean world. He points out that broad generalizations (like the public/private and male/female polarities) tend to overlook and obscure diverse ethnographic detail, resulting in claims that reinforce stereotypes rather than furthering scholarship.[78] He examines the honor/shame dichotomy and the symbolic use of horns and testicles to show that, while these symbols do occur throughout Mediterranean cultures (as well as many others beyond the Mediterranean world!), the meaning and application of the symbols varies considerably.[79] This is the dilemma he poses: anthropologists can either risk caricaturing the cultures of this geographical area through generalizations or risk dissolving this Mediterraneanist framework by prioritizing the particulars of ethnographic description.[80] In his assessment the risk of caricature is the greater evil, and too many scholars have fallen into the trap of imposing homogeneity on the cultures of the Mediterranean.[81] In a study focusing on the category of female in modern Greece, Herzfeld points out that many early ethnographies fruitfully employed sets of categories like male/female and public/private. However, these complementary oppositions rapidly became conventional descriptions that sacrificed "complementarity" for "opposition."[82] He then challenges ethnographers to study the *uses* of these categories in their historical setting,[83] which is one of the goals of the expanded classification offered below.

---

76. Lamphere, "Domestic Sphere," 90.

77. Cubitt and Greenslade, "Public and Private Spheres," 52–64; Stephen, *Women and Social Movements*, 7–12; Chiappari, "Conceptual Dichotomies," 14–21.

78. Herzfeld, "Horns," 440–43.

79. Ibid., 443–46. For a more detailed treatment of variations in the honor/shame and public/private dichotomies see Herzfeld, "Honour and Shame."

80. Herzfeld, "Horns," 446.

81. Ibid., 451.

82. Herzfeld, "Within and Without," 215.

83. Ibid., 216.

A Critique from the Theories and Texts of This Study

Thus, the public/private dichotomy has been dismantled from a variety of theoretical and historical perspectives. More particularly, such a dichotomization does not fit with the theoretical perspectives or biblical texts of this study. Echoing the sentiments of Herzfeld, Sack insists that we must have "geographically aware" positions that take context into consideration rather than applying one dominating paradigm. Similarly, he inserts the decisions and activities of human agents as part of his framework. In agreement with Cohen, Sack would claim that the categories of public and private are always deployed by particular agents in particular locations, and they must be examined accordingly. Sack's major contribution, again, is the insertion (or re-insertion) of space as a central consideration, and he points out that without a geographical ground one of the three forces is typically privileged and comes to dominate the others.[84] Sack moves beyond binary polarities such as time/space or nature/culture to make a triad the foundation of his relational framework (nature, meaning, social relations). Sack would probably view the application of the public/private dichotomy seen in some previous studies as an example of the way that meaning can come to dominate all the other forces in the absence of geography. He critiques the dominance of the realm of "meaning," focusing, in part, on the effects of Lévi-Strauss's cognitive and dualistic structuralism.[85] He concludes that the only way out of the conundrum of various perspectives either reducing or determining others is to bring them together with the integrating power of place and space.[86] Thus, Sack's theoretical perspective, which lies at the heart of this study, agrees with the criticism of the public/private dichotomy offered above and suggests a way forward.

The studies of political geographers likewise problematize the notion of a public/private dichotomy. Their work has shown that various political systems construct their own internal scale relations, defining how different political units are ranked and/or related to one another. This stands in contrast to the very broad and rough divisions imposed by a strong public/private dichotomy. We see just such an awareness of political scale in Plutarch's *Political Precepts*: "You rule a city, which is in turn subject to proconsuls, who are the agents of Caesar" (813e).[87] Thus, Plutarch reflects a widely held tripartite division of Roman administration: the imperial, the provincial, and the urban.[88] Cities could fall along a wide spectrum: smaller member cities in a league, *coloniae*, provincial capitals, and temple cities.[89] Furthermore, Plutarch distinguished between greater (μείζων) and

---

84. Sack, *Homo Geographicus*, 35–36.

85. Ibid., 44–52, and in particular 48–49 on Lévi-Strauss.

86. Ibid., 52.

87. The identification of the proconsuls as the agents of Caesar is interesting, given that Plutarch lived in Achaia. In Plutarch's day, Achaia was a senatorial province with a proconsul (ἀνθυπάτος, used here by Plutarch) and not an imperial province governed by a legate of Caesar. Nevertheless, Plutarch identifies the proconsuls as agents (ἐπιτρόπος) of Caesar. Practically, the distinction often collapsed, and provincials viewed the emperor as the highest authority. See Ando, "Administration of the Provinces," 179. Ando also distinguishes between holders of *imperium* and financial supervisors in the provinces.

88. This same tripartite division is articulated as the imperium, the provincia, and the Hellenistic cities in Marshall and Martin, "Government and Public," 410–14. See also Ando, "Administration," 179–82.

89. Gleason, "Greek Cities," 231–32.

lesser (ἐλάττων) or weightier (βαρυτέρος) and more trivial (μικρότερος) offices within a city (*Praec. ger. rei publ.* 813d). Hellenistic cities often had a ruling council made up of a variety of magistrates with particular duties.[90] This evidence demonstrates the scaling of politics and political space in the Hellenistic-Roman world. On a large scale, the Roman Empire was divided broadly into imperial, provincial, and local scales that were often centered around a city. Divisions of scale also took place on the local scale where insiders could rank and identify the roles of a variety of officials more meticulously. Thus, political geography demonstrates that one must first attend to the primary scale that frames a particular discussion or narrative and then analyze the various gradations and relations within that given frame. Within the realm of public space and politics, one must attend to a variety of spatial and social domains on various levels of scale.

The text of Luke 18:35—19:48 supports this same dissolution of the public/private dichotomy, for applying Neyrey's dichotomy of private and public-political space would result in several incongruities. First, the healing of the blind beggar in 18:35-43 must be classified as "private, non-household" space according to Neyrey's categories because it does not involve any political figures nor does it occur in a city *agora*. However, this event takes place just outside of the city on a major road, which was publicly traveled. A large crowd is accompanying Jesus, and the beggar must shout over them. The public nature of this episode is reiterated by the concluding response of the crowd in v. 43. Next, it may be possible that 19:1-5, set in Jericho, occurs in public space according to Neyrey's classifications, but this is far from certain. Jesus is now in a city, but he is not specifically in the *agora*, just passing through. Also, while Zacchaeus is a *chief* tax collector, he is not a political official and is only loosely tied to local government. In 19:6-10, Luke implies that Jesus has entered Zacchaeus's house, a private space for hospitality according to Neyrey's categories, yet the spatial and social zones are blended together seamlessly and public elements seem to prevail in this section. Zacchaeus as a host welcomes Jesus (a stranger and public figure) into his home as a guest. Such an act of hospitality where a host (generally a male householder) welcomes a relative stranger was common in the ancient world and created a bridge between the public and private spheres.[91] Zacchaeus appears to respond to publicly murmured criticism against Jesus (v. 7), and in v. 9 Jesus seems to be speaking both to Zacchaeus and to the public opponents who grumbled in the city. Then, who comprises the "they" (αὐτῶν) referred to at the beginning of v. 11? Only Zacchaeus and his family? The disciples of Jesus? The opponents? The parable that follows (19:11–27) addresses several audiences at the same time: hostile opponents, the crowds, the disciples, and presumably Zacchaeus and his household as well.[92] Finally, Jesus' entry into Jerusalem is more clearly political (and public), but a more nuanced perspective is needed to understand the social and spatial characteristics of Jesus' actions with regard to the disciples on

---

90. Marshall and Martin, "Government," 414–15.

91. Susan Ford Wiltshire emphasizes this interface of public and private through hospitality in her analysis of the Aeneid. See Wiltshire, *Public and Private*, 83–105. On 105 she says, "As the meeting place of public and private, hospitality can contribute to the transformation of both." She reviews several scenes in the Aeneid where hospitality involves the interaction of the spheres and concerns of public and private.

92. Johnson, "Lukan Kingship Parable," 145.

the road (v. 36–37), the Pharisees in the shadow of the city (v. 39) and the chief priests in the temple (v. 47). These points demonstrate the need for a more nuanced classification of public and private space to understand the social-spatial dynamics of Luke 18:35—19:48.

Building on the theoretical perspective set forth above, this section has demonstrated why it is necessary to move beyond the public/private dichotomy. Even though this binary polarity has served some heuristic usefulness, it has also imposed serious methodological limitations and resulted in problematic conclusions. The roots of such polarities lay in the intellectual traditions of structural anthropology and have been carried into contemporary studies. Structuralism has been critiqued and corrected by the contextual work of other anthropologists and by theoreticians like Bourdieu and Giddens. Neyrey's citation of Cohen is especially problematic, since Cohen has used the work of Bourdieu, Giddens, and Herzfeld to show why and how scholars must move beyond the constraints of such dichotomies. Sack's interdisciplinary triads, the study of scale by political geographers, and the data in Luke 18:35—19:48 also do not fit the public/private dichotomy. Thus, it is now time to present the classification of ancient space that will be described, defended, and deployed in this study.

The Classification Ancient Social-Spatial Categories

Qualifications and Complications

Before presenting the classification of ancient social-spatial categories, a few disclaimers are necessary. First, because places are culturally constructed it is quite possible for a space to be multivalent, a point reinforced by Cohen's work. Thus, different parts of an ancient house may be public or private given the time, purpose, and location.[93] Second, as Neyrey has argued with regard to John 4, forceful or friendly speech in a particular context may change the nature of that place from public to private or vice versa.[94] Thus, the very nature of the rhetoric can change the social-spatial setting (probably drawing on Sack's force of meaning). Third, the following classification posits a spectrum as the best way to move beyond the dichotomy of public and private, while maintaining the existence of the polar opposites. The spectrum has polarized extremes, but in-between those extremes lay many places that have various nuances between these two poles.[95] Combined with the preceding point, this means that a particular place may occur at various points along the spectrum of private to public with some limitations provided by the typical conception of places in the ancient world.[96] While places are often culturally located at a particular point on the

---

93. So Vitruvius comments on how certain rooms such as vestibules and courtyards are meant to be shared with visitors while others such as bedrooms and dining rooms are private and require an explicit invitation for a visitor to enter. See Vitruvius, *De Architectura* 6.5.1–2.

94. Neyrey, "What's Wrong," 85.

95. Several recent articles on the public-private distinction make explicit disclaimers about the fluidity of these categories and work against overgeneralizing polarities. See Benn, "Public and the Private," 3–7; Weintraub, "Theory and Politics," 2–6; D'Entrèves, "Public and Private," 1.

96. For instance, it would be difficult to place a city forum very far on the private side of the spectrum, though some private conversations may occur in such a space. Sahlins and Giddens both show how structure sets conditions for actions but also allows for transgressions and transformations of those norms.

public-private spectrum and assigned corresponding social norms, these can be adjusted, shifted, challenged, and changed in a variety of ways. Cohen's work demonstrates this in detail, and it is backed by the theoretical reflections of Bourdieu and Gidden. Fourth, when one identifies a place as public or private, a set of sociocultural rules follow close behind, but these are usually implied in Greco-Roman literature because it was a "high-context" society, recalling Hall's insight. A great deal of the necessary information is expected to be internalized in the recipient of the message and therefore is not explicit.[97] This high-context characterization of the ancient world is especially applicable to many of the spatial aspects of Luke's narrative, for he often makes comments like "once Jesus was in one of the cities" (5:12), or "they were going along the road" (9:57), or "Jesus entered Jericho and was passing through" (19:1), with very little explicit description of the place, the circumstances, or the norms in effect there. Again, a spectrum allows for more nuances in the analysis of these contextual clues and the accompanying social norms rather than forcing a particular setting into one of two extremes. Fifth and finally, while Neyrey speaks of developing a "native or emic" classification of space in the ancient world, the preceding points compel us to create a classification system that is both deeply conversant with ancient cultures and theoretically and heuristically sound in our contemporary context. The fluid and contestable nature of public and private space leads us to create a classification system that both takes seriously the basic public/private categorization and develops further categories that aid in the complex parsing and practice of ancient spaces.

A New Classification and New Categories

The following diagram of the classification of social-spatial categories draws some elements from studies that employed a public/private dichotomy. However, it also incorporates new categories for nuance, the triadic nature of Sack's theoretical framework, and indications of the interchange between the private and public/political spheres.

Figure 2.2: Diagram of Social-Spatial Classifications

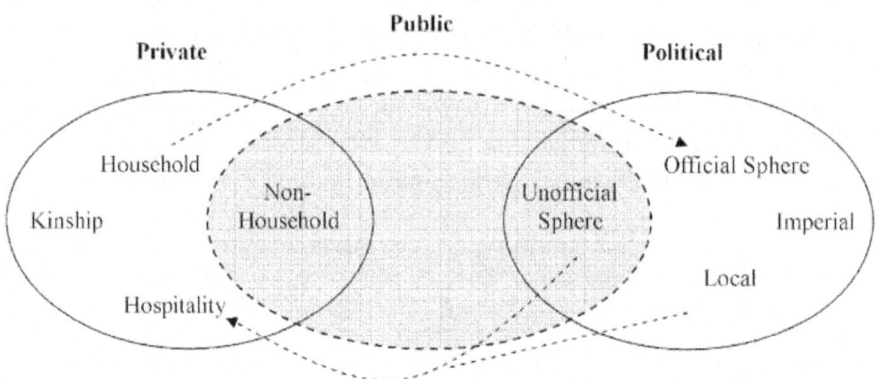

---

97. Hall, *Beyond Culture*, 91–92. Hall's description is also cited in Neyrey, "What's Wrong," 81.

Either extreme of the diagram is classified more minutely. In the ancient world (as is true today) such extremes were more isolatable, identifiable, and categorical. The extremes of the public-private spectrum tend to dominate philosophy and some rhetoric in the ancient world because they directly and clearly activate cultural values and thus have greater logical clarity and rhetorical impact. The extremes of private kinship space and imperial political space prevail in many characterizations of public and private, with the political sphere generally outweighing private concerns.[98] The identification and description of these extremes was and is a powerful way to depict and analyze the categories of public and private, but this does not eliminate the reality of the public-private *spectrum*. The Gospel of Luke falls in a variety of points on this spectrum between these two extremes, mostly beyond kinship-household but not on the level of imperial politics. Therefore, we must examine the muddier middle ground of this dichotomy in order to understand Luke's Gospel. The additional sub-classifications carry the caveat that they probably cannot have the same clarity and definition as the extremes. The following paragraphs will provide parameters and explanations for each of the categories, citing relevant examples along the way.

It is easiest to begin by defining one of the clearest categories, the private-household-kinship space on the far left of the diagram. This zone is clearly defined in two ways. The forces of place and social relations are determinative. It must occur in a household and only involve members of a given family (possibly including slaves), probably both male and female in their appropriate cultural roles. One of the best examples of this in the Gospel of Luke is found in 1:24–25, where Elizabeth conceives a child and remains in her home in seclusion for five months.

The private-household-hospitality zone is also easy to define and identify. Again, this must take place in a household, but in this case certain strangers/guests enter the home for personal or business reasons. Some further clarifications are needed at this point. First, this space of hospitality may have had tighter or looser gender restrictions given the particular culture in which the home was located.[99] Thus, in a specific cultural context, women of the family, female slaves, and/or female consorts may have participated more or less in hospitable gatherings within the home. While the social relations deemed appropriate may fluctuate, it is generally expected that the guest will treat the host and the family with due respect. Time becomes a more definitive factor here, since such dining

---

98. Note the classic division of the *Iliad* and the *Odyssey*. The former relates the story of public activity regarding men and their military adventures, while the latter tells of Odysseus (and his wife) reclaiming his home. Or, one could cite the division between Aristotle's *Politics* and *Economics*. For both Aristotle and Plato the public-political sphere has the greatest value. For a further look at this separation and the interaction of the two spheres in ancient Greece see Saxonhouse, "Classical Greek Conceptions."

99. Greeks seem to have rigidly maintained gender separation in their homes even when entertaining, while the Romans often prided themselves on not segregating their women. See Wallace-Hadrill, *Houses and Society*, 8–10. The situation seems to be more complex in the culturally volatile region of Palestine where Jewish norms predominated. The Mishnah erects strict guidelines about women's presence and behavior. However, Marianne Sawicki (*Crossing Galilee*, 89–94) claims that this was a form of literary cultural resistance against the Roman Empire attempting to preserve Jewish identity, since there is no hard archaeological evidence for segregated women's quarters in Jewish homes.

and entertaining were generally done in the evenings,[100] but hospitality could also be extended to allow a guest to stay in the home for a period of time.[101] An excellent example of private-household-hospitality space is found in Luke 10:38–42, where Jesus is welcomed to the home of Martha and Mary. Even though the gender roles are somewhat stretched by Mary and the disciples may or may not be present (contrast "they" in v. 38 with "him" in v. 39), this appears to be a private episode where Jesus is invited to dine and perhaps stay in a home.[102]

I concur with Neyrey's category of non-household private spaces.[103] These settings are determined more by the nature of the group at the encounter and the purpose of the gathering than by the space in which it occurs. The specific place can vary widely: workshops, the forum, baths, inside a city, outside a city. However, other forces gleaned from Sack help to identify private-non-household space: the nature of the social relationships (friends, neighbors, business partners), time (business transactions often occurred in the fourth to fifth hour, leisure and bathing began in the sixth), the meanings attached to such gatherings (personal business, leisure, pleasure), and human agency (how the participants shape the place and event). Many issues, while typically private, can take place outside of the home: personal interests, leisure, friendships and business dealings.[104] These can begin to blur into the public sphere (e.g., when leisure takes place at the public bath or business dealings in the *agora*). As we move toward the middle of the diagram the categories become more fluid and open to interpretation both in the ancient world and today. For example, even though Jesus directs the parable of the shrewd steward to the disciples in a generic non-household setting (Luke 16:1, seemingly private in nature), the audience learns in 16:14 that the Pharisees have been listening all along and then mock him (much more public due to the broader audience, the hostile social relationships, and the "challenge" nature of the rhetoric). These non-household spaces slide more easily along the spectrum of private to public, and specific instances must be examined in their cultural and literary context to assess how to categorize them.

The dashed arrows on the diagram represent the fluidity between the spheres, the way that they can interpenetrate one another. On one hand, hospitality was a ritualized social practice that created an opportunity for (unsafe) persons from the public sphere to enter into the private domain of the household.[105] Luke can import public persons, characteristics, and concerns into the traditionally private sphere of the household often through

---

100. Laurence, *Roman Pompeii*, 126, 131–32.

101. Neyrey, "In Public," 90.

102. However, many household hospitality scenes in Luke seem to be affected by matters from the public side of the spectrum. Take the dinner Jesus attends in Luke 11:37–53. At first, it appears that Jesus is simply welcomed into a Pharisee's home for a meal, but suddenly Jesus is rebuking the Pharisees as a whole (certainly not an act of respect!), and a set of lawyers (v. 45) and scribes (v. 53) also appear to be present for Jesus' attacks. This scenario of household hospitality has become more of a public event.

103. "In Public," 81.

104. See Demosthenes, *Tim.* 192–93, and the issue of the public role of personal friends in Plutarch, *Praec. ger. rei publ.* 812c–d.

105. This will be substantiated in detail in the next chapter. Wiltshire's study of the Aeneid makes thorough use of this idea (*Aeneid*, 83–105).

hospitality. For example, note the crowds present in (or at?) Simon's home in 4:38–41, the presence of the Pharisees at Levi's banquet (5:29–30), the way the crowd floods into Zacchaeus's home (19:1–10), and how Peter, a Jewish stranger, is welcomed by Cornelius (Acts 10:24–25). On the other hand, as argued by Moxnes, Jesus (particularly in Luke) appears to bring the standard of generalized reciprocity out of the household setting and apply it in a much broader way as a general ethical stance appropriate to both spheres.[106] Often in the ancient world, states, kingdoms, and empires were conceptualized as similar to a house, and the ruler could be called the father of the people.[107] In various parables in Luke, God is cast as a master of a household (14:15–24; 15:11–32; 16:1–8). This pattern brings a very private reality to bear on the conceptualization of the public-political realm. The arrows on the diagram reflect this capacity of the public and the private spheres in the Hellenistic-Roman world to affect each other in direct ways.

Now we move to the far right of the diagram and work from the clearer extremes of public space back again to the fuzzier middle ground. Again, imperial political spaces are relatively easy to identify through the forces of place and social relations: imperial triumphs in Rome, trials or embassies before the emperor, Augustus addressing the Senate, etc. Some spaces are almost exclusively political (the curia or the forum), but in other cases it is the persons present and the meanings (both political and religious) attached to such occurrences that demarcate them as public (e.g., events on roads or in cities). However, just as private-household settings at the one extreme can be further subdivided, so the political sphere should be further broken down in order to ascertain the appropriate scale of analysis: imperial, provincial, or local. Local politics encompasses the smallest end of the scale spectrum in the ancient world and captures both urban and non-urban settings. Socially, local politics deals primarily with the relationships of local political functionaries (e.g., Pharisees and centurions) who operate within groups and movements that are relevant to local citizens. Spatially, local politics affects a limited geographical area typically orbiting around an urban center. With regard to time, political exchanges typically took place during the daytime. Meaning is focused on local issues and often deals with group membership as a source of identity. The scale of politics in Luke's Gospel falls primarily into the local level. While the Gospel opens with a large, imperial horizon (2:1–2; 3:1–2), most of the action takes place in villages and cities throughout Galilee, a subdivision of a small province on the eastern margins of the empire.[108] The climactic material in Jerusalem at the end of the Gospel is exactly that—climactic. It is the highpoint of political and spatial development in the Gospel. Here, Luke reaches the level of a provincial capital, and the scale of analysis must adjust. Additionally, Luke's Gospel narrative tells two local political stories: the internal development of Jesus' movement (as it grows in both numbers and organization), and the relationship of this movement to external political realities (form local authorities to Jewish power structures in Jerusalem to the representatives of the Roman Empire).

106. Moxnes, *Economy*, 147.

107. Aristotle, *Pol.* 1269b; Aeschines, *Ctes.* 78; Augustus, *Res Gestae* 35.

108. Note how Jesus' trial is demoted politically by Pilate as a local matter better handled by Herod, the tetrarch of Galilee (23:6–7).

PART ONE: READING LUKE'S SOCIAL-SPATIAL CONTEXT

The last classification to be described is the most important for this study. Just as the private sphere should be subdivided into two more precise categories, so the public sphere must also be subdivided. However, it is not so easy to divide it into political and non-political. Public life was generally considered to be political in the ancient world, and it would be impossible to remove political overtones completely from any public action.[109] Yet, the preceding discussion demonstrates that a spectrum of public and private existed in the ancient world. Cohen rightly asserts, "the public sphere is larger than politics."[110] While any public action may have political ramifications (many private actions do as well), an action may be public without being directly or primarily political. As discussed above, the healing of the blind beggar, the meeting of Jesus and Zacchaeus, and the meal scenes in Luke have many public characteristics, but they are not primarily or directly political in nature (though political ramifications may be present).[111] Thus, the classification includes the category of the unofficial public sphere.[112] It is unofficial because, while it is public in many ways, it does not directly intersect the people, places, or topics of official politics. This investigation will distinguish this public sphere from the political sphere, which is more narrowly defined. This category is the least "native" or "emic" of all those in the classification, but it is necessary on several accounts. First, some places could be considered public or private on various occasions (e.g., parts of the house). Second, the people in the Hellenistic-Roman world often debated the public-private valence of places, people, roles, and rules. Third, the categories of public and private were defined in various ways by cultural insiders; there was no monolithic agreement.[113] The (unofficial) public sphere has the following characteristics. With respect to social relations, it can deal with the interactions of individuals up to large groups, but it does so without directly concerning major political functionaries or official laws. Societal norms are often still in effect, so public actions may still be governed by cultural rules of social interaction and be politically unofficial at the same time. The public sphere deals with places that are generally open and accessible to a wide range of people (cities, markets, roads), but more circumscribed locations (e.g., synagogues) can also be public if they admit a substantial representation of the populace. Actions in the public sphere generally occur at times when large or representative groups of people are present. The public sphere is characterized by audible words and visible actions that can be perceived by a large and broad audience. Meaning would be the most contested aspect of the unofficial public sphere: clues and perceptions could move an episode to the left or right on

---

109. The terms κοινός, δημόσιος, and πολιτεία derive from terms that refer to assemblies of people and came to connote the political activities that took place in these assemblies.

110. *Law*, 78.

111. The blind beggar calls Jesus the "Son of David," Zacchaeus is a tax collector, and the Pharisees are generally regarded local leaders. However, the content and form of these stories are not focused on these political characteristics.

112. Engberg-Pedersen identified a "sphere of ethico-political public discourse" that required further study (Hellenistic *Öffentlichkeit*, 33). This is exactly what I have in mind with the classification of an unofficial public sphere. Bachmann also uses the adjectives "official" and "unofficial" ("amtliche" and "nichtamtliche") with regard to activities in the temple (*Jerusalem*, 172).

113. These three points will be substantiated by examples in the following chapter.

the private-public spectrum.¹¹⁴ As with the private-non-household spaces in the middle of the diagram, the domain of the public sphere needs careful and contextual interpretation, since the adjudication of its valence is not as clear as other more sharply defined categories employed in Luke's milieu.

With all of the terms of the diagram now provided with a set of example and working parameters, we can see that a variety of places all along the private-public spectrum fill Luke's Gospel: temple, households, roads, countryside, cities, bodies of water, synagogues, public halls, wilderness, marketplaces, and others. Luke appears to have a preference for the public sphere. Luke emphasizes urban settings,¹¹⁵ and he often redacts Mark by eliminating or softening private elements and adding or highlighting public ones.¹¹⁶ Thus, it seems that in Luke many traditionally private settings (both in and outside of houses) are invaded or at least transformed by the public sphere. This study will argue that Luke typically places Jesus in the midst of the unofficial public sphere and on the edge of local politics. The fact that these two categories lie near the middle (and fuzzier) domain of the classification calls for careful comparisons and detailed exegesis in the examination of Luke's social-spatial characteristics.

Conclusion, Context, and Comparison

This chapter set forth a theoretical perspective for analyzing the social-spatial characteristics of Luke's Gospel, relying primarily on the framework of Sack and supported by insights gleaned from political geographers and Hall. This includes a set of forces that can be used to help discern the social-spatial valence of narrative events in Luke: nature, meaning, social relations, time, religion, place, and self. The triadic nature of Sack's framework and the research on various levels of scale leads us to reconsider the dichotomous public/private opposition. A look into the theoretical and historical underpinnings of this dichotomy showed that a public-private spectrum is more heuristically sound and suitable to analyze the Gospel of Luke in its ancient milieu. Thus, this chapter has closed with a presentation of a new classification of the private, public, and political spheres with a new set of categories to aid in the social-spatial analysis of Luke 18:35—19:48.

Now, it is necessary to examine the new classification and categories across a range of documents in the ancient world in order to offer supporting contextual evidence. This

---

114. For example, note the differences in the interpretation of the significance of Jesus' statement on paying taxes in Luke 20:20–26 and 23:2, the first being more concerned with religious devotion (and avoiding a trap) while the second is directly political and seditious.

115. Luke uses πόλις 36 times, Matthew 25 times, and Mark only 8 times. Rohrbaugh notes that Luke adds the word "city" in many places where the other Gospel writers do not ("Pre-Industrial City," 147).

116. For example, Mark employed the phrase κατ' ἰδίαν 7 times to refer to Jesus' private activity (4:34; 6:31, 32; 7:33; 9:2, 28; 13:3). Luke keeps only one of these (Mark 6:31 in Luke 9:10), omits the other 6, and then adds one of his own in 10:23. Luke recasts Jesus' retreats by asserting that Jesus withdrew for private prayer (5:16), not to escape the crowds (Mark 1:45).

Note how Luke softens the private nature of the explanation of the parable of the sower (8:9ff) in contrast to the explicitly private settings found in Mark 4:10–11 and Matt 13:36–37. Luke also places a crowd in the narrative to witness Jesus' crucifixion and death (23:48), while Mark and Matthew have no such group explicitly present and seem to stress the isolation of Jesus.

will be done in two ways. First, by setting a broad context of social-spatial characteristics in the ancient world, and second, by offering more focused comparisons to Luke's Gospel. Chapter 3 provides the context by conducting a broad survey that includes material drawn primarily from three geographical foci: Athens, Rome, and Jerusalem. It will include material that both predates and postdates Luke's Gospel to give a wide diachronic view. It will also include a variety of genres: history, biography, philosophy, drama, letters, etc. The analysis of literary works will be buttressed and enriched by archaeological material from three ancient sites: Ephesus, Pompeii, and a few sites in Palestine (corresponding to the three foci above). This will bring the evidence of real lived spaces to bear on the classification of ancient social-spatial zones. This literary and archaeological survey will demonstrate that the classification and categories presented in this chapter fit well with a broad swath of evidence in the Hellenistic-Roman world.

Alongside this more general survey work, chapter 3 will probe a small set of contemporaneous works that present themselves as excellent comparisons for the social-spatial characteristics of Luke 18:35—19:48. The first work is Plutarch's *Praecepta gerendae rei publicae*, or the *Political Precepts*. This essay is an excellent point of comparison to Luke's portrayal of Jesus on two accounts. First, it deals with someone who is entering political life, seeking to create a good reputation and popular support (e.g., *Praec. ger. rei publ.* 821a–e). Thus, it is quite analogous to Luke's depiction of how Jesus begins a movement around his own personal leadership in the Gospel. Second, the scale is similar to Luke's Gospel because Menemachus entered local politics in a corner of the empire under Roman supervision (*Praec. ger. rei publ.* 813d–e). The second piece is the *Vita Apollonii* by Philostratus, a narrative that has previously, and fruitfully, been compared to the Gospel accounts of Jesus' life.[117] Even though it was written approximately one hundred years later than the Gospel of Luke, this philosophical biography is relevant to Luke's portrayal of Jesus, but the contents of book 4 are especially pertinent to this study. In book 4, Philostratus recounts Apollonius's journeys from Ephesus through Greece and to Rome, a portion of the world with which Luke is familiar (as we know from Acts). A number of scenes in book 4 are comparable to Luke 18:35—19:48: Apollonius addressing the Smyrneans (4.7-8, like Jesus in Jericho), his grand welcome and rejection in Athens (4.17-18, like Jesus' reception in Jerusalem), the healing of a boisterous demoniac in Athens (4.20, like Jesus healing the shouting blind man), his presence at a wedding banquet (4.25, like Jesus in Zacchaeus's home), and on the road to Rome with his disciples (4.36, like Jesus on the way to Jericho and Jerusalem). Thus, both the subject matter and the particular social-spatial characteristics of book 4 of the *Vita* provide excellent comparative material for Luke 18:35—19:48.

---

117. Petzke, *Die Traditionen über Apollonius*; and Robbins, *Jesus the Teacher*, 105–7, 148–55.

3

Private, Public, and Political in the Ancient Contexts of Luke's Gospel

Introduction

THE PREVIOUS CHAPTER PRESENTED A NEW CLASSIFICATION AND NEW CATEGORIES OF private-public-political space in order to have a better tool to analyze the social-spatial characteristics of Luke's portrayal of Jesus in 18:35—19:48. The current chapter will explore the private, public, and political spheres in the ancient context of Luke's Gospel in order to substantiate and flesh out the categories of the new classification system in light of the theoretical perspective presented in the last chapter. This supporting evidence clusters around three geographical-cultural foci: classical Athens, Jerusalem, and Rome. These three foci represent three strains of influence evident in Luke-Acts: Hellenistic culture (Athens), Jewish traditions (Jerusalem), and Roman administration (Rome). Each section will follow the same pattern: a brief explanation of the focus and its relevance, an examination of several literary examples that illustrate the new classification, an analysis of selected archaeological remains, insights offered by another author who has studied the relation of private, public, and political space in that focus, and a conclusion using Sack's forces to help clarify the new categories on the spectrum. A few preliminary remarks will help set the stage for this examination.

First, the high-context nature of ancient communication means that one must sift through the evidence from the ancient world (both literary and archaeological) to glean the few occasions where the norm breaks and the extant record provides some explicit statements about what Luke and those of his shared milieu thought about private, public, and political spaces. Thus, the survey is both inductive and selective. It represents a thorough investigation of ancient literary sources, but the final results offer the most pertinent material for this study.[1] Casting the research net widely prevents a few selected works from exercising undue influence on the classification system and the exegesis of Luke. The survey will adduce some material that portrays dichotomized public and private spheres in the ancient world, but it will especially feature quotations that demonstrate how these spheres were contested, stretched, and overlapped in various ways. The extremes do exist

---

1. A much broader survey with many more examples and types of evidence was included in the dissertation, which served as the basis for this monograph. See Bruehler, "Public," 73–252.

but the variegated influences on Luke-Acts display a great deal of social-spatial variety and tension as well.

Any examination of the conceptions and categories of space in the ancient world must be linked to the actual structures of lived space in that world. This material provides insight into social and spatial specifics not always discernible in texts. Michael White, writing in honor of Wayne Meeks, states that "the full appreciation of the *realia* remains one of the most complex tasks still open to those who wish to explore the social world of the early Christians."[2] Despite the sporadic nature of archaeological remains, the selectivity of excavations, and the disciplinary specificity of archeological reports, it is necessary to ground the classification proposed above in some of the social-spatial *realia* of Luke's day. What did peristyles look like, and where were they found? How did people access such a public room in a home, and how many people could a sizeable peristyle hold? Meeks himself says, "To the limit that the sources and our abilities permit, we must try to discern the texture of life in particular times and particular places."[3] Since there is no consensus regarding the provenance of Luke, it is best to look at three representative sites that might provide helpful particulars. Ephesus, Pompeii, and Palestine will provide archaeological evidence corresponding to the three geographical foci.[4] Archaeology adds enriching and substantiating details to the new classification as well as providing specifics that may be applied to the exegesis of Luke's Gospel. While at times harder to "read" than ancient texts, the building patterns of the ancient world sometimes complement the "pictures" painted in texts, but at other times they challenge ideologically constructed descriptions of private, public, and political spaces.

Because of the scope of this survey, the focused analysis of comparative literary works will take place in the next chapter, which will deductively analyze Plutarch's *Precepts of Statescraft* and book IV of Philostratus's *Life of Apollonius*. The literary survey helps avoid myopia on the public-private spectrum and casts an analytical net very widely to capture the broad characteristics of the private, public, and political spheres in the ancient world. The narrower limits of these selected works will allow for deeper probing that will add further clarity to the spectrum and greater specificity to the implicit characteristics of the unofficial public and local political spheres that predominate in Luke's portrayal of Jesus. The in-depth analysis of specific works in the next chapter will help to avoid superficiality and show how the classification system can be applied to two works comparable to Luke's Gospel.

---

2. White, "Visualizing the 'Real' World," 234.

3. Meeks, *First Urban*, 2. In addition to Meeks and White see the comments by other prominent supporters of this position, including Strange, "First Century Galilee" and Horsley, *Archaeology*, 1–14.

4. This study has a similar approach to historical evidence (though a very different slice of that evidence) as found in Oakes's study *Reading Romans in Pompeii*. On p. 73, Oakes states, "Instead of using historical evidence to build specific situational theories and consequent readings, this study uses historical evidence to put flesh on to a more general situational scenario." Much the same could be said of this study and its approach to Luke's Gospel and the classification of private, public, and political. Rather than identifying on specific scenario, this study aims at understanding the cultural dynamics of space that influenced Luke's writing.

The First Focus: Classical Athens and Hellenistic Culture

Classical Athens was the birthplace of many ideas, practices, and institutions that have informed the history of Western culture, including the categories of public and private. As reflections upon society, law, politics, and philosophy burgeoned in the intellectual greenhouse that was ancient Athens, the categories of public and private emerged and developed. The famous speakers, thinkers, and leaders of Athens wrestled with these categories and deployed them in a variety of extant works. The culture, literature, philosophy, religion, art, society, and politics of classical Athens and Greece was spread throughout the Mediterranean world first by Alexander the Great and then many who came after him. This generated the Hellenistic era (c. 323–31 BCE), whose cultural influence was felt well into the period of Roman rule and the writing of the NT.[5] Luke is widely held to be a Hellenistic author and an inheritor of this Hellenistic cultural tradition.[6] Thus, it is appropriate to adduce evidence about the private–public–political spectrum that reaches back into the literature and culture of classical Athens and its progeny, Hellenism, to see how it shaped the understanding of social-spatial categories that operated in Luke's time and place. This investigation will begin by citing evidence from some of the influential classics of Greek literature and philosophy, then move to an examination of the city of Ephesus, and finally a brief look at Cohen's work on social dynamics in classical Athens.

The influence of the epic poems attributed to the hoary figure Homer on Greek culture is immense, and the *Odyssey* in particular illustrates some of the earliest thoughts about the nature of public and private that might have influenced Luke.[7] At the beginning of the *Odyssey*, Telemachus summons an assembly (ἀγορά) of the Achaeans. At the meeting, the aged Aegyptus speaks first to ask who summoned the assembly. "Has he heard some news of the army's return? . . . Or is there some other public matter (τι δήμιον ἄλλο) which he will address and speak to us about?" (*Od.* 2.30–32). The assembly sets the public tone of this meeting by the force of social relationships (and by the time of the summons), and this assembly deals typically with certain topics (the force of meaning) such as military matters. Then Telemachus stands and addresses the assembly, "I have not heard any news of the army's return that I can tell you plainly . . . nor will I address you and tell you about some other public matter. Rather, it is my own need, for evil has fallen upon my house in two ways" (*Od.* 2.42–46). The two private evils that Telemachus proceeds to name are the loss of his father and the unlawful wooing of his mother that threatens to ruin his home and his inheritance (2.46–59). However, even though concerns such as family and

---

5. Price, "Hellenistic Period," 309; the last 4 chapters of Boardman, Giffin, and Murray, *Greece*; and Betz, "Hellenism," 128–34.

6. Plümacher, *Schriftsteller*, 1–5; Moessner, "Reading Luke's Gospel," 125–32; Soards "Historical and Cultural Setting," 33–47; and all the articles in Moessner, *Jesus*.

7. Luke's use of *mimesis* as a Hellenistic author is widely attested. See Plümacher on Luke's imitation of predecessors like Polybius, Diodorus, and Josephus (*Schriftsteller*, 9–12) or his familiarity with the Septuagint (Fitzmyer, *Luke*, 109–25). MacDonald argues that Luke crafts some of the stories in Acts purely by imitation of Homer's Iliad (*Homer*, 146–48), giving credence to the notion that the portrayal of the private, public, and political spheres in the Odyssey are part of Luke's operative cultural heritage.

marriage are deemed private by the force of social relationships, Telemachus brings them into the public space of the assembly. He goes on to argue that this "private" evil, if ignored by them, will bring evil to their entire community (*Od.* 2.64–67), using the force of meaning to show why he has seemingly mixed public and private spheres. Thus, Telemachus's private matters have suddenly become public concerns because they have the potential to wreak havoc on the entire community.[8] Most of the assembly responds with due shame and sorrow, despite the seemingly inappropriate venue. This early and archetypal story already reveals the firm categories of public and private as well as the ways they impinged on one another.

The following examples come from some of the great orators of classical Athens. The first was already discussed in chapter 1, but a review is due here. In his defense of Mantitheus (speech 16), Lysias records Mantitheus's testimony on his own behalf, a testimony that is structured according to the categories of public and private. The private domain of Mantitheus's life deals with his family and personal wealth (16.10), largely matters of social relations. The public material (16.11–13) deals with three topics: the antagonism of his more profligate peers, the fact that he has never been tried in a criminal (public) or civil (private) suit, and his bravery in military service. Again these are largely matters of social relations, but also include place (courtrooms) and meaning (warfare). However under the category of public matters, he *also* includes how Mantitheus's behavior is superior to his non-kin peers (who are known to drink and gamble too much) as well as the absence of any private or civil charges against Mantitheus. This speech places Mantitheus's peer relationships and private suits under the category of public matters, employing it to substantiate his good reputation.

The following examples come from two colleagues, statesmen, orators, and enemies of fourth-century-BCE Athens, Aeschines and Demosthenes. Demosthenes uses the public/private dichotomy as a merism when he defends himself: "Nor did I abandon any honorable goal either in private matters (ἰδίας) or public matters (δημοσίας), and I delivered benefits both to the city (πόλει) and to friends (φίλος)" (*Cor.* 257). This clever chiasm shows Demosthenes dividing his laudable conduct into two spheres: the public, which concerns the whole city (identified primarily by the forces of place and meaning), and the private, which concerns his personal friends (identified primarily by the forces of social relations). Demosthenes explicitly states that there is a marked difference between evaluating public and private matters:

> I, for one, do not think that merit should be judged in the same way in political affairs [πόλει] and private matters [ἰδιώτῃ], because such evaluations do not deal with the same issues. In our private lives [ἰδίᾳ] each one of us tries to discern who is worthy to marry into our family, or something like that, and such questions are answered by custom [νόμοις] and opinion [δόξαις]. However, in public affairs [κοινῇ] the city and the people try to discover whom their benefactors and saviors are, and such questions are answered not by birth or opinion, but by actions. (*Lept.* 57)

---

8. Telemachus brings his private concerns to the attention of public and political authorities two more times in the Odyssey. He approaches Nestor and informs him that his mission is private rather than public (*Od.* 3.79–84), and confesses the same to Menelaus (4.312–30). See Wiltshire, *Vergil's Aeneid*, 9–10.

Private, Public, and Political in the Ancient Contexts of Luke's Gospel

Demosthenes begins with a strong demarcation between the private and political spheres both largely defined by social relations (the former dealing with a person's family and the latter with patrons). Furthermore, the two spheres have different standards of evaluation. Standards in the private sphere are defined by the force of meaning, here indicated by custom and opinion. However, such criteria are not permissible in the public sphere, where decisions about corporate well being must be based upon honorable actions evident to everyone, not personal opinions. Thus, self becomes the driving force here: the corporate self of the state decides this and it decides on the basis of action by other selves that might qualify as benefactors or saviors. Aeschines, Demosthenes's sometime opponent, confirms a clear division of the public and private spheres as seen in his portrayal of the proper public speaker in his prosecution of Timarchus (*Tim.* 21–36). He draws together several forces to argue that a public speaker (ῥήτωρ, the force of self) who addressed the people from the official platform (βῆμα, the force of place) on public matters (πρᾶγμα, perhaps the force of social relations) had to meet the legislated standards of morality and customs of public address (the force of meaning).

On the other hand, both men also demonstrate the flexible and contested nature of the private, public, and political spheres. Demosthenes claims that the same standard of private honesty should apply to the public-political sphere: "If we have a law that prohibits cheating in the marketplace, where a lie causes no public injury, then is it not disgraceful that the very same state does not abide by the same standards in public affairs as it enforces upon private persons, but instead cheats its benefactors?" (*Lept.* 9). Here the private arena is defined by the force of place combined with meaning (business occurring in the marketplace), but honesty is still the best policy across the entire private-public spectrum. Aeschines brings the values of the two spheres together as well, demonstrating how the private-kinship sphere can have direct influence on the distant political sphere (one of the arrows in our classification diagram). In his prosecution of Ctesiphon, Aeschines says, "A bad father who hates his children could never be a good leader, and a man who does not love his closest family will never care for outsiders like yourselves; nor would a man who is evil in his private life be any good in public life, and a man who is worthless at home could never be a man of honor as an envoy" (*Ctes.* 78). Aeschines mounts a lesser to greater argument here drawing on the force of social relations: If Ctesiphon was in fact a bad father who mismanaged his own home, he could never act wisely or bravely in the public sphere.[9]

The definition of social-spatial spheres plays an important role in trials. Demosthenes is forced to discuss his private life at trial because of the prosecution of Aeschines. He accuses Aeschines of wrongly portraying the whole tenor of his life and states, "As for his

---

9. This same cultural reasoning is expressed positively by Philo when discussing Joseph's role as a household steward: "The one who would become a political leader had to be trained and experienced first of all in the management of a household, for a house is actually a small and contracted city and household management is joined with politics, just as the city is like a large house and politics is quite similar to household management" (*Ios.* 38). Philo asserts that Joseph's time as a steward in a house was no accident but providential preparation for his future role. He makes an even stronger and more direct connection between οἰκονομία and πολιτεία, claiming that the two are practically the same thing on different scales. The leadership of a house comes first and prepares one for leadership in the public sphere, and Joseph manifested excellence in both.

abusive criticism of my private life, you will see that I have an honest and direct reply. I have never lived anywhere except in your midst. If you know that my character is such as he charges, then do not even tolerate my voice, but rise and condemn me immediately, even if my public conduct has been beyond praise" (*Cor.* 10). Demosthenes's defense is simple: every citizen present has a fair knowledge of his private life and knows that it is nothing like the outrageous assertions made by Aeschines. Thus, his private life must be accessible and observable by the general populace of Athens for this defense to be feasible. Demosthenes stakes his claim using the forces of place and social relations ("in your midst") and self (character and conduct).[10] His private life has become public business at the trial, but in some fashion it has been publicly evident throughout his life. Demosthenes has to prove in his speech *Against Medias* that it is appropriate for him to bring a public charge before the assembly because Medias insulted Demosthenes while the latter was serving as the city chorus master during an official festival. Demosthenes says, "If Medias had wronged me as a private citizen [ἰδιώτην] on any other day of the year, he would have had to pay a private [ἰδίᾳ] penalty, but if all of his attacks were actually against your chorus master during a holy festival, then it is fitting for him to face public [δημοσίας] punishment and pay a fair penalty" (*Mid.* 33–34). Demosthenes draws upon the combined forces of time (day of the year), self (the chorus master), and religion (the holy festival) to define a public event. What is crucial here is that Demosthenes has to argue this point or else he would make no mention of it at all. He is constrained to prove (probably against the counterarguments of Medias) that the assembly should in fact consider him to have been a public official in this circumstance.

Plato and Aristotle, the great representatives of classical Athenian philosophy, are the next contributors to the ancient conceptions of the public and private. Consider this revealing statement taken from Plato's *Laws*:

> No human being is naturally able both to perceive what is beneficial to the whole city, and after recognizing what that is, then to be able and willing to do what is best. For, in the first place, it is difficult for a person to recognize that true political action must care, not for private matters, but for public matters. This is because public interests [κοινόν] bind the city together while private interests [ἴδιον] tear it apart. Similarly, it is difficult to recognize that both public and private interests are benefited when public concerns are treated better than private concerns. (*Leg.* 875a–b)

Plato maintains that the public sphere contains the concerns of the city and official political business, while all else falls to the private sphere, and the two are defined in this case by the force of social relations. The difficulty of practicing true politics (πολιτικῇ καὶ ἀλεθεῖ τέκνῃ) is that the public and the private are not only separate spheres as they concern different sets of relationships, but to Plato they are also antagonistic to each other: "public interests bind the city together while private interests tear it apart." Given this state

---

10. Cohen claims that the social and physical living conditions in Athens made such familiarity possible. Moreover, Cohen extends Demosthenes' claim by asserting that any honorable man in Athens could assert that his whole life is lived out in the open because of the public nature of both domestic and political affairs in the city. See Cohen, *Law*, 80.

of affairs, Plato asserts that public/political/common (all possible connotations of κοινός) concerns are more important than private concerns and must be accorded greater care.[11]

However, despite this seeming prioritization of the public sphere, Plato also expresses dislike and distrust for public and political dynamics. He says,

> When the masses are seated together in assemblies [ἐκκλησίαις] or in courtrooms [δικαστήρια] or theatres [θέατρα] or military camps [στρατόπεδα] or any other kind of public gathering of a crowd [τινα ἄλλον κοινὸν πλήθους], they shout loudly and criticize some things that are said and done while approving others, but both are done with excess – by hollering and applause, and so the very rocks and land of the surrounding region echo and increase the noise of the censure and praise. In such cases, how do you think a young man's heart is moved within him, as the saying goes? What private teaching [παιδείαν ἰδιωτικήν] could possibly withstand this and not be swept away by the waves of censure and applause, and be carried off in its current so that the young man would affirm what they say is honorable and shameful, do what they do and even become like them? (*Resp.* 492b–c)

Plato begins using the force of social relations by emphasizing the size of the groups (πολλοί, πλῆθος) and then moves to the force of place by naming a variety of locations that have clear political connections (assemblies, courtrooms, military camps). The insertion of the theatre between courtrooms and military camps might seem odd to modern ears, but theatre in ancient Greece was a production of the state and was often performed during various Dionysian civic festivals; however, there were also other much less formal theatrical productions that took place within and without the city.[12] Plato also generalizes this list to other "public" (κοινός, not πολιτικός here) gatherings, probably because these other public areas were less official in nature. At the end of the passage, Plato deplores the behavior of these groups in a way that moves them away from organized political processes. The mention of theatres, generalized "other public gatherings," and the lowbrow behavior push the description in this passage beyond the realm of official civic politics into a more general public sphere. Plato closes by stating that philosophical instruction takes place in private (although specific locations are not given). However, this training in virtue is highly susceptible to the almost hypnotic power of the mob, which debases the young and leads them into folly by its clamor. Thus, the communication of meaning in the private sphere does not seem able to stand against the propaganda of the public crowd.

Many scholars, after wrestling with the complexities of discovering the authentic voices of Socrates and Plato in the extant dialogues, have concluded that Plato (unlike Socrates) rejected politics and the public life and retreated to the privacy of his garden academy to teach philosophy. This may have resulted from the "legal" trial and execution of his beloved mentor as well as from his own negative experiences with the Thirty.[13]

---

11. Drawing on her analysis of the *Republic*, Elshtain concludes that for Plato, "The achievement of the just state . . . can be attained only if private life, loyalty, and purpose are absorbed into the public domain" (*Public Man*, 31).

12. Green, *Theatre*, 7–9. In the Hellenistic world, the theatre lost some of its political character and became more of a part of the public sphere. The function of the theatre as a gathering place for the Ephesian crowd in Acts 19 is an excellent example of this development.

13. Elshtain suggests that it was the execution of Socrates that drove Plato to pursue a "nonpublic quest

PART ONE: READING LUKE'S SOCIAL-SPATIAL CONTEXT

Patterson points out that far from annihilating private life, Plato's political vision in the *Republic* portrays the polis as "one single family."[14] Plato re-envisioned the broken democratic politics that killed his mentor, casting ideal politics as the operation of a true family. This again reflects a direct influence from the private-kinship sphere into politics. Plato's repudiation of the political system of Athens led to two un-Socratic results. First, dealing with the force of place, Plato turned away from the public locations of Athens's gadfly, who spoke freely in the agora, palaestra, and gymnasia,[15] and moved his school from these public venues into his own private garden.[16] Second, dealing with the forces of self and meaning, he rejected the role of public social critic taken on by Socrates and focused his energy on private philosophical training. Ober has argued that the *Apology* and the *Crito* set out a portrayal of Socrates as an active citizen and social critic who sought to improve his fellow citizens.[17] However, in the *Gorgias* and the *Republic* we hear the voice of Plato claiming that the role of social critic is futile, like a doctor trying to defend himself against a pastry chef before a jury of children (*Gorg.* 521e).[18] Plato seems to conclude in the end that the philosopher has neither the ability nor the duty to do good to the city, and the best option is to retire into a private philosophical school and seek to improve one's own soul.[19]

Plato shares the ancient conception that the public sphere is the realm of official politics. However, he complicates matters by turning the traditional prioritization of the public sphere (see Aristotle) on its head in preference for the private sphere of individual philosophical training. Plato shows the importance of place by naming the locations of public gatherings and by relocating his own school from a gymnasium to his own private garden. A deep tension (or even contradiction) exists between the categories of public and private in Plato's writing, and many scholars agree that this tension has emerged from Plato's radical re-evaluation of the public and private spheres.[20] While Socrates embraced a public life for the sake of his fellow citizens, Plato scorned the public/political sphere because he personally witnessed its ignorance, incorrigibility, and injustice. Thus, Plato's writings are an excellent resource to explore how an author can reshape the portrayal of a hero based on particular views of the public and the private.

---

for justice, given a debased public world" (*Public Man*, 22–23). Ferrari cites the autobiographical comments in the *Seventh Letter* about Plato's dealings with the Thirty as well Socrates' execution to claim that Plato "came eventually to understand that no form of government in any existing state was satisfactory, and was driven to declare that there would be no end to the general wretchedness until philosophers . . . were given political power." See Plato, *Republic*, xii–xiii.

14. Patterson, *Family*, 180–82.

15. Veyne describes the gymnasium as "a second public square, a place where anyone could go" ("Roman Empire," 21). Thus, there was a dramatic shift in Plato's move from public gymnasia to private garden.

16. Donovan, "City and the Garden," 453 and 458–59. Debra Nails, *Agora, Academy*, 213–15.

17. Ober, "Gadfly on Trial," §§ 1–9, esp. § 3.

18. Ibid., § 6.

19. Ibid., § 7.

20. Thus, looking through the lens of Sack's framework, the force of meaning has come to dominate the forces of place, social relationships, and nature resulting in a recasting of the figure of Socrates.

Unlike the tension in Plato, Aristotle's writings have a thoroughgoing consistency about the public and private spheres. Aristotle's *Politics* is more a philosophical analysis of existing political realities than a utopian reflection as found in Plato's *Republic*. At the beginning of book 3 of the *Politics*, Aristotle draws together several forces to asseverate that public acts (πρᾶξις, meaning) and politicians (πολιτικός, self) have the state (πόλις, social relations) and its organization (πολιτεία, meaning) as their proper object (*Pol.* 1274b). Aristotle concludes that the life of virtue and happiness is best and that such a life, both individually and communally, is fostered by action in general and political action in particular (see *Pol.* 1324a—1325b). Aristotle places great value on the interconnectedness of the individual and the collective (see the end of 1325b), and while he prefers πόλις language over other terms for public and private (such as δημοσίος and ἴδιος), he does speak of the importance of "common" (κοινός) interests as one of the defining characteristics of the public sphere: "But it is necessary to manage public matters [τῶν κοινῶν] in a public manner [κοινήν]. At the same time, one must not think that any citizen belongs to himself, but rather all belong to the state for each one is a part of it" (*Pol.* 1337a). Social relationships come to the fore in this quotation for it the interrelatedness of all people that creates and prioritizes the public-political sphere.

Aristotle's views of the public and private spheres have also drawn some attention from modern scholars who have debated both the boundaries and valences of these two arenas. For Hannah Arendt, Aristotle was one of the foundational thinkers that cast the active life as a *bios politikos*, a life that produced beauty through excellent deeds.[21] Aristotle was the champion of one of Arendt's ideals, the truly political nature of the human condition. According to Arendt, Aristotle defined man as a *zōon politikon*, and drew a sharp line between the public/political sphere, where a man through action and (especially) speech could realize freedom and excellence, and the private/domestic sphere, where lesser matters of usefulness and necessity dominated.[22] Arendt's reflections on the human condition led to a number of later studies that have interacted with her strong claims, particularly from a feminist perspective.[23] The force of nature plays a very prominent role in Aristotle's classification, for the private and public sphere are definitively gendered according to nature: the public and political world was for men (*Pol.* 1253b, 1254b), while the home was the domain of the woman (*Oec.* 1343b).[24] Elshtain comments that such a division and Aristotle's preference for the public/male over the private/female emerges out of his teleological thinking, but that his view of participatory politics holds promise for feminist

---

21. Arendt, *Human Condition*, 12–13.

22. Ibid., 23–25. Arendt manifests the trumping of social relations by the force of meaning, for her teleological anthropology valorizes a particular type of spatial and social existence.

23. For instance see Habermas, *Structural Transformation*; Elshtain, *Public Man, Private Woman*, 41–54; D'Entrèves, "Public and Private"; and Swanson, *Public and Private in Aristotle*.

24. While the authorship of the *Oeconomica* is disputed, the female nature of the private sphere can be implied and inferred from Aristotle's comments on male and female nature at the beginning of the *Politics*. Patterson counters Arendt's use of Aristotle to demote the household claiming that while Aristotle preferred politics, he distinguished the two because he saw them as very different social entities (Patterson, *Family*, 182–83). Interestingly, Aristotle describes the household with public/political structures while Plato uses kinship terms to describe his ideal politics (ibid., 181–82).

thinkers.[25] However, Judith Swanson claims that Arendt and her intellectual descendants have overemphasized this difference in Aristotle, who actually envisioned a more dynamic relationship between the public and private spheres where both mutually support each other.[26]

The dramatists and historians have been absent thus far from this survey of classical Athens. Why is this so? The dramatists rarely comment explicitly on public and private matters, perhaps because they can rely on stage and setting to provide most of these cues. On the other hand, historians like Thucydides, Herodotus, and Diodorus use the whole gamut of terms that we have seen so far to reference private, public, and political affairs. However, while the dramatists can rely on stage and setting in their high-context society, the historians seem to rely on the terminology itself and rarely go into detail to explain why and how something is public or private. Furthermore, most of the historians write primarily about famous military and political events, which were naturally assumed to be public/political, and the private sphere is important only in the few instances when it impacts these more monumental events. However, Sophocles and Thucydides both have a contribution to make to this survey before it comes to a summary.

In *The Women of Trachis*, Sophocles portrays Deianeira standing in front of her home as a series of visitors report critical events that are transpiring. At one point a messenger enters bearing a report about Heracles that he had just heard spoken in the marketplace in the presence of many witnesses (*Trach.* 351–52). He says, "I heard this all from him, and there were several men in the marketplace who heard the same thing I did" (*Trach.* 371–72). Sophocles dramatically represents the marketplace (force of place) as a male space (force of nature) where news is pronounced to a large audience (force of social relations). Deianeira as a woman is excluded from this sphere and must be told what is going on because she and the other women remain near the home (*Trach.* 335–44). However, the news of Heracles's feats and fate are not political; they come closer to gossip. Also, the basis of the entire play is Deianeira's anxious marriage to Heracles. Thus, the issues discussed publicly in the marketplace are more personal than political on the basis of the forces of meaning (the content of the account) and social relations (the issue of a private marriage), though they are of interest to the entire community.

Next, Thucydides offers a couple of revealing remarks about private, public, and political matters. He says that most Athenians show interest in both private/domestic (οἰκείων, emphasizing the force of place in the identification of the private sphere) and public/political (πολιτικῶν) matters, being skilled in both personal business (ἔργα) and political practice (πολιτικά) (2.40.2). Of course, the public/political domain is accorded greater honor, for Athenians "regard the man who does not participate [in politics], not as a person who minds his own business, but as useless" (2.40.2). Thucydides also boasts that the Athenians do treat all men equally under the law in private disputes, but that a public reputation accrues to those who distinguish themselves by aiding the state (2.37.1–2). In both cases, the force of meaning determines the value of the self. Thucydides reiterates the

---

25. Elshtain, *Public Man*, 44–47.
26. Swanson, *Public and Private in Aristotle*, 1–4.

classical Greek identification of the public and the political as well as the prioritization of the public over the private. He also states that while private life has its proper place in business and law, public life is reserved for those who demonstrate honor and greatness through their words and actions.

Thus far this survey has focused on classical Athens. As stated above, this heritage is handed down to Luke's day through the spread of Hellenism. Dio Chrysostom is an excellent representative of a Hellenistic author who maintains these classical perspectives. Dio recommends that a young man who desires to be a proficient public speaker should consult many of the works discussed above: first and foremost Homer, and also Demosthenes and Aeschines. When mentioning the Socratics he focuses on Xenophon, who is an exemplar of the public speaker: one who commands armies, guides matters of state, addresses assemblies, and speaks in courts of law (*Dic. Exercit.* 14). This description comports very well with the depiction of public space found in the classical authors. Dio articulates the principle (similar to Demosthenes and Aeschines) that a person's values should hold across both the public and private spheres: "For just as you have words of praise for those in private life who are reasonable and prefer occasionally to submit to wrong rather than to quarrel with people, so also in public relations we find that cities of that sort are in good repute" (*2 Tars.* 44). Dio affirmed that public service was the highest calling, especially for a philosopher (*Rec. Mag.* 3), but like Plato he became skeptical about the public sphere (*Cont.* 2–3). Several other Hellenistic authors will be considered later in this study: Arrian in the section on Rome, and Josephus and Philo in the Jewish material. Most importantly, the work of two Hellenistic authors, Plutarch and Philostraus, are the focus of the in-depth analysis of the next chapter.

Now we turn to adduce the relevant work of David Cohen in his book *Law, Sexuality, and Society*. Cohen explores the social and legal mechanisms that structured and enforced sexual norms in ancient Athens. His starting point, after methodological considerations, is a careful analysis of the categories of public and private in classical Athens.[27] His poignant survey and expert explanation of the relevant material deserves a summary here. Cohen begins by pointing out that the public/private dichotomy was indigenous to classical Athenian society (as seen in the pair κοινός καὶ ἴδιος), so it is best to begin with the contrast itself rather than standing definitions of either sphere.[28] Throughout, Cohen skillfully connects buttressing polarities of male/female and honor/shame to show how they meshed with public/private, which he prefers to call a set of "complementary opposites" rather than a dichotomy to indicate their fluid and layered nature.

Cohen goes on to make three other interrelated points. First, Athenians identified the home as the paradigm of the private sphere and associated it with women (thus deploying the forces of place and nature). Second, the public sphere was generally male and involved political action (again featuring nature and also meaning). However, and third, these labels and their concomitant ideological generalizations were stretched, challenged, and manipulated in numerous ways through social and rhetorical practices to both gen-

---

27. Cohen's fourth chapter is devoted to this topic (*Law*, 70–97). The chapter is one of the very few (and definitely the very best) sustained study on this particular topic in the context of classical Athens.

28. Ibid., 70.

erate and preserve honor.[29] Thus, Cohen asserts that the application of these seemingly dichotomous terms in the honor/shame culture of Athens must be reconsidered in two ways. First, the domains of the two spheres themselves were not as rigid as generally assumed. With careful support from primary documents, Cohen concludes that "the public sphere is larger than politics and the private sphere is more extensive than the household."[30] Second, the terms "public" and "private" were in fact strongly relational and fluid so they could easily be shaped and applied to particular rhetorical purposes.[31]

Cohen moves on to examine privacy and hones in on the standards of sexual morality, but his points are still relevant to this more general survey of social-spatial zones in classical Athens. He states that "restrictions on the movement of women outside of the house have often been greatly exaggerated."[32] This exaggeration has had two causes: many scholars do not temper the cultural ideals of the ancient elite with evidence of actual social practice, and in practice the domestic boundaries of the ancient private sphere were far from impenetrable. This slightly demotes the force of place in classifying the private sphere and leads to the second illuminating point. One of the prominent exceptions to the barriers of privacy was the institution of friendship (φιλία). Friends often rivaled kin ties in loyalty, and close friends had intimate access to the private life of a family. Male friends of the head of the house, and often female neighbors/friends of the women of the household, were social forces that connected the privacy of the home to the larger community.[33] Thus, this social reality was one way that the public sphere entered the home and simultaneously made the οἶκος less private.[34] Finally, Cohen echoes that a man's reputation in classical Athens was indeed a state of honor derived from the opinion of the public. However, members of the household often protected that reputation by secrecy and deceit. Therefore, other members of the community frequently turned to gossip, innuendo, and inference (rather than observable public actions) in order to construct and destruct a person's reputation.[35] Thus, one's reputation was not a simplistic and direct result of public behavior. Rather, the "politics of reputation" was a coalescence of several social forces and

---

29. Ibid., 76–77. Cohen draws particularly on the work of Bordieu and other contemporary anthropologists who support this conclusion by claiming that cultural ideals must always be considered in light of actual social practice (84).

30. Ibid., 78. This point clearly reinforces the expansion of the classification of public and private space suggested in the first chapter of this study.

31. Ibid., 77. Cohen sites the example of a banquet. While representing a fairly stable social phenomenon, a banquet could be considered a public duty (such as a wedding feast) or a private prerogative (such as a symposium).

32. The sheer existence of cases of adultery indicates that privacy could be violated (willingly or unwillingly). Such sexual misconduct seemed almost commonplace and was problematic enough to be regulated by laws. Cohen covers this evidence in more detail in his sixth chapter.

33. Ibid., 85–88.

34. This institution was also somewhat suspect for the private access could be abused as in cases of adultery between a woman and a male neighbor/friend.

35. Ibid., 95–96.

techniques across the private-public/political spectrum that could be manipulated and deployed in a variety of ways in the attribution of honor and shame.[36]

The Hellenistic Space of Ephesus

Several aspects of the city of Ephesus qualify it for consideration at this point. A strong Hellenistic tradition molded both the architecture and social practices of this city.[37] The city layout and social structure were deeply indebted to its Hellenistic heritage, but also to the Roman emperors, beginning with Augustus, who increased the city's status and stature in innumerable ways.[38] The city was also a center of Roman administration and emperor worship.[39] Additionally, as a major seaport on the journey from the East to the West, Ephesus had an influx of cultural and religious influences from provincial Asia and the rest of the East that affected the character and makeup of the city.[40] Ephesus was a major seaport, a key economic market, a religious center (of both Artemis and the emperors), and a political/administrative hub of the Roman Empire. It was a cosmopolitan metropolis of the Roman Empire and an important seat for Hellenistic-Roman culture.[41] Thus, Ephesus is a good fit for the profile of the implied author of Luke as a cultured Gentile who lived in an urban area in the eastern part of the empire.[42] Luke is clearly well informed about certain specific details of the early history of the Christian movement at Ephesus, and he adds a number of brushes of local detail. Acts records that Ephesus was Paul's longest stop on any of his missionary journeys (two years according to 19:10). Furthermore, Acts claims that Paul's influence from this prominent city was province-wide (also 19:10). Luke includes a number of local specifics included in the long Ephesian narrative in Acts (18:24—19:41): the presence of Apollos, Priscilla, and Aquila, Paul's interaction with the disciples of John the Baptist, the episode with the Sons of Sceva, and the local color (including specific names, offices, and locations) included in the tale of the riot at Ephesus. On top of this, Luke has Paul give his farewell address to the Ephesian elders in 20:17–38, despite the fact that Paul still has quite a bit of living to do. While the provenance of Luke-Acts is highly debated and uncertain,[43] Ephesus could be considered a possibility, or at least representative of the character of cities in this part of the empire.

---

36. Ibid., 97.

37. Scherrer, "Historical Topography of Ephesus," 85–87; and DeVries, *Cities of the Biblical World*, 372–73.

38. For a survey of both the Hellenistic and Roman contributions to the city of Ephesus see Scherrer, "Topography."

39. Trebilco, "Asia," 308–9; and McRay, *Archaeology and the New Testament*, 257.

40. The possible impact of these influences particularly on the worship of Artemis is discussed in Baugh, *Paul and Ephesus*, 32–39. There also appears to have been a Jewish presence in Ephesus as well. See Kalantzis, "Ephesus ," 113–17.

41. Ephesus was probably the third largest city in the empire (Trebilco, "Asia," 307). The cosmopolitan nature of Ephesus is attested to repeatedly in most of all of the sources sited above.

42. For this representation of Luke see Robbins, "Social Location," 305–32.

43. Fitzmyer, *Luke*, 1:57. He says that the provenance is "anyone's guess."

PART ONE: READING LUKE'S SOCIAL-SPATIAL CONTEXT

Not only does Ephesus represent a cosmopolitan city that fits the profile of the author of Luke-Acts, it has also been well preserved and excavated. Since 1895, the exploration of this ancient site has been under the excellent supervision of the Austrian Archaeological Institute and has led to a plethora of detailed publications.[44] This stands in stark contrast to a site like Syrian Antioch, which has also been suggested as Luke's home. Very little is known about ancient Antioch because the modern city of Antakya rests on the ancient site.[45] Oster proclaims that the richly researched material remains of Ephesus cry out for serious use by NT scholars, a cry that has largely gone unheeded.[46] The city center of Ephesus has been preserved, excavated, and studied in magnificent detail (see the maps provided below). In addition to this, there have been a few recent attempts to interpret the remains of Ephesus in light of social and spatial dynamics. All of these external factors make Ephesus a suitable candidate to provide the social-spatial context for Luke's writing, alongside the internal indicators in Acts.

The site of Ephesus, near the mouth of the Cayaster River, was colonized by the Greeks in the ninth century BCE. An ancient sanctuary had existed on the site, but the first temple to Artemis was constructed by Croesus. This ancient sanctuary was burnt down and rebuilt with greater glory in the fourth century BCE. The city had to be moved due to the silting up of the river, and Lysimachos (one of the heirs of Alexander) refounded the city on its current site early in the third century BCE at the foot of Panayir Dag, a small mountain just to the east of the city center. Ephesus later came under the control of the Seleucids, and the Romans inherited the city in 133 BCE. However, Ephesus resisted Roman rule and participated in local rebellions (for which it paid heavily), but it came under full Roman control in 84 BCE. After this low period, Ephesus began to rise again. Octavian spent six months in the city and named it the new capital of Asia in 29 CE. This began an economic, cultural, architectural, and religious renaissance in Ephesus that would last for the next two hundred years under the Roman emperors, who tended to favor this increasingly prominent city. It became a center of Roman administration and a *neokoros*, or temple warden, for the official worship of the Roman emperors.[47] Thus, during the late first century and early second century CE (the most probable period for the writing of Luke-Acts), Ephesus was a thriving cosmopolitan center with a rich Hellenistic heritage and ongoing Roman favor. Two maps of the city as it looked in 104 CE are provided above and below.[48]

---

44. See Oster, *Bibliography of Ancient Ephesus*. For more selective and updated bibliographies see Koester, ed. *Ephesos*, xi–xv; and Scherrer, "Topography," 57.

45. DeVries, *Cities*, 374.

46. Oster, *Bibiography*, xii–xxiv. Two exceptions to this are Koester's edited volume and Baugh's dissertation. In addition to the structural remains that inform this study is a wealth of inscriptions that are used by Baugh as well as Horsley ("Inscriptions of Ephesos") and Van Tilborg (*Reading John in Ephesus*).

47. An overview of this history can be found in Scherrer, "Topography."

48. These maps are taken respectively from Rogers, *Sacred Identity*, 196 and 197. They are both reproduced here with the permission of the author.

Figure 3.1 Large View of Roman Ephesus in 104 CE

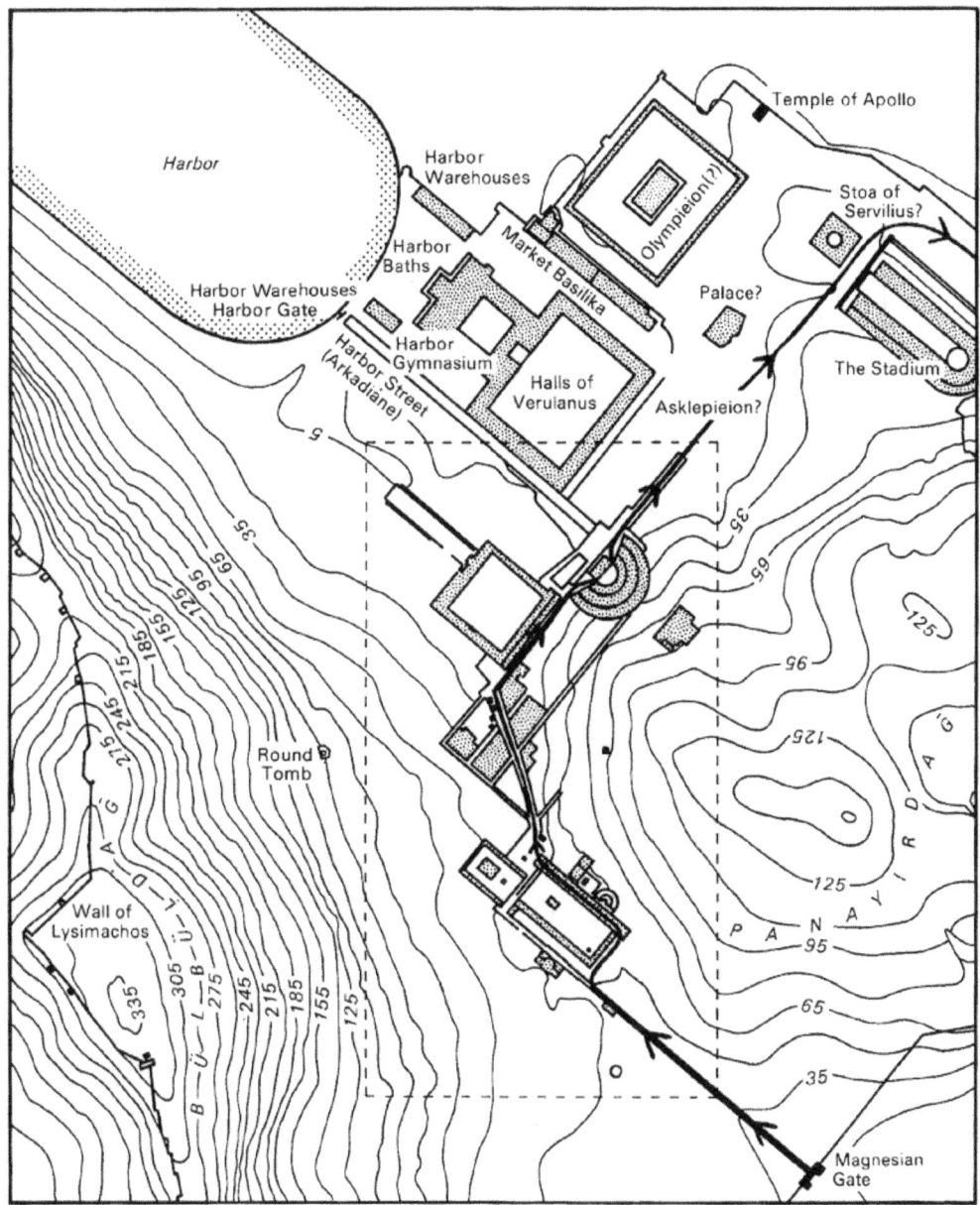

PART ONE: READING LUKE'S SOCIAL-SPATIAL CONTEXT

Figure 3.2 Streets and Hellenistic Agora of Ephesus in 104 CE
(detail from the dotted rectangle in figure 3.1)

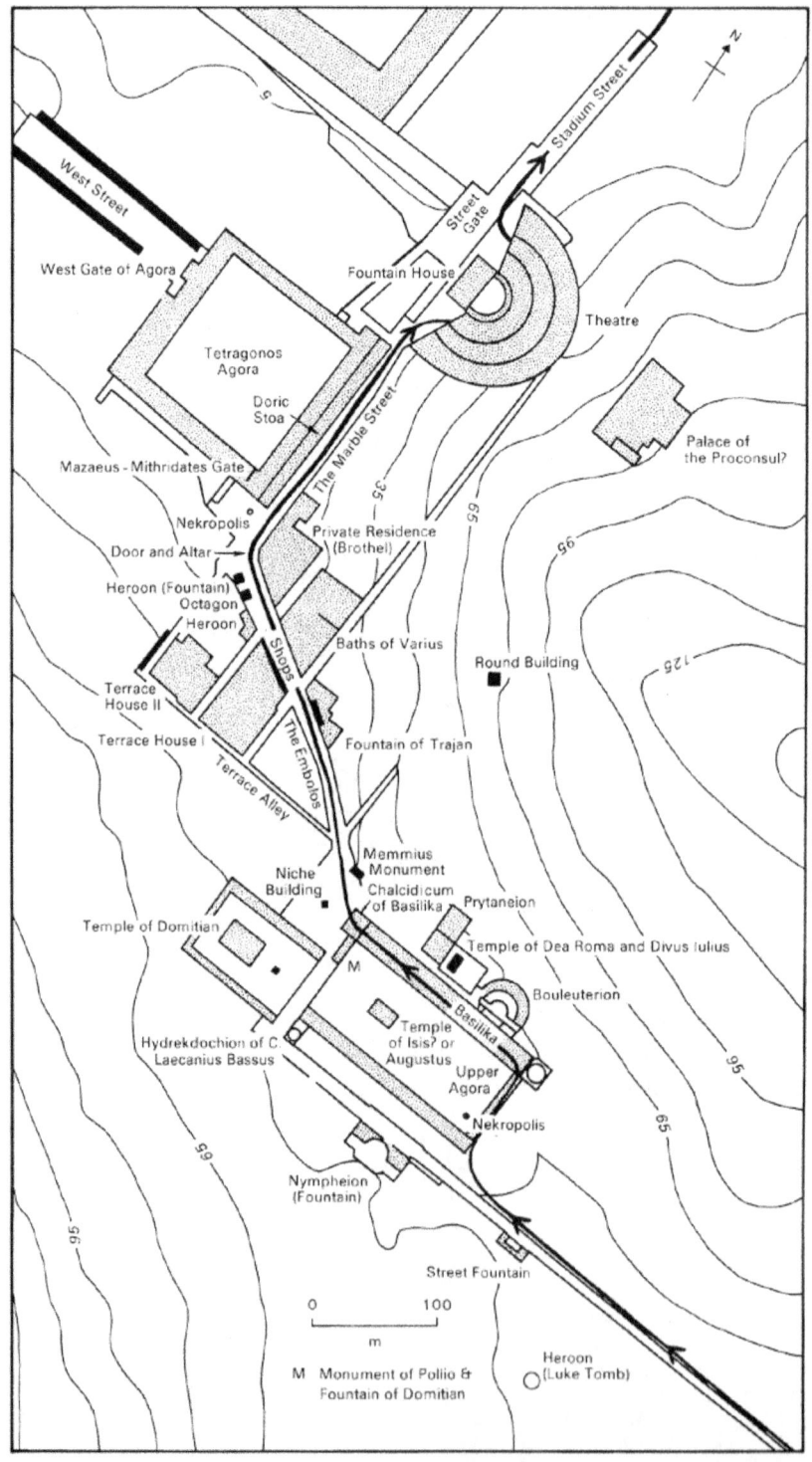

Private, Public, and Political in the Ancient Contexts of Luke's Gospel

These maps set the stage for a brief discussion of some of the salient architectural features of Ephesus. This will lead to a discussion of a few other suggestive studies and how this material might be employed in the social-spatial exegesis of Luke 18:35—19:48. The Curetes Street[49] leads from the Magnesian Gate on the southeast corner of the city up to the old Hellenistic or Upper Agora. From here the Marble Road (so called because it was paved with marble) moves along the eastern face of the newer Tetragonos Agora to the theatre. The Harbor Street or Arcadian Way was a colonnaded street that led from the theatre to the harbor perpendicular to the Marble Road. From the theatre, the Stadium Street continues to the northeast corner of the city and then leads out the Koressian Gate to the Temple of Artemis. Clear thoroughfares dissected the city. The main land trade route that stretched from the Euphrates through Asia Minor led into the Magnesian Gate and exited at the northeastern corner. From the northeastern corner, there was a branch that continued on to the temple and another that encircled sacred Mount Pion. This route from the temple to the Magnesian Gate, through the city, and back to the temple was used in various festivals and religious processions (often called the *via sacra*). One can retrace this common route through the city in order to point out the key structures in Ephesus.

The first buildings met on this route after leaving the temple and entering the Magnesian Gate are devoted to the worship of the emperors. A set of shrines and temples are clustered around the early Temple to Augustus (Isis?). Alongside these structures are a basilica as well as a *prytaneion* and a *bouleuterion* for official city meetings known as the civic agora.[50] The Ephesians' political identity included imperial elements (emperor worship) and local structures (like the *bouleuterion* for the city βουλή). These initial structures on the traveler's path through the city use space and architecture to proclaim the political and religious identity of Ephesus to both visitors and inhabitants. Following the course to the northwest, we come to the two only houses at Ephesus that have been excavated. The so-called "slope houses" or *hanghäuser* are large, grand, and diverse house complexes located on the slope of another hill to the south of Ephesus. Each of these "houses" was actually an entire insula containing several homes creatively built into this topographically challenging area. A row of shops and taverns face the road, but behind and above these are multiple stories, terraces, and rooms comprising several house units (called *Wohneinheit* in the Austrian excavations). The houses are decorated with fine mosaic floors and ornate wall paintings. This, along with their location in the heart of the city, indicates that they were probably inhabited by some of the most distinguished citizens of Ephesus.[51]

Near these grand homes are a set of baths, latrines, and a large brothel located across the corner from the city's commercial center. The Tetragonos Agora was the old Hellenistic agora that served commercial purposes in Roman Ephesus. So the traveler is guided first through the state agora (emphasizing Ephesian political identity) and then into the economic quarter of the city. This important turn in the road brought together homes, shops, markets, and establishments for personal comfort and entertainment. Continuing on the route, a series of cultural structures were either built or substantially rebuilt during the

---

49. Named for priests who represent the ancients who attended the birth of Artemis.
50. Yamauchi, *NT Cities*, 88; Erdemgil, *Ephesus*, 38–43.
51. Erdemgil, *Ephesus*, 75.

Roman period, largely through the generosity of the emperors or the wealthy imperial freedmen who dominated Ephesian society during the late first century CE. This includes the theatre (greatly expanded by Claudius and Nero), the harbor, the harbor baths (donated by a wealthy sophist), the market basilica, and a series of buildings devoted to athletics: the arena of Verulanus (sponsored by the high priest during Hadrian's reign), the harbor gymnasium, and the stadium (built during the reign of Nero). Many of these were built under the reign of the Julio-Claudian and/or Flavian emperors, and they served the growing population and famous festivals that were held at Ephesus.[52]

The final structure that must be mentioned is the Temple to Artemis or Artemesion. This is perhaps the most famous structure at Ephesus, located a short distance away from the city. This magnificent temple was completely destroyed by the Goths in 125 CE and has had to be reconstructed from literary accounts and less substantial remains. In addition, the Artemesion's location outside of the city (quite different from Jerusalem) makes it less applicable to how Luke and his audience might have imagined the temple in Jerusalem and Jesus' entry into it in light of any experience in Ephesus. What is eminently clear from this survey is that the urban layout of Ephesus was dominated by a series of public structures set on a circular route that linked to the temple and the trade road while navigating the steep hills on either side of the city. Ephesus also had two agoras (the lower or civic and the upper or commercial) as well as a rich set of cultural/athletic buildings in the northwestern quadrant of the city. The urban structures of Ephesus combined and interrelated private, public, political, commercial, and religious life.

Three preliminary conclusions can be drawn from this overview of Ephesus. First, the path through the city was clearly and grandly laid out for any traveler by a set of large, decorated streets. Major buildings are linked by a circular route with one spur leading out to the harbor. The buildings were carefully placed on this thoroughfare to introduce the traveler to the political/religious, economic, and cultural character of the city in that specific order. This throughway publicly proclaimed the identity and character of Ephesus as a Roman metropolis with a Hellenistic heritage. This was experienced daily by visitors, members of ritualized religious processions, and citizens on more mundane business. Thus, the force of place (and possibly nature in the architecture), combined with the force of meaning, helped create civic identity. Second, public buildings dominate the urban layout of Ephesus. The commercial agora was probably the pre-Roman heart of the city, but under Roman patronage in the first century CE the public buildings in Ephesus increased in number, size, and magnificence (e.g., the civic agora, the theatre, the arena of Verulanus, etc.). Thus, during the period that Luke and his audience probably lived (from the late first century into the early second), public space and public representations were coming to dominate the city of Ephesus in ever increasing ways. It is no surprise then that Luke would follow this trend by (perhaps intuitively or unconsciously) moving Jesus into the public sphere that was on the rise in Ephesus. The third and final conclusion is a corollary of the second. The extant remains and the dominance of public structures reveal a paucity of private space. The only structures we have to work with here are the slope houses,

---

52. Yamauchi, *NT Cities*, 90–92.

the brothel/latrine complex, and perhaps the baths and gymnasia to some degree. These structures are tightly integrated into the public structures of the city. From a brief look at the topography of Ephesus and its practical effects on the layout of the slope houses, one could conclude that the density of the homes due to the hilly surroundings reduced the natural availability of private space (more can be found in the less constrained city layout of Pompeii). Therefore, the domestic space was concentrated and small, lowering the spatial availability of privacy and perhaps affecting the social practices of privacy in these homes.

From this survey and a few initial conclusions, we can turn to experts who have analyzed the architecture and urban development of Ephesus with an eye on its social implications. The first piece is a recent article by Michele George, entitled "Domestic Architecture and Household Relations: Pompeii and Roman Ephesos." George opens her article with a statement that is in deep agreement with the perspective of this study. She says, "In Roman culture, in both the western and eastern parts of the empire, the public dimension to domestic space that is revealed in textual sources adumbrates the crucial role of the house as a vehicle for self-representation." George begins with social analysis of the homes at Pompeii. She comments that the remarkable number and preservation of Pompeian homes provides the best evidence for recovering some understanding of Roman domestic life as it was lived in typical Roman architecture.[53] She goes on to discuss two cases: gender and slaves. She concludes that gender divisions in the Roman home (when they did occur) were enacted by temporal rather than spatial means (e.g., the morning *salutatio* the atrium would have been avoided by the women of the house).[54] Clear divisions did exist between the service and reception areas of the home. Yet, slaves did not have designated quarters, and rather were omnipresent throughout the home in order to serve the needs of their owners.

Next, George examines the Ephesian homes, which differ so greatly from those found in Pompeii.[55] She notes several distinguishing characteristics of the Ephesian slope houses. First, they are actually apartment dwellings because the topographical situation demanded that more space be shared and closely linked, unlike the more discrete sections that could be built into Pompeian homes. The main entrances tended to be more subtle and indirect, which may indicate a favoring of the Greek preference for domestic privacy.[56] Furthermore, the great variety of the dwellings contained within these "homes" and the variation from the Pompeian examples makes it difficult to reconstruct social practices based on the extant domestic architecture at Ephesus.[57] Second, these homes lack the axiality of the homes studied by Wallace-Hadrill at Pompeii. Rather, these units generally reflect the Greek preference for a layout gathered around a central courtyard. Finally, much like Pompeii, owners attempted to decorate homes according to popular style. Wall paintings and floor mosaics fell into expected genres or type

53. George, "Pompeii and Ephesos," 11.
54. Thus, it is the force of time, not place that established these patterns.
55. George, "Pompeii and Ephesos," 15.
56. Ibid., 15.
57. Ibid., 18.

scenes and were commissioned to signal the wealth and status of the owner. From this she can conclude very little about the life of slaves in the Ephesian homes. On the other hand, the lack of specific male and female quarters (*andron* and *gynaikonitis*) may reveal how Roman influence pushed out this traditional Greek form of domestic architecture. However, George strongly cautions against dogmatic conclusions and ends by claiming that Roman influence varied widely throughout the eastern half of the empire.[58]

Michael White's article on "Urban Development and Social Change in Imperial Ephesos" does not cover the social-spatial specifics of the city but reinforces the larger cultural and architectural developments that took place at Ephesus from the first to the fourth centuries. Roman Ephesus was a thriving city that built upon its Hellenistic heritage. White points out that during this period Ephesus was the most important city of Asia, enjoying almost unmitigated growth and prosperity especially as reflected in frequent and magnanimous building projects.[59] White looks at the Ephesian narrative in Acts for examples of what might have been occurring in this burgeoning city. He notes the difficulties of using Acts as a historical source, but also states, "Acts portrays characterizations and conventions of urban life at the time when it was written as a part of its peculiar interpretation of the process of expansion of the Christian movement." Thus, in White's view Acts does a fair (one might say "verisimiltudinous") job of representing urban life and the change taking place in Ephesus during this period.

By examining the demographic, architectural, and epigraphic evidence, White concludes that Ephesus grew through an influx of immigrants during this period. Ephesus's population appears to have doubled from 100,000 to 200,000 between 50 and 150 CE, even though the evidence indicates that the high mortality rates at the time tended to keep general population growth at zero. Thus, this drastic increase can only be accounted for by immigration, which would radically alter the city's ethnic and cultural makeup.[60] The increase in building projects, the representation of a vibrant foreign presence (especially of freedmen), and the epigraphical evidence all point toward the same influx.[61] White notes that many people might have come to Ephesus in this period to enjoy status and honors that they could not receive at home (mostly due to their freed status). These immigrants brought a surge of wealth, creativity, and energy in this period which accounts

FIGURE 3.3

This large, composite structure faces the Curetes Street on its northeast side and a "house street" on the south with smaller alleys on the west and east. Shops, restaurants, and taverns lined Curetes Street. Behind these are 7 Wohneinheiten (WE) or dwelling units, essentially seven separate homes. The largest of these houses are WE 6 and 7, which both contain two large reception areas (an example of the developing peristyle house). However, the main entrances are reached from the side alley (WE 6 may have street access through T III). The entrances to the other houses are even more remote from the main street, and this placement may denote a heightened degree of access control (and privacy) or might represent the necessities of the topography. The houses behind 6 and 7 are denser and have smaller rooms (once again perhaps due to the requirements of the topography), but each house (with the possible exception of WE 3) incorporates a substantial reception area.

58. Ibid., 23.
59. White, "Urban Development," 34.
60. Ibid., 43–48.
61. Ibid., 57–61.

Private, Public, and Political in the Ancient Contexts of Luke's Gospel

for the bloom in building projects.[62] White's conclusions buttress the comments made above in two ways. It supports the cosmopolitan nature of Ephesus during this period and also helps to explain the increase in public architecture that came to dominate the urban space in Ephesus around the time that Luke wrote.

Figure 3.3 The Layout of Slope House 2[63]

62. This influx may have caused a reaction that stands behind the distrust of "foreigners" revealed in the riot at Ephesus in Acts 19.

63. Krinzinger, *Das Hanghaus 2*, 155. This illustration is used with the permission of the publisher. I have included the lines demarcating the separate homes following George "Pompeii and Ephesos," 17.

75

PART ONE: READING LUKE'S SOCIAL-SPATIAL CONTEXT

The last piece that must be examined here is Guy Rogers's monograph *The Sacred Identity of Ephesos: Foundation Myths of a Roman City*. Rogers's study focuses on a long and large inscription found in Ephesus that describes a special donation made in the very early second century CE by Salutaris to the city of Ephesus in order to fund an annual lottery and a biweekly procession. Rogers begins by describing how this moderately sized donation (others had made much larger contributions) was made by a private citizen. However, unlike many other donations, this particular one was meticulously negotiated and publicly approved by the city *Boule*. The inscription "relentlessly" reminds the reader that this was also a sacred donation closely associated with the temple, where the lottery took place and where the procession began and ended.[64] Thus, Salutaris's private donation set up a foundation for ongoing ritual lotteries and processions that were simultaneously very public and overtly sacred.[65] Rogers continues by describing the details of the lottery and the procession.[66] He concludes that this meticulous ordering and ranking of such small amounts of money served a social-symbolic function that reaffirmed or reasserted a very traditional version of the Ephesian social order, which recalled the Greek roots of the city.[67] At the same time, Salutaris included young adults of the city in with the male elders of the day.

The procession performed similar functions through spatial, temporal, and material means. The biweekly procession included 260 persons and 29 silver statues, which mostly portrayed figures from Ephesus's Greek and Hellenistic heritage. The procession left from the temple and followed the same route through the city as was discussed above: in the Magnesian Gate, through the civic agora, by the commercial agora and theatre, past the stadium and then out the Koressian Gate, which commemorated the ancient founding of the city by Androkolos. The route followed the "map of foundations" in reverse chronological order, from Roman power in the civic agora, through the Hellenized middle section of the city, and climaxing with the Greek founder. Thus, it left the ephebes with a lasting impression of the Ionian founding of the city resonating in their minds as they marched out with the elite elders whose places they would fill one day.[68] In Rogers's opinion, the primary purpose of this ritual was to enculturate the ephebes into the Hellenized cultural and social elite of Ephesus (while simultaneously raising Salutaris's honor). Thus, Salutaris established two sacred and public acts (a lottery and a procession) that served three interlocking purposes: to reassert the Greek and Hellenistic heritage of the city in a time of Roman authority, to reinforce the social hierarchy of the city that was based on this heritage, and to enculturate first the ephebes and second the entire citizenry into this sociocultural vision of Ephesus.[69]

What then does this examination of Ephesus add to the framework presented in this chapter and its potential as an analytical tool in the exegesis of Luke's Gospel? First, follow-

64. Rogers, *Sacred Identity*, 29.
65. Ibid., 25–29.
66. Ibid., 43–52.
67. Ibid., 72.
68. Ibid., 112–15.
69. Ibid., 136–40.

ing George, a serious examination of Ephesus's domestic architecture prevents facile and/or simplistic applications of local and contextual social-spatial realities to Luke's Gospel. The variations in domestic architecture and between Ephesus and Pompeii and within Ephesus itself make it difficult to directly deduce social practices or categories. Ephesus reveals some Roman elements and some Hellenistic elements, but there is no definitive pattern. Add to this the temporal variations in the use of space and the lack of substantiating literary resources and the picture becomes even murkier. However, Ephesus does show just how dense, contiguous, and integrated domestic, public, commercial, civic, and religious space could be in an urban area. What is clear, therefore, is that a flexible and nuanced heuristic is needed to begin to assess and classify the social nature and function of places and spaces in the Greco-Roman world. Ephesus provides an example of a complex, cosmopolitan city thriving during the time of Luke's writing.[70] Second, White's study of Ephesus reveals some of what could happen under the confluence of several social-spatial traditions: east and west, Greek and Roman, native and immigrant, local and imperial. These traditions came to bear on Ephesian society and space in creative and variegated ways. Finally, Rogers's work shows a creative combination of forces in the creation of identity. The biweekly procession (force of time) used a particular route (force of space) to create a specific, and very Hellenized, identity for the city and its inhabitants (force of meaning), which began and ended in the Artemision (force of religion). This demonstrates how identity was creatively constructed and challenged through social-spatial means in Luke's day. In particular, entering and/or passing through a city was often no mundane matter. City entrances and streets were organized, constructed, and decorated in the light of sociocultural realities and ideological aims. The layout of the streets in Ephesus not only gave visitors and inhabitants easy access through the city, but they also proclaimed important facts about how the Ephesian elite (in particular) construed their own identity. Thus, it may be no incidental matter for Jesus to "pass through" Jericho surrounded by a great throng and then invite himself to Zacchaeus's home. It also signals how the route to and entrance into Jerusalem might illuminate the identity of Jesus and his movement in Luke. Furthermore, Rogers's insight into the "enculturating" impact of such processions may provide a model for why Luke stresses the presence of the disciples as Jesus leads them through Jericho and up to Jerusalem.

Summary of Greek and Hellenistic Material

This conclusion will collect selected elements of the preceding survey under the various forces to show how they contributed to the construction of the private, public, and political spectrum in classical Greece and its ongoing influence in the Hellenistic world. Place is one of the most obvious forces and it appears quite frequently. Ancient evidence indicates

---

70. Thus, it is always important to pay attention to local subcultures and their particular social-spatial dynamics. The local influence of specific subcultures as well as particular historical and ideological factors on such systems is noted by Rohrbaugh, "Methodological Considerations," 521. Both George and Rohrbaugh rightly urge careful consideration of local specifics to balance sweeping generalization. The challenge with Luke-Acts is that we can only make educated guesses about its original local context and so this study seeks to balance some generalizations with attention to specific locations like Ephesus.

wide agreement about specific locations that were typically public or private. The city is the primary defining locus of the public-political sphere, and many authors mentioned specific public structures within cities: the assembly hall, courtrooms, military camps, theatres, gymnasia, and the marketplace (see Plato and Dio). A few authors made allowances for other general, unspecified public places or seemed to define a public place by reference to the fact that a crowd had gathered there, thus blending the forces of place and social relations. Homes were the ideal private space, and this too was strongly influenced by the force of social relations, for the home is the location of one's family (Isocrates). Gardens and marketplaces could also serve as private places. Urban public space was a powerful tool of identity formation (Rogers), and private architecture shows great flexibility (George). Time and nature played crucial but less frequent roles. The timing of a role or event could determine its valence as public or private (e.g., when Demosthenes was acting as the chorus master or how time affected the gendered nature of domestic space). Nature was critical in defining the public and private sphere, if one remembers that human nature should be included in this force for the ancient Greeks. Aristotle is clearest, but most of his contemporaries would agree, that the nature of the male calls forth public/political activity and speech, while the nature of the female naturally restricts her to the private sphere of the home. Religion often played an intensifying role, such as in the timing of Demosthenes's choir duties or the ideology of procession funded by Salutaris.

The forces of social relations and meaning appear repeatedly. Obviously, the presence of a crowd tended to make a specific scenario public in nature (Plato). Beyond this, specific sets of social relationships were defined as public or private. Family members, personal friends, business contacts, and some teachers were all considered private, embedded in the concerns of home and personal finance (Homer). On the other hand, public relationships took on much broader concerns. Military posts, political offices, and professional orators/prosecutors were widely public social roles. In a less official way, matters of common interest were likewise considered public (like reports about Heracles), but in this case there is more flexibility due to less specificity. For example, Telemachus urges the assembly of the Achaeans that his private situation should be a public matter because it concerns the honor of their community. Finally, speech was crucial in the realm of public social relations. Effective and persuasive public speaking was the key to winning honor, convincing crowds, and directing the life of the city. Rhetoric and persuasion were critical tools that defined and deployed the categories of public and private in specific cases. Public speech took place in public places at public times, was governed by law and custom (Aeschines), and was generally characterized by an agonistic struggle between two opposing parties (as indicated by Demosthenes's self-defense). Regarding the force of meaning, different standards of judgment operated in the different spheres (e.g., Demosthenes, Aristotle). Custom, personal advantage, and opinion governed the private sphere, while the public sphere demanded observable words and deeds, accountability, and accepted public norms of what is just and good. It was widely believed that the public sphere was more important than the private and that true fulfillment (for the superior male) came only through participation in the public and political life of the state (so Aristotle). Part of the ideological construction of these two arenas in classical Athens is that the public and the private *should* be kept separate from one another (e.g., a woman should not speak publicly and the state should not interfere with personal business).

Despite all of the ways in which these forces were deployed to construct private and public space, the boundaries were permeable and flexible in actual practice. Telemachus brings a private matter to the pubic assembly. The marketplace could be both public (so Sophocles) and private (so Demosthenes). Aeschines must specify standards to condemn Timarchus's *public* speaking, and Demosthenes needs to *prove* that Medias committed a public offense against him. Demosthenes's private life was publicly known. More than once, authors claim that character and values should remain consistent across the private and public spheres, and household management was held up as a model for political practice.[71] Plato's and Dio's mixed evaluation of the public/political sphere show how the valorization of the two could be inverted. As indicated in the diversity seen in the survey and reinforced by Cohen's analysis, these labels were not objectively assigned to universally accepted definitions but were intentionally and rhetorically deployed within cultural norms and structures for specific contextual purposes. Friends brought some element of the public sphere into the private home, and were one of the social mechanisms that linked public and private together. Finally, the dense construction of Ephesus brought private dwellings, public haunts (baths and stores), and political structures into very close proximity. Thus, the lived space of the city probably broke down stark dichotomies in practice, leading to more complicated spatial habits. Political and private were clear polarities that helped define social-spatial life; however it was not a rigid dichotomy. Rather, the public sphere already emerges here as part how persons negotiated the complex interaction of the social-spatial aspects of life.

The Second Focus: The Roman World

The second focus of investigation is Rome around the turn of the era. Some of these figures were active and influential at the end of the republic into the imperial period (Cicero and Vitruvius). Others wrote later in the first century CE, closer to the writing of Luke-Acts, about the greatness of Rome and the glory of the empire (Tacitus and Livy). Others, while being Greek and writing in Greek, also composed histories inspired by the greatness of Rome (Appian). Once again, as the literary record shows, Rome as a city and the seat of the empire was an almost mythic ideal that exercised great influence over the world that Luke and his audience inhabited. Scholarship has repeatedly shown that Luke is aware of, influenced by, and responsive to Roman values and government.[72] Thus it is appropriate to

---

71. A similar mixing of values is seen in a comment made by Socrates in Xenopon's *Memorabilia*: "The management of private concerns differs only in point of number from that of public affairs. In other respects they are much alike, and particularly in this, that neither can be executed without men, and the *one employed in private and public transactions is the very same person*" (3.4.12, emphasis added). Socrates's conclusion is that a just man is always just whether the matter is public or private. Thus, one should aim not for a person skilled in public affairs, but for a person who is just no matter what the social-spatial sphere. These comments articulate the common notion (incidentally both ancient and modern) that a person's behavior should be consistent across a variety of places and situations.

72. Walasky, *"And So We Came to Rome,"* 24–28, 63; Esler, *Community and Gospel*, 201–18; Walton, "State They Were In," 33–35.

PART ONE: READING LUKE'S SOCIAL-SPATIAL CONTEXT

consider the influence of the social-spatial dynamics of Roman culture on Luke. This will be complemented by a brief look at Wiltshire's study of public and private in the *Aeneid*, the foundation myth of Rome and its culture. Finally, Pompeii, one of the best preserved cites of Roman antiquity will provide the archaeological *realia* to ground the investigation of the literary resources. The consideration of the Roman focus will begin with the great statesman and orator, Cicero, who wrote frequently and insightfully about the nature of public and private space in his own turbulent life.

The separation and specification of the public and private spheres is a regular theme in Cicero's works. In a moving letter to his close friend Atticus, he poignantly articulates this dichotomy:

> I hardly know if I miss [your friendship] most in politics [*publicane re*], where I do not dare to neglect anything, or in my legal work which I used to practice for my personal honor and now maintain to preserve my position through popularity, or in my domestic affairs [*domesticis negotiis*].... Finally, neither my work nor my rest, neither my business nor my leisure, neither my legal affairs nor my domestic ones, neither my public life [*publicae*] nor my private life [*privatae*] can go on any longer without your most agreeable and affectionate counsel or conversation. (*Att.* 17)

Cicero sometimes divides his activities into three arenas as he does here: political, legal and domestic. Generally, however, the legal and political are subsets of the public sphere. This is implied in the beginning of the quotation but is made clear in the set of binary oppositions that close this quote. Cicero divides his life into public and private domains in order to express his comprehensive grief caused by Atticus's absence:

Table 3.1: Cicero's Public and Private to Atticus

Public (*publicae*)	Private (*privatae*)
Politics (*publicane re*)	Domestic affairs (*domesticis negotiis*)
Work (*labor*)	Rest (*requies*)
Business (*negotium*)	Leisure (*otium*)
Legal affairs (*forenses res*)	Domestic affairs (*domesticae*)

Thus, the two poles of the public (here in its most political color) and the private are distinct and separate spheres, and together they comprise the whole of Cicero's life. This list primarily employs the forces of social relations and meaning to identify the two spheres. Some tasks are culturally assigned to a specific sphere (e.g., legal matters are public, and leisure is private) as well as the social relations that take place in those spheres (e.g., politics is public and personal friendships are private).

In the following quote from his speech against Vatinius, Cicero explicitly adduces the force of place by deploying shared conceptions about public and private places to intensify his indictment of Vatinius's shameful treatment of Biblius:

> By your own criminal audacity you had Marcus Biblius driven from the forum, the senate building, the temples, and all other public places [*locis publicis omnibus*], and kept him secluded in his house. Now when the life of this consul was no longer pro-

> tected by the glory of his power or the authority of the laws, but only by the protection of a door and the security offered by the walls of his home—Did you not send a worthless bailiff to haul Biblius out of his house, so that even a home, which is always a place of safety for a private person, might not be a refuge for a consul while you were the tribune of the plebs? (*Vat.* 22)

Cicero identifies two spatial domains with specific locations. The forum, senate building (*curia*), and temples are all public. Added to this are a number of "other public places" that Cicero presumes his audience can supply for themselves (in this high-context situation). The home is the only private place identified, and this is common across much of Cicero's writing. The sheer number of public places (three, plus a large general category) outweighs the single private place (the home) and further illustrates Cicero's (and Rome's) preference for the public sphere by quantitative emphasis. The public places would have been the natural sphere of activity for a government official such as Biblius, yet he was barred from them. On top of that, the home is understood as a place of personal safety and refuge. Cicero implies that Vatinius's violation of the privacy of Biblius's home was his most heinous transgression in this matter. Thus, for Cicero, public places are the appropriate locations for honorable political activity, but the security and privacy of the home have an almost sacred quality that must not be transgressed.

Although Cicero and his contemporaries manifest a preference for the public life, they were not naïve about its dangers. In a statement reminiscent of Plato, Cicero points out the volatile nature of crowds:

> I repeatedly urge you to recall the irresponsibility of a crowd, the instable character of the Greeks and the force that a seditious speech can have in a public meeting [*contione*]. Even here in Rome, the most responsible and moderate of cities, where the forum is filled with courts, officials, noble and loyal citizens . . . think of the storms that you see raging in our public meetings [*contionum*]. (*Flac.* 57)

Cicero defends Flaccus's actions by pointing out that he is not responsible for mobs stirred up by the rabble of a city. The public sphere is a glorious space for eloquent speech and political action that accrue personal and national fame. However, it also contains the unruly crowds that can transform a properly political meeting into a public riot. The public-political sphere is made up of specific areas filled with rational citizens, but often these degenerate into less political, but no less public, gatherings.

One final quotation from Cicero reinforces his dichotomization of the public and private spheres while simultaneously revealing a small crack in this stark division:

> In those days when I fled from the sorrows of the state [*republica*], I had a home [*domus*] which comforted me, but now I cannot flee from my home and take refuge in her prosperity. Thus, I have removed myself both from my home [*domo*] and from the courts [*foro*], because the grief that the state causes is no longer consoled by my home life, nor are my private [*domesticum*] sorrows assuaged by the state [*respublica*]. (*Fam.* 4.6.2)

In this troubling case, Cicero sets up a strong dichotomy between state and home (public and private), and then exempts himself from it, placing himself in an unspecified "no-space" somewhere outside of both spheres. The power of the dichotomy in Cicero's thinking means that there is simply nowhere else he can turn once his public (political and legal) and private (domestic) activities both cause him pain and sorrow. For Cicero there is no spectrum between public and private, indeed, no place between public and private spaces. The most Cicero can do is to remove himself into limbo until his friend Sulpicius returns and restores some peace and wholeness to his private life (*Fam.* 4.6.3).

As with the historians of ancient Greece, it is difficult to find elaborations on the nature of public and private in the historians of ancient Rome. Again, this is due to two factors: the prevailing high-context form of communication common in history writing, and the fact that most historians deal primarily with political and military matters while recording private matters only when they are relevant to the larger story. However, both Tacitus and Livy have a few comments that illuminate how the concepts of public and private functioned in the Roman context. Livy tells an extended story about Rome's war with the Volsci (*Hist.* 6.24–25), and draws special attention to the interaction of two tribunes: the older and wiser Camillus and the younger and brasher Lucius. Lucius recklessly begins an early attack on the Volsci, but he is fooled by a simple ambush tactic and forced to call a retreat. However, Camillus covers for Lucius's mistake rather than publicly shaming him for it. Note how Livy intertwines the public and private spheres when describing the results:

> [Lucius] was assigned by lot to be [Camillus's] assistant, not so much for the good of the state (as it should be), but rather for the glory of his colleague. Camillus earned great respect in his public capacity [*publice*] because he reversed what Lucius's foolishness had caused, and in his private capacity [*privatim*] he used Lucius's mistake as an opportunity to earn his gratitude rather than to gain glory for himself. (6.24.6)

The public matters deal with interstate relations and military actions. Camillus's public respect was due to his martial wisdom and leadership. His private actions, while necessarily related to Lucius who was a public figure, deal instead with Camillus's intention to gain Lucius's personal gratitude. Thus, the same event has closely tied public and private results.

Two shorter comments from Tacitus demonstrate both the distinctiveness and the connections of the public and private spheres in ancient Rome. In book 12, section 8, Tacitus relates a backlash against new marriage laws that induced most of the Roman upper classes to exercise careful sexual control. Tacitus says, "It was a rigid, almost masculine hegemony: in public [*palam*] there was austerity and often arrogance; at home there was no trace of immodesty, unless it would contribute to power" (*Ann.* 12.7). Tacitus still divides the social world into public and private spheres, but in this case the reaction and social coercion was so strong that especially chaste sexual practices took effect in both arenas, public and private. In this quotation, Tacitus also reveals the power of public opinion to shape and shame both public and private behavior.[73] Another quote from Tacitus demonstrates the difference between public and private speech: "Mucianus had also sent a letter to the senate that caused some commotion. They said, 'If he is a private citizen [*privatus*],

---

73. See other examples of the power of public opinion on sexual and other matters in Veyne, "Roman."

why does he use this official [*publice*] language? He could have said the very same things when he was to address the senate a few days later'" (*Hist.* 4.4). The members of the senate immediately recognize two contradictory elements. Mucianus was purportedly acting as a private citizen; however, the language of his letter was obviously public and official. Political figures in ancient Rome could distinguish public language from private language and assess the propriety of its use. However, this situation results in a tension because the force of self (Mucianus's identity as a private citizen) and the force of meaning (the public nature of the language) point in different direction.

We get a different view from the satirists of Rome. Overcrowding in Rome was almost proverbial: apartments were crowded, noisy, smelly, and dangerous.[74] Juvenal complained about the regular disturbances in his apartment building (*Sat.* 3.195–202), the noise that kept him awake (*Sat.* 3.232–36), and the crowds that flooded Rome (*Sat.* 3.237–61). There was very little privacy to be had according to modern standards, but we must remember that the Romans had learned to accommodate the interrelation of public and private space in a way that they found satisfying or at least survivable.[75] The wealthy could afford to purchase the space that guaranteed privacy. Given the poor housing and the availability of public spaces, the vast majority of life in Rome and other cities of the empire took place out of doors in the open where it was publicly visible to anyone.[76] Horace reflects this when he speaks of people sycophantically seeking favors in the public crossroads (*in triviis*, *Sat.* 1.9.58–60). He also speaks about other satirists who bravely (or foolishly) broadcast their satires publicly (*per ora*) or purposefully withdrew from the crowds and the public scene (*a vulgo et scaena*) for private joking (*Sat.* 2.1.62–74). Both Juvenal and Horace speak more about an unofficial public sphere: places like crossroads in a crowded city where people could be seen and heard.

Next is Vitruvius, the architect who lived, worked, and wrote during the first century BCE. Vitruvius deals mostly with the impact of the force of place on the private, public, and political spheres. However, as with any good architect, he also has his eye on the social and economic functions of a building. The public/private distinction forms the basic framework in the introduction to *De Architectura*: "Building is divided into two parts: one concerns the placement of city walls and public buildings on public sites; the other concerns private structures" (1.3.1). Vitruvius goes on to state that public buildings have three purposes with specific structures assigned to each purpose. First, there are buildings for defense: walls, towers, and gates. Second, there are buildings for religion: shrines and temples. Finally, there are buildings for convenience (*opportunitatis*) and general public use (*usum publicum*): "harbors, forums, colonnades, baths, theatres, promenades and other buildings which are similarly intended for public occasions [*publicis locis*]" (1.3.1). Note that this list of public buildings includes several that are not directly political in nature (colonnades, baths, theatres, etc.). Kaiser provides two comprehensive charts to show how Vitruvius classified and identified both public and private buildings in his opus

---

74. Shelton, *As the Romans*, 63–65; MacMullen, *Social Relations*, 63–66.

75. Meeks, *First Urban*, 29. Meeks states that privacy was indeed rare and that the lack of privacy resulted in a thick network of social connections.

76. MacMullen, *Social Relations*, 62

PART ONE: READING LUKE'S SOCIAL-SPATIAL CONTEXT

(see below).[77] The public/private division (Category 1) is the most basic consideration in the classification of space for Vitruvius, followed by secular/religious (Category 2) and functional/social concerns (Category 3). Buildings should be fitted to their functional or social use (1.3.2), but in his high-context world he does not specify these exact uses except in a few cases.

Table 3.2: Kaiser's Categories of Vitruivius's Public Spaces

Category 1	Category 2	Category 3	Category 4
Public	Secular[78]	Defense	Wall / Storage / Tower
		Passage	Plaza / Portico / Street / Hallway / Courtyard / Stairway
		Administrative	Meeting
		Commercial	Bakery / Bath / Food / Market / Unspecified
		Entertainment	Viewing / Performing / Storage
		Educational	Portico / Exercise / Dressing
	Religious	Sacred	Ceremonial / Storage
		Passage	Courtyard / Stairway / Portico
		Funerary	Memorial / Burial

77. Kaiser, *Urban Dialogue* 19–22. These tables are reproduced with the permission of the author.

78. Kaiser's descriptive classification of Vitruvius is helpful but also interpretive at points. The application of the term "secular" is a prime example. Vitruvius has no direct equivalent for this term, and a sphere of life in the ancient world that was secular in the modern sense probably did not exist. Rather, Kaiser bases this category on the strong identification of sites as particularly and permanently sacred (treated in book 4; see *Urban Dialogue*, 20), which are literarily separated in Vitruvius's work from most other "public" sites such as forums, baths, theatres, etc. (treated in book 5).

Private, Public, and Political in the Ancient Contexts of Luke's Gospel

The charts below provide insight into Roman ideas about public and private as well as a specific list of structures that belong to each sphere. First, note again that several "public" structure have no direct political connection (especially commercial, entertainment, and educational buildings). "Commercial" spaces are public in Vitruvius while "industrial" sites are private. He does state that the forum is the (public) place where business transactions are made (5.preface.5). This somewhat agrees with Cicero's claim that "business" is public, but disagrees with the Greek notion of business as a private matter. It may reflect the fact that the actual manufacture of goods was private while their sale was public as well as the fact that the Roman culture further loosened the tie between politics and the public sphere.[79] Finally, note the frequency of "passage" elements in both charts. Passages are powerful because of their size, frequency, and the way they function as links between the public and private spaces.

Table 3.3: Kaiser's Categories of Vitruvius's Private Spaces

Category 1	Category 2	Category 3	Category 4
Private	Secular	Industrial	Metal Working Kiln Wine Production Garum Production Quarry Storage
		Elite Domestic	Reception Cooking Dining Garden Passage Bathing Sleeping Courtyard Service Storage
		Non-Elite Domestic	Sleeping Cooking Dining Garden Courtyard Passage Storage
	Religious	Elite Domestic	(none specified)
		Non-Elite Domestic	

79. Veyne has an excellent discussion of the mixed social and ideological nature of "business" in the ancient world ("Roman," 119–29). He describes a Roman mindset (primarily of the upper class) that viewed leisure and inherited land as the necessities of virtue and public life, whereas the person whose time and money was defined by work was considered naturally inferior. Thus, work had a mixed valence. The wealthy, high-status, public man could participate in it (both publicly and privately), but it never defined his character or being, while the "inferiors" were cast as slaves to their labor whether they were in fact slaves or not.

PART ONE: READING LUKE'S SOCIAL-SPATIAL CONTEXT

Vitruvius makes some interesting comments about the nature of homes. First, he seems to distinguish between public and private rooms in an elite home (6.5.1). Some rooms belong to the family (*propria loca patribus familiarum*) such as "bedrooms, dining rooms, baths, and other rooms with similar purposes." Thus, the activities of sleeping, eating, bathing, and other similar practices are the private nucleus of a private home. On the other hand, some rooms are shared with visitors (*communia cum extraneis*) such as "vestibules, courtyards, peristyles, and other rooms with similar purposes." Two factors determine the difference between public and private rooms in a private home: first and foremost the social relations (family vs. visitors) and secondly the tasks that take place there (bathing vs. meeting). Finally, Vitruvius points out that a person's social status will determine the nature of their home:

> Magnificent vestibules and alcoves and halls are not necessary for people of average wealth, because they pay their respects by visiting others, rather than being visited by others. But those who rely on rural produce must have stalls for cattle and shops in front. . . . The homes of bankers and tax collectors should be more spacious and imposing. . . . Lawyers and professors of rhetoric should have worthy homes that have sufficient space for their audiences. For persons of high rank who hold offices and magistracies, who serve the state out of duty, we must provide royal vestibules, lofty halls, and spacious peristyles. (6.5.1–2)

This is a classic example of how social and spatial forces can mutually reinforce one another. The type and style of home is dependent on the social role of the owner, and simultaneously the design of the home announces the social position of the owner. Once again, the primary division of spaces for Vitruvius is public and private (even within private homes), and this division is further specified and reinforced by social role and functionality.[80]

The home was represented as the ideal private place, but homes also took on a variety of public elements and functions. The peristyle house had a long history in the Greek east, going back to the fourth century BCE, and it was the peristyle and the various rooms contiguous with it that were specifically designed and decorated to entertain visitors.[81] Greek homes were generally more segregated into male-public and female-private space, but even the Greek homes reflect a range of accessibility and public to private valences, for even smaller Hellenistic homes had an *oecus maior*, a larger and more elegantly decorated room for welcoming guests.[82] The public aspects of Roman homes are even more common and better attested, and a couple of examples paint the picture well. In elite homes, Vitruvius says (6.5.1) that one must plan rooms for both invited and *uninvited* guests. It was apparently standard practice for uninvited guests to enter the home (generally through a guarded vestibule) for business or personal requests. Thus, even the private home had

---

80. Wallace-Hadrill makes several comments about the reciprocal effects of status and architecture (*Houses and Society*, 15, 36, 59).

81. Trümper, "Hellenistic Delos," esp. 24, 28–29, 37. Trümper attests that even smaller homes had an *oecus maior*, a larger and more elegantly decorated room for welcoming guests.

82. Trümper, "Hellenistic Delos," 37–39. As an example, Diodorus Siculus records an episode where homes in Syracuse were used to manufacture weapons (14.41.6)

certain areas that were expected to be accessible to the general public, with some controls of course. While the force of place predominates here through the location and decoration of specific rooms in the house, the force of time plays a role as well. Cicero describes the morning visitation, a common public event that generally took place at the homes of wealthy and powerful patrons. He laments Atticus's absence and says, "When my house is filled up with the morning visitors and I walk down to the forum among a throng of 'friends,' I cannot find one person in the whole group with whom I can joke freely or whisper intimately" (*Att.* 1.18). The *salutatio* was a common practice in which clients would come to greet their patron at home in order to show their grateful respect and receive favors.[83] This commonly took place in the atria and peristyles mentioned by Vitruvius, rooms in private homes that were designed as public spaces. In addition to these more formal meetings between clients and patrons, the homes of upper-class Romans were often filled with a variety of slaves, even in the bedrooms. Slaves were almost omnipresent and would have to be ordered away to secure pure privacy.[84] In Greek homes and especially in Roman homes of the upper classes, the public and private met and blended together through regular practices that linked the two spheres in various social and spatial ways.

The theatre was a common public location in Rome, one that often attracted not only a large but also diverse crowd. As Ovid says, people came to the theatre "to see and be seen" (*Ars* 1.99). The public nature of the theatre appears in one of Epictetus's discourses recorded by Arrian (*Epict. diss.* 3.4). The procurator of Epirus took the side of a comic actor in an undignified manner and was subsequently rebuked by the crowd who favored another actor. The procurator complained to Epictetus who retorts that the crowd had acted exactly as he had. The crowd just chose the other side, so why should the procurator complain about their behavior if it was essentially the same as his own (3.4.1–2)? Epictetus upbraids the procurator by saying, "You ought to know that when you enter the theatre, you enter it as a standard and example to the others, showing them how they ought to behave" (3.4.5). Epictetus concludes his advice by saying that the procurator could stage a number of private games and shows in his own house and crown whomever he prefers, "but in public [ἐν φανερῷ] do not overreach your station and do not snatch for your own what is common to all" (3.4.11). The procurator's political role (the force of self) creates the opportunity for this event. However, it is the force of place (entering the theatre) that dramatically shifts the event into the unofficial public sphere. The public place should shape the behavior (typically a part of the force of meaning) of the procurator, and this all occurs in a setting where the crowd adduces the force of social relations for this public scenario.

Two historians writing in Greek also give us insight into Roman culture. Polybius's long description of typical public funerals in Rome highlights the nature and the power of public events. Polybius tells us that when a famous man dies, he is carried into the forum for his funeral (6.53.1).[85] On such an occasion all the people (παντὸς τοῦ δήμου) gather,

83. Shelton, *As the Romans*, 14–15.

84. Veyne, "Roman," 72–73.

85. There is also evidence that indicates that women were sometimes honored with such public funerals. See MacMullen, "Women in Public, 211.

and a speech is given by the man's son or another relative (6.53.2). Often this speech moves the entire crowd to tears because the man's death is seen as "a common loss that affects the entire populace" (κοινὸν τοῦ δήμου φαίνεσθαι σύμπτωμα, 6.53.3). Thus, the force of social relations emphasizes the public nature of the event while the force of religion comes to the fore in the private domain. This public event is followed by proper religious rites in the home where an image of the deceased is set up, the proper private complement to the public rituals (6.53.4). Polybius concludes by saying, "The most important result is that the young men are inspired to endure suffering for the public good [ὑπερ τῶν κοινῶν πραγμάτων] in the hope of winning the glory that brave men receive" (6.54. 3). Note that Polybius features the language of κοινός and δῆμος in this description, perhaps emphasizing the public rather than the political importance of funerals. Polybius echoes many of the characteristics seen already: the public prominence of the forum, the role of public speech, the presence of a crowd, a sense of corporate identity at public events, and a private counterpart to public activities.[86]

Our next Greek historian of Rome, Appian, describes Caesar's building activity after a major victory:

> He erected a temple to Venus, his ancestress, as he had vowed to do when he was about to begin the battle at Pharsalus. He also framed an area around the temple which he intended as a forum [ἀγορά] for the Roman people, not for personal purchases but for the transaction of public business [πράξεσι] with each other, like the public squares [ἀγοράς] of the Persians, where the people seek justice or learn about the laws. (*Bell. civ.* 2.15.102)

Appian's description portrays how public-religious and public-secular space were intimately related and often contiguous in Rome. It is Appian's possibly editorial comment about the purpose of such public spaces that breaks the high-context silence and reveals some interesting information. Appian thought that economic interests had come to dominate the public spaces of his day in a way that was detrimental to the life of cities. He believes that the true purpose of such public arenas was not for money-making (questioning the presence of business in the public sphere) but so that people could gather to learn about and practice enlightened civil justice. Here the force of religion in the temple works together with the force of place (the forum) to create a sphere of legal justice (the force of meaning) for the good of the people (the force of social relations).

As with the survey of classical Athens, one secondary work on public and private stands out in its relevance to this study: *Public and Private in Vergil's Aeneid* by Susan Wiltshire. Unlike Cohen's more anthropological and historical description, Wiltshire's work is a socioethical reflection that emerges from a careful reading of the *Aeneid*. The Latin terms for public and private (*publicus* and *privatus*) are relatively rare in the *Aeneid*, but Wiltshire's analysis shows how Vergil formulates a reciprocal and vital tension that binds the two spheres together in his narrative.[87] Wiltshire's thesis is that "In the Aeneid

---

86. For more information on the emotive and symbolic power of public spectacles (such as triumphs or commissions) in ancient Rome, see Marshall, "Symbols and Showmanship."

87. This would be another excellent example of how modern scholars can employ the classification and analysis of social categories in a work of a high-context culture where the categories are rarely mentioned explicitly.

Vergil achieved a precarious balance between the public and the private. He knew that the two worlds usually conflict with one another but that this very tension is required for an individual life to be fully human and a civilization to be humane."[88] Furthermore, she claims that the Romans fixed the concepts that inform much of the contemporary debates about public and private in the West, so an analysis of this ancient epic is pertinent to our discussion of these categories. Wiltshire makes several comments in her introduction that support the summary of classical Athens above and anticipates several of the conclusions of this chapter. First, she asserts that public life was often "pre-political" and consisted of more informal interactions among acquaintances and strangers that did not require institutional structures.[89] Second, she echoes the characterization of Aristotle's dichotomized view of public and private given above.[90] Third, she points out how Roman ideas of public and private were definitively shaped by the legal code. Fourth, she states that Roman public goals included risk, change, and achievement while private ideals focused on perseverance and self-control. Finally, public life was the only life worth living for a man.[91]

In her third chapter, entitled "Self-distancing and the Capacity for Action," she gleans from the work of Arendt to discuss how both action and speech were means that enabled characters to distance themselves from their own needs, at least partially and temporarily, for the sake of the public good. This self-distancing that turns out to be necessary for the healthy functioning of both the public and the private spheres.[92] Without this self-distancing the public sphere would collapse into the private sphere and be determined by the private concerns of despair, passion, greed, and fear, which all rear their ugly heads in the *Aeneid*.[93] On the other hand, if the realities of private life are subsumed by the public sphere, it can become a vapid juggernaut that inhumanely dominates society.[94] A balance is necessary to maintain the integrity, in terms of both sustainability and morality, of both spheres. In the following chapter, thematized around the topic of home, Wiltshire moves through the whole of the *Aeneid* to reveal the complex interplay of private and public concerns at the heart of the narrative's pedagogical plot.[95] In books 1–2, Aeneas is dominated by private concerns. He is still emotionally tied to the old Troy and repeatedly yearns to have died there with his compatriots and family (see 1.94–96). Aeneas is so blinded by his grief over the loss of Creusa that he cannot hear her prophecy of his public role in the future and has to be urged on by Hector (see 2.776–84). In books 3–5 an uneasy, unhealthy, and unresolved imbalance between the two spheres throws Aeneas to extremes. On one hand, Aeneas makes several abortive attempts to prematurely refound Troy in some other location. Then, after the death of his father, another private loss, he settles in with Dido and

---

88. Wiltshire, *Vergil's Aeneid*, 4.

89. Ibid., 5.

90. However, she claims that Plato disdained private life seeing it as an escape from political action (ibid., 12) failing to notice the tension and development of Plato's thought on this.

91. Ibid., 14–15.

92. Ibid., 57–58.

93. Ibid., 63.

94. Ibid., 64.

95. Ibid., 72–80.

begins to help establish the *wrong* city, Carthage, which will one day be the rival of Rome. Mercury has to show up in person to awaken Aeneas and summon him onto his larger public mission (4.264–66). Books 6–8 narrate a degree of resolution with an appropriate remaining amount of tension and unrest to continue the story through to the end. Aeneas finally accepts his destiny as a public leader and founder of a new grand city that will be the rebirth of the old Troy. The dream of the rebirth of Troy gives Aeneas the vision he needs to make a home in this unknown land.

Chapter 5, entitled "Hospitality and the Transformation of Realms," is crucial to Wiltshire's book and to this study. Wiltshire asserts that hospitality was a cultural tradition that brought the public and private spheres together in transformational ways.[96] At the beginning of the chapter she says, "When a stranger from the public realm enters one's private space, changes occur in both host and guest."[97] A violation of private hospitality created the public repercussions that led to the Trojan War and ultimately fueled Aeneas's fate.[98] Aeneas and Dido suffer so much because of the way that her hospitality brought him into her private realm, where they formed a personal bond of *eros*, which Aeneas then broke.[99] In another case, Evander welcomes Aeneas as a guest-friend and distant relation and provides Aeneas with his first sense of home in the new land. Eventually, Evander offers his son Pallas as a personal guide for Aeneas. Later, when Pallas is killed by Turnus, Aeneas avenges the death of his now personal friend by slaying his public opponent Turnus with no mercy (an episode where public and private have gone out of a healthy balance). Regardless of the nature of the transformation, either beneficial or destructive, Wiltshire successfully convinces the reader that ancient hospitality was a key social mechanism that created an interface between the public and private spheres. As Wiltshire concludes, "As the meeting place of public and private, hospitality can contribute to the transformation of both."[100] This reinforces the addition of an arrow to the classification diagram that visually portrays how the public sphere could directly enter the private sphere of the household through the tradition of hospitality.[101]

In the final chapter, Wiltshire discusses how labor forms a bridge between the two spheres. Labor is required for the success of both spheres: agriculture in the private and politics in the domestic. The obligation and discipline implied by labor forms a way to link

---

96. There was a distinction between *hospitum privatum* and *hospitum publicum*. Private hospitality was devoted to the reception of personal friends and guests, who could also be political colleagues. Public hospitality was more generally open to citizens but focused on political leaders. See Wagner-Hasel, "Gastfreundschaft," 796–97.

97. Wiltshire, *Vergil's Aeneid*, 83.

98. Ibid., 87.

99. Ibid., 88.

100. Ibid., 105. This is very similar to the statements made by Cohen regarding the role of friendship in ancient Athens; the two were part of a related set of social practices that brought the public sphere into the private home.

101. Bolchazy has studied the theme of hospitality that runs through Livy (*Hospitality*, 61–62). He claims that Livy holds up hospitality (rather than the typical Augustan virtues of bravery, clemency, justice, and piety) because it tended more toward the peace and humaneness that he believed should characterize the Pax Romana (80–82).

the practices and lives that take place in both.¹⁰² If labor is the means of linking public and private, *pietas*, or loyalty to the other, is the motive. In the story of the *Aeneid*, Aeneas's *pietas* develops from personal loyalty to his family and city into a calling to found a new urban and political order.¹⁰³ Thus, at the end of her study, Wiltshire concludes that Vergil holds together in untidy tension the mutual necessity of the public and private spheres through a story that tells of how each realm impacted the other. Neither realm triumphs, both are problematic and disorderly, but both are also necessary and beneficial to human life and society.

Pompeii: Artifact of Roman Spatial Practice

The first reason for selecting Pompeii to represent the architectural trends of the Roman Empire emerges from the excellent preservation of this first-century-CE Roman city. Pompeii was frozen in time by the eruption of Vesuvius in 79 CE, and thus was preserved in more detail than any other ancient Roman site. This leads to a second reason for selecting Pompeii: the incredibly rich and accessible ruins at Pompeii have been a greenhouse that has nourished some of the most probing and insightful archaeological studies of the Roman world. More specifically, several scholars have focused directly on the relationship of space and society in Pompeii, proffering careful analyses of the categories of public and private. The investigation of the social use of space with a special focus on the role of public and private in Pompeii make it all the more applicable to the examination of public and private space in Luke 18:35—19:48. In addition to these reasons, the temporal proximity of the remains of Pompeii to the writing of Luke's Gospel (probably composed sometime in the late first century CE) strengthens the claim that this site may be used as a representative of the larger social-spatial trends that might have influenced him or his audience. Finally, many archaeologists either explicitly or implicitly treat Pompeii as an average-sized town that was typical of much of the historical, social, and architectural developments occurring throughout the Roman Empire during this period.¹⁰⁴ In light of these reasons, the social-spatial *realia* of Pompeii provide a good representative example that can be applied to the analysis of Luke's Gospel. The following map and description will orient the reader to the layout of Pompeii as well as some of the most important structures in the city.¹⁰⁵

---

102. Wiltshire, *Vergil's Aeneid*, 130–31.

103. Ibid., 135–36.

104. Wallace-Hadrill, *Houses and Society*, 15–16; Zanker, *Pompeii*, 4. Such a representative function is implied by the prominence of Pompeii as a case study that comprises more than half of Laurence and Wallace-Hadrill, eds. *Domestic Space*.

105. This map is adapted from "Cataline's Guess at What Pompeii Looked Like." A complete listing of all of the buildings coded to the map can be found online at http://users.ipa.net/~tanker/pompeii.htm.

PART ONE: READING LUKE'S SOCIAL-SPATIAL CONTEXT

Figure 3.4 Map of Pompeii

The archeological site of Pompeii has traditionally been divided into nine *Reggiones*. The *insulae*, or city blocks within the regions, are then further divided and numbered for reference (unnumbered areas have not been excavated). The *insulae* were grouped together in ancient times to make *vici* (neighborhoods), and these generally clustered around wells on street corners, marked with small squares on the map.[106] The *cardo* (the main street running roughly from north to south) transects Pompeii between the gates that lead to Vesuvius and Stabiae. The *decumanus* (primary east-west street) runs from the city wall (northeast of Reggio VII) to the gate that exits to Nola. In many cities, the intersection of the *cardo* and the *decumanus* was near the public heart of the city, and this is also true in Pompeii. The intersection of the *cardo* and *decumanus* is at the northwest corner of Reggio VII, which contains the forum and many public buildings. The main entrance to the city was from the Marine Road, which was used by visitors, inhabitants, and merchants; the visage of the Temple of Venus dominated the approach (VIII.b). This road led clearly and quickly to the forum (VII.7–9), which was filled during the imperial period with shrines and statues honoring the emperor. The main entrance to the city was designed to be aesthetically impressive, easily navigated, and ideologically powerful.[107] The other important public center of the city is Reggio II in the southwest corner, which contains the amphitheatre (II.6) and a large *palaestra* (II.7). Reggio VI (along the *cardo*, the *decumanus* and the *Via del Foro*) contained many homes for the elite. Reggio VII (which has one corner

106. Laurence, *Roman Pompeii*, 39–50.
107. Zanker, *Pompeii*, 78–81; Laurence, *Roman Pompeii*, 34–35; Kaiser, *Urban Dialogue*, 63–64.

Private, Public, and Political in the Ancient Contexts of Luke's Gospel

at the main entrance and one corner at the intersection of the *cardo* and the *decumanus*) was comprised of the forum, the baths and several commercial establishments. Reggio VIII (along both the Marine Road and the *cardo*) was filled with temples and other public buildings like a smaller *palaestra* and a small theatre or *odeon*. Finally, the Marine Road and the location of the amphitheatre made Reggio I an important and highly traveled part of the city as well, and this section will be explored in further detail below.

The pioneering scholar in the social analysis of the archaeological remains at Pompeii is Andrew Wallace-Hadrill. Wallace-Hadrill has written and edited a number of pieces that deal with the social and spatial elements of the city and citizens of Pompeii;[108] however, his most important work for the study at hand is his monograph *Houses and Society in Pompeii and Herculaneum*. This book opens with a methodological reflection about "Reading the Roman House," where Wallace-Hadrill claims that Roman domestic architecture is defined neither by gender nor by age, but rather by the intersection of two axes that stretch from public to private and from grand to humble.[109]

Figure 3.5 Grand-Humble/Public-Private Axes

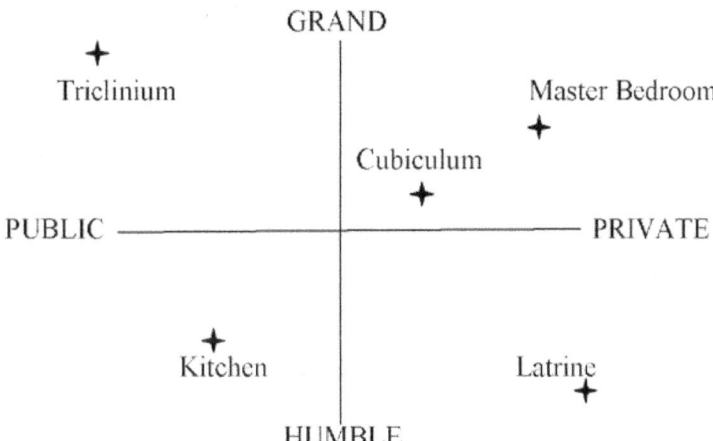

He uses the above graph to describe and analyze the use and meaning of rooms in the houses found at Pompeii. For example, a triclinium would be both public and grand because of its lavish decoration and use for guests, while the kitchen would be public (because anyone could enter it) but not presented as grand in any way to visitors. The "master" bedroom would often be grand but private, while the latrine would be private and humble. One of the most flexible rooms was the cubiculum, which could fall in many places on the chart depending on its usage, but would generally balance public-private and

---

108. See the bibliography for the long list of relevant works by Wallace-Hadrill.

109 Wallace-Hadrill, *Houses and Society*, 3–16, esp. 11. Grahame has responded to Wallace-Hadrill's axes by using access analysis to assert that the social-spatial categories of public and private must be informed by the distinction between inhabitants and strangers as well. See Mark Grahame, "Public and Private," 142–44.

grand-humble.[110] Shortly after this, he explicitly supports the conception of private and public as a spectrum rather than a dichotomy.

> Though archaeologists (who know their Vitruvius) are well aware of the public dimension of the Roman upper-class house, approaches have been based on a conception of the public/private antithesis in terms of a black/white polarity. But we are dealing rather with a spectrum that ranges from the completely public to the completely private, and with an architectural and decorative language that seeks to establish relativities along the spectrum.[111]

He goes on to apply these perspectives in the analysis found in later chapters.

In his third chapter, Wallace-Hadrill employs the public-private and grand-humble axes to illustrate how domestic architecture and ritual shaped social interaction among members of the household (e.g., slaves and family) and visitors to the household. Privacy was rare as many parts of the home were not only accessible through the vestibule and atrium but even visible to the passerby. However, Wallace-Hadrill concludes that as domestic architecture and decoration evolved, pri-vacy and luxury became commodities that were gathered and exploited by the wealthy.[112] In later chapters, Wallace-Hadrill claims that many structures actually contained "housefuls," that is, several layers and groups of families that form a larger composite, rather than simply a household. He also argues that domestic and commercial space was much more integrally connected than the elite literary sources would have us believe.[113] At the end of the book, Wallace-Hadrill concludes that the homes of Pompeii do not reveal a gulf between rich and poor structures[114] as much as they demonstrate how domestic structures in the Roman world facilitated the interaction of rich and poor, slave and free, young and old, male and female through a variety social rituals by using the fluid and flexible places of the home and city.[115] The examples below will adduce some *realia* to corroborate and exemplify the conclusions drawn by Wallace-Hadrill.

---

110. Riggsby claims that the cubiculum was a space that allowed for containment and secrecy. He demonstrates that activities like sex, rest, reception, art, and murder occurred in this more private space. These took place in contrast to the norms of public space and behavior. See Riggsby, "*Cubiculum*," 54.

111. Wallace-Hadrill, *Houses and Society*, 17.

112. Ibid., 51–52.

113. Ibid., 103 and 141.

114. Even very small homes such as the House of Fabius Amandino (I.7.a, only 125 sq. meters) could be lavishly decorated in the latest style. See Wallace-Hadrill, *Houses and Society*, 189.

115. Wallace-Hadrill, *Houses and Society*, 185.

Private, Public, and Political in the Ancient Contexts of Luke's Gospel

Figure 3.6 The House of Menander (Reggio I.10.b)[116]

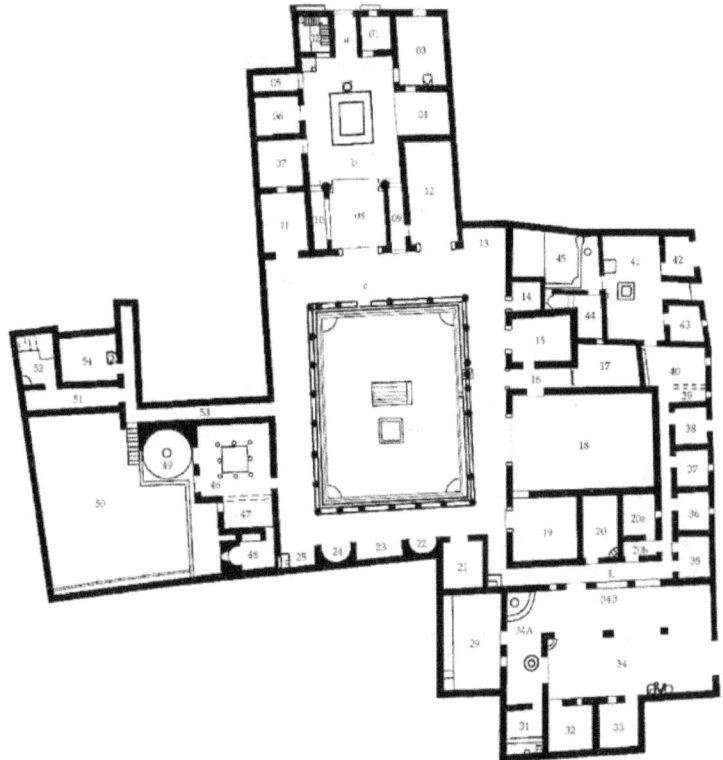

This large and grand house (approximately 1700 sq. meters) illustrates some of Wallace-Hadrill's points well. Note that a line of sight stretches all the way from the street (on the top of the diagram), through the vestibule (a), through the atrium (b), through the peristyle (c), onto a set of finely decorated alcoves in the back of the home (22–24). Another line of sight goes from the ornate reception room (18, the *tablinum*) through the peristyle to the bath area (46–49). Thus, this house would rank quite high on the public-grand scale, and many of the rooms of the house have easy access from either the atrium or the peristyle. The house appears to have some private areas, but these are few. Area 50 was a private garden, 51 contained a latrine and 52 and 54 were for food preparation and storage (kitchens and latrines were often located near one another so they could share access to water). Area 34 was a courtyard/stable, and the rooms surrounding it were used for feeding and housing animals as well as storage. Many of the rooms along corridor L and the far right side of the floor plan were for storage (20, 35–38) or commercial uses (40–43). The commercial area even has its own atrium for reception and business (41).[117] Therefore, this house deploys public space in a variety of ways. It incorporates a grand atrium and peristyle, a private garden, a stable area, several storerooms and a commercial unit, creating a very complex social-spatial arena that probably toward the public end of the spectrum. The size, organization and decoration of this house all indicate that a wealthy and prosperous "houseful" occupied this space—living, working, and entertaining in it.

---

116. This diagram is taken from Allison, *Pompeian Households*, 205 and is used with the permission of the publisher.

117. The identification and description of these rooms are taken from a web presentation of Mary Penelope Allison's work in Pompeii. See Allison, "Pompeian Households." Also see the excellent discussion of the rooms of this house by Oakes (*Reading*, 37–42).

PART ONE: READING LUKE'S SOCIAL-SPATIAL CONTEXT

Figure 3.7 The House of Stallius Eros (Reggio I.6.d)[118]

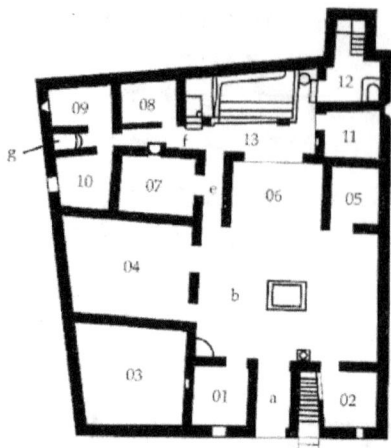

> This is a much smaller (275 sq. meters) and simpler house located just across the street from and slightly closer to the forum than the House of Menander. Its design is much more straightforward than the House of Menander. It reveals a basic orientation around the atrium (b) with a clear line of sight from the street. Rooms 5 and 6 were more well-decorated reception areas while 3 and 4 seem to have been commercial in nature. A loom and spinning materials were found in 8 and 9. There are smaller and more simply decorated rooms (1, 2, 11) and a garden (13). Also this home clearly had a second floor from the stairwells found in 2 and 12. This second floor probably contained more private living space while the bottom floor was apparently used primarily for commercial enterprises.[119]

Wallace-Hadrill's work focuses primarily on the construction and social use of domestic spaces in Pompeii, but other scholars have examined the city of Pompeii as a whole to explore how homes, streets, and public buildings interacted to create a social-spatial fabric for the entire city. Zanker opens his study of Pompeii by stating:

> Public buildings and their setting are then viewed as a kind of performance space, a stage created by society to meet its own needs. The public buildings, squares, streets, and monuments, together with the dwellings, cemeteries and their decorative art represent one key way in which the inhabitants could express who they were: the city as a combination of public stage and private living space.[120]

The first half of Zanker's book focuses on the role of public build-ings and space. He claims that streets, neighborhoods, and public buildings were used to hierarchically demarcate zones of the city according to class.[121] The above diagram demonstrates the complex public stage of the forum.

---

118. Alison, *Pompeian Households*, 209. This illustration is used with the permission of the publisher.
119. For room descriptions see Allison, "Pompeian Households."
120. Zanker, *Pompeii*, 3.
121. Ibid., 8.

Figure 3.8 The Forum of Pompeii (VII.7-9)[122]

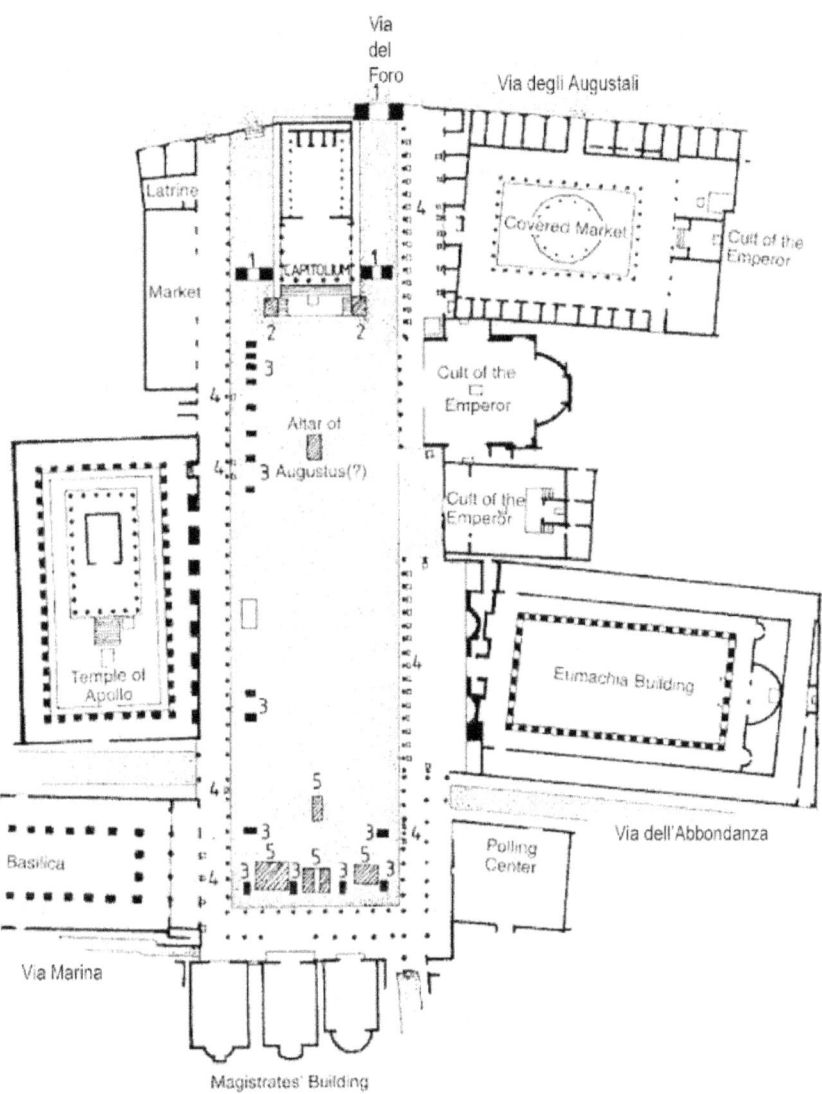

The large forum (50 by 200 meters) was at the intersection of several key streets, and the public baths are right around the northwest corner. The forum has an open area for public interaction as well as a latrine for public use. Note how Marine Road leads to the forum near a cluster of civic buildings where official political business was transacted: the basilica, the magistrates' building, and the polling center. Several religious sites surrounded the forum: the temple of Apollo and the temple of Venus as well as several altars and shrines devoted to the emperor cult. To balance this public space, the Eumachia Building (named after the wealthy patroness who paid for its construc-tion) provides several alcoves and halls for private space to serve small group meetings that were probably commercial or

122. Zanker, *Pompeii*, 86. This illustration is used with the permission of the author.

PART ONE: READING LUKE'S SOCIAL-SPATIAL CONTEXT

social in nature. The covered market provided space for merchants and the transaction of private business. The forum and its buildings are the social-spatial heart of the city, near major routes and with ample space for public display and private interactions.

The second half of Zanker's work focuses on domestic architecture. Similar to Wallace-Hadrill, he argues that the construction and use of public space declined as Roman cities moved into the second century CE, and that public functions (e.g., business or politics) were refit to the increasingly private nature of homes and villas. In the early imperial period, a variety of public structures (temples, theatres, *macella*) were built by wealthy local patrons to testify to their Roman loyalties and the greatness of the emperors, all the while reinforcing and expanding the hierarchical stratification of Pompeian society.[123] However, as the first century CE progressed, the wealthy withdrew from public building projects and public activity into their private villas. Large public buildings (theatres and temples) were left unrepaired, but smaller public sites like market streets and baths burgeoned under the influence of a growing middle class during this period.[124] The following samples provide specifics for the privatization of domestic space in Pompeii.

Figure 3.9 The House of the Moralist – floor plan (Reggio III.4.a)[125]

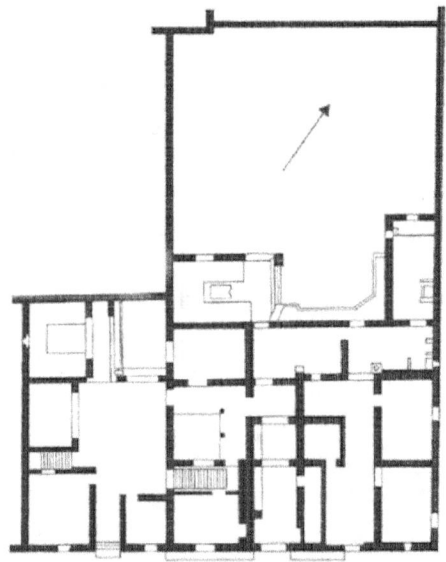

The floor plan of this house is moderately sized and not very elaborate. It was a combined structure made of two homes and only had one small shop at the bottom right corner (many other homes had multiple shops in the front of the house. The large garden in the back was a shrine to Diana, and the entire house is well decorated with images from the goddess's life. The front doors open onto Marine Road, but multiple doorways, turns, and small rooms remove any line of sight from the street and make the rooms more private. Also, note how the private garden is walled, set away from the street, and only accessible through a series of doorways.

123. Ibid., 100–114.
124. Ibid., 125–31.
125. Ibid., 164.

Figure 3.10 The House of the Moralist – reconstructed[126]

This reconstruction of the House of the moralist shows how the garden shrine fit onto the back of the house (in imitation of a villa) as well as how most homes in Pompeii (and many throughout the Roman world) included a second floor with further private living, storage and viewing space. Several windows look down from the more private second story onto the private garden enclosed by walls.

---

126. Ibid., 165.

PART ONE: READING LUKE'S SOCIAL-SPATIAL CONTEXT

Figure 3.11 The House of Sallust (Reggio VI.2.b)[127]

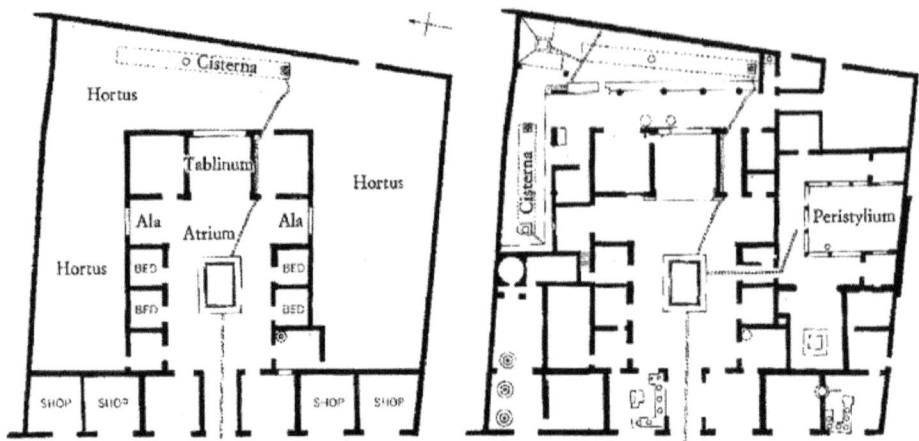

On the left, we see the ideal basic form of a Roman house from Pompeii in the 2nd century BCE (the time of the Roman colony). A vestibule leads from the decumanus to a central atrium. On either side of the vestibule, one finds shops or offices that also open onto the busy street. From the atrium one has immediate access to the main dining area in the *tablinum* as well as various bedrooms or *cubicula* and the *alae* ("wing" rooms) that lead to the garden that surrounds the living quarters.

On the right, we see a much more complex and privatized home from 79 CE. A peristyle for family and personal guests (reflecting the Hellenistic tastes of the day) with only one access point has been added as well as several other rooms which are more private due to the added passageways or the fact that they only open onto the back of the house. The atrium and front shops are still as public as they were before, but the hierarchical and demarcated nature of the space inside the home has increased greatly.

Working from another angle, Laurence uses statistical analysis to discuss the relationship of space and society in Pompeii. He presents detailed diagrams of the home sizes, streets, doors, and shops of the city and builds his conclusions based on the complex interaction of these various architectural elements.[128] Laurence reiterates that the main en-trance to the city was dominated by the appearance of the temple to Venus, and the city center with its agora and *macellum* were quickly reached by an easily navigated thoroughfare.[129] The size of streets and their intersections were carefully planned to guide a visitor

---

127. Ibid., 166. This illustration is used with permission of Ann Laidlaw, the original artist.

128. Kaiser uses similar tools to analyze the use of space in the ancient city of Empúries on the southeastern coast of Spain (Kaiser, *Urban Dialogue*). Kaiser focuses on the use of space for the dual purposes of inclusion and exclusion. He argues that while there may not have been strategic planning of public and private zones in a city, public and private in Greek and Roman areas do seem to organically cluster in certain predictable ways based on the analysis of the remains in Empúries. He concludes by saying, "The social norms that were translated into physical forms, however, were the result of a dialogue between the elite, the non-elite, the non-residents, and the supernatural constituents who used the city" (67). Thus, through such dialogue space was assigned to the public-private spectrum through specific architectural forms. Kaiser's study is useful for its theoretical and archaeological insight as well as an independent confirmation of many of the conclusions reached from other scholars' analyses of Pompeii.

129. Laurence, *Roman Pompeii*, 34–35.

to the public areas of the town. Wealthier homes were located close to but not directly on the agora to allow for easy (and widely visible) processions and departures. Grand homes were often on larger roads, but the most traveled roads (and most commercially active) were often indicated by the highest density of doorways opening onto it.[130] Doorways were important passageways throughout the city and often marked the linkage of public and private spaces. They could be guarded by porters, they allowed or restricted access to specific places, and they were often decorated to signify the status of the primary resident.[131] Many of the doors opened into shops, baths, brothels, and restaurants that lined the streets that led to the theatre and the amphitheatre; these were often key locations for non-elite public interaction.[132]

Laurence claims that the architecture of the city reinforced identities through the strategic deployment of public and private, elite and non-elite spaces. Thus, he focuses upon how the force of place affects social relations and self. The placement of streets, doors, shops and wells implies a neighborhood (*vicus*) identity that was reinforced by political representatives.[133] The buildings of Pompeii's forum have a similar function. The construction of the agora, temples, markets, porticoes, and other structures proclaimed the identity of Pompeii's elite and the imperial ideology of Rome.[134] Laurence also posits that the refined world of the elites and the poorly esteemed world of the commoner (who frequented brothels called *cauponae* or *popinae*) were spatially separated not by distance but by access. That is, the brothel might be contiguous with a large home, but one would enter them by very different routes. The elegant homes were presented grandly by doorways on large public streets, while brothels usually opened up onto side streets and alleys.[135] Some elite, probably merchants, incorporated their homes into commercial areas (as in Reggio I) while others distanced themselves from it (as in Reggio VI). Laurence also claims that time was a key element in the Roman creation of public and private space. At the end of his study, he claims that urban dynamics were often a result of the social use of time and space.[136] The public and private spheres were largely constructed and used by the wealthy, but this informed how the entire city populace interacted with each other. Above all, the public sphere with its events (plays, meetings, rituals) and places (theatres, streets, temples, markets) all served to reinforce corporate and individual identity.[137] The following example of a possible *vicus* in Reggio I will provide a sense of the *realia* that constituted a neighborhood in Pompeii and contributed to the lived and conceived public and private space of the city.

---

130. Ibid., 103–16.
131. Ibid., 88.
132. Ibid., 86–88.
133. Ibid., 50.
134. Ibid., 34–36.
135. Ibid., 84.
136. Ibid., 131.
137. Ibid., 135–37.

PART ONE: READING LUKE'S SOCIAL-SPATIAL CONTEXT

Figure 3.12 A vicus in Reggio I.6, 7, 10[138]

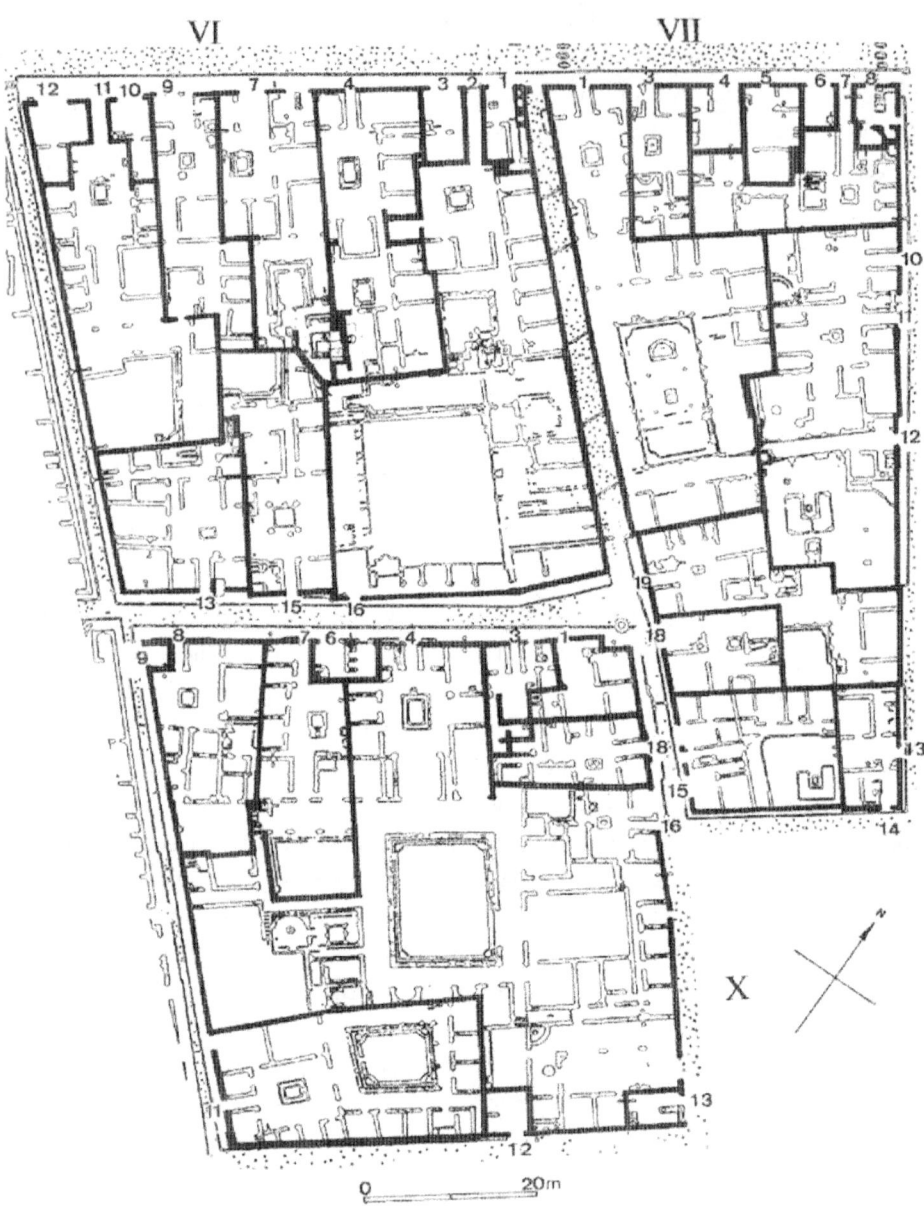

This picture shows three insulae clustered in Reggio 1 around a well at the northern corner of insula X. This clustering and the location of the well indicate that this might be an ancient *vicus*. This *vicus* contains the House of Menander (main entrance at X.4) and the House of Stallius Eros (main entrance at VI.13), which were both discussed above. This larger neighborhood shows the diversity of sizes and types of houses that multiplied the mixed valences of spaces within these houses. The top of the picture borders Marine Road and exemplifies the variety found along a busy street in Pompeii. The

138. Wallace-Hadrill, *Houses and Society*, 188.

following list describes the structures served by the numbered doorways and will move from the top left to the top right of the picture, as the average traveler would when moving through Pompeii in the ancient world.

VI.12 – Taberna, probably an iron worker's shop

VI.11 – House of Quadratus Teatralus (500 sq. meters with atrium and peristyle)

VI.10 – Taberna with back room and stairwell

VI.9 – Taberna, probably a drinking bar with living quarters in the back

VI.7 – Fullery of Stephanus, probably also a home with living quarters upstairs (325 sq. meters with atrium and peristyle)

VI.4 – House of the Lararium (400 sq. meters with atrium and refined decorations)

VI.3 – Workshop of Verus, possibly a coppersmith shop

VI.2 – House of the Cryptoporticus (a grand house of 1200 sq. meters with atrium, peristyle and bath suite)

VI.1 – Taberna, use unknown

VII.1 – House of Paquius Proculus (790 sq. meters with atrium, peristyle and rich mosaics throughout; cellar and upper floor)

VII.3 – House of Fabius Amandio (a small house of 125 sq. meters with atrium and lavish decoration throughout)

VII.4 – Officina, possibly a potter's shop

VII.5 – Officina, use uncertain

VII.6 – Taberna, use uncertain

VII.7 – House of Priest Amandus (230 sq. meters with atrium and peristyle)

VII.8 – Thermopolium, probably a drinking bar

This illustration highlights the diversity of types and degrees of public and private places along these two blocks: grand homes next to offices next to shops next to bars next to smaller homes. The use of space is quite flexible and fluid, but all of these places make the most of public access as well as incorporating some structures to control access (probably the purpose of the long vestibule at VI.2). In addition to the diversity found in these sequential doorways along the road, note that two *cauponae*, probably taverns and/or brothels, are located at VII.13–14 and X.13. Most of the brothels are located on street corners. These "unsightly" public places were located in close proximity to some of the finest houses in this insula, such as the House of Menander (X.4), the House of the Crytoporticus (VI.2) and the House of Paquius Proculus (VII.1). Even though the elite homes and the vulgar brothels are contiguous, the access routes to each are quite different and they are set as far apart as they can be in this configuration (so Laurence). Alongside these public structures (both elite and non-elite), note the relative lack of doorways on the east of insulae VI and X, the street between insulae VI and VII and to the south of insula X. This probably represents less-travelled, less prestiguous and, therefore, more private-humble areas. This single section represents a great diversity of public-private and grand-humble.[139]

The citizens of Pompeii found creative and routinized ways to negotiate the density and complexity of public and private spaces in their city. The remains of Pompeii and the scholarly interpretations of them reinforce the need for a more flexible and nuanced conceptualization of how persons in the ancient world defined and lived public and private space. Comments by Wallace-Hadrill, Zanker, and Laurence support the claim that Roman society existed across a spectrum, stretching from private to public to political. The classification system presented in this study describes and categorizes the diversity and fluidity of the archaeological remains at Pompeii better than a simple dichotomy between public and private spaces. The altars and shrines to the emperors in this forum reminded the city of imperial politics. However, the city was probably focused more on its own local politics, which took place in buildings at the public heart of the city like the basilica, the polling center, and the magistrates' building. Some parts of the forum (like Eumachia's macellum) and other public buildings (like theatres) fall outside of official politics and fit better in an unofficial public sphere. Prominent roads created public space for travel through the city. Monuments (like the temple to Venus), grand doors to homes, and hidden doors to brothels help travelers and residents identify sections of the city along with their public-private valence. Other roads linked carefully placed elite homes to the forum, allowing for unofficial public displays and processions following the morning *salutatio*. Other areas in the forum (such as the covered market) and places like *vicus* wells might have provided spaces for private interactions outside of the home. The homes ranged from grand and public (for welcoming business associates and friends) to the private and humble (for the non-elite). The House of Menander demonstrates a mixture of grand public spaces (like the large peristyle) and humble private spaces (like latrines and stables). Other homes, like the House of the Moralist and the House of Sallust depict more private and humble domeciles for family, religious, and economic activity. The city of Pompeii has a dense urban organization that illustrates categories all along the proposed spectrum, from imperial politics to private family space. These spaces emerged and developed in ways that revealed, reinforced, and created social and cultural identity. While Luke never describes urban or domestic structures in such detail, the city of Pompeii provides an example of what Luke and his audience might have inhabited and imagined as they heard the Gospel.

Summary of Roman Material

Again, Sack's framework of forces will organize the summary of the material from turn of the era Rome. Thanks largely to the work of Vitruvius, complemented by other authors, we have a clear representation of the force of place on the Romans' classification of public space. Vitruvius provides catalogue of public places, which he further subclassifies as sacred or secular and according to social location. Several public buildings have stood out

---

139. A similar "block tour" is hypothetically taken by Anderson (*Roman Architecture*, 293–97) around this same insula. He concludes that there was a "notable lack of discrimination" among economic levels in these contiguous dwellings. Furthermore, he notes the mixing of elite dwellings and even the most "noxious" forms of commerce (such as fulleries and taverns).

in our survey: the senate house, the temple, the forum, and the theatre. The first two had very specific political and religious functions respectively. However, the forum was more of a multipurpose space, and the theatre was set aside for entertainment. Both of these allowed for more informal and unofficial interactions that were still public.[140] In addition to these, one could add commercial sites (shops, baths, taverns) and a variety of passageways (roads, gates, doors). These were even less official and non-elite and come closer to bordering on the private sphere. Finally, there is the primary private structure, the home.[141] The home returns repeatedly in the survey above as the ideal private place, and many times the *dom-* word family is opposed to the category of the public (*publice*). The home is the place of safety and security. It can also be the place of love relationships (Aeneas and Dido) and family grief (Aeneas's loss of his wife and father). As the sole private refuge of many public persons, the home takes on an almost sacred and inviolable quality, which Cicero draws upon in his prosecution of Vatinius and which is referenced by Polybius's account of private religious rituals for a deceased family member. The survey of the remains of Pompeii demonstrates the complexity and density of various structures. The predominantly public areas of the city (forum, theatre) were dominated by public buildings surrounded by elite homes. Other neighborhoods combined grand houses with smaller homes, shops, and even brothels. Public and private structures could be contiguous or overlapping in very complicated ways.

The force of time plays a significant role. Cicero cites it as the time of the morning salutation and Laurence highlights its importance. The importance of time for the social activities that took place in public places is also attested by the frequent occurrence of sundials (or the like) in marketplaces and forums.[142] Martial supports this when he describes a typical day in Rome.

> The first and second hours wear out the morning greeters. The third hour taxes the talent of the strident lawyers. Rome continues her various labors well into the fifth hour. The sixth promises rest for the weary, and the seventh will bring an end to their work. The eighth hour provides time for the sleek gymnasia, and the ninth bids us to sink down on cushions which have been piled high. (*Epigrams* 4.8.1–6)[143]

The times allotted to specific tasks were assumed in the functions and activities discussed above. They seem to fall in to two large categories. Public time for greetings, legal proceedings, and other (political or economic) work extends from the first through the seventh hour. Then the eighth hour was a transition into the private time at home through the spatial passage of the gymnasia and baths. Private time typically lasted from the ninth hour

---

140. Although it appears that different ranks and classes were often seated in different parts of the theatres. See Dyson, *Community and Society*, 110, 170.

141. Vitruvius does list industrial buildings as private structures, but they are less prominent in the rest of the authors and are probably considered private by Vitruvius because they were built with private funds to manufacture goods for sale and personal profit.

142. Laurence, *Roman Pompeii*, 123.

143. See this quotation and a few other comments on Roman time in Shelton, *As the Romans Did*, 123–25. Laurence offers a good discussion and a visually helpful chart of the temporal allocation of daily activities based on the literary evidence (*Roman Pompeii*, 124–27).

to the next morning and involved family, rest, leisure, and hospitality. The force of nature seen in the gendering of space in classical Athens was not as prominent in Rome, which allowed more freedoms for women (see further below).[144] However, the force of religion appears more frequently. Vitruvius treated temples and shrines under public structures, and we saw how the temples to Venus and the emperors played key role in the entrance into Pompeii. Religion also played a private role in Rome (so Polybius), but its public role seems to predominate in the form of temples and official cults.

The force of meaning came into play in the characterization of various activities and functions in ancient Rome. Political and legal affairs were obviously public. Beyond this, military activity, commercial business, many religious rites, entertainment, visitations, meetings, and funerals were public events. Private activities were similarly delineated: rest, leisure, eating, bathing, sleeping, and managing household affairs. Furthermore, the meaning and morality of an action would be evaluated as to how appropriately it fit either the public or private location in which it occurred. Quite different from the modern world, legal and religious matters were considered public to Romans, as seen in Cicero's public legal and religious activity as well as the temple to Venus conjoining the forum built by Caesar. Like the Greeks, the Romans also gave great credence to public speaking, and the senators could immediately recognize public speech in Mucianus's letter. More importantly, public speech seemed to move the world in ancient Rome. Cicero was renowned as an orator, and the historians often recorded speeches and their dramatic impact. Wiltshire cited speech as one of the key resources in public self-distancing. Also, recall the effect that the funeral oration has upon the young in Polybius's account. Public speech had both a certain character and certifiable power in the Roman public sphere. Finally, and again somewhat similar to the Greeks, the Romans had very different standards for public and private behavior. Cicero said it best when he claimed, "At home they sought praise for self-restraint, but in public for grandeur" (*Flac.* 28). Fame was the aim of public life while moderation was the ideal in the home.

Last of all, social relations also played a key role in the definition of the public and private spheres in the Roman world. The private/domestic domain was for family and personal friends. The public domain was for political, legal, military, and economic relationships. Recall Livy's separation of the public and private dimensions of the relationship between Camillus and Lucius as well as Vitruvius's identification of private rooms for family and public rooms for visitors within homes. These public rooms within homes were often the locales of hospitality which enabled the public sphere and public persons to be inserted into private space. As could be expected, the crowd is often a prominent (and potentially problematic) character at public events (like plays, speeches, and funerals), and Epictetus's comments show that public persons were models for social and moral behavior, especially at public events in public places. Finally, place and social role often mutually reinforced one another. Those of senatorial rank would be found in the curia and

---

144. Although it was not specifically mentioned in the quotations discussed above, the Roman public sphere was largely male, as noted by Corley, *Private Women*, 15–18. However, Corley also points out that women entered the public sphere more and more during the early empire (24–30). This will be discussed further below.

appointed (elite) priests would serve in the public temples. Vitruvius's comments show how the very nature of the home was designed around the social position and social needs of the one who owned it. The grandeur and character of the structure was a major indicator of the height of a person's social status.

Private and public formed important poles in the ancient Roman construction of society and space.[145] The difference between these two zones can be so strong that Cicero cannot imagine any other place to be than the curia and the courtroom (public/political places) or his home (private place). While the Romans wanted to protect the peace and security of the home, they tended to place more value on the fame and honor that could be won by men in the public sphere. However, archaeological evidence also suggests that the private sphere began to eclipse the public sphere in the late first and early second centuries. The Romans had clear spatial boundaries that delineated and separated the public and private spheres, but on closer examination of the literary and archaeological evidence, it appears that they often found creative ways to negotiate the interpenetration and collision of the public and the private on a daily basis. The dichotomous poles of public and private were realities that existed, but most people in the ancient world had to manage the constant interfacing of the two spheres and a variety of nuances between the two extremes. Veyne even goes so far as to say about the Romans, "Neither in law nor in custom was there a clear dividing line between public life and private life."[146] Wiltshire's study emphasizes a "pre-political" public sphere, and she demonstrated how hospitality connected the well-defined private space of the home with the outside public world in crucial and recurring ways. Vitruvius and Wallace-Hadrill both comment on the complicated relation of public and private space within homes. While Roman culture often combined the public and the political spheres, the unofficial public sphere also appears frequently. Virtruvius indicates several public buildings that were not for political use (plazas, markets, porticoes, etc.). The theatre stands out as an unofficial public location where people mixed for entertainment and reputation. The satirists likewise portray a very public (not directly political) society where people meet at crossroads and in other public scenes. Finally, the remains of Pompeii display the complex interaction of public and private space in this densely organized city that set grand homes next to brothels and provided intricate means for the negotiation of various private, public, and political zones. The survey of Pompeii also display various other unofficial public places (main roads, *vicus* wells, the Eumachia building, baths, etc.). Thus, the literary and archaeological material from the Roman world substantiates the classifications put forth in this study.

---

145. Riggsby perceptively points out that the Romans defined the relational poles of public and private in the opposite manner from modern English. English language usage tends to begin with the core concept of private and defines public as anything beyond or outside the private sphere. Latin usage began with the concept of public (*publicum*) as that which related to the community, and defined private (*privatum*) as that which was not relevant to the community but dealt only with individuals. See Riggsby, "'*Cubiculum*," 49–50.

146. Veyne, "Roman," 105.

PART ONE: READING LUKE'S SOCIAL-SPATIAL CONTEXT

The Third Focus: Jewish Traditions and Places

The previous material comes from writers in the Greco-Roman world with little to no influence from Jewish life and culture. Given Luke's deep debt to the scriptures and history of Israel,[147] one should explore how this Jewish heritage, centered around Jerusalem, may have influenced the social-spatial milieu of Luke's narrative. The following brief survey of Jewish writings and the archaeology of Palestine add to this study in two ways. First, it will provide an opportunity to see if Luke's deep debt to the traditions of Israel includes some distinctively Jewish social-spatial characteristics. Second, it will contribute to our overall survey of the ancient world demonstrating the tripartite classification of space (private-public-political) proffered in this study.

Several stories from the Hebrew Bible express Jewish perspectives on public and private that predate the Hellenistic-Roman world, but may have still influenced Luke. The first set of these stories revolves around Moses, a key prototype of Jesus for Luke.[148] The social-spatial aspects of Moses' life operate in stark contrasts and sudden changes. He moves swiftly from the oppressed Jewish home of his birth to the palace of Pharaoh (Exod 2:1–10). Similarly, Moses goes from a city in Egypt to the wilderness of Midian (2:11–15). Later, Moses is thrust by the call of God from the wilderness (3:1) back into Pharaoh's court as the leader of Israel (3:16–18). In the next section of Exodus, Moses moves between the Jewish people and Pharaoh as the plagues come. After leaving Egypt, Moses still tends to alternate between contrasting social-spatial domains. Moses meets God alone on the mountain (19:3, 20) and returns to speak to the people (19:7, 25). Later, Moses alternates between the tent and the people (33:7–11; 34:29–35). The zones of sacred and profane space are more determinative in these cases rather than public and private. Also, the preponderance of the wilderness setting differentiates this narrative from most of the rest of the settings commonly found in Greco-Roman writing. Luke does mention the wilderness as a location for Jesus' private prayer (4:1, 42), but he briefly retreats to it and soon returns to the crowds (see Luke 9:10–11). This distinction probably comes into play in Luke's description of the Jerusalem temple, but in many other parts of Luke's Gospel Jesus breaks this religious dichotomy in various ways (e.g., 7:36–50, 19:1–10). For instance, the Jerusalem temple, which has a great deal of sacred valence in Luke's narrative, is still publicly available to the crowds whom Jesus teaches (20:1). For Luke the force of religion (sacred/profane) and the force of place (public/private) interacted in very different ways.

The Elijah-Elisha cycle, which manifests a slightly different set of social-spatial characteristics in Jewish tradition, was also known by Luke.[149] Like Moses, Elijah alternates between spaces, but now new places are introduced (indicated in italics) that emerge from the situation of Israel settled in Palestine. The prophet shifts from addressing King Ahab to staying at the *house* of a foreign widow whom he meets at a city *gate* (1 Kgs 17:1–10) and then to Ahab again (18:1). He calls a gathering of the people of Israel at Mt. Carmel (ch. 18)

---

147. See especially Moessner, ed., *Jesus and the Heritage of Israel*. This book is the first volume of a larger series on Luke as the interpreter of Israel. See also Rosner, "Acts and Biblical History"; and Bock, *Proclamation*, 261–79.

148. Johnson, *Luke*, 18–20; and practically all of Moessner, *Lord of the Banquet*.

149. Johnson, *Luke*, 13; and Brodie, *Luke the Literary Interpreter*.

but then flees into the desert to Mt. Horeb (ch. 19).[150] Elijah ventures into Samaria again to confront Ahab in Naboth's *vineyard* on God's command (21:18). Stark contrasts and swift changes are again the norm, but now the story adds homes, cities, and vineyards to the set of functioning places. Elisha differs from Elijah in that he tends to keep his activity to the "company of the prophets" and seems more active in this remnant community (2 Kgs 2:19–22; 4:38–41).[151] He too stays in a woman's home (4:8ff.; 8:1ff), but he also tends to stay in his own dwelling when dealing with leaders rather than going out to meet them as Elijah did (5:8–10; 6:32—7:2; 13:14–19). The stark and shifting contrasts bear some resemblance to the public/private dichotomy surveyed above, but the social groups involved, the importance of desert and mountain, and the relatively small role of cities differentiates this from the Mosaic material and from Luke's Gospel as well.

Much of the rest of the Hebrew Bible is dominated either by monarchial narratives or prophetic speech, which serve as weak social-spatial comparisons to Luke's narrative. However, a few other possible contributions could be mentioned here. Isaiah goes to confront Ahaz at a water source near the city (Isa 7:1–4), and Jeremiah has a number of public confrontations with the people in the temple (Jer chs. 7, 26), in various cities (11:6), and at a city gate (19:2). He denounces Hannaniah in the temple before the priests and people (ch. 28), and he moves from private to public in the section dealing with the Rechabites (ch. 35). The city gate is a key structure in the force of place, for it is perhaps the paradigmatic public place in much the Hebrew Bible, with dozens of references to it throughout various books in addition to those mentioned above (e.g., Gen 34:20; Deut 21:19; Ruth 4:1; 2 Sam 15:2, etc.). While it is clear that Luke has drawn on the traditions of Moses and Elijah/Elisha in his characterization of Jesus, Jeremiah might be the best scriptural precursor of Jesus' social-spatial activity, especially in and around Jerusalem.[152] One sees some overlap in the use of the forces of place and social relations. Like Jeremiah, Luke's Jesus had a number of confrontations specifically in the temple (e.g., Luke 20) and often spoke to large groups of people in cities (4:31–41; 13:22; 19:1–10).

The Apocrypha offer a few insights to this survey. Much like the Hebrew Bible, a great deal of the Apocrypha is filled with military matters (Judith, Maccabees) or discourse (Wisdom of Solomon, Sirach). However, there is some helpful material. Tobit intentionally invites poor neighbors from the public into his house for a meal (Tob 2:1–3). When he hears of a murdered man lying in the market place (ἀγορά), he removes the corpse from the city street (πλατεία) and brings it into his private home to bury it after sunset (2:4–6).

---

150. It is clear that mountains are an important place in the Hebrew Bible and often carry connotations of divine encounter. Luke has important material that picks up on this tradition. Jesus goes up the mountain to pray (6:12) and is transfigured on the mountain (9:28–37). What is interesting is that these locations seem to be considered private by Luke given, but then on both occasions Jesus comes down from the mountain to minister among the crowd (6:13–17; 9:37–45).

151. Thus, while the force of place plays a major role in the Elijah stories, it is somewhat eclipsed by the force of social relations in the Elisha stories.

152. This would be the primary limitation to the relevance of the material from Jeremiah. Almost all of Jeremiah's activity took place in and around Jerusalem, whereas only a small, but important, portion of Jesus' life (as recorded in the Synoptics) takes place in Jerusalem. Furthermore, Luke knows a Jerusalem (and a temple) that has been destroyed and rebuilt since the time of Jeremiah.

PART ONE: READING LUKE'S SOCIAL-SPATIAL CONTEXT

He crosses the boundaries of public and private out of his piety. The house dominates most of Tobit, as in this vignette, but there is some interaction with the public sphere. Regional politics and military matters dominate the Maccabean literature. Yet, it does mention particular public places (a city square in 2 Macc 10:2 and a public speaking platform in 2 Macc 13:26), public shaming (3 Macc 4:7, 7:14), and the public festival of Purim (3 Macc 6:36). The characters in these books mention the public and private spheres jointly, showing both a distinction and a connection between them. Onias appeals to the king in light of the private and public welfare of all the people (κοινῇ καὶ κατ' ἰδίαν παντὶ τῷ πλήθει, 2 Macc 4:5), and Antiochus refers to the public and private services he gave to the Jewish people (2 Macc 9:26). The Maccabean literature bears more resemblances to the Greek and Roman material covered above. For example, the city square supersedes the city gate as the common public space. In addition to the preceding examples, the εὐρύχωρον is the location in 1 Esdras where the people gather for worship (5:47) and to hear the reading of the law (9:38). Similarly, Nehemiah 8:1 (parallel to 1 Esd 9:38) mentions an "open area (πλάτο) in front of the Water gate." Part of the shift from the culture found in the Hebrew Bible to larger Hellenistic-Roman trends is seen in the fading of the city gate and the emergence of the city square as the ideal locale for public meetings and interaction. Some Jewish elements persist, but the social-spatial characteristics now share quite a bit with the rest of the Hellenistic-Roman world. City gates continued to be important monumental structures;[153] however their function as public gathering places became less prominent in Jewish Palestinian settings. This displays how cultural shifts (combining the forces of social relations and meaning) can affect how the force of place plays out. In keeping with this trend, Luke only mentions a gate twice in his Gospel. Once, Jesus almost incidentally meets a funeral procession at the city gate (7:12). The second instance is a gate to a house in the story of the rich man and Lazarus (16:20). It does not rank anywhere close to the importance of houses and cities, which are mentioned much more frequently.

Sirach has a mixed opinion about the public sphere. On one hand, the one who fears the Lord and has wisdom will be exalted "above his neighbors and will open his mouth in the midst of the assembly" (15:5, see also 21:17). Wisdom herself is described as speaking in the assembly in 24:2. These probably refer to official gatherings of the leaders of the people where political, religious, and military matters were debated and decided. On the other hand, farmers and artisans are so busy with their work that "they are not sought out for the council of the people, nor do they obtain eminence in the public assembly [ἐν ἐκκλησίᾳ]" (38:32b—33a); however, they are highly valued, for "they maintain the fabric of the world" (38:34). There is clearly value in life and activity beyond the public world of politics for Sirach. The scribe does "serve among the great and appear before rulers" (39:4). Yet, this is a side effect of the fact that the scribe studies the Law, seeks out wisdom, and preserves wise sayings (38:34b—39:3). The political activity of the scribe is derivative and secondary, based entirely upon the private tasks of study and learning. While the public sphere is certainly the seat of power and honor, Sirach notes that other occupations

---

153. See Segal, *Function to Monument*. As the title indicates, city gates shifted from functional public sites to monuments of architecture as Jewish society encountered Hellenistic and Roman influences.

(farming and crafts) have value as well, and that the scribe should first of all be devoted to his private (and group) study.

Philo and Josephus are two other writers shaped by Jewish historical, cultural, and religious traditions that must be considered here, partially because they have both been studied alongside Luke in the past.[154] As pointed out by Neyrey, Philo had a strongly dichotomized and gendered conception of the public and private spheres. Philo says:

> [The law] saw how unlike the bodily shapes of man and woman are and that each of the two has a different life assigned to it, to the one the domestic [κατοικιδός] life, to the other a civic life [πολιτικός], it judged it well in other matters too to prescribe rules all of which though not directly made by nature were the outcome of wise reflection and in accordance with nature. (*Virt.* 19)[155]

While the gendered natures of the public and private spheres are not dictated by nature, they do emerge from inspired application of natural physiology. This is strongly akin to Aristotle and draws upon the force of nature (here embodied in the law). Note also that for Philo public and private are divided into home and politics, similar to the dichotomy found in Cicero. A similarly gendered division of public and private is also made in terms of inside/outside by Philo:

> Marketplaces [ἀγοραί] and council-halls [βουλετήρια] and lawcourts [δικαστήρια] and gatherings [θίασοι] and meetings [σύλλογοι] where a large number of people are assembled, and open-air life [ὁ ἐν ὑπαίθρῳ βίος] with full scope for discussion and action—all these are suitable to men both in war and peace. The women are best suited to the indoor life in the home [οἰκουρία καὶ ἡ μονή], the entrance to the vestibule is the boundary for young women, and the outer door for the adult women; for there are two kinds of governance, the larger and the smaller. The larger unit is the city, but the smaller are homes. The management of these is divided to the two sexes separately. (*Spec.* 3.169–70)[156]

Philo's list of public places is quite similar to the list from Plato cited above (assemblies, courtrooms, theatres, camps, and public gatherings; *Resp.* 492b–c), and once again the house is the exclusive paradigm of the private sphere. Thus, the force of place features prominently as the expression of gendered space. While men do have some part in the household (they are at least allowed in it!), respectable women do not even cross the architectural boundaries of their domestic space. The spheres are explicitly gender-divided, but not only are the spheres divided, the management of those spheres is also divided by Philo, drawing in the force of meaning as well. Philo reflects elements already been seen in the Greek and Roman materials (especially the Greek division of men and women) and seeks to ground it in his own philosophical worldview and admiration of the Jewish law.

Philo can speak of some connections between the public and private spheres, but usually in an all-consuming negative sense. He says that male lovers are so consumed with their beloved young men that they forget all other public and private matters (πά-ντα

---

154. For examples see Borgen, "Philo, Luke and Geography"; and Sterling, *Historiography and Self-Definition*.

155. Neyrey, "Jesus, Gender," 49.

156. From Neyrey, "Jesus," 45.

PART ONE: READING LUKE'S SOCIAL-SPATIAL CONTEXT

ἴδια τε καὶ κοινάς, *Contempl.* 61), and idolators proclaim the great honors of their idols in both public and private (*Ebr.* 109). However, Philo does attribute pedagogical purposes to both the public and private spheres: "As parents teach wisdom to their children in private [ἰδίᾳ], so do [the poets] teach wisdom publicly [δημοσίᾳ] to cities" (*Prob.* 143). A clear division exists between domestic and civil audiences, but the poet occupies a place in the unofficial public sphere, for he is not an elected official and instructs the general populace. Finally, Philo also appears to consider synagogue meetings to be public events (contra Neyrey[157]). Philo says, "Thus, [Augustus] knew that [the Jews] had houses of prayer and met together in them, most of all on the sacred sabbaths when they are publicly [δημοσίᾳ] instructed in their ancestral philosophy" (*Legat.* 156).[158] Thus, for Philo, education has a very public and unofficial dimension either in cities or in synagogues.[159] Such gatherings are not cast as official political forums, nor are they described as private events that took place in homes. Even with his strong dichotomization of public and private, Philo implicitly recognizes and uses a domain of unofficial public space to portray the gathering of Jews for religious purposes and the people for education. The public valence of synagogues in Philo's presentation should be recalled when interpreting the social-spatial significance of Luke 4:44: "Jesus continued proclaiming the message in the synagogues of Judea." This is not private religious instruction, but public teaching by Jesus throughout an entire region.

The writings of Josephus have often been used as an analog to Luke's narrative and historical tasks. However, in the spatial analysis of Luke's Gospel the issue of scale makes the comparison much more distant, containing only a few illustrative passages relevant to the private-public-political spectrum of Luke's milieu. The prologues of both of Josephus's major works make the scope and scale of his writing clear. At the beginning of the *Jewish War* Josephus says, "The war of the Jews against the Romans was one of the greatest conflicts, not only of our own time, but of all the wars that have ever taken place between cities and nations that has been heard of before" (*J.W.* 1.1). Josephus prefaces his story of this conflict by setting it as one of the largest battles ever fought in the history of human civilization. Similarly, near the beginning of his *Jewish Antiquities*, he describes the scope of his writing: "It will embrace our entire ancient history and our political organization translated from the Hebrew records" (*Ant.* 1.2). Josephus is interested in world events, especially in their political and military manifestations. Luke does set his story with this larger political reality on the horizon (so 3:1a), but his narrative actually takes place on a much smaller scale (so 3:1b–2) mostly removed from these political and military realities until its climax near the end of Jesus' life.

---

157. Neyrey, "'Teaching You in Public,'" 88–89.

158. This portrayal of publicly accessible and open synagogue meetings serves an apologetic purpose (recall the rhetorical flexibility of these categories). However, Philo can credibly say to his audience that what took place in synagogues in Rome during this time was a public activity that Augustus knew of and approved.

159. Contrast this with Plato's emphasis on private education, but then compare it to the public buildings devoted to education in Vitruvius.

Josephus separates the private and public domains and prefers the public-political in his writing. Josephus replicates the traditional formulaic inquiry about the conduct of "public and private affairs" (τὰ κοινὰ καὶ τὰ ἴδια) referring to political and personal matters when describing the Jewish embassy's visit to Sparta (*Ant.* 13.166). Roman political leaders sometimes viewed private interactions as a hotbed for destabilizing, seditious, or murderous sentiments,[160] and Josephus features this often in his political narratives. Josephus describes how Herod left his "uncle" Joseph (private social relations) in charge of the public affairs when he left for a precarious meeting with Antony. Along with this public trust, Herod also left secret instructions that Joseph should kill Mariamme if Antony killed him (*Ant.* 15.65). Josephus even tells of a group of women who raised a public stir at court and then, after crossing the line by insulting the king's daughters, took to clandestine meetings in order to cause further problems for the king (*J.W.* 1.569). Private scenes among the royal family or among clandestine revolutionaries always predict trouble on the horizon.

Josephus also viewed the public-political sphere as the place of male leadership and distinction. He relates the following episode regarding Vespasian's rise to be emperor:

> Their general [Vespasian] had long shown concern for the common good, but never planned for his own promotion. Even though he was aware that his actions would justify such an acclamation, he preferred the tranquility of private life. But when he refused, the officers pressed him even more insistently, and the soldiers gathered around with swords and threatened to kill him if he chose to reject a life of honor. (*J.W.* 4.602–4)

Vespasian preferred a quiet private life over public power. He was forced to become emperor according to Josephus, and in fact this was the only way that he (an elite male) could avoid the most extreme form of shame, death. Moses won similar public acclamation with the opposite results according to Josephus's retelling of his flight from Egypt. After he had delivered the Egyptians from the Ethiopians and married an Ethiopian princess, certain powerful people began to fear that he would lead a revolution. Moses, faced with no other options, avoided the well-guarded public roads and fled through the desert to Midian. This tale reiterates Josephus's interest in the public-political sphere while simultaneously revealing the public status of roads (compare Luke 18:35–43), especially for a wanted man like Moses. Most of Josephus's historical narratives are occupied with political and military events. When private scenes do appear, they are often descriptions of malevolent political maneuverings (as with Herod and Mariamme) or brief excurses on the character and life of some political leaders (e.g., King Izates in *Ant.* 20.38–48). Josephus does replicate some of the characteristics of the Hellenistic-Roman public-private spectrum already discussed, but colors it with his own historical, political, and apologetic interests.

Finally, the body of Jewish literature that begins with the Mishnah and stretches through the Tosefta to the two great Talmuds must also be considered. These documents embody and relate a rather different sociocultural trajectory than that found in Luke's writings, and some are much later than Luke-Acts. Thus, they are not very suitable as

---

160. Many such examples can be found in MacMullen, *Enemies of the Roman Order*: the emperors' well-grounded paranoia that they might be assassinated (1–5), suspicions about philosophical movements (53–60), and the secret practices of magicians (107–8).

comparative pieces; however, they do illustratively demonstrate the flexibility and fluidity of the public-private spectrum among the Jews as they negotiated their faith in the midst of the larger Hellenistic-Roman world. The discussion of the boundaries and natures of different spaces is opened in *m. Šabb.* 1:1: "[Acts of] transporting objects from one domain to another [which violate] the Sabbath are two which are four [for one who is] inside, and two which are four [for one who is] outside. How so?"[161] This passage proceeds with a series of examples regarding the exchange of an object between a householder and a beggar with judgments based on who transported the object across a domain boundary. The spectral nature of the public and private is defined and applied in *t. Šabb.* 1:1–5 (found also in *y. Šabb.* 1:1 XIV and *b. Šabb.* 6a). In these passages four types of domains are enumerated and illustrated. The four domains are private, public, neutral (or *karmelith*), and alleyways (or places of legal non-liability). Thus, the Jewish sages classified spaces beyond the public/private dichotomy. Broad and wide ditches and tall walls were absolute private domains (*t. Šabb.* 1:1).[162] High roads (possibly camps), large public squares, and alleys that open on both ends were absolute public ground (*t. Šabb.* 1:2). The sea, plains, neutral spaces, and colonnades are neither public nor private domains, probably because they either generally do not or cannot contain a large number of people.[163] Size and general usage are determining factors for designating a place as neutral space. For example, the area between pillars, which usually contained goods for sale, was neutral because it was not large or convenient enough for the general use of the masses (*b. Šabb.* 7a).[164] Nevertheless, this was a true space with recognized boundaries, and transporting something across it represented a violation of the Sabbath (*t. Šabb.* 1:4). The rabbis expanded the classification of space based on the complexity of lived spaces, which required clear rulings about Sabbath regulations.

The next tractate *'Erubin* deals with mixtures or combinations of spaces that may be created to facilitate lawful movement on the Sabbath.[165] *'Erubin* 11b–12b of the Babylonian Talmud deals with how sideposts and cross beams should be employed to create appropriate connections between spaces and thus make them crossable on the Sabbath. The two primary cases are alleyways (places of non-liability), which often connected entryways to homes, and courtyards, which were often shared by multiple homes. These boundaries had to be able to be crossed in order to facilitate the sharing of traditional Sabbath meals. A height of ten handbreadths was the limit for an effective connection (*b. 'Erub.* 32b), and the majority of a person or event should be in a single domain rather than being divided (*b. 'Erub.* 20a–b).[166] This tractate (*b. 'Erub.* 22b) also raises an issue treated later in more detail in *Nedarim* and *Teharot*: how space affects the adjudication of cleanness or uncleanness. If a given case of pollution is in doubt, then the space in which it oc-

---

161. Neusner, *Talmud*, 15.

162. As well as homes, which are assumed. See Freedman, *Shabbath*, 17 n. 7.

163. Freedman, *Shabbath*, 18 n. 3.

164. Other spaces, such as a courtyard, shared by many houses and thresholds were even more complicated and required special accommodations to be discussed below.

165. Slotki, *'Erubin*, xi.

166. Places above ten handbreadths were either considered neutral space or private space (which extended to the sky) depending on the context.

curred becomes critical. If it took place in the public domain it is regarded as clean, but in a private place it is regarded as unclean (*b. Ned.* 3a, 5b). Several places actually switch their public-private valence according to the set of regulations to be applied. The following locations are considered private with regard to Sabbath laws but public with regard to the laws of uncleanness: neighborhood paths, valleys, basilicas, fora, colonnades, and shared courtyards (*m. Ṭehar.* 6–10). These examples demonstrate the flexibility of multiple spatial categories in antique Jewish culture. Public and private could be subdivided and both labels could be applied to the very same place in light of contextual clues, cultural norms, and religious standards. Once again, a simple dichotomy does not capture the complexity of the public-private spectrum. These later Jewish examples show how the ancient rabbis began to wrestle with and define this spectrum in their regulations for law-observant living with all of the variations and variability of social and architectural realities. By and large, their concerns and regulations are not shared by Luke, but this material provides a clear case of how the classification of public and private was nuanced and negotiated by Jewish subculture in the Hellenistic-Roman world.

No study of society and space in Jewish culture or Palestine focuses on the private-public spectrum like the work of Cohen and Wiltshire, but Sperber's study *The City in Roman Palestine* (modeled after *Daily Life in Ancient Rome* by Carcopino) does address some of these issues. Sperber's previous books covered agricultural and economic life in Roman Palestine from 200–400 CE, but he claims that there is enough evidence to stretch this book on the city back to 100.[167] In the last chapter (written by archaeologist Joshua Schwartz), the reader is reminded that

> Much mentioned in the literary sources of the time has not been uncovered in archeological excavations and even when perchance it has been, it has not always been correctly identified. In any case the limitations of present-day research often make such identification all but impossible. For example, literary sources, both Jewish and non-Jewish, mention buildings or monuments in Late Roman period Caesarea. We know, however, very little about what this city or the buildings in it looked like.[168]

Despite this realism and the limitations of the evidence, Sperber shows that at least some aspects of the architecture and functioning of a city in Roman Palestine can be known by integrating the evidence gleaned from both literary and archaeological remains.

Sperber's first chapter treats the nature of the market in Roman Palestine.[169] The market was regularly organized around a large open space surrounded by colonnades, shops, multistory homes, and other buildings. This was a bustling area where people from the city and satellite villages came frequently to buy and sell. One would often find public wells in a market as well as other more private services such as rest areas and brothels. In other cities where the geography or previous building demanded it, the market was often created by lining a wide and prominent city street with shops and stalls. The rabbis, in their various

---

167. Sperber, *City*, 3. Note once again, however, that the evidence for this period seems to be weighted late. It is a stretch to reach back into the second century, and Sperber makes no claims to reach back to the time of Jesus, but 100 CE is close to the writing of the Gospel of Luke.

168. Ibid., 149.

169. Ibid., 9–16.

rulings, assumed the public nature of these markets. They ruled that a shopper or passerby was not liable for damaging pottery or glass vessels that were placed outside of the shop in the market/street area, because that area was public and vendors placed their wares there at their own risk.[170] Later, Sperber discusses the variety of public buildings in Palestine: basilicas, theatres, hippodromes, and amphitheatres. Interestingly, all of these are noticeably absent from Luke's Gospel narrative (with the possible exception of Jesus' trial) though a few appear in Paul's travels in Acts. The theatres, hippodromes, and amphitheatres were strongly determined by Roman architecture and social practice. However, the basilica was one structure that was absorbed into Jewish life in Palestine and as such was a space that the rabbis frequently debated. A basilica was often located near the city center and served a variety of official (such as legal) and unofficial (such as economic) functions. It often covered such a large area that one could not see from one side to the other, and it was typically divided into one towering central hall and two side halls supported by columns. The rabbis argued where, how, and why transactions that took place in basilicas were either public or private and how such a valence affected Jewish life in these prominent buildings.[171] Finally, Sperber discusses roads and backstreets. The two main streets in the city (the *cardo* and the *decumanus*) tended to be wide, paved, and heavily traveled. The back streets were much narrower and may or may not be well paved. However, many legal discussions concern minor infractions and injuries taking place on side streets (often from items thrown off of balconies), which indicates that even these small side streets had a degree of public valence. They were frequently traveled and known to be dense areas of interaction where personal disputes and affronts had to be settled by legal rulings.[172] Thus, the main streets were clearly public (in an unofficial way), while the social-spatial valence of side streets had was contested.

Overall, Sperber presents Jewish and Roman evidence later than the writing of Luke's Gospel. However, the portrait that he paints from the intense examination of the rabbinic and architectural material is of a crowded, busy, and bustling city life where contested interactions and places tended to be placed in the unofficial public sphere. Furthermore, many of the rabbinic challenges and rulings were heavily determined by ongoing debates over the public and/or private valences of places in the city. Thus, even as the rabbis looked both back and ahead on Jewish life in Palestine, there was no easy and simple division of public and private. The two often overlapped or butted up against one another in awkward ways that drove both people and scholars into heated discussions. In light of this, the inflexible dichotomy of public/private (or male/female or urban/domestic) is not a helpful analytic framework for assessing the contours and claims of these debates. Conversely, the more diverse and flexible presentation of the public-private spectrum presented above offers a way forward.

---

170. Ibid., 12. Even though the vendors were aware of this, they did not like it and often accosted those who did damage their goods. Therefore, even this typical division of public and private was resisted and challenged.

171. Ibid., 74.

172. Ibid., 104–6.

The Archaeology of Palestine

When we come to Luke's Gospel the use of archaeological material is mired in a set of debated questions. Exactly how much did Luke know about the Palestine of Jesus' day, and how well did he represent it? How strongly does the quest for verisimilitude either cloud or clarify Luke's portrayal of Palestine? How does Luke's own social-spatial world relate to that of Palestine, and how does it shape what is portrayed in his Gospel? This section will seek to offer some tentative answers to these questions in order to explicate how the archaeology of Palestine can substantiate the framework presented in this chapter and illuminate Luke's Gospel.

The house is the natural place to begin, and when discussing houses in ancient Palestine, one must start with the work of Yizhar Hirschfeld, who has written a definitive compendium on the topic entitled *The Palestinian Dwelling in the Roman-Byzantine Period*. However, on the very first page of his introduction Hirschfeld proclaims a perspective that stands in stark opposition to the framework of this study and the evidence discussed the thus far. Hirschfeld says:

> In many societies, the division between public and private activities is regularly expressed in architectural terms. Large or imposing structures devoted to communal ritual, civic life, and administration stand in sharp contrast to the simpler structures used for domestic dwellings by the vast majority of the population. This sharp division between public and private architecture is a characteristic feature of the material culture of Palestine during the Roman-Byzantine period.[173]

Hirschfeld begins with the principle of a "division" between public and private in many societies. He moves from this grand assertion to particularize his claim in the material culture of Palestine in antiquity. Hirschfeld states that grander public buildings have received more attention in the past, and so he will focus on domestic architecture in order to explore the more private side of this division. After his brief introduction, Hirschfeld moves into a long chapter where he describes in detail and categorizes houses from ancient Palestine. From here he turns to a survey of traditional homes in contemporary Palestine, and finally he revisits all of this data in light of rabbinic sources. For this study, Hirschfeld's work and conclusions on ancient Palestinian houses are most crucial, and it is to that which we now turn.

Hirschfeld classifies houses in three categories. The *simple house* was a one-room structure located either behind or in front of a courtyard, which Hirschfeld claims created a barrier between the public and private domains.[174] The *complex house* was an expansion of the simple house created by adding new wings around the courtyard, which could have offered even greater potential for privacy. Finally, the *courtyard house* was a dwelling where various rooms surround the courtyard on all sides. Such a format was less common and was used only by wealthy families, but it could provide complete privacy for the inhabitants' courtyard activities. Some irregularities obfuscate neat archaeological classifications: the continued use and modification of dwellings, the lack of extant remains for

---

173. Hirschfeld, *Palestinian Dwelling*, 15.
174. Ibid., 21.

PART ONE: READING LUKE'S SOCIAL-SPATIAL CONTEXT

more humble homes, and the perishability or variability of materials. However, Hirschfeld maintains that the research and remains available allow for these three categories. The following is a selected survey of his work, which will provide examples of domestic architecture of Palestine. An analysis and critique of Hirschfeld's interpretation of domestic space will follow this sample of his presentation.

Figure 3.13 Plan and reconstruction of the Insula I house at Meiron, 2nd-3rd century CE[175]

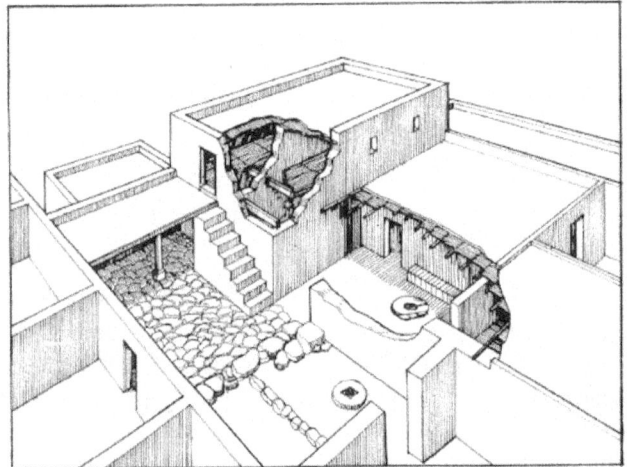

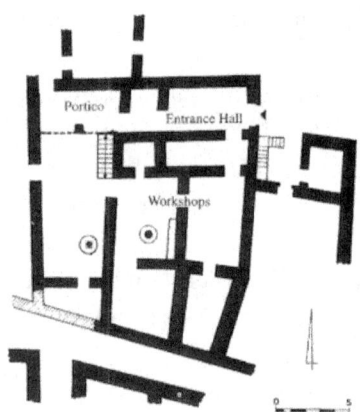

This 2nd-3rd century house follows the "two-wing" layout common at Meiron (two perpendicular sections). This house and many others at Meiron were well built with reinforced stone (which Hirschfeld thinks may have provided greater aural privacy). This construction also signifies some degree of economic prosperity. The total area of this house is approximately 180 sq. meters. The northern section has a roofed portico and an entrance hall, which probably had living space above it with access by a stairway in the courtyard. The portico led from one street directly into the courtyard while the entrance hall provided another route of access around the corner. The southeast wing was probably used for light industry or crafts. There is one *miqveh* in the courtyard and a second *miqveh* probably reserved for the family's private use in the southeast wing (denoted by circles with a darkened hole).

175. Hirschfeld, *Palestinian Dwelling*, 30. This illustration is used with the permission of the publisher.

The house from Insula I at Meiron is very typical for this village and this period in size, construction, layout, and function. This simple house type was more common in rural areas and less common in highly urbanized sites. Many homes had ground level rooms for storage and work, a roof level with living quarters, and a courtyard that was linked to all of the above. Hirschfeld comments that these simple two-story houses with a courtyard were common in upper Galilee, and that the courtyard often functioned to separate the house from the street.[176] Some of these simple houses also had shops attached to the front or side and/or a triclinium, which was used for family meals and receiving guests.[177]

The complex house came in two forms. The first is an urban apartment-style dwelling comprised of several units adjoining a common courtyard. The second form was the rural farmhouse, which consisted of several units and wings attached to a central courtyard.[178] Many of Hirschfeld's examples in this category are from later in the period (fourth–eighth centuries CE), are located closer to Syria or Arabia, or are from rural sites. Since all of these examples are rather distant from Luke's Gospel, no visual examples will be presented. Many of these complex houses in the country are large enclosed areas that contain living quarters, storage rooms, oil/wine presses, and areas for livestock.[179] Urban examples are less common in Hirschfeld's presentation; he has only a few examples of late apartment complexes. The urban apartments reveal more deliberate construction with repeating floor plans in multiple units, while the rural examples seem to reflect a process of gradual expansion and addition from the simple house form to more aggregate structures.[180]

The courtyard house also came in two types: a house with an inner courtyard without columns surrounded by rooms, and a house with an inner courtyard containing columns surrounded by rooms (peristyle house).[181] The first type preserves an ancient local traditional architecture in Palestine. The second, however, was imported from the building practices of the Hellenistic world. These peristyle houses were much less common and tended to be owned by wealthy landowners.[182] Examples from this category are found in rural areas, villages, and cities such as Samaria, Sepphoris, and Jerusalem.

---

176. Ibid., 29.

177. For an example of both of these see building no. 35 in ibid., 35–38. However, many of these examples are from the Byzantine period.

178. Ibid., 44.

179. Ibid., 54.

180. Ibid., 45–47, 50–51.

181. Ibid., 57.

182. Ibid., 57, 85–86.

PART ONE: READING LUKE'S SOCIAL-SPATIAL CONTEXT

Figure 3.14 Plan and reconstruction of the "Triple Courtyard House" from Capernaum, 1st-2nd Century CE[183]

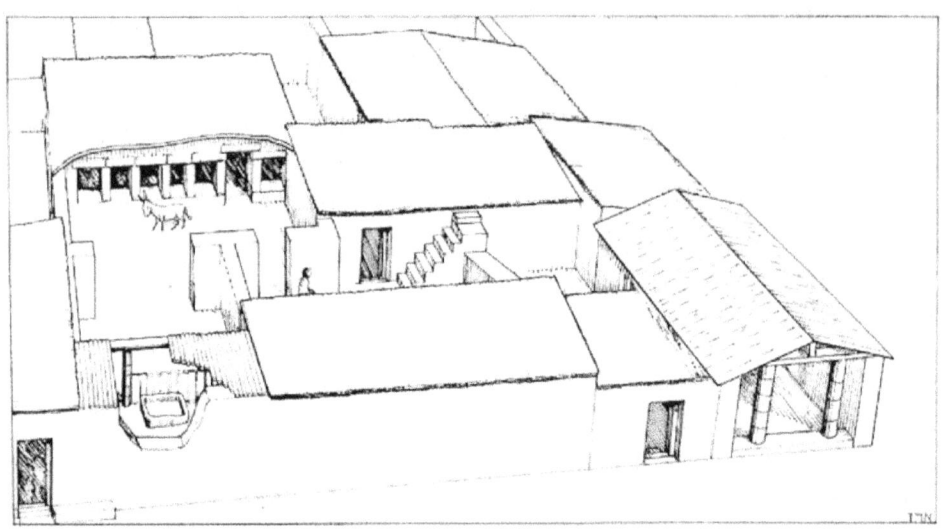

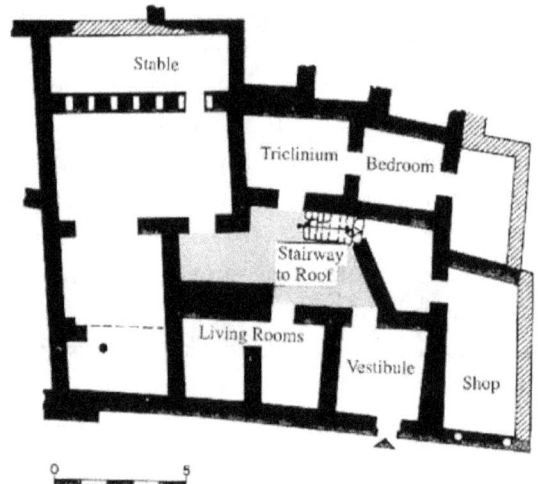

This house contains three courtyards separated by walls and connected by passageways (perhaps set aside for different purposes). The house can be entered by a doorway that leads to a vestibule and then to the central courtyard. Another entrance leads into the shop attached to the east side of the house (probably with a storage room on the northwest), and perhaps another entrance for livestock on the southwest corner. The house also has a triclinium, two "living rooms," and a more private bedroom off of the triclinium, all surrounding the central courtyard. This structure also incorporated a stable on its northwest corner. Finally, there is a stairway that leads to the roof, but no evidence of a second story structure is discernable.[184]

---

183. Ibid., 68. This is one example of the many homes found in Capernaum and originally documented by V. C. Corbo, *Cafarnao I*. This illustration is used with the permission of the publisher.

184. Hirschfeld, *Palestinian Dwelling*, 67.

Private, Public, and Political in the Ancient Contexts of Luke's Gospel

This home in Capernaum shares more similarities with the houses from Pompeii surveyed above. It incorporates a courtyard as well as commercial and livestock space, combining several functions into one structure (much like the House of Menander). The central courtyard of the house is at least partially visible through the vestibule, which provides access to it (as Wallace-Hadrill points out in many of the homes of Pompeii). The following example shows further similarities, and perhaps the increasing influence of Hellenistic and Roman forms of architecture taking root in Palestine.

Figure 3.15 Reconstruction of the "Peristyle House" at Aphek, 2nd-3rd Century CE[185]

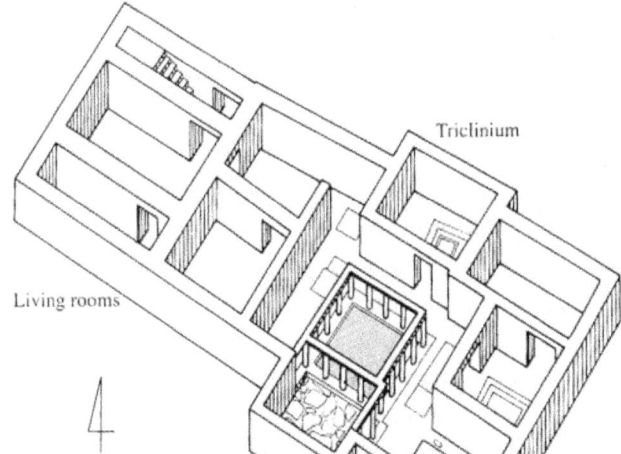

This home is approximately 450 sq. meters. Its southern side faces the *cardo*; however, the main entrance does not open onto the *cardo*, but rather a smaller alley on the eastern side of the house (potentially allowing for some privacy from the busy street). There is a short corridor which leads to a central courtyard with pillars. The peristyle has another paved courtyard just to its south, a triclinium on the northern side, and more guest rooms on the eastern side. These rooms fall on the grand side of Wallace-Hadrill's chart because they all contained elaborate mosaics which would demonstrate the wealth of the owner. More private living rooms (with much more indirect access) are found at the back of the house on its western side.

From this survey, Hirschfeld derives five conclusions. First, the simple house is characteristic of private rural construction. Second, the courtyard house is more characteristic of private construction in cities. Third, spacious Roman peristyle houses are rare in Palestine. Fourth, complex houses evolved to meet the needs of growing families. Fifth and finally, many homes had two stories. The lower story was used for domestic and workshop activities, while the upper story was generally used as living quarters. Shops were often

---

185. Ibid., 91. This illustration is used with the permission of the publisher.

located on the lower story while the upper story often included a triclinium. These areas of the house were connected by staircases, and many houses had a front portico as well.[186]

After this survey, and a corresponding survey of traditional homes in modern Palestine, Hirschfeld analyzes the architecture sociologically in light of rabbinic texts to deduce further important conclusions. First, the roof or second story should be understood as an extension of the courtyard where domestic/private activities took place.[187] Second, Hirschfeld asserts that "the house entrance marked the boundary between the public and private domains."[188] The main door was generally separated from the street by a courtyard, but it usually remained open to let in light and air. The entrances to homes were carefully designed and decorated (as noted by Wallace-Hadrill and Laurence); however, the courtyard entrance and house entrance were positioned differently to avoid a line of sight into the house (unlike Wallace-Hadrill's study). Finally, Hirschfeld closes with two important comments about the public-private spectrum. In his view the orthogonal construction of most houses was deployed to create and emphasize the separation of the more public triclinium and the private living quarters of most Palestinian homes.[189] Last of all he states, "The courtyard had the important function of serving as a barrier between the public and private domains, since the concern for privacy has been an important feature of both ancient and traditional dwelling cultures in Palestine."[190]

At this juncture, I will adduce some of my own criticisms of Hirschfeld's work before moving on to the responses and criticisms of expert archaeologists. Most of Hirschfeld's five conclusions from the archaeological survey are sound. However, in a few instances, Hirschfeld's conclusions are not substantiated by the evidence he lays out. I could find no examples indicating the presence of a second-story triclinium, and his comments on porticoes seem unwarranted given their rarity. This is even truer of the second set of conclusions at the end of the book, where Talmudic traditions and modern traditional homes are used to read the ancient archaeological evidence.[191] While several houses have no line of sight from the door into the house, Hirschfeld often fails to indicate this in his commentary, and he overlooks several examples that do have lines of sight through the house from the door such as the Insula I house at Meiron (displayed above), where a passerby can see straight to the back of the courtyard from the street, and the governor's house,[192] which has a line of sight to the back of the structure. Perhaps most importantly, aside from a few examples found in rural compounds, *no* ancient homes described in the book had a courtyard that served as buffer between the street and the door. Most often the main door led right into the courtyard, which served as the central point of access to the entire house. It appears that courtyards do function as a buffer in modern traditional homes

---

186. Ibid., 102.
187. Ibid., 246.
188. Ibid., 250.
189. Ibid., 289.
190. Ibid., 290.
191. The use of the Talmud to interpret daily life in the house and courtyard is particularly strong in ibid., 272–81. This material has deeply shaped Hirschfeld's interpretation of the remains.
192. Ibid., 74.

found in the Hebron hills (see pp. 150, 162, et al.), but Hirschfeld has apparently read this back into the ancient home and thus distorted his interpretation of the function of the ancient courtyard (for reception and entertainment). Most courtyards are an integral part of the interior of the home, rather than a mediating space between home and street. The variegated functions of ancient courtyards and the regular presence of shops and stables in ancient houses contradict Hirschfeld's strong dichotomization of public and private throughout the book.

Peter Richardson responds to Hirschfeld's work in a recent article called "Towards a Typology of Levantine/Palestinian Houses."[193] Richardson's first critique takes issue with the language of Hirschfeld's categories. Richardson says, "I aim for a nomenclature that derives from domestic architecture since the architecture is tangible; imprecise terms such as 'simple' or 'complex' seem intangible and ineffective."[194] Richardson also criticizes micro-geographical boundaries and family types as factors in such typologies, noting the great variety in both across the Levant.[195] Similar to a comment made above, Richardson points out that it is very difficult to speak of the form and functions of second stories since extant evidence is extremely rare.[196] Richardson proposes a much more precise typology divided into rural and urban houses, which is also attentive to the real influence of Roman and Hellenistic architecture that Hirschfeld seems to try to eschew. Richardson has the following categories for urban houses (the urban is more pertinent to Luke's Gospel): one room, shop dwelling, row shop, terrace house, side courtyard, central courtyard, peristyle, axial peristyle, communal courtyard, apartment, and insula.[197] Note that there are no *front* courtyard homes, as Hirschfeld implies in his conclusions. Also, Richardson goes on to point out the importance but lack of attention given to shop dwellings and terraced houses, which were very common in the Levant and adapted to the region's hilly geography and crowded urban areas.[198] He stresses that a broader typology is more helpful than narrow concentration on one type of structure in order to appreciate the fluid and dynamic use of space in early Christianity.[199] His comments suggest that a similar type of fluidity should break down Hirschfeld's simple and strong dichotomization of public and private space in the analysis of ancient Palestinian houses in favor of a broader and more precise typology such as the one argued for in this study.

The following two responses/critiques deal extensively with the question of gender in the light of ancient Palestinian society and archaeology. The first is taken from Marianne Sawicki's book, *Crossing Galilee*, which is not a direct critique of Hirschfeld, but seeks to offer a comprehensive interpretation of ancient material and mental "architecture" in order to explain how Jewish societies functioned in Jesus' day. Sawicki reinforces Hirschfeld's emphasis on the private nature of homes and the crucial role of doorways by her careful

193. Richardson, "Typology," 47–68.
194. Ibid., 48.
195. Ibid., 52.
196. Ibid., 48.
197. Ibid., 57.
198. Ibid., 60. Both of these receive very little attention in Hirschfeld.
199. Richardson, "Typology," 63–64.

examination of door technology. Doors were carefully and ingeniously engineered in the houses of Jesus' day, with two wooden panels set with pegs in stone frames that allowed the doors to swivel in a specific fashion. The doors were made so that they could only be opened from the inside. Furthermore, one panel could be opened enough to allow the inhabitant to see the visitor while still staying locked so as to deny entrance. That panel had to be opened to a particular point where the other panel could then be opened to allow full access to the house.[200] Sawicki claims that this meticulous and specific construction reveals a need and desire to control access to the house, reinforcing Hirschfeld's strong division between the public and private. However, Sawicki goes on to offer further evidence and interpretations that undercut Hirschfeld's conclusions.

First, she claims that later Jewish evidence as found in the Talmud should not be used to interpret the Palestinian architecture of Jesus' day for two reasons. First, these later Jewish sources reflect attempts to reassert gender control in an era when local control of kinship and commodities was becoming increasingly tenuous. A division of male-public and female-private simply is not found in the architectural record of the first century in Palestine.[201] Second, the concern over the flow and management of kinship (particularly women) and commodities (particularly water) manifests counter-colonialism rather than public/private concerns. That is, the stringent restriction of women's places and activities (such as the prohibition of women weaving in the marketplace) shows not only that such activities took place at some point, but more importantly emerges from a quest to preserve national and familial identity in the face of an ever encroaching and invasive Roman Empire.[202] Analogous reasons emerge in her analysis of the role of *miqvehs*.[203] The main concern in the Talmud was to be Jewish in the face of Roman enculturation. However, these are later developments. In the time of Jesus, she asserts that courtyards and *triclinia* were mixed-gender spaces where a variety of public and private business took place.[204] She extends this line of argument by claiming that the earliest synagogues (first–second centuries CE) were built in a semicircle to allow for face-to-face interaction (unlike the flow of crowds in the temple) and were open to both men and women (once again unlike parts of the temple).[205] While Sawicki does not comment directly on Hirschfeld's work, her interpretation of ancient domestic structures claims that the public-private valence of space in the pre-Talmudic era was much more mixed than Hirschfeld would allow.

The last piece to be considered here is an article by Eric Meyers entitled "The Problems of Gendered Space in Syro-Palesinian Domestic Architecture: The Case of Roman Period

---

200. Sawicki, *Crossing Galilee*, 15–18.

201. Ibid., 92, 98.

202. Ibid., 89–105.

203. Instead of accepting Roman water, which was collected in cisterns and transported by aqueducts, the *miqvehs* collected rainwater that fell from the sky and thus was pure because it followed the natural flow of water from God rather than human flows constructed by the imperial occupiers. Ibid., 23–25.

204. Ibid., 105.

205. Ibid., 130. It should be said at this point that as Sawicki moves along in her book, later conclusions are built on earlier ones and a great deal of inference and indirect evidence is employed, thus making her claims less convincing.

Galilee," which shares the gender awareness of Sawicki's work but is also a direct response to Hirschfeld at several points. Meyers covers examples of each of the type of house proposed by Hirschfeld. Out of this he concludes that the diversity of house layouts and the movability of most furniture (such as looms and couches) means that domestic space in Roman Palestine had to be more fluid and less gendered than Hirschfeld's analysis would allow.[206] From here, he asks whether or not the physical remains of domiciles reflect the construction of gender and space found in Rabbinic texts. His answer is a certain "no." Furthermore he states:

> One of the few criticisms that we may direct at Hirschfeld is that his otherwise commendable study of the house *presupposes a narrative of privacy* whether describing the courtyard as a "convenient barrier between the public and private domains" or characterizing the simple or complex house as offering "greater privacy." But as we have already noted, it is very difficult to ascertain the true nature of relationships that obtained among the residents of any particular domicile.[207]

The combination of work, sustenance, and production all in the same spaces (especially in courtyards) argues against the social-spatial division of gender. The interior of many excavated homes does not present private space separate from work space. "The public/private dichotomy simply cannot characterize this space where all manner of household, family and everyday activities were carried on."[208] At Meiron, homes and rooms were fluid spaces that adjusted to need, time of day, and season. Courtyards could function either to seal off private space or as common spaces shared by various households.[209] Meyers asserts that Hirschfeld's conclusion that the courtyard house was designed to maintain privacy must be rejected. The courtyard rather seems to have been a hub of a variety of activities that took place in the house.

Examining the rabbinic literature shows that men and women were located together in several contexts both in and out of the home: fieldwork, production, towns, and cities.[210] In Meyers's assessment, women had greater domestic and market freedom than many later literary sources portray. Thus, one must conclude that the valence of public and private places was not as simple as rigid gender divisions. This quality of space in ancient Palestine calls for more precise categories and more nuanced methods for ascertaining the public and/or private character of any given place, even of the Palestinian houses (and roads and cities) represented in Luke's Gospel. The framework defended in this study offers just such a way forward.

Most of Luke's Gospel takes place in smaller cities and villages in and around Galilee. Unfortunately, there are practically none of these locations from this period that have been excavated as thoroughly as Ephesus or Pompeii so as to provide a comprehensive understanding of urban public and private space in light of city plans and layouts in Palestine

---

206. Meyers, "Problems," 45–50.
207. Ibid., 60; emphasis added.
208. Ibid., 59.
209. Ibid., 60.
210. Ibid., 66.

PART ONE: READING LUKE'S SOCIAL-SPATIAL CONTEXT

during Luke's era.[211] In addition, many of the available remains come from later in the Roman Period (mostly after 135) when more imposing elements of Roman architecture were built into or on top of existing cities, covering over previous structures. Because of this state of affairs, only a few, limited studies of the nature of urban space and life in Palestine in the first–second century CE exist. The best that can be offered here is a glimpse at some of the incomplete remains and suggestive studies that may offer some additional insights about the nature of public and private space from an urban perspective.

V. C. Corbo headed Franciscan excavations at the site of Capernaum for many years, and his book *Cafarnao: Gli Edifici della Citta* has served as an invaluable resource for many scholars who have followed him. The ongoing work of Corbo and his team has provided one of the most comprehensive archaeological pictures of village life in Galilee around the time of Jesus, even though the excavations face all of the challenges discussed above and are still incomplete. The limited excavations display the presence of a *cardo* and *decumanus* as well as the dense conglomeration of domestic, commercial, religious, and civic structures seen in Ephesus and Pompeii. This generates complexly related public and private spaces, which were creatively negotiated by the inhabitants. This becomes clearer as we look at one of the central insulae.

Figure 3.16 Insula II at Capernaum[212]

Corbo provides general labels for the numbered areas in this diagram (*habitatzione*—living quarters, *corteile*—courtyard, and *vano*—space/area). Starting with the top right hand corner and moving clockwise the rooms may be categorized as follows:

59-63—A house with two large courtyards in 60 and 62, possibly with covered shop space in 60

58—Possibly a shop

45-56—This is the largest and most complex section which was shown above in the section on Herschfeld as the "triple courtyard house". 50 is a vestibule from the main entrance. 51 is the central courtyard with additional courtyards in 45 and 46 which probably served as work areas and for the care of the animals in the stable at 47. 53 is possibly a triclinium with 48 and 49 as general reception rooms off the central courtyard. 54 may have been a bedroom (55 is uncertain). 56 was probably a shop with 52 as storage.

42-44—House with courtyard and 2 entrances

64-67—This section is uncertain. There are a series of courtyards here with living spaces possibly in 64 and attached to the east.

---

211. Excellent archaeological remains exist for the ancient city of Jerusalem. These will be adduced later during the exegesis of Jesus' approach to and entry into Jerusalem.

212. Corbo, *Cafarnao*, tav. XIII. This illustration is used with the permission of the publisher.

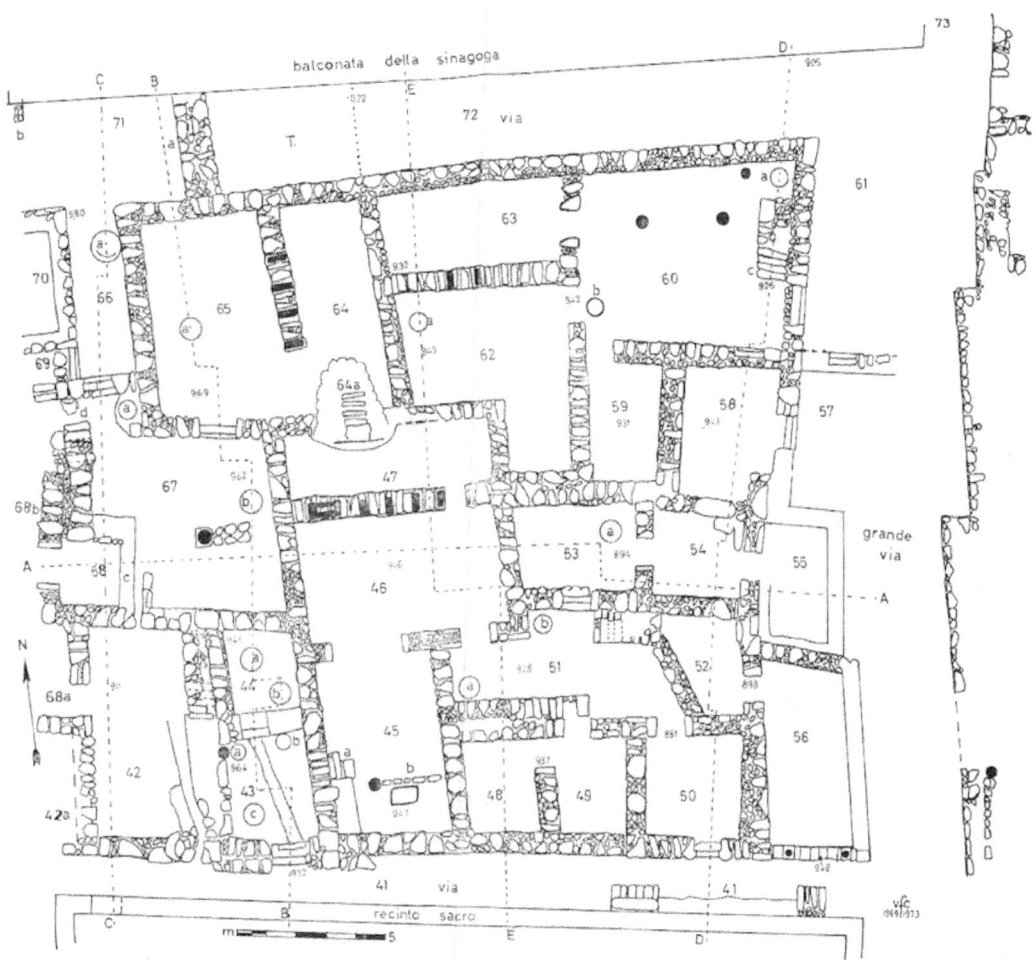

PART ONE: READING LUKE'S SOCIAL-SPATIAL CONTEXT

Figure 3.17 Reconstruction of Insula II[213]

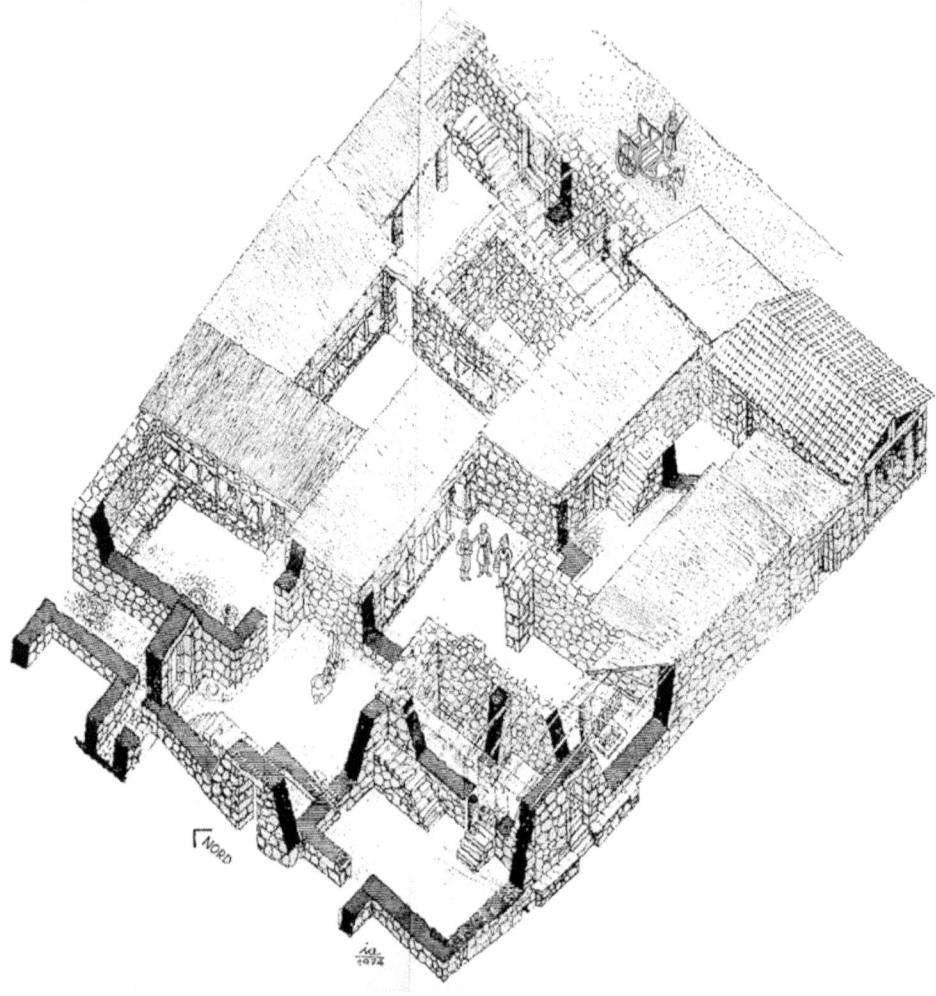

Capernaum has not yet been shown to have a city center anything like Pompeii or larger cities in Palestine (with a market, forum, etc.). However, these two selections from Corbo's work demonstrate once again the complex and densely integrated nature of space in ancient Palestine. Looking at insula II, living quarters, courtyards, shops, working areas, and even stables are all closely interlocked with each other. All of the possibly more private areas must have been shared within the household and are easily accessible, sometimes from multiple entrances. Furthermore, one must not forget that this insula is located right on the eastern side of the *cardo* that was lined with shops on the opposite side, to the north of the church (which probably would have been another dense insula in Jesus' and Luke's day), and to the south of the synagogue that was probably at the center of communal (and public) religious life in the village. The spaces in Capernaum as reflected in this insula

---

213 Ibid., XV. This illustration is used with the permission of the publisher.

were very flexible and stretched from intimate, domestic kinship relations up through the unofficial public sphere and perhaps into local politics.

Summary of Jewish Material

The Jewish material, in comparison to the Hellenistic and Roman, contains fewer passages that shed distinctive light on the social-spatial milieu of Luke's narrative. The material in the Hebrew Bible offers an interesting possibility but manifests cultural and spatial practices (e.g., assemblies at the city gate) that are quite different from those in Luke's writings. As one moves into the Apocrypha, Hellenistic-Roman social and spatial practices influence Jewish culture and architecture. Philo lived in a Hellenistic-Roman world and was deeply indebted to the Greek philosophical tradition. He reiterates the dichotomization of public and private already seen in previous (especially philosophical) works. However, even Philo with his philosophical background and political location created an unofficial public sphere focused on civic and religious education. Josephus was more strongly affected by Roman politics. His writings were set on a world stage with special focus on regional and imperial government. Thus, he often overshoots the social-spatial scale of Luke's Gospel. However, in a few places he also sheds some indirect light on Luke's portrayal of Jesus. Finally, the Mishnah and Talmud are not directly relevant to Luke, but they do exemplify how Jewish subculture in the Hellenistic-Roman world could stretch, subdivide, and manipulate the public-private spectrum in its classification of social-spatial practice. Sperber's study fills out the rabbinic discussions with an examination of illustrative archaeological *realia* that further supports the dense and contested interaction of private and public space as well as the existence of an unofficial public sphere.

The archaeological material supports what has already been seen at Ephesus and Pompeii, but on a smaller and less urbanized level. Despite the weightiness of Hirshfeld's study, several scholars have rightly objected both to his facile division of public and private and several aspects of his descriptions and classifications of Palestinian homes. Richardson and Myers point out that a more fluid and nuanced categorization of space is needed in light of the paucity and difficulty of the archaeological remains. Sawicki and Myers add the further point that the spaces of Palestinian homes cannot be easily gendered given their flexibility and lack of clear identification.[214] Contrary to Hirschfeld's claims, the courtyard (a prominent feature in much domestic architecture) appears to be a place where the public and private spheres interacted and overlapped, an unofficial public space. This all supports the nuanced and flexible classification system set forth in this study. Finally, the examination of the city layout and an insula of Capernaum reveal the same dense combination of domestic, economic, public, and religious architecture that characterized both Ephesus and Pompeii. This broad similarity further substantiates the need for a refined classification of space in the ancient world that can take into account the way that ancient peoples and cultures defined, debated, and navigated the categories of private, public, and political in their social lives.

---

214. A further examination of the breakdown of the association with female/private and male/public in the Hellenistic and Roman material can be found in Bruehler, "Public," 141–46.

PART ONE: READING LUKE'S SOCIAL-SPATIAL CONTEXT

Conclusion

We can now return to the diagram of social-spatial classifications presented in the previous chapter and connect it to the research of this chapter.

Figure 3.18 Diagram of social-spatial classifications

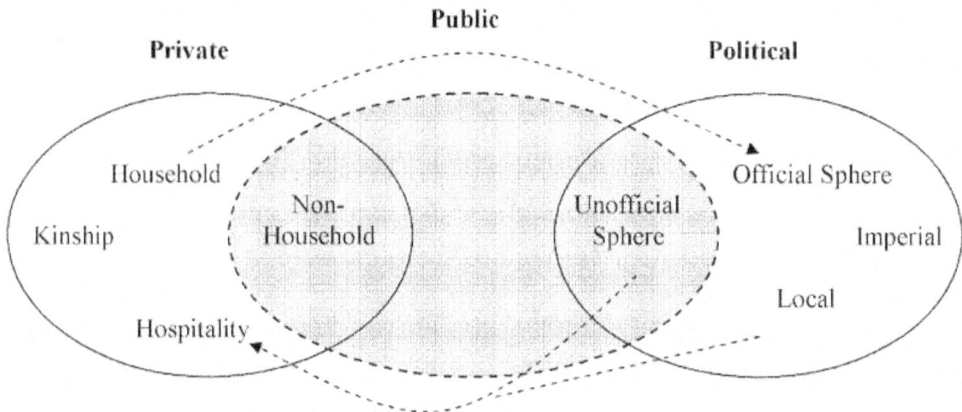

The extremes of the diagram are still evident and easiest to demonstrate. Starting with the private sphere, several citations in the preceding survey substantiate that the private sphere was strongly defined by its *spatial* character (the force of place). That is, the house itself was the key element of the private sphere in most of the Hellenistic-Roman world. Archaeological remains of houses in Ephesus, Pompeii, and Palestine demonstrate some variety of private quarters: those parts of the house cloistered from easy viewing and access that were often used by the family. Correspondingly, the private sphere was strongly oriented around kinship (the force of social relations), the people who lived in the house. We see this in a variety of authors. Homer speaks of the private/family concerns raised by Telemachus. Sophocles speaks of Deineira remaining at home. Cicero can speak of the home as an inviolable refuge from public life. The story of Tobit orbits around a few homes connected by a long journey. Other private places existed beyond the house, but these are much less defined than the house, which dominates the private category. The diagram above labels this private zone as "beyond the house." This zone in the public sphere is characterized more by issues (the force of meaning and social relations) than place. Thus, it is difficult to identify "non-household" private structures. It is more common that private social transactions could take place in more public spaces such as the baths in Ephesus, the Eumachia building in Pompeii, or the shared courtyards of homes in Capernaum. Friendship and leisure were often considered private matters (see Cohen and Cicero). These private interactions could take place in the public baths such as those at Ephesus and Pompeii. Both Demosthenes and Vitruvius indicated that personal economic interests were private in nature, even if they were transacted in "public" places. Business interests are perhaps one of the best examples of private activities that occurred outside the house (but also sometimes inside the house). Under this category one might also include private religious sites outside of the household, as well as private teaching that occurred in places outside of households like the gymnasium in Athens, the garden near Plato's home, or the schools of scholars envisioned by Ben Sira.

We now move to the other extreme of the diagram, the sphere of official politics, for it deals with official matters: rulers, officials, laws, the military, civic policy, and other government functions stretching from the local to the regional to the imperial. The political sphere of classical Greece, and specifically Athens, was focused on the assembly of male citizens in the city and upon the proper practice of rhetoric in such assemblies. Telemachus addresses an assembly of local elders using the language of neighbor (περικτίονας, *Od.* 2.65), men who know him and are known by him because of their proximity and shared history. Much later, similar local assemblies would have gathered in buildings like the Bouleuterion found in Ephesus. Demosthenes and Aeschines both discuss their public roles as rhetors. Plato and Aristotle depict distinct public and private spheres. Plato is more skeptical of the public sphere, and Aristotle strongly genders the two. This material is a good example of a more local political sphere, given that it deals primarily with people and issues in the city of Athens.[215] The imperial political sphere is common in the Roman material. The forum and the curia in Rome were the quintessential political places, but they were not just the heart of the city of Rome but of the government of the entire empire. These places were socially dominated by men of the highest rank, such as Cicero. The comments of Cicero emphasize the polar opposites of private and public space, suggesting that his home and the courtroom or curia are the only two places he can inhabit. Roman historians repeatedly focus on the political, legal, and military decisions and actions that took place in these arenas. On a more local scale, political matters within cities in the Roman Empire would have been transacted in the basilica and magistrates' building found in Pompeii's forum. Arrian's account of the procurator's behavior in the theatre is an excellent example of a local political official acting in the public sphere. Jewish social-spatial practices recorded in the Hebrew Bible and other writings stress the political assembly at the city gate, again more of a local political scenario. However, Josephus, a Jew writing from a Roman context, sets his Jewish history more in the regional or imperial political sphere, emphasizing military matters, royal leadership, and political events in cities, and larger geopolitical forces at work in Judea. Political places and concerns dominate the pages of the historians and rhetoricians; they are the best example of the official sphere of politics.

The public sphere stands between the two more well-defined spheres of private matters and official politics. The unofficial public sphere fills the gap along the spectrum between private dealings outside of homes and the category of local public politics. This sphere is "unofficial," for while it is public, it is not directly or primarily political in nature.[216]

---

215. Thus, while the πόλις was probably the original spatial zone defining politics in ancient Greece much as the house defined the private sphere, this ceased to be true when politics moved beyond the city into larger domains (leagues, provinces, empires) and into smaller segments within larger cities.

216. I fully recognize that it is nearly impossible to remove political ramifications or overtones from any public event in the ancient world (or in the modern world). However, this unofficial public sphere seeks to include those persons and events that clearly move beyond the sphere of the private without entering into the official realm of political offices, military endeavors, or legislation.

PART ONE: READING LUKE'S SOCIAL-SPATIAL CONTEXT

The area is shaded gray with a dashed border to reflect that it does not have the same direct clarity as the private and political spheres. Nevertheless, several examples cited above have shown that such a category is necessary to fully grasp the variety of social-spatial practices found in the literature and architecture of the ancient world.[217] Beginning with the classical Greek evidence, Mantitheus set his peer relationships under the category of "public" though they had no political ramifications (unlike his military service).[218] Recall how Demosthenes insisted that his "private" life was open and observable to the assembly gathered to hear the legal dispute between himself and Aeschines (*Cor.* 10). The character of Demosthenes's family life and business dealings (both "private" matters) was probably not table talk throughout the known world at the time or even in neighboring city-states, but he does claim that it was public knowledge in Athens, his city of residence.[219] In *The Women of Trachis*, Deianeira hears a report about the fate of Heracles from a slave who has just heard someone announce the story in the marketplace (371–72). These are not official political matters taken before an assembly, but rumors that are publicly proclaimed in the marketplace and later related in private.

Several other examples from the Roman material fit best in the (unofficial) public sphere. Vitruvius lists several structures under the category of buildings of convenience for general public use: harbors, open areas, porticoes, baths, theatres, promenades, and other similar sites. These are common public sites designed to serve the populace in their general life together, to facilitate social gatherings, and to enable common practices. They are not designed for political activity. Recall also the frequency of passageways in Vitruvius's classifications as public sites with no direct political connections. Roads and streets are common features that should also be emphasized under the category of passageways. These publicly traveled areas were surely a common place for social interaction that would be considered public while not being directly political.[220] Horace's and Juvenal's satiric insight reveal a crowded and bustling Rome full of busy, noisy streets, a place where most space was public and certainly not all of it was political. Appian envisions a public forum where people may gather for conversation and edification.

The Jewish material also demonstrates the existence of an unofficial public sphere. As Jewish culture came into more contact with the rest of the Hellenistic-Roman world, one sees fewer gatherings at city gates and the emergence of large gatherings in wide streets, open areas, and squares (see the material in the Apocrypha). Philo speaks proudly of the

---

217. Thus, while there is no label for this in the ancient world (no emic category), it clearly existed in a variety of cultural practices and so we can identify it and put language to it.

218. In her concluding remarks on "Public and Private in Early Hellenistic Athens," Patterson states that "Menander's plays reveal a new emphasis on the benefits of a community which stands between the public polis and the private individual (and his family). This is a community or society of interrelated and interdependent households . . ." (*Family*, 223). The category of the unofficial public sphere seeks to capture this "in-between" community and space.

219. Even more local spheres could be identified in classical Athens, such as demes, phratries, tribes, and neighbors. These various "localities" could be important in patron-client relationships and thus in political or legal contests as well. See Humphreys, "Public and Private," 102.

220. Streets are an important category for a socio-archaeological analysis of public social interaction. See Laurence, *Roman Pompeii*, ch. 6, "Street Activity and Public Interaction"; and Kaiser, *Urban Dialogue*, 47–57.

public gathering of Jews on the Sabbath for worship and education in the synagogues. Finally, the writings of the rabbis reflect a complex classification of space that included public spaces that were clearly not political. The navigation of public spaces in the market, on side streets, and on the Sabbath reflects a zone that is distinct from the private sphere but far from the sphere of official politics. Thus, material from all three provenances demonstrates the presence of the public sphere as a mediating space that existed between the private and political spheres.

Archaeological remains confirm this view of the unofficial public sphere. The sheer density of private, commercial, and social spaces seen in Ephesus, Pompeii, and Capernaum testify to the fact that much of life (which was not directly political) was carried out in the presence of others. One finds several archaeological examples of the unofficial public structures mentioned by Vitruvius. Ephesus and Pompeii had baths, markets, agora, stoa, porticoes, and streets[221] that provided plentiful public space for social interactions amongst a variety of people who crowded ancient cities. The partial remains at Capernaum reveal a similar concatenation of streets, shops, and religious cites that provided space for public interaction. One common setting for the unofficial public sphere would have been the theatre. As noted above, a wide variety of persons (male and female, slave and free, young and old) gathered in theatres and similar venues for entertainment events such as plays and musical performances. Ovid noted how people came to the theatre to see and be seen. Plato included theatres (along with other more official places) in his discussion of how the roar of the crowds can pull the young into its mob mentality. Arrian records the unofficial interaction of a procurator and citizens at a drama. The large entertainment events that often took place at theatres are excellent examples of episodes that are clearly public in nature without necessarily being closely connected with politics.[222] The public areas of homes demonstrate the overlapping of the private and public spheres, where time played a key role in determining the public or private nature of domestic space. Again, the written testimony of Vitruvius is borne out in the archaeological remains. The houses of Pompeii, as elucidated by Wallace-Hadrill, demonstrate clear planning to make specific parts of the home public, providing easy access and a line of sight leading from the street, through a vestibule into the atrium and then often into an interior garden. The Ephesian slope houses, while more dense and complex, also contain elaborate spaces for receptions. The open courtyards in the houses of Capernaum offer a setting for public interaction connecting the private and public spheres (contra Hirschfeld). The literary evidence points to the existence of the public sphere and the archaeological evidence provide several examples that suit this sphere well.

Finally, in some instances influence bypassed the public sphere, providing more immediate connections between the private and political spheres, as indicated by the arrows on the diagram. Again, the dashed lines indicate that these streams of influence were not as clearly defined by specific language in the ancient cultures surveyed above.

---

221. The public nature of streets will be explored in more depth in the exegesis of Jesus' encounter with the blind man in ch. 5.

222. Some games could be considered indirectly political when sponsored by a wealthy office holder to appease or win favor from the populace or when shows were determined and paid for by official civic bodies.

PART ONE: READING LUKE'S SOCIAL-SPATIAL CONTEXT

Recall how Telemachus brought his private concerns into a political venue. Demosthenes and Mantitheus cite their private behavior in official trials. Mucianus, writing as a private citizen, nonetheless addresses the senate with official language. Camillus turns his official military relationship with Lucius into a private friendship as well. Finally, some standards considered crucial to private life such as honesty, character, and good parenting were applied to the political sphere. As Aeschines points out, one certainly cannot expect someone who is a poor father at home to be a good leader in the city. Similarly, Philo asserts that Joseph's household management was crucial preparation for executing the same tasks on the larger scale of the Egyptian nation. In each of these cases, issues, people, or principles commonly considered private were inserted into the public sphere. Next, several examples demonstrate how the public sphere could reach into the private domain, illustrated by the other arrow on the diagram. Friendship and hospitality were two well-established cultural traditions that brought the public and political sphere into the private. These relationships allowed strangers from the public and political spheres access to the private sphere and linked the two together in mutually transformative ways (see Wiltshire). Cicero tells how Biblius's house was invaded by political order. Finally, one can see the political sphere reaching into the home in laws passed to regulate sexual and marital activity by the Romans. The arrows represent the dynamism of social-spatial zones in the ancient world. The private, public, and political spheres existed on a spectrum, but these skilled cultural agents could also skip across the spectrum creating connections between distant points.

Having substantiated and filled out this new classification of public space through a broad survey of literary and archaeological remains, we now turn to two specific works in order to further develop the public sphere and local politics, the two categories with the most relevance for Luke's Gospel.

4

The Public Sphere and Local Politics in Plutarch's *Precepts* and Philostratus's *Life*

Introduction

THE PREVIOUS CHAPTER FLESHED OUT AND SUBSTANTIATED A NEW CLASSIFICATION of the ancient private-public-political spectrum through a broad survey of literary and archeological evidence. The current chapter will complement this survey in a variety of ways. Instead of proceeding inductively through a large swath of material in order to find evidence to construct classifications, this chapter will proceed deductively by applying the classification system to two relevant texts, the *Political Precepts* of Plutarch (hereafter *Precepts*) and book 4 of *The Life of Apollonius of Tyana* by Philostratus (hereafter *Life*). Next, the provenance, date, and character of these two works help this examination begin circle in more closely on Luke's Gospel. Plutarch wrote from his hometown in Chaeronea in central Greece. Philostratus, while writing from Rome, was born on a Greek isle, educated in Athens, and familiar with Greece and Asia Minor. The *Precepts* and the *Life* fit well in the milieu of Hellenistic literature as does Luke-Acts. Also, rather than being earlier than Luke's Gospel like most of the literary material in chapter 2, the *Precepts* is roughly contemporaneous, and the *Life* was written in the early third century about a figure from the first century. Finally, each work respectively concentrates on one of the two categories on the private-public-political spectrum at the heart of Luke's social-spatial portrayal of Jesus: the public sphere (*Life*) and local politics (*Precepts*). Thus, this chapter will examine these two categories in more detail in preparation for the social-spatial exegesis of Luke. Each section will begin with a brief background on the particular work, follow with an analysis of selected passages, and close with a summary.

PART ONE: READING LUKE'S SOCIAL-SPATIAL CONTEXT

Local Politics in Plutarch's *Precepts*

Introduction

The *Precepts*, one of Plutarch's political treatises,[1] was probably written at the very beginning of the second century CE,[2] addressed to a young man of noble blood (εὐγενής) named Menemachus, who lived in the city of Sardis near Plutarch's own home. Menemachus decided to enter politics and sent to Plutarch for advice. Plutarch was a member of the Greek urban elite as was Menemachus, and Plutarch writes to him as one who shares his role in Greco-Roman society.[3] Plutarch assumes the right and authority of this upper class in the cities, and he believes that they must exercise control over the unruly masses for the benefit of everyone.[4] Plutarch writes out of his own experience as a local politician, and for him the urban elite have a duty to enter the public sphere, which is primarily, though not entirely, the arena of official politics on a local (municipal) scale.[5] Plutarch also writes as a philosopher engaged in public matters and intertwines moral, philosophical, and pragmatic concerns.[6] Plutarch's ideal form of leadership would be a moral monarchy, and his political treatises aim to inculcate justice, morality, and goodness in his peers. For Plutarch, the political order is a subset of the cosmic order and so should be governed by the same principles of justice and harmony.[7] Plutarch's ultimate goal in the *Precepts* is harmony (ὁμόνοια, 823f–825f). The harmony he seeks is politically practical, morally upright, and philosophically good. In order to help Menemachus achieve this goal he provides "precepts" or principles of action often supported by illustrative examples of paradigmatic political behavior selected from the classical past.[8]

Analysis of Selected Passages

Plutarch begins his treatise stating that he will gladly comply with Menemachus's request for guidance about entering politics in his "native city" (ἐν τῇ πατρίδι, *Praec. ger. rei publ.* 798a). Thus, he begins by establishing a local political setting. This treatise is not about imperial or even regional politics, but politics within the boundaries of a mid-sized Hellenistic city. Plutarch continues his introductory comments by admonishing Menemachus to enter public life (πολιτεία) only after making a clear, rational decision

---

1. Jones, *Plutarch and Rome*, 110. Plutarch has other political treatises including *Maxime cum principibus philosopho esse diserendum* (*Why a Philosopher Should Discourse with Men in Power*), *Ad principem ineruditum* (*To an Uneducated Ruler*), *An seni respublica gerenda sit* (*Whether an Old Man Should Engage in Politics*), and *De unius in republic dominatione, populari statu, et paucorum imperio* (*On Monarchy, Democracy, and Oligarchy*). These are often read along side Plutarch's *Lives*, as exemplified in the articles found in Nikolaidis, *Unity*, 317–37, 365–82.
2. Carrière, "Préceptes," 13.
3. Jones, *Plutarch and Rome*, 110–11; Carrière, "Préceptes," 29–33.
4. Jones, *Plutarch and Rome*, 111. See *Praec. ger. rei publ.* 818e–819b.
5. Aalders, *Political Thought*, 5–7, 26–27; Carrière, "Préceptes," 54, 60–62.
6. Aalders, *Political Thought*, 45–46; de Blois, "Ideal Statesman," 318.
7. Carrière, "Préceptes," 59.
8. Ibid., 57.

to do so (798c–799a). Then he instructs the future statesman to assess the character of the citizens and adjust his manner and diplomacy accordingly (799b—800a). Plutarch opens his treatise by calling the young Menemachus to reflect upon his decision in light of his own social-spatial context.[9]

After these introductory matters, Plutarch begins his advice regarding the life and activity of a political leader, and he begins with the character of the statesman. He opens with two examples of famous leaders (Themistocles and Pericles) who reformed their personal lives and habits with sobriety and composure upon their entrance into politics (800b). Plutarch continues this exhortation regarding personal character by saying, "For politicians are not only held accountable for what they do and say in public [ὧν λέγουσιν ἐν κοινῷ καὶ πράττουσιν], but people also meddle in their meals, love affairs, marriages, leisure, and any other serious interests" (800d). This statement contrasts private matters (meals, affairs, marriage, leisure, etc.) with public ones,[10] but in this case public is κοινός and not necessarily political (πολιτικός). While Plutarch manifests some disdain for this intrusion into a politician's private life, he acknowledges that a local politician must be prepared for people to know of and gossip about their leaders' private lives. Plutarch informs the young Menemachus that entering into politics brings not only scrutiny of all of one's public activities, but also of one's private activities, so both must be in moral order. Here, Plutarch portrays the porous boundaries between the three main divisions of the classification system offered in this study: private matters (meals, marriage, etc.), talk in the unofficial public sphere, and their impact on the careers of politicians in the local political sphere.

An ideal response to such constant attention to one's public and private life is provided by Livius Drusus.

> Therefore, Livius Drusus, the tribune, naturally gained an even better reputation because of the following situation. Many of the rooms of his home were openly visible to the neighbors [κάτοπτα τοῖς γειτνιῶσιν], and an architect offered to turn and reorient them for only five talents. However, Drusus replied, "Take ten talents and make the whole house open to view [καταφανῆ], so that all the citizens can see how I live," for he was a moderate and orderly man. (800f)

Rather than hide the private life of his home (once again the paradigmatic private place) from public view, Plutarch praises Drusus for opening his domestic life to the eyes of the city.[11] He can do this because of his personal integrity (the force of self in Sack's framework). Also, note that Drusus moves toward a larger public sphere by opening view from his most local "neighbors" to "all the citizens." Both the public and private spheres can be

---

9. Roskam points out that Plutarch purposefully placed these preliminary matters at the beginning of his treatise before diving into the actual precepts ("Two Roads," 325–26).

10. Note that this list fits well with the characteristics of the private-household-kinship category discussed at the end of the previous chapter.

11. Jesus may do this by welcoming the crowds in Luke rather than fleeing from them as in Mark (compare Luke 9:11 and Mark 6:30–32) or speaking in public what Matthew places inside a house with the disciples alone (compare Luke 8:4–20 with Matt 13:34–36).

perceivable to the general public, especially in a local context.¹² Furthermore, making the boundary more open benefits the rising statesman. Plutarch goes on to say, "Perhaps he did not need to expose his home to public view, for the people see through the characters, policies, actions, and lives of politicians . . . they love and admire one man and scorn and hate another for either their private [ἰδίων] or public [δημοσίων] behavior" (801a). Note Plutarch's list in the earlier part of this quote. The politician's "character" primarily indicates the private sphere, while his "policies" are directly political. This leaves the last two components, "actions and life," which probably fall into the intermediate zone of the unofficial public sphere. Thus, for Plutarch private integrity and public reputation are necessary for a successful political life. Public figures could expect that their behavior in both public and private would be judged according to a general moral code. Plutarch even states that the general citizenry has the ability to see through the public facades of politicians. In light of this, Plutarch advises his young protégé to order his personal life and general behavior in such a way that others may observe it and grant him greater honor for it. Once again, Plutarch advises Menemachus how to act given the porosity of the boundaries between these spheres.

Immediately after this section and still very early in the treatise, Plutarch discusses the speech of the statesman in detail (801c–804b). "However we should not in light of this [discussion of character] neglect the grace and power of the spoken word and ascribe absolutely everything to virtue," for both the character and the speech of the leader are persuasive (801c). In public rhetoric, the forces of meaning and social relations meet and mix in powerful ways. The local politician uses eloquent speech to steer the city (much like a rider uses the reins to turn a horse). In fact, an ordinary (ἰδιώτην) person cannot lead a city unless he is a persuasive and appealing speaker (801e), "for leadership consists of leading those who are persuaded by words" (802d).¹³ Plutarch quickly qualifies these statements by reminding Menemachus that the leader's speech must not be showy or overly subtle (and thus deceptive), like the various demagogues that he personally despises. Rather, it should be moderate, frank, insightful, and gracious as befits the speaker's office (802f–803a).

However, Plutarch is realistic about the speech contests of the ancient political sphere, and he believes that humor and ridicule can be useful rhetorical weapons for the statesman. Of course, they must be used appropriately and only for correction or self-defense when one is provoked (803b–c). Wit and humor can be effective so long as they do not go too far and offend the listeners or make the speaker look like a fool. An orator must be prepared to speak in public but also spry and quick witted because public life is full of occasions for rebuttals and apt responses (803f). Therefore, the statesman should not

---

12. This fits with the survey in the previous chapter, which demonstrated the dense organization and population of urban areas that greatly restricted privacy. A similar effect seems to take place in Luke when Jesus' "private" meals have public effects (e.g., 11:53–54), or his household discussions are extended into the public sphere (e.g., 14:25ff).

13. This is illustrated by examples such as two artisans competing for a building project. The one speaks well, but the other steps forward and says, "What this man has said, I will actually do" (802b). Plutarch also cites the persuasive power of Pericles. He says that Athens was a democracy in name but in fact ruled by Pericles alone because of the power of his speech (802c).

hesitate in a verbal contest but reply quickly and decisively (with appropriate humor) to shame his opponent and win over the crowd. Plutarch cites a number of examples of clever rejoinders (and failures) to drive home his point and thus demonstrates the frequency and importance of challenge-riposte contests in the local political sphere.[14] Plutarch's advice is also suitable for Luke's Jesus, who often silences his opponents with a barbed rebuttal.[15] In a local political context, the leader's speech is perhaps the most powerful means at his disposal to contend against opponents and win over the people. The previous chapter discussed the character and role of public speech in political life,[16] a role that Plutarch here depicts in greater detail. He portrays this as speech directed to fellow citizens, subjects, and other political leaders. Thus, these social relationships within the space of the city call for skillful speech in the local political sphere.

After his excursus on the statesman's rhetoric, Plutarch lays out to Menemachus the two paths into public life: the slow and safe or the fast and fiery (804c–806f).[17] This is followed by some comments on how to handle personal friends (806f–809b) and personal conflicts (809b–811a), and with this he closes his opening section.[18] Beginning in 811b and running all the way through 819e, Plutarch discusses the exercise of political power in a local context.[19] He begins with a few comments on how to be meticulous in the administration of municipal details without annoying the populace, primarily through the use of friends and colleagues (811b–813c).

In 813e Plutarch reminds Menemachus that "you are a leader who rules, but the city is also subject to the proconsuls, the agents of Caesar." Various indicators and admonitions in the treatise thus far have marked out its local or municipal character; however, at this point the local sphere defined by the space of the city is explicitly placed under the larger imperial political sphere. Plutarch warns Menemachus that to ignore this fact is to risk life and limb (813f), and he scorns those who drum up foolish pride by recalling the great exploits of the ancient Greeks (814a–c). How is one to handle authority in a local context under powerful (and potentially dangerous) imperial superiors? Plutarch advises Menemachus that he should not only be morally blameless before his superiors but also cultivate friendships with the Roman officials over him (814d).[20] Plutarch's pragmatic politics makes use of the patron-client system, so having friendships (or good client rela-

---

14. As noted by Malina and Neyrey, "Honor and Shame," 30–31, 38.

15. For examples see Luke 5:21–25; 13:15–17; 16:14–17; 20:23–25.

16. For example, recall Plato's comments about the power of public speeches (*Flac.* 57), obvious public nature of the language in Mucianus's letter (Tacitus, *Hist.* 4.4), and the importance of the funeral speech in Polybius (6.53.1–2).

17. See the examination of these two options in Geert, "Two Roads." Jesus appears to take the fast and fiery path in Luke. His baptism accompanied by divine signs (3:22), and news of his miracles precede him to Nazareth (4:22–27). However, this does not prevent other local leaders from envying him in contrast to what is said in *Praec. ger. rei publ.* 804d–e about the fast track eliminating envy (see also Geert, "Two Roads," 327).

18. The material on personal friends and conflicts will be combined with similar sections later in the treatise to be discussed below.

19. This breakdown is supported by Carrière, "Préceptes," 6–8.

20. Conquering rulers often extended benefits to states based on personal friendships, as Augustus was merciful to Alexandria because of his friendship with Areius (814d).

tions) with superiors will lead to the promotion of both personal and municipal political interests.

However, one should not be obsequious or obsessive in pursuing such friendships but make use of them for the sake of his native land: "while making his native city gladly obedient to its rulers, he must not demean it" (814e). Plutarch tells Menemachus that he does not have to get permission for every little thing like a man who asks his doctor every time he bathes (814f). Rather, the local and imperial spheres must be kept in balance and treated appropriately, and the good statesman recognizes where to draw the boundaries between local matters and imperial concerns. Thus, a good local politician is aware of scale and the various strategies appropriate to the various scales of politics: "The politician should soothe the ordinary citizens by granting them equality and the powerful through appropriate concessions in order to keep matters in the local government [ἐν τῇ πολιτείᾳ]" (815a). Local politicians should quickly cure any problems or dissensions at home in order to prevent external intervention (815b). The statesman must avoid generating contention at all costs, but also quell trouble when it arises (815c–d). He ends by citing a few key examples of men who prevented great evils by quieting local uproars and calming the rage of the powerful (815e–816a).

This section surfaces Plutarch's pragmatism and local consciousness. The political realities of Plutarch's day demanded that politicians like himself and Menemachus balance the demands of local and imperial spheres. To over-invest in either could bring dire consequences to one's homeland. Therefore, Plutarch advises his young colleague to balance the needs and demands of both sides of the political spectrum by preserving peace at home and friendships with superiors.[21] Local problems are generally caused by the greed and belligerence of prominent citizens whose clamoring for power threatens to induce imperial intervention (815a). When discussing the interactions between the local political and imperial spheres, Plutarch emphasizes the role of social relations: developing friendships with superiors and promoting harmony among peers and inferiors. The local political leader should manage relationships within the space of the city to promote the highest good (from the force of meaning): peace in the city, which allows for continued self-rule and prosperity. These precepts reflect his own attempts to work out the complicated realities of the local political sphere in light of his own political and philosophical commitments.

This same local political savvy is at work among the chief priests and scribes in Luke's Gospel. They had theological disputes with Jesus (e.g., 22:67), but pragmatically they feared that this popular figure would foment some type of rebellion among the crowds (22:2) and endanger their precarious political situation under suspicious Roman hegemony. Alternatively, they could be said to exhibit the pride and contentiousness of Plutarch's negative examples. In this case, they are jealous of Jesus' popularity and thus want to remove him. Either way, they surreptitiously arrest Jesus and present him to Pilate as a local rabble-rouser that the Romans should eliminate (23:1–2). They appear to exhibit

---

21. Roman authorities were apparently in favor of this policy as well. They preferred to reinforce the authority of municipal structures rather than expend their energy on local matters. See Carrière, "Préceptes," 54.

the wisdom of Plutarch's municipal statesman: dealing with local problems as quickly and neatly as possible and calling upon Roman power only when necessary to prevent more trouble or deal with serious threats. Note that Jesus' contact (and conflict) with regional leaders (like the Sadducees or Roman officials) occurs at the climax of his ministry. Jesus' activity only marginally gained the attention of a Roman agent like Herod (9:7-9; 23:8), who never acted on his curiosity about Jesus in the narrative. Thus, at the high point of his career, Luke places Jesus on par with political leaders in Jerusalem and plays out the final chapter of his life in a more regional political sphere.

Scholars of Luke's Gospel have long recognized that throughout most of the Gospel (5:17—19:40) Jesus' main opponents are the Pharisees and not the chief priests (who predominate following Jesus' entry into the temple in 19:47). Building on the previous paragraph, one can begin to assess the predominant social-spatial placement of Luke's Jesus in light of his primary adversaries. Plutarch recognized that the local political context of a city had a hierarchy of offices. He himself tried to exercise the utmost diligence even in minor or distasteful details like the city sewers (811a–c). Likewise, it appears that in Luke's view the Pharisees filled in the levels of local Jewish authority under the Sanhedrin, the ruling Jewish council in Jerusalem. Tax collectors and centurions represented the lower local manifestations of Roman authority, and Jesus was known to consort with such folk as well (5:30; 7:1–4). Therefore, the majority of Jesus' ministry in Luke deals with these minor local officials, and his identity in the Gospel is partially constructed through his interactions with these peers in the lower echelons of the local political sphere, bordering on the unofficial public sphere.

Plutarch also recognized that local officials must deal with one another in a variety of contexts, and he includes advice for Menemachus on this subject in 816a–817f. Here the force of social relations deals not with the statesman and the people but the statesman and his peers. He enjoins Menemachus to treat his political colleagues with honor and respect because they are his equals. Reciprocal displays of honor among officeholders build beneficial friendships and create stability in the city, as Plutarch's own experience as an embassy shows (816d–e). Practically, this involves higher officials showing respect for lower officials (817a), and occasionally requires enduring undue anger from a colleague (817c). Nevertheless, this does not mean that the local leader should lack initiative or vehemence. Plutarch says, "One should always confront any official with zeal, wisdom, and forethought for the common good" (817d). If that official is a worthy man, thoughtful and respectful speech from any citizen should convince him. Yet, if the official is reticent or bad tempered, a leader should come forward and address the people because he has a duty to his city regardless of whether or not the matter falls under the administration of some other designated official. "For the law always gives preference in politics to the one who does what is right and recognizes what is beneficial" (817d–e). Plutarch cites the example of Xenophon heading up the Greeks' return from Persia in the *Anabasis*, despite the fact that he was not a military leader. The one who knows what is best must take the reins of leadership when it is left undone. This is Plutarch the philosopher speaking to the political sphere. But more than that, it justifies the spontaneous emergence of local leadership outside of (and sometimes in conflict with) official authorities. Here the unofficial public sphere presses into the local political sphere. Plutarch opens the way for popular and "public" men to influence the official political domain because their cause is just and good, despite the fact that they do not hold the appropriate office.

This is probably how ancient audiences, especially friendly ones, may have perceived Jesus' conflict with the Pharisees. According to Luke, Jesus believed that the Pharisees as local semi-officials failed the test of good leadership and ended up harming the people (e.g., Luke 11:37–52). Thus, Jesus took it upon himself to oppose them and tried to lead the people in accordance with God's will. Jesus' conflicts with the Pharisees are a manifestation of Plutarch's realization that often a noble man must take a leadership role for the benefit of the people when the current local leaders are mistakenly or selfishly doing more harm than good. This naturally results in conflict, but it is incumbent upon the good man who knows what is right to step into the local political sphere and oppose local officials if they do not respond to more respectful overtures.

Plutarch has advice scattered throughout the treatise on how to choose, treat, and employ friends as a skillful leader.[22] Friends should neither be renounced nor unfairly favored (806f). The statesman should not put his friends above the well-being of the community and so "subordinate the community and public matters to private favors and interests" (807b). To do so would put the private and local political spheres in hazardous conflict. The statesman needs friends like an architect who designates specific tasks to skilled craftsmen, "for friends are the living and thinking tools of politicians" (807d). While the statesman should employ his friends in specific tasks, he must be vigilant about their character and performance. One can grant favors and leniency to one's friends, but it must not go too far, and it must not harm the state (808b–d). These favors can and often should include appointments to municipal assignments and minor offices. Employing a boat metaphor, Plutarch explains that the captain uses a variety of different crew members to steer the ship just as the statesman should incorporate others into his administration in a variety of ways (812c–d). This brings efficiency to one's administration and also disperses power so as to diffuse potential enmity. For example, Pericles appointed Menippus and Cimon as generals in order to add to the success of his reign and prevent accusations of tyranny (812d). Such delegation is even more important when "something great and advantageous must be done that necessarily entails a great deal of conflict and strife" (819b). In such cases, the leader must choose powerful friends who are willing and able to cooperate, especially those who complement the strengths and weaknesses of the leader.[23]

Jesus appears to have similar purposes for the disciples, his friends and associates. His commission for them is very similar to his initial statement of his own public mission to proclaim the Kingdom of God (Luke 4:43 and 9:1–2). They cover more territory and reach more people than Jesus could on his own and possibly draw negative attention

---

22. Also see the survey of this material in Blois, "Ideal Statesman," 318–21. Once again, the force of social relations comes to the fore in this topic.

23. Plutarch seems to end his discussion of local administration with these comments about the usefulness of skilled friends in 819c–d. A new section regarding the goals of political action begins in 819e. See Carrière, "Préceptes," 8.

away from Jesus (such attacks appears to be rising in 9:7–9). The seventy have a similar role in 10:1–12 where they extend the public ministry of Jesus. Finally, Jesus delegates the task of collecting the colt for his entry into Jerusalem to two of his disciples (19:28–30). Therefore, by incorporating close associates into his work, Jesus once again manifests the characteristics of a local political leader in Plutarch.

In the final section of the treatise, Plutarch discusses some of the goals and pitfalls of political leadership. One should avoid greed (819e), ambition (819e–820a), bribing the multitude (821f–822a), and debt due to public donations (822d–823e). Conversely, one should garner a good reputation (821a–e), give to public causes if one has the funds (822a–c), and pursue peace and tranquility in the city (823f–825f). Plutarch returns to the recurring themes of character and virtue in 820f–821f, where he discusses how and why a statesman should garner a good reputation among the people.[24] Plutarch says that "the man of politics should not look down upon the genuine honor and favor that is based upon the good will and disposition of those who remember [his character]" (820f). Of course, there is false honor based on bribes, games, and doles that should be avoided, but it is both useful and pleasant to develop a positive reputation among the people (820f). Plutarch reveals a bit of his social bias by citing the example of trainers (compared to leaders) who instill affection and good will in their dogs and horses (compared to the people). The statesman can only lead the people once he has won them over. He can use techniques comparable to painful horse bits and restrictive dog collars, "but nothing makes a man freely submissive and meek except a firm belief in the leader's good will, noble reputation, and righteousness" (821b).[25] In Luke's Gospel, Jesus appears to win the trust and admiration of (most of) the people through his healing activity (see 4:38–42, 6:17–19, 19:37, and Acts 10:38); his reputation as a healer wins him public honor.

A good reputation is largely a function of the unofficial public sphere, and Plutarch goes on to say that there are two invaluable benefits associated with such a reputation. The good will of the people can grant a person entrance into public affairs, and it can serve as a weapon against malicious and evil opponents (821c). A good reputation is actually a dynamic power that can raise the commoner to the level of the nobles, the poor to the level of the rich, and private citizens to the level of leaders (τὸν ἰδιώτην τοῖς ἄρχουσι) (821c). In fact, when a good reputation is mixed with honesty and virtue, it paves the way for a man to receive a political office (821d). Here again, Plutarch displays a person crossing the boundary from the unofficial public sphere into local politics. If any person has a virtuous character and popular recognition to go along with it, he can move quite easily from being a regular citizen to being a political leader in the city. This emphasis at the end of the treatise, exemplifies the importance of honor as part of the force of meaning that characterizes unofficial public and local political spheres.

---

24. On the subject of good will and its relation to other topics such as ambition and virtue in the *Precepts*, see Alexiou, "*Eunoia* bei Plutarch," 367–72. He notes that ambition is particularly destructive to the political community (367).

25. Virtue and goodwill are very closely intertwined in the *Precepts*. See Alexiou, "*Eunoia* bei Plutarch," 369.

PART ONE: READING LUKE'S SOCIAL-SPATIAL CONTEXT

Again, these characteristics fit the portrayal of Jesus in Luke's Gospel. Jesus was probably invited to speak in his home synagogue because of his reputation (4:16–17, 22–23). This wave of public acclaim presses Jesus into the local public sphere. As his popularity grew he gained the attention of Pharisees (4:17 et al.), centurions (7:2), Herod (9:7–9), synagogue leaders (13:4), and eventually the chief priests (19:47). Thus, his character and reputation as a beneficial healer (and powerful speaker) energized Jesus' public career. Jesus' reputation in Luke's Gospel also serves the purpose of defense as well. Throughout the passion narrative, the chief priests, scribes, and leaders are unable to arrest or harm Jesus in any way because the crowd was captivated with him (19:48; 20:19; 22:2). Therefore, Jesus' public reputation in Luke's Gospel fulfills both of the functions mentioned by Plutarch with regard to the statesman's honor in a local political context. Jesus' popularity as a healer and miracle worker gains him ever-increasing notoriety and gradually pushes him toward the public end of the public-private spectrum. At the same time, the adoration of the crowds serves a prophylactic purpose as his enemies attempt to plan his demise.

Conclusion

Plutarch's advice to Menemachus in the *Precepts* emerges out of and focuses on the realities of the local political sphere. This treatise depicts the characteristics of the local political sphere with a stress on the force of social relations: goodwill among the citizenry, dealings with other officials, the importance of public honor and reputation, and the role of patron-client relationships with political superiors. Plutarch emphasizes the importance of friends to the politician: they can help establish one in politics, protect one from enemies, and cooperate in accomplishing important deeds. With regard to the force of place, Plutarch says very little about the specific public places in which local politics occurred.[26] He briefly mentions the theatre and gymnasium (799f), the public areas of homes (800f), courtrooms (810a), the market (811c), and temples (816c, 825b). However, he does not develop them; they are incidental details for his high-context instructions. The force of meaning appears in the vital role of public speech, which is also the focus of a great many of the precepts in the treatise. The character, contents, and techniques of the politician's speech are all important, for it is the primary implement by which the politician leads the people and bests his opponents. Social relations and meaning meet when the public citizenry attributes honor to the statesman on the basis of his public rhetoric.

Two other observations should be noted. First, Plutarch is very aware of political scale. The large central section of the treatise reveals Plutarch's local political consciousness in light of imperial rule, a given fact of the world Plutarch inhabited (and perhaps part of the force of nature). The local leader must serve his native state and simultaneously cultivate friendships with Roman superiors for the good of his city. Thus, the local leader must work for justice and concord, solving local disputes as quickly as possible and aiming to preserve peace for the sake of the city and its citizens. Second, Plutarch portrays the porous boundaries between the private, unofficial public, and local political spheres. A local politician must have a virtuous private life because of public scrutiny, and a "public"

---

26. Thus, he is very similar to Luke's narrative, which also rarely labels specific public places.

man may step into local politics to do what is right for the city. Good character must be manifest in all spatial domains, and it is often the way that one moves from one sphere into another. The following chart is a concise list of elements of various forces culled from the previous chapter and this survey of the *Precepts* that use elements of the various forces to classify the local political sphere as a category in the ancient social-spatial spectrum.

Table 4.1: Forces in the Local Political Sphere

	Nature	Social Relations	Meaning	Religion	Time	Place
Public—Political-local	Males in organized human society; city government within the Roman Empire	Local political assemblies, citizens, political peers and superiors (affected by scale), friends who help in public matters	Attribution of honor, public speech, conflict, political functions determined by scale	City shrines and local patron deities	Mostly daytime	Cities, theatres, courts, fora, basilicas, *bouleteria*, official residences

Points of relevant comparison with Luke also arose in this analysis. Jesus often acts like Plutarch's ideal local politician. He initially gains a good reputation through his words and deeds. His reputation fuels his public career and also protects him temporarily near its end. He interacts with other local leaders, primarily the Pharisees but also the chief priests, often confronting them over issues of justice for the sake of his people. In these confrontations, Luke portrays Jesus as a skillful speaker who knows how to rebut and refute his opponents with a quick rejoinder. He gathers friends around him who help to further his mission and diffuse opposition. In comparison with Plutarch's *Precepts*, Jesus seems to straddle the border between the unofficial public sphere and local politics, a border mentioned a few times by Plutarch himself. Jesus intersects the local political sphere (much more than the regional or imperial) in Luke's Gospel. However, his activity in most of Luke's Gospel falls on the very lowest levels of that sphere (interacting with Pharisees and local synagogue leaders), and only near the end of the Gospel does he come to the attention of the Sadducees and chief priests and the regional authority of the Roman government. Therefore, in order to understand the social-spatial contours of Luke's portrayal of Jesus, we must turn to another work that fills out the domain of the unofficial public sphere more fully as a complement to Plutarch's representation of local politics.

PART ONE: READING LUKE'S SOCIAL-SPATIAL CONTEXT

The Unofficial Public Sphere in Book 4 of the *Life of Apollonius* by Philostratus

Introduction

This introduction will explore the hero, the author, and the scholarly study of this work in order to frame its usefulness for the investigation of the public sphere in Luke's Gospel. Apollonius hailed from Tyana in Cappadocia (*Vit. Apoll.* 1.4). He was probably born sometime early in the first century CE and is reported to have died during the reign of Nerva (96–98 CE).[27] He was renown as a traveling philosopher and ritual expert and especially for his ability to foresee the future and perform healings. He took up the Pythagorean tradition (vegetarianism, reincarnation, no animal sacrifice) and encountered various political officials in the course of his journeys and actions. Philostratus is our primary source for the sage, and so little more can be said for certain; however, more can be said about Philostratus and his aim in the *Life*.

Philostratus was born around 170 CE. He was descended from a line of sophists from Lemnos, but he himself was primarily associated with Athens. He eventually came into the literary circle of Julia Domna, empress of Syria and wife of Septimus Severus. She was a devotee of Apollonius and commissioned Philostratus to write a biography of the holy man/philosopher.[28] Philostratus also wrote the *Lives of the Sophists*, which reveals his own social location. Philostratus was a sophist—an educated, literary man who prided himself on skill in rhetorical display more than intellectual profundity; this is readily apparent throughout the *Life*.[29] Bowersock says, "In writing about Apollonius, Philostratus was himself practicing the sophistic arts."[30] The work combines several available genres: biography (details of the life of Apollonius), aretology (magnification of the wisdom and great acts of the sage), romance/novel (travels and intrigue), and history (accounts of emperors and foreign lands) all stirred together by a literary artist displaying his sophistic prowess in the glorification of a holy philosopher.[31]

Koskeniemmi says, "Wer das Neue Testament mit Hilfe der Apollonius-Tradition auslegen will, ist dazu verpflichtet, sein Vorgehen methodisch zu begründen und darzulegen, wie er einen Zirkelschluß vermeidet."[32] The best way to accomplish this here is to pro-

---

27. Bowersock, "Introduction," 10–11.

28. Unfortunately, she committed suicide in 217, and the work was probably not finished until c. 220 after her death. For some of these basic details and the complexities of sorting them out see Anderson, *Philostratus*, 1–17.

29. Anderson, *Philostratus*, 9–10, 127–28. One of the best examples is the apology that Apollonius supposedly composed but never delivered in his trial before Domitian (8.6–7). This rhetorical display is most likely a demonstration of Philostratus's own skills of presentation. Knoles comments that Apollonius's philosophical discourses lack depth and detail in the *Life*. See Knoles, "Literary Technique," 293–94.

30. Bowersock, "Introduction," 15.

31. For a discussion of the spectrum of genres that the *Life* relates to see Anderson, *Philostratus*, 227–36. Philostratus references the (debated) notes of Damis, a disciple of Apollonius, as one of his sources. His charge from Julia was to rewrite these notes (and other available sources) with more careful attention to diction and style (*Vit. Apoll.* 1.2).

32. Koskenniemi, *Apollonios von Tyana*, 206.

vide a very brief survey of previous work on the *Life*: how it both leaves room and paves the way for a comparison of its social-spatial characteristics with Luke. The comparison of Apollonius and Jesus has its roots far back in the early church. Hierocles posited the superiority of Apollonius to Jesus based on their miracles and teachings. Eusebius wrote a sharp rejoinder attacking his claims. Origen and Augustine were also compelled to comment on the comparison of the two figures. F. C. Baur launched the modern study of the two figures by claiming that Philostratus deliberately attempted to trump the portrayal of Jesus with his own hero, Apollonius.[33] Modern comparisons of the Apollonius and Jesus, especially in Germany, heavily employ form- and tradition-critical parallels with some history of religions analysis. The primary example of this vein is Petzke's *Die Traditionen über Apollonius von Tyana und das Neue Testament*. Koskenniemi writes in this same tradition.[34] None of these studies attend to place or social dynamics.[35]

More recent studies employ literary and narrative criticism to illumine the *Life* and compare it to the Gospels. Knoles examines the use of narrators, time, characterization, and thematic development in the *Life*, but gives little to no attention to social-spatial matters.[36] Robbins uses the narrative sequence of the teacher-disciple relationship in the *Life* to cast light on the relationship between Jesus and the disciples in Mark.[37] Finally, Reimer uses a narrative-critical approach to study the role of magic and miracles in the *Life* and Acts. His approach bears more resemblance to the current study. Reimer says, "I will use the premises of narrative-critical approaches to construct a 'narrative world' from our text."[38] This study adds the qualification that this "narrative world" of Luke relates to the social-spatial world and the *realia* of its context in complex and illuminating ways. Reimer also points out that ancient writers assumed that their audience would supply quite a bit of implicit, necessary information when hearing the story (a high-context society), and that historically and culturally distant interpreters must go in search of such information.[39] This is precisely what this study aims to do with regard to ancient understandings and practices of space and place, which are not part of Reimer's analysis, using a similarly eclectic mode of investigation.

What aspects of the *Life* and the Gospel of Luke merit a comparative study of their social-spatial characteristics? First, no scholar has explored the spatial features of each of these texts in their ancient contexts. Reimer explores the social worlds but with a specific focus on the meaning of miracles and magic. Thus, there is a gap in scholarship that should be filled, at least to see if such a comparison of the social-spatial portrayals of Apollonius

---

33. Bowersock, "Introduction," 21. Almost no scholars still hold this position.

34. Koskenniemi, *Apollonios*, esp. 169–229.

35. Petzke gives one brief passing remark that "Apollonius lebt überwiegend in Tempeln" and notes only that Apollonius and Jesus both taught as they traveled (*Traditionen*, 169). Reimer correctly notes that Petzke's desire for objectivity results in his comparison being merely lists of parallels with little to no analysis or interpretation (*Miracle and Magic*, 17–18).

36. Knoles, "Literary Technique," vi–vii.

37. Robbins, *Jesus the Teacher*, 147–66.

38. Reimer, *Miracle and Magic*, 24.

39. Ibid., 28.

and Jesus is viable and useful. Second, Luke-Acts may stand in closer affinity to *Life* than the other canonical Gospels to Philostratus's portrayal of Apollonius. Note that Hadas and Smith include the *Life* and the Gospel of Luke along with Porphyry's *Life of Pythagoras* and Philo's *Life of Moses* in their sample of spiritual biographies from antiquity.[40] Koskenniemi includes a selection from Luke in each of his sections on the possible literary relationship between the Gospels and the *Life*, while Mark and Matthew are sometimes left out.[41] Reimer fruitfully compares *Life* and Luke's second volume to each other. He admits the chronological distance between the two works (a little over a century); however, he argues that there is some connection to the first-century Apollonius and that many cultural trends and perspectives remained relatively unchanged over this period.[42] Third, and finally, some scholarship indicates the public nature of Apollonius's activity, suggesting some affinity with Luke's public emphasis. Petzke has an entire section on "Die öffentliche Wirksamheit" of both Jesus and Apollonius.[43] Furthermore, Robbins has labeled all of books 4–6 of the *Life* as public material. He says that in this stage of the work Apollonius "addresses the major public issues and performs major public actions that set the stage for the final phase of the teacher/disciple relation."[44] However, he does not set out to demonstrate how either of these narrative sections manifests the social-spatial characteristics of public activity, which is the aim of this study. Both of these scholars intuitively label material in the *Life* as public without demonstrating how and why that is the case. In Petzke, politics is not in view at all, while Robbins points out how the public activity brings increasing political attention. In light of this, it is both viable and relevant to compare the social-spatial characteristics of the unofficial public sphere in the two works to cast light on Luke's portrayal of Jesus.

For reasons of both relevance and manageability, this comparative survey of the *Life* will be limited to book 4. First, the *Life* is an expansive work and boundaries must be drawn somewhere to make the comparisons less superficial. Selecting specific passages from one book allows for more depth and coherence. Second, in book 4 Apollonius travels through a part of the Mediterranean world that is also traveled by Paul in Acts. In fact the two figures visit many of the same locations: Ephesus, Athens, Corinth, and Rome. It makes sense to focus on a section of the work that relates a part of the world that Luke uses in the second volume of his own narrative, rather than far off lands like India and Spain. Third, both Jesus in Luke, and Apollonius in book 4 of the *Life*, add disciples, travel from city to city, minister in public venues, perform public acts, and encounter increasingly more important political figures as the narratives progress. This emphasis on the unofficial public sphere in the *Life* complements the role of the local political sphere in the *Precepts* in preparation for the analysis of Luke's Gospel.

---

40. Hadas and Smith, *Heroes and Gods*, 101–4.
41. Koskenniemi, *Apollonios*, viii.
42. Reimer, *Miracle and Magic*, 19–23
43. Petzke, *Traditionen*, 167–82. However, once again, this amounts to little more than a list of parallels.
44. Robbins, *Jesus the Teacher*, 153.

Analysis of Selected Passages

Book 4 opens with material relevant to the unofficial public sphere and local politics. In the first chapter, three groups respond to the return of Apollonius to Ionia. First, when he arrives in Ephesus, even the lowest of artisans (βάνουσοι) leave their work, drawn to his beauty and lifestyle.[45] Second, several religious oracles of the area affirm Apollonius's wisdom and powers. Finally, embassies (πρεσβεῖαι) come from the surrounding cities to invite Apollonius to instruct them about life and religious matters. Apollonius's fame crosses the breadth of urban society (the unofficial public sphere), the sacred sphere of oracles, and the political sphere of official delegations from nearby cities. However, before moving on to other locations, Philostratus begins by reporting Apollonius's activities in Ephesus.

Apollonius delivered his first public discourse to the Ephesians "from the platform of the temple [ἀπὸ τῆς κρηπῖδος τοῦ νεώ]" (4.2). Apollonius often used temples both as a place of proclamation and as a place of residence.[46] Given the fact that there are no other labels (other temples could be found in Ephesus, especially for emperor worship), the reader would naturally assume that this gloss refers to the famous Artemision, which was located a short distance outside of the city (recall the high-context communication scenario). Thus, Apollonius locates his activity not in the center of the city's political or commercial activity, but at its religious heart, which was outside of the city in this case. The forces of meaning and religion work together to stress the importance of this location to the Ephesians and thus its public nature. Due to the course of history we know only a little about this magnificent temple. We do know it was common practice in the ancient world to build temples on a raised platform (κρηπίς) with steps leading up from the ground.[47] The enormous platform of the Artemision was 127 meters long and 73 meters wide, while the actual temple sanctuary was 110 meters long and 55 meters wide.[48] The main sanctuary at the center of the platform was surrounded by sets of pillars, providing walkways for worshippers around the shrine. The text says that Apollonius spoke from the platform to the Ephesians, who probably gathered in the large area around the base of the platform. This temple was frequented by huge numbers of local residents and pilgrims on a regular basis, making the place public by means of the force of social relations. Furthermore, the physical structure of a raised platform in a level area (an element of the force of place) created an ideal setting for addressing a crowd.

---

45. The term βάνουσος probably refers to the lowest imaginable class of artisans/craft workers. It is often translated as "mechanic" and has cognate meanings of "mean, vulgar." See "βάνουσος," LSJ, 305. This comment implies that Apollonius's appeal stretched across all classes of people in the city.

46. Apollonius frequently stayed in temples during his travels (see the examples from Rome below). Additionally, a letter preserved by Philostratus records a request from Apollonius to the Ephesians requesting to stay in their temple (*Ep.* 66).

47. For a classical description of temple buildings and especially their foundations or platforms see Vitruvius, *Arch.* 5.2.

48. The figures for the platform and sanctuary are cited in Yamauchi, *NT Cities*, 103. A similar description, with a slight variation in the numbers, can also be found in Erdemgil, *Ephesus*, 30–32.

PART ONE: READING LUKE'S SOCIAL-SPATIAL CONTEXT

A crowd is not explicitly mentioned in the first chapter; however, this first discourse seems to be directed at the city as a whole, and further evidence gathered below supports this. In 4.2 the Ephesians are mentioned in the plural twice as the audience of this first speech. Apollonius urges them to "fill" Ephesus with zeal rather than laziness, and he accuses the city of being full of dancers, pipers, effeminate men, and noise. Thus, he rebukes the city as a whole. Finally, this brief chapter concludes by noting that Apollonius risked "offending the Ephesians" by upbraiding them so sharply. Yet, he decided it best to air these criticisms and clear the way for further instruction. According to Philostratus's narration, Apollonius takes full advantage of one of the most prominent public religious locations in Ephesus to address a large, representative group of residents about the ills of the city as a whole. Apollonius speaks to large crowds in Ephesus but has no explicit contact at this point with any priests of the cult or government officials. His social-spatial location at the temple is certainly public, but the forces of place and meaning make it much more religious and philosophical than political and thus places him in the religious domain of the unofficial public sphere.

The following chapter is a representative report of a discourse that Apollonius spoke to the Ephesians (a technique also employed by Luke). Chapter 3 of book 4 opens in this way: "He delivered his other discourses around the sacred groves near the covered walkway" (περὶ τὰ ἄλση τὰ ἐν τοῖς ξυστοῖς δρόμοις). The following speech concerns the topic of community sharing (κοινωνία), using a coincidental act of a sparrow as an example. Strabo reports that the area around the temple was occupied by a grove of trees called the Ortygia, where Leto was purported to have given birth to Artemis (14.1.20). Thus, the presence of groves is not surprising, but Philostratus provides further information about the public valence of these groves "near the covered walkway." Near the end of the *Life*, Philostratrus records another episode where Apollonius preaches in this setting with additional details. Apollonius was speaking "around the groves of the covered walkway" (περὶ τὰ τῶν ξυστῶν ἄλση),[49] when he supernaturally perceived the murder of Domitian in Rome (8.26). This passage states that he spoke from a small platform or pulpit (βῆμα). Moreover, Philostratus plainly states that "The Ephesians were shocked, for *all* of them were present when he spoke" (ἐκπεπληγμενῆς δὲ τῆς Ἐφέσου, παρῆν γὰρ διαλεγομένῳ πᾶσα). We can read this same description back into the earlier account of Apollonius's public preaching at Ephesus. Therefore, these groves were a common public gathering place near the temple where Apollonius probably regularly addressed the populace of Ephesus. Philostratus has no qualms about employing the hyperbole that all of Ephesus was present to hear Apollonius at these groves on this occasion, and the same is probably true of his first visit to the city.

Philostratus provides more background information about this place in the *Vitae Sophistarum*. He recalls one of the building projects of a noble sophist from Ephesus named Damianus: "And even more, he connected the temple to Ephesus by stretching a walkway along the road to the Magnesian gate. It was a stoa nearly two hundred yards long made entirely of marble, and the idea of this structure was that the worshippers would not be

---

49. In this case the term δρόμος is omitted, but this was a common practice. The full phrase ξυστός δρόμος was often abbreviated just to ξυστός. See LSJ, 1193.

kept from the temple in case of rain" (*Vit. soph.* 2.23).⁵⁰ Philostratus envisions Apollonius preaching among the trees near this long covered walkway lined with pillars and built for pilgrims and residents coming to worship at the shrine of Artemis.⁵¹ Thus, Apollonius's activity makes the most of two public-religious structures, drawing on the combined force of these places. The first is the temple and the crowds that were gathered around it, and the second is the covered promenade leading to the temple. Persons traveling to or from the temple might stop in the comfortable shade of the trees or the walkway to listen to Apollonius speaking from a pulpit. Being in proximity to the temple itself on the sacred ground of the groves might also attract worshippers to hear his discourses, bringing the force of religion to bear. Philostratus portrays Apollonius in public places thick with religious overtones, a viable alternative to the public spaces of urban politics, and more compatible with the thrust of Apollonius's lectures.⁵² Philostratus places Apollonius in the religious domain of the unofficial public sphere.⁵³ After his first speech from the platform of the temple, Apollonius moves to the main route leading to the heart of the sacred precinct, the groves that surround the temple. Perhaps this provided a space away from the officials of the temple, who might have objected to his presence and use of the space.

The following chapter (4.4) relates how Apollonius foresaw a plague in the city and interspersed his regular speaking with exclamations to ward it off. However, the Ephesians did not understand and thought his behavior foolish. Because of this, Apollonius left Ephesus for Smyrna (4.5–9). However, when the plague started to overwhelm Ephesus, the city sent an official delegation (ἐπρεσβεύοντο) to Apollonius, asking him to come and rescue them from it (4.10). Apollonius immediately and miraculously appeared in Ephesus ready to help them. When he arrived he "called together the Ephesians [ξυναγαγὼν οὖν τοὺς Ἐφεσίους] . . . and led all the people to the theatre [ἦγεν ἡλικίαν πᾶσα ἐπὶ τὸ θέατρον]." Philostratus presumes that Apollonius had the honor and authority to execute a city-wide summons and manage the crowd that would gather. This time, instead of situating himself near the temple, Apollonius draws the populace to the heart of the city itself. The theatre was a semicircular building at the intersection of three of the most

---

50. Philostratus personally knew of Damianus's exploits, for Damianus was one of his teachers (Anderson, *Philostratus*, 4).

51. In this case, στοά and ξυστός (δρόμος) are interchangeable labels. Given the parity of these structures, the terms stoa, portico, and xystus are all defined very similarly by Dinsmoor, *Architecture*, 394–97. Lawrence comments that a xystus might be externally indistinguishable from a stoa (*Greek Architecture*, 269). Thus, Philostratus is probably referring to the same structure in both the *Life* and the *Vitae Sophistarum* even though he employs different architectural terminology.

52. Knoles ("Literary Technique," 292–94) concludes that the *Life* primarily draws on the philosophical tradition in its portrayal of Apollonius but that it also draws strongly from the traditions about "holy men" in antiquity. Both philosophical and religious topoi fill Apollonius's speeches.

53. Once again, there was no stark division between religion and politics in the ancient world, and the two interfaced quite frequently. However, these episodes from the life of Apollonius are fraught with explicit comments, topoi, and implicit cues related to religion and philosophy, but there is almost no mention of political places, matters, or officials. The one exception is when Apollonius's vision of the slaying of Domitian interrupts his discourse in *Vit. Apoll.* 8.26, but even this is immediately surrounded by talk of trances, sacrifices, religious oaths, and prayer. Interestingly, Apollonius also appears religiously "unofficial" as his audience is made up of crowds of (nameless) worshippers, and he has no interaction with cultic officials in these stories.

prominent streets in the city: the Harbor Street, the Marble Street, and the Stadium Street.[54] The theatre stands between the Tetragonos Agora (economic center of the city) and the complex of athletic and political buildings around the Halls of Verulanus. Furthermore, a theatre (as discussed in ch. 2) was one of the most common unofficial public structures in Hellenistic cities. Additionally, theatrical performances were often dedicated to the gods for religious festivals and treated religious themes, making it more appropriate for Apollonius's activity.

Philostratus further specifies the spot by parenthetically indicating that it was the place where "the Averting god has been set up." Apparently, this statue or image must have been well known to his readers. At the end of 4.10, Philostratus explains that a statue of Herakles was set up precisely on the spot where the demon causing the plague (disguised as a beggar)[55] was stoned to death by the people on Apollonius's command. Later in the *Life*, Apollonius retells this incident in his defense before Domitian. He explains that he had prayed to Herakles to purge the city of the plague, and so he set up a statue-shrine to him to commemorate the event (8.7).[56] After a brief review of this story, the public nature of Apollonius's activity is manifest. He has the authority to call the populace together at a moment's notice. He chooses a very public structure, the theatre, at the heart of the city for the assembly.[57] Here, he presides over the public execution of a demon in front of the theatre. Once again, most of these public actions are in the unofficial sphere, since this public event took place during the day in front of a theatre surrounded by crowds. The only official element is the dispatching of an embassy, which was presumably sent by some political body like the βουλή of Ephesus. However, no other officials play any role in the story after this opening request. Thus, the unofficial public sphere is the best classification for this event.[58]

In 4.17–22 Apollonius visits Athens. His arrival there is a public event and bears interesting similarities to Jesus' arrival in Jerusalem. Apollonius comes to Athens during a popular festival with his companions, drawing on the force of time (the occasion of the festival) to stress his public arrival. Then, a mass of philosophy students recognize

---

54. Rogers, *Sacred Identity*, 196. See also the discussion of Ephesus in ch. 3.

55. The demon turned out to be some kind of huge dog once it was dead. Dogs, along with other animals, were often associated with the plague and other evils in the ancient world. See Faraone, "Talismans," 100–112.

56. Herakles was a common apotropaic deity. Apollonius cites his saving activity in 8.26, but Faraone argues that it was his horrific form that frightened demonic forces away ("Talismans," 112–15). Faraone also mentions that apotropaic images could be set up by legendary philosophers/holy men (274–75), as would seem to be true in this instance.

57. The text is unclear whether the people gathered *inside* the theatre or *in front of* the theatre. Philostratus only states that Apollonius called them "to" (ἐπί) the theatre. It was most common for apotropaic images to be set up at boundaries, entrances, and thresholds (Faraone, "Talismans," 9–10), so in this high-context narration it would seem most probable that the image was set up at the entrance to the theatre which was where the people assembled in the streets and subsequently killed the demon.

58. Even though Apollonius has now moved into the city from the temple, Philostratus still provides a religious color to the social-spatial character of this event by initially describing the location as the place of the Averting god and closing the whole story by mentioning that a statue of Herakles had been set up where the demon was killed.

him and form a throng welcoming him into the city, drawing on the force of social relations to reinforce the public setting (see 4.17). In the city during the crowded festival, the people hang around Apollonius and eventually accompany him to his own initiation into the mysteries. The priest refuses to initiate him at first, but then bows to the pressure of Apollonius's riposte and pressure from the crowd. Apollonius's entry is unofficial since he is accompanied by only his own disciples and local philosophy students who recognize him. The publicity continues into the city when Apollonius does run afoul with a (religious) official, but the crowd makes its presence felt again and sways the priest to admit him (which Apollonius then refuses). This unofficial, public entry will be discussed in more detail in chapter 7 in comparison with Jesus' entry into Jerusalem.

Next, Philostratus recounts a few episodes of Apollonius preaching in Athens. As at Ephesus, Apollonius addresses the populace of the entire city (τοὺς Ἀθαναίους, 4.19), though the social-spatial specifics are left for high-context readers to recognize and fill. In 4.20 Philostratus relates a story about the exorcism of a demon-possessed man with a reputation for rowdy living. Apollonius was speaking on libations to his audience when a boisterous youth interrupted him with raucous laughter. Apollonius exorcised the demon, which marked its departure by knocking over a nearby statue in the royal stoa (βασίλειον στοάν) where the whole event took place. The royal stoa was an ancient structure (sixth century BCE) connected to the office of "kingship" in ancient Athens (Pausanias, *Descr.* 1.3.1). This was not the largest of the stoas surrounding the Athenian agora, but it was strongly associated with public events and political functions.[59] When the statue fell, the crowd cheered and applauded, and the youth was well again. This is much like the account of Jesus exorcising the boy with the demon in Luke 9:37–43. Jesus encounters the crowd in a public place, the demon puts the boy into convulsions, Jesus rebukes the demon, the boy returns to normal, and the crowd responds with awe. In both cases, the exorcism takes place in the public sphere where a large crowd can witness and respond to the hero's demonstration of spiritual power and its physical effects.

The next we hear of Apollonius in Athens, he is present for the festival of Dionysius (4.21). Apollonius saw the Athenians "converging on the theatre," and he presumed they were going to hear traditional hymns and solos from the great dramas. It turns out that they were dancing jigs, acting like bacchants, and generally desecrating this sacred occasion by their "effeminate" behavior. As in Ephesus, the theatre is a convenient and typical place for unofficial public (and religious) actions. Apollonius does not encounter any officials, but the acrid speech that follows uses military metaphors and events to shame the Athenians into better behavior. The last account of Apollonius in Athens deals with the theatre as well. 4.22 begins by saying that "the Athenians flocked together in the theatre" (οἱ Ἀθηναῖοι ξυνιόντες ἐς θέατρον) in order to watch gladiatorial fights. Apollonius demonstrates his disdain of this public debacle by refusing to attend an official public assembly (ἐκκλησία) of the Athenians and sending a letter that criticized these barbaric spectacles instead. Here, Apollonius withholds his public presence in this official setting to note his disapproval of their public behavior.

---

59. Coulton, *Architectural Development*, 10–13, 41.

PART ONE: READING LUKE'S SOCIAL-SPATIAL CONTEXT

In 4.25 Philostratus recounts in detail Apollonius's encounter and defeat of a lamia or vampire. This is one of the few meal scenes to be found in book 4, and it is relevant because Luke includes several meal scenes with Jesus. In Philostratus's story, Apollonius has come to Corinth and won over a philosopher named Demetrius and several of his students. One of these students, the young and fine-looking Menippus, was in love with a rather suspicious foreign woman whom he visited frequently in the suburbs. Apollonius confronted Menippus about the relationship and told him, "you cherish a snake, and a snake cherishes you." Upon his challenge, Menippus decides to marry the woman and arranges for the ceremony to take place the very next day. The following line establishes the public valence of this event and foregrounds Apollonius's intentional timing: "Therefore, Apollonius waited for the time of the wedding banquet and stood up in front of the guests who had just arrived." This draws upon the force of time, place, and social relations to create a public scenario. Apollonius induced Menippus to marry the woman by challenging him (presumably in public). Then, he waits for all of the guests to arrive at the banquet and proceeds to publicly confront the woman-lamia. When he does so all of the goblets, decorations, food, and servants at the banquet, which are said to belong to her, dissolve and disappear. At this point, Apollonius forces the lamia to confess what it is and that it was planning to devour Menippus after fattening him up. Philostratus ends and marks the public valence of the episode by stating that it was one of the best-known stories about Apollonius (τοῦτον τὸν λόγον γνωριμώτατον τῶν Ἀπολλωνίου, perhaps drawing on the force of meaning), and that it had occurred right in the middle of Greece (καθ' Ἑλλάδα μέσην, clearly drawing on the force of place). While this is not as public (or religious) as Apollonius's speeches at temples and theatres, it is far from private and demonstrates how homes could take on a public valence. This unofficial public event begins with a public challenge and climaxes in the public area of a home (place) during a wedding banquet (meaning and time) in front of all the guests (social relations). Philostratus's portrayal capitalizes on these characteristics to reinforce the publicity and popularity of this story.

While Jesus is less intentional about arranging such meal confrontations in Luke (he is usually invited by a Pharisee), he does take advantage of the setting to confront and teach in a public way. He forgives a sinful woman and challenges the hospitality of Simon the Pharisee in Luke 7:36–50. He reprimands the scribes and Pharisees as a whole at a dinner in 11:37–54. In 14:1–24, he heals a man just before the meal and proceeds to teach his host and fellow guests about humility, hospitality, and their own failure to accept the invitation to God's great banquet. The rhetoric in all of these household banquets, both in Luke and the *Life*, is agonistic and challenging, speech that is more apropos to the public sphere.[60] In each case the hosts and guests are challenged and corrected by the hero, violating the normal stipulations of hospitality and respect. Finally, each case involves a large group gathered in a home: the wedding guests in *Life* 4.25, the Pharisees and the sinful woman in Luke 7:36–50,[61] a host of scribes, lawyers, and Pharisees in Luke 11:37–54, and

---

60. Neyrey, "'What's Wrong,'" 84–85.

61. Even though no one else besides Jesus, Simon and the woman are mentioned, the presence of this "woman of the city" in the house of Simon strongly suggests that the public sphere of the city has penetrated the potentially private boundaries of the meal. This will be discussed further in ch. 6.

a similarly large group of guests in Luke 14:1–14. These scenes fail to abide by the typical standards of hospitable respect and privacy, and instead emphasize the presence of large groups of people who are either challenged by the hero or witness his power and authority. This technique employs the force of meaning to make a typically private setting (a home) into more of a public venue. Thus, such meal scenes still belong in the domain of the unofficial public sphere. However, they slide farther to the left toward the public areas of homes and the private sphere rather than butting up against local politics as Apollonius does in Athens and even more so in Sparta.

In 4.31, Apollonius preaches again from the platform of a temple, this time in Olympia. He taught about all of the virtues and "amazed everyone" (πάντας ἐκλήπτων, drawing on social relations). Some Lacedaemonians in this crowd gathered around him and invited him to be a guest of honor in their city. When Apollonius arrives in Sparta, the authorities (τέλοι) ask him how to honor the gods, heroes, and men. This vignette represents a rather smooth crossover from the unofficial religious public sphere (preaching from a temple platform in Olympia) to a local political sphere (the leaders of Sparta). Apollonius is invited to Sparta by some residents and then becomes an advisor to the leadership on moral and political matters. He has entered the local political sphere as an invited guest.

In the next scene (4.32) Apollonius sought out a young Spartan man who had forsaken public affairs (τὰ κοινά) and spent all of his time sailing and trading on the high seas. Apollonius found such conduct in a Spartan reprehensible and upbraided the young man before his official trial (ἀγών) began. Apollonius asks the man if his ancestors were sailors. The man confesses that they were not but were "all leaders of the gymnasium and ephors and council members." Thus, Apollonius led him to acknowledge his official political heritage. He admonishes the young man to give up seafaring business and take up politics instead. After this rebuke, the man is overcome, repents of his ways, takes to a life on land, and is officially acquitted by the ephors. Here we see Apollonius arguing for public-political involvement and against sea trade. He even has some access to and clout with the council of ephors to obtain an acquittal. Apollonius actively supports local political involvement and takes action to convert this man into a politically active citizen in his home city.

The last incident in Sparta (4.33) rises from the local to the highest political scale. While Apollonius is still in Sparta, the Lacedaemonian assembly (τὸ κοινόν) receives a letter from the emperor criticizing them for their pride and abuses. The letter was induced by several complaints lodged by the governor of Greece. The local practices of city government roused the ire of a regional official who convinced the emperor to issue an official reprimand. The city was divided over how to respond. Should they try to appease the emperor or reply with a sense of their own superiority? Philostratus says, "Under these circumstances, they asked Apollonius for counsel." Apollonius perceived the severity of the division, entered their official public assembly, and delivered one sentence of advice urging them to be neither too bold nor too cowardly. Here, Apollonius responds to an official request for guidance on a political matter that stretches from the local through the regional to the imperial. He even enters the political space of the assembly to deliver his advice, terse though it may be. This set of stories about Apollonius and the Spartans is transitional.

It portrays Apollonius moving from activity located primarily in the unofficial (religious) public sphere, to the local public sphere (note that Apollonius visits no temple in Sparta only their official assembly), and even touching matters that reach to imperial politics. In each case he supports the life of local politics in Sparta, and these traditions of Apollonius in Sparta prepare the reader for his arrival in Rome, the seat of imperial politics.[62]

At the beginning of 4.34, Philostratus mentions Apollonius's intent to visit Rome. However, due to a dream he takes a brief detour to Crete and arrives in Rome in 4.35. The tone for this Roman section of Apollonius's activity is set in 4.35, where Philostratus highlights Nero's opposition to philosophy, exemplified by the imprisonment of Musonius. On the way to Rome, Apollonius and his disciples are warned by a cowardly rhetorician named Philolaus to avoid Rome because of Nero's rabid hostility toward philosophers (4.36). Because of Philolaus's tirade about the madness of Nero, twenty-six of Apollonius's thirty-four companions desert him, leaving only eight (4.37). In 4.38 Apollonius exhorts his disciples and explains that the truly wise man need not fear any human being, even one with such a horrible reputation as Nero. Apollonius and his companions enter Rome in 4.39 and take up residence at an inn near one of the gates of the city. Almost immediately, during dinner that evening, they encounter the first of Nero's excesses, hired harpists who travel throughout the city playing his compositions. Anyone who ignored or refused to pay these official performers could be arrested. Of course, Apollonius and his disciples pay little attention to the droning of this second-rate harpist, who accuses them of violating the honor and authority of Nero. Nothing happens at this juncture, but Apollonius demonstrates his opinion of Nero in this first encounter with a very minor representative of the deranged emperor in a small public inn on the edge of the city. More serious meetings with higher-ranking officials loom just around the corner.

The next morning Apollonius is summoned by the consul Telesinus for an interview (4.40).[63] Telesinus questions him about his dress, teaching, and religious opinions. Telesinus himself was a religious man and was deeply impressed with Apollonius's answers. So, he granted Apollonius official permission to visit and reform any of the temples in the city. Apollonius acknowledges his generosity and adds, "I would like you to know this about me as well: I also prefer to make my home in the temples that are not closed up, and none of the gods objects to me sharing their dwelling." Later, Tigellinus, Nero's deputy, has Apollonius arrested on trumped up charges (4.44). In a private, but very official, interview Apollonius amazes and frightens Tigellinus with a rhetorical display of his wisdom and insight. Tigellinus closes the interview by saying, "You may go wherever you like, for you are too powerful to be controlled by me." This demonstrates that Apollonius continued his habit of visiting and dwelling in temples even in the metropolis of Rome. Also, his

---

62. This study will argue that Luke 18:35—19:48 serves a similar transitional function, preparing the reader for the transition from local politics earlier in the Gospel to higher and more official political encounters in the passion.

63. The consuls were elected officials who were in charge of security in the city of Rome. They were the chief administrators of public affairs in the city and also led military expeditions. The public renown and political power of such elected officials was only superceded by that of the emperor. See Shelton, *As the Romans Did*, 207–11.

encounters with these two figures bring him into some of the highest levels of the imperial political sphere in Rome.

As a result of his religious discourses in the temples, the gods were worshipped with greater zeal and frequency (4.41). Then, Philostratus provides a general summary of Apollonius's activity in Rome that highlights its public character:

> And people flocked to these places [temples], supposing that they would receive more benefits from the gods, and no one objected to his conversations because he spoke seriously in public and addressed all people, for he did not hang around the doors of rich men, nor did he bother the powerful, though he welcomed them if they came to him, and he talked just as much with them as he did with the people as a whole. [καὶ ξυνῄεσαν οἱ ἄνθρωποι ἐς ταῦτα, ὡς τὰ ἀβαθᾶ πλείω παρὰ τῶν θεῶν ἕξοντες, καὶ οὕτω διεβάλλοντο αἱ ξυνουσίαι τοῦ ἀνδρὸς διὰ τὸ σπουδάζεσθαί τε δημοσίᾳ λέγεσθαί τε ἐς πάντας, οὐδὲ γὰρ θύραις ἐπεπόλαζεν, οὐδὲ ἐτρίβετο περὶ τοὺς δυνατούς, ἀλλ᾽ ἠσπάζετο μὲν ἐπιφοιτῶντας, διελέγετο δὲ αὐτοῖς ὁπόσα καὶ τῷ δήμῳ]. (4.41)

This summary breaks the high-context silence and informs the reader of several forces that make Apollonius's actions public. Furthermore, the public nature of this activity serves an apologetic purpose: no one objected to his discourses because he conducted them openly with all people. At the beginning of this summary, Philostratus says that the people of Rome flocked to these places (καὶ ξυνῄεσαν οἱ ἄνθρωποι ἐς ταῦτα). As we have already seen, Apollonius lived, worked, and preached in temples.[64] The forces of place and religion set the unofficial public stage: Apollonius was preaching openly in *temples*. Next, with a bit of redundancy for emphasis, Apollonius "spoke seriously in public and addressed all people" (σπουδάζεσθαί τε δημοσίᾳ λέγεσθαί τε ἐς πάντας). Philostratus draws on the force of meaning by describing his teaching as δημοσίᾳ (referring to a cultural description of public activity) and on the force of social relations by specifying that he spoke to *everyone*. Apollonius did not dote on the powerful (τοὺς δυνατούς), but he welcomed them and spoke to them just as willingly as he spoke to the general populace (τῷ δήμῳ), which probably consisted of the masses who had much less status, wealth, and power. Part of the public nature of Apollonius's work, in Philostratus's eyes, was that it stretched across all of the social groups and classes found in Rome. Apollonius's did not discriminate or show favoritism but welcomed and spoke with anyone (rich or poor, high or low) who sought him out. This may have included some political officials, but they are not given special mention, making this description unofficial in nature. In this short summary, Philostratus employs elements from the forces of place, religion, meaning, and social relations to place Apollonius in the unofficial public sphere. This statement serves as an excellent summary of Apollonius's public and religious activity not only in Rome but throughout the cities of the Mediterranean world.

In 4.45 he recounts a tale of a public miracle in Rome. A young woman died at the time of her wedding, leaving her husband-to-be in mourning. Philostratus says, "Even Rome mourned along with him, for the young woman belonged to the consular class."

---

64. The demonstrative ταῦτα probably refers back to the temples that were discussed in the preceding chapter (where Apollonius was granted permission by Telesinus to enter them).

Apollonius interrupts the funeral procession, reassures the crowd, and asks what her name was. The crowd (οἱ πολλοί) thought he was about to deliver a funeral oration when he bent over, whispered something, and the girl woke up and began talking. This story bears strong resemblances to the raising of the widow's son in Luke 7:11–17. Here again is a socially tragic death: the death of a widow's only son instead of a bride-to-be. Jesus approaches the crowd in the funeral procession, meeting them near the gate of the city—a high-context formula for a public event. He stops the procession and speaks to the young man. Suddenly the dead youth gets up and begins to speak to the amazement of the crowd! Similar public dynamics will be discussed in the healing of the blind beggar just outside Jericho (Luke 18:35–43), dynamics that characterize many of the miracles recounted in Luke's Gospel.

Conclusion

Plutarch's *Precepts* primarily concerns the local political sphere while dipping occasionally into the unofficial public sphere. In balance to this, the *Life* primarily concerns the unofficial public sphere while also showing how Apollonius interacted with political matters and figures starting with the local and moving all the way up to the imperial level. Plutarch explicitly considers the realm of official politics. However, Apollonius never holds (nor intends to hold) a political office of any kind. When he does intersect the political sphere, he is an outside consultant or an object of suspicion. The different genres also lead to different social-spatial emphases. The *Precepts* is a didactic piece that expounds on local politics and gives advice using exemplary stories with little accompanying detail. The *Life* is a narrative (like Luke's Gospel) and requires more contextual investigation and interpretation of implicit clues to deduce how Philostratus marks Apollonius's actions as public. Apollonius is strongly located in the religious-philosophical arena of the unofficial public sphere, especially by the content of his discourses (force of meaning) and his presence in temples (force of place).

Luke and Philostratus share many similar scenes in their portrayals of their respective heroes, scenes that have long generated comparisons between the two figures. Apollonius preaches in and around the Artemision. Jesus preaches in the Jerusalem temple. Apollonius is welcomed by philosophy students into Athens. Jesus' own disciples shout and rejoice as he approaches Jerusalem. Apollonius is rejected by the priest at Athens. Jesus is rejected by the chief priests in Jerusalem. Both exorcize boys possessed by demons. Apollonius confronts a student and his demon-lover at a wedding banquet. Jesus confronts his hosts and other unexpected guests at banquets. Apollonius acts as a consultant to the Spartan assembly. Jesus is regularly interviewed by the Pharisees. Apollonius is interviewed by Telesinus and Tegillinus. Jesus is interviewed by Pilate and Herod. Apollonius raises a bride-to-be who tragically died. Jesus intervenes in the equally tragic death of a widow's only son.

Philostratus's methods of characterizing these episodes as public events sharpens our understanding of the unofficial public sphere and provides heuristic hints for the exegesis of Luke. Place is a critical factor. First, Apollonius frequents cities in book 4, much as Jesus does in Luke's Gospel. Book 4 is organized around the various cities that

Apollonius visits, and Luke generically states that Jesus was often in cities (e.g., 4:43; 5:12; 7:11; 8:1, etc.). In both cases, the city creates a local and public setting. Within the cities in the *Life*, Philostratus makes frequent use of theatres and roads/passageways as unofficial public places but also acts publicly in city assemblies and banquets. Second, Apollonius often chose temples both as his pulpit and his place of residence. In 8.7, Apollonius says, "I lectured publicly in temples" (δημοσίᾳ διελέχθην ἐν ἱερῷ), in contrast to wizards who avoid such public religious places.[65] Jesus employs the religious space of the synagogue, and Luke portrays him as regularly preaching there (cf. 4:44). Furthermore, Philostratus often says that he spoke to the Ephesians, or Athenians, or Romans as if the entire city was present at Apollonius's temple addresses.

These temples were accessible to the general public and commonly visited by the masses. They provided an ideal location for Apollonius to publicly address the population of entire cities. Therefore, social relations also affect Philostratus's accounts. He repeatedly points out the presence of large and diverse crowds. The entire cross-section of society, from the rich and powerful to the lowest artisans and residents, hears Apollonius and benefits from his instruction. Apollonius speaks freely to all people, and the generalized crowd is Apollonius's most common audience. However, he also deals with his disciples such as Menippus, Demetrius, and those who bravely enter Rome with him. Thus, the range of people in the force of social relations stretches across a broad scale. The same is true of Apollonius's interaction with the political sphere. The selected passages show a steady increase from the level of the general populace through local governments to imperial officials through the course of book 4. In Ephesus he deals with the general populace and no officials (not even cultic ones) at all. At Athens, he is joyfully welcomed by a crowd of students but is scorned by the initiatory priest of the mysteries. He is invited to Sparta and speaks to their city leaders, who consult him on matters of first local and then imperial scope. Finally, he proceeds to Rome where he encounters powerful figures in Nero's imperial regime. The actual content of this increase is slightly different from Luke's Gospel, but a general social-spatial incline can be noted in both, especially how both heroes rise to higher and higher levels of political attention.

Finally, other forces come into play as well. The subject matter of Apollonius's speeches addresses ideological themes of public concern: religious worship, public entertainment, virtues, community sharing, political involvement, and others. Thus, the force of meaning contributes to the public atmosphere. Apollonius takes advantage of the timing of the festival in Athens and the arrival of guests at the wedding banquet to increase the public valence of his actions. The force of nature does not play a prominent role here (possibly because of the fuzzier nature of this middle ground); however, the development in book 4 of the *Life* does clearly move to higher degrees of scale. The distinction between *unofficial* public space (seen in the earlier part of book 4) and the *official* political sphere (which develops as the story moves toward Rome) perhaps fits best under the force of nature. Most of his speech and action occurs during the day, the time of public interaction. Apollonius is portrayed as an intentional agent who seeks to intersect and interact with the public

---

65. Apollonius's public locations and activity have an apologetic function. This alerts us to the fact that Luke's public portrayal of Jesus could have a similar apologetic function.

sphere, while his political encounters are often initiated by others. Philostratus consistently places Apollonius in the domain of religion. He lives and teaches in public temples. He reforms and restores ancient rites. He speaks about the gods frequently. His public activity is strongly colored by his religious character, practices, and preaching. However, he emerges as an unsanctioned religious figure outside of (but eminently wise about) cultic establishments. Finally, Philostratus's portrayal even emerges from its high-context style and explicitly describes Apollonius's activity in Rome as public. Four characteristics mark this explicit commentary: Apollonius was in various temples, people flocked there to see him for some religious benefit, he spoke openly there, and he welcomed all classes of people.

This analysis fits the characteristics of the unofficial public sphere examined in the previous chapter. This survey of the *Life* confirms the existence of the unofficial public sphere in the ancient world and demonstrates how an author might go about depicting and deploying that sphere in his narration of the life of a religious hero. The following chart highlights some of the most common elements of the various forces that help to identify the unofficial public sphere as a category within the ancient social-spatial spectrum.

Table 4.2 Forces in the Unofficial Public Sphere

	Nature	Social Relations	Meaning	Religion	Time	Place
Public – Unofficial	Public activity outside of official politics	Wide variety including friends, clients, opponents, crowds, onlookers, mixed gender, often in large groups	Speech concerning public topoi, challenge-riposte rhetoric, local attributions of honor	Local cults, unofficial religious figures, popular festivals, crowds of worshippers	Varies, but generally daytime and perhaps during festivals	Cities, theatres, temples, stoas, roads, markets, public areas of homes

Philostratus's writing differs from Luke in various ways, but his use of the unofficial public sphere provides indicators of what to look for as we assess the social-spatial characteristics of Luke's own portrait of Jesus.

Summary

This chapter examined Plutarch's *Precepts* and Philostratus's *Life* as two specific works that illuminate local politics and the unofficial public sphere, respectively, with some preliminary comparisons to Luke's Gospel. This analysis serves three interlocking purposes. First, it confirms the existence of the unofficial public and local political spheres presented in the preceding chapter. Second, the analysis in this chapter used these categories deductively to describe and explain the unofficial public sphere and local politics in more detail. The emphasis on local politics in the *Precepts* and the unofficial public sphere in the *Life* has allowed the two to be clarified in greater detail through the closer study of a single work. Finally, the analysis throughout this chapter has shown various motifs, descriptive details, contents, settings, and literary techniques that might be employed when writing about the unofficial public sphere and local politics in the Greco-Roman world. This comparative survey provides a set of possible means at Luke's disposal as he casts Jesus in the public sphere, and shows how those available means were used by other authors in the same milieu to achieve a similar social-spatial character in their writings. Thus, these comparative works show, on one hand, *that* the unofficial public sphere and local politics were active social-spatial categories in Luke's literary and social-spatial milieu. On the other hand, these comparative works show *how* Luke might shape his narrative in order to portray Jesus in the public sphere. The exegesis of Luke 18:35—19:48 in the following chapters will illustrate both that Luke emphasizes the public sphere and local politics and how he did so in one representative section with ramifications for the Gospel as a whole.

PART TWO

Social-Spatial Exegesis of Luke 18:35—19:48

5

The Healing of the Blind Beggar (18:35–43)
A Public Miracle Story and Its Political Implications

Introduction

PART 1 SITUATED THIS OF LUKE 18:35—19:48 BY EXAMINING THE RELEVANT HISTORY OF interpretation, considering theoretical issues related to the construction of space and society, and examining the social-spatial milieu of Luke's Gospel through broad survey and focused comparison. Part 2 of this study will examine the social-spatial characteristics of each pericope through careful exegesis. These chapters will employ the theories and classification system presented in Part 1 to cast light on the implicit clues about space in Luke's stories, the way particular spaces function, and how Luke features public and political elements in his portrayal of Jesus. After a brief review of the previous interpretation of 18:35–43, this chapter will examine the social-spatial characteristics of the healing of the blind beggar, focusing on the characterization of the blind beggar, the portrayal of Jesus, and the role of the crowd. The chapter will close with a brief summary of the results organized by the forces discussed in Part 1 (place, social relations, time, meaning, and religion) and then preview the implications of the public and political characteristics of this passage that will be discussed in Part 3.

A Brief Review of Previous Interpretation

Many studies of the healing of the blind man focus on Mark's redaction of this traditional story in light of that Gospel's theological themes.[1] Others have treated it as a case for examining the form of miracle stories.[2] The blind man addresses Jesus as the "Son of David," which has generated both historical and theological questions.[3] However, the particularly Lukan form and context of this story have received little attention, apart from standard treatments in commentaries. Busse discusses it in his monograph on

---

1. Robbins, "Healing"; Achtemeier, "'And He Followed'"; Johnson, "Mark 10:46–52"; Dupont, "L'aveugle de Jéricho." Paul, "La guérison de l'aveugle," treats the redactional work of Matthew and Luke before going into more detail on the form of the story in Mark.

2. Steinhauser, "Form."

3. Fisher, "'Can This Be'"; Burger, *Davidssohn*, 107–12; Duling, "Solomon"; Strauss, *Davidic Messiah*, 306–7.

miracles in Luke,[4] and a few other articles cite this passage in larger thematic studies of Luke-Acts.[5] Roland Meynet seeks out theological significance by applying a chiastic form of rhetorical analysis to Luke 18:35–43.[6] Finally, Porter wrestles with Luke's placement of this story on Jesus' entrance into (rather than exit from) Jericho.[7] While the works of all of these scholars contain pieces of useful information for this study, none of them has a sustained treatment of the literary or social-spatial characteristics of this passage in Luke's Gospel.

The Social-Spatial Characteristics of 18:35–43

The healing of the blind beggar serves Luke's portrayal of Jesus in the unofficial public and local political spheres in six ways. First, the first half of v. 35 establishes that Jesus is approaching Jericho, setting an urban and local scene that bears several parallels to Jesus' entry into Jerusalem. Second, the second half of v. 35 creates a public setting through the characterization and location of the blind beggar. Third, the blind beggar takes the initiative to question the crowd and cry out to Jesus, turning a public setting into a public scene (vv. 36–39). Fourth, the passage employs publicly announced titles to characterize Jesus as a public and royal figure with political undertones. Fifth, the interaction between Jesus and the blind beggar takes place in the full view of the crowd (vv. 40–43). Sixth, the passage as a whole exemplifies Luke's view of the crowd/people at public events and implies Jesus' authority over members of his own movement in the crowd. Each of these points will be discussed below.

Jesus Approaches and Enters Jericho: An Urban and Local Public Setting

The story begins in 18:35 with a reiteration of the journey motif: ἐγένετο δὲ ἐν τῷ ἐγγίζειν αὐτὸν εἰς Ἰεριχώ. Most commentators agree that this refers to Jesus' approach toward Jericho;[8] however, Porter resists this translation in order to remove a conflict in the synoptic tradition about the location of the episode.[9] The directionality of the even in Luke is important both to the location of the beggar and the development of a public scene, so it is critical to evaluate Porter's argument and decide on the social-spatial implications of this introduction. Porter examines all of the uses of ἐγγίζω in Luke-Acts and concludes that this verb primarily denotes location rather than movement.[10] While Luke does employ ἐγγίζω to designate spatial proximity,[11] Porter also claims that ἐγγίζω oc-

---

4. Busse, *Die Wunder*, 227–34.
5. Kodell, "Luke's Use of Laos"; Hamm, "Sight to the Blind"; Speckman, "Beggars and Gospel."
6. Meynet, "L'Aveugle de Jéricho."
7. Porter, "'In the Vicinity.'"
8. Fitzmyer, *Luke*, 2:1211–13; Johnson, *Luke*, 283; Bovon, *Luc*, 3c:223.
9. Porter, "In the Vicinity." Mark 10:46 and Matt 20:29 state that the healing occurred while Jesus was leaving (ἐκπορεύομαι) Jericho, whereas Luke's redaction and placement of the story implies that it occurred before Jesus entered the city.
10. Porter, "In the Vicinity," 95.
11. Perhaps the best example (considered more difficult by Porter on p.100) is in Luke 15:1. Here ἐγγί-

curs near verbs of motion and thus cannot indicate movement in these contexts because such a combination would be redundant or difficult to understand.[12] He concludes that Luke chose the term ἐγγίζω in 18:35 to designate only the proximity of Jericho and not any sense of direction. Therefore, this locational sense prevents any direct conflict with the tradition as preserved in Mark and Matthew.[13]

However, Porter's argument has several flaws regarding the analysis of ἐγγίζω and its application to 18:35. Porter argues that Luke associates ἐγγίζω with verbs of motion in Luke-Acts and that in most of these cases it must have a locational sense to avoid redundancy or strained meaning. However, the frequent association between ἐγγίζω and other verbs of motion (twelve of twenty-four uses in Luke-Acts) actually implies the opposite. In these cases, ἐγγίζω connotes proximity (location) in conjunction with motion—motion that is generally directed toward a nearby goal that is reached in the future, rather than having already been reached in the past.[14] This is eminently clear in 18:35–43. While Jesus is ἐγένετο δὲ ἐν τῷ ἐγγίζειν αὐτὸν εἰς Ἰεριχώ, he is said to be "passing by" (παρέ-χεται, v. 37), when he then stops (σταθείς). Here, as in other examples, the situations of proximity and motion must be occurring simultaneously (e.g., "moving toward while being near") to make any sense of the verbs that follow the introductory phrase in 18:35a (ἐγένετο ἐν τῷ + infinitive).[15] Furthermore, the present tense of the infinitive ἐγγίζειν can imply an ongoing process of drawing near. The next problem is Porter's interpretation of the use of ἐγγίζω in 18:40. He says that this clearly cannot mean "when or while he was approaching," since Jesus and the blind man would have to be face to face in order to speak to one another.[16] However, the aorist active participle ἐγγίσαντος in this context should be translated "after he approached Jesus," signifying that the process of drawing near to Jesus was completed before Jesus questioned him in this public setting.[17] Finally, and most problematically, Porter offers only four very weak reasons why the placement of this story

---

ζοντες is used in a construction with ἦσαν, an adjectival sense referring to the physical closeness of the tax collectors and sinners. See Smyth, *Greek Grammar*, # 1961.

12. Porter, "In the Vicinity," 98–99, 102.

13. Porter fails to argue why Luke placed this story *before* the account of Zacchaeus for literary or theological purposes. He also fails to note that this passage does not use other words in Luke-Acts that denote approaching or coming near to something such as προσάγω or συντυγχάνω. Both of these may have strengthened his argument.

14. Only an unusual circumstance prevents the older brother from entering the house after Luke 15:25. Jerusalem is soon reached after 19:41. Jesus and the two disciples arrive in the village after 24:28. The same implication with ἐγγίζω is present in Acts 9:3; 10:9; and 22:6.

15. Luke often uses this construction to set scenes. See Fitzmyer, *Luke*, 1:119–20; 2:1214. Fitzmyer states that the dative articular infinitive with ἐν usually has a temporal sense. The introductory action mentioned in this transitional construction often continues throughout the scene (1:8; 2:6; 5:1; 17:11, etc). The same thing takes place in 18:35–43: Jesus is approaching Jericho throughout the narrated events until Luke states that he stopped in v. 40.

16. Porter, "In the Vicinity," 101.

17. This is a temporal usage of the genitive absolute referring to antecedent action, especially since its subject (the blind man) is different from the subject of the main verb (Jesus). See Wallace, *Greek Grammar*, 623–25, 655.

PART TWO: SOCIAL-SPATIAL EXEGESIS OF LUKE 18:35—19:48

before 19:1–10 does not imply that it occurred on Jesus' way into (and not out of) the city.[18] While Luke can use a free hand that does not always match narrative time to historical events (4:16–30 is a famous example), the order of these events creates a narrative timeline in which the healing occurs before Jesus enters the city. The grammar of 19:1 confirms this, for εἰσελθών must be read in temporal relation with διήρξετο: "after he entered, he was passing through Jericho." This indicates that Jesus did not come to Jericho before 19:1 and binds Jesus' entry to his subsequent movement through the city, disallowing an entry in the indeterminate past. Finally, 18:35 is part of the string of reminders of Jesus' journey, found at the beginning of each pericope (ἐγγίζω also occurs at 19:29, 37, and 41).[19] In light of all this evidence, 18:35a should be translated "as he was approaching Jericho."[20] As Jesus comes near to the city, he (and his entourage; see below) encounter a blind beggar sitting on the side of the road, and with this Luke begins to paint a public setting for Jesus' entry into Jericho.

Why does Luke retain Jericho as the location of this public incident? Jericho was the location of this healing in the tradition preserved by Mark, even if Luke did shift it from Jesus' exit to his entry. Luke could have omitted the name of the city and said that it occurred on the way into "some city" (cf. 10:38 or 13:22). First, 18:35 introduces cues that create a public setting for the following encounter. Jericho is the only named city on Jesus' journey to Jerusalem, and it does not lie on a normal route from Galilee or Samaria to Judea (see 17:11), so it is difficult to understand Jesus' movements as an efficient journey to Jerusalem.[21] After several chapters of general travel with very few specified geographical markers, the force of place is activated by the naming of Jericho: it awakens the audience's spatial attention to the urban (and public) setting. Second, Luke has already mentioned a road between Jericho and Jerusalem (10:30) and apparently understands Jericho to be somewhat near to Jerusalem. Thus, this also helps to create the setting for the following parable (so 19:11). Third, the location of Jericho allows Luke to connect this healing with Jesus' encounter with Zacchaeus (this be explored in depth in the following chapter).

Fourth, by arranging these two particular stories with these unique touches, Luke has created a preparatory triumphal entry into Jericho with several parallels to the entry into Jerusalem. Luke places the healing of the blind beggar just *before* Jesus enters Jericho and *adds* the material in v. 43b about the crowd joining the man in public praise. Immediately afterward, Jesus enters Jericho, where a large crowd welcomes him (19:1, 3). In both cases,

---

18. Porter, "In the Vicinity," 103–4. These are his reasons: Luke has merely retained the travel language from his source in 19:1; 19:1 is merely another generic notice of the journey motif; the aorist participle εἰσελθών could mean that Jesus entered in the past before the previously narrated healing; finally, there simply may be no chronological order here. These are offered very briefly and are far from convincing, but the explanation of this problem is crucial for his argument to be persuasive.

19. The cognate adjective ἐγγύς appears in 19:11 where it designates location not associated with movement (no complementary verb). Thus, if Luke had wanted to mark only location in 18:35 he could have employed this construction.

20. Thus, this construction communicates a temporal circumstance associated the main verb (with Fitzmyer, *Luke*, 1:120); however, I have chosen to omit the superfluous translation of the ἐγένετο δέ (contra Fitmyer, *Luke*, 1:119).

21. Evans, *Luke*, 657; and Rengstorf, *Lukas*, 212.

The Healing of the Blind Beggar (18:35–43)

Luke describes Jesus approaching and entering a major city. In both cases, large crowds welcome Jesus, though the make up of the crowds is different. In both cases, at least part of the crowd praises God for Jesus' miracles. In both cases, Jesus encounters some opposition from the crowd at his entry.[22] Both stories emphasize Jesus' royal identity as "Son of David" and "king." One clear difference is that the entry into Jericho is mostly unofficial with some political implications, while Jesus' entry into Jerusalem draws the attention of the high priests, the leading Jewish officials of the land. Luke's geographical and narrative placement of this healing generates illuminating comparisons with the entry into Jerusalem that will be explored after examining this pericope itself. Fifth, parallels with the entry into Jerusalem highlight several public indicators: a nearby city, Jesus' procession, the presence of a crowd, and public conflict (challenges to Jesus' honor). However, the noticeable absence of any religious or political officials at Jesus' entry into Jericho indicates its unofficial status. Placing it at the entrance into Jericho makes the healing and its effects more of a local phenomenon, limited to the city of Jericho.[23] Luke's audience can already begin to create a mental picture of a public scene: a busy trade road filled with travelers and others surrounding Jesus as he approaches one of the main gates of the city.

A Blind Beggar: The Public Space and Public Shame of Begging

Luke 18:35b reads τυφλός τις ἐκάθατο παρὰ τὴν ὁδὸν ἐπαιτῶν.[24] These seven words contain social and spatial information that identifies the status of the blind man (social) and specifies the public stage for the miracle that will follow (spatial). Luke nominalizes the adjective τυφλός (in Mark) and identifies this person as "a certain blind man" (τυφλός τις).[25] Many scholars have pointed out how this story fulfills the infrequent but important motif in Luke's Gospel that Jesus will restore sight to the blind (4:18; 7:21–22).[26] Additionally for Luke, a blind person belongs to the category of "the poor" as revealed by the repeated list πτωχούς, ἀναπείρους, χωλούς, τυφλούς (7:21–22; 14:13, 21).[27] Such physically disabled and impoverished persons would have generally fallen into the lowest

---

22. At the entrance to Jericho, this occurs when the crowd grumbles at Jesus' encounter with Zacchaeus (19:7).

23. Recall that Mark and Matthew place this story right before the entry into Jerusalem, using it as a springboard into a larger, more regionally noticed event.

24. Luke omits any mention of the disciples as found in Mark 10:46 and moves the mention of the crowds (found in the setting before the story in Mark 10:46 and Matt 20:29) into the body of the story in 18:36.

25. Mark calls him a "blind beggar" (τυφλὸς προσαίτης) and Matthew speaks of two blind men (δύο τυφλοί).

26. Fitzmyer, *Luke*, 2:1214; Bovon, *Luc*, 3c:226; Hamm, "Sight." Hamm insists (following Meynet) that the recovery of sight stands at the center of a chiasm in 4:16–18, highlighting its significance. Roth concludes that the blind were the subject of special protection and generosity because of their vulnerability. They could be healed by God or God's agent, especially in the eschaton. See Roth, *Blind*, 103–6.

27. The term τυφλός usually referred to total and permanent physical blindness, while it could be used for metaphorical blindness as well. This term is disproportionately common in the NT, while other terms for blindness or partial loss of sight (e.g., ἀλαός, ἀθέατος) are missing. See Just, "Social Role." 44–60.

stratum of society in the ancient world.[28] This is clear in Luke, for in addition to being blind, the man is also begging.[29]

Luke 18:35 implies that the man is destitute because he is begging (ἐπαιτῶν) as he sits by the side of the road. His begging is a public manifestation of desperation and need, which was probably a result of his blindness (see further below). Luke mentions begging as one of the options rejected by the shrewd steward because it was too shameful (16:3). He also tells the story of a lame beggar who is healed by Peter and John in Acts 3:1–6.[30] The beggar of Acts 3:1–6 is lame, thus also physically disabled like the blind beggar under consideration here. In the setting for the story in Acts, Luke provides additional background information about this disabled beggar. He was lame from birth, while no such specification is given to the man's blindness in Luke 18:35. The beggar in Acts 3 is carried from his (nearby?) home and placed at the Beautiful Gate of the temple, a good public place to beg for alms.[31] We can presume a similar scenario for the blind beggar in Luke's narrative world. Someone led him to a highly traveled section of the road leading to Jericho where he would find available public space to beg from those who walked by him.

Other descriptions of beggars in the ancient world fill in social and spatial details that would have been supplied by Luke's high-context audience. Ancient sources preserve stories of some (in)famous beggars. The first is Homer, the blind poet of the Iliad and the Odyssey. While his blindness is nearly proverbial, ancient accounts also represent him as desperately poor, one who received a double curse of both blindness and poverty from the gods (see Dio Chrysostom, *Troj.* 15). Pausanius states that after he received the (private) affliction of blindness, the gods further vexed him with the (public) shame of begging (*Descr.* 2.33.3). A similar series of events was probably presumed about the blind beggar in Luke: his blindness led to his begging. In addition to Homer's poetic gifts, blind persons in the ancient world exercised supernatural insight as seers (e.g., Tiresias), often speaking their prophecies in public settings.[32] A more infamous blind beggar is Oedipus, who put out his eyes in grief and agony and was then consigned to a life of wandering and begging (Sophocles, *Oed. col.* 421–59). While blind persons were not *necessarily* understood to be cursed or socially outcast for their physical handicap, the addition of begging to blindness moves such a person to the bottom of society, forcing them to shameful action

---

28. Green, *Luke*, 663.

29. Just's dissertation, "Social Role," explores the social status of blind persons in the ancient world. He illustrates the variety of social roles taken by blind persons and the diversity of attitudes toward them (see esp. his ch. 4). He states emphatically and repeatedly, "we will find sightless individuals in a wide variety of social situations, not just as the stereotypical blind beggar" (72). Just admits that there are blind beggars mentioned in ancient literature (Diogenes Laertius 6.56, and below) and in the NT (but only three: Mark 10:46; Luke 18:35; and John 9:1, 8), but he correctly asserts that blind persons in the ancient world fell along a rather wide spectrum of social status. Just claims that there would have been a variety of attitudes toward the blind in the members of the crowd that was passing by in the synoptic accounts of this healing (219). However, the fact that this man was not only blind but also a beggar would have defined his low social status and probably elicited a generally negative response.

30. For a discussion of the symbolic significance of many of the details of this healing in Acts see Hamm, "Acts 3, 1–10."

31. Ch. 7 will demonstrate the public nature of the Beautiful Gate in Luke's account in Acts.

32. Just, "Social Role," 130.

in the public arena. This fits well with Luke's collocation of the blind with the poor, lame, and crippled. In addition to ancient blind characters, the activity and location of public begging requires examination in order to elucidate the social-spatial dynamics evoked by the description in Luke 18:35b.

Begging cast shame over the public life and literary portrayals of all beggars but in slightly different ways. Speckman classifies four different types of beggars:[33] structural beggars, moira-type beggars, voluntary/philosophical beggars, and physically disabled beggars, each of which had slightly different public manifestations. In 18:35b, Luke presents a paradigm of Speckman's final category. The man is first identified as blind. His blindness reduced him to poverty, and so he is now publicly begging on the side of the road.[34] Furthermore, beggars were portrayed as shaggy and unkempt, covered with filth, grime, and insects. Their clothes were ragged and a general stench followed them wherever they went. They were miserable sights to behold.[35] Aristophanes provides a long account of the life and characteristics of beggars in *Plutus* 527–54. He describes beggars as a "hollow-cheeked rabble of destitute hags, and brats on the verge of starvation. And the lice, if you please, and the gnats and the fleas whom I can't even count for their numbers.... For a robe but a rag, for a bed but a bag."[36] Entering the public arena of a beggar was a particularly distasteful act.[37] Furthermore, many ancient writers viewed begging as the result of the person's own laziness, and anyone who gave money or provisions to such people only enabled their idleness. As Plutarch quotes, "But if I give something to you, you will become a beggar all the more, and your shameless conduct is due to the first person who gave to you; he made you lazy" (*Apoph. lac.* 235e).[38] Even though they were viewed as wretched and destitute, beggars were also said to be greedy and gluttonous (*Od.* 18.1–3; Martial, *Ep.* 12.32). Beggars became a trope representing unbecoming pleading for political or personal favors (Juvenal, *Sat.* 4.116–117; Horace, *Ep.* 1.17.43–44). Therefore, the public evaluation of Jesus' benefaction to this beggar could have ranged from very positive to very negative: either Jesus could have been showing kindness and mercy or he could have been encouraging the man's shameful activity. However, Jesus does not give to the man, but publicly heals him, rescuing him from a degenerate public life.

The terms ἐπαιτέω and προσαιτέω are very rare in the LXX, as are depictions of beggars or begging. In Psalm 108:10 (LXX), the author prays that God will curse his enemy by forcing his children to go out to beg (ἐπαιτησάτωσαν). Job affirms that the

---

33. Speckman, "Beggars and Gospel," esp. 316–21. Structural beggars were those pressed into begging by systemic social and economic forces apart from any physical impairment. Moira type beggars were those doomed to poverty and begging because of the decrees of the gods (e.g., Odysseus). Voluntary/philosophical beggars were those who chose a life of poverty because of their philosophical commitments (e.g., the Cynics).

34. Speckman, "Beggars and Gospel," 320–21.

35. These characteristics are found in the descriptions of beggars in Homer, *Od.* 17.197–203; Euripides, *Rhes.* 710–18; and Martial, *Ep.* 4.53.

36. This quote is taken from *Aristophanes*, 139.

37. This would probably represent the extremely "humble" end of Wallace-Hadrill's "grand-humble" axis, which intersects here with a public setting (*Houses and Society*, 3–16, esp. 11).

38. Also see Plautus, *Trin.* 339–40 and the discussion in Hahn, "Beggars."

PART TWO: SOCIAL-SPATIAL EXEGESIS OF LUKE 18:35—19:48

children of the ungodly will end up begging (προσαιτήσουσιν, Job 27:14 LXX).[39] Sirach mentions begging a few times, mostly with regard to food. In a set of prohibitions warning the reader to avoid spurning the poor (4:1–6), Sirach counsels his readers, "Do not delay giving to the one in need" (4:3b),[40] which implies a duty to give to those who ask for help in their desperation.[41] On the other hand, Sirach also seems to have a negative opinion of those who beg. He hates "the poor man who boasts" (πτωχὸν ὑπερήφανον, 25:2), and he admonishes his readers in 18:33, "Do not become a beggar (πτωχός) by feasting from borrowed money."[42] Most telling, and most derogatory, is the advice contained in 40:28–30:

> Child, do not live the life of a beggar [ἐπαιτήσεως]; it is better to die than to beg [ἐπαιτεῖν]. When a man constantly looks at the table of another, such a life is not a way of life. His soul is demeaned by another man's food, but the man who is intelligent and educated keeps this from happening. In the mouth of the shameless [ἀναιδοῦς], begging [ἐπαίτησις] is sweet, but it lights a fire in his belly.

What could be more condemning than the statement, "It is better to die than to beg"? Sirach reveres God's commands to help those who are genuinely poor. However, he seems to view begging as the public result of some combination of pride, gluttony, and laziness. Note that he uses the word group ἐπαιτ- (the verb used in Luke 18:35) when he pens his most stringent denunciation of begging in 40:28–30. Sirach agrees with the general representation of beggars in Greco-Roman sources.[43] Typically, beggars were perceived to be despicable people who had lost their self-respect and turned to a shameful practice out of laziness just to fill up their stomachs. The man of Luke's story who was both blind and a beggar would have been at the bottom of the social ladder, an outcast scorned for his wickedness and laziness. The prevalent characterization of beggars draws upon the force of meaning to place them in the humblest, the most dishonorable, part of the public sphere.

Luke draws upon the force of place to confirm this beggar's public location by stating that he is παρὰ τὴν ὁδόν.[44] Fitzmyer states that this blind beggar "was probably sitting

---

39. In Ps. 37:25, the author says that he has never seen the children of the righteous "begging bread" (ζητοῦν ἄρτους). The term προσαιτέω is not found anywhere else besides Job 27:14, and ἐπαιτέω is only found again in a passage from Sirach that will be discussed below.

40. "One in need" translates the word προσδεομένου, which can mean "to be in need" or "to beg."

41. The "hungry" are mentioned just before in 4:2a.

42. It may be debated whether "begging" is associated with πτωχός in 25:2, but it definitely makes contextual sense in 18:33 with the mention of borrowed money. Hands suggests that πτωχός had a wide semantic range, including the designation of "beggar" (*Charities and Social Aid*, 62–63).

43. Later Jewish sources agree as well. Beggars who went from door to door were given very little, while the "registered" poor of a Jewish village were to be given regular provisions (*b. B. Bat.* 9a). See Hamel, *Poverty and Charity*, 218.

44. The same exact phrase is found in Mark 10:46 and Matt 20:30. This unusual prepositional phrase occurs in the NT only in this story and the parable of the sower (Mark 4:4, 15; Matt 13:4, 19; Luke 8:5, 12). It is much more common to find ὁδός with ἐν or εἰς and sometimes κατά. In light of this, the phrase is a bit difficult to translate. In the parable of the sower, it is usually translated "on" the path, which refers to the fact that the seed fell in the middle of the path as the sower walked along. This cannot be the meaning of the phrase in Luke 18:35 and parallels, for it would be quite dangerous for a blind beggar to sit in the middle of

on the roadside near the entrance to the town."⁴⁵ Nolland says, "The blind man would be on the pilgrim route through Jericho to Jerusalem—a good place to beg."⁴⁶ However, he does not supply any supporting material to justify that such a location was normal or advantageous for a beggar in the ancient world. Since there is little information about beggars in the LXX and Apocrypha, they cannot shed light on the blind man's location; however, there are a few comments in the Odyssey that reflect the public locations of beggars. Telemachus tells his swineherd to lead a certain beggar (Odysseus in disguise) to the city (ἐς πόλιν) where he can beg for food and water (*Od.* 17.10-12). Odysseus affirms this public destination by replying, "It is better for a beggar to beg for his food in a city than in the fields" (πρωχῷ βέλτερόν ἐστι κατὰ πόλιν ἠὲ κατ' ἀγροὺς δαῖτα πτωχεύειν). Soon after this Irus appears as a "public beggar who begged throughout the town of Ithaca" (πτωχὸς πανδήμος, ὃς κατὰ ἄστυ πρωχευσκ' Ἰθάκης). The Odyssey portrays cities and towns as the characteristic locations of beggars and even describes one beggar as a "public" (πανδήμος) figure, probably because he regularly frequented heavily populated places in order to ask for alms.⁴⁷ The setting in Luke 18:35-43 conforms to these expectations, for Jesus publicly heals the beggar near a city, not in a rural area. More specifically, Jesus encounters this beggar as he nears the city, and he enters immediately after the healing. The examination of ancient Ephesus in chapter 2 showed that a city generally had only a few main entrances that were linked to highly traveled roads and carefully designed to create a public, aesthetic impact on the traveler. We can probably assume the same for Jericho, or how Luke and his audience would imagine Jericho. Thus, as Jesus approaches Jericho, he comes into public space on the road near an entrance to the city, a public space that is also occupied by the public character of a shameful beggar (and no honorable political officials).

Several authors from Rome also provide illuminating comments about the spatial habits of beggars. The Sublician Bridge (also known as the Bridge of Sculpicius) was among the named haunts of beggars. It was an ancient wooden bridge that led across the Tiber River directly into the Forum Boarium, a crossroads at the heart of Rome. Seneca speaks of the crowd of vagrants at this bridge, "Take me to the Sublician Bridge and toss me among the destitute . . . in the company of those who reach out for alms" (*Tranq.* 25.1). Juvenal also speaks of beggars lurking around a bridge at the Arician Hill near the Appian Way to accost the chariots as they descended (*Sat.* 4.116-18). A bridge would have been a convenient place to find shelter, and the heavy nearby traffic promised plenty of opportunities to beg. Juvenal more generally locates beggars along curbs (*crepides*) and bridges (*pontes*) (*Sat.* 5.8-9), but beggars were so commonplace around bridges that

---

the road. The translation "on the side" is supported by similar uses of παρά with different objects in Luke-Acts (Luke 5:1—"by the lake"; Luke 9:47—"by his side"; Acts 16:13—"by the river").

45. Fitzmyer, *Luke*, 2:1215.

46. Nolland, *Luke*, 901. Jericho would have surely been a natural station on the way to Jerusalem for those traveling from Perea or other areas east of Jerusalem; however, there is no direct evidence for a regular pilgrimage route through Jericho.

47. Hands suggests that πανδήμος refers to the fact that beggars were expected to travel from city to city (*Charities*, 64), but Irus is located habitually in Ithaca and is not said to travel around. It makes better sense in context for this term to refer to the fact that Irus, as a beggar, spent most of his time in urban public areas.

he could use the turn of phrase *aliquis de ponte* ("someone from a bridge") to refer to a beggar (*Sat.* 14.134). Martial confirms that bridges and hills were frequented by beggars. He too uses the trope that beggars swarm around bridges (*Ep.* 5.5.4–5 and 12.32.23–25) and mentions the Arician Hill in particular (*Ep.* 2.19.3; 12.32.9–10). Plautus adds one more location to this list. In the *Trinummus*, Philto states that Lesbonicus's father will have to live at "Beggar's Gate" (*in portast locus*) because of his son's profligate spending (*Trin.* 422–24). This should probably be identified as the Porta Trigemina, a gate also near the Forum Boarium that was on the heavily traveled route to Ostia.[48] These roadside locations were public areas busy with human traffic and located near or in a city, and they provided a handy explanation for why the stereotypical beggar loitered in such places.[49]

Therefore, Luke's public location of the beggar on the side of the road near a city entrance would have fallen into widely held cultural expectations. Such easily accessible and heavily trafficked areas generated the best chances for a beggar to receive something due to the sheer number of people passing by the spot. Moreover, beggars preferred locations like cites, roadsides, bridges, and gates because of their public quality. These public places were accessible to a variety of people, sometimes offered a degree of shelter, and were heavily traveled during the day. A number of the quotations above also cited the "localization" of beggars in Rome. They infamously hung around particular bridges and hills. The blind beggar of Jericho may have been a similar local figure, similar to the beggar who was carried "daily" to the same gate of the temple (Acts 3:2). Thus, the setting retains a local flavor relevant to Jericho and its environs. However, none of the quotations above mentioned politics, official agents, or laws. Thus, they place beggars in the category of the unofficial public sphere as discussed in chapter 2, which already pointed out the unofficial public nature of roads and other spaces related to travel. The large number of people present on these passageways reinforces their public nature with the force of social relations.[50] Thus, Luke 18:35 sets an unofficial public stage for Jesus to perform the miracle that follows.[51]

The Blind Beggar and the Crowd: The Meeting of Public Arenas

After the introductory material in 18:35, the rest of this pericope falls into two sections: 18:36–39 (focusing on the blind beggar and the crowd) and 18:40–43 (focusing on the blind beggar and Jesus). In the first section (vv. 36–39), two issues shape the social and

---

48. See the translation and note in Riley, *Plautus*, 1:23 n. 2.

49. Hahn concludes that the Roman authors generally testify to the "presence of beggars in busy places and roads" ("Beggars," 580).

50. This also resonates with Apollonius preaching publicly "around the sacred groves near the covered walkway" (*Vit. Apoll.* 4.3), another public roadside location.

51. While the setting for this miracle is almost identical in Mark 10:46 and Matt 20:29–30, they both use it as a way to prepare for the crowds that accompany Jesus into Jerusalem (Mark 11:8–9 and Matt 21:8–9, despite the nearly ten mile walk through the desert that separates the two cities!). Thus, its public valence is deployed specifically to prepare for Jesus' grand entrance into Jerusalem. Luke, on the other hand, separates this story from the triumphal entry, but retains its public valence and even increases it by foregrounding the role of the crowd in v. 36 and adding the praise of the crowd in 18:43b. In Luke, this story helps to prepare for Jesus' entry into Jericho and fits into the public nature of many of Luke's miracle stories (see ch. 9).

The Healing of the Blind Beggar (18:35-43)

spatial character of this story: the interaction of the blind beggar and the crowd and the two titles applied to Jesus. The blind beggar is the center of the action in vv. 36-39: he inquires, he is answered, he cries out, he is rebuked, he cries out more. At the very beginning of this story, Luke emphasizes the initiative of the blind man in two ways.[52] In v. 35, Luke verbalizes the noun προσαίτης found in Mark into the present (continuous) participle ἐπαιτῶν. The man is not just a beggar sitting, but one who actively begs. Second, in v. 36 the blind beggar does not overhear some people in the crowd talking about Jesus (as seems to occur in Mark 10:47). Rather, when he hears[53] the crowd passing by[54] he directly asks (ἐπυνθάνετο) what is happening (τί εἴη τοῦτο, literally "what this might be").[55] Luke does not leave the crowd as part of the setting (cf. Mark 10:46 and Matt 20:29) but inserts it at the beginning as a secondary character in the story.[56] Usually, when Luke uses the verb πυνθάνομαι, it is typically a request for more information based on some preliminary indicators.[57] Thus, Luke's story implies that the blind man recognizes that something of public importance is taking place, and he asks for more information about it. Instead of merely remaining part of the background, the blind beggar takes action. His actions take his dishonorable public status as a beggar (discussed above) and thrust it into the midst of this scene.

The crowd accompanying Jesus on his approach to Jericho creates another (more honorable) public arena that collides with the (shameful) public arena of the beggar, intensifying the public valence of the scene. Luke moves the crowd into the foreground and makes it a secondary character that causes the blind man to ask what is happening (18:36).[58] The presence of the crowd marks an unofficial public setting through the force of social relations.[59] Because of the ruckus, the blind beggar addresses the crowd, and they tell him, "Jesus of Nazareth is passing by" (18:37), quite unlike Mark and Matthew where the blind man/men merely appear to "overhear" this information (ἀκούσας ὅτι . . .).

---

52. Burger says that Luke tells the story from the perspective of the blind man (*Davidssohn*, 108). Marshall says more generally that Luke has added "vigour" to the story (*Luke*, 693).

53. A temporal translation of the participle ἀκούσας, which also incorporates causal overtones ("because he heard the crowd passing by").

54. Luke uses the word διαπορεύω on two other occasions to indicate purposeful travel (Luke 13:22; Acts 16:4).

55. Nearly the same exact phrase is found in Luke 15:26, where the older brother asks "what is happening" because he hears something (some MSS insert ἄν after τις and before the optative εἴη in 18:36, making the two passages even more alike). Johnson cites this verse and uses this translation as well (*Luke*, 284).

56. Luke has also omitted any specific mention of the disciples at this point (see Mark 10:46), which results in a more generalized crowd (Green, *Luke*, 662).

57. See Acts 4:7; 10:18, 29; 21:33; 22:39. The similar usage in Luke 15:26 was just noted, but perhaps the clearest example is in Acts 23:20, where it is reported that the Jews are coming "to inquire more carefully about him" (ἀκριβέστερον πυνθάνεσθαι περὶ αὐτοῦ).

58. The scenario is different in the other Synoptics, Mark indicates that Jesus' disciples and the crowd left Jericho with Jesus (10:46), and Matthew states that the crowd was "following" him (20:29). Then, the crowd (πολλοί in Mark 10:48 and ὄχλος in Matt 20:31) tries to rebuke the man and silence him. Finally, the crowd in Mark tells the man that Jesus is summoning him (10:49, not in Matt), and after this, they have no further role in the episode.

59. Recall the role of crowds as markers of public events in the evidence of ch. 3.

PART TWO: SOCIAL-SPATIAL EXEGESIS OF LUKE 18:35—19:48

Their answer in v. 37, prompts the blind man to cry out to Jesus, creating the possibility for the intersection of these two public arenas. At first however, when Jesus and the crowd come into a public space also occupied by the beggar, those "leading" the way (the προά‐γοντες) try to *prevent* Jesus' public entourage from socially intersecting the (less honorable) public arena of the beggar. Nevertheless, Luke's Jesus forces the issue, stops, and calls for the blind man. By doing so, Luke expands the boundaries of Jesus' public activity beyond the borders of his own honorable "group" to include the roadside rabble and other travelers entering Jericho. The two public arenas meet through the initiative of the blind man, the (unwilling) mediation of the crowd, and the active response of Jesus. Thus, the public nature of Jesus' procession (indicated by the force of social relations) and the public setting of the blind beggar on the side of the road (indicated by the force of place) come together to create a thick public event.

Verse 37 opens with the impersonal third-person plural form ἀπήγγειλαν, implying that some persons in the passing crowd heard the blind beggar's question and were well-disposed enough to answer him. The first words spoken to the blind man are not hostile and come from an unspecified element in the crowd (contrast with v. 39 below).[60] The crowd tells the blind man that this Jesus the Nazorean is "passing by" (παρέρχεται), signaling the journey motif once again and causing the blind beggar to realize that he has a short window of opportunity to attract the attention of the famed miracle worker.[61] Luke can use the term παρέρχομαι to refer to simple travel (Luke 12:37; 17:7), but more often it refers to something that has already passed (Acts 16:8; 27:9) or to something that is neglected or negated (Luke 11:42; 15:29; 16:17). Thus, it may have an overtone in this case that Jesus was about to pass by the man with no intent on stopping (as with Mysia in Acts 16:8), excluding the blind beggar (and his dishonorable public arena) from his public entrance into Jericho. If such a connotation obtains, then it adds even more believability to the initiative of the blind beggar. Luke paints a scene where the blind man's one chance to get the attention of the powerful Jesus of Nazareth may be slipping away, and where the beggar, with understandable zeal and persistence, instigates a public encounter with Jesus.

By the end of v. 37, Luke's audience can now envision the following scene. Jesus, with a crowd surrounding him, is traveling on a major thoroughfare approaching the city of Jericho. The presence of the crowd indicates the public nature of Jesus' procession using the force of social relations. As he comes near to the city, Jesus naturally encounters a heavily traveled part of the road where beggars might sit on the side to ask for alms. The force of meaning (ancient characterizations of beggars) and the force of place (the side of a road near a city entrance) combine to make a public (but dishonorable) setting for the beggar. The two public arenas meet when the beggar takes the initiative to ask what is happening. Through the dialogue that follows in vv. 38–39 the meeting becomes a collision that results in Jesus summoning the beggar and healing him.

---

60. The verb ἀπαγγέλλω in Luke-Acts typically, but not always, has an indirect object who receives the news. In this case, the presence of αὐτῷ keeps the blind beggar in the narration of the story.

61. Luke has this verb of movement in contrast to the predicative statement of identity in Mark 10:47: ὅτι Ἰησοῦς ὁ Ναζαρηνός ἐστιν. Matthew uses παράγω at this point in his version.

The Healing of the Blind Beggar (18:35-43)

Nazorean and Son of David: The Public and Political Significance of Titles for Jesus

In their interaction, both the crowd and the beggar apply a title to Jesus in vv. 37-39. The first, Ἰησοῦς ὁ Ναζαραῖος, is spoken by the crowd to tell the blind man who is coming. This title specifies an individual public persona. The second, υἱὲ Δαυίδ, is shouted out twice by the blind man in an attempt to get Jesus' attention. The blind man's public label for Jesus focuses not on his individual public persona (note that he does not use Jesus' name) but rather on a public identification of his (Jewish and royal) heritage.[62] Much of scholarship has focused on the use and meaning of the second title (generally using Mark's form of the story) without attending to the social status of the one who is using it, the blind beggar. Before turning to this important title however, we must first consider the significance of Jesus being identified as "the Nazorean."

Luke changes Mark's Ναζαρηνός (Nazarene) to Ναζωραῖος (Nazorean), but the two forms are not differentiated in Luke-Acts (or the rest of the NT), and both refer to Jesus more specifically as the Jesus who is from Nazareth.[63] This label associates Jesus with his hometown, but both forms of the label are also commonly found near representations of Jesus as a public miracle worker in Luke-Acts. After four uses of the name Nazareth in the infancy narrative to identify the home of Jesus and his family (1:26; 2:4, 39, 51), it appears in 4:16, when Jesus returns to this town "where he had been brought up." Immediately after his citation of Isaiah (4:18-19, which speaks of release and recovery of sight), Jesus' miracles become a point of contention (4:23-27) that causes a public riot engulfing "everyone in the synagogue" (4:28). The first public healing narrated in the Gospel occurs immediately after this, the healing of the demoniac in Capernaum (4:31-37). The demon addresses Jesus as "Jesus the Nazarene" (4:34) in the midst of the public meeting of the crowd in the synagogue, and the people wonder who this person is who has authority and power over unclean spirits (4:36). Already, the title "Jesus of Nazareth" identifies Jesus as a public figure, linking him with a ministry of public miracles.

Jesus is not identified as a Nazarene again in the Gospel until the pericope under discussion in 18:37. After this, in Luke 24:19 and Acts 2:22, the label again designates Jesus' publicly visible miracle-working powers. In Luke 24:19, Jesus of Nazareth is "a prophet, powerful in deed [ἔργῳ, probably referring to miracles] and word before God *and all the people*" (the emphasis reiterates the public nature of his ministry). In Acts 2:22, Peter pro-

---

62. To say it another way, the crowd emphasizes Jesus' "acquired honor" noting his public acts of power and generosity, while the blind man emphasizes Jesus' "ascribed honor" which Jesus receives through his ancestry. See Malina and Neyrey, "Honor and Shame," 28-29.

63. The latter of the two forms has puzzled interpreters for some time despite the fact that it is more common in the NT. Ναζαρηνός is only found in Mark 1:24; 10:47; 14:67; 16:6; and Luke 4:34; 24:19, while Ναζωραῖος occurs at Matt 2:23; 26:71; Luke 18:37; John 18:5, 7; 19:19; Acts 2:22; 3:6; 4:10; 6:14; 22:8; 24:5; 26:9 (more times in Acts than either form in any of the Gospels). Ναζαρηνός more clearly refers to one from Nazareth, a "Nazarene," but the presence of the omega in Ναζωραῖος raises questions about the formation and implications of this form. See the discussion in Schaeder, "Ναζαρηνός, Ναζωραῖος," 4:874-79; Wise, "Nazarene," 571-74; Davies and Allison, *Matthew*, 1:275-84; and Fitzmyer, *Luke*, 2:1215-16. Though some reflection on the Hebrew terms נצר or נטר is not out of the question, I prefer Fitzmyer's conclusion that "Nazorean" is possibly a gentilic adjective—"one from Nazareth."

claims to the international crowd in Jerusalem that Jesus the Nazorean is "a man attested to you by God through powers and wonders and signs [all words designating miracles], which God worked through him *in your midst as you have seen*" (the emphasis again reveals the public visibility of Jesus' actions). In Acts 3:6 and 4:10, it is by the name of "Jesus Christ the Nazorean" that the lame beggar at the temple is healed, probably in the midst of a throng of people entering the temple.[64] Peter, in Acts 10:38, speaks of Ἰησοῦν τὸν ἀπὸ Ναζαρέθ, who was anointed with the Holy Spirit and power and went about doing good (εὐεργετῶν) and healing (ἰώμενος).[65] Finally, in the first recounting of the Damascus road experience in Acts, Paul speaks of "Jesus the Nazorean." This is the only account of the Damascus road experience that attaches Nazareth to the name of Jesus in a positive sense, and it is the only retelling of the event that includes Paul's blindness and restoration of sight (22:11–13).[66] When characters in Luke-Acts positively identify Jesus as the "Nazorean" or "Nazarene," they also mention his ministry of public miracles. Thus, when some part of the crowd told the blind man that "Jesus the Nazorean" was passing by, they were not merely specifying which Jesus this was by linking him with his hometown, but probably also identifying him as the Jesus who was famous for performing miracles.[67]

While the crowd specifies Jesus' public identity as an individual in the title "Jesus the Nazorean," the blind beggar publicly identifies Jesus as "Son of David," a title that refers to Jesus' heritage with royal and political overtones. Before continuing on to the analysis of the "Son of David" title shouted by the blind beggar, we must explore the meaning and use of the adjectives, royal and political. First, we consider the adjective "political." Kinman subtitles his work on Jesus' entry into Jerusalem: *In the Context of Lukan Theology and the* Politics *of His Day* (emphasis added). He does not explicitly define what he means by "politics," but a few hints appear in the introduction. Kinman speaks of interest in the political issues surrounding Jesus' life as a manifestation of contemporary scholars wrestling with the relationship of "church" and "state."[68] He argues that Luke shaped his presentation of the entry to distance Jesus from "Jewish nationalists."[69] Finally, he explains that the phrase "'Political apologetic' refers to Luke's interest in demonstrating that loyalty to Jesus does not mean disloyalty to the Roman Empire."[70] Therefore, Kinman uses "political"

---

64. Two occurrences of the label in Acts (6:14 and 24:5) are found on the lips of opponents who are attacking the "sect" that has organized around Jesus the Nazorean (see 24:5). In another instance, Paul speaks of his past life when he was convinced that he should do "many things against the name of Jesus the Nazorean" (26:9).

65. In vv. 36–37, Peter mentions the broad scope of Jesus ministry as well as the way in which news about him has spread, again casting a public sense over the events.

66. Of course, some narratives and summaries about miracles in the Gospel and Acts do not identify Jesus with Nazareth, but every positive mention of Jesus' hometown occurs in relation to his miraculous powers.

67. Therefore, no contrastive polarity exists between Jesus the Nazorean (an insignificant little village) and Jesus the Son of David (king of an entire country), contra Meynet, *Luc*, 2:180–81. Rather, the blind man simply raises the honorific title applied to Jesus by a couple of degrees, from a divinely empowered miracle worker to a divinely appointed royal figure.

68. Kinman, *Jesus' Entry*, 1.

69. Ibid., 4.

70. Ibid., 10.

in the narrow sense of government or national power structures.[71] Cassidy also employs "political" in a narrow sense when he speaks of Luke as an "empire historian" and closes his study by asking, "Was Jesus Dangerous to the Roman Empire?"[72] However, Cassidy also believes that Jesus' stance on socioeconomic issues impacts his political position, opening the realm of politics beyond the scope of what governments do.[73] On the other side of the spectrum, Yoder speaks dismissively of studies that limit themselves to "traditional . . . state-oriented politics."[74] For Yoder, Jesus' social ethic is political,[75] a perspective that fits into the broader understanding of politics as the social exercise of power.[76] For the sake of this study, I will use this broader understanding of the term "political": politics is the study of the social exercise of power among groups and individuals.[77]

Kinman initially insists on labeling the "Son of David" traditions as "political";[78] however, later, in the analysis of the entry, Kinman prefers the term "royal." Some articles on Luke's Gospel focus on the royal or kingly identity of Jesus.[79] Nevertheless, almost no scholars reflect on the definition and implications of the label "royal." Without careful reflection, "political" and "royal" seem to imply two different, but related, types of authority: "political" is more city-centered and bureaucratic while "royal" is more nationalistic and hegemonic. The examination of Luke's use of the title "Son of David" will show that it calls upon Jewish heritage (with its divine backing) as a marker of Jesus' public authority and identity. For the sake of this study, the adjective "royal" will refer to a complex set of symbols, ancestry, and identity markers that imbue a person or family with both authority and high status for a particular group of people. The title "Son of David" employs ancestry (a descendant of King David) to communicate royal connotations. Thus, "royal" refers primarily to the status and authority ascribed to a person by means of their ancestry (ascribed honor), while "political" refers primarily to the use of that status and authority at work in the public arena (achieved honor).

The two terms overlap in the domain of authority/power, for both royal and political figures have and exercise power. However, royal connotations tend to emphasize the right to and dignity of that power while political connotations emphasize the possession and execution of power. Even if the two conceptual domains overlap at points, they are not identical and have different indicators and implications.[80] To clarify, "political" describes

71. Tansey says that the "narrow" use of the adjective "political" refers exclusively to official state power structures (*Politics*, 4).

72. Cassidy, *Jesus, Politics*, vi–vii.

73. See chs. 2 and 3 in Cassidy, *Jesus, Politics*.

74. Yoder, *Politics of Jesus*, 14.

75. Ibid., 2, 8–13.

76. Tansey, *Politics*, 4.

77. Ibid., 6. Tansey prefers this perspective as well, with special attention to the dynamics of cooperation and conflict.

78. Kinman, *Jesus' Entry*, 12–24, 68–77.

79. Tannehill, "What Kind of King?," 17–22; Plevnik, "Son of Man"; Johnson, "Kingship Parable"; George, "La Royauté."

80. I would say that the label "imperial," which is used to identify the highest level of political power in my social-spatial classification, represents the ultimate fusion of the two semantic ranges.

the pragmatic and public use of social power, while "royal" has more to do with the symbols, status, and identity publicly attached to a person by means of his or her heritage and/or divine appointment. Luke more prominently uses βασιλ- (i.e., "royal") language in 18:35—19:48 to refer to Jesus (19:11-12, 14, 38, plus the "Son of David" references in 18:38-39), while πολιτ- (i.e., "political") language only appears in the description of the hostile citizens in 19:14. On the other hand, Jesus also exercises "political" power in a number of ways that are not directly tied to his royal identity (e.g., ordering the blind beggar to be brought to him, requesting Zacchaeus's hospitality, instructing two disciples to fetch a colt for him). The two terms intertwine at points, but I will attempt to use them specifically to identify the two domains outlined above whenever possible.

To return to the titles applied to Jesus, after the crowd identifies Jesus as "the Nazorean," the blind man suddenly cries out to Jesus as the "Son of David" (18:39).[81] The appearance of this title in this story has generated pages of scholarly debate. First, considerable discussion has transpired about the origin and use of this title in the Markan account.[82] Rather than probe the pre-Lukan roots of the title "Son of David" and its possible meanings,[83] it is more fruitful for this study to see how and why Luke employs it.[84] Most of the references to David before this pericope in Luke specify him as an important Jewish forefather for Joseph (1:27) or Jesus (1:69, 3:31) or use his name as part of the identification of Bethlehem (2:4, 11), and in one case David is referred to in an example story told by Jesus (6:3). Jesus is clearly a descendant of David in Luke's account, but what is the significance of that descent? Perhaps Berger is right to claim, "Daß Jesus dabei als der Sohn Davids angerugen worden sei, bleibt zwar erhalten, spielt jedoch keine besondere Rolle."[85] Yet, this label must have some meaning for Luke, even if it plays no "special role." It enables Luke to root Jesus in the royal ancestral traditions of the Jewish people and their divine authentication.[86] For Luke, David is a marker, drawn from Jewish tradition, for a more general royal theme. In Luke 1:32, the only prior reference to David not mentioned above, the angel Gabriel tells Mary that "the Lord God will give to him the throne of his ancestor David." This reference identifies the royal status of David (his throne) and affirms God's right to assign this royalty. This is the only substantial clue provided by Luke in the Gospel about the significance of Jesus' Davidic heritage, a heritage bestowed by God that communicates royal status

---

81. Burger rightly demonstrates how Luke both shortens and smoothens out Mark's account at this point. See Burger, *Davidssohn*, 109.

82. Some have insisted that "Son of David" was associated with healing traditions about Jesus prior to Mark's Gospel. See Hahn, *Titles of Jesus*, 254–55; and Lohmeyer, *Gottesknecht*, 76. However, I agree that Mark probably inserted the title into this story. See Robbins, "Healing," 234–36.

83. Fisher argues that the title makes sense because extant traditions portray Solomon as a great miracle worker ("Son of David"). On the other hand, Robbins claims that this title associates Jesus with David and Jerusalem ("Healing," 241–42). In either case, Bovon is right to wonder, "Si tel est le sens traditionnel, Luc en est-il encore conscient?" (*Luc*, 3c: 227).

84. Meynet claims that Luke emphasizes the center of the story ("Son of David, have mercy on me") through chiasm and repetition ("L'Aveugle de Jéricho," 700).

85. Burger, *Davidssohn*, 111. Conzelmann agrees (*Theology*, 172 n. 1).

86. The reference to David as a key Jewish forefather here is complemented by the reference to Abraham in the next pericope.

The Healing of the Blind Beggar (18:35–43)

to Jesus. In Acts, David is primarily a prophet (2:25, 34; 4:25) and an example of death (13:34–36). However, as an ancestor of Jesus, David is a divinely appointed king. In Acts 13:21–23, Paul says to a mostly Jewish audience, "Then they asked for a king, and God gave them Saul . . . when he had deposed Saul, he made David their king . . . from this man's [David's] lineage God has brought to Israel a savior, Jesus." Once again, Luke emphasizes David's royal identity as Jesus' ancestor and God's initiative: just as God made Saul king, just as God made David king, so God made Jesus to be a royal savior.[87]

The implications of these sparse clues are confirmed by Luke's combination of material in 18:35—19:48. The "Son of David" acclamation is the first sounding of a royal theme that emerges again in the parable of the pounds (19:11–12) and the triumphal entry (19:38).[88] In spite of this recurring royal theme, an overwhelming consensus insists that Luke omits the reference to David in 19:38 (contrast Mark 11:10 and Matt 21:9) in order to subdue any possible political overtones that might have been attached to a Davidic figure entering Jerusalem.[89] Luke does not portray Jesus arriving in Jerusalem to re-establish a Jewish political state. On this point, he agrees with the majority of the NT. However, Luke does not diminish the royal identity of Jesus. Instead, he clarifies and intensifies it, showing how Jesus publicly manifests his royal heritage. First, Luke elongates this section between the last passion prediction and the entry, including a Q parable retold with distinctively Lukan elements that feature royal rights and power (19:11–28). Second, Luke does not only omit the name of David in 19:38, he also *adds* the noun βασιλεύς as a designation for Jesus. In Mark, it is the coming of the βασιλεία not the βασιλεύς that is celebrated. Therefore, Luke has not toned down the royal overtones of this passage; rather, he has focused them precisely onto the person of Jesus. Third, as Jesus enters Jericho, he is hailed as the "Son of David"; then as he enters Jerusalem, he is hailed as "the king." The parallels between the two entries place "Son of David" next to "king." The two terms are functionally equivalent and clarify one another. By the time of Luke's writing in the late first century, "king" was fading away as a viable political office under the hegemony of the Roman Empire, and few client kings were still appointed by the Romans in the first half of the first century CE (e.g., Herod Agrippa, 41–44 CE).[90] Thus, the title "king" appears to be more important for its connections to Jesus' ancestry and the divine honor bestowed upon Jewish royalty rather than for its implications of active political power in the empire of Luke's day. Thus, the blind man publicly addresses Jesus as "Son of David" to beseech him as one who is authorized by God and dignified by his royal Jewish ancestry to grant mercy to a handicapped beggar.

---

87. Kinman concludes that "political" expectations regarding the "son of David" were dominant in the HB and intertestamental literature (*Jesus' Entry*, 73). If that is in fact the case, then Luke shifts the emphasis from political to royal in his writing.

88. Strauss, *Davidic Messiah*, 306–7.

89. Conzelmann, *Theology of St. Luke*, 139; Burger, *Davidssohn*, 127; Fitzmyer, *Luke*, 2:1245–46; Strauss, *Davidic Messiah*, 315. Kinman now changes his language and emphasizes the "royal" elements present in the entry according to Luke (*Jesus' Entry*, 94–98).

90. Jacobson, "Roman Client Kings," 34; and Goodman, *Roman World*, 110–12. Goodman also points out that many of the children of appointed client kings were incorporated into the Roman ruling class, which is surely not part of Luke's connotation here.

PART TWO: SOCIAL-SPATIAL EXEGESIS OF LUKE 18:35—19:48

Then why does Luke omit the name of David in 19:38? First, he has already mentioned it in the opening pericope of this section, so he need not specify it again.[91] Second, he may have omitted it because it would have been stylistically awkward to include it.[92] Finally, and perhaps most likely, the double reference to the title "Son of David" in 18:38 and 39 firmly ties Jesus to royalty in Israel's heritage, but in the rest of the section and specifically in 19:38, Luke orients the presentation toward his predominantly gentile audience. While a gentile audience might have cognitively understood the implications of the appellation "Son of David" due to some familiarity with Jewish traditions, such a title has no cultural resonance for them. Thus, Luke does not unnecessarily repeat a Jewish title for Jesus later in the same section, but adds another title, "king," which both Gentiles and Jews would have understood. When the (Gentile) audience arrives at 19:38, they can be certain that Jesus (the "Son of David") is a royal figure ("king") for his followers. By employing "king" in 19:38, Luke clarifies and specifies the royal content of the blind man's address, "Son of David, have mercy on me!"

Luke uses this title in his development of the royal identity of Jesus. However, Jesus is not hailed as "Son of David" by a respectable, dignified member of society, but rather by a blind beggar, a veritable outcast. So then, how does the public acclamation of the beggar in this public setting serve to shape the public perception of who Jesus is? The man's status would have cast some suspicion on the accuracy of his address for many in the Greco-Roman world, but Luke uses the man's status in a surprising way to endorse his use of the title. Recall that beggars could be characterized as overly importunate (Sirach 25:2; Martial, *Ep.* 53) or sycophantic (Juvenal, *Sat.* 4.116–17; see also the description of clients in *Ep.* 1.17.43–44). His status makes him eminently unworthy of the attention of Jesus, which the προάγοντες seem to recognize in their attempt to silence him. He fulfills the stereotype of an annoying beggar by continuing to shout despite the rebuke of some in the crowd. Furthermore, his public address to Jesus, "Son of David," could certainly seem overly flattering to the crowd (especially any potentially hostile elements in it). Such a cry might seem to be a ploy to attract an attention-seeking benefactor in this public setting. One can easily imagine some people in the crowd wishing to say, "Lord, order this man to stop," much as the Pharisees do in 19:39.

However, we must also recall the traditions that present blind persons as gifted or prescient: the poetic wisdom of Homer, the prophetic insight of Tiresias, or the righteous but blinded Tobit. Luke's portrayal of the blind man activates these implications more than the stereotype of the annoying, lazy beggar. When this blind man publicly cries out in a public setting, he "sees" the identity of Jesus in a way that is unseen by those around him. For Luke and his audience, this man stands in a line of those in the third Gospel who have unexpected insight given the prejudices against their social status: the centurion in

---

91. Luke writes similarly in other places. In 4:44, Jesus is said to preach in the synagogues of Judea, and yet he is rarely in a synagogue in the rest of the narrative. This is because the representative story in 4:16ff serves to make the point well enough. Note also how Peter's speeches about Cornelius' conversion in Acts 11:1–18 and 15:6–11 presume certain details of the story from ch. 10 and add clarifying interpretations to it.

92. Strauss, *Davidic Messiah*, 315 n. 1.

7:1–10, the sinful woman of 7:36–50, and the lepers (and a Samaritan) in 17:11–19.[93] Luke states the principle behind this in 10:21: "I thank you Father, Lord of heaven and earth, because you have hidden these things from the wise and intelligent and revealed them to infants."[94] Jesus accepts the man's recognition of his royal identity by heeding his cry, not denying the title, and honoring his request in this public scenario. Comparing this herald with Jesus' reception at Jerusalem reveals an ironic barb. Jesus' true identity is acclaimed by unlikely, low-status agents (such as blind beggars, tax collectors, "sinful" women, and centurions), whereas those who should have recognized Jesus' royal arrival publicly oppose him (19:42).

Kinman states that a secondary function of the healing of the blind beggar is to foreshadow a growing association between Solomon and Jesus.[95] However, Solomon is only explicitly used as a preliminary or negative example that is superseded by Jesus in most of Luke-Acts. In Luke 11:31, Jesus is the one greater than Solomon, and in 12:27 even the lilies are dressed more finely than Solomon. Finally, in Acts 7:47–50, Stephen has nothing positive to say about the temple built by Solomon, the very temple that must be cleansed by Jesus (Luke 19:45).[96] A striking contrast emerges in Luke's account between the wealth and royal pomp that mark Solomon's reign (e.g., the temple and the palace built by conscripted labor) against the unassuming figure of Jesus who does not personally claim royal status (the disciples must attribute kingship to him in 19:37) and includes beggars and commoners in his following.[97] In light of this, it makes sense that a blind beggar would be the first human being to hail Jesus as royalty, for Jesus' rule will restore and include the dregs of society rather than use them to construct extravagant buildings. Thus, Jesus is a king *unlike* Solomon: he has no royal pomp and wealth to attend his rule, but instead he

---

93. Green makes a similar argument with this evidence (*Luke*, 663).

94. In my analysis of the literary structure of Luke's Gospel the passage in Luke 10:21–24 is the conclusion of transitional material in 9:1—10:24 that sets up the travel narrative, which then properly begins in 10:25. Thus, there would be an inclusio here between this verse and the insight of the blind man near the end of the travel narrative.

95. Kinman, *Jesus' Entry*, 79–80. Kinman uses the Solomonic associations to support his claim that Luke distances Jesus from political aims (113–15).

96. Chance argues that Luke intends Stephen's speech to critique the way that the temple could be used to limit God's presence rather than the temple cult itself, which he speaks of positively in several places (*Jerusalem*, 40–41). This is why the tabernacle is portrayed more positively (Chance, *Jerusalem*, 126). Maddox claims that Stephen's speech is a caustic (but accurate) narration of Israel's rebellion in Luke's eyes, a rebellion that is ironically and climactically exemplified in the temple (*Purpose*, 53–54). Stephen's critique echoes Solomon's own admission about the inadequacy of the temple (1 Kgs 8:27), and Jesus identifies the temple as a house of prayer much as Solomon does (1 Kgs 8:30). Luke's view of the temple and its cult is layered and complex, but Stephen's speech is the one occasion that clearly associates Solomon with the temple, and it is clearly derogatory.

97. Kinman interprets the story of the struggle for succession in 1 Kgs 1 as illustrating the humble passivity of Solomon in contrast to his brothers (*Jesus' Entry*, 52) and then compares this to Jesus (112). However, he misses the point that 1 Kgs 1 focuses on the political maneuverings executed by Bathsheba and Nathan on Solomon's behalf (Solomon appears to be a pawn). However, as soon as Solomon obtains the throne, he ruthlessly and violently consolidates his power, eliminating all rivals (1 Kgs 2:13–45). This differs starkly from Jesus' initiative in obtaining the colt which is followed by his more passive stance and ultimately his self-sacrifice in the passion.

is publicly heralded by impoverished outcasts, whom he welcomes into his movement (rather than putting them to forced labor).[98]

Having gained Jesus' attention through his persistence and his honorable address, what does the man request of Jesus? Mercy: "Son of David, have mercy on me!" (vv. 38 and 39), a cry with both social and spatial implications. The terms for mercy (ἔλεος, ἐλεάω) are not common in Luke-Acts. The noun appears in the infancy narratives to refer to an attribute of God that leads to acts of divine kindness and protection for Elizabeth in particular (1:58, a more private concern) and Israel in general (1:50, 54, 72, 78, more public concerns).[99] The noun appears once again in the punch line to the story of the good Samaritan. The lawyer recognizes that the man who acted as a neighbor was ὁ ποιήσας τὸ ἔλεος μετ' αὐτοῦ.[100] There are four occurrences of the verb in Luke-Acts—all in the Gospel and all in the aorist imperative form ἐλέησον. Two of these occur in the story under consideration here (vv. 38 and 39). Prior to this, the word appears in the story of the rich man and Lazarus when the rich man cries out, "Father Abraham, have mercy on me!" (16:24). Next, the ten lepers of 17:13 utter the plea publicly: "Jesus, Master, have mercy on us!" Luke's audience might have understood such a cry from a blind beggar as a request for alms.[101] This would be akin to the "mercy" received by the robbed and beaten man in the parable of the good Samaritan or the beggar in Acts 3. However, the audience has recently heard the identical request of the lepers who are healed in 17:11–19, so Luke has prepared his audience to anticipate a healing after such a cry for help to Jesus.

All three requests for mercy in Luke (16:24; 17:13; and 18:38–39) are shouted out from some distance. In the case of the rich man, he calls out to Abraham who is "far away" on the other side of a great "chasm" (16:23, 26). The setting for the healing of the lepers is even more like that of the blind man. As Jesus enters the city, the lepers approach him but address him while still "standing at some distance" (ἔστησαν πόρρωθεν, 17:12). So, Luke uses this cry for help in cases of spatial separation. Furthermore, in all three cases the request follows an honorific title. The rich man calls Abraham "father" (16:24). The lepers address Jesus as "master" (ἐπιστάτα, 17:13). The blind beggar uses "Son of David." All three titles attribute dignity and authority as a prelude to a cry for help. Thus, the blind man uses a formulaic cry found in two previous passages in Luke. He cries out from some distance, addressing Jesus with an honorific title, asking for mercy in a public setting like the lepers. Then, like the lepers, he is healed.

Jesus' lack of response to the title itself introduces an ambiguity about Jesus' claims to royal authority that is quietly resolved in the rest of 18:35—19:48. Put simply, does Luke cause Jesus to simultaneously refuse the royal honor and possible political implications

---

98. Though he does not refer to this passage specifically, the contrast between Solomon and Jesus is insightfully expounded by Brueggemann, *Prophetic Imagination*, 25–34.

99. Similar to the use in the LXX where mercy is a characteristic quality of God (Ex 33:19; 2 Sam 24:14; Ps 86:15; Hos 2:19).

100. Interestingly, the figure who needed mercy in this case was also found on the side of the road (ὁδός).

101. Johnson, *Luke*, 284.

of the title "Son of David"?[102] The fact that he stops, calls the blind beggar, and grants his request (noting the man's faith) indicates an implicit acceptance of the title. However, Jesus makes no reference to the title and appeals to no royal status, symbols, or ancestry on his own behalf in the rest of this passage. Instead, in 18:35–43 Luke portrays Jesus as a royal figure deserving of the title "Son of David," for he has the divinely bestowed royal authority to grant mercy and heal the man. Jesus' royal identity could be bolstered when Luke casts him as a merciful and beneficent figure who publicly cares for the poor and needy.[103] Set on the outskirts of Jericho, this healing is a local display of Jesus' Davidic status, a status confirmed by his authority within the procession that enters Jericho "triumphantly" with him. In the next verse (v. 40), Luke will portray Jesus exercising political authority in the *local* sphere by issuing an order to his followers in the surrounding procession. The same balance of implicit royalty and local political action obtains in the rest of 19:1–48. Jesus makes no royal claims when he meets Zacchaeus (he labels himself as the "Son of Man" not "of David"), but he claims the right to determine true Jewish heritage (a royal prerogative) by labeling Zacchaeus as a "son of Abraham." Furthermore, he exercises the authority of a local leader by inviting himself into the home of Zacchaeus, the local chief tax collector. In the parable of the king and his subjects (19:11–27), Jesus indirectly casts himself in the role of the crowned nobleman, but the story focuses on a very local exercise of power (politics) in the king's house and among his own citizens. At the entry into Jerusalem, Jesus implies kingship by orchestrating his own arrival on a donkey, while the explicit acclamation is left to his disciples. Then, he comes into conflict with Jewish (religious) leaders. The Pharisees are local leaders, and they object to Jesus' implicit acceptance of his disciples' royal acclamation. The chief priests are regional leaders with more political authority. They do not object to any of these titles or symbolic acts (perhaps viewing them as negligible). Their animosity is roused when Jesus interferes in the temple, the center of their power. Thus, beginning with the blind beggar's appeal to Jesus as the "Son of David," Luke portrays Jesus as a royal figure who does not assertively claim royalty for himself, but confidently exercises the power and authority of a local (and unofficial) leader. Royal terms (rather than political ones) are more common in 18:35—19:48, and Luke uses them to support Jesus' authority and divine authorization. When the narrative mentions Jesus' own exercise of power (a form of politics), it is for salvific purposes in local contexts and among his own followers.

---

102. Kinman claims that the healing of the blind beggar forces the audience to consider whether or not Jesus will fulfill the political hopes of the nation, and then he argues that the tenor of the account communicates that Jesus will not fulfill such nationalist hopes (Kinman, *Jesus' Entry*, 79). I believe that Kinman constructs and answers the question wrongly because he does not carefully parse out the connotations of royal and political.

103. A precedent for this might be seen in the healing performed by Vespasian (Tacitus, *Hist.* 4.81). Tacitus reports that while Vespasian was in Alexandria a blind man and a man with a diseased hand beseeched him repeatedly to heal their infirmities. They probably saw him as a royal figure who enjoyed the favor of the gods. After consulting with physicians, Vespasian consents and heals both men. Tacitus closes this episode by explaining that both healings were performed in the presence of a multitude of witnesses who could attest to the veracity of his account.

PART TWO: SOCIAL-SPATIAL EXEGESIS OF LUKE 18:35—19:48

The two titles applied to Jesus use the force of meaning to express public and political characteristics. When the crowd tells the blind beggar that "Jesus the Nazorean" is passing by, they identify him as the Jesus who is famous for his ministry of public miracles. The blind beggar recognizes the import of the moment and relentlessly cries out to Jesus from some distance, intensifying the public scene. The blind beggar exercises unusual insight (paradoxically contrasting with his blindness and social status) by calling Jesus the "Son of David." This term raises royal connotations that grant public honor and authority to Jesus by associating him with a kingly Jewish ancestry that received its right to rule from God. Such a royal label may have some limited political connotations. However, in 18:35—19:48, Jesus never explicitly claims his own royal status; instead he accepts and implies his royal identity through his actions (healing the man, portraying himself as the king of the parable, riding the colt). The public domains of Jesus' procession and the blind man each issue their own public acclamation of Jesus' identity. The crowd affirms Jesus as a public miracle worker, and the blind beggar casts him as a royal figure, one who then exercises authority publicly in a variety of local contexts.

A Public Miracle and Public Praise

The focus of the story in vv. 40-43 is Jesus, who now initiates the action and heals the man. The initiative of Jesus transforms the collision of the (dishonorable) public sphere of the beggar and the (more honorable) procession surrounding him. Jesus summons the blind beggar and heals him. Now, instead of conflict between the beggar and the crowd, the crowd will follow the man's lead and join in his praise. One must also remember that the interaction between Jesus and the blind beggar, and the resulting healing, takes place in full view and hearing of the surrounding crowd. This could easily be forgotten since the crowd is only implied in the passive verb ἀχθῆναι and is not mentioned explicitly again until v. 43b. Beginning with v. 40, Jesus would have drawn the attention of everyone in the procession by stopping (σταθείς) and ordering that the man be brought to him (ἐκέλευσεν αὐτὸν ἀχθῆναι). After the blind beggar comes near (ἐγγίσαντος) to Jesus, Jesus asks him what he wants. The blind beggar replies, "κύριε, ἵνα ἀναβλέψω."[104] This request itself contributes to the public nature of the scene, for it is a positive honor challenge to Jesus.[105] Jesus is called upon to demonstrate his authority and power by granting the request for healing in the presence of the crowd.

Two important literary connections to earlier miracle material are relevant here. The man asks Jesus to see again (ἀναβλέψω). Jesus then commands the man to see again (ἀνέβλεψον), and the narrator reports that the blind beggar regained his sight (ἀνέβλεψεν). The threefold reiteration of this word in the short space of vv. 41-43 connotes that this story is the fulfillment of the scriptural promise that Jesus' mission would bring good news to the poor by proclaiming recovery of sight for the blind (τυφλοῖς ἀνάβλεψιν, 4:18 and

---

104. The blind man now addresses Jesus as κύριε instead of "Son of David." This is a respectful form of address present throughout the Gospel (5:8, 12; 7:6; 10:17; 11:1, etc.), and it does not appear to have special significance here as a title for Jesus. He is simply using a common title for addressing a social superior.

105. Malina and Neyrey. "Honor and Shame," 51-52.

The Healing of the Blind Beggar (18:35-43)

7:22). Luke also reports that the man recovered his sight "immediately" (παραχρῆμα). This is one of Luke's favorite words for designating the direct and instantaneous effects of Jesus' miracles, and it is one way that this final miracle of Jesus' public ministry encapsulates previous stories.[106] In many cases, this adverb can imply both temporal *and* spatial immediacy, a case that will be further argued in the analysis of 19:11. In this setting, the adverb connotes not only that the beggar received his sight without delay, but that it also occurred "on the spot" as a public event in the full view of the multitude of the halted procession. Jesus speaks the word of healing, "See again!", and the man regains his sight immediately.

After receiving his sight, the beggar ἠκολούθει αὐτῷ δοξάζων τὸν θεόν. Mark tells of the man following Jesus,[107] but Luke adds the participial phrase about the man's public praise. The man "follows" Jesus and "praises" God. Both words have public implications. The language of "following" Jesus is found in two contexts in Luke's Gospel: to describe a (potential) disciple's response to Jesus (5:11, 28; 9:23, 61; 18:22) or to refer to the crowds that followed Jesus (7:9; 9:11).[108] Perhaps, this instance recalls both uses. First, it marks the fact that this man publicly joins Jesus' movement as a disciple.[109] This physical and social outcast is not merely restored, but he also becomes both a herald of Jesus' royalty and his follower. Second, this verb may remind the audience that the crowd was still following Jesus as well, continuing the socially public nature of the event. The verb δοξάζω often takes place in public settings in Luke-Acts,[110] and in this case, the man's public praise is contagious. The crowd returns to the scene right after the beggar's praise at the very end of the story, emphasizing the public nature of the healing once again. Verse 43b reads, καὶ πᾶς ὁ λαὸς ἰδὼν ἔδωκεν αἶνον τῷ θεῷ. Form-critically, miracle stories often close by describing the amazement of the surrounding crowd, as this story does.[111] Yet, neither Mark nor Matthew reports the crowd's astonishment. Luke adds this statement to reiterate the public nature of the event, reminding the reader that the interaction between Jesus and the blind beggar did not escape the notice of the crowd. On the contrary, they all saw what

---

106. He adds it to Mark's accounts in 4:39 and 8:47 substitutes it for Mark's εὐθύς in 5:25; 8:44; 8:55; 18:43, and uses it in his own special material in 13:33. Thus, Luke uses παραχρῆμα in seven miracle stories (and three non-miracle stories: 1:64; 19:11; 22:60).

107. Luke probably omits Mark's tag ἐν τῇ ὁδῷ because Jesus immediately arrives in Jericho city right after this episode. Compare Fitzmyer, *Luke*, 2:1217.

108. Curiously, this word does not occur between 9:61 and 18:22. Thus, its use here primarily recalls chs. 5–9, which is also where Jesus performs most of his miracles.

109. Contra Fitzmyer, *Luke*, 1:242, who lists 18:43 as one of the "generic" instances that simply describes physical following.

110. Jesus was "praised" *by all* when he taught in the synagogues (4:15). The paralytic "praised" God as he got up and walked out of the over-crowded house (5:25). Then like the crowd of 18:43, the surrounding crowd also "praises" God when they see the paralytic walk (5:26). The healing of the widow's son causes the people to "praise" God, and the report goes out to the surrounding area (7:16-18). The crippled woman "praised" God in the midst of the crowded synagogue assembly (13:13). The centurion "praises" God in the midst of the multitude that gathered to witness Jesus' crucifixion (23:47-48). All the people "praised" God because of the healing of the lame beggar in Acts (4:21). After the Gentiles "praise" God in Acts 13:48, the Gospel spread throughout the entire region (13:49).

111. Bailey and Vander Broek, *Literary Forms*, 137, 142.

happened and joined the man in praising God for the miraculous cure. Indeed, this former disabled outcast now becomes the leader of Jesus' entourage (a position not properly filled by the προάγοντες), the one who initiates the chorus of praise.¹¹²

The encounter of Jesus and the blind man results in a public miracle, which leads to public praise. The presence of the crowd brings in the force of social relations, for the large group of followers and travelers surrounding Jesus witness the miraculous healing. Similarly, Philostratus records the presence of a crowd (οἱ πολλοί) at the raising of the dead girl (*Vit. Apoll.* 4.45). The force of time comes into play as well. While Luke's audience probably assumed that this healing occurred during the day, the drama of Jesus halting the entire procession and calling the blind man to him brings in an element of time, a pause in the normal procession, that intensifies the public setting. Again, Philostratus portrays Apollonius halting a public procession to raise a dead girl in Rome (*Vit. Apoll.* 4.45). When he is healed the blind man begins to praise God publicly. Luke alone brings the crowd back at the end of this story and has them join in the man's praise, creating a throng that rejoices over Jesus' miracles as he enters the city of Jericho.

The Composition of the Crowd and the Local Politics of Jesus' Movement

The group of people surrounding Jesus intensifies the public character of this brief episode in Luke's version. While v. 35a states that "he" (αὐτόν, referring to Jesus) was approaching Jericho, v. 36 reminds the audience that the crowd (ὄχλος) was traveling with him. Luke places the crowd in the midst of the action, emphasizing their role more than Mark or Matthew. Luke makes the crowd a character that speaks to the blind beggar in v. 37. Luke's version is the only one that names the "leaders" (οἱ προάγοντες, v. 39). Finally, only Luke reiterates the presence of a large group called "all the people" (πᾶς ὁ λαός) in v. 43. Despite its importance, the composition and role of the group surrounding Jesus is not immediately clear because of the three different labels. The ὄχλος appears in 18:36, indicating a large (Jewish) crowd that has attended Jesus throughout the Gospel (4:42; 5:1; 6:17, etc.). This ὄχλος follows Jesus throughout the travel narrative, and he regularly admonishes them.¹¹³ In v. 39 Luke further identifies a specific group, οἱ προάγοντες, that is presumably part of the larger crowd. It is "those leading the way" that rebuke the blind beggar and attempt to silence him. The identity of this group is not immediately perspicacious because this is the only time Luke uses this verb in his Gospel.¹¹⁴ Finally, Luke uses the term λαός in v. 43. The labels for the crowd (ὄχλος and λαός) reinforce the public

---

112. As ch. 9 will show, this is not an unusual or isolated occurrence. Luke often highlights the presence or activity of crowds at Jesus' miraculous event in ways not found in the parallel synoptic accounts. It is one way that he uses the force of social relations to place Jesus in the public sphere.

113. Johnson highlights the way Luke interchanges three specific audiences for Jesus in the travel narrative: the disciples, the Pharisees, and the crowd (*Literary Function*, 107–11). Moessner emphasizes that throughout the travel narrative Jesus repeatedly admonishes the crowd, which is characterized as "this evil generation" (11:29; *Lord of the Banquet*, 92–96). Tannehill demonstrates the complex nature of Luke's portrayal of the crowd/people, which includes both positive and negative elements. Jesus' relationship with the crowd grows increasingly tense as the crowd continues to fail to heed the call to discipleship (*Narrative Unity*, 145–58).

114. It does occur four times in Acts (12:6; 16:30; 17:5; 25:26), but in each case it means to "bring someone out" before a crowd or an official. This cannot be the meaning here.

The Healing of the Blind Beggar (18:35-43)

nature of the event and prepare the audience for the public support and opposition that Jesus receives in the passion narrative. Next, a closer examination of οἱ προάγοντες will show that this term refers to leaders within Jesus' growing public movement.

The presence of a crowd uses the force of social relations to indicate the public sphere (see ch. 3 above). The references to the crowd in this Jericho section (18:35—19:10) reflect Luke's typical, but not rigid, usage of the terms ὄχλος and λαός in the Gospel which gives a negative flavor to the first term and a more positive flavor to the latter. The crowd (ὄχλος, v. 36) initially functions as the means by which the blind man knows that Jesus is approaching. They signal a public event. After that they turn into an obstacle, and at least part of the crowd (οἱ προάγοντες) attempts to repress the man. However, by the end of the story the miraculous healing has won over the crowd (now λαός, v. 43), which then follows the man's example by praising God. In the story about Zacchaeus, the public gathering (ὄχλος again in 19:3) begins as an obstacle for Zacchaeus. However, they do not berate Zacchaeus (as they did the blind beggar), but publicly attack Jesus instead.[115] Finally, at the conclusion of the Zacchaeus pericope, there is no resolution in which the crowd publicly affirms the actions of Jesus. Luke allows the complaint of the crowd to echo, rather than narrate a change of heart at the end of the Zacchaeus story.

Throughout the Gospel, Luke uses both λαός and ὄχλος to designate a large group of people gathered around Jesus; it is one of his favorite devices for signaling a public event.[116] The term λαός generally refers to the Jews as God's people and is portrayed more positively (e.g., 1:68: 3:15: 7:16: 20:1). The term ὄχλος is more common in chsapters 3-18 and implies a negative portrayal of a crowd around Jesus with fewer explicitly Jewish connotations (e.g., 3:7; 5:29; 8:45; 11:14; 12:13).[117] Luke uses λαός more frequently in the infancy narrative (chs. 1-2) eight times with no occurrences ὄχλος) and in the "Jerusalem Narrative" (19:29—24:53) where he uses the term λαός eighteen times as opposed to only five occurrences of ὄχλος.[118] In chs. 20-21, λαός is used exclusively and refers positively to a public gathering of the Jewish people who hang on Jesus' every word. The juxtaposition of the two terms indicating the crowd/people in 18:36 and 43 builds on Luke's previous usage of the two terms and helps to prepare the audience for the public material in the passion. It re-establishes a positive sense for λαός from the infancy narratives that has been subsumed by the frequent use of ὄχλος in chs. 3-18, and it illustrates the fickle nature of the crowd/people in public settings. When Luke speaks of the ὄχλος in 18:36 and 19:2, they create obstacles and object to the actions of Jesus and his associates. However, when Luke speaks of the people's praise in 18:43, he calls the public gathering "the people"

---

115. While the complaint is "murmured" it takes on the nature of a public challenge, to which Jesus and Zacchaeus both respond.

116. Tannehill begins his discussion of ὄχλος and λαός by pointing out that the two terms can function synonymously in Luke. He cites 18:35-43 as an example of this, but briefly refers to the passage only one other time in the rest of his discussion (*Narrative Unity*, 143).

117. Kodell, "Luke's Use," 328-31, 340. Kodell sites exceptions to this positive use of λαός, but his explanations do not deny their presence and impact on the narrative. I agree that λαός is generally positive, but it must not be pushed much further than that as the two terms are also interchangeable in parts of Luke's Gospel.

118. Ibid., 328-29.

PART TWO: SOCIAL-SPATIAL EXEGESIS OF LUKE 18:35—19:48

(λαός), rather than just a crowd. The interplay of the two terms in 18:35—19:10 sets up both the positive portrayal of the public gatherings in chs. 20-21 (associated with the praise of the λαός in v. 43) and the interplay that occurs between the terms λαός and ὄχλος at public events later in the passion narrative.

The parallels between Jesus' entries into Jericho and Jerusalem cast further light on the meaning of these two terms. Jesus publicly enters (εἰσελθών) both Jericho and Jerusalem (19:1, 45) to the shouts of a joyful throng celebrating his miracles (18:43; 19:37). In 18:43 the joyful throng is the people, while in 19:37 it is the disciples and not the general crowd who accompany Jesus. The only explicit mention of the crowd at the entry into Jerusalem associates them with the Pharisees (καί τινες τῶν Φαρισαίων ἀπὸ τοῦ ὄχλου),[119] who object to the acclamation of the disciples (not the acclamation of the crowd as in Mark 11:8-9). So, as Jesus approaches Jericho the "crowd" has turned into the "people" who celebrate Jesus' entry (18:43), while at the entry into Jerusalem the only active element of the crowd (the Pharisees) is vociferously opposed to the acclamations from the disciples about Jesus' arrival. Furthermore, the larger group in view reverses its opinion about Jesus at both entries. After rejoicing over Jesus' miracle in 18:43, the crowd/people suddenly turns on Jesus for going to the house of a known "sinner" (19:7). However, after the neutral to negative portrayal of the crowd at Jesus' entry to Jerusalem (19:39), they appear in 19:48 as the "people" who become Jesus' adoring audience. The response of the crowd/people to these public actions of Jesus establishes their positive status in some cases and their negative status in others. The abrupt reversal of public opinion about Jesus portrayed here has occurred before in Luke's narrative (4:22-29), and it will occur again.

The changing role of the crowd/people in these two entries prepares the audience for their changing public roles in the latter half of the passion narrative. After several positive appearances of the people (λαός) in chs. 20-21, ὄχλος appears again in 22:47-53, now associated with the hostile Jewish leaders at Jesus' arrest. After this, "crowd" and "people" appear in tandem much as they did in 18:35 and 43. In 23:4 Pilate speaks to the ὄχλος,[120] but in 23:13-23 the people (λαός) join with the Jewish leaders and give a public answer to Pilate. Surprisingly, they now demand Jesus' death, even though they were recently captivated by his public teaching (see 21:38).[121] This sudden reversal has puzzled scholars,[122] but Green has pointed out that it is prefigured in the citizens of the parable of the pounds (see 19:14).[123] It is also prefigured in the way the praising "people" of 18:43 turns quickly into the obstructing and murmuring "crowd" of 19:2. Later, the λαός stands by watching the crucifixion in 23:35, and they do not scoff like the "leaders." Then in 23:48 the text says

---

119. A similar construction can be found in Acts 12:1. It probably simply indicates that the Pharisees were part of the larger crowd (Wallace, *Greek Grammar*, 368).

120. Pilate, as the Roman prefect in charge of Judea, makes the scene explicitly political, though it is still politics on a regional scale. Pilate's referral to Herod in 23:6-12 and mention of Herod in 23:15 reinforces the regional political nature of Jesus' case and this episode in general.

121. Luke may be "playing down" the culpability of the λαός in the passion (so Kodell, "Luke's Use," 333), but he does not eliminate their culpability (also admitted by Kodell, ibid., 338-39).

122. Marshall, *Luke*, 858. Fitzmyer explains it as a case of "mob psychology" (*Luke*, 2:1488-89).

123. Green, *Luke*, 809.

that the ὄχλος (presumably the same group of people) witnesses Jesus' death and then beats their breasts in public remorse.[124] In this case, the pair of terms is more favorable. While the crowd does not actively approve of Jesus in this public setting, they are differentiated from the scorning leaders and even show a sign of public regret.

The connection of these two "triumphal entries" in Luke 18:35—19:48 prepares the audience for the passion narrative by revealing the fickle nature of public gatherings. The sudden reversals juxtaposed by the entries into Jericho and Jerusalem demonstrate that the crowd/people are in the habit of "flip-flopping" in Luke's narrative.[125] The crowd has no consistent public persona but fluctuates in a variety of public settings. First, in 18:35—19:10, they change from a "crowd" gathered around Jesus that answers the blind man (18:36) to the "people" who praise God for the miraculous public healing performed by Jesus (18:43) and then back to a crowd that objects to Jesus' choice of hosts in Zacchaeus (19:2). Then, in 19:29-48, they change from neutral-negative (associated with the hostile Pharisees) to Jesus' ardent public admirers throughout chapters 20-21. It is no surprise that they unexpectedly change again in 23:13-23 and demand Jesus' death in an official public setting before Pilate after hanging on Jesus' every word in chs. 20-21 only to show regret over his death later in chapters 23. With this complex and developing portrayal of the crowd/people, Luke has prepared his audience well for the public portrayal of Jesus in the midst of crowds in the passion narrative.

Luke singles out one group within the crowd/people, whom he calls οἱ προάγοντες in 18:39. This unusual term has puzzled interpreters and resulted in three divergent explanations. First, it may simply indicate those who were at the front of the crowd.[126] The second two possibilities rely on a more metaphorical connotation for this word by which it refers to some group of "leaders." Johnson is "tempted" to read it as a subtle reference to the Pharisees who try to silence the cries of the disciples in 19:39, much like οἱ προάγοντες try to silence the blind man here.[127] The final option is offered by Green. While he appreciates Johnson's insight about the indication of leaders, he retorts that it may very well indicate the "leaders" of Jesus' own movement, the disciples.[128]

Several pieces of indirect evidence support the final option. In Luke, Jesus has already sent his disciples ahead of him (ἀπέστειλεν . . . πρὸ προσώπου, 9:52 and 10:1) into various public (urban) and private (domestic) settings on two previous occasions in the Gospel. Thus, the audience is familiar with Luke portraying the disciples as those who go ahead of Jesus as he travels. The very same thing might be happening here as Jesus publicly

---

124. Fitzmyer, *Luke*, 2:1520.

125. This portrayal of the crowd is consistent with Plutarch's portrayal of a crowd in a local political context in the *Precepts*. The populace makes judgments about a politician based on private matters like meals and hospitality (800d), much like the crowd objects to Jesus entering Zacchaeus's home. He comments that the people are persuaded by the leader's words (802d), much like the crowds hang on Jesus' words in the temple. However, Jesus has won a good reputation among the crowds who then protect him from his opponents (821c).

126. Marshall, *Luke*, 693; but note that Marshall thinks that Luke might have taken this term from its use in Mark 10:32 or 11:9 (see more below). This is also Green's initial suggestion (*Luke*, 664).

127. Johnson, *Luke*, 284. The verb ἐπιτιμάω appears in both 18:37 and 19:39.

128. Green, *Luke*, 664 n. 173.

PART TWO: SOCIAL-SPATIAL EXEGESIS OF LUKE 18:35—19:48

enters Jericho: the disciples lead the way, preparing the city for his arrival. The preposition πρό connects these two verses to the title οἱ προάγοντες in 18:39. Then, Green points out that the disciples "have recently demonstrated their tendencies toward controlling who has access to Jesus (18:15–17),"[129] yet the connection is even stronger than Green indicates. In 18:15, Luke states ἰδόντες δὲ οἱ μαθηταὶ *ἐπετίμων* αὐτοῖς (emphasis added). It is the disciples who rebuke those bringing children to Jesus in this recent story, and so it seems reasonable to suppose that it is also the disciples who rebuke the blind beggar in 18:39.[130] Next, Marshall wondered if Luke took οἱ προάγοντες from Mark's use of it in 11:9 (or 10:32). Mark 11:9 reads, "Those who went ahead (οἱ προάγοντες) and those who followed were shouting . . ." Luke's version of this in 19:37 reads, "The whole multitude of the disciples were praising God joyfully in a loud voice." Thus, Luke understands οἱ προάγοντες (and οἱ ἀκολοθοῦντες) in Mark's account to be disciples. Finally, if οἱ προάγοντες are the disciples, it fits well into the parallels between the entries into Jericho and Jerusalem, for the disciples fluctuate much as the crowds do. At Jericho, the crowd changes from positive to negative while at Jerusalem they do exactly the opposite. This reading of οἱ προάγοντες means that the disciples who here do not appear to understand the ministry of Jesus (cf. 18:34) later change and acclaim its proper significance in 19:37–38. This parallel reading reinforces the complex interweaving of Luke's portrayal of the crowds and the disciples. In light of this evidence, it seems most likely that Luke's οἱ προάγοντες refers to Jesus' own disciples, some part of the large group of followers traveling with him.

Jesus' interaction with οἱ προάγοντες adds a political nuance to Luke's account of the healing of the blind beggar. Luke's account is shorter and less detailed than Mark's,[131] but it becomes political when Jesus orders (ἐκέλευσεν) that the man be brought to him.[132] This is the only occurrence of κελεύω in Luke's Gospel. However, Luke uses it several times in Acts for orders issued by local political leaders. The leaders of the Sanhedrin "order" Peter and John to be taken out of the council proceedings (Acts 4:15), as does Gamaliel (Acts 5:34). Herod "orders" sentries to be put to death (12:19), and local magistrates (στρατήγοι) give "orders" for Paul and Silas to be beaten (Acts 16:22). The word is even more common in Acts 21–25. Several times the tribune (χιλίαρχος) issues "orders" about Paul's imprisonment and treatment (21:33, 34; 22:24, 30; 23:10). Felix and Festus issue a series of "orders" as well (23:35; 25:6, 17, 21, 23). Finally, a centurion "orders" the men to swim for land after the shipwreck (27:43). Luke frequently employs this word when depicting an order given by a range of local leaders, mostly political, some military, and one royal. The range stretches from minor military commanders like a centurion through the ranks of tribunes up to procurators and a regional king. However, this verb is applied only once to Herod, who is far from a role model of proper royalty in Luke-Acts, and such ordering

---

129. Ibid., 664 n. 173.

130. It is true that the Pharisees ask Jesus to "rebuke" his disciples in 19:39, but they are not the ones doing the actual rebuking, and the contexts of 18:15 and 19:39 are much more similar. Jesus is the only other person who has done any narrated rebuking before 18:15.

131. Marshall calls it "distinctly colourless" (*Luke*, 694).

132. In Mark, Jesus simply "tells" (εἶπεν) them to call the man. Luke has changed this to κελεύω.

about appears to be below Agrippa and is handled by Festus on his behalf.¹³³ In most cases, this verb describes the action of a mid-level political or military authority in Acts. Thus, by depicting Jesus issuing an order with the verb κελεύω, Luke casts him as a local political leader who commands his subordinates to carry out a specific action for him.

The content of the command introduces politically tinged irony. Jesus gives an order that the blind man is to be brought to him (αὐτὸν ἀχθῆναι πρὸς αὐτόν). In agreement with Plutarch's advice, Jesus employs associates in minor tasks and monitor their activities in order to correct them when necessary (*Praec. ger. rei publ.* 807b–808d). Jesus most likely issues this command to οἱ προάγοντες, those disciples in the larger crowd that have (or are at least taking) a leadership role. Thus, Jesus has to tell these leaders (προάγοντες) that the blind man is to be brought (ἀχθῆναι). The replication of the ἄγω stem in these two words generates the political irony. Because these disciples are not "leading" in accordance with the tenor of Jesus' mission, Jesus must stop and command them to "lead" the blind man to him. Colloquially, Jesus says, "You think you are "leaders" (προάγοντες)? Then act like it and "lead" (ἀχθῆναι) that blind man to me!" This may reflect Plutarch's suggestion that humor and ridicule are powerful tools in the hands of a leader when used aptly (*Praec. ger. rei publ.* 803b–f). Jesus acts as a local political leader who delegates duties to his disciples; however, he also exercises his power by correcting them publicly and ordering them to bring the very man to him that they had recently attempted to silence.

This final section features the force of social relationships in Luke's portrayal of the crowd. The crowd/people is a complex and layered character in Luke's Gospel, and it is one of Luke's favorite tools for marking a public event. Luke typically employs ὄχλος in a neutral-negative sense and λαός in a more positive (and Jewish) sense, but the interplay of the two terms in 18:35—19:10 reveals the fickle nature of the crowd/people in the various public scenes of the passion narrative. While the crowd always signals a public event, they fluctuate between support for and hostility toward Jesus. In v. 39, Luke specifies one group, οἱ προάγοντες, within the larger crowd. A look at the broader context indicates that this is probably a group of leaders in Jesus' movement. This identification helps to bring out the local political nature of this story. Jesus acts as an authoritative leader who "orders" members of his movement to "lead" properly. Jesus exercises power (politics) among his own followers (locally) by issuing them an order and correcting their mistaken behavior.

Conclusion and Preview

The healing of the blind beggar in Luke 18:35–43 is an unofficial public event with local political implications. This concluding summary will organize the data about the public and political nature of the healing of the blind beggar around the forces based on Sack's framework. Let us begin by recalling the characteristics of the unofficial public and local political spheres developed in chapters 3 and 4.

---

133. See 25:22, 23, and 32, where Festus handles logistical matters for Agrippa, and compare Agrippa's more dignified issuance of "permission" in 26:1.

PART TWO: SOCIAL-SPATIAL EXEGESIS OF LUKE 18:35—19:48

Table 5.1 Forces in the Unofficial Public and Local Political Spheres

	Nature	Social Relations	Meaning	Religion	Time	Place
Public—Unofficial	Public activity outside of official politics	Wide variety including friends, clients, opponents, crowds, onlookers, mixed gender	Attribution of honor, local popularity, impact beyond the private; sometimes scorned by elite	Local cults, unofficial religious figures, popular festivals, crowds of worshippers	Varies, but generally daytime	Homes: atria and peristyles; Cities: theatres, basilicas, fora, roads, macella, temples
Public—Political-local	The polis; organized human society (male); city government within the Roman empire	Local political officials relating with citizens, political peers and superiors and friends who help in public matters	Attribution of honor, speech for persuasion and conflict daily city life, minor political functions; determined by scale	City shrines and patron deities	Mostly daytime	Cities, theatres, courts, fora, basilicas, bouleteria, official residences

The force of place (and nature) comes into play at the very beginning of the pericope with the mention of Jericho. Luke casts this scene as Jesus *approaches* Jericho, bringing the public sphere into play by associating the entire episode with a city. At the same time, this is a local scene that stays within the bounds of Jericho and its environs. The mention of a city could bring in a local political coloring with the force of nature.[134] However, Luke does not mention any political officials, places, or systems in association with Jericho at this point, leaving the audience with a distinctly *unofficial* public event (unlike the entrance into Jerusalem). The force of place continues to influence the scene, when Luke describes a blind beggar sitting on the side of the road near the entrance to Jericho. Roads are typical unofficial public locations. This road would have been heavily traveled by those entering and exiting the city, and Luke employs it as a public setting for the business of begging.[135]

The force of meaning (and religion) also emerges with the characterization of the beggar. Evidence from the Greco-Roman world (especially Rome) revealed a standard set of characteristics that were culturally associated with beggars, particularly their public

---

134. This is especially true of a city like Jericho with its military and political history, which will be discussed in the next chapter.
135. This roadside setting is unofficial for no laws or government agents come into play. Similarly, ancient evidence about beggars makes no mention about political agents or official intervention among beggars (as we might see today).

The Healing of the Blind Beggar (18:35–43)

presence and shameful behavior. The force of meaning intensifies the interaction of the blind beggar and the crowd as the dishonorable public arena of the beggar collides with the honorable public procession surrounding Jesus. The surprising and somewhat hostile interaction between the blind beggar and the crowd intensifies the public nature of the scene.[136] At least some part of the honor-conscious crowd scorns the blind beggar's attempt to summon Jesus, reflecting the public concern with honor and status under the force of meaning in the unofficial public sphere. Then, the blind man's request functions as a positive honor challenge to Jesus in this public setting. The crowd and the blind beggar both publicly apply titles to Jesus that are loaded with cultural significance (the force of meaning). When the crowd identifies Jesus as "the Nazorean," they specify him as the Jesus who is famous for his ministry of public miracles. When the blind man calls to Jesus as the "Son of David," he brings in the forces of meaning and religion. This appellation recalls the royal authority and divine authorization associated with King David. However, the low status of the blind beggar highlights the fact that Jesus is an *unofficial* religious figure. He receives no official sanction for this title (the Pharisees object to a similar acclamation when Jesus enters Jerusalem), and he is differentiated from Solomon by welcoming this poor blind man. Finally, in this passage and throughout Luke, Jesus implicitly accepts the honors of royal status but acts politically in the way he exercises power locally among his followers and the surrounding crowd.

The force of social relations dovetails with the force of meaning, for the cultural status of the characters (beggar and crowd) overlaps with their social functions. The prominence of the crowd in Luke's version of the story brings the force of social relations to the fore in establishing the unofficial public nature of this event. Luke emphasizes the role of the crowd by giving them the status of a secondary character as the beginning of the story and reiterating their amazement as witnesses to this public event at the end of the story.[137] The change from ὄχλος (v. 36) to λαός[138] (v. 43) calls up the variety of public roles that the crowd has in Luke's Gospel, and prepares the audience for the fickle public actions of the crowd in the passion. The role of the crowd also adduces the ironic political implications of this story, for Jesus must *order* the "leaders" of his movement in the crowd to "lead" the blind man to him. Here, Jesus orders his subordinates just as other political officials give orders in Acts. This also helps to clarify the identity of the οἱ προάγοντες within the crowd as leaders in Jesus' movement, implying a developing power structure among Jesus' followers and his authority over it. This implies local politics, for Jesus only exercises this power among his followers. Therefore, the forces of place (and nature), meaning and religion, social relations, and time all work together to create a thick portrayal of Jesus who heals the blind beggar in an unofficial public setting and acts in ways that imply local political authority.

---

136. This may also draw in the force of time, implying the daytime setting and dramatically adding to the public nature of the event.

137. Additionally, the force of time may come into play when Jesus halts the procession to heed the blind beggar's call.

138. The use of λαός may also bring in the force of religion given Luke's preference for using this term to refer to the *Jewish* people in accordance with its usage in the LXX.

PART TWO: SOCIAL-SPATIAL EXEGESIS OF LUKE 18:35—19:48

The import of this passage extends beyond its public nature and local political implications. Chapter 9 will demonstrate that this pericope functions as a microcosm of previous miracle stories in the Gospel: summing up the healing and exorcisms and climaxing them with the healing of a blind person. Building on the importance of the urban roadside, the characterization of the blind beggar, and the presence of a crowd, chapter 9 will explore how the elements of locations, characters, and crowds appear throughout Luke's miracle stories to make them public events. Furthermore, other miracles in Luke's Gospel contain political implications regarding Jesus' authority over spirits and his own followers, as well as the nature of the movement that developed around him. Chapter 10 will consider some of the historical and contemporary implications of the public and local political character of Luke's portrayal of Jesus in 18:35–43. This passage may cast some light on the historical circumstances of Luke's context and community. First, the title employed by the crowd, "Jesus the Nazorean," appears several times in Luke and Acts where it assumes that the general public knows about the ministry of Jesus. This may imply that certain elements of the life and death of Jesus were common knowledge to the general (non-Christian) public in Luke's context. Second, identifying the οἱ πρόγοντες as leaders within Jesus' movement may reflect the development of political organization or hierarchy in Luke's Christian community. Finally, this passage raises comparisons with the contemporary functions of roads. While being public (in terms of publicly accessible), roads today actually discourage public interaction to provide specific space for travel. Are there contemporary places of travel that do or could function as places where Christian acts of power and politics (both in a positive sense) might foster public interaction?

Jesus' journeying in Jericho is not finished for Luke. In 19:1–10, Jesus meets another person along the road, Zacchaeus, and ignites public conflict by accepting his hospitality.

6

Jesus Meets Zacchaeus (19:1–10)

City and House as Public Settings for Conflict and Salvation

Introduction

AFTER JESUS HEALS THE BLIND BEGGAR, HE ARRIVES IN JERICHO AND BEGINS TO PROCEED through the city when he meets Zacchaeus in a tree looking over the crowd. A few public elements already stand out: the city, Jesus' procession, and the crowd. The story opens with conflict between Zacchaeus and the crowd in the city. The potential for conflict and salvation increases when Jesus meets Zacchaeus and accepts his hospitality. The conflict intensifies when "everyone" complains about Jesus' choice of hosts. However, Jesus' encounter with Zacchaeus initiates a process of salvation that culminates with Jesus' public pronouncements at the end of the story. The conflict and salvation begin publicly in the streets of the city, but Luke seamlessly shifts the scene to Zacchaeus's home, which becomes a public setting for the resolution of the conflict and the climax of salvation. This chapter will open with a review of the previous interpretation of 19:1–10 that demonstrates how this story summarizes several important themes in Luke's Gospel, especially the topics of conflict and salvation and the places of city and house. The social-spatial exegesis of this passage will show how Luke brings out the public and local political characteristics of Jesus' encounter with Zacchaeus in the city and in a home.

A Brief Review of Previous Interpretation

This appealing and memorable vignette is unique to Luke and reprises many of Luke's prominent themes. Therefore, unlike the healing of the blind beggar, Luke's story about Jesus meeting Zacchaeus has been broadly and deeply probed by many interpreters. This review will cover two recurring elements in the interpretation of this passage: the Zacchaeus story as an epitome of Luke's Gospel and the identification of the literary form of this pericope.[1]

---

1. Three other elements appear in many interpretations of this story. First, the debate over the nature of Zacchaeus's statement (defense vs. resolve) will be considered in the course of the social-spatial analysis below. Second, Zacchaeus also appears in discussions of "tax collectors" in Luke (and the synoptics). These are important studies for the discussion below; however, they are focused topically on taxes and tax collectors rather than on the meaning of this particular pericope, so they will not be examined here. Third, the mention of "the Son of man" (v. 10) often comes up in thematic studies of that title, but like the material on tax collectors, most of these studies do not focus on its import for this particular story.

PART TWO: SOCIAL-SPATIAL EXEGESIS OF LUKE 18:35—19:48

The story of Zacchaeus sounds several important themes in Luke's Gospel. This fact, intensified by its placement near the end of the travel narrative, has led many scholars to see this story as an epitome of Luke's Gospel of salvation for the outcast. Marshall claims that it is the "supreme example of the universality of the Gospel offer" in Luke, an offer that is accentuated by Jesus' initiative.[2] Bovon emphasizes the placement of the story at the end of the travel narrative in a section that has been labeled "the Gospel of the outcast," and he points out that several Lukan themes come together in this one story (the journey, wealth, seeing, the reversal of values, the day of salvation, and the mission of Jesus).[3] For Green, this story is a paradoxical and surprising illustration of "good news for the poor," where Luke eschews all status stereotypes and includes a rich toll collector in Jesus' mission.[4]

Loewe claims that the encounter between Jesus and Zacchaeus "does seem to condense much that is peculiarly characteristic of Lk."[5] He focuses on Luke's vocabulary in this story to display the redactional touches, and then turns to thematic considerations, paying special attention to connections with the infancy narrative. He concludes by claiming that this pericope climactically sums up five major themes in Luke's Gospel.[6] O'Hanlon proceeds similarly, documenting the Lukan vocabulary, style, and theology of the story. Based on this and the placement of the story at the end of the travel narrative, he asserts that this pericope "is a fitting summation of many of the themes" of Luke's Gospel.[7] Two later articles in Spanish continue this same stream of investigation. Molinà begins by analyzing the Lukan vocabulary and redaction of this story and then places it in its literary and theological context at the end of the travel narrative.[8] From here he proceeds lexically, examining some of the key words in this vignette in the light of Luke's Gospel as a whole (πλούσιος, δεῖ, σήμερον, σωτηρία, ἀπολωλός).[9] A later article by Nuñez begins with a similar literary analysis but then moves into the semiotic and ethical dimensions of the story.[10] Lastly, Paul Kariamadam has published a monograph on 19:1–10, which is an excerpt from his longer dissertation on the end of the travel narrative. Kariamadam demonstrates the characteristically Lukan vocabulary and style of this passage, claiming that

---

2. Marshall, *Luke*, 694.

3. Bovon, *Saint Luc*, 3c:234.

4. Green, *Luke*, 667. Green, however, goes on to support this by claiming that Zacchaeus defends his regular beneficent actions (rather than pledging a new course of action), a position with which I will disagree.

5. Loewe, "Towards," 321.

6. The five themes are Jesus as the manifestation of divine power, mercy unto forgiveness, the fulfillment of the promises to Abraham, the reversal of expectations, and Jesus as the cause of division (ibid., 330–31). In mild criticism of Loewe, I would say that some of the themes he highlights are not characteristic of Luke as a whole (e.g., the promises to Abraham, found rarely in the Gospel) and that others are so broad (e.g. Jesus as the manifestation of divine power) as to be able to cover almost anything in any of the Gospels.

7. O'Hanlon, "Zacchaeus," 9–10. However, unlike Loewe's emphasis on the infancy narratives, O'Hanlon attends to special connections with the sermon on the plain. He concludes that, while there are shared topics (especially regarding the poor and the use of wealth), the themes of the Zacchaeus story are found throughout the Gospel and even in Acts.

8. Molinà, "Zaqueo."

9. Ibid., 23–46.

10. Nuñez, "Zaqueo."

Luke has thoroughly reworked an oral tradition.[11] He concludes that this story features Zacchaeus's conversion and renunciation, two themes that run through the entire Gospel.[12] Finally, by setting the story of Zacchaeus next to that of the blind beggar, he explores how these two stories reveal Jesus' mission to offer salvation to the lost.[13]

The present study resonates with these analyses, affirming that this pericope is a microcosm of previous material in the Gospel. The following analysis will focus on the literary connections to the preceding content of the Gospel with more specific attention to the spatial settings (a city and a house) and a clearer understanding of the form of the story (see below). While these previous studies have probed the literary connections thoroughly, none of them has attended to the spatiality of the story or its public nature. Attention to these will open up new connections to previous material in Luke's Gospel.

Other interpreters have concentrated on the literary form of Luke 19:1–10. In his magisterial study of the Synoptic tradition, Bultmann classifies this story as a biographical apophthegm because of the "legendary" nature of the story and the fact that a saying of Jesus closes the pericope.[14] Dibelius calls it a personal legend because of the colorful details (e.g., Zacchaeus's height), and Taylor considers it a "story about Jesus" moving emphasis from the words to the drama of the tale.[15] Talbert regards it as a conflict story, seeing a precedent in Luke 5:27–32.[16] Culpepper claims that it has the form of a miracle story.[17] Finally, Tannehill, with later endorsement from O'Toole, identifies Jesus' meeting with Zacchaeus as a quest story, a particular form of the pronouncement story.[18] The quest story portrays a person, generally an outcast, seeking out Jesus to meet a critical human need. Tannehill points out that these are common in Luke and that four of the nine Synoptic quest stories are unique to Luke, such as the episode with Zacchaeus.[19]

The story of Jesus' encounter with Zacchaeus appears to be an amalgam, containing the characteristics and themes of a variety of different forms.[20] This pericope draws together conflict, quest, pronouncement, and salvation into a story set initially in the city

---

11. Kariamadam, *Zacchaeus*, 53.
12. Ibid., 57–58.
13. Ibid., 73. See further below.
14. Bultmann, *Synoptic Tradition*, 55–57.
15. Dibelius, *From Tradition*, 50–51, 118; and Taylor, *Gospel Tradition*, 75–76.
16. Talbert, *Reading Luke*, 176–77.
17. Culpepper, *Luke*, 9:357. However, Culpepper seems to draw this conclusion from the content of the story ("the power of God at work", an accurate observation) rather than its formal characteristics. The best connection between the Zacchaeus pericope and the miracle stories in Luke's Gospel is the use of σώζω, which will be discussed below.
18. Tannehill, *Narrative Unity*, 122–25; and "Story of Zacchaeus," 205–6. Also see the more focused examination of this discussion by O'Toole, "Literary Form." The quest stories in Luke are the healing of the paralytic (5:17–26), the healing of the centurion's servant (7:2–10), the "sinful" woman (7:36–50), the healing of the Samaritan leper (17:12–19), the rich ruler (18:18–25), Zacchaeus (19:1–10), and the criminal crucified next to Jesus (23:39–43).
19. Tannehill, *Narrative Unity*, 111–12.
20. Bovon, *Saint Luc*, 3c:237. Yet, I do have more skepticism than he does about the possibility of reconstructing the tradition history of the story in order to determine its genre.

and then in Zacchaeus's own home. Tannehill's "quest story" provides the best framework for such an amalgamation. Many quest stories recount dramatic conflict (5:20–22; 7:38–40; 23:39–40) comparable to the conflict Zacchaeus faces in the objections of the crowd as he "quests" to see Jesus.[21] Three of the other conflict stories in Luke also speak explicitly of salvation (7:50; 17:19; 23:39) and three more contain the concept if not the term.[22] This is also seen in the emphasis on salvation in the pronouncements of 19:9–10. Therefore, the story about Zacchaeus, like many other quest stories, tells a tale of conflict and salvation. Three of the Lukan quest stories appear early in Jesus' ministry (chs. 5–7) and three at the end (chs. 17–19), emphasizing their importance in Luke's portrayal of Jesus.[23] This places Zacchaeus in a climactic position that can serve as a microcosm of the previous five stories and a preparation for the final quest story in the passion.

Most of Tannehill's quest stories also take place in public settings. The healing of the paralytic occurs in a house (5:19) taken over by a crowd from the surrounding cities (5:17). The healing of the centurion's slave transpires in the presence of the Jewish elders and a crowd (7:3, 9). Then, the elders return to the house (7:10) to find the slave well. The woman from the *city* (7:37) enters Simon's house (7:36) making it a public event. The healing of the ten lepers occurs as Jesus enters a village (17:11–19). Jesus' encounter with the rich ruler (18:18–25) takes place immediately after he is surrounded by children and is overheard by bystanders (18:26). Finally, Jesus' dialogue with the crucified criminal occurs at their public execution (23:39–43). Furthermore, both cities and villages function as public venues. Several conflict and quest stories in Luke's Gospel take place in homes (5:17–26, 29–32; 7:36–50; 11:37–52; 14:1–24), or they stretch across both city and house much like 19:1–10 (7:1–10; see also 7:36–37; 8:39; 9:4–5; and 10:5–11 where Luke adds material about cities). Therefore, Luke 19:1–10 tells a story of conflict and salvation that stretches across both city and house. The social-spatial exegesis of 19:1–10 will show how Luke employs both city and house as settings for the public interaction between Jesus, Zacchaeus, and the crowd.

The Social-Spatial Characteristics of 19:1–10

Jesus' encounter with Zacchaeus illustrates the public and political character of Luke's portrayal of Jesus in the following ways. First, the parallels between Zacchaeus and the blind beggar reiterate the intertwining of conflict and salvation in the presence of the crowd and create one extended public event that occurs in Jericho. Second, Jericho's history of political, military, and economic importance sets an apt stage for an event with public

---

21. Tannehill, *Narrative Unity*, 111; O'Toole, "Literary Form," 108. One could also say that the centurion and the lepers faced obstacles (social and/or religious status), if not outright conflict, that kept them from Jesus in some way. This would be similar to the obstructing role of the crowd in 19:3.

22. Tannehill, *Narrative Unity*, 112. The rich ruler asks about "eternal life," which is analogous to salvation. While the terms for "salvation" do not appear in the healing of the paralytic or the centurion's slave, their restoration falls under Luke's larger understanding of the significance of salvation (Marshall, *Historian & Theologian*, 95–96).

23. Tannehill, *Narrative Unity*, 118. Also, as the last quest story of Jesus' public ministry, the episode with Zacchaeus prepares for the final quest story in 23:39–43.

characteristics and political overtones (19:1). Third, the characterization of Zacchaeus displays his prominent but liminal position: he is Jewish with connections to the Romans, an unofficial businessman with political links (19:2). Fourth, Luke begins his story of the public interaction of Jesus, Zacchaeus, and the crowd in the city as Jesus encounters Zacchaeus in the midst of a crowded procession (19:3–6a). Fifth and finally, the public story of conflict and salvation invades Zacchaeus's home. Zacchaeus offers hospitality to Jesus, and the resulting objection from the crowd is met with public pronouncements by both Zacchaeus and Jesus.

Zacchaeus and the Blind Beggar

Social and spatial elements bind these two stories together in Luke's Gospel. Geography connects them from the very beginning: both stories open with a reference to Jericho and both speak of Jesus traveling on a road (18:35; 19:1). Both stories display public settings of conflict and salvation: the blind beggar confronts Jesus' entourage (18:39–40); Jesus and Zacchaeus must respond to the accusations of "everyone" watching (19:7). Both men face conflict because of their outsider status: one for his poverty and disability and one for his greed and wealth. Despite the obstacles they face, both stories climax when Jesus announces "salvation" to these social outcasts (σώζω in 18:42 and σωτηρία in 19:9). Many scholars note that Luke conjoins the blind beggar and Zacchaeus in complementary ways. Johnson points out that each story offers an answer to the question, "Who then can be saved?" (18:26).[24] These two characters are both foils to the rich ruler in 18:18–23: the blind beggar is the paradigm of one who is free to follow Jesus because he has no wealth whereas Zacchaeus dispenses his wealth properly and receives salvation even though he is rich. Further comparisons and contrasts reveal the tight interaction between these stories set up by their geographical association. The following chart lists several well-established connections.[25]

---

24. Johnson, *Luke*, 286–87.
25. Meynet, *Saint Luc*, 2:187; and Paul, "La guérison," 57–58. See also Kariamadam, *Zacchaeus*, 62–64.

PART TWO: SOCIAL-SPATIAL EXEGESIS OF LUKE 18:35—19:48

Table 6.1: Comparison of Luke 18:35–43 and Luke 19:1–10

Luke 18:35–43	Luke 19:1–10
1. Jesus is near Jericho (18:35)	1. Jesus is in Jericho (19:1)
2. The blind beggar cannot see Jesus (18:35)	2. Zacchaeus cannot see Jesus (19:3)[26]
3. He asks about Jesus (18:36)	3. He runs ahead to find Jesus (19:4)
4. Jesus passes by (παρέρξεται, 18:37)	4. Jesus passes through (διέρξεσθαι, 19:4)
5. Some rebuke the blind beggar (18:39)	5. Crowd murmurs about Zacchaeus (19:7)
6. The beggar perseveres despite opposition (18:39)	6. Zacchaeus perseveres despite opposition (19:8)
7. Jesus is the Son of David (18:37)	7. Jesus is the Son of Man (19:10)[27]
8. The blind man is healed (σέσωκεν, 18:42)	8. Zacchaeus receives salvation (σωτηρία, 19:9)

Some additional observations build on these insights and clarify the narrative impact of the juxtaposition of these two stories. First, in both cases a physical limitation prevents the character from seeing Jesus (blindness and shortness, respectively). Nonetheless, each one somehow recognizes the significance of Jesus' arrival (unlike the leaders and residents of Jerusalem who have no such physical limitations, cf. 19:41–44). The blind man actively seeks Jesus' attention and asks Jesus to heal him. Zacchaeus is more passive. He only intends to catch a glimpse of Jesus; it is Jesus who initiates contact with Zacchaeus and invites himself to Zacchaeus's home. Thus, both those who approach Jesus and those whom Jesus approaches can receive salvation. The crowd opposes both men and judges both to be dishonorable despite their radically different socio-economic positions. Finally, the presence of the crowd in both stories highlights their public nature, and both men make public declarations before the crowd. The conjunction of the two stories implies a series of public moments in temporal succession as Jesus traveled into Jericho. This extended public event stretches from a road outside of the city, to a passage through the city, and finally into Zacchaeus's house.

The literary connections between these two stories emphasize the role of several forces in creating a public event. The dual mention of Jericho draws upon the force of place to reinforce the urban and public setting of both stories. The parallels between the blind beggar and Zacchaeus as well as the reiteration of the presence of the crowd employ the force of social relations to depict a public scene with public characters. Finally, the literary and narrative connections of the two stories adduce the force of time as Luke tells of one

---

26. Luke drops the name (or at least the patronymn) of the blind beggar from Mark 10:46 and adds a different named character in 19:2. Thus, Zacchaeus, the second of the two figures and the only one given a name, is perhaps the more important of the two in Luke's arrangement.

27. Robbins explains that Mark may have located this story at this point in his narrative in order to connect the suffering Son of Man (in 10:33–34, 45) with the triumphant Son of David (10:47–48; 11:10) ("Blind Bartimaeus," 225–26). The same connection carries over into Luke's order as well with some shift in emphasis. Luke omits the story about James and John in Mark 10:35–45 that specifically associates the Son of Man with suffering. Instead, Luke reiterates the Son of Man title in 19:10 but now in reference to his salvific mission.

The Social-Spatial Connotations of Jericho

Luke names Jericho in 18:35 and 19:1, and this double specification of Jesus' location stands in contrast to the generalized geographical reports in the rest of the travel narrative, which never locate Jesus in a specific city. So, why does Luke specify this city at this point in the story and what might it mean for Jesus to "enter and pass through" this particular city? From the setting of the good Samaritan (10:29–35), Luke's audience knows that Jericho is near Jerusalem and that a well-traveled route connects the two cities. Given that a priest and a Levite were traveling from Jerusalem to Jericho (10:31 and 32), one might conclude that Jericho is a major urban center with connections to the temple and its hierarchy in Jerusalem. For more insight into the status of this city, one must turn to other sources.

Jericho had an abundant water supply and a tropical climate making it a prosperous agricultural center.[28] It was an important stop (with an oasis) on the east-west route from lands beyond the Jordan into Palestine.[29] Additionally, Jericho was well known as the winter resort for Jerusalem's aristocracy.[30] Josephus confirms these points (see *J.W.* 4.459–75) and adds other insights. Jericho was one of the cities fortified by Bacchides in Judea (*Ant.* 13.15 and 1 Macc 9:50), and Josephus tells of many battles taking place there (*J.W.* 1.120, 297, 323, etc.). Later, Jericho was the headquarters for one of the five administrative districts set up by Alexander, son of Aristobulus (*Ant.* 14.91, *J.W.* 1.167), and it remained an administrative and military center (*J.W.* 2.567; 3.55) even when the Romans controlled the area (*J.W.* 4.486; 5.67). Thus, Jericho had a history of being a significant military and political center. Herod the Great had built three grand palace complexes in Roman-era Jericho (which was different from the earlier location of the city) as well as a theatre and a racing track.[31] Josephus tells us that before his death, Herod gathered a large number of "leading" Jews in Jericho's hippodrome, ordering that they be killed upon his own death so that mourning would follow (*J.W.* 1.659–60). After his death, Salome and Alexas mercifully dismissed these leaders and made Herod's death public (ἐφανεροῦτο) by summoning the soldiers to the theatre and announcing it to them there (*Ant.* 17.193–95).

Jericho had the potential to be rich with public and political connotations that bear on the story through the force of place. Luke knew Jericho as an important urban center linked with Jerusalem and temple officials. It was a seat of regional government, and the winter home of many in the local political system. Both the Jews and Romans used it as an administrative center, and military campaigns often sought to capture Jericho as a point of regional control. This history might have implied official overtones to Luke and his audience. Herod's winter palaces added a royal element to the city, which contributes a very subtle note to the royal theme found through most of 18:35—19:48 (note that this would

---

28. DeVries, *Cities*, 282.
29. Ibid., 282–83.
30. Netzer, "Jericho," 739.
31. Ibid., 738–39.

be the only suggestion of this theme in 19:1–10). The reputation of this city also has many unofficial public characteristics. Jericho had a long history as a hub for travel, agriculture, and trade. It had a major theatre and hippodrome complex, which hosted large public gatherings, especially associated with Herod's death according to Josephus. Therefore, as Jesus enters Jericho, Luke's audience might understand this to be a regional center of religious, economic, political, and military activity with dynamic official and unofficial public spheres. It makes a feasible setting for a "tax" collector like Zacchaeus with his lucrative business, local authority, and ties to both Jewish and Roman officials. The bustling city of Jericho with its heavy traffic makes perfect sense as an unofficial public location for Jesus to meet Zacchaeus, a man with some official connections.

The verbs in 19:1 set expectations for what Jesus will do in the city. Luke states that Jesus "entered and was passing through Jericho" (εἰσελθὼν διήρχετο τὴν Ἰεριχώ).[32] The main verb, διέρχομαι, can have several different connotations in Luke-Acts: to spread out, to go across, or to walk by. In this case, Jesus seems to plan to go straight through the city on his way to Jerusalem (e.g., Luke 4:30; Acts 12:10). However, εἰσελθών may signal a different intent. The most common location that is "entered" in Luke-Acts is a household (Luke 1:40; 4:38; 7:36; Acts 9:12; 16:15; et al.). In several cases though, a person or persons "enters" a city (or village) as Jesus enters Jericho in 19:1.[33] In most of these passages, the entrance into the city is followed by a reception, or expected reception, into a home.[34] For example, as soon as Jesus "enters" the village in 10:38, he is welcomed into Martha's home. Similarly, Peter arrives in Caesarea only to be found immediately in Cornelius's home (Acts 10:24). When Paul and his companions "enter" Caesarea, they go straight to the house of Philip the evangelist and stay with him (Acts 21:8). Thus, in Luke-Acts, when a character enters a city, the audience can presume that hospitality in a home will follow. This naturally raises the expectant question: who might welcome Jesus in Jericho? The answer to this question appears in v. 2.

The Characterization of Zacchaeus

In v. 2, Luke introduces the unlikely character who will welcome Jesus into his home. We are told four things about this person: he is a man, his name is Zacchaeus, he is a "leading tax collector" (ἀρχιτελώνης), and he is rich (πλούσιος).[35] The fact that he is a man is not surprising, and, while Luke does not often name secondary characters in his stories about

---

32. This construction probably indicates that Jesus had already entered Jericho (prior time temporal participle) and was currently passing through the city (progressive imperfect) when the following narrated events took place.

33. Luke 7:1; 9:52; 10:8, 10, 38; 17:12; 22:10; Acts 9:6, 10:24, 14:20, 21:8, 28:16.

34. The only exceptions to this are Luke 17:12 and Acts 14:20.

35. Green asserts that there are four characteristics here also. Zacchaeus "is a Jew, a ruler, a toll collector, and wealthy" (*Luke*, 668). He does not see it necessary to specify his gender, and I would disagree with the way that he separates the term ἀρχιτελώνης into two separate categories. By doing so, he locates Zacchaeus in the official public sphere. He sees Zacchaeus as a "ruler" in the Greco-Roman world and compares this label to the use of ἄρχων for a "magistrate" in Luke 12:58. Zacchaeus is a "leading" figure, but I will claim that he is a "leading" businessman, not a politician.

Jesus Meets Zacchaeus (19:1–10)

Jesus,[36] the name does not seem to have any special significance beyond the fact that it is clearly Jewish.[37] That leaves two labels: ἀρχιτελώνης and πλούσιος. These two terms are the best evidence available to understand Zacchaeus's public status and whether or not he was a political official.

Luke ends his description of Zacchaeus with the adjective πλούσιος, perhaps for emphasis as the story develops. Luke's Gospel has several "rich" characters:[38] the centurion (7:1–10), two landowners (12:16 and 16:1), the rich man (16:19ff), and the rich ruler (18:18–30). Several more appear in Acts: Barnabas, Cornelius, Herod, Lydia, Felix, and Festus. All of these rich characters have a public persona, while some are official and some unofficial. They are wealthy and influential citizens, military commanders, holders of political positions, and community leaders. In Luke-Acts, "wealthy" is largely a negative description, but not always so. The pejorative power of this term is best summed up in Luke's version of the beatitudes: "Woe to you who are rich [πλούσιος], for you have received your consolation" (6:24). However, Luke's portrayal of the rich is not monolithic.[39] The rich landowner in the parable of the shrewd steward is not chastised in any way, and instead comes across rather favorably (see 16:1ff).[40] The centurion of Luke 7 and Cornelius were wealthy men (given their public benefactions) and righteous as well. Luke's depiction of charitable giving in the early church is another good example. Barnabas has enough wealth to sell a piece of property and offer it publicly to the apostles for the church's use (Acts 4:36–37). Barnabas goes on to become a leading character in Acts, while Ananias and Sapphira, who also have disposable wealth, are struck down.[41] Having wealth is not the problem for Luke. What matters is whether or not you use that wealth in just and compassionate ways.[42]

---

36. There are a number of unnamed characters: the paralyzed man of ch. 5, the widow of Nain, the crippled woman. However, Luke does name Simon the Pharisee, Jairus, and Lazarus, so it is not uncharacteristic of Luke to name Zacchaeus.

37. "Zacchaeus" is the Grecized form of the Hebrew name Zakkai, which means "clean, innocent." I agree with Bovon who points out that here, as elsewhere, Luke does not attend to the etymology of names (*Saint Luc*, 3c:239).

38. Not all of these characters are explicitly labelled πλούσιος, but their description or status would mark them as rich in Luke's cultural context.

39. The term is used with positive overtones outside of Luke: Josephus, *J.W.* 1.61; Diodorus Siculus, *Library* 13.83.1; Cicero, *Planc.* 86. Various good characters in the LXX and Apocrypha were "rich" as well: Abraham (Gen 13:2), Tobit, and Judith.

40. See Scott, "Master's Praise," 184, 187–88.

41. Gillman notes the contrast set up between Barnabas and Ananias and Sapphira as well as between Barnabas and the man too preoccupied with his "field" to accept the invitation to the master's banquet (Luke 14:18). Barnabas "puts the needs of the community above preoccupations with holding onto personal possessions: (*Possessions*, 97–98). Interestingly, Gillman does not consider the examples of the centurion or Cornelius. Their disposition to their possession is an important part of their characterization (e.g., Acts 10:2). Johnson, also, does not comment directly on how wealth plays into the positive portrayal of the centurion, Barnabas, or Cornelius (*Literary Function*, 97, 203–4).

42. Gillman, *Possessions*, 109–11.

PART TWO: SOCIAL-SPATIAL EXEGESIS OF LUKE 18:35—19:48

Being wealthy would have placed Zacchaeus in the small minority at the top of the social hierarchy.[43] While the adjective πλούσιος might have cast a suspicious shadow over Zacchaeus's character for Luke's audience, it does not completely determine the public honor attached to his social position: the rich could be despised for their greed and dishonesty[44] (as Zacchaeus might have been by the crowd) or deemed worthy of their wealth as a blessing from God (as with the rich ruler of ch. 18).[45] The rich ruler is a recognized member of the honored Jewish elite, while Zacchaeus (also rich) is despised by his fellow citizens. Two factors in Luke's narrative cast Zacchaeus in a good light. First, many characters who approach Jesus in the Gospel (other than the Pharisees) are healed/blessed/honored by Jesus (e.g., the leper, the centurion, the sinful woman, the blind beggar). Second, Luke's audience knows that other τελῶναι have responded rightly to Jesus (5:27-32; 7:29). Luke presents some rich persons as corrupt and greedy (12:13-21; 16:19-31), but other rich persons are characterized positively in the narrative (the centurion, Barnabas). Thus, calling Zacchaeus "rich" evokes a complex set of strong, but potentially very different, connotations.

The rich ruler in 18:18-30 is a critical precursor for the interpretation of Luke's portrayal of Zacchaeus.[46] Both stories use some element of ἄρχων and πλούσιος to describe the person encountering Jesus, but the "ruler" of ch. 18 is most likely a respected local official in the Jewish community,[47] while Zacchaeus is marginalized from his community (c.f. 19:7) and not an official leader in it (see below). Furthermore, their encounters with Jesus have opposite results. The story of the rich ruler is a tragedy—while portrayed positively (18:18-22) and apparently respected by the crowd (18:26), in the end he cannot enter the kingdom because he cannot release his wealth (18:23). The disciples seem to be shocked that this, or any, rich man would not enter the kingdom, presuming that the man was publicly honored as one blessed by God (18:26). Zacchaeus, in contrast to the rich ruler, has nothing going for him: he cannot see Jesus, he is publicly called a "sinner," he does not know what to say to Jesus, and yet God overcomes Zacchaeus's attachment to his wealth and he receives salvation (compare 18:26 and 19:9). The contrast between these two figures could imply that Zacchaeus was not a political figure, unlike the official status of the rich *ruler*. Concluding the tragic story of the rich ruler with Jesus' assertion that "everything is possible with God [even the salvation of the wealthy]!" might have prepared the audience to hope for a better resolution in Jesus' interaction with the next

---

43. MacMullen, *Roman Social Relations*, 88-92.

44. The free, landed elite of the Roman world despised upstart merchants (who were often freedmen) who became rich. The classic example is Petronius's Trimalchio. See also Garnsey and Saller, *Roman Empire*, 44-45. Green emphasizes this perspective in his comments (*Luke*, 668-69), but again we must remember that it is how one uses wealth, not wealth itself, that often impacts public opinion. Jesus may have precisely been overturning this "elite bias" in his interaction with tax collectors. See Schottroff and Stegemann, *Jesus*, 13.

45. Several passages in the LXX state that wealth is a blessing given by God for obedience: Deut 28:1-14; Job 42:10-17; Prov 10:22, etc. Of course, the portrayal of the wealthy is complex. Sirach perhaps puts it best when he states that the "blameless" rich man (not the greedy one) is most blessed (Sir 31:1-11).

46. Green, *Luke*, 666-67; Fitzmyer, *Luke*, 2:1222; Johnson, *Luke*, 287.

47. Green describes him as a high-status leader in the religious community, like the synagogue ruler of 13:14 (*Luke*, 654). Bock states that he was a representative of the wealthy lay leadership (*Luke*, 299).

rich "leader," Zacchaeus. Because Luke's portrayal of the rich is complex and broad,[48] we must look further to understand Zacchaeus's social-spatial place in Luke's narrative and in the eyes of Luke's audience.

Unfortunately, when we turn to the title ἀρχιτελώνης for more information, we run into a wall of obscurity. This term never appears prior to Luke's Gospel, and after Luke's Gospel it is almost exclusively found in Greek works commenting on this unique Lukan story. However, excellent studies have more generally illuminated the role and status of "tax" collectors in Palestine during the time of Jesus.[49] Two conclusions from this research must be rehearsed before moving forward. First, the τελῶναι of the Synoptics were not "tax" collectors in the sense that they collected population or agricultural taxes as local political officials in the Roman bureaucracy. These direct taxes were typically assessed and collected by Roman officials (censors, procurators, or their charges). Rather, the τελῶναι of the Gospels were minor "toll" collectors, employees of city administrations or businessmen who exacted indirect taxes: customs duties at ports, boundaries, and markets throughout the empire.[50] Thus, the τελῶναι of the Synoptics were not Roman officials. This would place them outside of the official public sphere. They were also not "publicans," the elite Romans who ran large tax farming corporations that disappeared by the end of the second century.[51] Second, these toll collectors were generally despised throughout the ancient world for their greed and dishonesty.[52] In Rabbinic literature, toll collectors are compared to thieves because of their financial misconduct; they do not appear to have been hated because of some purported connection to the Romans that was tantamount to treason.[53] This overview of τελῶναι implies that Zacchaeus is outside of the official public sphere and that he would have been hated for his deceitfulness and greed. However, Zacchaeus's public and official status is complicated by the addition of the prefix ἀρχι- to his title. What might the title ἀρχιτελώνης imply about Zacchaeus's public and political status to Luke's audience? Before answering that question we must add two qualifications.

First, history records several exceptions to the general animosity leveled at tax collectors. Rabbinic literature mentions both *gabba'in* (tax collectors) and *mokhsin* (toll collectors). Donahue concludes (with some appropriate reservations) that the *gabba'in*

---

48. Zacchaeus does not overturn a staunch, stereotypical presentation of the wickedly rich (contrast with the claims of Green, *Luke*, 667); rather, he is one more example of the amazing power of God at work in the person of Jesus, bringing salvation to unlikely people (including the wealthy) and unlikely people to salvation.

49. Donahue, "Tax Collectors"; Michel, "τελώνης"; Badian, *Publicans*; Walker, "Tax Collectors"; Schottroff and Stegemann, *Jesus*, 7–13; Herrenbrück, *Jesus*.

50. Badian, *Publicans*, 11–12; Donahue, "Tax Collectors," 48–49; Herrenbrück paints a very complex picture of the terminology involved in designating various officials involved in ancient tax systems (101–3), but he also agrees that the synoptic τελῶναι were minor hirelings in the Hellenistic tax bureaucracy (*Jesus*, 291–92).

51. Garnsey and Saller, *Roman Empire*, 21, 87–88; Malmendier, "Roman Shares," 33.

52. Michel, "τελώνης," 8:101–2; Donahue, "Tax Collectors," 52–53; Schottroff and Stegeman, *Jesus*, 11–13.

53. Donahue, "Tax Collectors," 53, 59.

collected direct taxes and were generally officials in the Roman administration, while the *mokhsin* were minor employees renown for their deceitfulness.[54] Herrenbrück paints a more complex picture of the two terms, showing that they were applied to a variety of different political officials as well as minor employees.[55] Nevertheless, while the evaluation of the *mokhsin* (and the less common *gabba'in*) was largely negative, one must be very careful to differentiate various layers in the rabbinic traditions and recall that these documents are shaped by an ideological interpretation of the past.[56] The complexity can be seen in *b. Sanh.* 25b. At the beginning of this section, both tax collectors (*gabba'in*) and toll collectors (*mokhsin*) are condemned for overcharging, but then qualifications are made: *gabba'in* are permitted to serve as witnesses in official trials, and a story is told of a *gabbai* who once helped the Jews avoid some heavy taxes. Another example of a positively portrayed Jewish tax collector is John the τελώνης, a leading Jewish citizen of Caesarea, who interceded with the obstinate procurator, Florus, to restore some dignity to the synagogue there (Josephus, *J.W.* 2.287, 292). John had ties to the official public sphere, possibly because of his occupation. Thus, while "tax" collectors of all varieties were widely disdained, reproach was not cast at every τελώνης without exception.

The second qualification is that we must differentiate between the situation of the historical Jesus in Palestine and the situation of Luke's audience, for they might have had dissimilar views of, experiences with, or language about tax collectors.[57] Assessing the tax situation within Palestine during the Roman era is exceedingly complex for several reasons: records are sparse and conflicting at points, different areas of Palestine were controlled by different administrations with different policies at different times, the *societates publicanorum* were disappearing around the empire, and variegated local taxation systems were being revived.[58] The situation of Luke and his audience, not the situation of the historical Jesus, will guide the social-spatial interpretation of Zacchaeus's status in this study. This leads one to attempt to understand the context of Luke's audience and what the characterization of Zacchaeus as an ἀρχιτελώνης might have meant for their social-spatial understanding of the man in a high-context world.

Herrenbrück offers an interpretation of Zacchaeus as an ἀρχιτελώνης in his recent and very thorough study on Jesus and the τελῶναι in the Synoptics. He focuses on the historical role and status of the τελῶναι, going back to the oldest strata of the Synoptic Gospels.[59] Problems with this approach for understanding Zacchaeus were noted above;

54. Ibid., 53.

55. *Jesus*, 196–98.

56. Herrenbrück, *Jesus*, 205–11.

57. Kinman, *Jesus' Entry*, 84–85. However, after making this astute observation, Kinman states that τελῶναι is the Greek equivalent for *publicani* in Latin. Thus, he implies that this Greek word would have probably meant "publicans" to Luke's audience and signaled support for or collaboration with the Roman Empire. He does not pursue other possibilities raised by the context of Luke's audience or the unusual term ἀρχιτελώνης.

58. One only needs to survey the table of contents in Herrenbrück, *Jesus*, to get a glimpse at the diversity. He generally works with two categories: the Roman system (with its direct and indirect taxes) and the varieties of Hellenistic tax systems (as found in Greece, Egypt, Palestine, etc.) (98–104).

59. Ibid., 228.

however, we must still examine Herrenbrück's comments on 19:1–10. He argues for a "hebräische" source for the story of Zacchaeus on three grounds: the tradition history allows for it, Luke does not coin words and so ἀρχιτελώνης cannot be a neologism (despite the fact that it never appears before this passage), and the best explanation for this title is that it is Luke's translation of *rav mokesh*, a term for the leading member of a tax business partnership in Mesopotamian sources.[60] Herrenbrück concludes that Zacchaeus would have been the ἄρχωνης or "first among equals" in one of the taxation organizations that were common in the Hellenistic world. There are two serious problems with his interpretation of this passage in its Lukan context. First, even if there is an Aramaic tradition behind this passage, Herrenbrück must then assume that Luke and his audience are familiar with earlier tax systems in Judea, an assumption that is far from demonstrable. Second, he must hearken back to sources from the reign of Tiglath Pilieser I, reaching back before 1000 BCE for a reference to a *rav mokesh* rather than looking for sources that are much closer chronologically and geographically to Luke's Gospel. Herrenbrück does not explore the social-spatial ramifications of his research, and while his conclusion is similar to the one offered below, his approach must be rejected from the perspective of this study.

This study proceeds on a working assumption that Ephesus serves as a useful example for the social-spatial world of Asia Minor, which is a plausible (though not provable) location for Luke and the original audience of his Gospel. Therefore, we will look to evidence from this area to evaluate the social-spatial valence of the title ἀρχιτελώνης. Herrenbrück very briefly discusses publicans in the Roman province of Asia, but limits his discussion to the situation c. 130 BCE.[61] Sources on taxation in this area during the late first to early second century CE (the era in which Luke was written) are very limited, but they do provide some useful information, especially regarding the official status of tax collectors and usages of the stem ἀρχ- in the context of tax collection (such as we have with Zacchaeus).

The official status of tax collectors was in flux in the provinces in the late first–early second century CE. As early as 44 BCE, Julius Caesar had ended the publicans' role in collecting direct taxes (population and land taxes) in Judea, and he put the collection of these direct taxes into the hands of cities, which were responsible to gather the dues and pay them to the *quaestor* of the province.[62] In general, with the decline of the republic and the rise of the empire, the *societates* were increasingly restricted and their collection activities were closely supervised[63] and assumed by imperial agents.[64] However, the indirect taxes (customs, duties, purchase taxes) were still farmed out to the *societates publicanorum* in

---

60. Ibid., 276–77.

61. Ibid., 103–4.

62. Direct and indirect taxes were collected differently. During the imperial era, cities and local rulers (like Herod) or local administrative bodies (like the Sanhedrin) most often collected the direct taxes and paid them into the imperial treasury (in imperial provinces), while indirect taxes (like tolls) were still farmed out to private business enterprises. See Magie, *Roman Rule*, 1:406–7, 2:1260; and Michel, "τελώνης," 8:96–97.

63. Laet, *Portorium*, 375–76.

64. Malmendier, "Roman Shares," 33.

the first century in Asia (and Judea).⁶⁵ The *publicani* who formed these organizations were powerful, wealthy, elite businessmen who had regular contacts with Roman officials (particularly the senate and censors). While they had and used these political ties, they were not themselves part of the Roman administration, but cooperative partners that served the needs of the Roman state. The head of a *societas* was called a *manceps* or *magister*.⁶⁶ He lived in Rome and dealt directly with the censors. The head representative of the *societas* on the ground in the provinces was called the *promagister*, who reported to the *magister* (and thus the title).⁶⁷ *Promagister* was most often translated by ἀρχώνης in Greek, which shares the lexeme ἀρχ- with Zacchaeus's title (ἀρχιτελώνης) in Luke 19:2.⁶⁸ The *societas* responsible for the collection of the indirect taxes in Asia was based in Ephesus, and the *promagister* resided in and worked from there.⁶⁹ The *societates* and their agents were despised in Ephesus and most of Asia for their abusive plundering of the province in the first century BCE.⁷⁰

Evidence confirms that the *societates* were still actively collecting indirect taxes in Asia Minor at the beginning of the first century CE;⁷¹ however, by the second century the *publicani* had disappeared in Asia, and Roman officials collected both direct and indirect taxes.⁷² During this transition, the first Roman official put into place was also known as the *promagister* (again ἀρχώνης in Greek).⁷³ This official was attached to a central office in Rome and could be a freedman of the emperor.⁷⁴ Later, by the time of Trajan, subordinate procurators were appointed over particular districts and were under the supervision of a general procurator stationed in Rome. This bureaucracy reflects a centralizing tendency that probably goes back to the policies of Vespasian.⁷⁵ This centralization was furthered by emperors annexing land and adding taxes in the province of Asia. However, any animosity raised by such imperial intrusions was overcome by gratitude for Vespasian's generosity and good policies in the region. He was honored throughout Asia as "Benefactor."⁷⁶

---

65. Magie, *Roman Rule*, 1: 407, 567; and Michel, "τελώνης," 8:97–98.

66. Herrenbrück, *Jesus*, 100; Magie, *Roman Rule*, 1:165.

67. Magie, *Roman Rule*, 2:1424; Rostovtzeff, *Staatspacht*, 480 n. 233.

68. Mason, *Greek Terms*, 27. In the inscriptions at Ephesus the title is usually ἀρχώνης λιμένων, and it is listed this way in Mason. See also Herrenbrück, *Jesus*, 100.

69. Laet, *Portorium*, 278–79; Magie, *Roman Rule*, 1:165; Cicero, *Fam.* 5.20.9.

70. Broughton, "Part IV: Roman Asia," 535–43.

71. An inscription found at Ephesus in Greek and Latin with corrections made in 5 CE provides guidelines for the activities of the *societates*, confirming their ongoing activity in the province. See Malmendier, "Roman Shares," 37.

72. Magie, *Roman Rule*, 1:567.

73. This translation is confirmed by a bilingual Latin-Greek inscription found at Ephesus and dating to 104 CE. See McCabe et al., *Ephesos Inscriptions*. Ephesos 765 (and related copies, only in Greek) are very similar to 823 and come from the same time. A much longer inscription (Ephesos 4*5) contains tax regulations from the first century BCE and some additional material from the early first century CE. This inscription is discussed by Malmendier ("Roman Shares," 34–35, translated in part on 41–42).

74. Magie, *Roman Rule*, 1:567; 2:1423.

75. Ibid., 1:567–68.

76. Ibid., 1:568–72.

Jesus Meets Zacchaeus (19:1-10)

Thus, while these tax officials with Roman and imperial ties might have been disliked, they were part of a beneficial regime that was regarded favorably. Members of the official public sphere in this era might have enjoyed relative respect and approbation because they belonged to a much-liked imperial administration. Consequently, right around the time Luke was writing, the taxation system (and its relation to the official public sphere) was changing in the context of Asia Minor, our proposed home for Luke and his audience.

The first conclusion from this evidence is that Luke's title for Zacchaeus, ἀρχιτελώ-νης, probably signaled the office of the *promagister* to an audience in Ephesus in the late first–early second century. However, this creates a chronological quandary. The latest clear evidence of the presence of a *promagister* connected to a *societas publicanorum* comes from an inscription dated to 26 CE, though there are hints of them being active in Asia in the middle of the century.[77] The earliest mention of an imperial *promagister* (not part of a *societas*) is dated to 104 CE.[78] The sparse evidence, compounded by the changing situation right around the time of the writing of the third Gospel, makes it difficult to decide which one of these two different *promagistri* would have been referenced when Luke's audience came across the title ἀρχιτελώνης. The decision is critical however, for the *promagister* of the *societas* would have been a hated businessman with loose ties to the official public sphere defined mostly by social connections and economic dealings, whereas the imperial *promagister* would have been an appointed political official working for an emperor currently in the good favor of the people. Two factors indicate that Zacchaeus would have probably been associated with the despised *societates publicanorum* rather than imperial tax officials. The first is the public vitriol directed against Zacchaeus in 19:7. Luke's audience would have taken this (and his admission of extortion in v. 8) as a sign that Zacchaeus was one of the contemptible members of one of the despicable *societates* that bought the rights to collect (or extort) indirect taxes.[79] Second, Luke's Gospel seems to be written by 90 CE,[80] during a time when the "publicans" were either still active or a fresh memory in Asia. If we can presume that the audience has some historical consciousness, they would have understood that the events Luke records in his Gospel took place earlier in what we call the first century CE, when the *societates* were still the primary indirect tax agents in Asia Minor. Luke's audience would recognize that the events of the life of Jesus occurred *before* their current time and thus make them recall the operation of the *societates* from their recent past. Operating with their own social-spatial maps and Luke's sense of verisimilitude, Luke's title for Zacchaeus, ἀρχιτελώνης, probably would have signaled the office of the *promagister*, a regional manager of customs collection for a hated *societas*

---

77. Ibid., 2:1424.

78. Ibid.; McCabe, *Ephesos Inscriptions*, Ephesos 823. This inscription cements the official nature of the imperial *promagister*. Salutaris, the first known imperial *promagister*, who is named in this inscription, is called a φιλόκαισαρ, a "friend of Caesar" (lines 5–6).

79. It is possible that the fact that Zacchaeus is "short" (τῇ ἡλικίᾳ μικρός) may reinforce a negative portrayal of Zacchaeus according to ancient physiognomic principles. See Parsons, "Short in Stature."

80. Fitzmyer, *Luke*, 1:57. However, there has been significant debate on this point with some placing the writing of Luke and/or Acts much later. See Tyson, *Marcion and Luke-Acts*.

publicanorum. As such, Zacchaeus would have been part of the unofficial (business) public sphere but with some ties to political officials.

Three forces converge here to help determine Zacchaeus's social-spatial location in the eyes of Luke's audience. First, the force of place locates him in Jericho, a city known as a political, transportation, military, and economic hub in Judea with active official and unofficial public spheres.[81] Second, the force of social relations employs a partially inconclusive portrait of this wealthy businessman. The fact that he is rich places him in the upper echelons of public status but introduces some ambiguity because wealth could be a sign of either public honor (the wealth of a leader blessed by God, e.g., the rich ruler) or dishonor (the result of a businessman's greed and dishonesty). Thus, a "rich" person could either be a respected political official or a prominent (or infamous) private citizen. Third and finally, the force of meaning comes into play with the title ἀρχιτελώνης. This title had cultural associations in Ephesus that would have probably led Luke's "Ephesian" audience to identify Zacchaeus with the leading local representative of the despised *societas publicanorum*, which had earned the ire of the populace and had relatively loose connections to Roman and local officials.

Zacchaeus is a liminal and ambiguous figure. He has one foot in Jewish culture and one foot in the Roman tax system, high status but publicly despised, at home in the unofficial public sphere but connected to politics on various levels. Zacchaeus's infamy appears to be local in nature. He is a leading toll collector in Jericho, and its inhabitants have come to despise him. Luke's audience would have been similarly swayed by their own local experience of the *societates* when they encounter the character of Zacchaeus in Luke's narrative. Zacchaeus comes across as an unofficial public figure, a Jewish man ostracized, but publicly known in the local context because of his business dealings. When Jesus personally encounters Zacchaeus, he encounters the intersection of Jewish and Roman, wealth and status, official and unofficial. Thus, the complex and liminal nature of Zacchaeus's social standing becomes part of the force of social relations in Luke's portrayal of Jesus. Zacchaeus's questionable status and mostly unofficial standing informs Luke's audience about the person and status of Jesus, especially when Jesus requests and receives hospitality from Zacchaeus. As Garnsey puts it, "you are with whom you eat."[82] Therefore, Luke's characterization of Zacchaeus also characterizes Jesus as one who has a mixed public status and stands in between the unofficial public and local political spheres. Luke casts the encounter of these two characters in the public domains of both city and house, intensifying the effect of their association.

Jesus in Jericho: Public Encounters with Zacchaeus and the Crowd

From a spatial perspective, the rest of the story (vv. 3–10) can be divided into two parts. Verses 3–6 take place in the city of Jericho: Jesus enters the city amidst a crowd, encounters Zacchaeus, and speaks to him. Verses 7–10 take place in Zacchaeus's home:

---

81. Both the force of place (the city of Jericho) and the force of meaning (his name) mark Zacchaeus as a Jewish man.

82. Garnsey, *Food and Society*, 128–38.

everyone grumbles, Zacchaeus pledges new charity and fairness, and Jesus concludes with a double pronouncement. The public encounters in the city of Jericho take place between three sets characters: Zacchaeus and the crowd, Jesus and the crowd, and Jesus and Zacchaeus. This section will consider the public interaction of these three characters in the setting of the city.

The portrayal of Zacchaeus in v. 2 sets him up as a liminal figure stretched across various social and cultural boundaries, a figure that could have aroused both sympathy and animosity in Luke's audience. Zacchaeus's actions clarify his status and evaluation in the narrative. First, Zacchaeus "seeks to see Jesus" in v. 3. However, this allows ambiguity and suspense to remain in the story, for people seek Jesus in the third Gospel for many reasons, some good and some bad. Herod "seeks to see" Jesus (9:9 reads ἐζήτει ἰδεῖν, exactly the same phrase as in 19:3), but obviously not for good reasons. Others wrongly seek after a sign (11:16, 24). Some "seek" to enter the kingdom but are unable (13:24). On the other hand, people rightly seek out Jesus for healing (5:18; 6:19), and Jesus tells people to "seek" the kingdom (11:9-10; 12:31; 15:8). Finally, at the end of this story, Jesus casts himself as one who "seeks." The audience is not clear *why* Zacchaeus is seeking to see who Jesus is. All that we are told is that he is initially unable to do so.

The first public encounter presented in this story comes at the end of v. 3: "and he was not able (to see) because of the crowd, for he was τῇ ἡλικίᾳ μικρός." Many interpreters take this as a straightforward statement that Zacchaeus's shortness prevented him from seeing over the crowd.[83] However, Green has suggested (with strong lexical support) that ἡλικία usually means "age" not "size/stature," and he reads the ἀπὸ τοῦ ὄχλου as causative. Thus, Zacchaeus could not see Jesus because he was young (and insignificant) and the crowd purposefully pushed him away.[84] However, this interpretation does not hold, for Luke can say clearly when someone is prevented from doing something by someone else (e.g., κωλύω or ἐάω with a negative; see Luke 11:52 and Acts 16:6-7 et al.). Here, instead, he speaks of Zacchaeus's "ability" with the verb δύναμαι. Furthermore, Green's interpretation assumes a concerted effort on the part of a large crowd that appears to be focused on Jesus. Such an organized attempt to block his view could have certainly kept him from climbing a tree as well. Regardless, Zacchaeus does not have the social or official status to command the people in the crowd to stand aside and let him through to see.[85] It is not that the crowd intentionally blocks Zacchaeus. Instead, Zacchaeus does not have the authority to command them to do so both because of his lack of official standing and his lack of a good (unofficial) reputation. Zacchaeus's spatial marginality (on the outside of the crowd looking in) reflects his social liminality, and the two work together to add yet more drama to the story: will Zacchaeus ever be able to see Jesus?

Jesus does not have any direct interactions with the crowd in vv. 1-6. Yet, they are clearly part of the scene, marking it as a public event. Luke takes the opportunity to re-

---

83. Fitzmyer, *Luke*, 2:1223; Marshall, *Luke*, 696.

84. Green, *Luke*, 669-70. Alternatively, Parsons may be right that some in the ancient world might have been prejudiced against short people ("Short," 53-54), but it would have to be just one more piece in the complex and conflated puzzle that makes up Zacchaeus's characterization.

85. Tannehill, "Story of Zacchaeus," 206.

PART TWO: SOCIAL-SPATIAL EXEGESIS OF LUKE 18:35—19:48

mind the audience that a crowd is present, portraying them as an obstacle to Zacchaeus's aim in v. 3. Luke reiterates that Jesus was "passing through" (διέρχομαι) Jericho (vv. 1, 4) and states that Zacchaeus had to run ahead and climb a tree to see Jesus (v. 4). The crowd lining the road around Jesus is so large that Zacchaeus cannot see over them. Furthermore, Zacchaeus cannot simply run ahead to where the crowd thins out. No, such a large crowd has gathered along the entire length of the road that even when Zacchaeus does run ahead he must still climb a tree to get a glimpse. The material on Ephesus from chapter 3 examined the procession established by Salutaris, which followed a clear thoroughfare (the *via sacra*) from the Artemesion through the city and back to the temple.[86] Other cities in the ancient world followed a similar street pattern: they had few entrances/exits and a few main roads that connected major public areas/buildings and moved travelers through the city (generally a *cardo* and a *decumanus*; examples can also be seen at Pompeii and Jerusalem). Thus, Luke's audience would supply the following social-spatial map for this event based on the high-context clues: Jesus is following one of the main thoroughfares through Jericho, a road lined with public buildings, markets, and other open spaces where crowds could easily gather to watch. The crowd has lined the street to behold Jesus and his entourage as they pass through the city. Apparently, the throng is so large that Zacchaeus cannot see over them anywhere along the route. Zacchaeus easily anticipates where Jesus is "about to pass by" (ἤμελλεν διέρχεσθαι, v. 4) because Jesus is traveling a well-worn thoroughfare through the city. Therefore, Zacchaeus can run ahead on the route, find a tree, and perch himself in it as Jesus approaches. While this story does not delineate any interactions between Jesus and the crowd, Luke's readers would have understood this to be a busy, bustling, public scene with the masses scrambling along the main thoroughfare of the city to watch Jesus as he passes.

The first and most important aspect to notice regarding Jesus' public encounter with Zacchaeus is that it takes place right in the midst of the lively public scenario described above. As in the story of the blind beggar, Jesus comes to a halt, but in this case Luke emphasizes the spatial factor, for his meeting with Zacchaeus occurs "when he came to the place" (ὡς ἦλθεν ἐπὶ τὸν τόπον) where Zacchaeus had perched in a tree. Jesus suddenly stops in the middle of the road, surrounded by his entourage and the people of Jericho, and unexpectedly addresses a most unlikely character in the full sight and hearing of everyone. Jesus states his intentions publicly and succinctly: "Zacchaeus, come down quickly, for I must stay at your house today" (v. 5).[87] Jesus here acts on the very advice that he gave to his own disciples (9:4; 10:7) to stay (μένω) with those who welcome them in the cities that they visited. The term μένω connotes extended hospitality in the house of a host (see Luke 1:56; Acts 9:43, 18:20). It would have been evident to everyone within earshot that Jesus had prompted Zacchaeus to host him at his home. Zacchaeus should gain public honor for himself (and the entire community) by hosting a guest with such high honor as

---

86. See Rogers, *Sacred Identity*, 112–15.

87. Many commentators have noted the theological weight that δεῖ carries in Luke's narrative, emphasizing the divine imperative behind Jesus' mission. See Bovon, *Saint Luc*, 241; Fitzmyer, *Luke*, 2:1224 (and 1:180). Both also mention that this is intensified by the use of σήμερον here as well.

Jesus Meets Zacchaeus (19:1–10)

Jesus;[88] however, it is far from enough to overturn the community's negative stance toward Zacchaeus (cf. v. 7). At the same time, the fact that Jesus publicly (first invites himself and then!) accepts Zacchaeus's hospitality means that he recognizes Zacchaeus as a relative social equal, including him in his movement, and this is precisely what shocks the crowd.[89] The *urban* public interactions of Jesus, Zacchaeus, and the crowd set the stage for the *domestic* public interactions that follow.

Verses 3–6 cast a very public scene that employs several forces. The force of place sets a stage for the first part of the story as Jesus travels a main thoroughfare of Jericho, a route that was constructed for public interactions and frequently filled with bustling traffic. The force of meaning probably impacts the understanding of this space, given the cultural associations with processions in the Greco-Roman world. Social relations add to the public nature of the scene with the reminder of the crowd (v.2), a crowd so large that Zacchaeus cannot see over or around them. Time plays a role in two ways. First, this event continues the public scene already begun in the healing of the blind beggar, and second, Jesus' procession through the city must take some time if Zacchaeus is able to run ahead on the route and wait for the famed prophet to pass by.[90] Finally, no political officials, legal matters, or military officers impinge on this entire episode other than the very loose connection of Zacchaeus to the Roman taxation system.[91] Luke portrays Jesus at the heart of an unofficial public event as he proceeds down the city street surrounded by crowds gathered to meet and see him.

Jesus in a House: Public Encounters with Zacchaeus and the Crowd

The process of hospitality, the bridge between public and private,[92] begins in the public sphere with the interaction between Jesus and Zacchaeus in the presence of the crowd. Luke extends this bridge into Zacchaeus's home. Zacchaeus responds to Jesus' command and "comes down quickly" from the tree. Next, Luke writes that Zacchaeus ὑπεδέξατο αὐτὸν χαίρων. "Joy/rejoicing" is an important theme in Luke-Acts,[93] but the critical

---

88. Gowler, "Hospitality," 220–21. Recall the quotation from Cicero: "It is most appropriate for the homes of famous men to be open to distinguished guests. The fact that foreigners in our city never fail to receive hospitality also brings great honor to our city. Furthermore, it is very advantageous for those who want to obtain political power through honorable means to increase their popularity and influence abroad by welcoming guests" (*Off.* 2.18.). It is possible that Zacchaeus saw this as an opportunity to gain honor in the eyes of his estranged community.

89. Neyrey, "Ceremonies," 364, 378. Again, Jesus' association with Zacchaeus casts some of Zacchaeus's liminal and unofficial status onto Jesus.

90. It is also quite likely that Luke's audience would have imagined this event transpiring during the day, the time for public interaction.

91. Contrast this with the unofficial public riot that occurs in Ephesus at the instigation of grumblers in the crowd (Acts 19). In Luke 19:1–10, no officials ever step into the narrative, but in Acts 19:35–41 a "town clerk" (ὁ γραμματεύς) appears, advises them to take proper legal action, and warns the crowd that they might be breaking the law. The official public sphere comes into play here in a way that it does not in the story of Zacchaeus.

92. Recall the work of Wiltshire, *Public and Private*, esp. ch. 5, "Hospitality and the Transformation of Realms."

93. Green, *Luke*, 670 n. 206.

PART TWO: SOCIAL-SPATIAL EXEGESIS OF LUKE 18:35—19:48

social-spatial element is the fact that Zacchaeus "welcomed" Jesus. While some commentators assume that the events following this "welcome" take place in Zacchaeus's house,[94] Fitzmyer insists that this is "far from clear."[95] Part of the problem is the tight interaction of the public and private spheres in this story. Verses 7–10 still appear to be occurring in public: the crowd murmurs against Zacchaeus and both Zacchaeus and Jesus respond. This probably induces Fitzmyer to claim that this dialogue takes place on the way to Zacchaeus's house. However, several high-context clues in the story tell the audience that Jesus does enter Zacchaeus's home. The same term ὑποδέξατο (aorist of ὑποδέχομαι in v. 6) occurs in 10:38 where Martha "welcomed" Jesus into her house and prepared a meal. Therefore, just as in 10:38, this verb signals that Jesus has entered into Zacchaeus's home.[96] This is strengthened by the connotations of μένω (v. 5) indicating household hospitality in Luke as discussed above. Further confirmation is found later in the passage when Jesus proclaims, "Today salvation has come to this house [τῷ οἴκῳ τούτῳ]" (v. 9). The term οἶκος can mean "house" (a physical structure as in Luke 4:38, 7:10, et al.) or "household" (the members of Zacchaeus's family as in Acts 10:2; 11:14; et al.). In either case, it would be odd for Jesus to make an utterance about "*this house*" (or household) if he was not already in Zacchaeus's home.[97] In a high-context society, the audience would presume that Jesus has entered Zacchaeus's house at the end of v. 6 based on the clues provided by Luke.

Verses 7–10 transpire in a "publicized," private domain. Jesus and Zacchaeus are not the only ones to enter, for it appears from vv. 7–10 and the following parable that Jesus' entourage and the grumbling crowd enter as well. The report of the crowd's objection, Zacchaeus's public riposte/pledge, and Jesus' definitive pronouncements about Zacchaeus to the crowd all take place within Zacchaeus's home. This presence of a large, mixed group is confirmed by the following parable (19:11–27), which speaks to the general crowd, teaches Jesus' followers, and warns Jesus' opponents, all within Zacchaeus's home.[98] The unofficial public sphere has invaded and saturated Zacchaeus's home (cf. Wiltshire). Zacchaeus's hospitality has gotten him more guests than he probably expected, and his home becomes the setting for the public events that follow in vv. 7–10. Therefore, next we will set forth a plausible model for how Luke and his audience might have envisioned Zacchaeus's house. From there, we can unpack the objections raised in v. 7, Zacchaeus's response/pledge in v. 8, and Jesus' pronouncements in vv. 9–10. The seeds of this public conflict are planted in vv. 3–6, they come to full bloom in v. 7 as Jesus enters Zacchaeus's home, and they prompt the public responses in vv. 8–10.

94. Ellis, *Luke*, 221; and Green, *Luke*, 670.

95. Fitzmyer, *Luke*, 2:1225. Johnson, much like Fitzmyer, says that Zacchaeus stopped (σταθείς, v. 8) while they were on the way to his house to defend himself (*Luke*, 285–86).

96. The aorist tense implies the occurrence of the entire event of hospitality. See Wallace, *Greek Grammar*, 557–58. The translation "welcome" is infelicitous in the sense that ὑποδέχομαι refers not just to words of greeting (as "welcome" often does in modern parlance), but to actual reception and entertaining in the home. Hamm cites further evidence from Acts and papyri to prove that ὑποδέχομαι refers to a full welcome of hospitality ("Luke 19:8," 343–45). The verb occurs again in Acts 17:7, but the context is less instructive.

97. The demonstrative adjective here probably has a deictic function, pointing to the house/household that was present. See Smyth, *Greek Grammar*, #1241; and Blass and Debrunner, *Greek Grammar*, #290.

98. The next chapter will discuss the various audiences of the following parable.

Jesus Meets Zacchaeus (19:1–10)

The events of this story transform Zacchaeus's home not merely into a hostel for Jesus and his companions but into a venue for public exchange and teaching. As such, it must host a large number of people including Zacchaeus and his "household," Jesus with his companions, and part of the city crowd from Jericho, which seems to contain people hostile to Jesus. It would naturally be assumed that Jesus, and probably his close companions, would meet with Zacchaeus and his household through the rituals of hospitality. However, we also hear of an objection (19:7) and a question (19:11) that are raised in Zacchaeus's house but do not come from either Zacchaeus's family or Jesus' followers. Furthermore, the following parable answers a question from the crowd (v. 11), while speaking to Jesus' own disciples (vv. 13, 15) and opponents (v. 14), which Luke's audience would probably assume to be in the home listening to Jesus. Thus, Zacchaeus's house must be able to hold a large crowd in such a way that there could be social interaction and conversation among the various groups there. What would such a house have looked like to Luke's audience?

Unfortunately, the houses at Ephesus offer slim and atypical evidence. The "slope houses" are the only excavated domiciles, and, while they reflect some standard architecture from the Greco-Roman world, they are also strongly determined by the hilly geography of Ephesus. Therefore, it seems best to look to other relevant geographical centers, Pompeii and Palestine, for examples of houses that might have been called to mind as the setting for this public encounter in Zacchaeus's home.[99] Zacchaeus, because of his wealth, would have been able to own a substantial home within the city of Jericho, which was no architectural backwater.

The first example is taken from Palestine, the peristyle house found at Aphek.[100]

Figure 6.1: Reconstruction of the "Peristyle House" at Aphek

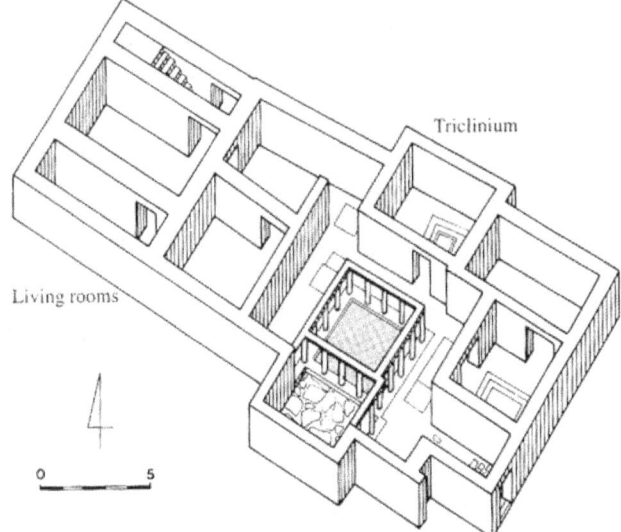

---

99. George, "Domestic Architecture." She states that Pompeii offers the best evidence for typical Roman homes (11) and that Ephesian homes are unusual and more difficult to interpret (15). She also notes the potentially public nature of homes (7).

100. Hirschfeld, *Palestinian Dwelling*, 91. This illustration is used with the permission of the publisher.

PART TWO: SOCIAL-SPATIAL EXEGESIS OF LUKE 18:35—19:48

This style of house with an inner courtyard/garden surrounded by columns became popular in the early second century and eventually became the model for the classical Roman house (though only a few examples have been found in Palestine).[101] As with many houses of this era, the central courtyard was only accessible through a narrow entrance and vestibule (on the bottom right hand corner). The vestibule was designed to control access to homes, and would have been a bottleneck for a crowd trying to enter Zacchaeus's house. The entrance of this house opens onto a small alley that led quickly to a major thoroughfare in the city.[102] This would allow for some privacy while still providing easy public access. The vestibule leads to a hallway that winds around a square courtyard that was approximately five meters on each side (twenty-five sq. meters). Next to the courtyard is a paved area approximately three meters long and five meters wide (fifteen sq. meters). This makes a total area of forty sq. meters, which should be reduced to thirty sq. meters to allow room for furniture and permanent garden area. On the conservative estimate that one square meter could hold two people (perhaps more if everyone were standing), this courtyard and pavilion together could have held sixty people with additional space provided by the passageway surrounding it, allowing for a total of eighty people. It is feasible that Zacchaeus, Jesus, and their closest companions and family would have gathered in the paved patio and addressed the crowd gathered in the garden. Thus, even this modestly sized Roman villa in Palestine could hold a gathering of approximately eighty people, quite enough to constitute a public event occurring in this home. It shows what Luke's audience might have imagined as an urban home for a rich Jewish businessman. It also demonstrates some practical issues when the public invades a home, such as the difficulty of access through the vestibule and the variability of public space in a home: peristyle, passageway, and pavilion.

The next example is the "House of the Labyrinth" from Pompeii.[103] This house has the popular atrium-peristyle design that was widespread in cities across the Greco-Roman world in the first and second centuries. It allowed several layers of access and public presence in a home.[104] The main entrance to this house is near the lower right hand corner. Like many elite houses in Pompeii and the house examined above, this entrance did not open right onto a main thoroughfare but was on a side street two blocks from two of Pompeii's main streets (one north-south and one east-west). This kind of location allowed for greater privacy while still allowing quick passage to more public areas, a popular way for elites to maintain their privacy and retain the opportunity for public display.[105] This home has a very small vestibule (only about two meters by two meters), which opens quickly onto an atrium (with six pillars and an opening in the roof) that would have served as a reception area.[106] On the other side of a few small chambers beyond the atrium

101. Ibid., 85–86.
102. Ibid., 91–92.
103. See the detailed report on this home in Michel, *Casa del labirinto*.
104. Wallace-Hadrill, *Houses*, 17, 38–44.
105. Laurence, *Pompeii*, 112, 137.
106. Wallace-Hadrill speaks of the layers of the "grandness" of the public space in this house based on the quality of the decorations (*Houses*, 28). As one moves from the front to the back of the house, the decorations become more impressive (and expensive).

Jesus Meets Zacchaeus (19:1-10)

Figure 6.2 The House of the Labyrinth

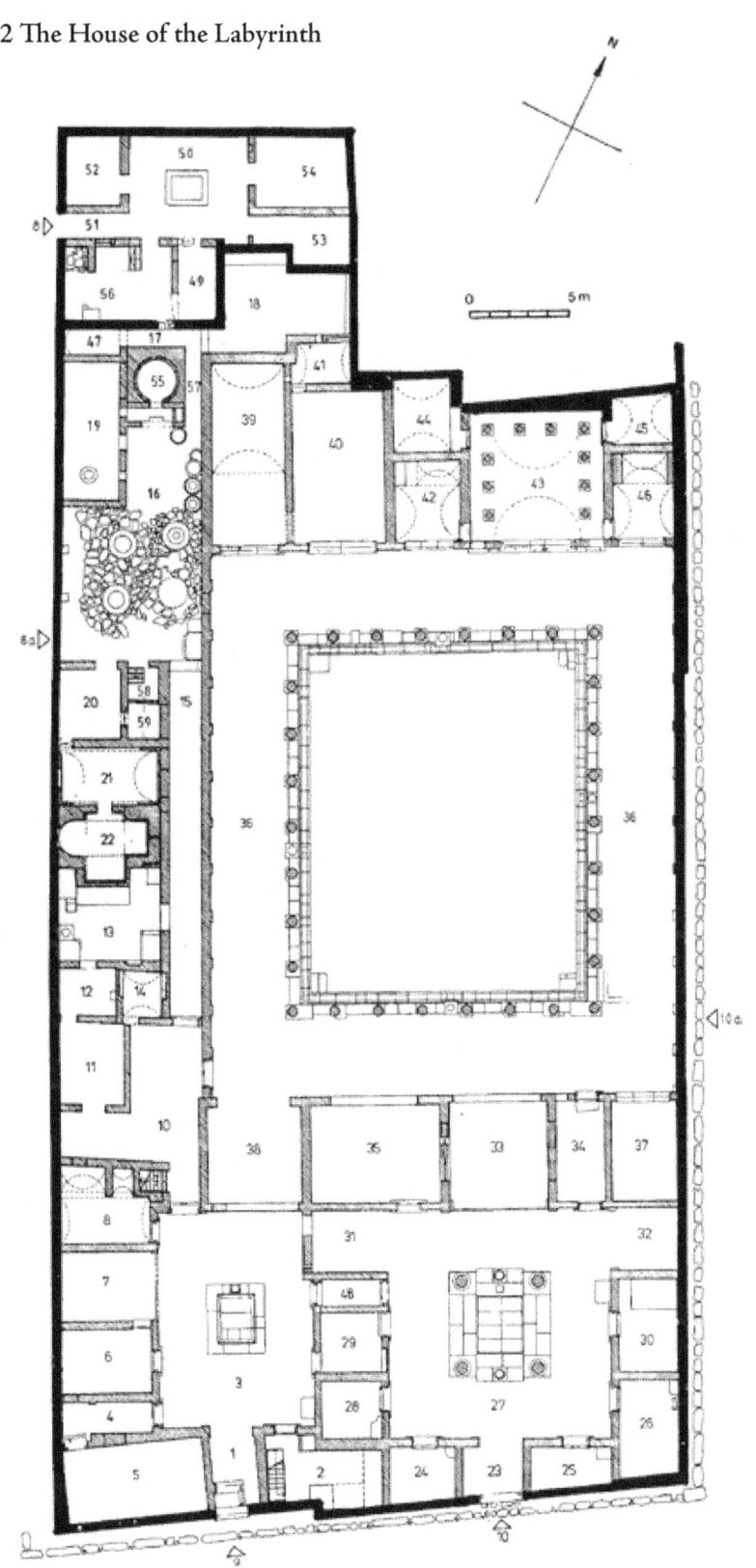

219

PART TWO: SOCIAL-SPATIAL EXEGESIS OF LUKE 18:35—19:48

was the large peristyle garden.[107] This large area (approximately four hundred sq. meters) could have held five hundred people.[108] If filled with people, it would have easily turned this private domicile into a public setting for the events that follow. Luke's audience might imagine Zacchaeus welcoming Jesus and his entourage into the home while the crowd from the streets flowed (almost uncontrollably) into the house through the vestibule, then the atrium, and finally into the garden. It might have been during this bustling invasion of the house that people in the crowd began murmuring about Jesus accepting hospitality from a "sinner" like Zacchaeus.[109] This house provides another good example of a typical urban domicile with available public areas that could have hosted a large crowd.[110]

The text of v. 7 lays out the timing of the events as people flooded into Zacchaeus's home: καὶ ἰδόντες πάντες διεγόγγυζον λέγοντες ὅτι παρὰ ἁμαρωλῷ ἀνδρὶ εἰσῆλθεν καταλῦσαι. "After everyone saw" (prior time temporal participle ἰδόντες), they "were murmuring" (durative imperfect διεγόγγυζον, emphasizing the ongoing complaining). They were upset that Jesus had "entered" the house. The aorist tense of εἰσῆλθεν may be "dramatic" emphasizing the recent entry of Jesus in the narrative timeline.[111] The use of εἰσέρχομαι further supports the fact that the audience would envision Jesus going into Zacchaeus's house and enjoying hospitality there as the events of vv. 8–10 (and 11–28) transpire. However, it was not just that Jesus entered but that he entered "with a sinful man" (παρά indicating association with ἁμαρωλῷ ἀνδρι, the "sinful" Zacchaeus). Finally, Jesus did not simply enter, but he entered "to stay" (καταλῦσαι) with Zacchaeus. Luke uses this word in 9:12 for finding food and lodging in nearby cities and it reinforces the fact that Jesus both entered and planned to stay in the house of Zacchaeus. The crowd saw and heard the public interchange between Jesus and Zacchaeus, and they were already suspicious. When Jesus actually enters the house, they crowd begins to complain about it, but at least some portion of the onlookers follows them into the home to see what would happen next.

Two further observations about v. 7 must be stated here. First, many have noted the climactic element in the fact that "everyone" (πάντες) saw and grumbled, a designation that would presumably include Jesus' disciples, the crowd in general, and any of the stauncher opponents of Jesus.[112] Luke sets a public scene for this entire story in vv. 1–3,

---

107. The far left of the house appears to be used for storage, servants' quarters, a bath area, and later a bakery. The square room at the back of the house with a three-sided colonnade was a finely decorated Corinthian oecus. See ibid., 208, 210.

108. The estimate of two persons per sq. meter should be reduced to allow for space taken up by actual gardens and other accoutrements like furniture or statues.

109. The irony is that the grumbling crowd ends up in the house much like Jesus does. However, they are not "invited" guests but uninvited guests. Ch. 3 discussed the appearance of uninvited guests in homes (see especially Vitruvius, *Arch.* 6.5.1).

110. Luke rarely specifies parts of a house (atrium, peristyle, triclinium). He does mention roofs (Luke 5:19; Acts 10:9), an upstairs room (Luke 22:12; Acts 1:13), and a gate door (Acts 12:13–14). This lack of specificity calls for attention to archaeological evidence to both understand how such a house might have looked and how Luke's audience might have envisioned it.

111. Wallace, *Greek Grammar*, 564–65.

112. O'Hanlon, "Zacchaeus," 15–16; Johnson, *Luke*, 285; Green, *Luke*, 671. Fitzmyer, *Luke*, 2:1224, calls it "hyperbole" without noting its function here, and others cite this "hyperbole" dismissively as well (see Nolland, *Luke*, 905).

mentioning Jesus' procession through Jericho and the presence of the crowd. Here in v. 7, after Jesus' encounter with Zacchaeus in the streets of the city, he reminds the audience of the presence of the amalgamated crowd, emphasizing yet again the public nature of this story. The use of πάντες maintains the public valence of the story as the scene shifts from the streets of Jericho to Zacchaeus's home. "Everyone" is still present and watching, making even the interaction in the home public in nature. Second, what "everyone" does is "grumble" about Jesus' association with a sinner. This marks the public conflict at the heart of the story. The last people to "grumble" against Jesus were the Pharisees (15:2; see also 5:30), and such grumbling is tied to the label "sinner" in Luke (see 5:30; 7:34, 39, 15:1–2). However, Jesus himself uses the label "sinner" throughout the Gospel, turning it back on his opponents by reevaluating it (5:32; 6:32–34; 7:34; 13:2; 15:7, 10), and in this story Jesus reevaluates Zacchaeus's status as a "sinner" not by his words but by his actions when he accepts hospitality from him. As is the case through most of the Gospel, the exact offenses that earn Zacchaeus the label of "sinner" are left unspecified, though it is clear that the identification marks him as one who has been marginalized from the community.[113] Donahue has shown that "tax" collectors in Jesus' day were disdained for their dishonesty (not treasonous tendencies or specific religious violations).[114] The discussion of Zacchaeus above emphasized how agents of the *societas publicanorum* in the late first century CE in Asia Minor (with whom Zacchaeus would have probably been associated by Luke's audience) were hated both for their dishonesty and their greed. Therefore, Luke's audience probably would have supplied some content to the label "sinner": assuming that Zacchaeus had been habitually dishonest (confirmed by v.8) and that his deceptive dealings had made him unfairly rich. Jesus does not only accept poor "sinners" (like the blind beggar) but rich ones as well. He accepts them publicly and openly enjoys their hospitality.

Plutarch's comments cast further light on the conflict that Jesus faced in Jericho. Plutarch warns Menemachus that "every public office [πολιτεία] brings forth some conflicts and disagreements" (809b). Jesus was certainly no stranger to conflict, and the conflict that arises in 19:1–10 is a result of his public acceptance of Zacchaeus's hospitality. As a public figure (on a public procession through a city), people observed what he did and made judgments for or against him: in this case on the basis of his choice of hosts. This is an example of what Plutarch says: "Those in public life [οἱ πολιευόμενοι] are not only held accountable for what they say and do in public [ἐν κοινῷ], but people also watch their meals [δεῖπνον] and their bed and their marriage and their amusement and every other serious concern" (800d). Thus, as a public figure, Jesus would be evaluated based on a wide range of factors, including with whom he ate (such as tax collectors). The fact that the inhabitants of Jericho were hostile toward Zacchaeus is no surprise, since Plutarch states that the masses will dislike a rich man who does not share his private possessions (822a). Furthermore, Plutarch says, "(Gifts) should be given at a time that has an elegant

---

113. Green, *Luke*, 671; and Neale, *None but the Sinners*, 183. Neale says that the actual content of this label/accusation is irrelevant, for the lesson is simply that Jesus alone receives such persons. I would counter that audiences supply such "gaps" in the text to understand the ramifications of those whom Jesus accepts.

114. Donahue, "Tax Collectors," 59–60.

PART TWO: SOCIAL-SPATIAL EXEGESIS OF LUKE 18:35—19:48

[ἀστείαν][115] and good setting, a setting connected to the worship of God which leads everyone to piety" (822b). Zacchaeus takes advantage of such an occasion in 19:8. On this public occasion, when the famous prophet Jesus deigns to stay in his house, Zacchaeus stands up[116] in front of the crowd gathered in his home to announce his generous gift to the poor and to pledge a new life of honest dealings. Jesus affirms the religious effects of Zacchaeus's announcement by proclaiming the arrival of salvation in the house and tying the entire event to the nature of his mission, probably in the hope of winning over the crowd to both accept Zacchaeus and affirm his own message.

Tannehill is right to note that "the rest of the story [vv. 8–10] is a response to the crowd's objection."[117] However, it is not only a response to the objection of the crowd (narratively and rhetorically), but it also takes place in the presence of the crowd. Verse 7 portrays the transition of this public event from the city streets to a house and maintains the presence of the crowd. The complaints of "everyone" probably began when they "saw" Jesus stop and talk with Zacchaeus. They continued as Jesus walked to the house and climaxed when they "saw" Jesus enter the "sinner's" home. Thus, the pronouncements in vv. 8–10 are uttered publicly within Zacchaeus's house with the crowds present. This is signaled at the beginning of v. 8, for Luke frequently uses the participle form of ἵστημι (here in the aorist σταθείς, but elsewhere in other tenses) to mark public speech.[118] Two different forms of the participle are applied to the Pharisee and the "tax" collector in 18:11 and 13, describing prayer in the temple (where the Pharisee prayed for the hearing of those around him by Luke's account). The examples from Acts are even clearer: Peter "stands" to address the crowd at Pentecost (2:14), God commands the apostles to "stand" in the temple and preach (5:20), Paul "stands" to speak before the Areopagus (17:22), finally Paul "stands" on the steps of the temple to speak to the crowd (21:40). Exactly when or where Zacchaeus "stood" is not made clear,[119] but Luke uses the term here to reiterate the public nature of Zacchaeus's statement. Zacchaeus stands up in his own home and publicly resolves to donate to the poor and reform his deceitful business practices.

---

115. This term originally meant "of a city" in opposition to rural behavior and came to mean "refined, elegant, courteous." It speaks to behavior that is proper for public actions (LSJ, s.v., 260).

116. Plutarch also notes times when public speaking is marked by the person standing up (804a, c), much as Zacchaeus does in v. 7.

117. Tannehill, "Story of Zacchaeus," 206.

118. Hamm states that σταθείς "nearly always signals a public pronouncement" ("Luke 19:8," 435). However, both Fitzmyer (*Luke*, 2:1224) and Johnson (*Luke*, 285–86) state that σταθείς here indicates that Zacchaeus "stopped" as he was walking to his house to defend himself against the denunciation of the crowd. This term does mean "stop" in the immediately preceding narrative, where Jesus "stops" (σταθείς, v. 40) and orders the blind man to be brought to him. However, 18:40 is the only occasion in Luke-Acts where the participle form of ἵστημι means to "stop/stand still" rather than "stand/stand up." Luke might have employed σταθείς in 18:40 under the influence of the use of στάς in Mark 10:49. In light of the argument above, the end of v. 6 marks the entry into Zacchaeus's home, v. 7 describes a continuing stream of grumbling from city into home, and v. 8 takes place inside Zacchaeus's home. This order of events means that σταθείς must take place inside of Zacchaeus's home, where the meaning "stand" makes good sense in the context of sitting for a meal of hospitality.

119. Ellis describes it as "at or after dinner" (*Luke*, 221). The same is suggested by Hamm ("Luke 19:8," 435 and n. 21).

Jesus Meets Zacchaeus (19:1-10)

Zacchaeus's statement in 19:8 has generated a recent debate: does Zacchaeus defend or resolve? Does he defend himself by asserting his generous habits, or resolve to live a new life of justice and beneficence? Hamm traces the history of this debate, citing the majority of scholars who have supported the traditional interpretation: Zacchaeus pledges a new course of generous giving after his dramatic encounter with Jesus. Hamm also traces the origin and history of the alternative interpretation (incited by the present tense verbs in v. 8), which asserts that Zacchaeus defends himself by proclaiming his typical behavior in front of Jesus and the crowd.[120] In either case, Zacchaeus makes a *public* statement: either to vow overtly a new course of action or to present his generosity as a defense against open objections to Jesus' visit.[121] While either position could support the thesis of this study by affirming the public nature of the story, the traditional interpretation is more convincing for three reasons. First, the strength of the term συκοφαντέω makes it improbable that Zacchaeus is talking about unintentional overcharges.[122] Second, if Zacchaeus was in such a habit of generous donations and restitutions, then he would have eventually won over the favor of his countrymen.[123] Finally, the portrayal of the τελῶναι in Luke is a picture of those who recognize their need for repentance and act on it in the narrative (3:12; 5:29-31).[124] It is not a picture of those who are typically and customarily righteous.[125]

A similar phrase found in both v. 8 and v. 9 might seem to negate the public nature of these statements by Zacchaeus and Jesus. Verse 8 states that Zacchaeus spoke πρὸς τὸν κύριον (to the "Lord," not to the crowd). Similarly, v. 9 states that Jesus spoke πρὸς αὐτόν (to him, that is Zacchaeus, and again not to the crowd).[126] Furthermore, v. 8 is

---

120. Hamm, "Luke 19:8," 431-32.

121. Ibid., 435 (arguing for resolve); Ravens, "Zacchaeus," 21 (arguing for defense); Mitchell, "Zacchaeus," 157-58 (arguing for defense). Tannehill suggests that the end of the episode contains "indirect" statements meant for the broader hostile audience ("Story," 207-9, favoring resolve).

122. Neale, *None but the Sinners*, 185-86.

123. This is especially true since the reigning charge against toll (not "tax") collectors was dishonesty (not treason), and higher-level figures (who collected "direct" taxes for the Romans) were not so universally condemned. Zacchaeus surely would have escaped the charge of dishonesty by such a practice, and he might have even been associated with the higher-level (and more honorable) tax collectors. See Donahue, "Tax Collectors," 51-53.

124. That is, they are the ones who are sick and in need of a physician (c.f. 5:31). See also Hamm, "Luke 19:8," 437.

125. To put it another way, the proper analog for Zacchaeus is the "sinful woman" of ch. 7 who is forgiven by Jesus, not the centurion of ch. 7 who already appears to have spiritual insight and no apparent cause to repent (much like Cornelius in Acts). Green suggests (*Luke*, 667-68) that with Zacchaeus Luke is undoing the stereotypes that have been developed in his own narrative (of ruler, wealthy, toll collector, and sinner). This is an interesting, but unnecessary, device. The "wealthy" and "rulers" can be righteous figures in Luke-Acts. The centurion of ch. 7 is wealthy, having donated funds for a synagogue. The same could be said of Cornelius as well. Later, in Acts, the proconsul Sergius Paulus (a "ruler") believes Paul's message. Green is right to attend to the complexity of Luke's own characterization, but it is so complex as not to allow the rigid stereotypes that Green seems to require here in order to make Zacchaeus the dismantling of them. Rather, Zacchaeus is a climactic and complex figure, and as such further attests to Luke's theme of repentance (24:47; Acts 2:38).

126. This phrase in v. 9 probably does not mean "about him" (O'Hanlon, "Story," 17). Luke frequently uses the construction εἶπεν/λέγω + πρός with the accusative to indicate the recipient of the speech. Fitzmyer notes this possibility of "about him" as well, justifying it by the odd third person nature of Jesus' statements. He rightly notes in conclusion that these pronouncements were "made to both Zacchaeus and the crowd—or better, to the crowd through him."

clearly directed at Jesus with the use of the singular imperative ἰδού and the vocative address κύριε. On the other hand, Zacchaeus must be responding to the complaint of the crowd, for Jesus has not raised any problems regarding his wealth or business practices.[127] Thus, while directed to Jesus, Zacchaeus's statements are in response to the public criticism of the crowd, which both he and Jesus have overheard. Interestingly, Jesus' statements are all in the third person, never address Zacchaeus by name, and instead refer to Zacchaeus with a deictic pronoun (αὐτός). Tannehill is right to note that Jesus' response addresses two audiences at once, Zacchaeus and the crowd.[128] Likewise, Zacchaeus's statement addresses both Jesus and the crowd. Thus, the addressees of these announcements may be somewhat opaque because these statements form a social bridge between a public audience and a private audience, much like Zacchaeus's hospitality opened a spatial bridge to link the public streets of Jericho with his own house.

How can these statements address both private and public audiences, individuals and crowds, at the same time? Tannehill employs the rhetorical category *insinuatio* to describe the function of these pronouncements. A speaker uses an *insinuatio* to address a thorny issue with a hostile crowd. It speaks indirectly to an objection as a way to answer the objector while minimizing the risk of alienating the audience.[129] Zacchaeus's statement functions in this way: while directed to Jesus, it indirectly responds to the complaint of the crowd, which he presumes Jesus has heard (and might believe). Jesus' statements are spoken to Zacchaeus, but their third person, almost gnomic, formulation moves the rhetoric away from Zacchaeus and toward the objecting crowd. Jesus announces the coming of salvation to Zacchaeus's house and reaffirms his status as a child of Abraham. Jesus substantiates the proclamation of v. 9 by citing his own divine mission to save the lost in v. 10. Through the technique of the *insinuatio*, Luke has Zacchaeus and Jesus address public and private audiences at the same time within the now public space of Zacchaeus's private home. Jesus' pronouncements in vv. 9–10 echo back over the story and transform this house from a public setting of conflict to a public setting of salvation.

Jesus' pronouncement draws upon several powerful terms and images to drive the point home. Jesus begins with the word "today" (σήμερον) using the force of time to emphasize what he is about to say. What has occurred "today" is the coming of salvation, signaling the forgiveness and full inclusion of this representative figure in Luke's Gospel. Jesus links this salvation to Zacchaeus's identity as a son of Abraham. Doing so probably challenges the opinion of the grumbling audience who would have presumed that Zacchaeus's life and business excluded him from the people of God. However, Jesus publicly reaffirms Zacchaeus's Jewish identity and his concomitant salvation. Finally, Jesus grounds this radical public pronouncement in the very nature of his divine mission in v. 10.[130] This saying about "the Son of man" falls into the category of Jesus referring to himself

---

127. Although, it would not be uncharacteristic of Jesus to do so (c.f. 18:22).

128. Tannehill, *Narrative Unity*, 124.

129. Tannehill, "Story of Zacchaeus," 207–8. The *insinuatio* is particularly useful when the audience is already prejudiced against the speaker, as in this case when "everyone" grumbles against Jesus. See also Kennedy, *Rhetorical Criticism*, 36.

130. For an analysis of the relationship and argumentative force of Jesus' pronouncements in vv. 9–10, see Tannehill, "Story of Zacchaeus," 208–9.

and his divinely authorized mission.[131] A few similar sayings appear before the travel narrative in scenarios of public conflict.[132] In 5:24, Jesus publicly answers the objections of the crowd gathered in the house when he pronounces forgiveness on the paralytic by saying, "So that you may know that the Son of man has authority on earth to forgive sins." In 6:5, Jesus answers the Pharisees' objection to plucking grain on the Sabbath by stating, "The Son of man is Lord of the Sabbath."[133] In 7:34, Jesus publicly addresses his opponents who rejected John the Baptist for his asceticism but who also decried Jesus for his enjoyment of food and drink (note the reference to the surrounding crowd in 7:24). In this case, "the Son of man" (Jesus himself) is accused of being a glutton, a drunkard, and a "friend of sinners." Here, as in 19:7, Jesus' association with "tax collectors and sinners" earns him the ire of some, and he responds by affirming the nature of his mission. Thus, the phrase "the Son of man," the setting of public conflict, and the affirmation of Jesus' mission in 19:10 harkens back to Jesus' public retorts about "the Son of man" in chs. 4–9 (before the travel narrative). Jesus silences the grumbling crowd gathered in Zacchaeus's house with these climactic pronouncements, putting an end to the public conflict and publicly declaring salvation for one who also deserves to be called a son of Abraham.[134]

Jesus' pronouncements also fit well with Plutarch's advice about public speaking. Plutarch advises frank and straightforward speech (803a), which describes Jesus' "self-invitation" to Zacchaeus's home in front of the crowd. Plutarch also provides several guidelines about how to respond to public challenges. First, one should avoid offending one's audience (803d), and thus Jesus' use of an *insinuatio* is apropos in this situation of public conflict. Second, Plutarch notes that a quick and apt reply is often the perfect remedy for public challenge or criticism (803f–804a), and this is exactly what Jesus gives to the "grumblers" in vv. 9–10. Finally, Jesus appeals to the moral and religious sentiments of his audience by announcing salvation for a fellow "Son of Abraham" (809e–f), while at the same time summoning this great ancestor of the Jewish people to shame the narrow-mindedness of his audience and affirm the ancestry and actions of Zacchaeus (810a–b). Jesus seems to follow Plutarch's middle way in this episode of public conflict: he seeks resolution by clearly, but indirectly, challenging his audience with an apt reply that calls upon their own deeply held sentiments.

This analysis of the public interactions taking place inside of Zacchaeus's house features several forces. The force of place comes to the fore as Jesus accepts Zacchaeus's

---

131. I agree with Kingsbury's conclusion that "the Son of man" is a technical term in Luke's Gospel. This phrase does not reveal who Jesus is (like the titles Messiah, Son of David, etc.). Instead, Jesus uses it exclusively to refer to himself (i.e., "this particular man or human being"). Thus Jesus says, "'This man' has come to seek and save the lost" ("Observations," 283–90).

132. These are followed by several references to either the suffering (9:22, 44; 18:31) or the eschatological return of "the Son of Man" (11:30; 12:40; 17:26).

133. This saying nicely serves Kingsbury's point, though he does not cite it. In 6:5, Jesus is clearly referring to himself (i.e., "this man here" is lord of the Sabbath). However, the phrase "the Son of man" serves only a deictic function referring to Jesus, the content of the identification follows the copula. Jesus is the "lord of the Sabbath."

134. Ch. 9 will explore the significance of the use of σωτηρία in 19:10 as a climax to the theme of salvation in Luke's Gospel.

hospitality and enters his home. Luke casts a scene where the public sphere invades the home of Zacchaeus, a wealthy businessman who could own a large house. Luke's audience might envision a house with a door near one of the major thoroughfares, a tight and crowded vestibule, and a large peristyle or garden where a crowd could gather. The force of meaning intensifies this scene because the custom of hospitality becomes the means by which the crowd (v. 2) and "all" the grumblers (v. 7) could flood into the house, transforming this potentially more private space into a setting for public interaction and speech. The crowd and its actions bring in the forces of time and social relations. Social relations play a recurring role beginning with the mention of the crowd in v. 2 and climaxing with the reference to "everyone" grumbling in v. 7. The crowd helps to set a public scene at the beginning of the story and is present through its denouement. The force of time comes into play in v. 7, which connects the urban and domestic scenes. This verse describes the ongoing presence of the crowd as it witnesses, complains about, and follows Jesus and Zacchaeus as they enter the house. The public pronouncements in vv. 8–10 weave together the forces of place, social relations, time, meaning, and religion. The text cues the audience to imagine a household scene for these pronouncements (place) but a scene that has been transformed into a public setting by the presence of the complaining crowd (social relations). Furthermore, both the conflict that Jesus faces and the way he responds to it fit the parameters of local politics as described by Plutarch. In the midst of the conflict, Zacchaeus stands and utters a declaration to Jesus and the crowd using an *insinuatio*, which allows the orator to speak publicly and indirectly at the same time (meaning). Jesus speaks in the same vein, addressing both Zacchaeus and the crowd. He publicly proclaims that "today" (time) salvation has come to this son of Abraham (religion). Jesus puts an end to the public conflict by publicly announcing salvation for Zacchaeus and his house.

Conclusion and Preview

Jesus' encounter with Zacchaeus is an unofficial public event with subtle overtones of public-political sphere. Luke has portrayed Jesus as he enters a city, initiates conflict by associating with Zacchaeus, and ends that conflict by announcing salvation. This summary will again turn to the forces and the characteristics of the public sphere and local politics to draw together the previous analysis and prepare for the implications discussed in the last part of this study.[135]

The force of place appears at the beginning of the story, tying it to the story of the blind beggar. Luke reiterates that these events occurred in Jericho, a city of significant standing. Jericho had an important role to play in regional political and military history, but it was also a prosperous unofficial center of trade, agriculture, and culture.[136] The city is a suitable setting for a figure like Zacchaeus with his mixed status, both official and unofficial. Jesus proceeds through the city on one of the major thoroughfares, which would have called up associations with public processions in the ancient world. While

---

135. The reader might find it helpful to review the chart displaying the characteristics of the public and local political spheres found at the end of ch. 5.

136. The history of and associations with Jericho may draw upon the force of meaning as well.

the setting of the city dominates the first half of the story (vv. 1–6), Luke transitions the story to Zacchaeus's home while maintaining the public nature of the interaction. Thus, the force of place operates in both a predictable and an unpredictable way. The opening urban setting creates a public scene to Luke's audience, but the public characteristics do not end when Jesus enters Zacchaeus's house. Instead, Luke employs several clues like the ongoing presence of the crowd and the nature of the pronouncements in vv. 8–10 to imply that the events that transpire inside of Zacchaeus's house are just as public as those that took place on the city streets. The surprising transformation of Zacchaeus's home into a public place through the ritual of hospitality throws the public nature of the entire event into sharp relief.

The force of social relations enters first with the characterization of Zacchaeus. The fact that he is rich places him in the upper echelons of society and yet he is despised by the local Jewish community because his wealth was taken as a sign of dishonesty, not blessing. The label ἀρχιτελώνης has a sparse and complicated history, but an audience in Asia Minor would have probably associated such a figure with the regional head of a *societas publicanorum*, which collected indirect taxes and often cheated or extorted money from the local populace.[137] Luke's portrayal of Zacchaeus stretches him across several boundaries: Jewish and Roman, wealth and dishonor, official and unofficial. Despite his mixed status, Jesus stops and asks Zacchaeus to host him in his house, accepting him as a social equal in the full view of the crowd. Zacchaeus's characterization then spills over to characterize Jesus as well: by accepting Zacchaeus, Jesus also accepts his liminal cultural, social, and official standing. The crowd is the other element in the force of social relations. It appears at the beginning of the story (v. 2), where Zacchaeus encounters them as an obstacle to seeing Jesus. He is a social outsider and lacks the authority to order the crowd aside. Luke reiterates the presence of the crowd by stating that "everyone" grumbled against Jesus (v. 7). This crowd captures a wide variety of people: city residents, disciples, and opponents. The crowd both lined the streets as Jesus walked through the city and filled the home of Zacchaeus, following on the heels of Jesus.

The force of nature establishes that this episode is predominantly, but not purely, a local and unofficial public event. The healing of the blind beggar was entirely unofficial, and many of the same characteristics carry through to this scene (road, crowd, outcast, conflict, salvation). Jesus' encounter with Zacchaeus is primarily unofficial; however, Zacchaeus's liminal status as a chief tax collector introduces subtle overtones of the public-political sphere. The complicated and liminal nature of Zacchaeus's character comes into play here. While Zacchaeus is primarily a Jewish businessman, his connections as a chief tax collector link him to the official public sphere where he would come into contact with local and regional authorities associated both with Jewish leadership and Roman administration. Thus, Zacchaeus serves as a subtle beginning of the increase of the public-political sphere that will develop in the next two pericopes (19:11–28 and 29–48). While Zacchaeus has these links to the administrative structures of the Roman Empire, Jesus' encounter with Zacchaeus is primarily an unofficial and local phenomenon. No other officials step into

---

137. Again, the force of meaning may come into play here because of the cultural understandings of a man in Zacchaeus's position.

the story, and the local knowledge of the crowd causes them to object to Jesus' association with this locally infamous "sinner." This event does not spill over into regional events (like the entry into Jerusalem) and is confined to the city of Jericho.

The force of time runs across the entire story, supporting its public characteristics in two ways. First, the connection of the blind beggar and Zacchaeus in the narrative establishes one public event that begins outside of the city and then grows as Jesus triumphantly enters and processes through Jericho. Second, the transitional material in vv. 6–7 and the public force of the declarations in vv. 8–10 give the impression that the crowd was present for the entire event, watching everything as it transpired. Jesus enters the city, meets Zacchaeus, enters Zacchaeus's home, and pronounces salvation. Time stretches across this event maintaining public characteristics throughout.

Finally, the forces of meaning and religion contribute to the public nature of this episode. Meaning colors the portrayal of Zacchaeus and the understanding of Jesus' procession through a major city. Meaning sets the parameters for Zacchaeus' act of hospitality. An ancient audience would have known that this custom allowed a certain degree of the public sphere to enter into the private domain of the home. However, Luke multiplies this effect of hospitality: not only do Jesus (and his associates) enter Zacchaeus's house, but the floodgates are opened and the entire (hostile) crowd enters as well. The force of meaning provides a way to understand the public and rhetorical nature of the pronouncements of vv. 8–10 by classifying them as an *insinuatio*. Finally, the force of meaning and religion help to climax this public event when Jesus publicly declares that salvation has come to this son of Abraham and that all this is in accordance with the public mission of the Son of man.

The social-spatial character of this pericope has implications for Luke's Gospel, Luke's audience, and the contemporary world. Chapter 9 will demonstrate how this story serves as microcosm of previous public episodes of conflict and salvation as well as preparing for the role of the Romans in the passion narrative. The double reference to Jericho in 18:35 and 19:1 signals the importance of this city in these two stories. A broader analysis of Luke's Gospel reveals his overriding preference for cities in his portrayal of Jesus. Luke balances this urban emphasis by also portraying Jesus in several significant household scenes. Like the story of Zacchaeus, these earlier scenes involve hospitality and burst the private boundaries of the houses, making them too into public settings of conflict and salvation. Many other stories in Luke reflect the importance of the city and the household as public settings for Jesus' mission, and these will be explored in chapter 9.

Chapter 10 will articulate the historical and contemporary implications of this passage. Luke's treatment of cities and houses as public settings for Jesus' ministry leads us to consider how this portrayal interacts with urban and domestic trends experienced by Luke's community. Urban growth had isolated power in the hands of the political and economic elite, reducing democratic participation as the influence of the empire and the gap between rich and poor both increased. Thus, the average person in the city was largely excluded from the political life of the city but still immersed in its public places. Many of the elite in this era seem to intensify the privacy and luxury of their personal homes, perhaps signaling a retreat from the public sphere and a heightening of private control.[138] Luke may be responding to both of these trends. His portrayal of Jesus as a popular figure interacting with a large populace in a city fits the urban growth of the early Roman Empire. Also, Luke may be rejecting the retreat to and increased control of homes. He adduces the ancient custom of hospitality, intensifies it, and portrays Jesus creating public episodes in homes that become settings for both conflict and salvation.[139]

Finally, Luke's use of cities and houses as settings for the ministry of Jesus raises interesting comparisons and contrasts with these places in the contemporary world. First, Luke portrays cities as thriving urban areas rich with opportunities for public interaction (and conflict). However, the exponential growth of the population of cities in the contemporary world has resulted in depersonalization and a loss of the unofficial public sphere. The gaps between those with wealth and power and those without are increasing. Political participation is decreasing. Public events (concerts, fairs, rallies) offer little opportunity for personal interaction or dialogue. Does Luke offer a way forward for Christian action and interaction in the urban domain? Second, while hospitality is alive and well in the contemporary world, it is often limited to personal friends and associates. The idea of welcoming a relative stranger into one's house as an act of hospitality is considered unusual and unsafe. What happens to Zacchaeus's home would certainly be considered trespassing. At the same time, the notion of the home as a private, inviolable retreat from the public sphere is on the rise. Luke's portrayal of Jesus in homes runs against this grain and suggests a radically different role for Christian hospitality.

The events in Zacchaeus's home do not end in 19:10. The parable that follows continues in this public and domestic setting. However, it is not only the external setting and function of the parable, but also its internal setting and function, that illustrates Luke's emphasis on the public sphere and local politics.

---

138. The same increase of private control may have been taking place in the various "house churches" in urban Christianity.

139. Moxnes claims that the household became the spatial heart of the transforming and inclusive presence of the kingdom of God (*Putting Jesus*, 105–6). However, he focuses on the historical Jesus and does not consider how the typically private household is burst open by Luke's portrayal of Jesus.

7

The Story of a King and His Subjects (19:11–28)
Public Pedagogy through a Political Parable

Introduction

WHILE JESUS IS STILL IN THE NOW PUBLIC SPACE OF ZACCHAEUS'S HOUSE, HE PROCEEDS to tell a parable to the gathered audience. The public scene of salvation and conflict in Zacchaeus's home changes to a scene of public pedagogy. Luke mentions the nearness of Jerusalem and the expectations of the large, mixed crowd as a transition to Jesus' parable of a king and his subjects. The parable deals with a nobleman who departs to be crowned as king. Before leaving, he charges ten of his servants to do business with part of his resources. A group of disgruntled citizens opposes his appointment and sends an embassy to protest. Upon his return, the king evaluates the performance of his servants and executes his enemies. Jesus speaks this parable in a public setting, and the parable deals with political matters (kings, servants, cities). A closer examination will reveal that Luke and his audience would have envisioned a grand public scene when the king judges his servants and enemies. Also, most of the story's political action takes place at the local scale with only necessary references to higher levels of politics. In 19:11–28 Luke presents Jesus teaching publicly with a parable that emphasizes local politics and the public sphere.

This parable has a long and complex history of interpretation. Much of the debate focuses on topics that are foundational to the following social-spatial exegesis. Therefore, the review of previous interpretation of this pericope will not be as brief as others in this study. The social-spatial exegesis of the passage will begin by reiterating the public setting of this parable and building upon previous interpretation to sharpen the understanding of the public purpose of the parable. Next, the exegesis will examine the local nature and public valence of the politics that takes place in Luke's version of this story. Finally, the public pedagogy of this parable deals with the four political characters in the story: the master-king, the faithful servants, the wicked servant, and the citizen-enemies. After the social-spatial exegesis, the conclusion will summarize the forces that make this parable local and public, and preview the literary and historical implications that will be covered in chapters 9 and 10.

The Story of a King and His Subjects (19:11–28)

A Review of Previous Interpretation

The parable of the king and his subjects is not unique to Luke (like the story of Zacchaeus), but Luke's distinctive placement and version of the story has drawn significant scholarly attention.[1] Three recurring elements in previous interpretations are relevant to the following social-spatial analysis. First, many have noted connections between the parable and the immediate narrative context, both the story of Zacchaeus and the entry into Jerusalem. Second, interpreters often employ historical/political parallels about other client kings in the Roman world to illuminate the events of the parable in Luke. Third and most prominently, scholars have debated the purpose of the parable at this juncture of the Gospel narrative.

Many interpreters observe that the grammar of v. 11 ties the entire pericope to the preceding story.[2] Luke's redactional touches on this verse are obvious, and he has inserted the parable into Mark's framework.[3] Many commentaries and articles repeat the axiom that Jesus' bold statements in 19:9–10 about the arrival of *salvation, today*, for a *son of Abraham* fueled eschatological expectation and prompted the following parable.[4] However, scholars have failed to see the spatial connection between the two stories. Many simply ignore the implication that this story is told while Jesus is still in Zacchaeus's house before he leaves for Jerusalem in v. 28. Some note it but do little to develop its significance.[5] Others try to explain the public nature of the parable (addressed to the crowd) by claiming that Jesus told it before he arrived in Zacchaeus's house.[6] However, the previous chapter demonstrated that Luke places several clues in his story of Jesus' encounter with Zacchaeus to indicate that Jesus did enter Zacchaeus's home to enjoy his hospitality. Connecting the story in the other direction, many interpreters have fruitfully read the parable in light of Jesus' entry into Jerusalem. However, they do not attend to how the crowd adds to the public valence of both stories. Therefore, they miss how the third servant in the story illuminates the role of the crowd at Jesus' entry (see further below).

---

1. Scholars in the first half of the twentieth century sought to unravel the tradition history of 19:12–27 in comparison with the similar story found in Matt 25:14–30. Both pericopes share similar elements, but the Lukan version differs not only in minor details (e.g., ten servants instead of three), but also by adding unique material about the "throne-claimant" (19:12, 14–15a, 27). Most scholars now accept that Q material lies behind both versions. See Denaux, "Parable of the Talents/Pounds." This conclusion requires a decision regarding the provenance of the unique material in Luke. Was the "throne-claimant" a second parable merged here into the Q parable by (or before) Luke, or was it a Lukan composition added to the existing Q parable? While the question is not critical to this study, I will proceed on the hypothesis that Luke has adapted a tradition to create 19:12, 14–15a and 27, combining these elements with his redacted version of the Q parable. For a defense of this position, see Denaux, "King-Judge," 51–53.

2. Plummer, *Luke*, 438; Green, *Luke*, 677; Nolland, *Luke 18:35–24:53*, 912; Aletti, "Parable," 323–24.

3. Denaux, "King-Judge," 46.

4. Plummer, *Luke*, 438; Nolland, *Luke*, 913; Green, *Luke*, 677. Differences emerge over whose expectations are raised. Is it the (Jewish) crowd (Denaux, "King-Judge," 47) or the disciples more specifically (Green, *Luke*, 677)?

5. Ellis, *Luke*, 221; Hamm, "Luke 19:8," 435 and n. 21.

6. Fitzmyer, *Luke*, 2:1224–25; and Johnson, *Luke*, 285–86.

PART TWO: SOCIAL-SPATIAL EXEGESIS OF LUKE 18:35—19:48

Many interpreters employ historical and political parallels about client kings in the early Roman Empire to clarify the plot and meaning of the parable.[7] Interpreters claim that Luke's audience knows the contours of such a story from cultural patterns and typified literary accounts about client kings and their accession to power.[8] These parallels do help us fill in some information that would have been supplied by Luke's high context audience. However, scholars fail to note how Luke's parable diverges from the loose set of elements that characterize these accounts. Most importantly, they do not see that, in contrast to the imperial focus of Roman historians, Luke concentrates on local politics and the public sphere as the nobleman-become-king publicly doles out rewards and punishments to his own servants and citizens after returning home.

Finally, several recent articles on the parable of the king and his subjects have wrestled with the function of the parable, especially in light of v. 11. The "traditional" interpretation reads it as an allegory directed at Luke's audience. In this case, Jesus (the nobleman) goes to a distant land (heaven, at the ascension) where he receives a kingdom and then returns (at the Parousia) to judge his servants and opponents. This reading exhorts Luke's audience to accept Christ as King and to utilize divine or ecclesial resources during his absence.[9] Some authors have moved away from allegorization, but still emphasize the paranetic function of the parable for Luke's audience, calling them to faithful obedience during Christ's absence.[10] However, this perspective falls short on two related accounts. First, several points of the allegorization misfire and cannot make sense (e.g., How could the opponents follow Jesus to heaven to object to his kingship? Is the third servant ejected from the kingdom, or not?). Second, this perspective has difficulty interpreting the parable as a whole, especially Luke's version with the additional throne-claimant material.[11]

A small number of commentators object to this view claiming that Luke does not associate Jesus with the nobleman-become-king. On the contrary, the "king" in the parable is an ambitious, exploitative, vengeful foil to the humble and peaceable king, Jesus.[12] Herzog and Culpepper assert that the royal figure of the parable is an antitype to Jesus. The master-king of the parable fits a Palestinian peasant's view of oppressive absentee landlords, while Jesus' reign as king contradicts the political and economic practices of the aristocracy.[13] This perspective fails for several reasons. First, Luke's urban audience did not share the same peasant view of absentee landlords as argued by Herzog. Second, if the political violence of 19:27 is unfitting for the Lukan Jesus, then one must also reject texts like Luke 17:27–38 and 20:16 that frankly speak of the destruction of God's enemies. Finally

---

7. The contemporary discussion of these parallels was launched by Weinert, "Throne Claimant." See also Bock, *Luke*, 2:1532; Nolland, *Luke*, 918; and Denaux, "King-Judge," 53–54.

8. Busse, "Dechiffrierung," 432–33. Culpepper says that client king stories are part of a "cultural type scene" (*Luke* 9:362).

9. Marshall, *Luke*, 702. Also see the list of supporters cited in Busse, "Dechiffrierung," 424 n. 5. Busse cites a monograph as late as 1996 that takes this position (see 434–35).

10. See ibid., 440; Bovon, *Saint Luc*, 3c:265–66; and Fusco, "Point of View," 1691.

11. See Johnson, *Luke*, 293–94.

12. Green, *Luke*, 675–77; Herzog, *Parables*, 150–68; Culpepper, *Luke*, 9:361–64.

13. Herzog, *Parables*, 160–61.

in v. 26, the king announces his rationale for transferring the one pound to the servant with ten pounds: "To all those who have, more will be given; but those who have nothing, even what they have will be taken away." Jesus employs the same principle (with many of the same words) in Luke 8:18, which suggests an analogy between the two characters. The analogy between Jesus and the nobleman-king is not perfect and complete, but it is the comparison, not the contrast, between the characters that is most illuminating.

Interest in Luke's political apologetic has led a few interpreters to argue that this parable fits Luke's desire to distance Jesus from Jewish revolutionaries. They maintain that the "delay" portrayed in the parable does not attempt to solve a theological dilemma for Luke's audience as they await the Parousia (as in the traditional interpretation). Instead, the delay functions to relocate Jesus' kingship (and kingdom) to another time and realm away from the present.[14] Jesus will reign, but the political consummation of his kingdom lies in the future. Thus, the parable deals with Lukan politics more than Lukan eschatology. This perspective appropriately attends to the political nature of this parable, but if Luke wished to distance Jesus from royal implications, he has botched the job. Jesus is proclaimed king in 19:38 and several royal characterizations of Jesus follow (23:2, 37–38, 42). Furthermore, even if his reign is temporarily postponed, Jesus (as implied by the parable) is still a king who judges his servants and executes his enemies, hardly details that would quell anxiety about his political ambitions.

While most interpreters use the immediate literary context (especially the entry story) to interpret the parable, the last two perspectives outlined below emphasize this connection more robustly. The most radical revision of the traditional view insists that the parable does not refute the imminent expectation expressed in 19:11 but confirms it, setting the stage for the explicit proclamation of Jesus as king when he enters Jerusalem. This interpretation was suggested by Tiede,[15] more completely developed by Johnson,[16] and extended by Potterie.[17] Proponents of this view discount traditional allegorizing and revisit the relationship of the parable to the introduction in v. 11.[18] This verse can be read as an expectation about the kingdom that is confirmed in the parable and in Luke's larger narrative because Jesus is declared king in 19:38 and his servants/apostles exercise authority in Acts. This perspective is intriguing and insightful, yet also runs into obstacles. First, the explanations of παραχρῆμα and ἀναφαίνεσθαι are in tension since the first must be tangible and palpable[19] while the second is transformed into a mere "proclamation" (a very strained reading of ἀναφαίνω).[20] Second, some elements of the parable's timeline and its relation to Luke's narrative break down. The parable does not require a long delay,

---

14. Nolland, *Luke*, 918; and Kinman, *Jesus' Entry*, 89.
15. Tiede, *Prophecy and History*, 79–80.
16. Johnson, "Kingship Parable." Also see his commentary (*Luke*, 292–94).
17. La Potterie, "Parabole du Prétendant."
18. Johnson, "Kingship Parable," 146–51.
19. Ibid., 148.
20. Nolland calls Johnson's interpretation of the term "impossible" but without further explanation (*Luke*, 913). Denaux is more correct to explain the use of ἀναφαίνω in 19:11 by how Luke uses it in Acts 21:3, "coming into view" with emphasis on the spatial aspect ("King-Judge," 47).

but it does require the master's *absence*, and this perspective allows no time for absence.[21] Finally, this reading must contend that Jesus' audience in v. 11 has a nuanced view of the kingdom of God. However, in Luke's account the disciples (Acts 1:6–8), the crowds (Luke 12:54–56), and the Pharisees (17:20–21) all misunderstand the eschatological significance of the ministry of Jesus. The narrative does not support the sudden enlightenment of the mixed crowd in v. 11, which would then be confirmed by the parable.

However, Johnson does offer a way forward by examining how parables in Luke relate to the perspectives of Jesus' audiences. He cites one case where Jesus tells a parable to refute the view of his audience (18:9, 10–14) and one case where Jesus tells a parable to confirm his own previous statements (13:6–9). Unfortunately, Johnson creates a false dichotomy by offering these as the only functions of parables in Luke: they either counter or confirm.[22] Johnson's own examination suggests a third alternative: shift or correct.[23] Jesus can speak to correct or redirect comments from the crowd (11:27–29; 12:13–21; 13:22–29), the disciples (9:46–56; 10:17–20), and his opponents (14:15–24; 16:14–31). Most of Jesus' parables correct, shift, subvert, or redirect the comments of the audience, offering a new way of viewing the situation. The implications of the Zacchaeus story and the content of the parable imply that all three audiences (crowd, disciples, and opponents) are present for this public teaching in Zacchaeus's house. Jesus' publicly teaches this amassed audience as he has addressed each discretely before, by correcting their mistaken notions about the kingdom.

The final perspective also emphasizes the conjunction of the parable and the entry to Jerusalem while attempting to hold the present and future implications of the parable together. Guy articulates the paradox well: "The kingdom will not appear immediately. And yet it will, for the king has come."[24] Proponents claim that the parable, especially in relation to v. 11, attests to a delay of the coming kingdom, a delay implied by the *distant* land of v. 12.[25] This "future" element of the kingdom in the parable corrects the Jewish expectation of the (political) arrival of the messianic kingdom at Zion,[26] which may have been activated by Jesus proclaiming salvation "today" in 19:10.[27] This does not imply the "problem" of a long delay of the Parousia in Luke's day, but the kingdom does not arrive as anticipated by

---

21. Carroll notes that even the idea of distance must be overlooked by this perspective, for Jesus does not receive his kingship "in a distant land" but nearby in Jerusalem (*Eschatology*, 102).

22. Johnson, *Luke*, 292. A similar critique is mentioned by Carroll, *Eschatology*, 101 n. 247.

23. He speaks of the subtle "rebuff" of the Pharisees in the parable of the rich man and Lazarus (16:19–31), the implicit subversion of the lawyer's question in the parable of the good Samaritan (10:30–35), and a shift in perspective achieved by the parable of the great banquet (14:16–24). Johnson is technically correct when he says that the "lost" parables of ch. 15 confirm the Pharisees' description of Jesus' ministry (15:2, "This fellow welcomes sinners and eats with them."). However, these parables upend the Pharisaic *evaluation* of his ministry, shifting the focus from the wickedness of the "lost" to the joy that comes when the lost repent. See Johnson, "Kingship Parable," 146–47.

24. Guy, "Interplay," 133.

25. Ibid., 127; Fusco, "Point of View," 1687–89; Busse, "Dechiffrierung," 439.

26. See Zech 9:9–10 and Tg. Isa. 31:4–5.

27. Busse, "Dechiffrierung," 433; Guy, "Interplay," 126–27; Denaux, "King-Judge," 48–50. Fusco adds that such an explanation might have had apologetic significance for Luke's readers, explaining to their contemporaries why the kingdom did not come when Jesus arrived at Jerusalem ("Point of View," 1690–91).

the crowd and may serve Luke's community as an apologetic to certain Jews.[28] Through this story, Luke has Jesus correct the audience by disassociating himself from the immediacy of the kingdom (the force of time) and from the nearness to Jerusalem (the force of place), but the parable still underscores the presence of the kingdom in the person of Jesus, the king (the characterization of self). This perspective handles the issue of delay (and absence) and the identity of the king more satisfactorily than the others.

The social-spatial exegesis will build on this final perspective to clarify the meaning of v. 11 and the purpose of the parable as a whole. In preparation for the social-spatial exegesis of 19:11–28, this review of previous interpretation highlights three matters that need further clarification. First, the narrative setting of this parable must be established and considered when interpreting the parable. The mixed audience gathered in Zacchaeus's house illuminates the characters in the story. Second, scholars often recount historical and literary parallels to this parable, but they fail to consider the public implications of this material and the way Luke focuses on local (not imperial) matters in his account. Finally, grasping the public and political nature of the parable clarifies the message of the story in Luke's account.

The Social-Spatial Characteristics of 19:11–28

The exegesis of 19:11–28 raises a special question for this study. What does social-spatial analysis have to say about a pericope that has very little setting or action (limited to v. 11) and instead is mostly comprised of a story told by Jesus? Given this scenario, v. 11 will function prominently in the analysis, for it does contain several high-context clues that indicate the public setting of the parable. Additionally, the nature of the story itself in Luke's version may be read as a mirror of Luke's own social-spatial situation. The parable told by Jesus reflects the same social-spatial verisimilitude that characterizes Luke's retelling of the story of Jesus. That is, both stories about Jesus and stories by Jesus within that story have implications for the social-spatial character of Luke's narrative. Therefore, the social-spatial analysis of 19:11–28 falls into three sections. First, v. 11 maintains the setting of 19:7–10, where a large, mixed crowd flooded into and "publicized" Zacchaeus's home. Understanding this public setting helps to clarify the meaning of v. 11 and the purpose of the parable. Second, Luke's version of the parable portrays a public setting for the local politics that take place in the story. Finally, this parable and the audiences it addresses highlight the public nature of Jesus' pedagogy.

Verse 11: The Public Setting and Purpose of the Parable

Verse 11 connects the parable that follows to the preceding story about Jesus' encounter with Zacchaeus. Luke achieves this with specific grammatical forms at the beginning of the verse. These connections establish social and spatial continuity between vv. 7–10 and 12–28, indicating that the location and the audience stay the same: a large, mixed crowd gathered in Zacchaeus's home. This understanding of the setting casts new light on the

---

28. Fusco, "Point of View," 1690; Denaux, "King-Judge," 48–49.

meaning and implications of the latter half of the verse, which clarifies the purpose of the parable.

Verse 11 begins with ἀκουόντων δὲ αὐτῶν ταῦτα.[29] This is a textbook example of the genitive absolute. The subject of the participle (αὐτῶν, the crowd) is different from the subject of the main clause (Jesus). Furthermore, the genitive absolute is (concurrent) temporal, and thus the present participle connects what follows to the events and pronouncements in vv. 7–10.[30] The most likely grammatical antecedent for αὐτῶν is the πάντες of v. 7, which refers inclusively to the general crowd, Jesus' opponents, Jesus' disciples, and Zacchaeus's household.[31] Thus, the αὐτοί at the beginning and later in the verse recalls the large crowd gathered in Zacchaeus's house. The (neuter, plural) pronoun ταῦτα typically points to immediately preceding material,[32] and in this case it refers to Jesus' two closing pronouncements in vv. 9–10. The participle and (main) verb that follow this opening clause support the continuity of location and time. The combination προθεὶς εἶπεν παραβολήν can be translated, "Jesus went on to tell a parable."[33] The combination of προστίθημι with εἶπεν indicates that Jesus simply continued speaking publicly in Zacchaeus's home without interruption, flowing from the end of v. 10 to the beginning of v. 12.[34] Therefore, v. 11 establishes a continuous scene between 19:1–10 and 19:12–28. Jesus follows his public pronouncement of salvation in Zacchaeus's home (19:9–10) by immediately speaking a parable in this public setting. The connection of these two pericopes has implications not only for the location of the parable but also for its audience and purpose.

As stated above, the αὐτῶν in the first clause of v. 11 refers back to the πάντες of v. 7. Thus, the audience of the parable is the same as the audience of the events surrounding Zacchaeus, an audience that was unanimously hostile to Jesus (19:7) and ignorant about his mission to bring salvation to the lost (19:10). However, not all commentators agree on this. Some scholars identify "they" as the disciples[35] or stress the eschatologically confused Jewish crowd.[36] However, Johnson and Denaux are right to say that the αὐτοί at the beginning of v. 11 refers to the entire audience gathered in Zacchaeus's home, which consists of three groups: crowd, opponents, and disciples.[37] The parable also features three

---

29. Many commentators note that v. 11 ties the following parable to the story of Zacchaeus, but few note the specifics of how this occurs. See Nolland, *Luke*, 912; Green, *Luke*, 677 (who simply notes the genitive absolute); Carroll, *Eschatology*, 97. Others only note part of the following evidence.

30. Wallace, *Greek*, 655; and Marshall, *Luke*, 703.

31. Deneaux, "King-Judge," 49; Johnson, *Luke*, 289.

32. Wallace, *Greek Grammar*, 333. See a similar usage of ταῦτα in Luke 14:20 and also the comments by Bock, *Luke*, 2:1531.

33. This is probably an attendant circumstance construction, literally "and he continued and said." See Wallace, *Greek Grammar*, 640–43; and Marshall, *Luke*, 703 and 149.

34. Johnson makes a similar point (*Luke*, 289). The best analog to this use of προστίθημι in Luke-Acts is in Acts 12:3, where Herod "continues" his persecution of Christians by arresting Peter after executing James.

35. Bock, *Luke*, 2:1531. Green specifically reiterates the presence of the disciples at this point, but includes them as part of the larger crowd (*Luke*, 677–78).

36. Nolland, *Luke*, 913. Denaux, "King-Judge," 49–50. Fusco calls them "other people who are not better identified" ("Point of View," 1678).

37. Johnson, "Kingship Parable," 145; and Denaux, "King-Judge," 49. The second use of αὐτοί later in the verse refers to this same large, mixed group. Fitzmyer speaks of a "vague audience" including the crowd,

sets of characters that interact with the nobleman-king: the hostile citizens (v. 14 and 27), the two faithful servants (vv. 16–19), and the "wicked" servant (vv. 20–23). Luke sets up several parallels between Jesus' trifold audience, the actions of various groups at the entry into Jerusalem, and the characters in the parable which demonstrate that all three groups (crowd, opponents, disciples) are gathered in Zacchaeus's house to hear the parable.

All three of the groups that make up this public audience are mistaken about the presence of the kingdom and its relationship to Jesus earlier in the Gospel. In ch. 11, the crowds (v. 14) fail to recognize the presence of the kingdom in the power behind Jesus' exorcisms (vv. 19–20). Later, Jesus upbraids them for properly interpreting meteorological signs but missing the significance of τὸν καιρόν of Jesus' ministry (12:54–56). Therefore, the crowd in Luke is guilty of not recognizing and acting on the eschatological significance of Jesus and his ministry. Not surprisingly, Jesus' opponents are also mistaken about the presence and coming of the kingdom. They berate Jesus because they fail to recognize the days of the bridegroom (5:34–35) and maintain the stubborn perspective of old wineskins (5:36–39). They mistakenly ask for observable signs (17:20–21) and miss both the present (v. 21) and future (vv. 22ff) dimensions of the kingdom. Therefore, Jesus' opponents not only fail to see the presence of the kingdom, but their failure leads them to reject Jesus as well. Finally, and somewhat surprisingly, the disciples are also wrong on this topic. In 12:35–48, Jesus warns his disciples to be active and alert like a slave awaiting the return of the master.[38] Recently, in 18:31–34, they are privy to Jesus' prediction of the final phase of his ministry, but they are prevented from understanding its full significance. Even after the resurrection in Acts 1:6–8, they are still asking the wrong questions about the kingdom, dreaming of its immediate (and national) restoration by Jesus. Therefore, Jesus' disciples recognize that their master is the agent of God's kingdom, but they must be rebuked for focusing too much on the present when they need to prepare for service in the future. Each audience (crowd, opponents, disciples) has its own particular way in which it does not grasp the kingdom of God, and a similar pattern obtains in Jesus' parable and at the triumphal entry.

Many interpreters have noted and probed the connection between the parable and the entry story,[39] and this connection has led interpreters to see the parallels between the connections between the faithful servants and the disciples as well as the hostile citizens and the Jewish leadership.[40] This fits well with the characteristic misunderstanding of each group earlier in the Gospel. Just as the Pharisees failed to recognize Jesus' kingdom mission in the past and consequently complained against him, so they do at the

---

disciples, and opponents (*Luke*, 2:1234). Busse similarly states that the parable answers Jesus' critics and quells the enthusiasm of his disciples ("Dechriffrierung," 434). Johnson goes on to note that the eschatological hopes of each group would be energized by the statements in vv. 9–10. Yet, this begs the question as to whether or not Jesus' words (and actions) in 19:1–10 are the source of fresh eschatological fervor in the crowd, which likewise bears upon the purpose of the parable.

38. Jesus takes the initiative in this case. No statement or action on the part of the disciples appears to prompt him. However, Luke makes it clear that he is addressing his disciples in 12:22 and 41.

39. See especially Johnson, "Kingship Parable"; Guy, "Interplay"; and Denaux, "King-Judge."

40. Johnson, "Kingship Parable," 156–58; Denaux, "King-Judge," 54–55; La Potterie, "Parabole du Prétendant," 636–37; Aletti, "Parabole des Mines," 325–26; Guy, "Interplay," 120–25.

entry once again (v.39). By the end of the entry story, Jesus earns the murderous ire of the Jewish leaders, stepping up both the scale of leadership and the degree of animosity. The citizens in the parable similarly reject the nobleman, verbally oppose his reign, and face the ultimate sentence from the returned king-judge much like the ultimate sentence against Jerusalem in 19:41–44. Therefore, the character of the hostile citizens in the parable functions as a warning to Jesus' opponents (typically Jewish leaders) in the audience gathered in Zacchaeus's home. On the contrary, the disciples honor Jesus as king at the entry (19:38), similar to the first two servants who obey their master as the future king (19:17–19). The good servants already work for their master; he entrusts his resources to them during his absence, and rewards them with greater authority upon his return. The disciples are already following Jesus, but here he once again exhorts them, as he has before and will again in Acts, to focus on their patient service in the near future while awaiting his return in full authority.[41] This confirms that Luke envisions both Jesus' opponents and his disciples as part of the audience gathered in Zacchaeus's house.

However, this leaves the important (and somewhat perplexing) figure of the third servant with no analogous character in the immediate or larger narrative.[42] The critical link is inaction. Just as the third servant does nothing with the resources entrusted to him, so the crowd says nothing about Jesus' entry in Luke. The only mention of the crowd in 19:29–44 is that some of Pharisees are among the crowd (v. 39). The crowd "listens attentively" (19:48) to Jesus but says nothing as he comes into the city.[43] Their presence protects Jesus while he teaches in the temple, but they never publicly act or speak in support of Jesus. Later, they fall in with the Jewish leadership, demanding Jesus' death (23:13–23). The third ("wicked") servant of the parable is paralyzed by his fearful perception of the master-king as the crowd is subdued by the competing voices of acclamation and rejection at the entry. Jesus previously rebuked the crowd for failing to recognize and respond to the eschatological significance of his ministry. Sadly, the parable (and the rest of the Gospel) demonstrates that this warning fell on deaf ears. The crowds still fail to act (by acclaiming Jesus at the entry) as the "wicked" servant fails to act in the parable. Chapter 5 discussed Luke's portrayal of a fickle crowd. At Jesus' entry, their fickleness, uncertainty, and fear reduces them to silence, a silence that will earn them no approbation from the king, just like the third servant in the parable. The third servant is stripped of his place in the kingdom (19:24); so the crowd joins Jesus' opponents in demanding his death (23:13–23), and

---

41. Green asserts that "issues of alertness and faithful allegiance are at center stage" in the parable (*Luke*, 679).

42. Johnson, Denaux, and La Potterie make almost no mention of the "wicked" servant at the end of their articles. Fusco suggests that the third servant warns Christians to stay faithful ("Point of View," 1691). Some discuss the third slave's harsh characterization of the master-king (Green, *Luke*, 679–80; Busse, "Dechiffrierung," 436–47). Nolland sees a kind of "nominalism" in the third servant who simply manages risk without commitment (*Luke*, 918–19). Bock has the best discussion of the identification of the third servant (*Luke*, 1541–43). The third servant could point to the Jewish leadership (following Jeremias), one like the "carnal believer" of 1 Cor 3 (following Danker), or the eschatologically condemned third slave of the Matthean version (following Plummer and Klostermann). Bock opts for the last option, but doing so forces him to read Matthew into Luke and fails to read the story as part of Luke's narrative.

43. In contrast, both Mark and Matthew (11:9 and 21:9 respectively) depict the crowd crying out to welcome Jesus to Jerusalem.

they become part of the "city" that is destroyed for its blindness (19:41–44). Therefore, the character of the "wicked" servant relates to the "crowd" element of the audience in Zacchaeus's house.

Understanding the threefold makeup of Jesus' audience as he publicly tells this parable casts light on the remainder of v. 11 and the purpose of the parable in Luke's Gospel. The rest of v. 11 gives two reasons for why Jesus goes on to tell the following parable:[44] (1) Jesus is near Jerusalem, and (2) "they" expect to see the kingdom imminently. The typical explanation requires an interpretive rephrasing of this long articular infinitive clause: (after Jesus spoke the pronouncements of 19:9–10) "he told this parable *because they thought the kingdom of God was about to come into sight immediately because he was near Jerusalem.*" Thus, most claim that the combination of the powerful language in v. 9 ("today, salvation . . . has come") and the nearness of Jerusalem prompt a burgeoning of eschatological expectation among Jesus' audience. However, three points argue against this reading. First, the preceding analysis of v. 11a showed that Jesus speaks continuously from 19:10 to 19:12. Luke does not narrate any change of heart on the part of the crowd, and they say nothing. Despite the redactional introduction in v. 11, no one in the crowd speaks, no events transpire, and nothing changes. There is no (narrative) time for the crowd to "mumble" their eschatological expectation for Jesus to overhear and answer. Second, both occurrences of αὐτοί in v. 11 (including this latter one) refer to the large, trifold audience that was thoroughly disgusted with Jesus' actions only five verses ago (19:7) and repeatedly misunderstands Jesus' eschatological significance in the Gospel. Does the narrative make it feasible to believe that this "grumbling" audience (with crowd, opponents, and disciples) was so impressed by Jesus' proclamations in vv. 9–10 that they now think that Jesus will usher in the kingdom of God? No. We hear of no reversal in the crowd's opinion of Jesus.[45] They are still mistaken, and Jesus knows it. Finally, the reading above switches the primary agency of the infinitives to the crowd. The main verb of the sentence (εἶπεν) has Jesus as its subject; therefore, he should be the focus of the substantiating material in the rest of the verse. The impetus behind the parable lies with Jesus. Luke has Jesus tell this parable because of what he knows about the crowd. The situation is analogous to Jesus' supernatural perception in the story of the paralytic (5:21–24). It is more apropos to supply an ellipsis and translate v. 11b as "because *he knew that* he was near Jerusalem and that they thought the kingdom was about to come into sight immediately."

Throughout Luke-Acts, Jewish characters eagerly await the appearance of the kingdom. As shown above, each element gathered in Zacchaeus's home (crowd, opponents, disciples) has a record of (mistaken) eschatological expectation in Luke-Acts.[46] The birth of Jesus excites eschatological hopes in the infancy narrative (1:32–33, 68–70; 2:25–32, 38;

---

44. The causal function is marked by διὰ τό (Wallace, *Greek Grammar*, 596–97). This preposition and article govern both of the following infinitives (εἶναι, δοκεῖν) which are linked by the conjunction καί. Each interpreter has a different perspective on the precise significance of this clause, but they largely agree that this is what it says. See Nolland, *Luke*, 913; Johnson, *Luke*, 292–93; Green, *Luke*, 677–78; Bock, *Luke*, 1531; Bovon, *Luc*, 3c:256; and Guy, "Interplay," 126.

45. Fitzmyer says, "There is no connection between this expectation [in v. 11] and Jesus' words to Zacchaeus" (2:1234), but he does not substantiate this claim.

46. Luke 2:25, 38; 3:15; 14:15; 17:20; 21:5–7; Acts 1:6–7; 3:19–21.

3:15–17). Sometimes Jesus' words or actions arouse expectations (5:34–37; 7:16, 18–23; 9:18–20; 14:15; 24:19–24), and sometimes Jesus asserts his own eschatological significance (4:18–21; 10:23–24; 11:20, 19:41–44; 21:7–36). However, not all eschatological expectation emerges from Jesus, for Luke also establishes such anticipation as a general Jewish attitude during Jesus' ministry.[47] Many people were *already* "looking for the redemption of Jerusalem" (2:38) when Anna told them about Jesus. The people's *already*-existing expectation is excited by John's preaching (3:15). The Pharisees spontaneously ask Jesus about the coming of the kingdom with no impetus from him (17:20). Peter speaks about "times of refreshing," a "universal restoration," and a prophet like Moses to a Jewish crowd that appears familiar with such topics (Acts 3:19–23). Adding 19:11 to this matrix, Luke regularly portrays the Jews of Jesus' day as a people with heightened eschatological expectations. Jesus' person and ministry intensify existing hopes. Thus, in this story, Luke does not tell us that the crowd suddenly changes their opinion, sees Jesus as the messianic agent of God's kingdom, and begins murmuring about his climactic nearness to Jerusalem. Rather, in v. 11 Luke says that Jesus perceives that his nearness to Jerusalem and the prevalent eschatological expectation among his amalgamated Jewish audience provides an excellent opportunity for a parable that addresses each group in the audience and corrects their mistaken conceptions about the eschaton and their place in it. Verse 11b gives the two reasons cited by Luke to explain why Jesus, without a break, moves from his final words in v. 10 to tell the parable at this public gathering in Zacchaeus's house.

Luke's description of the crowd's expectation in v. 11b fits with Luke's overall portrayal of the eschatological mistakenness of Jesus' audiences in the Gospel. Luke says that δοκεῖν αὐτοὺς ὅτι παραχρῆμα μέλλει ἡ βασιλεία τοῦ θεοῦ ἀναφαίνεσθαι. It is true that δοκέω does not necessarily connote mistakenness, only a subjective opinion.[48] Therefore, one must rely on the context to provide the positive or negative connotation of this term. Johnson states, "It depends on content whether it (δοκέω) is a mere 'supposition', or a 'consideration.'" However, this is only partially true, for it also depends upon the subject who holds the opinion. When Luke speaks of the crowds and δοκέω, they are typically mistaken. In Luke 12:51, Jesus asks the crowds (see 12:54), "Do you think that [δοκεῖτε ὅτι] I have come to bring peace to the earth?" The question presumes that they do think so, but Jesus' answer is a firm "No!" Soon afterwards (13:1–5), Jesus addresses another crowd about their mistaken conceptions: "Do you think that [δοκεῖτε ὅτι] . . . they were worse sinners than all other Galileans?" (13:2); and "Do you think [δοκεῖτε ὅτι] . . . they were worse offenders than all the others living in Jerusalem?" (13:4). In both cases, the answer reflects their mistaken opinion, for Jesus again asserts, "No!" The mistakenness of the crowd throughout the Gospel colors Luke's use of the term δοκέω in 19:11—as the crowd has thought erroneously before, so they do again in 19:11.

Furthermore, the content of the supposition also supports its mistakenness (contra Johnson and Potterie). However, the content is difficult to understand given the unusual

---

47. Many scholars refer to this general expectation but with little attention to Luke's indications of it in the Gospel. See Denaux, "King-Judge," 50; Guy, "Interplay," 126; Fusco, "Point of View," 1690.

48. Johnson, "Kingship Parable," 146; and La Potterie, "Parabole du Prétendant," 622–23.

The Story of a King and His Subjects (19:11–28)

word choices and syntax.[49] The crowd thinks that παραχρῆμα μέλλει ἡ βασιλεία τοῦ θεοῦ ἀναφαίνεσθαι. This is only one of two instances in Luke-Acts (and five in the whole NT) where μέλλω is complemented by an aorist infinitive.[50] Even though ἀναφαίνεσθαι is aorist, it combines with μέλλω to form a periphrastic future.[51] Regarding the complements for μέλλω, Smyth states that "the aorist is used when it is important to mark the action as ingressive, resultative, or complexive."[52] The emphasis here is probably complexive, concentrating the entire manifestation of the kingdom into a single point.[53] The verb μέλλω can refer to future events that are at hand (Luke 19:4; Acts 5:35; 16:27) or that still lie at some distance in the future (Luke 9:31, 44; 10:1; Acts 12:6; 17:31). This verb can also connote nearness and/or certainty: that an event will definitely and/or soon occur.[54] This combination establishes the certainty of the event, but the timing of its realization remains ambiguous in the near to not so near future. Finally, the only other occurrence of μέλλω with an aorist infinitive in Luke-Acts refers to an event that does not obtain (Herod's exhibition of the imprisoned Peter in Acts 12:6). Thus, the combination μέλλει . . . ἀναφαίνεσθαι encapsulates the entire occurrence of the future coming of the kingdom, but this coming does not occur as anticipated.

Luke fronts παραχρῆμα, probably for emphasis, even though it modifies ἀναφαίνεσθαι several words away at the end of the clause.[55] Luke often employs παραχρῆμα to describe the physical manifestation of Jesus' miracles (Luke 4:39; 5:25; 8:44, 47, 55; 13:13; 18:43; Acts 3:7).[56] On two occasions a person dies "on the spot" (Acts 5:10; 12:23). It also appears to refer to other immediate, observable events in Luke 1:64 (Zechariah speaks) and 22:60 (cock crows) as well as Acts 13:11 (blindness falls), 16:26 (doors open), and 16:33 (people are baptized). An event is παραχρῆμα for Luke because it is tangible, observable, and happens without delay, on the spot. Recalling that the combination μέλλει . . . ἀναφαίνεσθαι refers to a future event, this is the only instance in Luke-Acts (or the NT as a whole) where παραχρῆμα modifies a future instead of a past event.[57] What then is the nature of this event in light of the verb? Luke's other use of ἀναφαίνω (in the active

---

49. The reordering of words in the textual tradition for both halves of the διὰ τό clause reveals that even the ancients were somewhat confused.

50. Smyth states that μέλλω is usually completed "with the present or future (rarely the aorist) infinitive" (*Greek Grammar*, #1959). The other three instances occur in Revelation.

51. Smyth, *Greek Grammar*, #1959.

52. Ibid.

53. Ibid., #1927. This works against La Potterie's interpretation that the entrance proleptically reflects the ascension ("Parabole du Prétendant," 632–34). The ingressive is unlikely because ἀναφαίνω is not a verb that connotes a state or continued action (Smyth, *Greek Grammar*, #1924). The resultative is possible, but the end or effect of the kingdom does not seem to be the focus.

54. Luow and Nida, *Greek-English Lexicon*, 637 and 672.

55. A look at παραχρῆμα in Luke-Acts shows that this adverb is next to or only one word (typically just a particle) away from the verb it modifies thirteen times. The only exceptions are Luke 19:11; 22:60; and Acts 16:33 where more than three words separate verb and adverb.

56. Note that it is missing in the healing of the centurion's servant (7:1–10), which happens at some distance.

57. A brief look at the uses of παραχρῆμα cited above shows that they all refer to (very recent) past events.

PART TWO: SOCIAL-SPATIAL EXEGESIS OF LUKE 18:35—19:48

voice) in Acts 21:3 refers to the sighting of Cyprus as Paul sails to Jerusalem. In the passive, the prefix ἀνα- often intensifies the root of this verb, giving the meaning "to appear *plainly* or *clearly*" (consistent with παραχρῆμα).[58] This meaning fits well with the active use in 21:3, for both refer to actual appearances. Finally, this meaning correlates with a Jewish view that the kingdom of God would appear dramatically at Jerusalem (Zech 14:4–5; Tg. Isa. 31:4–5).[59] The combination παραχρῆμα μέλλει . . . ἀναφαίνεσθαι suggests that the kingdom would appear observably (tangibly and visibly) with an immediacy that had both a spatial component (nearby in Jerusalem) and temporal component (in the immediate future).

However, this implication of παραχρῆμα is in tension with μέλλω, because the former implies absolute immediacy, while the latter implies certainty and temporal nearness but not necessarily absolute immediacy. Luke also uses μέλλω to refer to what is supposed to or destined to happen, especially with reference to eschatological events (Luke 9:31, 44; 21:7, 36; 24:21; Acts 11:28; 17:31; 24:15). Recall that this expectation of the eschaton is common among Jews in Luke and that Luke's narrative in 19:7–12 gives no reason or time for the (hostile) crowd to suddenly see Jesus as the agent of God's eschatological kingdom. Thus, μέλλει . . . ἀναφαίνεσθαι refers to the conviction that the kingdom will arrive, and at a point in the not too distant (but also not too immediate) future. One could say the kingdom is "on the horizon."[60] Combined with παραχρῆμα, the phrase means that the future coming of the kingdom (in the crowd's view) is certain, very soon (not necessarily immediate), tangible, and observable.[61] Thus, we can translate the phrase as "they believed that the kingdom would most certainly appear clearly and observably." Jesus knows (in 19:11) that this is the general conviction of his audience in Luke about the coming of the kingdom, a conviction that is generally mistaken.

Given this interpretation of 19:11b, Luke has Jesus tell the following parable both to correct and redirect the audience's understanding of the kingdom. Luke wants to maintain that the arrival of the kingdom is certain and near (12:54–56; 16:16; 21:31–32). However, Luke wants to modify the crowd's view because part of the nearness of the kingdom consists of its proleptic presence in the ministry of Jesus (4:21, 43; 11:20; 17:20). He achieves this in the parable when the nobleman's coronation becomes known in his home country *before* he receives the authority in the distant land (vv. 13–14). While the nobleman goes away (he must be absent for the drama to unfold), he is not gone for long and returns to hand out judgment and reward.[62] Thus, the crowd is correct to expect the coming of the

---

58. LSJ, s.v. ἀναφαίνω.

59. Thus, it is unnecessary to search for other less common meanings of ἀναφαίνω as Johnson does ("Kingship Parable," 149–150). La Potterie is right to emphasize the spatial nature of the verb as Luke also uses it in Acts 21:3 ("Parabole du Prétendant," 623–24). This links this last half of the διὰ τό clause to the first half's reference to Jerusalem.

60. An appropriate nuance for ἀναφαίνω, cf. Fitzmyer, *Luke*, 12:1234.

61. Thus, I am in general agreement with Denaux's conclusion ("King-Judge," 50), while my interpretation offers more specificity and evidence.

62. Interpreters are right to note that Luke does not dwell on this point and that journey to a distant land does not necessarily imply a long delay. See Johnson, "Kingship Parable," 143–44; Fusco, "Point of View," 1690; Carroll, *Eschatology*, 100.

kingdom, but mistaken for missing its imminence already in the present kingship of Jesus (see 19:38). The crowd is also partially wrong and partially right about the "observability" of the kingdom. They have repeatedly failed to observe the signs of the presence of the kingdom in Jesus' ministry (11:20, 29–32; 12:54–56), and Jesus reproves the Pharisees' (reasonable) question about the coming of the kingdom by stating that "the kingdom of God does not come with observable signs (μετὰ παρατηρήσεως)" (17:20).[63] Even with the observable signs that Jesus outlines (17:24; 21:20–28), the "coming of the Son of Man" (as the agent of God's kingdom) still catches people by surprise (17:26–30; 21:34–36). Therefore, Luke has Jesus eschew the popular preoccupation with eschatological events and timetables in order to focus on more important issues in the parable. Instead of dwelling on when and where, Jesus redirects his audience to consider the *whos* and *whats* of the present and immediate future. I have labeled this story "the parable of the king and his subjects" to draw attention to the *whos*: king, good servants, bad servant, and enemies. Jesus' story forces the audience to take sides and identify with one of the various characters.[64] The corollary to this is *what* each character in the story does between the proleptic announcement of the nobleman's coronation and his return in power. In the same way, Jesus repeatedly refocuses his audience onto their current behavior leading up to the time of the eschaton (12:35–48; 13:1–9; 14:12–14, 21:7–19; Acts 1:6–11). Therefore, the purpose of the parable is to correct the audience's understanding of the immediacy of the kingdom and redirect their attention from eschatological events to proper behavior in light of the coming kingdom.

In summary, the beginning of v. 11 establishes continuity with the places, people and pronouncements in 19:7–10 using the force of time. Therefore, the force of place (Zacchaeus's publicized house) and the force of social relations (the large mixed crowd) carry over from the preceding events and continue to characterize the telling of the parable in 19:11–27 as a public event. The addressees implied within the parable confirm the presence of the general crowd, Jesus' disciples, and opponents, maintaining the public emphasis in the force of social relations. The public setting of the parable casts light on the meaning of v. 11b and the purpose of the parable, drawing in the force of meaning. The recurring eschatological mistakenness of the various audiences in Luke and the unusual grammar of this portion of the verse combine to reveal that Jesus spoke the following parable publicly to correct and redirect the audiences' skewed understanding of the coming of the kingdom. In the parable, Jesus focuses on whos and whats that are inherently political.[65] This emphasis leads us into the public setting and (very local) politics of the parable. After examining the public and political nature of the scene envisioned in the parable, we will summarize the message of Jesus' public pedagogy in this story.

---

63. On the interpretation of this statement see Fitzmyer, *Luke*, 2:1160; and Marshall, *Luke*, 654–55.
64. Aletti, "Parabole," 326–31.
65. Johnson, *Luke*, 292.

PART TWO: SOCIAL-SPATIAL EXEGESIS OF LUKE 18:35—19:48

The Local Politics of Luke's Parable

Political elements flavor Luke's version of this parable. The nobleman goes off to obtain a βασιλεία. He is opposed by a group of πολῖται who send an official πρεσβεία to protest his appointment. Finally, the successful servants are awarded with authority over πόλεις. This raises the question of the nature and scale of the politics portrayed in the story as well as the places in which such political activity occurred. The following social-spatial analysis will begin by setting Luke's version alongside the material in Plutarch's *Precepts* to establish its local scale. Comparing Luke's retelling of this story with the client king system under the Romans further confirms that this story focuses on local politics. Finally, Luke paints a highly public scene within the parable itself when the newly crowned king sits in court to judge his servants and execute his enemies. These comparisons will reveal the local political and public nature of both the social and spatial relations portrayed in the story of the king and his subjects.

Luke's version of the parable in 19:12–27 fits well into the local political sphere as described by Plutarch in his *Precepts*. Both Menemachus (*Praec. ger. rei publ.* 798b) and the master-king of the parable (19:12) are described as εὐγενής and both live under the power of greater authorities. Thus, they stand in comparable positions as local political figures. As discussed in chapter 4, Plutarch is conscious of the political position of local officials in the Greek cities of his day: they are under the authority of the Romans and must deal with their superiors kindly and wisely (see 813c–814e). He advises Menemachus to remind himself: "You rule as one who is ruled over; you are subject to the proconsuls, the agents of Caesar" (813e). This position is similar to the client ruler depicted in Jesus' parable of the king and his subjects, for he depends on authority over him to validate his own rule.[66] Plutarch asseverates that a political leader will face conflict (809b), but states that the one who fails to do good for the state out of personal hatred (μισέω) is in the wrong (809d). Furthermore, the statesman should restrict his enemies (ἐχθρός) to those who harm the state (809e). In the parable of the king and his subjects, the hostile citizens hate (ἐμίσουν, 19:14) the king and thus are blameworthy characters. The king counts the protesting ambassadors[67] as his enemies (τοὺς ἐχθρούς μου) because their seditiousness destabilizes the state. Plutarch warns Menemachus that the leader who is constantly "exact and obsessive" (ἀκριβὴς καὶ σφοδός) will earn the ill will of the people. This is very similar to the accusation of the third servant who fears the master-king because he is "harsh" (αὐστηρός). Plutarch tells Menemachus to entrust some political duties to friends who demonstrate skill in a given arena (812b–c). The statesman should share political affairs with others (ὁ πραγμάτων ἑτέροις ἐν πολιτείᾳ μεταδιδούς) in order to make the government run more smoothly (812d–e), but he must choose capable and likeminded associates and test their work (807d). The future king of Jesus' parable puts this advice into by testing the character of his servants in practice (διαπραγματεύσαντο in 19:15), and then placing the faithful and capable ones in positions of authority. Plutarch states that a

---

66. Note that Luke deals with royal images and uses the verb βασιλεύειν while Plutarch uses ἄρχειν more often.

67. Plutarch also describes the local political activity of sending πρεσβεῖαι (*Praec. ger. rei publ.* 808b, 809b, 816d, 819c).

The Story of a King and His Subjects (19:11–28)

good reputation can vault even the low-born into high office (821c–d) as the slaves of the parable are appointed over cities because of their character and capabilities (19:17–19). Luke's story of the king and his subjects corresponds to the world of local politics as described by Plutarch.

Luke's parable reflects cultural information about client kings in the ancient world.[68] However, two factors complicate Luke's use of the client king pattern. First, both time and space separated Luke and his audience from client kings. Most client kings had been deposed over forty years before the Gospel was composed (c. 80–90 CE) because the Romans viewed these appointed rulers as untenable risks. Also, many client kings had ruled lands far away from Luke's possible home in Ephesus.[69] Second, no two client kings have identical stories, and many of them do not correlate well with Luke's depiction. The closest match is Archelaus's attempt to secure the kingship of Judea when his father, Herod the Great, died: Archelaus is named as king in Herod's will, he travels to Rome seeking confirmation of his new title, a delegation of Jews follows to oppose him, and he mass murders his opponents.[70] Yet, Archelaus was not appointed king (only ethnarch), and the massacre occurs *before* he leaves for Rome, not after his return. Even more variables emerge in the stories of other client kings. Herod (the Great) flees from Judea and the Parthian regent there seeking refuge in Rome; Antony takes the lead to make him king. He returns with popular support to oust the Parthians (Josephus, *J.W.* 1.268–96). This is unlike the peaceful departure of Luke 19:12 accompanied by local displeasure. Perhaps the nobleman in Luke's story would have been viewed as an outsider, since many client kings (like Herod) came from territories neighboring the one they ruled.[71] Some kings were appointed by letter while they remained at home instead of traveling to Rome.[72] Many, like Agrippa (I) and Juba II, lived in Rome where they were groomed among the aristocracy for future rule.[73] Their appointment involved only travel from Rome, not travel to Rome, unlike the nobleman of the parable. While Luke's high-context audience would have certainly noticed the marks of a client kingdom in this story, this cultural practice varied widely and would have lost some of its relevance by the time Luke's Gospel was written.[74] These two factors give Luke

---

68. Busse, "Dechiffrierung," 432–33; Culpepper, *Luke*, 9:362.

69. Jacobson, "Client Kings," 34. Almost all client kingdoms came under direct Roman control by 50 CE. Furthermore, Luke appears to write from (and to) the heart of the eastern empire, focusing on Asia Minor and Greece in Acts. The closest client kingdoms would have been Cappadocia and Thrace, and both were on the limits of the empire far from Luke and his audience in Ephesus.

70. Weinert, "Throne Claimant," 508, 512–13; Culpepper, *Luke*, 9:363. These events are narrated in Josephus, *Ant.* 17.237–318.

71. Jacobson, "Client Kings," 24. Citizens were often hostile because they viewed the appointed king as an outsider.

72. Braund, *Friendly King*, 25.

73. On Agrippa (who was well received at home) see Bruce, *New Testament*, 258–59. On Juba II (also not a native of Mauretania, which he ruled) see Roller, *World of Juba II*, 98–100. Other client kings were appointed, not in Rome, but in cities much closer to their own homes, such as Archelaus, who was appointed king of Cappadocia by Antony while he was in nearby Armenia (Dio Cassius 49.32).

74. Therefore, while interpretations of parables such as those put forth by Culpepper and Herzog are valid and interesting, they fail to be adequate interpretations of *Luke* because of their focus on Jesus' context in early first century Palestine.

flexibility in the telling of his story; he does not have to bow to cultural norms but can shape elements of the story to fit his own aims.

Luke's version of the accession of a client king demonstrates how he selected, altered, and ignored certain elements of this cultural pattern for his own purposes. Luke has adopted the typical description of a client king who already qualifies as part of the aristocracy (εὐγενής in v. 12). He also makes use of the motif where the appointed king (like Archelaus) must travel to Rome (the "distant country") to be confirmed by Caesar.[75] However, the departure and absence of the appointed king from his home territory is not a necessary part of the pattern. As seen above, some kings were appointed by letter, others in nearby locations, and some were already in Rome before their appointment. Luke selectively inserts the departure and absence of the master-king, during which his slaves must carry out his orders. Absence is a necessary part of Luke's story. It must be addressed in any interpretation and seems to fit the situation of Luke and his audience, who lived during the absence of Jesus between the ascension and the Parousia.

The fact that the nobleman was going to obtain a kingship must have been publicly known before he left for the distant country.[76] His servants certainly know of it and so do the hostile citizens who send a delegation to oppose his appointment. Josephus tells how Herod's will was read publicly in Jericho's hippodrome to the soldiers, who then acclaimed Archelaus as king before his official investiture at Rome, which ultimately failed (*Ant.* 17.200–205).[77] This proleptic recognition of a king is comparable to the disciples' acclamation of Jesus as king in 19:38, but the parable assumes that the faithful servants affirm their master's future accession by their active obedience in his absence. The close association of the parable with the entry allows the audience to see that the faithful servants of the parable must have rejoiced at their master's nomination as king (as the disciples did at Jerusalem). Yet, the parable focuses attention on the servants' behavior in the absence of the king, which directs the audience's attention to the actions of the disciples in Acts and to their own situation during Jesus' absence. Recognition of Jesus' kingship among the faithful is a given in Luke's parable. Luke uses the absence motif to exhort his audience to active obedience during Jesus' absence, an obedience modeled on the disciples in Acts.

Finally, Luke omits two common elements in accounts of client kings. He makes no mention of dynastic infighting at the regional level, and he has no account of the formal appointment to power, the *appellatio*, in Rome. These are often the meat of the story in Josephus or Dio, but Luke passes over them in silence. Instead, almost all of the action is more mundane and takes place in the "province" that the king will rule over: the summoning of the slaves, the original complaint of the opponents, the reckoning with the slaves, and the slaughter of the enemies. Like the servants in Luke's story, slaves owned by wealthy

---

75. As the empire developed in the first century, emperors guarded control of succession more and more closely (Braund, *Friendly King*, 26). Thus, the strongest control would have been closest to Luke's time of writing.

76. This is not the case with Herod the Great. Josephus says that he did not go to Rome seeking kingship (*Ant.* 14.386).

77. Josephus states that Herod's death was widely known and narrates the reading of the will to the soldiers in the hippodrome, a location with a strong public valence.

aristocrats were often entrusted with financial and political responsibility, and the emperor used his own slaves to govern the empire.[78] However, this pragmatic reality is often passed over in silence in the stories of client kings.[79] Occasionally, an author will note how a newly appointed king rewarded his loyal subjects. Judean client kings often appointed new high priests, and Agrippa lifted the house tax (Josephus, *Ant.* 19.299). However, we do not hear of the dramatic promotion of previously minor servants. This inverted emphasis reveals Luke's local political interests. While this story deals with a king on the regional scale of politics who must be approved by imperial power, these larger-scale matters are passed over as briefly as possible to make way for the local actions and consequences of the king and his subjects. The actions and places that truly matter in this political tale are local.

Luke also includes opposition against the client king. Most client kings were not natives of the lands that they ruled, and "many of their subjects regarded these Roman surrogates as illegitimate usurpers."[80] These kings faced various layers of opposition from discontent, to troublemaking, to outright revolt.[81] Thus, the citizens' opposition to the nobleman's appointment in Luke 19:14 would have been no surprise. However, the violent retribution upon his return as king is surprising. Most ancient historians, like Dio and Tacitus, passed over such local events in their focus on a higher scale of politics, but Luke again includes the local enactment of the king's authority. Furthermore, no parallel to the slaughter in Luke 19:27 occurs in Josephus. Herod is welcomed gladly when he returns as king and sets out to defeat the Parthians (*Ant.* 14.394). Archelaus does slaughter unpredictable rebels, but he does so *before* he goes to Rome (*Ant.* 17.213–18) and yet is still opposed by a delegation of Jews in Rome (*Ant.* 17.299ff). When Archelaus and Agrippa return to Judea, Josephus briefly mentions that they depose the current high priest (*Ant.* 17.339–41)—hardly comparable to a massacre. Finally, Agrippa (I) was embraced by the Jewish populace for his Hasmonean heritage and respect for Jewish religion.[82] Therefore, the slaughter in Luke's retelling would have stood out to an ancient audience as atypical.[83] This added detail comports with Luke's focus on local political matters regarding the king and his subjects. It also connects this story to Luke's most conspicuous addition to the entry story: Jesus' prediction of the destruction of Jerusalem in 19:41–44 (not in Mark or Matthew). In 19:27, the king returns home and has his "enemies" (ἐχθροί) slaughtered in his presence, and in vv. 43–44 the "enemies" (ἐχθροί) of Jerusalem surround the city and crush the people. Here, Luke retains a local element that refers not to his own community,

---

78. Luke gives us a picture of the high responsibilities of slaves in 12:41–48 and 16:1–9. See also Jeffers, *Greco-Roman*, 224–26; and Harris, *Slave of Christ*, 35–36.

79. Thus, it is hard to cite this aspect as a part of a typical "cultural scene." Josephus sometimes mentions revolt or unrest at home during the absence of the king-to-be and may note rewards to personal friends at the king's return (*Ant.* 17:250–98; *J.W.* 286–89). Dio almost entirely ignores provincial events outside of their relevance to imperial rule.

80. Jacobson, "Client Kings," 24.

81. Most Jews, like Josephus, disliked Herod (*J.W.* 1.521; 14.403). Archelaus of Cappadocia faced formal charges before Tiberius (Suetonius, *Tib.* 8), and Juba II faced a revolt in Mauretania (Tacitus, *Ann.* 2.52).

82. Bruce, *History*, 258–59.

83. Thus, the "slaughter of enemies" upon return is *not* typical of this "cultural type scene" (contra Culpepper, *Luke*, 9:362), and Busse can cite no historical parallels in his discussion.

PART TWO: SOCIAL-SPATIAL EXEGESIS OF LUKE 18:35—19:48

but to one that was local for Jesus' audience in Jericho. Luke's Jesus does not relate tales about distant political machinations, but brings the king's vengeful power close to home to cast light on the coming destruction of nearby Jerusalem. The hostile citizens of the parable refuse the king at the announcement of his coming coronation, so the city of Jerusalem fails to recognize the proleptic royal visitation of Jesus (19:38–39). The fate of both sets of citizens is the same: destruction in their local context.

Luke emphasizes local politics in his presentation of this client king, and these local political matters transpire in a public venue. The bulk of the parable tells of the king holding court upon his return to judge his subjects (vv. 15–27; twelve out of fifteen verses). Once again, as a good high-context author, Luke does not explicitly state the public nature of this scene, but an ancient audience would have envisioned a public scenario for these local political matters.[84] Luke indicates the public emphasis near the beginning of the parable. Instead of Matthew's three servants, Luke has ten (19:13). Near the end of the parable some group present at the scene states their amazement at the king's actions (note the plural εἶπαν in v. 25). Already, the group gathered around the king has grown in Luke, and a brief survey of comparative material will further demonstrate the public valence of this scene in Luke's retelling of the parable.

The most pertinent information comes from three scenes portraying client rulers in the rest of Luke-Acts. First, Jesus is brought before Herod Antipas (the tetrarch of Galilee) in Luke 23:8–11. Luke does not specify the location of this episode (perhaps Antipas's own residence in Jerusalem?), but the scene is more than a private meeting between Antipas and Jesus. Antipas interviews Jesus (v. 9), but Luke adds that the chief priests and scribes were present to accuse him. Furthermore, Antipas's soldiers are present as well, and they join with him in mocking Jesus. While access to Antipas's residence (palace? headquarters?) would have been controlled, Luke paints a picture of a client ruler judging one of his subjects surrounded by local leaders and his own soldiers. This is a public scene in a local political context. Later in Acts, Luke tells of King Herod Agrippa's visit to Tyre and Sidon, another local and public episode. Agrippa takes his seat on the platform (βῆμα, v. 21) before the citizens of the city (the δῆμος, v. 22) and delivers a public address (δημηγορέω, v. 21) to them.[85] This time Luke places the client ruler in a fitting public location, a βῆμα, and the king speaks publicly to the gathered citizens in this local context. Already, Luke displays a pattern of public appearances and actions by client rulers in local contexts, but the best example occurs in Acts 25.

In Acts 23 Paul is taken to Caesarea (Maritima) and held prisoner in Herod's praetorium. This praetorium was built by Herod the Great and probably continued as the political headquarters and residence of the Roman governor of the region. Paul's trials

---

84. The scene is clearly political in nature, so the question is whether or not the audience would have viewed it as public or private. In this case the public-private spectrum must be laid on top of politics, rather than the political sphere being more public than the unofficial public sphere as my framework visually suggests. The following discussion will consider how the obviously political scenario in the parable is also public and not private.

85. Josephus tells a slightly different story that leads to Agrippa's death. Josephus narrates Agrippa entering the theater (another public location) at Caesarea where he was proclaimed a god by the crowd. He died soon after (*Ant.* 19.343-52).

in chs. 23–26 all take place in this seat of regional political government. In ch. 25 King Agrippa (II) comes to meet Festus, the new Roman governor, in Caesarea, probably in the praetorium. Festus asks him about Paul (Acts 25:13–22). Agrippa then asks to hear Paul, and they make arrangements for the next day. In 25:23 Luke provides his vision of the court of a client king. Luke describes the arrival of Agrippa and Bernice "with great display" (μετὰ πολλῆς φαντασίας). Then he states that they enter the "auditorium" (τὸ ἀκροατήριον) with a large retinue that includes military commanders (χιλιάρχοις) and the chief men of the city (ἀνδράσιν τοῖς κατ' ἐξοχὴν τῆς πόλεως). Luke specifies that a large group of local and regional political leaders is present at King Agrippa's entrance, using the force of social relations to emphasize the public nature of the event.[86]

Luke also provides a specific location for this public event, the ἀκροατήριον. Unfortunately, we cannot shed much light on this *hapax legomenon*. Most often this term refers to a lecture hall for philosophers (Epictetus, *Diatr.* 3.23.8; Plutarch, *Rect. rat. aud.* 45f) or the audience gathered to hear a lecture (Plutarch, *Curios.* 522e and *Fac.* 937d).[87] On one occasion, Philo speaks of "auditoriums" and "theatres" in the same breath, for both are public arenas for philosophical discourse (*Congr.* 64). No other ancient author, independent of Luke, uses this term to refer to part of a praetorium, but its valence is clearly public.[88] Luke portrays this scene as a large public event in the praetorian auditorium attended by the prominent leaders of this seat of regional government. This arrival of a Roman client king at the headquarters of a neighboring province to hear a prominent prisoner is portrayed as a momentous public occasion. The public nature of this most explicit portrayal of a client king at court in Acts, supported by the two other scenes, helps to construct what Luke and his audience envisioned as the king of Luke 19 returned to judge his subjects. However, material outside of Luke-Acts offers further evidence for the public valence of such scenes in the ancient world.

In 4 Maccabees 5:1–2, King Antiochus sets up a scene of royal judgment in order to punish the Jews. He takes his seat "on a certain high place" (ἐπί τινος ὑψηλοῦ τόπου, perhaps another way of referring to a βῆμα). He is joined by his counselors and armed soldiers to execute his orders. From this public vantage point, Jews are brought before him and commanded to eat pork on pain of death. The elderly priest, Eleazar, publicly proclaims (δημηγορεῖν, 5:15) that he will not do so. Then a local leader speaks publicly against the king's wicked policy. In another scene from Josephus (*Ant.* 17.200–205), Archelaus sits "on a high platform" (ἐπὶ ὑψηλὸν βῆμα, 201) near the Jerusalem temple after seven days of mourning for his father. There he acknowledges the "masses" (ὁμίλους, 201) and eventually convinces the "crowd" (ὄχλος, 204) of his good will. In these two scenes, a king and a

---

86. As was noted above, such a scene implies that access was limited to political elites. Thus, it is not public in the sense that anyone in the street could witness the events. It is public because it involves a large crowd made up of various important officials. While access is one of the indicators of public valence, it is not the only one, and the limited access is a function of the elite nature of this event.

87. The Vulgate of Acts 25:23 uses the Latin term *auditorium*, which also typically refers to a public lecture hall (Seneca, *Ep.* 52.11; Suetonius, *Tib.* 11.3) or a public audience (Tacitus, *Dial.* 9.3).

88. Unfortunately, archaeology is no help, for the remains of Herod's praetorium in Caesarea have not been discovered.

potential king sit on a raised platform surrounded by their attendants and people to speak publicly to a crowd. Both scenes are made public by the location and the people (the forces of place and social relations), and both demonstrate a cultural view of audiences before client rulers (the force of meaning).

Therefore, a typical picture emerges of a client ruler sitting in a public place on a raised platform surrounded by attendants, soldiers, local leaders, and a crowd. From here he speaks publicly to issue judgments and rewards. Luke has not related all of these details in his narration of the nobleman-become-king when he returns, but he does not need to in a high-context society, for his audience will fill in the details of this typically public scenario. Luke tells us that there are at least ten servants of the king present, those entrusted with resources in his absence. However, the king also appears to have attendants with him, those who execute the order to summon the ten servants (note the passive verb φωνηθῆναι in v. 15). These attendants might be the same ones who are shocked by his decision to give the third servant's pound to the one who already has ten in v. 25. Furthermore, this king appears to have soldiers with him, those who carry out the order to arrest his enemies and slaughter them in his presence. This might be an elite scene with limited access, but it is a very public scene with servants, attendants, soldiers, and doomed citizens. This setting seems to fit best with the other trial scenes before kings in Luke-Acts: Jesus before Antipas and Paul before Agrippa. Therefore, Luke and his audience would imagine a large auditorium where the king sits surrounded by his attendants to judge his servants and subjects in the local area.

The traditions about client kings in the ancient world provide the force of meaning to summon images of stately public scenes. The force of place comes into play as we apply the spatial details of Acts 25 and similar episodes to the public scene cast in Luke 19. Finally, the force of social relations contributes to the public nature of the scene as similar literary accounts clarify the presence of attendants, soldiers, and citizens at these local political events. For a high-context audience, Luke's clues in this story of a king and his subjects call up public elements from all three of these forces as they envision this scene. Finally, the events that transpire in this public (and elite) space focus on local politics. Jesus does not narrate any events that transpire outside of the king's country. This is in stark contrast to other ancient historians who focus on events at Rome or before the emperor and ignore more local happenings. Rather, all of the events in Luke 19:12–27 take place at home (perhaps in the king's home), and most of the story focuses on the king in relation to his own servants and subjects. Therefore, Jesus is not only addressing a public audience himself, but the story he tells is firmly set in context of local politics and the public sphere.

The Public Pedagogy of This Political Parable

What then is the public pedagogy of this political parable? Or to put it another way: What message does Jesus communicate to his mixed audience with this story about a king and his subjects? Jesus' parables should generally not be allegorized by assigning meaning to each detail. However, this parable has several layers and so is a partial exception to the rule for the following reasons.[89] First, Jesus addresses three distinct groups that comprise the large audience gathered in Zacchaeus's home: the crowd, his opponents, and his disciples. Therefore, specific elements in the parable are relevant to each group. Second, this parable summarizes various eschatological teachings found in Luke's Gospel.[90] Finally, Luke has Jesus redirect eschatological concerns about when and where to discuss who and what: the characters and their respective actions. Thus, the parable contains a lesson bound up with the following characters: the nobleman-king, the hostile citizens, the faithful servants, and the wicked servant. Each one expresses a part of the composite message. These political players are embedded in two layers of public pedagogy. First, the narrative setting surrounding the parable marks it as a public event, especially with the various functions of v. 11 discussed above. Second, the setting of the events inside the parable relate a common scene of the public actions of political officials.

Jesus is the well-born nobleman-king. The king's high social status fits ancient expectations for client rulers, who were drawn from the aristocracy. While predictable, this also reflects the honorable status of Jesus in Luke throughout his public ministry. Despite questions about his birth and abilities (e.g., 4:22–23), Luke consistently upholds Jesus as a person of high honor in the eyes of both God and people (2:52), a reputation that is demonstrated publicly and locally in his powerful words and deeds (e.g., 7:6–10; 13:17). The proleptic public announcement of the nobleman's appointment to the kingship is implied by the citizens' organized response in 19:14. It must have been known that the nobleman was going to become king before his official investiture. This points ahead to the proleptic public proclamation of Jesus as king in 19:38 as a partial realization of the presence of the kingdom. The official investiture of royal power occurs during the nobleman's absence, most likely indicating the status granted to Jesus after the ascension (Acts 2:36).[91] Thus, summarizing Luke's eschatology, the kingdom is proleptically present during Jesus' earthly ministry (11:20; 17:21), but it will not be fully realized until after his resurrection, ascension, and return (Luke 17:22–37; Acts 3:21).

The hostile citizens correspond to Jesus' opponents among the Jewish leadership. The citizens are first mentioned as a united block who hate the king-to-be (v. 14).[92] Their hatred implicitly includes all citizens and is unexplained. This fits Luke's portrayal of the leaders who oppose Jesus: they are united against him, and their vitriol is simply self-evident (6:11; 11:53–54). Even though "all" of the citizens hate the master, a select few are chosen to form a delegation (πρεσβεία) that officially oppose the future king's appointment: "We do not want this man to rule us" (v. 14b). This points to the hostility and culpability of the Jewish *leaders* in Luke's narrative. This delegation echoes events surrounding the accession of Archelaus (*Ant.* 17.299–303). Note that the Jewish delegation opposes

---

89. Other scholars have also broached limited allegorical readings of this parable: Denaux, "King-Judge," 54–55; and Johnson, "Kingship Parable," 158–59.

90. This can be seen in the numerous cross references to previous eschatological material in the Gospel and will be demonstrated further in ch. 9.

91. See also Busse, "Dechiffrierung," 439.

92. The article on οἱ πολῖται is generic, referring to the citizens of the country as a class. See Wallace, *Greek Grammar*, 227.

Archelaus because they desire *autonomy*. They want to rule themselves rather than live under a client king (*Ant.* 17.299). This might illuminate the motivation of the hostile citizens and the Jewish leaders: they do not want to lose their own power to this new upstart ruler (see Luke 11:43 and Acts 5:17). Implicitly but obviously, their protest fails (unlike the case of Archelaus), and the nobleman returns as king. They disappear from the story while the king settles accounts with his servants. When the citizens reappear (v. 27), the king calls them "enemies." The king summons "those who did not want me to rule them" (citing the language of the official protest in v. 14) and orders them to be slaughtered. Only these "leaders" in the embassy appear to be killed; the rest of the hostile citizens do not face the same immediate fate.[93] On one hand, the citizens as a whole and those in the embassy are combined as the Jewish people and their leaders are at the destruction of Jerusalem (19:41–44) or Jesus' sentencing before Pilate (23:13–25) or in the sermons of Acts (2:23, 13:27). On the other hand, a distinction is made and only the leaders in the embassy face execution as special judgment is aimed at Israel's leaders (for this distinction see Luke 20:19 and Acts 5:30–31). The fate of the citizens functions on three levels. In the immediate context, their execution points to the destruction of Jerusalem because the city as a whole disregarded Jesus' entrance as king-to-be (19:41–44). In Luke's narrative, it points to the judgment on those who reject Jesus (Acts 3:23), especially the Jewish leaders. Finally, it points to the eschaton, where the ultimate price will be paid by those who do not acknowledge Jesus as king (17:26–30; Acts 13:46).

The faithful servants speak a word of hope to the loyal followers of Jesus both in and beyond Luke's narrative. Once again, Jesus' followers are portrayed as slaves who are given responsibilities by their master (12:35–38, 41–48). Luke reflects the large movement of disciples by increasing the number of servants from three (in Matthew) to ten (v. 13). The followers of Jesus can rest assured that he will receive his royal power despite the opposition arranged against him and that they will be rewarded for their perseverance during his absence. The disciples in the narrative hear this promise as they still do not understand Jesus' rejection in Jerusalem (18:31–34), and the disciples in Luke's audience hear it as they await Jesus' return. The task of the slave/disciple is to increase the king's resources in his absence. Luke has Jesus dismiss speculation about possible wheres and whens among the audience to refocus attention on the whos and whats of the present. Specifically, with whom do they associate within the story and what are they doing to obey the absent king's directions? This comports with Jesus' emphasis on active obedience in Luke 12:35–48 and and Acts 1:6–8. Luke's ecclesial audience is not treated to an account of Jesus' coronation in heaven.[94] Rather, they are called to examine their behavior in their present, local context in the absence of their master-king. The ministry of the apostles in Acts adds believers to the church (Acts 2:41), and they serve as a model for Luke's own audience. The faithful servants are granted a part of the master-king's own political power by being placed over

---

93. Note that πολῖται is not qualified in v. 14. Presumably, "all" (or at least most) of the citizens of the country hated the nobleman, but it is improbable to imagine the king slaughtering all the citizens, a representative group makes better sense and fits the story of Archelaus as well.

94. I agree with Busse that the ascension probably represents Jesus' accession to the throne and that his reign is currently in heaven according to Luke ("Dechiffrierung," 439).

cities, and Jesus grants a share of his royal authority to the apostles (22:28-30). Yet, much like the proleptic proclamation of Jesus as king (at the entry) precedes his coronation (at the ascension), so the apostles will exercise authority in the church (Acts 5:1-11 and 6:1-7) while they await the full and future consummation of the kingdom (Luke 18:28-29; Acts 1:6-8; 3:21). Their ministry stands as an example for believers in Luke's community who will follow the same pattern (see Acts 20:32-35) of present faithfulness and future reward.

Finally, the parable speaks a word of warning to the crowd—those who listen to Jesus but fail to act on his call to discipleship like the third servant. The third servant is attached to the master but fails to increase his resources out of fear and misperception (19:21). Jesus has already warned his disciples and the crowds that they must act on his words or face catastrophe (6:46-49). The crowds are in danger of missing the significance of Jesus (11:29-32), and must repent and produce appropriate fruit (13:1-9). Within the immediate context, the crowd does nothing at the entry, neither joining the affirmation nor voicing their rejection. In the passion narrative, they shout for Jesus' death (23:23) but later express remorse (23:48). Throughout Acts, the Jews are in danger of missing God's offer of salvation if they do not respond (Acts 13:46; 28:24-28). Inaction is not an option, for it will result in judgment. While the third servant is not slaughtered, he is cut off from the king's house. He can only join with the other citizens of the realm who hated the king and will eventually face judgment as well (cf. 19:41-44), for the little that he has will be taken away (19:26 and 8:18), leaving him destitute. Again, the parable points to the inaction of the crowd at the entry (Jesus' context), to the precarious place of the Jews in Acts (narrative context), and to the situation of Luke's audience. In Luke's context, the third servant is a warning against indecision during the master's absence, for such a stance will result in judgment at Jesus' return.

Conclusion and Preview

Once again, we will conclude by summarizing the findings of the social-spatial analysis with the chart of characteristics put forth in chapter 4. However, in this case we will see how the forces affect the public and local character of the external setting and the internal nature of the parable. Finally, we will preview some of the implications that will be discussed in Part 3 of this study.

The force of time serves to connect the material in 19:11-28 with what preceded it in vv. 7-10. The introductory material in v. 11 reveals that Jesus continued to speak after his dramatic pronouncements in vv. 9-10. He goes on to tell the parable that follows in vv. 12-27. This temporal connection maintains the public scenario of Zacchaeus's home. Therefore, the forces of place (perhaps a peristyle garden in Zacchaeus's home) and social relations (the large, varied crowd) carry over from the previous story to characterize Jesus' teaching in 19:12-27 as public. Luke's narrative timeline connects the two scenes in the same location before the same crowd, attributing public characteristics to both and creating a public setting for the telling of the parable.

PART TWO: SOCIAL-SPATIAL EXEGESIS OF LUKE 18:35—19:48

The force of social relations forms an explanatory bond between the narrative setting of the pericope and the internal drama of the parable. The three groups in the audience (crowd, disciples, and opponents) have corresponding characters in the story. Luke shapes his unique version of the parable to address each element in the audience. Luke builds a public scene by increasing the number of servants to ten (from Matthew's three) and adding attendants and soldiers who respond to and act on the king's orders in vv. 25–27. Evidence from Luke-Acts and other ancient historians reveals the public nature of client kings sitting at court. They often took their place on raised platforms or in official residences surrounded by their entourage of attendants, commanders, and aristocracy as they addressed and judged their people. The scene inside Jesus' parable provides the cultural clues for the audience to imagine a grand public scene when the king returns home to judge his servants and his enemies.

The force of social relations combines with the force of nature to cast a political and local scene. A royal note is sounded at the beginning of the story when the nobleman is to receive a kingdom (βασιλεία, v. 13) and resurfaces when he returns with royal authority (again βασιλεία, v. 15). However, these royal characteristics are overshadowed by political characteristics. Luke chooses the word πολῖται to describe the residents under the authority of the king-to-be.[95] Later, the king gives his faithful servants authority over cities (πόλεις, vv. 17–18) and executes the enemies of his rule (v. 27). These elements use terms related to the polis and deal with official, governmental matters—the stuff of politics. The politics portrayed in the parable are local in nature. In contrast with other ancient historians, Luke passes over imperial scenes and events in the "distant country" (i.e., Rome) in order to focus on the events that happen in the king's home setting: the opposition of the citizens, the judging of the servants, and the execution of the enemies. Luke's parable of the king and his subjects is a story about local politics that casts light on Jesus, the kingdom, and the fate of the various groups in the audience.

Finally, the force of meaning affects the story in two ways. First, Luke and his audience are familiar enough (but not too familiar) with client kings and stories about them to fill in some of the implicit material appropriate to their high-context setting. Luke can draw on details like a nobleman being appointed king, servants being entrusted with resources, and hostile citizens, but also select and alter them in ways that further the point of his story. Second, Luke himself appears to be embedded in the public sphere and local politics. His own familiar life settings provide the material for the parable that Jesus tells. Thus, not only do Luke and Luke's Jesus inhabit the public and local political spheres, but they also are most comfortable telling stories set in those very same spheres.

This analysis has implications for the nature of Luke's Gospel as a whole. The social-spatial character of this episode reflects the public and political nature of Jesus' teaching throughout the Gospel. As an example, take the parable of the good Samaritan. Jesus has just been speaking to the Seventy upon their return (10:17–22). Then he turns to his disciples "privately" and speaks to them (10:23–24),[96] presuming that others are around who

---

95. Luke could have used a word like λαός instead. See Acts 4:25–26 and LSJ, s.v. λαός.

96. This is one of two instances (and the only one unique to the third Gospel) where Luke uses κατ' ἰδίαν.

The Story of a King and His Subjects (19:11–28)

might have overheard if he spoke aloud. In v. 25, Luke has a representative of those others speak. A lawyer (a local leader) stands up[97] to publicly question Jesus, a classic example of a challenge-riposte exchange. Jesus meets his challenge, and then the lawyer wants to "justify himself" (that is, defend his honor), so he challenges Jesus with another question, which Jesus answers with a parable. As with the setting in 19:11–28, we see Jesus implicitly surrounded by a mixed crowd including his disciples, opponents, and probably a crowd before whom the challenge-riposte takes place. Jesus answers the explicit challenge (it is implicit in 19:11) by publicly teaching with a parable as he does in 19:12–27. Furthermore, like the parable of the king and his subjects, the parable of the good Samaritan makes its point using local political characters (a Levite and a priest) associated with cities (Jerusalem and Jericho). This story reveals how Luke often uses the force of social relations (implying a large, mixed crowd) to cast Jesus' pedagogy as public, just as he does in 19:11–28. Finally, it also exemplifies Jesus' interaction with and stories about local leaders. Throughout most of the Gospel, Jesus interacts with leaders in the local political sphere (Pharisees, a centurion, a synagogue leaders), and his teaching sometimes features such characters. Chapter 9 will explore the public settings and local political characters in Jesus' teaching leading up to the climactic story of the king and his subjects.

The historical and contemporary implications of 19:11–28 to be discussed in chapter 10 overlap with those mentioned at the end of the previous chapter since the location and audience carry over from 19:1–10. The setting, audience, and parable of 19:11–28 can cast further light on Luke's social-spatial perspective. Jesus rarely teaches his disciples privately in Luke. Instead, he teaches them while others (both general crowds and opponents) stand by listening, or he teaches them by warning these other groups in their hearing. This has implications for the catechetical settings that Luke might have either been familiar with or desired to see develop in his own Christian community. Jesus does not privately instruct a new order of Christian scribes (contrast Matt 13:36, 51–52). Rather, he teaches his disciples in the midst of the variegated public. The local political flavor may provide further confirmation for the social status of Luke and his audience (exemplified in the "most excellent" Theophilus). Luke demonstrates an awareness of and preference for the local political sphere, possibly reflecting his own social (and political) standing. These implications raise questions about the places and audiences of contemporary Christian catechism. Luke has very little time for "preaching to the choir" and challenges the leaders of his community to take their teaching into the public sphere where it may be heard by disciples and crowds alike. This forces one to consider the places and times where similar activity might occur today. Finally, Luke casts Jesus as a local nobleman-king and uses a story about this figure to illuminate the nature of the kingdom. Luke's familiarity (and seeming approval for) the local political sphere might have implications for Christian participation in, and borrowing from, the political sphere in the contemporary world. Yet, as we move into the final pericope of this study (19:29–48), Jesus' disciples and the political leaders have opposite reactions to Jesus when he publicly enters Jerusalem.

---

97. Recall how the use of various forms of ἵστημι signals public speech (see the discussion of v. 8 in ch. 6).

8

The Procession into Jerusalem (19:28–48)

The Public Culmination of Jesus' Movement and its Political Ramifications

Introduction

AFTER PUBLICLY HEALING A BLIND BEGGAR, AFTER MEETING ZACCHAEUS IN PUBLIC, AND after telling a parable to a gathered crowd inside Zacchaeus's home, Jesus begins the last leg of his journey to Jerusalem. Verse 28 is a transitional statement that forms an inclusio with 19:11 and prepares the audience for Jesus' public entry into Jerusalem. Luke's account of Jesus' entry begins by focusing on Jesus and his disciples in vv. 29–38. He sends two disciples to fetch a colt, and this act initiates a series of royal allusions applied to Jesus. The disciples respond and publicly treat Jesus as royalty: placing him on the colt, spreading their garments on the road, and announcing his arrival as king. In vv. 39–48, the tone changes to one of increasing conflict and doom. The Pharisees in the surrounding crowd rebuke Jesus one last time, and Jesus speaks a word of destruction against the city that will not recognize him. Finally, after Jesus cleanses the temple and begins to teach there publicly, the highest Jewish officials (chief priests, etc.) plan how to eliminate him, yet they are prevented by the public influence of the crowd that hangs on Jesus' every word.

The review of previous interpretation will focus on the nature of Jesus' entry and the place of Jerusalem and the temple in Luke-Acts. Then social-spatial exegesis of 19:29–48 starts by examining the route that Jesus took into the temple in Luke's account. This leads to an analysis of the politics within Jesus' movement and the public nature of the disciples' action at Jesus' entry. Finally, the social-spatial focus will illuminate the public and political characteristics of the opposition that Jesus faced as he entered Jerusalem and took a public stand in the temple. Through this analysis, problems with the typical "entry" material compared to Luke's account will emerge, creating a need to find other entries of an *unofficial* nature that are more appropriate parallels to Luke's account. The conclusion of this chapter will summarize the public and political characteristics of 19:29–48 according to the forces of Sack's framework and offer a preview of the implications discussed in Part 3.

The Procession into Jerusalem (19:28–48)

A Review of Previous Interpretation

Luke's retelling of Jesus' arrival at Jerusalem has drawn scholarly attention on three main fronts: the scriptural fabric of Luke's account, the place of Jerusalem and the temple in Luke, and the ironic nature of this "triumphal" entry. These last two areas (the place of Jerusalem and the nature of Jesus' entry) directly impact the social-spatial analysis of this passage and will be dealt with in more detail.

The scriptural fabric of Luke's account of Jesus' arrival plays some role in most studies of 19:29–48. Many of these allusions and their implications have been debated by scholars. Riding a colt into Jerusalem is a symbolic act that recalls Solomon, who rode the royal ass to his coronation (1 Kgs 1:33–37).[1] The colt also may recall the entrance of the peaceable king depicted in Zech 9:9–10.[2] However, Luke's omission of the citation of Zech 9:9 might signal an attempt to quell suspicion about Jesus' political aims (see further below).[3] The fact that Jesus must *borrow* the colt might indicate an ironic contrast with the extravagant royal figure of Gen 49:11–12.[4] Then, the spreading of the cloaks in 19:36 recalls a similar honor bestowed upon Jehu at his coronation (2 Kgs 9:13).[5] The main thread of this scriptural fabric, according to Sanders, is the use of Ps 118:26, the only direct quotation of the Hebrew Bible in vv. 29–44.[6] Sanders explores the use of this Psalm as a re-enthronement liturgy, showing how Luke portrays the disciples (*not* the priests) as the ones who acclaim Jesus as king.[7] Sanders claims that the allusions to Zech 9:9, the spreading of the garments, and the exclamation from Ps 118 make this a scene of "a king riding to his coronation" in Luke.[8] One of the unresolved questions raised by these allusions is whether Luke portrays Jesus as a king arriving at a city to celebrate a victory (as in a typical triumphal entry) or as one who is coming with pomp and circumstance to be crowned king (as with Solomon). Royal connotations abound in these allusions, but scholars differ over their meanings and implications in Luke.

The scriptural allusions and citations continue past v. 40. Jesus' lament (19:41–44) draws upon depictions of the fall of Jerusalem in the Hebrew Bible, particularly from Jeremiah.[9] Nothing here qualifies as a direct citation, but the allusions are plentiful. The cleansing of the temple could allude to Mal 3:1–2 and Zech 14:21.[10] 19:46 is a direct cita-

---

1. Kinman, *Jesus' Entry*, 92; and Sanders, "Fabric," 142. I have borrowed Sanders's textile analogy in my description of this passage.

2. Sanders, "Fabric," 140. On the "peaceable" and eschatological nature of this portrayal see Ganser-Kerperin, *Das Zeugnis*, 153–54.

3. Fitzmyer, *Luke*, 2:1244–45; Johnson, *Luke*, 301; Kinman, *Jesus' Entry*, 109, 113–14.

4. Nolland, *Luke 18:35–24:53*, 924.

5. Fitzmyer, *Luke*, 2:1246; Kinman, *Jesus' Entry*, 95.

6. Also see Ganser-Kerperin, *Das Zeugnis*, 155–57.

7. Sanders, "Fabric," 143–48.

8. Ibid., 148.

9. Dodd, "Fall of Jerusalem," 79; and Gaston, *No Stone*, 359.

10. Fitzmyer, *Luke*, 2:1266 and Johnson, *Luke*, 299. On this episode as a fulfillment of Zech 14:21 see Catchpole, "Entry," 333. Kinman disagrees and says that Luke is following the conventions of entrance stories rather than portraying a fulfillment of Mal 3:1. The questions surrounding the possible allusions to Zech 9

tion: the first half from Isa 56:7 and the second half from Jer 7:11. Luke has omitted the last phrase of Isa 56:7, which states that the temple will be a house of prayer "for all nations," reflecting his view that the temple has no lasting role for Gentiles.[11] Instead of being a house of prayer, Jesus states that the temple has become a "den of robbers" (Jer 7:11).[12] The identification of these "robbers" varies,[13] but scholars almost unanimously agree that Luke uses the cleansing to prepare the temple for Jesus' final teaching ministry.[14] Again, while many scholars employ these allusions and quotations, their interpretation is debated. The social spatial analysis below will help resolve some of these debates.

The account of Jesus' approach and entry contains frequent and specific geographical references: Bethphage, Bethany, the Mount of Olives, the descent down the mountain, Jerusalem, and the temple.[15] The reference to the Mount of Olives might also allude to Zech 14:3–4. The density of scriptural allusions and citations in this passage combined with the specific geography leads Catchpole to say that in the account of Jesus' entry (in Mark) "space has given way to time, geography to eschatology, and all in the interests of Christology."[16] Similarly, Sanders critiques those who state that the stones Jesus refers to in v. 40 are rocks along the road down the mount. He says, "Such a view puts geography above theology; here as in much of the rest of the Gospels, we have theological or eschatological geography."[17] These allusions and citations certainly color the entire episode. However, Sack's theoretical framework demonstrates the dangers of reductionism, reducing some forces (space and social relations) to mere subsets of one dominating force (time or meaning/theology). Catchpole and Sanders have reduced place and geography, for they are entirely determined by Luke's eschatology or theology. Instead, Sack's framework holds that the forces of nature, place, social relations, and meaning (to which we have added time and religion) work together in complementary and interdependent ways to shape our understanding of people and actions.[18] Thus, this study will incorporate the importance of sacred tradition and theological perspective in Luke's retelling of the triumphal entry

---

and 14 are simultaneously questions about the eschatological nature of Jesus' arrival in Luke. If the allusions to Zechariah obtain, then the event is cast as an eschatological fulfillment of the Jewish scriptures.

11. Johnson, *Luke*, 300. Parsons describes Luke's use of Jerusalem in this way: "Jerusalem was, on one hand, an ending to the story of Jesus and, on the other hand, the beginning of the church's endtime witness." While Luke sees the importance of Jerusalem, especially in the life of Jesus, Jerusalem is only the beginning of the story of a centrifugal (not centripetal) mission ("The Place of Jerusalem," 168).

12. Note that part of Jesus' rebuke involves a re-labelling of the space of the temple from a "house" to a "den." I will discuss this further below.

13. Nolland claims that this reference more generally recalls Jeremiah's indictment (*Luke 18:35–24:53*, 937). Kinman opposes Barrett's view that the λησταί are Jewish nationalists and claims that Jesus ejects corrupt merchants demanding unrealistic prices (*Jesus' Entry*, 152). Green claims that this is an insulting reference to the Jewish leaders (*Luke*, 693).

14. Fitzmyer, *Luke*, 2:1267; Johnson, *Luke*, 307; Green, *Luke*, 691–95.

15. See the brief comment on this in Fitzmyer, *Luke*, 2:1247.

16. Catchpole, "Entry," 325.

17. Sanders, "Fabric," 150.

18. *Homo Geographicus*, 30–34.

while injecting a more robust investigation of the role that place plays in Luke's portrayal of Jesus' public entrance.

Studies of the place of Jerusalem and the temple in Luke-Acts also contribute significant insights to Jesus' entry. Ganser-Kerperin breaks 19:29–48 into four scenes based on geography. The Mount of Olives dominates the first two scenes, which focus on the obtaining of the colt (vv. 29–36) and Jesus' descent down the mount (vv. 37–40). The third scene (vv. 41–44) focuses on Jerusalem and records Jesus' lament upon seeing the city. The fourth and final scene (vv. 45–48) portrays Jesus in the temple and sets the stage for the passion narrative.[19] He claims that Luke employs the symbolic weight of Jerusalem and the temple to highlight the tragic nature of the rejection of Jesus. The high hopes set by verses like Luke 2:32 collapse when Jerusalem fails to recognize the divine visitation. The fateful repudiation of Jesus in the temple and by temple leaders underscores the calamity in store.[20] In his study of the role of Jerusalem and the temple in Luke-Acts, Chance has just a few words to say about 19:45–48. Jesus does not cleanse the temple as a condemnation of the cult (like in Mark). Instead, Luke depicts a conflict over authority. Jesus claims authority by teaching in this "climactic encounter with Israel," which takes place in the temple in the next two chapters.[21] Chance notes how Luke uses 19:47–48 and 21:37–38 to frame this section, emphasizing the centrality of Jesus' teaching and the presence of the people.[22] Bachmann develops these same observations further. He points out the use of λαός in 19:48; 20:1, 9, 19, 26, 45; and 21:38 and concludes that "the people" that Jesus teaches in the temple represents the entire Jewish people.[23] Thus, Jesus' temple teaching, set up and framed by 19:47–48, climactically addresses all Jews as Jesus draws near to his death and resurrection.

Bachmann's point, however, is a conclusion to a more comprehensive examination of the public valence of Jesus' teaching in Luke. Bachmann begins by questioning the "official" nature of teaching in the temple, and he points out that many "teachers" (such as John the Baptist and Jesus) do a great deal of teaching *outside* of the temple.[24] After examining relevant teaching scenes and summaries, Bachmann concludes that Luke regularly puts Jesus in places where large crowds gather to hear him teach, and he does not limit the audience as Mark and Matthew do at times.[25] The same is true, but even more so, in Jesus' temple teaching. As Jesus taught publicly before, so he teaches publicly in the temple. This public temple teaching is reinforced by Jesus' appearance in the temple in Luke 3 and by the close association of the public cleansing and teaching in 19:45–48.[26] Bachmann concludes that since teaching itself is a public event in Luke, so teaching in the temple (the

---

19. Ganser-Kerperin, *Das Zeugnis*, 149–52.
20. Ibid., 163, 167.
21. Chance, *Jerusalem*, 58–59.
22. Ibid., 61.
23. Bachmann, *Jerusalem*, 278–79.
24. Ibid., 262–63.
25. Ibid., 265.
26. Ibid., 268–75.

center of Luke's world) is public to a superlative degree.[27] Bachmann primarily employs the force of social relations (the presence of crowds) to demonstrate his point. The following examination will build on his study looking at the public and political ramifications of the people, places, and meanings employed by Luke throughout 19:29–48.

Finally, a few interpreters assert that Luke casts Jesus' entry as "a-triumphal" or as an ironic use of ancient triumphal entry standards. Catchpole was the first to make such a claim. Though his study employs Mark's account (since it was the earliest), many of his comments are relevant to Luke as well. He begins his short analysis with the axiom that ancient audiences were familiar with a "family of stories" that tell of the joyful entry of a hero figure into a city after a victory.[28] He continues with a concise survey of twelve such stories and concludes that they share a set of standard features: an achieved victory, a ceremonial entry, praise directed to God, a climactic entry into a temple, and finally either positive or purgative activity in the temple. He states that Jesus' healings are the victory celebrated at his entry (Luke 19:37). Catchpole references several of the scriptural allusions cited above to buttress his argument and emphasizes how the evangelists portray Jesus as king.[29] Catchpole doubts several historical details because Markan Christology dominates the story. He also claims that the historical cleansing of the temple must have been a minor event, since it did not evoke an official response from the temple authorities.[30] Catchpole concludes that the cleansing exhibits Jesus in his pre-Easter role as prophet, but the entry casts Jesus from a post-Easter perspective as the Davidic Messiah.[31]

Duff builds on Catchpole's comparison of Jesus' entry with Greco-Roman entrance processions. He furthers the claim that these stories were part of a literary form that raised specific expectations in the audience's mind.[32] Duff presents a minimal structure for these stories: the king is met at the gates by the citizens, escorted into the city with hymns and acclamations, and then performs a ritual in the temple. He also cautions that rigid distinctions cannot be made among the variety of entrance stories (from conquering foreign ruler to the return of a city's own victorious general).[33] Duff contributes to the interpretation of this literary form by arguing that the conquering king's action in the temple symbolically asserts his appropriation of the entire city.[34] Duff argues that Mark separates the entry and the cleansing in order to demonstrate Jesus' ironic rejection of Jewish temple worship.[35] He concludes that Mark "teases his readers with what seem to be triumphal allusions but

---

27. Ibid., 283–85.

28. Catchpole, "Entry," 319.

29. However, Catchpole does not see any tension between Greco-Roman triumphs that celebrated the victory of one who is already king and the coronation stories from the Jewish Scriptures alluded to in the Synoptic accounts. While precise distinctions can be hard to make (see more below), one must decide whether Jesus is already king or becoming king at this entry.

30. Catchpole, "Entry," 332–33.

31. Ibid., 334.

32. Duff, "Divine Warrior," 56.

33. Ibid., 61, 64.

34. Ibid., 61.

35. Ibid., 67–68.

never satisfies their expectations which might have been built up by those allusions."[36] His comments on the ironic nature of Jesus' entry in Mark resonate with Kinman's analysis of the entry in Luke.

Kinman's monograph on Jesus' entry in Luke was discussed at length previously, but it deserves mention here again. Kinman provides a more probing and wide ranging survey of triumphal entries in the Greco-Roman world. He discusses the arrival of a distinguished person, the yearly assize of the governor, the Roman triumph, and Jewish royal and military precedents.[37] He proffers the following list of typical elements: a royal figure, meetings outside the city, political leaders and citizens, ceremonial accoutrements, speeches, and a climactic escort to the temple.[38] Kinman claims that 18:35—19:48 "serves to emphasize that Jesus is king and, at the same time, to play down any possible connection between him and Jewish nationalists."[39] Jesus does not exert control over any mundane affairs, and Luke disassociates Jesus from the prophecies of Zech 9 and omits the nationalistic waving of palm branches.[40] Instead, Luke associates Jesus with Solomon (a peaceful king) through the story of the obtaining and riding of the colt and adding "king" to the acclamation of the disciples.[41] In the lament (vv. 41–44), Jesus speaks judgment against Jerusalem (not Rome) like one of the "prophets of old," and finally Luke abbreviates the cleansing to eschew any possible political implications.[42] In the end, Jesus' entry is "a-triumphal" because the city does not welcome Jesus, while his disciples rejoice at his royal and peaceful arrival.[43]

These studies on the "a-triumphal" nature of the arrival of Jesus at Jerusalem move the discussion forward significantly, but they also present unresolved interpretive problems. The first set of problems occurs with their use of form criticism. The various examples of "entries" present such diversity that scholars cannot agree on the necessary or possible elements of the form. Several of Catchpole's examples do not reflect the form well. For instance, when Simon enters Jerusalem (1 Macc 13:49–51), he militarily *expels* the current residents (rather than being welcomed by them) and his own soldiers sing hymns and praise God.[44] Archelaus's royal activity in Jerusalem after his father's death is also problematic (Josephus, *Ant.* 17:194–239),[45] for no *entrance* is narrated. Instead, Archelaus appears to be in the city already when he processes ceremonially to the temple. Duff has the most minimal list of elements: met by citizens, escorted with acclamations, and ritual in the temple. However, the final element of temple activity does not appear in many triumphal entry stories, and Luke's account does not portray any citizens coming out to welcome

36. Ibid., 70.
37. Kinman, *Jesus' Entry*, 27–64.
38. Ibid., 33–34.
39. Ibid., 91.
40. Ibid., 105, 113–17.
41. Ibid., 91–97.
42. Ibid., 144, 153–55.
43. Ibid., 97–98.
44. See Catchpole, "Entry," 320
45. Ibid., 321.

Jesus.⁴⁶ Furthermore, though Duff rightly states that we cannot make rigid distinctions among this family of stories, all three of these scholars combine coronation stories from the Hebrew Bible with Greco-Roman triumphs, which are mostly not coronations, but the arrival of one who is already king. Therefore, the variability of the "form," the missing elements in Luke's account, and the failure to distinguish between coronations and triumphs problematize the application of this material to Luke's portrayal of Jesus' entry.

The second set of problems emerges from Duff's and Kinman's similar conclusions that the accounts of Jesus' entry use these traditions ironically or contrastively. Duff states that Mark fails to fulfill the audience's expectations of an entry, and Kinman argues that Luke's political apologetic leads to an entry that is *not* triumphal. Neither considers at what point the comparison breaks down. When so many elements fail to obtain in Luke's account and others are so variable, is it possible that an ancient audience might have seen this as something else altogether? Kinman argues that while Luke intensifies the royal dimensions of this account, he plays down any potential political overtones. At one point, he wonders whether such a division between the religious and secular could have obtained in the ancient world. He grants that Luke's audience might not have comprehended the distinction, but he insists that Luke himself did divide them and "*sought* to depoliticize Jesus."⁴⁷ Kinman is right to note that ancients did not bifurcate these spheres, and we must consider their relationship in Luke more carefully.

The social-spatial framework presented in this study helps to diagnose and resolve these problems. First, the issue of scale rarely rises in the analyses of Jesus' entry. It is inappropriate to compare Jesus' entry to Pilate's assize⁴⁸ because the two figures operate at very different levels of the political scale. Jesus was a popular unofficial figure who interacted with minor, local officials. Pilate was a provincial governor appointed by the Roman Empire. This stark difference should warn us to avoid comparing apples and oranges (or one might say a grape and a grapefruit). This study also argues that a distinction did exist in the ancient world between the official and unofficial public spheres.⁴⁹ Again, Pilate's entry would have been an official event, anticipated by the leaders and citizens of Jerusalem who responded appropriately. On the contrary, Jesus' entry was largely unofficial. He is welcomed only by members of his own movement, and the leaders of Jerusalem are not mentioned until after the cleansing of the temple (vv. 47–48). Thus, the examination below will seek to apply better and more nuanced categories to the analysis of Jesus' entry and find better comparisons that fit its unofficial nature.

The Social and Spatial Characteristics of 19:29–48

The following social-spatial examination of 19:29–48 will focus on four areas: the public significance of Jesus' route to Jerusalem, the social and political nature of Jesus' relation-

---

46. Fitzmyer says, "The Lucan story knows nothing of a crowd coming out of Jerusalem to meet Jesus" (*Luke*, 2:1243).

47. Kinman, *Jesus' Entry*, 107.

48. Ibid., 170–72.

49. This distinction was not held equivalently or universally, but ch. 2 demonstrates that it did exist.

The Procession into Jerusalem (19:28–48)

ship with his disciples (focusing on 19:29–38), the public and official conflict at Jesus' entry (focusing on 19:39–48), and finally a critique and comparative analysis of the political nature of Jesus' entry.

The Public Significance of Jesus' Route to Jerusalem

Luke reminds his audience several times that Jesus is purposefully traveling to Jerusalem (9:51–53; 13:22, 33–34; 17:11), and these reminders increase in both frequency and intensity as Jesus nears the end of his journey (18:31–34; 19:1, 11, 28, 41). It is quite odd, then, that at the climax of the journey Luke never explicitly states that Jesus arrives in the *city*.⁵⁰ In 19:41, Luke says, "As Jesus came near he saw the city and wept over it." Next, Luke states, not that Jesus entered Jerusalem, but that he entered the temple area (καὶ εἰσελθὼν εἰς τὸ ἱερόν, 19:45).⁵¹ Exactly where and how did Jesus enter the temple and/or Jerusalem? An ancient (high-context) audience would clarify this scene by supplying information about Jesus' arrival based on a few clues in Luke's text and some awareness of the geography and architecture of Jerusalem.

Previous commentators have wrestled with this question. Lake suggests that Luke envisions Jesus coming through Bethany, over the crest of the Mount of Olives, descending toward the city, and entering immediately into the temple through the eastern Shushan Gate.⁵² Conzelmann resolves this dilemma by claiming that Luke redacts the story of the entry in order to disassociate it from the Parousia. Thus, Jesus arrives in and takes possession of the temple, *not* Jerusalem.⁵³ Jesus cleanses and claims the temple as the arena for his teaching. Conzelmann thinks that the first mention of the city in 22:10 coincides with the true beginning of Jesus' passion, the return of Satan and the messianic sufferings. Thus, for Conzelmann, Luke separates Jerusalem and the temple for literary-theological purposes. Bachmann, in direct opposition to Conzelmann, proposes that the temple and the city are one in Luke's mind and thus an entry into the temple is, in fact, an entry into the city.⁵⁴ Bachmann does not need to go into further specifics because his claim that Luke sees the city and temple as one dissolves the dilemma.

---

50. Conzelmann notes the same phenomenon stating that Luke "does not connect the entry with the city at all . . . , but he connects it exclusively with the temple" (*Theology*, 75). At this point, Conzelmann also says that Jesus never enters the city until the last supper according to Luke, but even this entry is implied. Jesus merely instructs Peter and John to arrange for the meal in a house that they find "when they enter the city" (22:10), and he later joins them there with no explicit mention of his entry into the city (22:14) unlike the parallel in Mark 14:17. Bachmann also notes the lack of an explicit entry (*Jerusalem*, 146 n. 53).

51. In the Gospel the temple has only been mentioned thus far in the infancy narrative (1:9, 21, 22; 2:27, 37, 46), the temptation (4:9), and as a setting for the parable of the Pharisee and the tax collector (18:10). This only augments the unexpected mention of the temple rather than Jerusalem in 19:45. Of course, the temple will become much more important as a location for events in the early chapters of Acts.

52. Lake, "Localities," 476. Lake claims that Christian tradition depicts Jesus entering through the eastern gate but provides no references. This route over the northern slope of the Mount of Olives seems so certain to Lake that he is forced to conclude that the location of Bethany must be reevaluated in light of it.

53. See Conzelmann, *Theology*, 74–80. Conzelmann also believes that Luke has a sorely misguided conception of the layout of the city and temple (75 n. 1), so it would be nearly impossible for him to describe Jesus' entry accurately.

54. Bachmann, *Jerusalem*, 146–48. In a long and detailed footnote, Bachmann dismantles Conzelmann's argument and concludes that "mit dem Entritt in den Tempel das Ende des Wegs nach Jerusalem und damit

PART TWO: SOCIAL-SPATIAL EXEGESIS OF LUKE 18:35—19:48

The spatial specifics of Jesus' arrival according to Luke establish both its social dynamics and its public valence. Archaeological information about the road to Jerusalem and the entrances into the temple will set some of the boundaries of feasibility for this analysis (as it did in the latter half of chapter 2). The goal is not to critique Luke's historical accuracy, but to see what social-spatial picture his narrative creates within the parameters of plausible verisimilitude about Jerusalem and the temple. Luke maintains the tradition of Jesus traveling from Jericho to Jerusalem found in Mark and Matthew.[55] However, all three Synoptics recount different geographical details at Jesus' entry. A few key details in Luke help us to reconstruct his route for Jesus' entry. To do this, one must answer two interrelated questions. On what road did Jesus approach Jerusalem, and how did he enter the temple (and city)? The following maps of Jerusalem will serve as guides to the discussion.[56]

Figure 8.1: The Eastern Side of Jerusalem

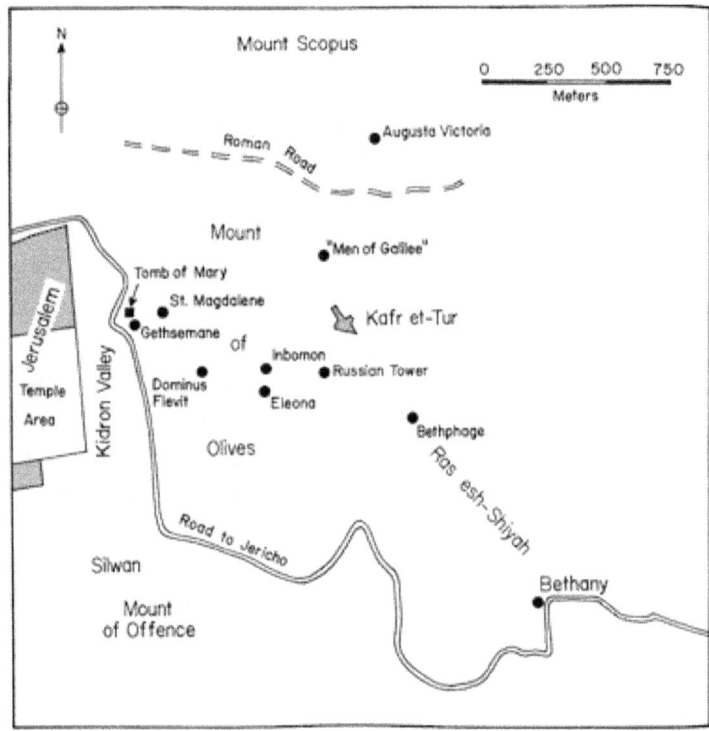

das Betreten der Stadt unzweideutig angesprochen sieht" (ibid., 147 n. 54). On the other hand, Bachmann also comments on the fact that Luke emphasizes temple scenes in 19:45—21:38 and city scenes in 22:1—23:55, which indicates (contra Bachmann's overriding thesis) that Luke can distinguish the city from the temple, even if the two are bound together.

55. Luke makes Jesus' visit to Jericho a significant event in itself as well as preparation for the journey to Jerusalem. Mark and Matthew, on the other hand, use the healing of the blind man/men pericope as a springboard directly into the triumphal entry with quite different results. For the role of Mark and Matthew's use of this story see Verseput, "Jesus' Pilgrimage," 115.

56. The first map in figure 8.1 is from Finegan, *Archaeology*, 154. The second map in figure 8.2 is found at the back of Meeks, ed., *Harper Collins Study Bible*, color map 16. This second map is reproduced with the permission of the publisher.

The Procession into Jerusalem (19:28–48)

Figure 8.2: Jerusalem in Jesus' Time

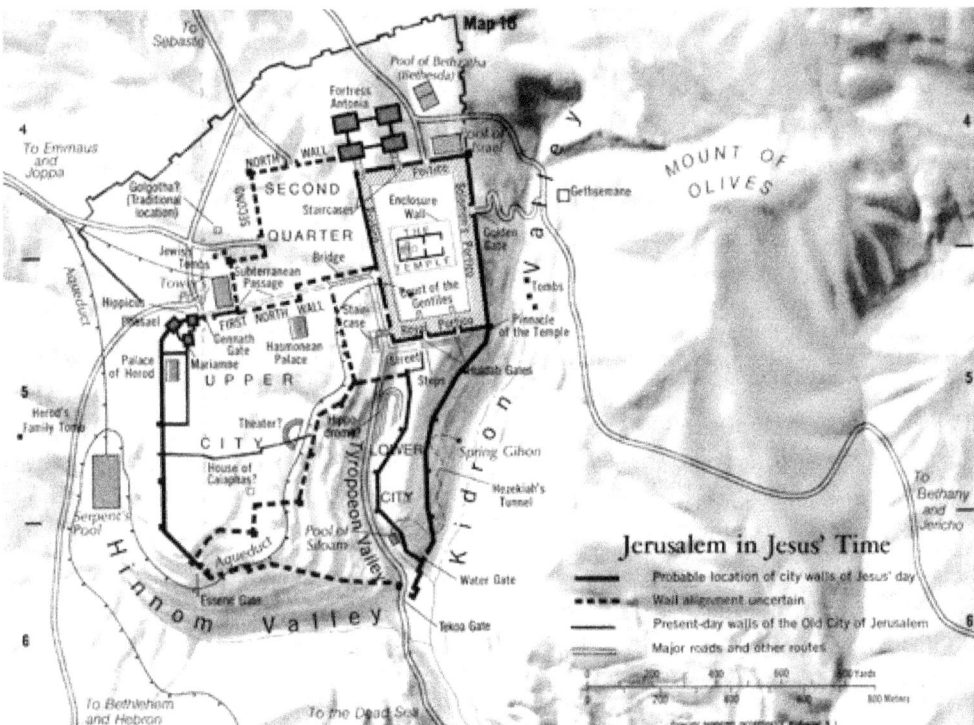

The road between Jericho and Jerusalem was an ancient and well-used route.[57] Yet, archaeological and literary evidence offer two possible routes of final approach to Jerusalem from Jericho. One branch breaks off to the south approximately ten miles east of Jerusalem. It follows a path of least resistance through valleys and passes to navigate the mountain ridge east of Jerusalem. Ancient Bethany lies on this road (with Bethphage probably nearby), and it is often the only road depicted on many Bible atlases.[58] This branch could have led travelers up through the Kidron Valley to the eastern or northern sides of the city[59] or connected to other roads that led to the southern and western sides

---

57. The Roman road in Figure 8.1 probably followed an ancient route. See Dorsey, *Roads and Highways*, 204–5. Wilkinson also points out references to this route in the Hebrew Bible and Josephus ("Way," 10). The distance from Jericho to Jerusalem on the Roman road is not quite twenty miles (Finegan, *Archaeology*, 152). Thus, it probably would have taken the better part of a day's journey to walk from Jericho to Jerusalem on the Roman road given average travel times of the day. See Chevalier, *Roman Roads*, 194; and Wilkinson, *Jerusalem*, 32–33.

58. This southern branch is the only option depicted on Figure 8.2. This slightly easier route makes sense given the fact that Jerusalem's elevation is over half a mile higher than Jericho. The traveler would have to face this incline as well as rugged desert-like terrain for most of the journey. See Wilkinson, "Way," 11. Some commentators conclude that this was the probably the route taken by Jesus because the steep descent down the Mount of Olives simply could not have accommodated the crowds described at Jesus' entry. See Perot, *Land of Christ*, 77–78. Finegan raises this issue as well but prefers the traditional descent down the mountain (*Archaeology*, 171).

59. Finegan, *Archaeology*, 155. This way through the Kidron is depicted on both maps above. The *Macmillan Bible Atlas* depicts Jesus entering by a northeasterly route. However, it does not follow the road up through the Kidron Valley and implies that Bethany is northeast, rather than southeast, of Jerusalem. Such a sugges-

of the city.⁶⁰ Note that this road *avoids* the summit of the Mount of Olives; a modern road follows this path because it is the least precipitous route. The other branch was the route of the Roman road. It approached the northeastern corner of the city, crossing a higher point in the ridge between Mount Scopus and the Mount of Olives.⁶¹ This road probably delivered travelers to Jerusalem by skirting to the north of the Mount of Olives near the top of the Kidron Valley, and from here they could have entered the city from either the north or the east.⁶² Both routes are historically feasible. Jesus could have followed the less arduous southern branch and then entered the city a variety of ways, or he could have taken the steeper Roman road and entered the city from the east or north.

One critical and unique detail in Luke's account (not found in Mark or Matthew) makes an approach along the Roman road most likely. Luke 19:37 portrays Jesus descending down the western slope of the Mount of Olives and into Jerusalem: "when he [Jesus] had come right up to the descent of the Mount of Olives . . ." (ἐγγίζοντος δὲ αὐτοῦ ἤδη πρὸς τῇ καταβάσει τοῦ ὄρους τῶν ἐλαιῶν).⁶³ The next geographical marker appears in v. 41 where Luke says that Jesus "came near and saw the city." Therefore, in Luke's account, Jesus descends down the Mount of Olives toward Jerusalem. This is very similar to the route taken by the Roman road, while the southern branch avoided the higher points of the range.⁶⁴ With Luke's description, Jesus could have only taken the southern branch if he then left that road, climbed the mountain, and then descended—a most unlikely scenario. The more likely scenario, according to Luke's description, is that Jesus followed the Roman road (by Bethphage and Bethany), left it to go the short distance up to and over the Mount of Olives, and then headed down toward the city.⁶⁵ He would have entered Jerusalem by a gate on the eastern or possibly the northern side of the city.

The gates to the city adduce another set of evidence and probabilities. An entrance from the west or northwest seems most unlikely, despite the density of roads and gates

---

tion was made by Lake ("Localities," 476). Yet, most scholars consider the southeastern site (near the modern village of el-'Azariyeh, derived from the name of Lazarus) to be most likely, with Bethphage lying slightly to the northwest and closer to the Mount of Olives. See Finegan, *Archaeology*, 155–57; and McRay, *Archaeology*, 195–97.

60. The archaeological evidence for the connection to the south and west is less certain, but its existence is probable. See Dorsey, *Roads and Highways*, 205–6.

61. Some of the paving of this road has survived and helps in reconstruction of its path. However, it is missing from most Bible atlases and maps. See Finegan, *Archaeology*, 155; and Wilkinson, "Way," 23.

62. Finegan, *Archaeology*, 155.

63. This is also noted by Fitzmyer, *Luke*, 2:1250. Green calls this description "topographically realistic," while others have doubted it (*Luke*, 686). Marshall notes several distinctively Lukan elements in this verse (*Luke*, 714).

64. Luke does say that Jesus came near to Bethphage and Bethany (19:29), but this does not mean that Jesus had to be on the road that went to these cities. Luke preserves Bethphage from the Markan tradition and adds Bethany (as Matthew does). The two cities would have been the best markers of nearness to Jerusalem, even from the Roman road. Bethphage was probably located between the two roads near the southern ridge of the Mount of Olives. The addition of Bethany might have helped to locate this little known village. Bethphage was also most likely the place where the disciples found the colt, and it would have been just as accessible from either route. See Finegan, *Archaeology*, 162–63.

65. If Jesus diverted off the road toward Bethphage, a climb over the Mount, down the valley, and to the city would have been the most direct route (Finegan, *Archaeology*, 171).

on the northwest corner of the city, for this would have been an unnecessarily circuitous and long route when approaching Jerusalem from the east. Entering through a western gate of the temple also would have been unusual.[66] Similarly, an entrance from the south would have involved extra travel: after arriving at the northeastern corner of the city, Jesus would have had to go south through the Kidron and then take another road leading to one of the southern gates (the Water Gate or the Tekoa Gate).[67] The Roman road could lead travelers to the north, and the gate in this area was most likely the Sheep Gate (Neh 3:32; John 5:2), which may be identical with the Tadi Gate mentioned in the Mishnah (*Mid.* 1:3, 9; 2:3).[68] An entrance from the north is possible but faces three difficulties.[69] First, no hard archaeological evidence exists for a northern gate to the temple in Jesus' (or Luke's) time.[70] Second, this gate might have been used for the traffic of animals into the temple and possibly as an exit for impure priests, so it is unlikely as an entryway for Jesus.[71] Furthermore, Luke never mentions a gate on the north and has a preference for the eastern side of the temple throughout Luke-Acts, as will be shown.

Luke's interest in the Mount of Olives and differences from Mark and Matthew make the Roman road and an entrance from the east more likely. For Luke, the Mount of Olives is an important place at the end of the Gospel and the beginning of Acts, and it definitively shapes his portrayal of Jesus' entry. The Mount of Olives is Jesus' pilgrim residence throughout his last week in Jerusalem: at the end of each day of teaching, Jesus would retire to the Mount of Olives and spend the night there (21:37).[72] Luke even identifies this as Jesus' custom, adding the phrase κατὰ τὸ ἔθος to the traditional material preserved in 22:39, which describes Jesus departing to the Mount of Olives after the last supper (see Mark 14:26).[73] This is in contrast to both Mark and Matthew who identify Bethany

---

66. The western side of the temple had four gates (Josephus, *Ant.* 11.5), and these gates open onto the crowded western section of the city with its growing elite suburbs (Finegan, *Archaeology*, 211). However, they were mostly used by priests who lived in this area (Levine, *Jerusalem*, 230). In light of the more distant location (force of place) and their elite character of the gates (the force of social relations), Jesus probably did not enter the city or the temple from the west.

67. The southern entrance would have lead through the Tyroponean Valley section of the lower city, one of the most densely populated areas of the city, to the southern gates of the temple, which were the most commonly used. Such an entry would have been undeniably public, and may fit Matthew's account best. Matthew specifies that Jesus entered the *city* (21:10), then the crowds speak (21:11 as Jesus approaches the temple through the Tyroponean Valley), and then Jesus enters the temple (21:12).

68. Finegan, *Archaeology*, 214–15, 227–28; Levine, *Jerusalem*, 230 n. 50. Figure 8.2 suggests that this gate could be reached by the southern branch, but it would have been more direct to take the Roman road.

69. Some maps definitively show Jesus entering through this gate. See Dowley, *Kregel Bible Atlas*, 77.

70. Levine, *Jerusalem*, 230. A northern gate is mentioned very briefly in Josephus's account of the Roman's siege of Jerusalem (*J.W.* 2.537).

71. However, some evidence points to a pilgrim camp on the northeast corner of Jerusalem due to the availability of water in that area. See Tsafrir, "Jewish Pilgrimage," 371.

72. Luke's Jesus returns to the Mount of Olives in order to teach the apostles after his resurrection (Acts 1:12).

73. On the other hand, Luke omits the statement found in Mark 13:3 and Matt 24:3, which specifies that Jesus delivered the Synoptic apocalypse to his disciples on the Mount of Olives. However, the most probable reason for this omission is that this verse in Mark and Matthew describes the Mount as a location of private (κατ᾽ ἰδίαν) instruction. By omitting this reference, Luke subtly changes the social-spatial valence of this en-

as Jesus' place of lodging (Mark 11:11–12; 14:3; Matt 21:17; 26:6) and so imply that Jesus triumphally and regularly entered Jerusalem (and then the temple) from this village (and perhaps from the south).[74] Jesus' entry into Jerusalem is affected by the preference for including Bethany (so Mark and Matthew) or the Mount of Olives (so Luke). Luke creates a different impression of Jesus' entrance into Jerusalem. Luke modifies the tradition in 19:28–29. He includes all of the places mentioned in Mark and Matthew, but clarifies that Jesus "comes near" to Bethphage and Bethany on his way to Jerusalem. Instead of ἐγγίζουσιν/ἤγγισαν εἰς Ἱεροσόλυμα (Mark 11:1 and Matt 21:1), Luke has Jesus ἐπορεύετο ἔμπροσθεν ἀναβαίνω εἰς Ἱεροσόλυμα. Jesus heads toward the city instead of coming near to it. What Jesus "comes near to" in Luke is Bethphage and Bethany, which are close to (πρός) the Mount of Olives.[75] However, Luke merely uses these as a spatial setting for the sending of the two disciples: "And it happened, when he came close to Bethphage and Bethany which were near the Mount of Olives, he sent . . ."[76] Luke never mentions these two villages again, but the Mount of Olives reappears several times in Luke-Acts and is the last geographical marker (v. 37) before Jesus enters the city. This mention of the Mount of Olives in 19:37 is unique to Luke and is the determining factor in reconstructing Jesus route into the city, for the Mount lies due east of the temple. Therefore, Luke envisions Jesus continuing on the main Roman road until it met the crest of the ridgeline near the Mount of Olives. It would have then been a short distance off the road to the summit of the Mount of Olives with the descent toward the temple and city on the other side.

Given the route of Jesus' arrival in Luke and the problems with entering from the north, one must ask: how would Jesus enter the temple from the east? Luke seems to assume that there was a gate on the eastern side of the temple that opened directly onto the Kidron Valley near the bottom of the Mount of Olives. However, no hard evidence exists for an eastern gate in Jesus' time. Josephus does not mention an eastern gate. Levine thinks there was probably no gate to the east because of the inaccessibility of the topography.[77]

---

tire section, transforming it from Jesus privately teaching selected followers on the Mount to Jesus delivering another public discourse as the climax of his temple activity (Luke 21:5–36 with the conclusion to this section coming in vv. 37–38). This is also noted by Conzelmann, *Theology*, 79.

74. Bethphage and Bethany play more significant roles in Mark's and Matthew's accounts of the entry and passion. When describing Jesus' entrance, Mark says (somewhat awkwardly) that Jesus was approaching Jerusalem at Bethphage and Bethany near the Mount of Olives when he sent his disciples into the village (perhaps Bethany in Mark given the fact that Jesus stays there later) to fetch a colt for him (Mark 11:1–2). Matthew, on the other hand, has Jesus draw near to Jerusalem and enter Bethphage, which is at the foot of the Mount of Olives (21:1). These geographical clues would place Jesus on the southeastern side of Jerusalem, making an entrance from the south more likely (especially according to Matthew 21:10–12). Luke only states that Jesus enters the temple (no mention of the city as in Mark and Matthew). Bachman sees this as part of Luke's habit of associating the temple and the city (*Jerusalem*, 147–48), but the explanation provided below shows why Luke has Jesus enter the temple with no mention of the city.

75. Mark does not mention Bethany. I have taken the πρός as indicating that the two villages are "close to" the Mount of Olives in Luke's view (compare Mark 5:11 and John 20:11–12)

76. Fitzmyer, *Luke*, 2:1248; and Bock, *Luke*, 2:1552.

77. Levine, *Jerusalem*, 229. Many maps of Jerusalem in the time of Jesus show no gates on either the northern or eastern walls of the temple.

However, other evidence indicates that there might have been a gate on the eastern side of the temple in the early first century and that Luke *thought* there was a gate in the eastern wall. Jewish sources may speak of a gate on the eastern side of the temple called the "Shushan Gate."[78] Comments from medieval times mention a gate on the eastern side of the temple called the "Golden Gate" (*Porta Aurea*), which Christian tradition designated as the gate of the triumphal entry.[79] At this point, some scholars adduce Luke's mention of a gate called "Beautiful" (ὡραία) in Acts 3:2 and 10. The identification of a supposed eastern gate with Luke's Beautiful Gate (which is never mentioned by any other ancient record) has been discussed at least since Lake posited this solution with some reserve.[80] This solution has three difficulties. First, no archaeological evidence supports the existence of this gate in Jesus' day.[81] Yet, this study presumes that Luke was not bound to historical veracity but to historical verisimilitude, and the existence of an eastern gate does not seem to lie beyond the bounds of the believable. Second, scholars repeatedly suggest that such a location would have been quite inauspicious for a beggar (Acts 3:2) since it would have received far less traffic than the gates on the west and south.[82] Again, it is within the bounds of historical possibility for Luke and his audience to believe that any gate to such a magnificent temple would have received plenty of traffic, and Luke does not make the geography sound overly arduous. Third, some scholars point out that the apostles were typically in the city (Acts 1:13) as Jesus commanded, and thus probably would not have entered through this eastern gate, which led into the temple and not the city. However, the importance of the Mount of Olives in Luke's story (see Acts 1:12) makes it feasible that the early Christians in his account would have visited this nearby sacred location on the eastern side of the city often. Peter and John may have been entering the temple precincts from one of their visits to the Mount of Olives.

Several pieces of evidence suggest that Luke's Beautiful Gate should be identified with the eastern gate. First, Luke's use of the term ὡραία is phonetically similar to the early medieval Latin name *aurea*, suggesting that the Greek appellation used by Luke slipped phonetically over into the later designation (or the two mutually influenced one another).[83] In Acts, Luke depicts the apostles entering through this eastern gate into the courtyard of the Gentiles in the larger temple complex (ἱερόν, Acts 3:1) and not the sanctuary itself (ναός, which Luke uses exclusively for the actual temple building).[84] After

---

78. Levine is quite skeptical of this reference (*Jerusalem*, 229 n. 49), while Finegan gives it more credence (*Archaeology*, 209).

79. Finegan, *Archaeology*, 210. This gate is labeled on Figure 8.2.

80. Lake, "Localities," 485–86; and Finegan, *Archaeology*, 209–10.

81. Some scholars insist that the "Beautiful" Gate of Acts 3 should not be identified with a gate into the temple precincts (the Shushan Gate) but a gate into the sanctuary. See Bahat, "Jesus," 301–2. However, this would not comport with Luke's saying that this was τὴν θύραν τοῦ ἱεροῦ, a gate to the temple precincts and not the sanctuary (which Luke always calls the ναός).

82. Both of these objections are found in Haenchen, *Acts*, 198 n. 12. Many subsequent commentators site the same problems.

83. Finegan, *Archaeology*, 210.

84. Hamm, "Acts 3,1–10," 309–11. Hamm carefully examines Luke's use of ἱερόν and ναός to show that the former *never* refers to the sanctuary in Luke-Acts. Hamm admits that Luke is probably mistaken about

healing the lame man and entering the temple, a crowd gathers at Solomon's portico (Acts 3:11) on the eastern side of the temple.[85] After being healed at the eastern gate, the blind man would have entered the temple and created a public scene in its eastern court around Solomon's portico. Thus, Luke-Acts implies a gate on the eastern wall of the temple called the Beautiful Gate (whether or not one actually existed in his time).[86] According to Luke, after descending down the Mount of Olives, Jesus could have entered directly into the temple through the eastern gate.[87] This explains why Luke does not state that Jesus entered Jerusalem, but rather the temple, at the climactic completion of his long journey. Luke probably knows that the temple complex is part of the larger city of Jerusalem; however, his comment in 19:45 is precise, for Luke thinks that Jesus entered straight into the temple precincts through an eastern gate rather than entering one of the city gates first and then proceeding to the temple (as implied in Matthew). Therefore, clues in Luke's account, especially the mention of Jesus' descent down the Mount of Olives, and a set of historical probabilities make the following scenario most likely for Luke's narrative: Jesus stayed on the (more northern and steeper) Roman road as he traveled from Jericho to Jerusalem. When he neared the city, Jesus made the short ascent up the Mount of Olives from the topographically higher Roman road and then descended down the Mount of Olives toward the eastern side of the temple. Finally, Jesus entered directly into the temple through an eastern gate, probably the Beautiful Gate of Acts 3.

What are the social ramifications of the spatial details of Jesus' entry in Luke? First, the route proposed above lends some credibility to the order of the groups that acknowledge Jesus at his entry. Following Luke's account, Jesus takes the more northerly Roman road up to the Mount of Olives. He passes through no towns but sends his disciples into the nearest village (Bethphage?) to fetch a colt for him. They do not tell anyone in the village that Jesus is traveling on the nearby road.[88] Thus, the only people present with Jesus as he proceeds from Jericho to the descent down the Mount of Olives would have been his own disciples and possibly a few other pilgrims taking the same route with him. Note that the disciples are the only other characters in the entry until 19:39. The disciples are the ones who lay their cloaks in the road in 19:36, and then the disciples alone acclaim Jesus as king in vv. 37–38 (see further below). The crowd and some Pharisees appear in Luke's

---

this eastern gate, but then in resonance with this study he says, "Such an error is understandable in an author writing quite probably after the destruction of the temple and at some distance from the scene. What Luke the historian may have been working with is (a) a story about the healing of a well-known crippled beggar at a familiar gate, (b) a tradition about the original Jerusalem Christian community commonly meeting in Solomon's Portico, and (c) a vague knowledge of the temple layout. That very distance in time and space and that incomplete knowledge gave Luke the freedom to combine the fragments as he wished." The same reasoning can be applied to Jesus' entry.

85. Josephus, *Ant.* 20.220–21. See also Finegan, *Archaeology*, 209–10.

86. Barrett concludes much the same. He thinks that Luke's narrative strongly implies that the Beautiful Gate was an eastern entrance the opened onto Solomon's Portico despite some textual problems and the lack of historical verification (*Acts*, 1:191–92).

87. Although argued somewhat differently, the same conclusion is reached by Finegan, *Archaeology*, 171–72.

88. The somewhat cryptic reply, "The Lord needs it," may have resonated with early Christians who revered Jesus as Lord, but would have had no such connotation to these villagers.

retelling after Jesus has completed at least part of his descent down the mountain (19:39). While no independent evidence exists for pilgrim camps on this rather steep hillside or the valley below,[89] Luke states that Jesus went out to stay on the Mount of Olives (with other pilgrims in Luke's view?) each evening and implies that this gate had enough traffic to support a beggar. Thus, the side of the Mount of Olives near the city would have been the first place for a crowd (with some Pharisees) to gather around as Jesus descended the slope to the shouts of his disciples.

Second, given this spatial analysis of Luke's narrative, Jesus would have entered the temple precincts at Solomon's Portico and immediately begun driving out the merchants in the Court of the Gentiles. This court was a public area. Conzelmann says, "According to Luke, Jesus addresses the speakers of xxi, 5 publicly in the temple."[90] Such public address characterizes the entire temple teaching in Luke's account of the passion and can also probably be localized more specifically in Solomon's Portico, which has a strong public valence in Luke's narrative. While merchants might have set up shop in the Court of the Gentiles and while Jesus could have easily roamed and taught throughout this area, Luke's narrative emphasis on the eastern side of the temple and his specific mention of the Beautiful Gate and Solomon's Portico may imply that Jesus was most active in this area. Notwithstanding other possible allusions,[91] this scenario is very public in nature. Solomon's Portico was located immediately across from the entrance to the Court of the Women and the main sanctuary. Luke states that a crowd gathered there after the healing of the lame man (Acts 3:11–12). Luke counts five thousand in this crowd who believed because of Peter's address in 3:11–26 (see 4:4), even more converts than at Peter's Pentecost sermon (2:41). Thus, Luke's larger narrative casts the Court of the Gentiles and especially Solomon's Portico as public space, and Jesus would have publicly arrived in this area of according to the entry account.

This analysis of Jesus' entry into the temple in Luke is more than an exercise in the vague minutiae of historical topography and archaeology, for Jesus' arrival through the eastern gate of the temple aligns with Luke's view of the public nature of this area and explains the absence of any mention of Jesus' entry into the city. Some (like Sanders and Catchpole) have sought to downplay or reduce Luke's geography in light of theological concerns. However, when examining the force of place in this passage, one sees Luke employing specific geography to mark Jesus' route to the temple and simultaneously illuminate its public valence. Grasping the role of the places casts light on the force of time and social relations, for Jesus' route into the city makes good sense of the sequence and composition of the various groups that appear along the way in Luke's account. Finally, other examples in Luke use the force of social relations to portray large crowds present in the outer courts of the temple, especially the eastern portico. Therefore, intertwining

---

89. Tsafrir says there is evidence for pilgrim camps on the north, west and south of the city near water sources, but his only source for this is Josephus (*J.W.* 2.44). See Tsafrir, "Jewish Pilgrimage," 371.

90. Conzelmann, *Theology*, 79.

91. For instance, the "Son of David" (Luke 18:38) now occupies *Solomon's* Portico and Jesus primarily teaches in an area named after the fount of Israel's wisdom traditions. It is also quite probable that Luke depicts the apostles teaching in precisely the same location that their master did (Acts 3:11; 4:1–2).

PART TWO: SOCIAL-SPATIAL EXEGESIS OF LUKE 18:35—19:48

the spatial specifics of Jesus' entrance with Luke's social characterization of the eastern portion of the temple precincts reinforces the public nature of Jesus' entry and the events that follow.

Jesus and His Disciples (19:29–38)

After examining the route of Jesus' entry and its public nature, we can consider the public and political emphases in the two major sections of Luke's account, 19:29-38 and 39-48. Jesus and the disciples are the main characters in 19:29-38. The disciples play a role in obtaining the colt, preparing elements for Jesus' approach to the city, and rejoicing as he draws near to the city. The following social-spatial analysis will explore these three parts of vv. 29-38 to understand the politics of Jesus' movement. This material will lead the way to comparisons drawn from Plutarch's *Precepts*.

Luke casts Jesus as an effective leader of his movement of disciples in vv. 29-34. Jesus heads out for Jerusalem in v. 28 (note the singular verbs). When *he* came near (again a singular verb in v. 29) to the villages of Bethphage and Bethany, he dispatched two of his disciples on an important task (implying that his disciples were following his lead toward the city). The language of the command in vv. 29b-31 recalls the commissioning of the Twelve and the Seventy earlier in the Gospel.[92] Jesus takes the initiative to prepare for the final leg of his journey, and he issues a comprehensive order complete with hypothetical objections and responses. These verses demonstrate the complete control of Jesus.[93] The "sent ones" leave and find the colt "just as he had said to them" (v. 32). Jesus' hypothetical obstacle comes to pass in v. 33, and the disciples' response, "The Lord needs it," effectively silences the owners' objection in v. 34. Interpreters almost unanimously agree that ὁ κύριος in vv. 31 and 34 refers to Jesus as "Lord."[94] However, the next use of κύριος in v. 38 clearly refers to God (not Jesus). Also, unless the owners (and other villagers) in the narrative somehow know that assume that the disciples were followers of Jesus, most Jews would have taken the absolute use of this term as referring to God. Identifying ὁ κύριος as God makes Jesus the authorized delegate or agent of God who then delegates tasks to others, a portrayal that is consistent with Luke's depiction of Jesus (cf. 4:43 with 9:1-2; 22:28-29). Jesus initiates the obtaining of the colt (under God's authority), precisely predicts the course of events, and is obeyed by his disciples without variation or question. The politics here are mostly internal and local, dealing with Jesus' leadership of his own movement (under God's authority). Thus, as Jesus prepares to enter Jerusalem, Luke casts him as an effective leader with divinely bestowed authority and insight, who is in full control of the events surrounding his own arrival.

However, after v. 34, the disciples become the protagonists in Luke, and they are the subject of most of the verbs in vv. 35-38. The disciples bring the colt to Jesus. They

---

92. Jesus "sends" (ἀποστέλλω) his disciples here just as he "sends" them in 9:2 and 52. They "go" (ὑπάγω) as they "go" in 10:3. Nolland states that the use of ἀποστέλλω in v. 29 characterizes the disciples as Jesus' "authorized delegates" (*Luke*, 925), adding a political tinge to his description.

93. Bock also notes that this episode displays Jesus' control over the events in preparation for his entry (*Luke*, 2:1546, 1554).

94. Marshall, *Luke*, 713; Fitzmyer, *Luke*, 2:1249; Green, *Luke*, 685.

The Procession into Jerusalem (19:28-48)

throw their cloaks on it,[95] and they place Jesus on it (Luke 19:35). Mark and Matthew state that Jesus sat (ἐκάθισεν) on his mount(s). Luke, however, states that the disciples "seated" (ἐπεβίβασαν) Jesus on the colt.[96] Then the disciples throw their cloaks on the road before Jesus (Luke 19:36). Both Mark and Matthew note that the disciples placed their cloaks on the animal(s) for Jesus (Mark 11:7 and Matt 21:7), but then they specify that a crowd (πλεῖστος ὄχλος in Matt 21:8 and πολλοί in Mark 11:8) spread their cloaks on the road as Jesus approached the city. However, Luke does not change the subject of the actions in 19:36: the disciples (not the crowd) take the initiative to spread their garments on the road before Jesus.[97] As Jesus descends down the Mount of Olives, the disciples (not the crowd as in Mark 11:9 and Matt 21:9) declare Jesus to be king (v. 38). Jesus does not initiate any of these actions, and instead is the object of the disciples' actions.[98] After Jesus' first command, the disciples shower Jesus with royal honors that have precedents in the Hebrew Bible.

Kinman argues that Luke was attempting to distance Jesus from the Jewish revolutionaries of his era, while emphasizing his royal status.[99] However, Luke has failed to curtail the revolutionary implications of the actions of Jesus' followers, for they act like the loyal followers of a rival king. Riding on a colt into Jerusalem could recall both Solomon (1 Kgs 1:33) and the eschatological king of Zech 9:9. In 1 Kgs 1:32-33, David, the current king, gives the order for the procession. While in Luke, the disciples take it upon themselves to bestow this honor upon Jesus. The stark difference lies in who takes the initiative to place the "heir" on the animal. The disciples bestow royal honors by placing Jesus upon a colt, and by doing so usurp the royal right of kings to name a successor. They act very much like the revolutionary followers of Simon the slave who proclaimed him as king (Josephus, *Ant.* 17.273-74). While the garments on the colt have no known parallels, the placing of garments on the road echoes the acclamation of Jehu (2 Kgs 9:13). Like Jehu, Jesus is acclaimed king by his own followers. However, Jehu is a poor point of comparison if Luke wants to downplay any revolutionary overtones of Jesus' entry.[100] Jehu is a rival king who is anointed to annihilate the ruling house of Ahab and take over the throne (2 Kgs 9:4-10). The actions of Jesus' disciples recall this rebel king and thus color Jesus' entry.

---

95. The verb here is plural, but it is not entirely clear if Luke means that the two disciples sent on the task do this, or if more members in the band of disciples also participate.

96. Kinman wants to disassociate the use of ἐπιβιβάζω here and in 1 Kgs 1:33 from the use of ἐπιβαίνω in Zech 9:9 (*Jesus' Entry*, 94-95). However, the two words are philologically and semantically related, since ἐπιβιβάζω is the causative form of ἐπιβαίνω (LSJ, s.v. ἐπιβιβάζω). Luke never uses ἐπιβαίνω for sitting on an animal, only for entering a geographical area (Acts 20:18, 21:4) or getting on a ship (Acts 21:2, 27:2), whereas ἐπιβιβάζω is Luke's verb for riding an animal (Luke 10:34, Acts 23:24).

97. The NRSV translation is quite misleading when it says "people kept spreading their cloaks on the road." The noun "people" is supplied by inference from the third person plural forms in the clause ὑπεστρώννυον τὰ ἱμάτια αὐτῶν (Luke drops Mark's subject, πολλοί). However, the natural antecedent to these is the larger group of disciples mentioned in 19:29. This is noted by Marshall (*Luke*, 714), but Green sees them as functionally equivalent (*Luke*, 686).

98. Nolland also notes the shift of initiative (*Luke*, 925).

99. Kinman, *Jesus' Entry*, 21.

100. Thus, if Luke was downplaying political/national overtones by omitting the waving of palm branches (ibid., 115-17), then he should have omitted this detail as well.

PART TWO: SOCIAL-SPATIAL EXEGESIS OF LUKE 18:35—19:48

Finally, a scene with fanatical disciples following a prophet down the Mount of Olives recalls the route of another revolutionary: "The Egyptian" and his followers (Josephus, *J.W.* 2.261–63). Again, the actions of Jesus' followers echo the actions of the followers of other revolutionaries. While Luke does not specifically cast Jesus as a political revolutionary, he does a poor job of modifying the actions of Jesus' disciples to distance Jesus from Jewish uprisings.

Instead of focusing on how outsiders (especially politically sensitive Romans) might have viewed Jesus' entry, Luke concentrates in vv. 29-38 on how Jesus' own disciples rejoice at his entry into Jerusalem. Thus, Luke's aim is more epideictic than apologetic.[101] He highlights the disciples' actions to reveal something about Jesus and discipleship to his Christian audience, not to convince outsiders that Jesus is no political threat. While Jesus initiates a train of royal allusions by instructing his disciples to fetch an unridden colt, the disciples follow through zealously, heaping royal honors upon their master in vv. 34–36. In v. 37, Luke brings out the role of the disciples as "witnesses" who rejoice over Jesus' "acts of power," a role that Jesus' disciples continue to play in Acts (1:21–22; 2:32, 5:32, 10:39). In Luke's view, the disciples of Jesus who witnessed his teaching and healing are the best interpreters of the significance of these events. Thus, the disciples rightly "praise God" for the actions of Jesus with a surge of excitement as they draw near to Jerusalem. The disciples (not the crowds or the Pharisees or the chief priests) recognize Jesus as king with Luke's edited recitation of Ps 118:26.[102] Most others lamentably miss his true identity (and so the lament of 19:41–44). Finally, Luke ratifies the witness of the disciples when they proclaim peace and glory in heaven at the arrival of Jesus (v. 38b). This cry echoes the announcement of the angelic choir in 2:14 when they proclaim glory in heaven and peace on earth.[103] Thus, the disciples share the same perspective and insight as the angels. At the climax of Jesus' movement of discipleship as he draws near to Jerusalem, the disciples exult and acclaim Jesus as king verbally and symbolically. By doing so, Luke urges his (mostly Christian) audience to adopt the disciples' attitude and actions toward Jesus in their own day.

Luke's account of Jesus' entry in 19:29–38 has little to do with official politics. Luke does not place Jesus in relation to the Jewish hierarchy or the Roman Empire. Rather, Luke focuses on Jesus and the disciples. The (royal) politics of this episode are local and internal to Jesus' own movement. The focus of Luke's narrative cautions us to select comparative materials more precisely. While Luke does employ allusions to coronation traditions from the Hebrew Bible, Jesus' identity is not constructed by or for Jewish national structures. He is proclaimed "king" by his disciples within his movement, and that kingship has primary relevance for that movement. Jerusalem and the official Jewish establishment bear the negative relevance of this proclamation, for not joining it seals the city's doom (cf. vv. 41–44). Similarly, Jesus' kingship is not cast against the backdrop of the Roman Empire, but

---

101. See the discussion of the difference between these two aims in ch. 1.

102. As Sanders noted, Luke's version contrasts the acclamation of the disciples with the lack of recognition on the part of the Jewish leaders ("Fabric," 149).

103. The locations and circumstances have changed slightly, for peace is now "in heaven" instead of "on earth." This probably presages the doom that awaits Jerusalem because it did not recognize Jesus.

against the backdrop of the growth of his followers (now a "multitude") and his ministry of miracles. In this sense, Kinman is correct that Luke's Jesus does not look like the Jewish revolutionaries of his day, and his entry is "a-triumphal." However, that is not because Luke purposefully moves his account of Jesus entry *away* from nationalistic or political concerns, but because he moves Jesus *toward* ecclesiological concerns and christological confession (the disciples and their response to Jesus).

This high point in Jesus' relationship with his movement of disciples calls up several comparisons with Plutarch's *Precepts* that reinforces the local politics of vv. 29–38. Plutarch urges Menemachus to strike a balance between favoritism to one's friends and rejection of one's friends when entering political office (807a–b). Plutarch says that the wise statesman should choose friends as an architect selects employees and craftsmen who will cooperate to bring the building to an excellent completion (807c), "for friends are the living and thinking tools of the statesman" (807d). Jesus has done this. Jesus acts as a leader initiating a string of royal allusions when he instructs the disciples to fetch an unridden colt. The disciples quickly adopt this line of thinking, add further royal honors, and ultimately acclaim him king. The disciples, as Jesus' well-chosen followers, perceive his intent and follow through on it enthusiastically. Plutarch also warns Menemachus against overscrupulousness, for obsessive involvement in the affairs of people sours their perception of the statesman (811d–812b). One of the best ways to defray public annoyance is to "put faithful and good men to work in particular tasks according to their ability" (812c). Instead of commandeering the colt and claiming royal honors for himself, Jesus starts the ball rolling and allows his followers to further the process. In this public climax to his ministry and his movement, Jesus entrusts the important task of celebrating his arrival to his disciples. This is similar to Plutarch's advice that the statesman should select his most powerful and most cooperative friends to achieve goals that require effort and struggle (819b). Luke's portrayal of this important moment in Jesus' movement squares with Plutarch's advice on how a local political leader should regard and employ his friends. Jesus' movement is unofficial, unlike Plutarch's official purview; however, the political wisdom transplants well as Luke portrays Jesus as one who appropriately employs his own friends/followers at his approach to the city.

The force of nature and social relations come to the fore in this part of the analysis. In vv. 29–38, Jesus encounters no political officials, judges, or military commanders. Luke constructs his portrayal at the beginning of the entry by using his relationship with his disciples. Thus, at this point Luke casts Jesus' entry as more unofficial than political. However, there is a type of politics (the social exercise of power) at work here, for Jesus is an effective and authoritative leader among his disciples. He entrusts tasks to them, and they faithfully carry them out. Furthermore, they pick up on his (royal) intentions and magnify them by their own initiative. Luke does not portray Jesus in relation to the empire or the Sanhedrin as he approaches Jerusalem; instead he focuses on the local and internal politics of Jesus' movement.

PART TWO: SOCIAL-SPATIAL EXEGESIS OF LUKE 18:35—19:48

The Public and Official Conflict at Jesus' Entry (19:39–48)

The characters and tone of Luke's account change at v. 39. The disciples disappear from the narrative and a variety of other (mostly hostile) characters appear. The royal accolades and jubilation fade as Jesus faces, predicts, and precipitates conflict. A series of brief scenes comprise vv. 39–48: Jesus' conflict with the Pharisees (vv. 39–40), Jesus' lament over Jerusalem (vv. 41–44), Jesus' cleansing of the temple (vv. 45–46), and the final summary/preparatory statement about Jesus' teaching and his official opposition (vv. 47–48). Each scene contributes a piece to Luke's public and political portrayal of Jesus and each scene adds an element of conflict to the entry. With these scenes, the royal Jesus enters into the political sphere where he faces his greatest opposition.

In v. 39, the Pharisees step onto the narrative stage, telling Jesus to rebuke his disciples. They have not appeared as a character since 17:20 and have not been mentioned since the parable in 18:9–14. The Pharisees are part of the crowd (ἀπο τοῦ ὄξλου) present on the descent down the Mount of Olives.[104] Luke does not say that the crowd or the Pharisees came out to meet Jesus.[105] Rather, they happen to be in this area when Jesus descends down the mountain to the acclamations of his followers. The Pharisees address Jesus as teacher, reflecting their ongoing assessment of him as a peer and part of the unofficial public sphere.[106] The Pharisees then command Jesus to command his disciples to stop. They use the aorist imperative ἐπιτίμησον, a word which appears in exorcisms (4:35; 9:42) but also refers to a command to stop doing something, especially to stop speaking (4:41; 9:21, 55; 18:39). Thus, Luke's Pharisees focus on the acclamation of the disciples (reported in vv. 38–39) and want Jesus to tell them to stop proclaiming such religious and royal honors for Jesus. The Pharisees issue Jesus a command as a peer, but they expect him to issue a command as the leader/teacher of his disciples, for they recognize his local and unofficial authority within his movement. The precise meaning of Jesus' reply has been debated by scholars, but Kinman's interpretation seems the most plausible: Jesus asserts that his entry is so momentous that someone or something must acknowledge it.[107] Furthermore, it must be acknowledged *publicly*. The disciples shout with a "loud voice" (φωνῇ μεγάλῃ), and the crowd near Jerusalem hears their vociferous acclamation. If they do not shout publicly, then the stones would "cry out" (κράζω). Luke has recently used κράζω to describe the public cry of the blind beggar in 18:39, and he uses it in Acts to refer to public shouting (14:14; 16:17; 19:28, 32, 34; 21:28, 36). The acclamation of Jesus as king at his entry into Jerusalem cannot remain private; it must be proclaimed publicly by someone or something for all to hear.

---

104. Luke specifies that only "some" (τινές) of the Pharisees voiced their opposition. Others might have been opposed and silent or perhaps even in favor of the acclamation.

105. Furthermore, it is inappropriate to read this mention of the "crowd" in v. 39 back into the preceding verses, for if that were the case, the Pharisees would still be a part of the "crowd" that had spread its garments on the road before Jesus (cf. 19:36) only to object here. No, Jesus travels with his disciples who honor him as king, and at v. 39 Jesus and his entourage encounter a crowd with some Pharisees in it.

106. Recall Bachmann's comments on the unofficial but public nature of "teaching" in most of Luke-Acts (*Jerusalem*, 262–65). The complex unofficial and official nature of the Pharisees will be discussed in ch. 9.

107. *Jesus' Entry*, 100.

The Procession into Jerusalem (19:28–48)

When the audience comes to v. 41, Jesus is surrounded by a crowd with his disciples proclaiming his royal arrival and some Pharisees objecting to it all. In the midst of this bustling, public scene Jesus speaks to the city before him in vv. 42–44.[108] Luke says that Jesus came near to the city and wept over it.[109] Rather than addressing the people or the nation or the leaders, Jesus addresses the personified city.[110] However, Luke typically places the burden of blame for the rejection of Jesus on the leaders of Israel,[111] so the official leaders of the Jewish nation are primarily responsible for not recognizing "the things that make for peace" in v. 42. Later in the lament Jesus centers on the πόλις of Jerusalem as a corporate entity including the people who live in it (Jerusalem's children, v. 43) and the city as an architectural reality (the stones that will be thrown down in v. 44). Thus, Jesus' lament deals with a humanly constructed city (the force of place), which represents all of its inhabitants (the force of social relations) and particularly the Jewish leaders (the force of meaning).

According to vv. 42–43, Jerusalem, with its citizens and leaders, encounters two outside powers that determine its fate. First, Jesus arrives bringing peace from heaven (2:14 and 19:38). Heaven stands both spatially and politically over Jerusalem, for Jerusalem is both (physically) under heaven and under the authority of God. However, the city (with its leaders and people) fails to recognize the significance of Jesus' arrival and therefore cannot receive the heavenly peace that he brings.[112] This causes a second outside power ("your enemies") to wage war against the city, destroying it and its inhabitants. Luke and his audience would have probably understood this to be the Roman Empire's sack of Jerusalem, which adduces the imperial political sphere.[113] This brief prophetic oracle from the lips of Jesus intertwines several social and spatial dimensions. Jesus addresses the city as a spatial entity that includes the social realities of its inhabitants and its political structures. The local (and climactic) rejection of Jesus at his entry into the city by the representative leaders is a rejection of the divine peace that Luke locates spatially in heaven. The local rejection of this heavenly peace by the city causes drastic consequences executed by forces on earth from the imperial political sphere. Jesus' lament condenses these social and spatial forces to create a powerful prophetic warning just before Jesus enters the city.

In 19:45, Jesus arrives in the temple (and in the city as argued above). Ancient sources and contemporary interpreters affirm the public valence of temples in the Greco-Roman

---

108. Jesus' lament in vv. 41–44 is unique to Luke.

109. Weeping (κλαίω) often takes place publicly in Luke (7:13, 32; 8:52; 23:28).

110. Jesus addresses his lament in the second person singular (σύ) and speaks of the destruction that will befall the city. See Borg, "Luke 19:42–44," 104 and n. 10.

111. See Johnson, *Luke*, 302 and passages such as Luke 24:20 and Acts 7:52; 13:27. Kinman views the entire city as culpable since the citizenry did not come out to welcome Jesus as they should have at an entry (*Jesus' Entry*, 142). However, the "triumphal entry" traditions are poor comparisons to Luke's account at precisely this point.

112. Kinman is right to say that this "peace" probably includes peace with God (salvation) as well as a more mundane form of peace (absence of earthly warfare). See *Jesus' Entry*, 138–40.

113. Borg classifies vv. 42–44 as a "threat oracle," which involves "the coming destruction of the present order through military conquest, seen as a judgment against the ruling elites of politics, wealth, and religion" ("Luke 19:42–44," 104).

PART TWO: SOCIAL-SPATIAL EXEGESIS OF LUKE 18:35—19:48

world and the Jerusalem temple in particular. After his survey of the public nature of teaching in Luke, Bachmann concludes that for Luke, "the Jewish sanctuary is guaranteed to be a place that is public to a superlative degree."[114] Jesus' ministry of public teaching in Luke reaches a social-spatial climax in the temple teaching of the passion narrative. Acts recounts several public scenes in the temple.[115] The discussion of Jesus' route into Jerusalem already highlighted the public valence of the beggar's location at the Beautiful Gate (Acts 3:1–10) and the public nature of the following speech in Solomon's Portico (Acts 3:11ff). After their imprisonment, God orders the apostles to "stand in the temple and tell the people the entire message about this life" (Acts 5:20). The presence of "the people" in the temple continues to mark its public valence. No more scenes occur in the temple until the account of a riot surrounding Paul's presence in the temple in Acts 21:27ff. An accusation against Paul rouses a mob that drags him out of the temple and begins to beat him. After this, Paul makes a speech from the steps to the crowd below.[116] Bachmann is correct: Luke employs the temple as a public place throughout his two-volume work.

Archaeological and comparative material confirms this description. While Herod maintained the modest size of the sanctuary according to canonical guidelines, he added an enormous and ornately decorated platform to create a stunning temple precinct. The platform was over 172,000 square yards, the largest site of its kind in the ancient world.[117] This platform contained courts, gates, porticoes, the Antonia fortress, and other buildings, providing ample room for crowds of people and reinforcing the sacred and public nature of the space. Chapter 3 cited the following statement from Appian about one of Caesar's building projects:

> He erected a temple to Venus, his ancestress, as he had vowed to do when he was about to begin the battle at Pharsalus. He also framed an area around the temple which he intended as a forum for the Roman people, not for personal purchases but for the transaction of public business with each other, like the public squares of the Persians, where the people seek justice or learn about the laws. (*Bell. civ.* 2.15.102)

Herod's temple reflects the same incorporation of public space into the temple precinct (if not the same high ideals). Philostratus also displays the public nature of temples in his portrayal of Apollonius. He delivered his first public discourse to the Ephesians "from the platform of their temple" (*Vit. Apoll.* 4.2). Later, Apollonius delivers more public speeches to large crowds from the platform of the temple in Olympia (4.31). Finally, when Apollonius arrives in Rome, Philostratus reminds us that he frequented the temples there (4.40). Then he states, "And people flocked to these [temples], supposing that they would receive more benefits from the gods, and no one objected to his conversations because he spoke seriously *in public and addressed all people*" (4.41, emphasis added). The public nature of temples is clear in the *Life*, a work that offers several apt social-spatial comparisons

---

114. *Jerusalem*, 283–85.

115. Bachmann cites Jesus in the temple as a boy in ch. 3 as another example of public teaching in the temple (*Jerusalem*, 271–72). However, he fails to note exactly why and how this scene is public.

116. Note references to the crowd in 21:27, 34 and 36.

117. Meyers, "Temple, Jerusalem," *ABD* 6:367.

The Procession into Jerusalem (19:28-48)

to Luke's Gospel. Thus, when Luke casts the temple as a public venue for Jesus' words and deeds, he concurs with a common cultural perspective that regarded temple precincts as public spaces.

When Jesus arrives in the courts of the temple, the first thing he does is to begin "to drive out those who were selling there" (19:45). Luke has abbreviated his account of the cleansing, removing the details found in Mark 11:15b-16 about the overturning of tables and the prohibition of commercial traffic.[118] Interpreting the cleansing is difficult due to its brevity in Luke's Gospel; however, Luke's editing provides three clues that color the significance of the event. First, Luke states that Jesus drove out "those who were selling" (τοὺς πωλοῦντας),[119] omitting any mention of "those who were buying" (τοὺς ἀγοράζοντας, Mark 11:15). The only people forced to leave the temple are the merchants, probably only a handful in comparison to the throngs of worshippers. Jesus allows everyone else, including the large number of people who were doing business with the merchants, to remain. Rather than emptying out the temple as in Mark and Matthew, Jesus halts the economic activity, leaving "the people" to listen to his teaching. Second, Luke has omitted the phrase "for all nations" from the citation of Isa 56:7 in v. 46a and concluded his account of the cleansing by juxtaposing Isa 56:7 with an allusion to Jer 7:11 (σπήλαιον λῃστῶν).[120] This editing emphasizes the stark spatial contrast between the "house of prayer" and the "den of robbers" (19:46) by allowing it to echo at the end of the brief account.[121] These two spaces represent two extreme characterizations of the sacred space of the temple precincts. On one hand, the temple and its precincts can be a "house of prayer," a place where people serve the Lord, rejoice, and make sacrifices the way God intended (cf. Isa 56:6-7).[122] Or, the temple can be a "den of robbers," a place where stealing, murder, adultery, and idolatry go on unchecked (cf. Jer 7:8-9).[123] The recipients of this accusation (the "you" of ἐποιήσατε) are probably the "chief priests, scribes, and leaders" who plot against Jesus in 19:47.[124] The Jewish leaders bear the brunt of culpability in Luke-Acts, and they (not the merchants) react with hostility to Jesus immediately after the cleansing in 19:47.[125] The chief priests and other leaders are the source of conflict and the object of

---

118. Mark's version of Jesus' entry portrays it more as a portent of the temple's rejection and destruction. See Duff, "Divine Warrior," 67-69.

119. This term has no negative connotations in Luke (12:6, 33; 17:28; 18:22; 22:36) or Acts (4:34, 37; 5:1). This weighs against an economic motivation for the cleansing (i.e., the merchants were cheating the buyers).

120. Part of the reason for the omission of "for all nations" has to do with Luke's understanding that the temple has no lasting significance for Gentiles (cf. Johnson, *Luke*, 302).

121. In Luke's construction of this combined quotation, the two spatial labels occur at the end of each stich, highlighting the parallel and the contrast.

122. Note the contrast here: Zacchaeus's house is ready for Jesus to teach in it (because of Zacchaeus's repentance), but the temple (God's house) must be cleansed first.

123. Nolland says that the text from Jeremiah "makes a general protest against the lives of people coming to worship" (*Luke*, 938). I agree with this assessment, but the accusation in Luke is about the nature of the place, and responsibility falls upon those who have charge over it (the chief priests, etc.).

124. The chief priests and others seem to be the object of his accusation here as they are in the parable of the wicked tenants (see 20:19). Stephen similarly indicts the Sanhedrin in Acts 7. This is contra Kinman, *Jesus' Entry*, 151.

125. Catchpole concludes that this must have been a minor event because there was no official response

PART TWO: SOCIAL-SPATIAL EXEGESIS OF LUKE 18:35—19:48

Jesus' rebukes throughout the next chapter (20:1–2, 19, 20, 27, 45–47), and the preparatory function of these verses implies that they are the addressees in 19:46 as well. These leaders, who should have preserved the proper function and purity of the temple, have instead allowed it to degenerate to a place of moral and religious depravity. They are rebuked by Jesus for allowing God's house to turn into a robber's den. Third and finally, Luke inserts v. 47a into the Markan tradition: "and he was teaching every day in the temple." Scholars have long noted that Luke casts the cleansing as Jesus' preparation of the temple for his final teaching in chs. 20–21.[126] Luke's Jesus drives out the merchants from the temple in order to restore the space to its proper function, a place of prayer (Luke 18:10; 19:46a; Acts 3:1) and public teaching (Luke 2:46–47; 19:47; Acts 5:21).

In vv. 39–48, the scale and degree of hostility against Jesus intensifies. The appearance of the Pharisees in v. 39 recalls the opposition that Jesus faced from them previously in the Gospel (the Pharisees do not appear again until Acts). Then in 19:47, Luke introduces "the chief priests, the scribes, and the leaders of the people" and so establishes a new level of official opposition against Jesus. When Jesus enters the temple (and the city), these regional religious/political leaders replace the Pharisees as Jesus' primary opponents at this point, and their opposition to Jesus is more destructive and more political than that of the Pharisees. The Pharisees are hostile to Jesus and try to catch him in some misstep (11:53–54), but it is not until Luke introduces the chief priests and leaders that we hear of plans to murder Jesus (19:47). Also, while the Pharisees have some political connections (as seen more clearly by their participation in the Sanhedrin in Acts), these are downplayed in the Gospel where they appear more as locally popular leaders. The chief priests/scribes/leaders/elders, however, hold power in the seat of regional administration (Jerusalem) and they interact with the Roman governor of the region (23:1–2). Thus, the degree of opposition (from hostility to murder) and the political scale (from local to regional leaders) increase when Jesus' movement climaxes with his entrance into Jerusalem.

This increased hostility fits with Plutarch's portrayal of the local politician. Plutarch predicts that conflict will emerge in the course of a local leader's career in the *Precepts*: "Every public career [πολιτεία] will bring forth enmities and conflicts" (809B). Plutarch, who seeks "concord" in the state throughout the treatise, urges the statesman to deal with political conflicts fairly and generously, not allowing them to spill over into the private sphere or disturb the local government (809b–810a). However, such peaceful resolution is impossible in Luke's Gospel, for the Jewish leaders in Luke are stubbornly wrong-headed and must be opposed. Plutarch describes such a conflict in 817d–f. He states that any citizen should challenge the official leaders (ἀρχήν) for the sake of the common good. If the local leaders are reluctant or hostile, then one (even one who does not hold office) must speak for the public good, "for the law always gives primacy to the one who does what is right and knows what is beneficial in public affairs" (817e). Similarly, Jesus (a popular, unofficial leader) denounces the degeneration of the temple into a marketplace, drives out

---

("Entry," 332; Nolland, *Luke*, 936, has a similar view). However, Luke makes it clear that there was no response because they feared the reaction of the crowd that hung on Jesus' every word (19:48).

126. Conzelmann, *Theology*, 77–78; Fitzmyer, *Luke*, 2:1269; Johnson, *Luke*, 301–2: Ganser-Kerperin, *Das Zeugnis*, 165–66.

the merchants, and accuses the regional officials (chief priests, etc.) of failing to maintain the sacredness of the temple space. To correct this, Jesus restores the holy function of the temple by teaching the people in the public courts. Jesus fits the role of one who stands up against the local leadership, calling them to task for their errors and presenting a better way to the people. While Luke's overall portrayal of Jesus casts him as a leader in the unofficial public sphere, Jesus does finally come into conflict with the ruling authorities of the land, and he rebukes them in public for the sake of his people, similar to Plutarch's advice.

19:47–48 is a preparatory summary that sets the stage for the passion narrative and forms an inclusio with 21:37–38.[127] Verse 48 states that the people are "captivated" (ἐξεκρέματο) by Jesus' teaching and prevent the leaders from taking action against him. When Luke recapitulates the temple ministry he recalls Jesus' teaching and the presence of the people in 21:37–38. The adulation of the people stands in stark contrast to the murderous hostility of the Jewish leaders in 19:47–48. However, Luke does not find that hostility important enough to reiterate in 21:37–38. What is important is that Jesus taught in the temple every day,[128] and that this teaching was public, for it took place before the people (ὁ λαός), a fact that 21:38 emphasizes by adding that "all" (πᾶς) the people came to hear Jesus. The temple scenes of the passion climax Jesus' public teaching in Luke. The space of the temple becomes the most public place of the Gospel, where Jesus addresses "all the people," indeed all of Israel.[129] Thus Luke concludes this final and transitional stage of Jesus' journey to Jerusalem by setting the stage for his final stint of public teaching in the temple at the social, spatial, and religious heart of the Jewish nation.

In vv. 39–48, Luke densely combines all of Sack's forces to present a thick public event. The emphasis shifts from Jesus and his disciples (vv. 29–38) to display increasing tension and hostility toward Jesus in vv. 39–48. The Pharisees among the crowd publicly voice their final complaint against Jesus in vv. 39–40, and Luke uses the force of social relations to intensify the public scene by obliquely mentioning the crowd. Then, the force of nature recalls the local and largely unofficial status of the Pharisees, and the force of meaning sets the parameters for this public challenge-riposte scene, which Jesus wins. In vv. 41–44, Luke weaves together several forces to portray how Jerusalem's rejection of heavenly peace (force of place in both) results in destruction for the city and its inhabitants (force of social relations) by (Roman) enemies (drawing in the imperial political sphere). Finally, Jesus enters the temple, which he must publicly restore to its status as a "house of prayer" before he teaches in it (force of religion and place). Doing so raises the ire of the highest Jewish religious/political officials of the land (the force of social relations and religion bringing in the official public sphere). However, the crowd (force of social relations) protects Jesus

---

127. Plummer notes this and labels vv. 47–48, "The Publicity and Popularity of Christ's Final Teaching" (*Luke*, 454).

128. 19:47a and 21:37a state that "Jesus was teaching in the temple every day" and are only slightly different in the Greek.

129. Recall Bachmann's statements about the "superlative" degree of the temple as public teaching space in Luke (*Jerusalem*, 283–85).

and he proceeds to teach publicly in the temple every day. Jesus' entry is clearly public (and royal), but appropriate parallels and its political ramifications remain unclear.

Parallels and Political Ramifications

After assessing the social-spatial nature of Jesus' entry in Luke, one can consider corrective suggestions regarding the best comparative material and the political ramifications of Jesus' royal entry and public actions. Catchpole, Duff, and Kinman offer several examples of other entries in the ancient world to illuminate Jesus' entry into Jerusalem. Their examples mostly fall into three categories: Solomon's coronation procession in 1 Kgs 1, the entries of Greco-Roman rulers, and the arrivals of Maccabean leaders. Catchpole, Duff, and Kinman each offer their own set of typical characteristics for these entries. The previous review discussed problems with their specific examples and lists of standard characteristics. Ancient authors and audiences probably (unconsciously) recognized a cluster of characteristics that could appear in the arrival of any distinguished person at a city: the distinguished figure, the figure's victory or royalty, the figure's entourage, citizens and officials meeting the figure outside of the city, a ceremonial welcome into the city, shouts of rejoicing or acclamation, speeches, and climactic action in the temple. No one story exhibits all these characteristics, and wide variety exists across the stories. Some cultural patterns emerged in the welcome of distinguished figures in the ancient world; however, historical and local details varied greatly. As Duff noted, one should not make rigid distinctions given the variability.[130]

Granting that this is a loose literary form, several problems persist when attempting to illuminate Luke's account of Jesus' entry by comparing it to these other entries. First, all of the previously cited arrivals occur in the *official* public sphere: Solomon is a prince becoming king, the Maccabees are political or military leaders, most Greco-Roman entries concern kings, governors, or conquering military commanders. However, Jesus' entry in Luke primarily takes place in the *unofficial* public sphere (all the way up to 19:45). Luke does not mention "citizens" (as he does in 19:14); the Pharisees are part of the unofficial public sphere (a "crowd" in 19:39); and Jesus does not encounter any officials until after the cleansing of the temple when he begins teaching (19:47). Luke does not portray an official entry, because Jesus is not an official. He is the leader of a popular movement in the unofficial public sphere. Second, most of the proffered examples occur on the wrong scale for they are far too grand.[131] Based on comparisons at mismatched scales, interpreters have called Luke's account "a-triumphal,"[132] a "tragic irony,"[133] or a minor arrival of pilgrims.[134] However, if Jesus is not a grand, distinguished, official figure, then it is inappropriate to expect his arrival to be accompanied by citizens, local officials, grand parades, lavish ceremonies, and formal speeches. Finally, the people gathered at Jesus' entry in Luke do not

---

130. "Divine Warrior," 64.
131. Here, I recall Wallace-Hadrill's spectrum of humble—grand (*Houses and Society*, 11).
132. Kinman, *Jesus' Entry*, 172.
133. Green, *Luke*, 688.
134. Marshall, *Luke*, 710–11.

The Procession into Jerusalem (19:28-48)

comport with ancient entries. Fitzmyer notes that Luke does not mention any reception by the citizens of Jerusalem.[135] Kinman notes that Luke has the "multitude of disciples" welcome Jesus (not a more general crowd as in Mark and Matthew). He suggests that this would have been a smaller group that might not have captured the attention of the city and its officials and thus not have represented a political threat.[136] However, he does not consider whether the composition or the size of the group in Luke problematizes his comparison with Pilate's assize or Solomon's coronation. Jesus' arrival in Luke is a large public event signaled both by the spatial specificity and the social impact of Jesus' large movement. However, it transpires in the unofficial public sphere, and therefore more suitable comparisons must be found.

In order to select better comparative material, one must interpret the significance of the royal indicators at the entry, which climaxes the royal theme peppered throughout 18:35—19:48. First, does Jesus enter Jerusalem as one who is already king,[137] or as one who is becoming king?[138] Unfortunately, this dichotomized question fails to capture the complexity and fluidity of Luke's presentation of the kingship of Jesus. The interpretation in chapter 7 of the parable of the king and his subjects argued that the truth lies in between these two alternatives, for the nobleman is announced (and recognized) as king before his departure but later returns in full royal (and political) authority. Similarly, the disciples celebrate Jesus' victory as demonstrated in his miracles (19:37), and yet Jesus will not attain his final victory until the resurrection (Luke 24:26; Acts 2:24). The disciples acclaim Jesus as king (19:38), and his kingship is real and recognized but not yet complete, for he will not come into his full reign until his ascension (Acts 2:34-36) and return (Acts 1:11). In terms of the parable in 19:11-28, the public announcement of Jesus' kingship has occurred (cf. 19:12-14); however, his full investiture and return has not yet transpired (cf. 19:15). Jesus is the one destined to be king over Israel (1:32). He should be received by the city as the one who will become king when he enters Jerusalem (tragically, he is not), but he still must pass through death, resurrection, and ascension (these are passed over quietly in the parable and thus also unmentioned at the entry) before receiving his royalty in full at his return. Therefore, the appropriate political metaphor might be that Jesus arrives as a crown prince: he is already royalty and is sure to become king, but his full royal identity and authority is not yet realized.[139]

A similar type of tension and complexity exists in Jesus' relationship to another crown prince: Solomon. Kinman rightly notes connections between Luke's account and Solomon:

---

135. Ibid., 2:1243.

136. Kinman, *Jesus' Entry*, 172.

137. Green takes this position but supports it by comparing Jesus' arrival with the entries cited by Catchpole where "entry presupposes and already achieved victory" (ibid., 683). As just argued, these examples are poor comparisons.

138. Kinman leans toward the latter by emphasizing the similarities between Jesus and Solomon in Luke's account (*Jesus' Entry*, 107-15).

139. One might ponder how Luke's theological and political perspectives intertwine on this point. Does Luke's theological timeline of the royal investiture of Jesus provide the grounds for his "not yet" kingship to be less of a political threat to the Romans, or does his desire to ameliorate political fears cause him to subtly defer Jesus' final investiture? Perhaps the two mutually influence one another.

PART TWO: SOCIAL-SPATIAL EXEGESIS OF LUKE 18:35—19:48

the title "Son of David," riding of the colt, and the emphasis on peace.[140] Considering the disciples' use of Ps 118 (an enthronement psalm) and Luke's addition of the title "king," a strong royal theme colors Luke's entry account in vv. 29–38.[141] These elements connect the portrayal of Jesus and Solomon. However, several discontinuities exist between the two figures. As mentioned in chapter 5, Jesus' ministry includes poor outcasts rather than creating a system of conscripted labor among the impoverished populace. Solomon's reign is a period of mundane peace without any foreign wars, but the rejection of Jesus just before his accession to royal power brings catastrophic foreign invasions (19:42–44). The arrivals of the two figures in Jerusalem, while similar in that both may be called "crown princes," are different. Solomon's arrival takes place with official accoutrements and authorities (1 Kgs 1:32–40), but Jesus' entry takes place in the unofficial public sphere as an event within his own movement. The initiative of the two characters is inverted. Jesus takes the initiative at the beginning of Luke's account with the command to fetch the colt for his entry, but from that point on the disciples take the lead placing Jesus on the colt, spreading out their cloaks, and acclaiming his royal arrival. Solomon, on the other hand, takes no initiative in the orchestration of his entry and coronation, which David plans on his behalf. When Solomon does come to power, he then initiates a bloody purge of all of his rivals (1 Kgs 2, far from a king of "peace"). Finally, Solomon's entry is also his coronation, while Jesus' full and final coronation lies in the future. Luke sets up (or allows) a parallel between Solomon and Jesus, but the differences, not the similarities, between them illuminate the kingship of Jesus.

Given the lack of fit with other triumphal entries, the complex nature of Jesus' kingship, and the differences between Solomon and Jesus, scholars should search for better comparative material to illuminate Jesus' (unofficial) entry into Jerusalem in Luke. The *Life of Apollonius* offers a promising parallel, for in 4.17–18, Philostratus tells of Apollonius's arrival and reception at Athens during a festival. He reports that Apollonius and his companions sailed to Piraeus (the port city for Athens) at the season of the mysteries, which took place in the fall generally around the autumnal equinox. This temporal marker (the force of time) supports the public nature of the story, for Philostratus goes on to say that this was "the most crowded of the Hellenic festivals" (πολυανθρωπότατα Ἑλλήνων) (4.17). Therefore, Apollonius arrived in Athens, the heart of Greek culture and philosophy, during the largest and most bustling religious festival held in the city. Similarly, Jesus came to Jerusalem, the heart of the Jewish nation, during the crowded festival of Passover (Luke 22:1). As Apollonius was going up (πρόειμι) to the city, he came upon a large group of philosophy students (πολλοῖς τῶν φιλοσοφούντων) on their way to Phalerum.[142] At this point, the force of social relations comes to the fore. They recognize Apollonius, and

---

140. *Jesus' Entry*, 110.

141. Note that these royal indicators fade after v. 38. No specific royal characteristics emerge in the Pharisees' complaint, Jesus' lament, or the cleansing of the temple.

142. Phalerum was another port area for Athens to the east of Piraeus. Apollonius must have been relatively close to the city at this point, close enough to meet them before their path diverged from the road to Piraeus. Note that even though time is a critical force here, Philostratus still provides several geographical details to set the public nature of the story also.

The Procession into Jerusalem (19:28–48)

"all of them turned around together and welcomed him gladly" (ξυνανεστρέφοντο τε καὶ ἠσπάζοντο χαίροντες). Then ten more young men joined the group. In good processional ceremony, these ten lifted up their hands to the Acropolis and cried out that they were heading to the port to travel to Ionia to see Apollonius. Philostratus paints an unofficial public welcome by a group of philosophy students who recognize Apollonius as a distinguished figure and rejoice at his arrival. Similarly, Jesus' own disciples are the primary "welcomers" who rejoice at his arrival in Luke 19:36–38.

Philostratus provides further details about the time and public nature of the festival in 4.18. Apollonius arrived in Athens on the day of the Epidauria, the fourth day of the mystery festival dedicated to Asclepius.[143] The ritual for this day was based on the tradition that Asclepius once missed the rites at the beginning of the festival and was initiated into the mysteries nonetheless. Thus, for Epidauria, the initiation rites were repeated and Asclepius was worshipped. Apollonius's appearance at this time was such an event that "most of the people skipped the second initiation and hovered around Apollonius." Apollonius, in line with his concern for ancient rites, urged the people to attend to their religion and he himself went to be initiated. Then the joyful tone of the story changes sharply, much like the tone of Jesus' entry changes at v. 39 where the joyful shouts of the disciples give way to the complaints of the Pharisees. The priest refuses to initiate Apollonius, whom he accuses of being a wizard. Apollonius boldly and capably meets this public challenge with his riposte: "You have not mentioned my primary offence—that I come to you for initiation even though I know more about the rites than you do!"[144] Similarly, the Pharisees publicly challenge Jesus who successfully answers them (19:39). Then in v. 46, Jesus publicly challenges the regional leaders, but they have no reply and so are publicly shamed. Those gathered around (τῶν παρόντων) applaud Apollonius's response, and the priest gives in when he recognizes that his exclusion of Apollonius was "not appreciated by the crowd" (οὐ φίλα τοῖς πολλοῖς). In the same way, Jesus' adoring crowd prevents the Jewish leaders from carrying out their destructive plans (19:48). Finally, after the entry, Philostratus describes the various discourses Apollonius gave in Athens, paralleling Luke's account of Jesus' temple teaching in Luke 20–21.

Apollonius's entry into Athens is a better analogy for Jesus' entry into Jerusalem on several accounts. Both are public and *unofficial* entries. In both cases, disciples of the sage accompany him into the city with joy and acclamations (the force of social relations). In neither case is the sage greeted on the outskirts of the city by religious or political officials who come out specifically to welcome the visitor. Both entries are into major urban and cultural centers (the force of place) and take place during crowded religious festivals (the force of time), allowing for throngs of people to be present and making the entry more public (the force of social relations). Both sages proceed to the cultic heart of the city (the force of place) where they encounter public conflict in the form of a typical

---

143. This is fitting given Apollonius's association with the cult of Asclepius and various healings (e.g., *Vit. Apoll.* 1.9).

144. This story is an excellent example of Philostratus's apologetic aim in the *Life*. In this case, Apollonius is directly accused of being a wizard who deals with impure divination. Apollonius rhetorically bests the man, is supported by the crowd, and predicts the demise of the priest.

PART TWO: SOCIAL-SPATIAL EXEGESIS OF LUKE 18:35—19:48

challenge and riposte (the force of meaning). Jesus and Apollonius both incur the ire of priests based on their actions, more specifically their insistence that they know the true function of the rituals and places better than those who have official oversight (the force of religion). Finally, a crowd gathers around both Apollonius and Jesus, and their public influence constrains the actions of the officials (the force of social relations). Apollonius is not a conquering king or official governor, and his arrival is not "a-triumphal." Instead, his arrival reveals his support among two groups: students of philosophy and the general populace. Similarly, Luke's account highlights the disciples' recognition of Jesus' power and authority, and he too finds support among the people in 19:48. Apollonius is not viewed as a threat to imperial rule when he arrives in Athens, though he will be when he arrives in Rome (4.40, 43). Rather, local officials look down upon him as an outsider and usurper and wish to exclude him. The royal elements in Luke's account cast more political suspicion over Jesus' arrival, but again we find local (or regional) officials taking offense at his claim to authority and seeking to undo him.[145] In both cases, the people validate the authority of the sage, forcing the official authorities to give way, and the sage goes on to teach publicly in the city. This comparison illuminates the unofficial and public nature of Luke's account. Furthermore, it reinforces the role of officials (Pharisees and chief priests), while adding realism to how the public masses exerted pressure on the political/religious officials enabling Jesus to teach in the temple.

Finally, given the royal indicators in Luke's account (not found in *Vit. Apoll.*), one must consider the possible political ramifications of Jesus' unofficial, but royal, entry. Three (previously discussed) principles set guidelines for the following conclusions. First, religion and politics were not separate spheres in the ancient world; they overlapped and reciprocally influenced one another. Luke's own narrative presents chief *priests* as the primary party in the Sanhedrin, the highest Jewish *political* body. Second, the unofficial and official public spheres are different, but they are also related and contiguous on our social-spatial spectrum. Third, Luke's narrative addresses Christian insiders first and interested outsiders second. Thus, it is more epideictic historiography than apology. The preceding analysis demonstrates that Luke places Jesus' entry in the *unofficial* public sphere. Furthermore, he casts it as an event that has primary significance for his own followers (vv. 29–38) and only later gains the attention (and rebuke) of local leaders (the Pharisees) and regional officials (the chief priests). Therefore, the acclamation of Jesus as king is both by and for his own disciples within his movement. It is not instigated or acknowledged by any level of local or regional authority. The same holds true for Luke's audience. Worshipping Jesus as king is relevant for the Christian community; it is neither directed at nor fully intelligible to outsiders.

That being said, the public nature of Jesus' entry causes it to spill over into the official sphere, especially after Jesus cleanses and teaches in the temple. The public acclamation of Jesus as king, while appropriate within his religious movement, is misunderstood by politically sensitive outsiders (such as the Pharisees). The issue is as much social as it is semantic. It is not only the meaning of the title "king" but also who uses and hears that

---

145. None of the royal elements in Luke occur in the *Life*. This is the main difference between the two accounts.

title.¹⁴⁶ Luke and other ancient persons might have been able to distinguish the religious and political spheres in some ways, and Luke might have exploited this in his portrayal of Jesus. However, the preceding analysis hints that the identity of the audience (force of social relations) makes the difference as to whether the title "king" is heard as a (non-seditious) christological confession or as a threat to the sovereignty of Caesar. Jesus is (properly) acclaimed as "king" in the section focused on his disciples (19:28-38). When outsiders call Jesus "king" in the remainder of the Gospel, it is either sarcastic (23:37) or in reference to potential treason (23:2, 3, 38). In 23:2, the Jewish assembly offers a combined accusation of Jesus as one guilty of political crimes (perverting the nation and forbidding the payment of taxes) and religious claims (being "Messiah, a king"). However, Pilate dismisses the stock political charges by not mentioning them. Instead, he focuses on the question of kingship, but nothing seems threatening about Jesus' acceptance of the title of "king" (23:3-4). Thus, Pilate (and Herod) simply releases Jesus (23:13-16), deeming his purported "royalty" to be no threat to the empire. Other instances in Acts confirm the importance of the audience when judging the political ramifications of religious claims. A hostile crowd accuses the Christians of proclaiming Jesus as another "king" (Acts 17:7), a sign of political insubordination on the part of his followers that flies in the face of the "decrees of the emperor" (ἀπέναντι τῶν δογμάτων Καίσαρος). Luke, however, considers these "royal" claims as a part of internal "Jewish" matters not worthy of Roman attention. Later in Acts 19:38-39, the city clerk (a local political official) urges Demetrius and his associates to bring a (valid) legal complaint against the Christians instead of fomenting a riot (yet, they cannot do so). Luke puts this principle clearly in the mouth of Gallio when he tells Paul's Jewish accusers, "If this were a matter of injustice or some crime, then Jews, I could accept your complaint, but since it is a dispute about words and *names* and your own law, see to it yourselves" (Acts 18:14-15, emphasis added).¹⁴⁷ The tribune Claudius Lysias expresses a similar notion in Acts 23:29: "I found that he [Paul] was accused about questions concerning their [the Jews'] law, but he was charged with nothing deserving death or imprisonment."¹⁴⁸ Therefore, some hostile persons take the Christians' royal claims about Jesus and try to turn them into evidence of treason (so the Jewish leaders and the mob in Thessalonica). They are outsiders and do not understand the religious significance of such christological claims. More discerning outsiders (like Gallio and Claudius Lysias) recognize that these were internal Jewish matters, not political threats worthy of Roman attention. Christians use and understand these terms correctly, but those outside of the followers of Jesus may either (belligerently) misconstrue the meaning of "king" or ignore it as insignificant (so Pilate).

---

146. This insight might help resolve Kinman's uneasy bifurcation between the religious and political spheres in the ancient world (*Jesus' Entry*, 107).

147. The closest "name" in context is Paul's preaching that Jesus is the "Christ" in 18:5. However, this could also include debates over the title "king," especially since the Jewish assembly connects the two titles in Luke 23:2.

148. Agrippa, Bernice, and Festus agree that Paul had done nothing to deserve "death or imprisonment" (Acts 26:30-31).

Thus, the title "king" has social and semantic multivalence. Despite the potential for the title of "king" to be exploited for political ends, Luke refuses to drop it. It remains an appropriate appellation for Jesus within the Christian community. Luke allows Jesus to cast himself as a type of client king in the preceding parable, and he alone among the evangelists has the disciples acclaim Jesus as king when he enters Jerusalem. While Jesus (and his disciples) does not seek to overthrow official authorities anywhere on the political scale, Luke also insists that Christians follow a higher divine authority that can include (Acts 26:29), transcend (Acts 4:19–20), or judge (Acts 12:20–23) the existing political system. By acclaiming Jesus as king, the disciples recognize him as the agent of God's kingdom and affirm his authority and dignity. However, outside of the Christian community, the title "king" can have political implications. By cleansing and teaching in the temple, Jesus (the "king") accuses the temple leadership of failure and steps into their sphere of religious/political influence (compare with Plutarch). The Pharisees object to the disciples' outrageous use of "king" (19:39), but the chief priests are most disturbed by his actions and criticism in the temple (19:47–48) and say nothing about his royal claims in chs. 20–22. When the Jewish assembly questions Jesus, they ask him if he is "the Messiah" (22:67), but when they bring him before Pilate, they accuse him as one who claims to be "the Messiah, *a king*" (23:2, emphasis added). They find the political implications of royal (religious) claims politically useful when they come before Roman officials. Because of its intensely public nature, Jesus' entrance into Jerusalem, while primarily intended to declare his royal lordship among his followers and before God, gains the attention of the authorities. Jesus' actions in the temple intensify the potential political ramifications of his royal entry and bring Jesus into direct conflict with the highest official Jewish assembly which then exploits the political implications of the disciples' royal acclamation.

Conclusion and Preview

The entry into Jerusalem is the public climax of Jesus' movement as the multitude of disciples rejoices over his ministry and acclaims him king. Luke's account of Jesus' entry also climaxes the spatial and political elements of the Gospel. The long awaited arrival in Jerusalem has finally come. At this moment, Jesus meets his familiar opponents, the Pharisees, who voice their objections one last time, but ultimately Jesus enters the official public sphere and meets his death through the political workings of Jewish and Roman officials. We will now examine how each of the forces work together in 19:29–48 and preview some of the implications to be discussed in Part 3.

The force of place comes into play through a variety of specific and momentous locations in this section. The mention of Jerusalem in v. 28 sets the stage for all that happens in vv. 29–48, and the Mount of Olives signals the very last step toward Jerusalem. While Luke shares the geographical material in 19:29 with Mark, v. 37 is unique to the third Gospel. Jesus approaches the "descent down the Mount of Olives," adding to the drama with more geographical specifics. The nearness and finally the sight of Jerusalem intensifies all of the other forces. The climactic events that have been anticipated by the audience since 9:51 are about to come to pass and the proximity of Jesus' passion energizes this last step of his journey. Approaching the city evokes contrasting responses, however. First, as Jesus rides toward the city on his royal mount (the colt), the disciples cannot contain themselves. They joyfully praise God for the powerful acts of Jesus' ministry, shower Jesus with royal honors, and publicly announce his arrival as king with the glad refrain of an ancient enthronement psalm. Second, Luke uses the descent down the mountain as the location where the public actions of the "multitude of disciples" encounters the first public element associated with the city, a crowd containing some upset Pharisees. Their complaint contrasts with the disciples' joyful acclamation. Finally, the city evokes weeping and lament from Jesus (v. 41). Instead of joining the chorus of joy, celebrating the deliverance and wholeness that his ministry has brought, Jesus speaks of rejection and destruction. Jesus' arrival at Jerusalem induces penultimate joy and grief. The ultimate joy of victory will come after Jesus' resurrection (Luke 24:41, 52). The ultimate grief will come with the razing of Jerusalem. Jerusalem is the spatial climax of the Gospel, a place that induces grief and joy, and a place where Jesus' movement and its opposition both culminate.

The temple is the final place that plays a role in this section. The most likely route of Jesus' entry into the temple reinforces the public valence of the cleansing and teaching. Jesus descended down the Mount of Olives and entered the temple through an eastern gate into an area that appears repeatedly in Acts as a public location. Luke frames the Gospel with the space of the temple, and several early events in Acts take place there. In Luke's version of the cleansing of the temple, the combined citations of Isaiah and Jeremiah use scriptural images of space to describe the true function and degeneration of this sacred place. The temple should be a "house of prayer," a safe and familial place where worshippers come to speak with God and be taught. However, the unfaithful leadership has allowed the temple to become a "den of robbers," a place where every kind of iniquity flourishes. Luke portrays Jesus restoring the purpose of the temple. First, he drives out those who muddle the sacredness of the space (the merchants, v. 45), and then he proceeds to teach publicly in the temple for the next two chapters (20–21). Finally, as Bachmann concluded and as this study confirmed, the temple is a public place where Jesus addresses the whole of Israel. When Jesus enters the temple (and city) he enters the spatial and religious heart of the Jewish nation, a superlative public place where he encounters the highest Jewish officials and teaches all the people.

Other characters in 19:29–48 bring the force of social relations into Luke's portrayal of Jesus as a public and local political figure. Luke emphasizes the role of the disciples in vv. 29–38. Recalling the commissioning stories, Jesus authorizes two disciples as his delegates to fetch a colt for the final leg of his journey. They do so obediently and successfully. Jesus takes the initiative in sending the two disciples, but then the disciples take the lead. They put Jesus on the colt, spread their cloaks on the road, and acclaim his royal arrival. Jesus' own followers recognize him as king and honor him as such at this climactic moment (and place) in contrast to those in official leadership (the Pharisees, chief priests, etc.). Luke alone states that a "multitude" of disciples rejoices at Jesus' arrival, highlighting the climax and public significance of Jesus' popular movement. Luke also mentions a general crowd in v. 39, perhaps to reinforce the public nature of the event. However, the crowd itself is silent, in contrast to the crowd/people of 18:36 and 43 who identify Jesus and then praise God. The crowd does nothing for or with Jesus at his entry; much like the third servant did nothing with the money left with him in the parable of 19:12-27. However, Luke points out the presence and prophylactic power of the crowd that hangs on Jesus' teaching in v. 48. They are present throughout his temple teaching (see 21:37-38) and reinforce its public nature.

Finally, Jesus encounters new and old opponents in vv. 39-48. First, he meets his familiar foes, the Pharisees. These local leaders are primarily part of the unofficial public sphere in Luke's Gospel. They appear here for the last time with familiar objections: they see Jesus overreaching the appropriate boundaries of religious and political authority. The shouts of the disciples attribute too much to him, and he should act as their "teacher" and leader to quell their overzealous acclamation. Jesus, as always, rebukes the Pharisees with an apt (and public) reply and therefore accepts the royal identity and authority that the disciples proclaim. The mention of these familiar opponents prepares for a new level of political and religious opposition. After the cleansing of the temple (and the implicit rebuke of v. 46), Jesus faces the hostility of the "chief priests, scribes, and leaders of the people." Jesus, the local leader of a popular movement who typically faced off against other local and popular leaders (the Pharisees), now comes into the purview of the highest religious and political body of the Jews. Ultimately, the religio-political leaders of the Jews will bring Jesus to Roman officials who will cooperate in his death. The Pharisees and the chief priests with their associates, demonstrates the contiguity of the unofficial public sphere and the local political sphere. After the cleansing, Jesus, who spent most of the Gospel in the unofficial public sphere, enters the political sphere where he encounters local and regional officials who plan his execution.

The forces of place and social relations overlap with the force of nature to set the unofficial, political, local, and regional nature of this section. As Jesus begins his approach to the city, Luke shows him acting as a local leader within his unofficial movement. The orders, actions, and acclamations in vv. 29-38 all occur within Jesus' multitude of disciples. With the appearance of the Pharisees in v. 39, Luke continues the local emphasis but adds a dimension outside of Jesus' movement that has some official standing among the Jews. When Jesus arrives in Jerusalem and the temple, the new place provides a setting for a new level of opposition. Jesus now takes action to purge and then teach in the social, spatial, and religious heart of the nation. By doing so, he angers and threatens the official leadership of the Jews (v. 47). Jesus now faces the highest levels of Jewish religious and political authority. These regional and national leaders plot against Jesus and bring him before imperial Roman officials in the passion.

This study complemented Sack's three forces (place, social relations, and meaning) with the forces of time and religion (the latter a subset of meaning). The force of time comes through in the narrative compression of these events. Jesus and his multitude of disciples come upon a crowd on their descent down the Mount of Olives; Jesus then immediately heads into the temple. He cleanses the temple and begins to teach there all in the presence of the crowd of disciples and others gathered there. Later, Luke adds another element of time that reinforces the public nature of these events. In 22:1, the audience finds out that all this transpired during Passover, when throngs of pilgrims attend to his teaching in Jerusalem.

The force of meaning and religion intertwine in many ways throughout 19:29–48. Luke adduces a number of allusions and citations of Hebrew Scripture in this passage: the Mount of Olives, the colt, placing Jesus on the colt, spreading out cloaks, the disciples' acclamation, Jesus' lament, and Jesus' statement at the cleansing all recall or recite portions of the Hebrew Bible. In vv. 29–38, these allusions and citations help to cast Jesus as a royal figure (a "crown prince") arriving in Jerusalem. In the second half of the passage (vv. 39–48), the allusions take on a more ominous tone and become a vehicle for communicating the conflict and destruction that lies ahead for both Jerusalem and Jesus. Many of these allusions and citations come from public scenarios themselves: the coronation of Solomon in 1 Kgs 1, the proclamation of Jehu as king (2 Kgs 9), the ritual (re-)enthronement of the king in Ps 118, prophecies of the destruction of Jerusalem,[149] and Jeremiah's temple sermon (Jer 7). The forces of meaning and religion appear in two public challenge-riposte episodes. The Pharisees object to the disciples' royal acclamation and Jesus shames them with an apt reply. The chief priests and leaders (whose social status is colored by the force of religion) are shamed when they have no reply to Jesus' accusation in v. 46. The force of meaning and religion centers on the royal allusions and religious officials and accentuates the public and political nature of this section.

Finally, many of the forces call for a deeper investigation into the meaning, function, and implications of the royal title "king" in v. 38 and a search for better parallels to Jesus' unofficial entry into Jerusalem. The disciples' rightly acclaim Jesus as king, recognizing him as the agent of God's kingdom and the leader of the Christian community (force of meaning and religion). However, the royal symbols and labels also have political ramifications and do not escape public and political notice (23:2, including the force of nature). The meaning of the title "king" takes on different meanings and ramifications depending on the social context in which it is employed (the force of social relations). Even with the royal allusions and the climactic official opposition, Jesus' entry in Luke is primarily an *unofficial* event. Thus, many "triumphal entries" from the ancient world are in the wrong sphere (political and imperial) to illuminate Luke's account. Philostratus's account of Apollonius's entry into Athens is a viable alternative that portrays an unofficial arrival attended by disciples that is clearly public and ends with official conflict. Luke brings together place, social relations, time, and meaning to portray the meeting of the unofficial public sphere and regional political at the climax of Jesus' public ministry in preparation for the passion.

The previous pericopes in 18:35—19:48 served primarily as microcosms of previous related material in the Gospel and secondarily as a preparations for the passion. That order reverses with the story of the entry into Jerusalem. The juxtaposition of the acclamation of the disciples in 19:29–38 and the opposition of Jewish leaders in vv. 39–48 recalls the contrasting episodes of acceptance and rejection that have occurred already in Luke's Gospel. More importantly, though, Jesus' entry into Jerusalem marks the dramatic increase of the

---

149. For a list of various Hebrew Bible allusions in vv. 41–44 see Fitzmyer, *Luke*, 2:1258–59.

PART TWO: SOCIAL-SPATIAL EXEGESIS OF LUKE 18:35—19:48

scale and animosity of the official public sphere, a trend that will continue into the passion narrative. The analysis of vv. 39–48 has already shown how this opposition rises from the Pharisees to the chief priests and leaders. Chapter 9 will explore the meaning and parameters of the term "official" more fully and explore the official status and scale of the Pharisees, chief priests (and their associates), and finally the Roman officials who appear in the passion narrative.

Several historical and contemporary implications also issue from the preceding analysis. While the vast majority of Jesus' ministry in Luke's Gospel transpires in the unofficial public sphere, Jesus encounters and challenges the highest Jewish authorities in the land at the climax of his movement. This and supporting evidence from Acts indicate that Luke and his Christian community had begun to intersect political figures and structures in his own day. This signals a rise in the social and political status of Christianity and calls for a new level of theological (and narrative) reflection that Luke grounds in the story of Jesus. Luke also manifests an understanding of insider and outsider status (around the title "king") that takes place in the public sphere. Luke's version of identity formation takes place through engagement with the public and political structures of his day, not in isolation from them. Luke begins to formulate a complicated (but perhaps not fully coherent or systematic) perspective on Christianity's relationship to political authority that involves separation, challenge, apology, and transcendence. Also, Luke's portrayal of the entry encourages the contemporary church to reflect on its practices and preaching from outsider and insider perspectives. While the disciples' acclamation of Jesus as "king" is true and appropriate, it bears different implications to those outside the community, where it might be misunderstood, ignored, or attacked. The hostile response of the Pharisees and the violent plans of the chief priests remind contemporary followers of the responsibilities and risks of encountering varying degrees of the political sphere as members of Jesus' movement.

PART THREE

Implications for Luke's Gospel and Our World

9

Luke's Emphasis on the Public Sphere and Local Politics in the Gospel as a Whole

Introduction

CHAPTERS 5–8 EXEGETED THE FOUR PERICOPES FOUND IN 18:35—19:48 IN ORDER TO reveal the social-spatial characteristics of each passage. Though the particular contents and emphases of each pericope varied, they all placed Jesus in the unofficial public sphere with some connection to the local political sphere. This chapter will demonstrate that the emphasis on the public sphere and local politics is characteristic of Luke's Gospel as a whole. The following analysis will look first at the literary functions of the pericopes in 18:35—19:48, illustrating how each serves as a microcosm of previous related material in the Gospel and as a preparation for the passion narrative. Then, it will turn to the social-spatial implications by bringing together the literary functions and the public/political characteristics of each pericope. For example, Luke's emphasis on the role of the crowd as a marker of the public nature of the healing of the blind beggar in 18:35-43 turns out to be characteristic of miracle stories throughout the Gospel where Luke highlights or adds crowds. Careful social-spatial exegesis of the representative material in 18:35—19:48 raises topics and techniques that Luke uses throughout the Gospel to emphasize the public sphere and local politics in his portrayal of Jesus.

The Literary Functions and Social-Spatial Implications of 18:35–43

Chapter 5 established the public nature and political implications of this story. Jesus meets a beggar (known for their public loitering) on a road near an urban center (Jericho)—all marks of a public episode. Throughout the story Jesus is surrounded by a crowd, who witnesses the events and confirms their pubic nature. Within these public indicators, we also found political implications regarding Jesus' authority over his movement. We can now turn to examine its literary functions and social-spatial implications for the Gospel as a whole. Regarding the literary functions, the narrative placement and nature of the healing in this pericope help it serve as a microcosm of the previous miracle material in the Gospel. Also, this final miracle prepares the audience for the triumphal entry and several specific elements in the passion narrative. Regarding the social-spatial implications, this healing highlights three elements that mark the public nature of most miracles in Luke's

PART THREE: IMPLICATIONS FOR LUKE'S GOSPEL AND OUR WORLD

Gospel: location, characters, and crowd. Finally, many miracle stories have similar political implications for Jesus' authority and identity.

A Microcosm of Previous Material: The Final Miracle of Luke's Gospel

The healing of the blind beggar is the last typical miracle story found in Luke's Gospel, and this positions it to have summative and climactic functions.[1] This has been noted by several scholars. Busse, in his extensive study of the miracles in Luke's Gospel, labels the healing of the blind beggar a "paradigmatischen Wunderepisoden."[2] Green notes that 18:35–43 is the final healing narrative in Luke's Gospel and says that this healing "epitomizes" Jesus' work on behalf of the poor as a sign of the kingdom.[3] Likewise, Marshall claims that this pericope, along with the Zacchaeus story, functions as a "climax" of Jesus' ministry to the poor and outcast.[4] Others, like Bovon, observe that this story evokes the prophecy of Isaiah, cited in Luke 4:18, that the blind will see again.[5] This healing represents a capstone to Jesus' ministry to the poor and outcast in Luke's Gospel. The man's status as both impoverished and impaired makes him an excellent figure to represent both the financially poor (cf. Luke 6:20) and the physically disabled (cf. Luke 14:13), who are the special recipients of good news and divine favor (4:18–19). The healing of the blind beggar epitomizes the fulfillment of Jesus' mission as set forth in the programmatic prophecy of 4:18–19.

Collecting several insights from Busse's work demonstrates how the healing of the blind beggar sums up the miracle traditions recorded in Luke's Gospel. The vast majority of the miracles in Luke (and the other Synoptics) are healings and/or exorcisms, with the calming of the storm (Luke 8:22–25) and the feeding of the five thousand (Luke 9:10–17) being the major exceptions.[6] Busse distinguishes two intertwined motifs developed in the Lukan miracle stories: the "Befreiungsmotiv" that is typical of exorcisms, and the theme of "Wohltat" where Jesus graciously restores the ill.[7] In the case of the blind beggar, Busse claims that this story draws both of these motifs together into one healing: "Jesus schenkt dem Blinden vor Jericho *wohltätig* die Sehkraft und *befreit* ihn damit zugleich aus der beschämended Lebenswiese eines Bettlers."[8] Thus, while this healing does not explicitly

---

1. While miraculous events occur in Luke after Jesus' entry into Jerusalem, they do not appear in the form of a miracle story. Luke mentions the restoration of a soldier's ear in 22:51, but only in passing. Several supernatural events surround the crucifixion (cf. Luke 23:44–45), and the resurrection itself counts as a miraculous event. After this, Luke narrates two miraculous appearances of Jesus (24:13–35, 36–49) and the ascension as well (24:50–53). Yet, all of these are of a different order, quite unlike the miracles narrated in Luke 3–19.

2. Busse, *Die Wunder*, 333–34.

3. Green also notes that there is one other healing mentioned in the Gospel: 22:51, which is not a typical miracle story (*Luke*, 661–62).

4. Marshall, *Luke*, 691.

5. Bovon, *Saint Luc*, 3c:226. Also, Busse, *Die Wunder*, 332.

6. The vast majority of the healings/exorcisms in Luke's Gospel are public as well with the raising of Jairus's daughter (9:49–56) as the exception.

7. Busse, *Die Wunder*, 181–82. He initially bases this distinction on the use of the two verbs θεραπεύω and χαρίζομαι in Luke 7:21 and develops it further in his interpretation of Acts 10:38 (428ff.).

8. Busse, *Die Wunder*, 332; emphasis added.

deploy the demonic dimension characteristic of the "deliverance-motif," Busse recognizes that the man is "delivered" from a life of poverty and shame as well as receiving his sight again, so it draws together both healings and exorcisms. The majority of the miracle stories in Luke occur before the travel narrative (thirteen out of seventeen).[9] Busse labels the miracles of 4:44—7:50 as the "Die Errettungstaten Jesu der judäischen Stadtmission," and he asserts that "Lukas wahrt so die inhaltliche Kohärenz der Erzählverlaufs."[10] Part of this "internal coherence" is that Jesus "mit dem Bekanntwerder des Wunders seine missionarischen Aktivitäten in den Städten aufgeben muß." Thus, Busse recognizes the public impact of the largely "urban" miracles of Jesus. Later, Busse says that by joining the healing of the blind beggar and the encounter with Zacchaeus (in the "Stadt" of Jericho), Luke "gemeinsam ... faßt ... das öffentliche Handeln Jesu."[11] Busse recognizes the public dimension of this final miracle and implies its connection to the concentration of miracle stories in 4:14—9:50, a connection that will be developed further below.

As a Preparation for the Passion: Entries, Miracles, and the "Son of David"

The social-spatial exegesis of chapter 5 indicated two ways that the healing of the blind beggar prepares Luke's audience for the passion. First, Jesus' entry into Jericho forms an illuminating parallel with the entrance into Jerusalem, which sets the stage for the passion. This final miracle is the most recent of Jesus' "deeds of power" (19:37), prompting the disciples to acclaim Jesus as king. Second, the juxtaposition of terms for and roles of the crowd/people (ὄχλος/λαός) at the entries into Jericho and Jerusalem prepares the audience for the fickle behavior of the crowd throughout the entry and passion. First, they say and do nothing (19:37). Then they hang on Jesus' every word while he teaches in the temple (19:47–48 and 21:37–38). Next, they turn on Jesus and demand his crucifixion (23:13–25), only to later express grief at his death (23:48). With this complex and developing portrayal of the crowd/people, Luke has prepared his audience well for the public portrayal of Jesus in the midst of crowds in the passion narrative.

The miracle and the mention of the Son of David remind the audience of two specific political issues that reappear in the passion after not being heard of for some time. This final miracle in 18:35–43 provides context for Herod's desire to see Jesus perform a sign (23:8),

---

9. These are the miracles as I count them in Luke's Gospel: (1) 4:31–37, man with an unclean spirit; (2) 4:38–39, Peter's mother-in-law; (3) 5:12–16, man with leprosy; (4) 5:17–26, the paralytic; (5) 6:6–11, man with a withered hand; (6) 7:1–10, the centurion's servant; (7) 7:11–17, raising the widow's son; (8) 8:22–25, calming the storm; (9) 8:26–39, the Gergesene demoniac; (10) 8:40–42a, 49–56, raising of Jairus' daughter; (11) 8:42b–48, the hemorrhaging woman; (12) 9:10–17, feeding the 5,000; (13) 9:37–43, the epileptic boy; (14) 13:10–17, the crippled woman; (15) 14:1–6, the man with dropsy; (16) 17:11–19, the ten lepers; (17) 18:35–43, the blind beggar. Busse treats twelve passages in the section from 4:14—9:50, dividing them into three sections (4:14–43, 4:44—7:50; and 8:1—9:50). See Busse, *Wunder*, ii–iii. My list does not include the summaries in 4:40–41 and 7:21–22, nor the brief mention of the healing of a mute man in 11:14, which serves to set up the Beelzebul controversy, nor the restoration of the soldier's ear in 22:51. These two latter examples are miracles but not developed miracle stories.

10. Busse, *Die Wunder*, 113. Busse does little to develop the social or spatial significance of the fact that in Luke's Gospel this mission is specifically directed to the "cities" of Judea (4:43–44).

11. Ibid., 334.

PART THREE: IMPLICATIONS FOR LUKE'S GOSPEL AND OUR WORLD

an interest that has not been mentioned since 9:7-9 (near most of Jesus' other miracles). Thus, as this miracle recalls prior miracles earlier in the Gospel, so it also provides a link to the role of Herod in 23:6-12. Finally, the mention of the Son of David in 18:38-39 recalls Jesus' royal identity, which Luke has not sounded since the infancy narrative (1:32-33) but which now proliferates in the remainder of the Gospel.[12] Jesus casts himself as a king in 19:12-27. The disciples pick up on the bind beggar's attribution of royalty and acclaim Jesus as king in 19:38. He is accused of being a king (23:2) and is derided as a "king" on the cross (23:37-38). Finally, he grants royal rule to his closest disciples (22:29). Perhaps most importantly, Jesus himself alludes to the title Son of David in his own teaching in the temple (20:41-43). Therefore, the healing of the blind beggar prepares for some political elements of the passion by portraying a miracle and mentioning the Son of David right before Jesus enters Jerusalem.

Miracles in the Public Sphere: Locations, Characters, and Crowds

Location, location, location. One of the most critical factors that determines the public nature of an event is its location (and the characterization of that location). The healing of the blind beggar takes place on a road as Jesus nears Jericho. Various pieces of evidence presented in chapter 3 demonstrated the public nature of roads. Vitruvius discusses roads and passageways under the heading of buildings for public convenience (1.3.1). Laurence and Kaiser both cite roads as indispensable locations for analyzing public social interaction.[13] Rabbinic sources also mention the heavy traffic and public interaction that occurred on roads.[14] Archaeological evidence from Pompeii and Ephesus displayed entrances to cities that were heavily traveled and architecturally crafted for public access and aesthetic impact. Finally, one should also note how Apollonius took advantage of the masses that followed the covered walkway from Ephesus to the Artemesion. He spoke in the sacred groves near the covered walkway where throngs of people would pass by and could be drawn to his public discourses (*Vit. Apoll.* 4.3). Luke uses the road as a location (the force of place) that casts events as public. Luke's audience also would have known that beggars would often gather in highly traveled areas (like roads and bridges) hoping for a better opportunity to solicit money. Designating the location of the beggar on the side of the road connects with widely held cultural knowledge. Not only that, but this healing occurs on the side of a road just outside of a major city. Jericho was the site of Herod's winter palace in addition to being an agricultural center and an important transportation juncture.[15] The size and political importance of this city would have added to the public nature of this healing. Therefore, Luke uses the road, the city, and cultural knowledge about beggars to deploy the force of place and characterize Jesus' healing of the blind beggar as a public event.

---

12. This is noted by Marshall, *Luke*, 70; Ellis, *Luke*, 222; and Johnson, "Kingship Parable," 155.
13. Laurence, *Roman Pompeii*, 88-103; and Kaiser, *Urban Dialogue*, 47-57.
14. See *t. Šabb.* 1.2; and Sperber, *City*, 103-6.
15. Netzer, "Jericho," 740; DeVries, *Cities*, 282-83.

Luke's Emphasis on the Public Sphere and Local Politics in the Gospel as a Whole

An examination of other miracle stories in the Gospel shows that Luke repeatedly employs specific locations to create a public setting. We begin with the synagogue, the site of Jesus' first narrated miracle. Recall Philo's comments about the public nature of synagogue meetings (*Legat.* 156) as well as the public nature of Luke's presentation of Jesus' inaugural sermon in the Nazareth synagogue (4:16–30). The role of synagogues in Acts reinforces their public quality.[16] Synagogues, for Luke, were public places where crowds gathered for religious rituals and teaching. In this light, the healing of the man with the unclean spirit in the Capernaum synagogue (4:33, taken from Mark) and the healing of the crippled woman in the synagogue (13:10–13, from Luke's special material) both occur in public venues. Luke also portrays Jesus' miracles as public events by placing them in cities. Luke specifies that the cleansing of the leper (5:12-16) occurs when Jesus was in a city (5:12, πόλις is not found in either Mark or Matthew). In Luke's unique story of the raising of the widow's son, he specifies that Jesus is in the πόλις of Nain. Like the healing of the blind beggar, Jesus stops a procession near the entrance of the city and publicly heals the man (7:11-12). Luke alone notes that the Gergesene demoniac is a man from the city (ἀνήρ τις ἐκ τῆς πόλεως, 8:27), linking this lakeside healing to the local population center. Luke softens the private nature of Jesus' retreat upon the return of the twelve by stating that Jesus withdrew to the πόλις of Bethsaida (9:10), rather than to the ἔρημος (Mark 6:32 and Matt 14:13). One can only conclude that the feeding of the five thousand occurred publicly in the vicinity of Bethsaida according to Luke's retelling, rather than in the isolated wastelands of the desert as implied in Mark (see 6:35, missing in Luke). Finally, Jesus is hailed by a group of ten lepers as he enters an unnamed village (κώμη). The miracle takes place as the lepers depart for the priests, but Jesus issues his directions to them on the road as he enters this village, another public setting for another miracle in Luke.

Luke also transforms healings that transpire in households into public events. Take, for example, the healing of Simon's mother-in-law. Mark specifies that Jesus entered the home only with Simon and Andrew, James and John (1:29). Luke also narrates Jesus' entrance into Simon's home (4:38) but then says that "they asked" (ἠρώτησαν) Jesus about the sick woman. The last character mentioned in the narrative that could supply the unspecified subject here is the crowd of Capernaum that was amazed by Jesus' authority in v. 36. Next, while Mark does state that the whole city gathered at the door of the house that evening (1:33), the crowd still remains outside of the house. In contrast, Luke states that "all" the sick and diseased were brought to Jesus (πρὸς αὐτόν), presumably while he was still in the home since Luke does not say that he left the house (4:40). Thus, Jesus heals Peter's mother-in-law apparently at the behest of the crowd that has followed him into Peter's home, and later the crowds continue to flood into the home bringing the sick to be touched by Jesus. The potentially private nature of this domicile bursts open with the influx of people who request, receive, and witness Jesus' healing touch. In the healing of the

---

16. The public effect of Paul's synagogue preaching in Pisidian Antioch is one example. Notice that the "whole city" gathered in the synagogue on Paul's second Sabbath there (13:44). Also, ch. 1 demonstrated how the Ephesian synagogue and the lecture hall of Tyannus were both considered public settings by Luke in light of the comments in 19:10 and 21 (contra Neyrey's private classification of synagogues).

paralytic, Luke stresses the public nature of the gathering by stating that people had been drawn from "every village in Galilee and Judea" to hear Jesus preach (5:17). Then, Jesus heals the paralyzed man who had to be lowered through the roof because the enormous crowd barred all the normal entrances (see Luke 5:19 and Mark 2:4). This house too becomes a public location for another healing miracle. Finally, Jesus heals the man with dropsy while he is on the way to the home of a Pharisee (14:1–2). While the exact location of the miracle is debated, Jesus heals the man either in or near the house, and the healing becomes the introduction to a series of interrelated debates with the Pharisees in the house that then leads directly to another discourse with the crowds.[17] Luke has transformed these private homes into public settings for more of Jesus' healings.[18]

Place is one of the critical forces in Sack's framework. Most of the miracles in Luke occur in humanly constructed spaces (roads, synagogues, cities), and so take on the character of culturally constructed places with public valences.[19] Not only is Luke's depiction of the healing of the blind beggar on the side of the road a public miracle, but it stands as an excellent example of the public locations of miracles throughout Luke's Gospel. Roads, synagogues, cities, and even homes become public venues for Jesus' healing ministry. These locations strongly determine the public valence of many of these miracles, but the actions and interactions of the characters reinforce it as well.

The characters (part of the force of social relations) also contribute to the public nature of an event,[20] and the actions of the blind beggar and his interaction with Jesus reinforce the public nature of 18:35–43. He was attempting to grasp what might have been his one chance to get Jesus' attention and so he publicly cries out for the Son of David to have mercy upon him, much as the lepers cried out to Jesus in 17:12–13. He got someone's attention, for the leaders of the procession rebuked him and told him to be quiet. Nevertheless, he persisted, probably to the dismay of his rebukers, and he was successful on the second attempt. At this point, the (honorable) public procession surrounding Jesus meets the (dishonorable) blind beggar on the side of the road near Jericho. This entire scene must have attracted the attention of nearly everyone in the entourage, especially when Jesus stopped the group and had the man brought to him. The crowd would have had their eyes and ears riveted on the two as they talked, and ultimately they witnessed the blind man's restoration and joined in his public praise.

The actions and interactions of other characters in Luke's miracle traditions similarly intensify the public valence of these stories. In the healing of the demoniac at Capernaum, Luke relocates the demoniac's loud voice (φωνῇ μεγάλῃ) from the moment of the exorcism (Mark 1:26, later in the story) to the beginning of the story when the man first disrupts the Sabbath gathering in the synagogue by shouting at Jesus (ἀνέκραζεν, compare

---

17. Braun, *Feasting*, 22–23, 162–68. Luke 14:1–25 will be explored more fully below.

18. The one exception to this is the healing of Jairus' daughter in Luke. Here, Jesus only allows Peter, James, John, and the girl's parents to witness the miracle and then orders them to tell no one (8:51–56).

19. This also draws Sack's force of meaning into the analysis.

20. Neyrey, "'What's Wrong,'" 84. Neyrey notes how the very nature of the rhetoric between the woman and Jesus characterizes the space as first public and then private. Recall the excellent analysis on how interactions between host and guest brought the public sphere into the home in Wiltshire, *Public and Private*.

Luke 4:33 and Mark 1:23). This sets a public stage for the entire episode that follows, rather than being a closing outburst. Furthermore, Luke changes Mark's account and states that the demon threw the man down in the midst of the crowd (ῥῖψαν αὐτὸν τὸ δαιμόνιον εἰς τὸ μέσον, 4:35), instead of Mark's general description of a convulsion (1:26). Again, Luke stresses the public nature of the episode with the presence of the crowd and the visibility of the action. In addition, even though it is shared with Mark, what could be more noticeable than a paralyzed man being lowered down into an overflowing house through a hole dug in the roof (Luke 5:19)? Another subtle change arises in the healing of the man with the withered hand. While Mark reports that the man "got up in their midst" (Mark 3:3), Luke has Jesus command the man to "get up and stand in our midst" and then reports that he did so (Luke 6:8). Thus, Jesus summons the man to join him at the head of the synagogue where he is teaching on the Sabbath (Luke 6:6) so that he can heal him in front of everyone.[21] In the raising of the widow's son, Jesus walks up to the woman in the midst of the funeral procession and tells her not to weep. Then he steps forward, touches the bier, and tells the man to rise. Not only does the man sit up, but he begins to speak, and Jesus restores the man to his mother in the full view of the entire crowd (7:13–15). Luke also retains the public indicators in Mark's healing of the Gerasene demoniac: the swineherds report the news in the city (Luke 8:34), the people go out to see what happened (8:35), and the man is sent off by Jesus to declare what was done for him (8:39). Luke adds the detail that "all the people of the surrounding region" ask Jesus to leave (8:37), a public marker not found in Mark 5:17.

Both positive and negative interactions reinforce the public nature of Luke's miracle scenes. He retains the crowded scene to create drama in the healing of the hemorrhaging woman (see Luke 8:40, 42, 45 and Mark 5:21, 24, 31), but he opens the story by stating that the crowd gladly "welcomed" Jesus (8:40), rather than Mark's more general statement that a crowd had gathered. Then, Luke adds several public touches to the story: the woman comes and falls at the feet of Jesus and publicly "announces" (ἀπήγγειλεν instead of Mark's more mundane εἶπεν) "in the presence of all the people" (ἐνώπιον παντὸς τοῦ λαοῦ, no parallel in Mark) what Jesus has done for her (compare Luke 8:47 with Mark 5:33).[22] However, after Jesus heals the crippled woman, the synagogue leader becomes angry and challenges him in the midst of the gathered assembly (13:14). In this case, the healing has occasioned a challenge-riposte contest in the midst of this Sabbath gathering.[23] The leader challenges Jesus by insisting that he has violated the law of the Sabbath (13:14). Jesus responds by labeling the leader a "hypocrite"[24] and counters with practical agrarian wisdom ("don't you give your ox water on the Sabbath?"), which he then applies to the situation in a lesser to greater argument by assigning the woman the dignity of a "daughter of Abraham" (13:15–16) in order to trump the legal citation of the leader. By this apt reply,

---

21. Having this and other events take place on the Sabbath uses time to intensify the public valence of this religious gathering.
22. The public nature of Luke's version of this story is pointed out by Robbins, "Woman," 197.
23. Malina and Neyrey, "Honor and Shame," 29.
24. Malina and Neyrey, "Conflict in Luke-Acts," 99 and 108.

PART THREE: IMPLICATIONS FOR LUKE'S GOSPEL AND OUR WORLD

the leader was publicly put to shame in the presence of the entire crowd who then rejoiced over Jesus' amazing words and deeds (13:17).[25]

The actions and interactions of the characters in Luke's miracle accounts draw on the force of social relations to exhibit the public nature of these events. The actions of the blind beggar and his interactions with Jesus serve as an excellent sample of the public nature of various characters in many of Luke's miracle accounts. Often, Luke highlights or emphasizes the public visibility or audibility of a character's actions in ways that are not found in Mark. The public effect carries over into dramatic interactions with Jesus, adding to the public nature of the event. Luke also omits miracle stories in Mark that stress the private nature of the episode.[26] Some of Luke's miracles combine the force of time with the force of social relations to mark the event as public. Jesus heals the blind beggar as he *enters* Jericho, allowing the public event to carry over into the city (rather than dissipating as Jesus leaves the city). Also, the repetition of the man's cry and the question and answer session that follows extends the length of this public interaction in the presence of the crowds. The duration, sequence, and pace of other miracles contributes to their public valence (e.g., the hemorrhaging women falling down before Jesus in the presence of the crowd right after Jesus asks who touched him), and the timing of synagogue healings on the Sabbath (i.e., the Capernaum demoniac and the crippled woman) intensifies the public valence of these two miracles. Luke intertwines characters and timing in the healing of the blind beggar to emphasize its public character—a technique he uses repeatedly in other miracle stories.

The presence of a crowd is a common marker of public miracles in Luke, one with a substantial cultural background. Examples of crowds in the public sphere abounded in chapter 2. Isocrates spoke of dealing with crowds as a necessary part of public life (5.81). Plato spoke of the psychological impact of roaring crowds in public assemblies (*Resp.* 492b–c). Crowds could be found in all types of public settings, but the theatre seems to have been almost paradigmatic (Ovid, *Ars.* 1.99; Arrian, *Epict. diss.* 3.4). Marketplaces and the forum were also common locations for crowds (Plato, *Theaet.* 173c–d; Sophocles, *Trach.* 371-72; Livy, *Hist.* 34.1.5), and Juvenal lamented the noisy overcrowding of Rome (*Sat.* 2.237-61). The crowd also shows up several times to color Socrates' public activity (e.g., Plato *Apol.* 19d; Xenophon; *Mem.* 1.2.30; 2.5.1). Finally, Plutarch noted the importance of managing the crowd as part of public-political life (*Praec. ger. rei publ.* 815a–816a), and crowds frequently gather to hear Apollonius's public discourses (*Vit. Apoll.* 4.2, 10, 18, etc.). In the Greco-Roman world, the crowd was a cultural trope that indicated a

---

25. Malina and Neyrey, "Honor and Shame," 36–38. Malina and Neyrey emphasize the public nature of the challenge-riposte exchange and the necessity of public evaluation. On p. 36 they say, "Again, publicity and witnesses are crucial for the acquisition and bestowal of honor. Representatives of public opinion must be present, since honor is all about the court of public opinion and the reputation which that court bestows. Literally, public praise can give life and public ridicule can kill."

26. In the healing of the Syrophoenecian woman's daughter, Mark notes that Jesus "did not want anyone to know" that he was in the house (7:24). In the next story in Mark's account, Jesus takes a deaf man aside privately away from the crowd (ἀπὸ τοῦ ὄχλου κατ' ἰδίαν) before healing him (7:33). Finally, Mark notes that Jesus took a certain blind man out of the city of Bethsaida before healing him (8:23). Luke does not include any of these stories, perhaps because of the private emphasis in Mark's accounts.

public event using the force of social relations.²⁷ Mentioning a crowd became a culturally accepted way to dramatize and color a public event that was immediately understood in Luke's high-context milieu.

Returning to the healing of the blind beggar, chapter 5 noted that Luke moves the crowd out of the background of the story to make it a secondary character. The crowd and the blind man speak to each other, and the leaders of the crowd quickly attempt to silence him. By placing an active crowd at the beginning of the story, Luke sets a public stage where the crowd is present for the interaction between the main characters: the blind man and Jesus. Luke brings the crowd back at the end of the story, a move that neither Mark nor Matthew make. Luke says that when "all the people" (πᾶς ὁ λαός) saw the miracle, they joined the healed beggar in a chorus of praise as Jesus publicly entered Jericho. Thus, not only are the crowds mentioned again in a way not found in the other Synoptics, but Luke also emphasizes their role as witnesses and worshippers. Their presence surrounds and saturates the entire event and unmistakably marks the public nature of this healing. The ubiquity and actions of crowds in Luke's other miracle stories could, on its own, make them into highly public events. He retains the presence of the crowd in the healing of the Capernaum demoniac with slight variations.²⁸ At the end of the story, both Mark and Luke note, with minor linguistic variations, that the news about Jesus spread throughout the country (Mark 1:38 and Luke 4:37); however, the evaluation of this notoriety is quite different.

At the beginning of the cleansing of the leper, Luke notes that Jesus is in a city (5:12), while Mark gives no such setting. Both Mark and Luke begin the conclusion of this story by describing how the report about Jesus spread even more widely (Mark 1:45a and Luke 5:15a, again with slight variations). Yet, at this point their evaluation diverges subtly but importantly. Mark states that the healed leper went out and proclaimed the news with abandon, and the result was that "Jesus could no longer enter a city openly, but instead he stayed out in the countryside and people came to him from everywhere" (Mark 1:45). Thus, Mark paints a picture of a Jesus who is so harried by the crowds that he had to flee them by withdrawing from the cities into the country, and yet, even there, the crowds pursue him. The increased notoriety forces Jesus' unsuccessful retreat from the masses in Mark. In Luke however, the notoriety causes "great crowds" (ὄχλοι πολλοί) to gather to hear Jesus and be healed of their diseases (Luke 5:15). Thus, while the notoriety and the crowds are an annoying obstacle to the Markan Jesus, in Luke the notoriety leads to the presence of even more crowds who receive the benefits of Jesus' public mission of teaching and healing!²⁹ Although the changes are subtle, the resulting evaluation of the relationship

---

27. It could also have a share in the force of meaning. On the surface, a crowd is simply a large group of people, but as one probes deeper, it is seen to be a "marker" of a public event. See Sack's discussion of the "surface/depth" loop in the force of meaning *Homo Geographicus*, 94–97). Later, he also speaks of our culture "assigning" a meaning to the term home (194). This would be similar to Greco-Roman culture assigning a meaning to the crowd.

28. Both Mark and Luke note the gathering on the Sabbath (Mark 1:21; Luke 4:31) and the astonishment of the crowd (Mark 1:22; Luke 4:32).

29. Luke does remind the reader that Jesus still retired to the desert to pray in 5:16.

PART THREE: IMPLICATIONS FOR LUKE'S GOSPEL AND OUR WORLD

of Jesus and the crowds is remarkable.[30] Jesus wants to escape the crowds in Mark, while the crowds become the object of Jesus' mission in Luke. Luke's positive evaluation of Jesus' interaction with the crowds, and simultaneously of Jesus' place in the public sphere, is undeniable.

The crowds repeatedly appear as witnesses to Jesus' public acts in Luke's Gospel. Note the crowd in the packed house that causes the friends of the paralyzed man to take such extreme measures (Luke 5:19, very similar to Mark 2:4). In the Q story of the healing of the centurion's servant, Luke stretches out the drama by adding messengers and exchanges to the basic frame of the story. Near the end of the story, Luke makes another subtle change that brings the crowd back once again. Jesus, amazed at the centurion's faith, turns and speaks. In Matthew, Jesus addresses "those following him" (τοῖς ἀκολουθοῦσιν, i.e., the disciples in 8:10), but in Luke Jesus addresses "the *crowd* that was following him" (τῷ ἀκολουθοῦντι τῷ ὄχλῳ, 7:9, emphasis added). Luke uses the crowds as a witness again in his unique story about the healing of the widow's son in 7:11 and 16. In the Q story of John the Baptist's inquiry about Jesus, Luke sets the stage for Jesus' answer by adding material about large groups not found in Matthew 11:2–6. Luke states that Jesus had just healed many (ἐθεράπερσεν πολλούς) and given sight to "many blind people" (τυφλοῖς πολλοῖς) when the messengers ask their question (Luke 7:20–21). Crowds also function as witnesses in several miracle stories: at the healing of the hemorrhaging woman (given special emphasis in Luke 8:47), just before the second passion prediction (9:43b), as the occasion for the Beelzebul debate (Luke 11:14, also in Matt 12:23), and at the healing of the crippled woman (13:17, unique to Luke). When Jesus heals someone in Luke, the crowds are almost always present to witness the cure and express their amazement, adding public touches to Luke's telling of the story. Jesus' public ministry of healing became so well known that characters in Luke-Acts refer to it as common public knowledge (Luke 24:18–19; Acts 10:36–38).

The crowds stand out at two other events in Luke's Gospel that may be considered supernatural but are not healings. In the feeding of the five thousand, Luke, along with Mark and Matthew, narrates Jesus' private retreat.[31] However, Luke then qualifies it in two ways. First, in Luke, Jesus and the disciples withdraw to the city of Bethsaida (9:10), while in Mark and Matthew Jesus escapes into the desert (Mark 6:32 and Matt 14:13). Second, when the crowds hear about it and go to find him, Jesus welcomes them in Luke (ἀποδεξάμενος αὐτούς).[32] In contrast, Mark asserts that Jesus had to withdraw because the crowds were overwhelming him and the disciples (Mark 6:31b, 33). Luke appreciates the presence

---

30. A similar difference emerges in the portrayal of the crowds in the healing of the possessed boy. Both Mark and Luke note the presence of a crowd (Mark 9:14; Luke 9:37). While the crowd is more active in Mark's story, they are also more troublesome. The disciples appear to be arguing with the crowd (Mark 9:16, not in Luke), and Jesus has to rebuke the spirit quickly when the crowd rushes him (Mark 9:25, again not in Luke). Finally, Luke omits Jesus' private explanation to the disciples (Mark 9:28–29) and instead concludes his story with the refrain that "all were amazed" (Luke 9:43).

31. This is the one occasion that Luke keeps the κατ' ἰδίαν found in the Markan tradition.

32. Luke omits the mention of Jesus' compassion on the crowds (Mark 6:34), which casts them as a ragtag band of lost souls. Luke can be rather positive in his portrayal of the crowds, except when Jesus is directly rebuking them, which he does on occasion.

of the crowd, while Mark portrays them as a nuisance. The second supernatural event is Jesus' death. Luke, like Mark and Matthew, mentions that the women in Jesus' movement witnessed this event (23:49, but he does not name them as does Mark 15:40 and Matt 27:56). To emphasize the public nature of this tragic event, Luke adds, "When all the crowds who had gathered [πάντες οἱ συμπαραγενόμενοι ὄχλοι] for this spectacle saw what happened . . ." (23:48), a comment that is found in neither Mark or Matthew. Thus, even as they were present at Jesus' great deeds throughout his life in Luke, so the crowd stands as a witness of his public demise.

The crowd is a marker of public events both in the broad survey of the ancient world and in the accounts of Jesus' miracles in Luke. The actions of the crowds are first and foremost part of the force of social relations in defining these public events, but they also took on the force of meaning as a trope in the ancient world, indicating a public event simply by being present. Luke brings the crowd to the fore at the beginning of the healing of the blind beggar, and he alone reintroduces them at the end of the story to join the beggar's praise. Over and over, throughout the Gospel, Luke uses these two methods to emphasize the public nature of Jesus' miracles: he makes subtle changes to highlight the crowd (as he does when he moves them to the foreground), and he adds crowds where they did not exist in the tradition previously (as he does in 18:43). Luke portrays Jesus as constantly interacting with the crowds and performing most of his miracles in the presence of crowds who witness the amazing deeds and rejoice over them. Luke often portrays the crowd positively and sets Jesus publicly in their midst.

Luke's uses of location, characters, and crowds bring together the forces of place, social relations, time, and meaning in his accounts of Jesus' public miracles. This was shown to be true in a detailed investigation of the healing of the blind beggar in 18:35–43, but it did not end there. The role of the location, the characters, and the crowd in this episode reflects standard techniques that Luke employs repeatedly throughout the Gospel to mark the public nature of most of Jesus' miracles. Luke has recounted and redacted the miracle stories at his disposal to portray Jesus and his actions in the public sphere.

The Political Implications of Public Miracles: Authority, Disciples, and the Movement

The portrayal of Jesus in the local political sphere emerges from the implications of Jesus' public actions in 18:35–43. The same holds true for many of the miracle stories in Luke's Gospel. The public miracles contain subtle hints and indicators of the political nature of the portrayal of Jesus in Luke. Therefore, I have entitled this section the political *implications* of public miracles. The best way to analyze the political portrayal of Jesus is to set it next to the advice and stories set forth in Plutarch's *Precepts*, rather than filtering them through the forces outlined by Sack.

The blind beggar's cry of "Son of David" is the first potentially political reference in 18:35–43. For Luke, this is primarily a marker for Jesus' royal identity with regard to his Jewish heritage. However, this identity carries with it implications of political power.

PART THREE: IMPLICATIONS FOR LUKE'S GOSPEL AND OUR WORLD

The end of the blind man's cry, "Son of David, *have mercy on me!*," may imply that the blind man was requesting some type of benefaction from Jesus. Given Jesus' reputation as a public miracle worker (probably connoted by the crowd when they identify him as Jesus "*the Nazorean*"), the man asks Jesus to restore his sight when Jesus asks him what he wants. Thus, the blind beggar uses this title to attribute honor to Jesus, who is his social superior. At the same time, the blind beggar's address implies that he believes that Jesus has the power and authority to heal him, and the gracious character of a beneficent king who is willing to do so.[33] When the blind man addresses Jesus as the Son of David he identifies him as one with the authority and character to grant his miraculous request.

The early miracles in Luke's Gospel deal with the interrelated issues of Jesus' authority and identity. In the healing of the demoniac at Capernaum, the demon identifies Jesus as "the Holy One of God," and at the end of the story the people are amazed and wonder what kind of authority (ἐξουσία) and power (δυνάμις) Jesus must have to command demons in this way (Luke 4:34, 36).[34] Right after this story, Jesus is identified as the "Son of God" by the demons whom he exorcises in Peter's home (4:40), a comment that is unique to Luke, but similar to the cry of the Gerasene demoniac recorded in all three Synoptics (Luke 8:28 and par.). In another statement shared in all of the Synoptics, Jesus responds to the scornful Pharisees just before healing the paralytic: "The Son of Man has the authority to forgive sins" (Luke 5:24 and par.). Luke also retains the Q tradition in which the centurion compares Jesus' power to heal to his own understanding of military authority (Luke 7:8 and Matt 8:9). When the disciples of John the Baptist come to question Jesus regarding his identity, Luke first reports the healings that Jesus had just performed (Luke 7:21, no parallel in Matt), and then repeats this information in Jesus' answer to them (Luke 7:22, compare Matt 11:4–5), emphasizing the link between Jesus' identity and the authority/power required to perform such miraculous deeds. Finally, when Jesus sends out the Twelve he gives them "power and authority over all demons and to cure diseases" (9:1). Luke alone mentions "power" again in this passage (compare Mark 6:7 and Matt 10:1). Luke is also the only one who records Jesus giving similar "authority and power" to the seventy when they are sent out ahead of him (Luke 10:19). Thus, when Jesus sends out his followers to cure and heal, he delegates his own power and authority to them as agents who act on his behalf, an act befitting political figures for Plutarch (see below).

The exegesis in chapter 5 argued that οἱ προάγοντες of 18:39 were disciples who had some type of leadership role in Jesus' movement, and so were leading the crowd into Jericho. The very fact that levels of leadership emerged in the movement (the Twelve, the Seventy, the προάγοντες) indicates that it was large and organized enough to require and sustain these roles during Jesus' lifetime according to Luke. This suggests some development in Jesus' movement. Three elements emerge from the story of the blind beggar to illustrate how Jesus exercised social power (a form of politics) over his movement and the leaders in it. First, Jesus did not closely manage all of the members of his movement, even

---

33. Recall the example of Vespasian's healing activity (Tacitus, *Hist.* 4.81).

34. Luke mentions Jesus teaching with authority prior to this healing (4:32). The Markan parallel to Luke 4:36 has people wondering about Jesus' "teaching and authority" rather than his "authority and power." Luke adds the second mention of authority in 4:36 and the term power is unique to Luke.

those who seem to be exercising some leadership role. This is seen in the fact that οἱ προά́γοντες take the initiative to attempt to silence the man without asking Jesus about it first. Second, we see a group of leaders in Jesus' movement who apparently do not do as Jesus would have wished. This is illustrated in the irony that Jesus must tell the προάγοντες that the blind beggar should be "led" (passive of ἄγω) to him. They were not doing the very thing that this label implies they should be doing, and so Jesus must correct them. Third, and finally, Luke narrates Jesus issuing an order (κελεύω) to his disciples, commanding them in a way very similar to other local political authorities in Luke-Acts (centurions, tribunes, and procurators). In this way, Luke shows that Jesus does have authority over these members of his movement, and he exercises it to correct them and achieve the goals of his mission when necessary.

The preceding miracle traditions in Luke support this picture of Jesus' leading and correcting his disciples. The disciples do not appear very often in Lukan miracle stories, but when they do, they do not grasp the significance of Jesus' mission, and their master must correct and instruct them.[35] Jesus rebukes the disciples for their lack of faith after he calms the storm, and they are left asking each other, "Who is this?" (Luke 8:25). In the healing of the hemorrhaging woman, Luke places the lack of understanding on Peter (rather than the disciples in general as in Mark 5:31). In the healing of the boy with a demon, Jesus probably calls the disciples the "faithless and perverse" generation that he must endure (9:41).[36] In the feeding of the five thousand, the disciples respond with astonishment to Jesus' instructions to feed the crowd in all the Synoptics, but it is only in Luke that they go on (somewhat foolishly) to suggest that they would have to travel to the city to buy the people food. After this, in Mark 6:39 and Matt 14:19, Jesus himself orders the crowd to sit down, but in Luke Jesus assigns this task to his disciples. He tells them to make the crowd sit down (9:14), instead of doing it himself. Finally, Luke tells twice how Jesus delegated authority to his disciples (the Twelve and the Seventy), sending them out to expand his mission of teaching and healing, while Mark and Matt only record one such commissioning. In Luke's miracle stories, the disciples are employed by Jesus as his agents in both mundane (ordering the crowd to sit) and supernatural (healing others) ways; however, they do not appear to fully grasp the nature of Jesus' identity or mission in these accounts much as they fail to do so with the blind beggar.

Luke's portrayal of Jesus supervising his disciples during public miracles fits with the portrayal of a local political leader. Jesus' actions resonate with Plutarch's advice to delegate authority to trusted friends in order to achieve one's aims (*Praec. ger. rei publ.* 812c–d), a political move that is especially warranted when "something great and advantageous must be done that necessarily entails a great deal of conflict and strife" (819b), an apt description

---

35. The exception to this would be the miraculous catch of fish in 5:1–11. Simon appears to have very keen insight after the miracle and then follows Jesus.

36. Note that Luke omits Mark's material referring to the father's lack of faith (Mark 9:21–24). Furthermore, Luke specifies that Jesus gave the boy back to his father (9:42b), which is not stated in Mark. Thus, the father is not cast in a negative light in Luke as he is in Mark. The only ones who fail to have faith in Luke's account are the disciples who could not cast the demon out right after a successful healing tour (see 9:1, 10). Green (*Luke*, 386) says that this barb is directed at the disciples.

of Jesus' public mission. On the other hand, Jesus does not gloss over the mistakes of the disciples but calls attention to them and corrects them. Similarly, Plutarch cautions that a local political leader should not be indulgent toward his friends. While granting one's friends appropriate authority and favors, one must not overextend leniency and so harm the state (808b–d). Jesus sees the need to admonish his disciples and he does so when necessary. Once again, this local political material is not prominent in Luke's miracle stories, but the indicators that are present do cast Jesus as a local political leader.

Some further political implications can be gleaned by comparing the role of Luke's miracle stories with material in Plutarch's *Precepts*. Plutarch advises his protégé to earn a good reputation among the people in order to rise in political power and resist one's enemies (*Praec. ger. rei publ.* 821c). Jesus' merciful acts of healing not only cull the gratitude of those healed, but the crowds are amazed at his power and pleased by the wonderful things he does (4:42; 7:16; 13:11). Thus, through his public miracles, Jesus garners a good reputation with the crowd. Eventually, their public support will prevent the Jerusalem leadership from acting openly against Jesus (20:19). The inclusion of former outcasts (like a crippled woman, lepers, and a blind beggar) into Jesus' movement may fit Plutarch's aim for "harmony" (ὁμόνοια, 823f–825f). Plutarch speaks of the dangers of factions (824a) and considers the absence of conflict a blessing (824Cc). Such peace and concord requires the relative well-being of all citizens (824d). While Plutarch pursued a type of political stability that guaranteed the safety and security of the Greek cities, Jesus seems to purse peace by raising up those excluded from society and restoring them to health and community.

Luke's account of Jesus healing the blind beggar in 18:35–43 functions literarily as a microcosm of the previous miracle material in the Gospel, and it also prepares Luke's audience for some elements found in the entry and passion. The social-spatial exegesis of this passage revealed specific elements and techniques that Luke used to highlight the public and local political nature of this episode: the location, the characters, the crowd, and politics within Jesus' movement. Surveying the other miracle stories in Luke's Gospel in this light demonstrates that Luke also employed these same elements and techniques throughout the Gospel. One finds locations, characters, and crowds appearing repeatedly to emphasize the public nature of Jesus' miraculous acts, and some of these stories also tell of Jesus' authority and identity as local leader similar to 18:35–43. Therefore, the public and local political character of the healing in 18:35–43 is true of miracles in the Gospel as a whole.

The Literary Functions and Social-Spatial Implications of Luke 19:1–10

Chapter 6 demonstrated the public and local political nature of Luke 19:1–10. The opening of this story contains obvious and predictable public markers: Jesus is in a city on a major thoroughfare surrounded by a crowd. However, the introduction of Zacchaeus complicates matters. A careful investigation of his characterization in 19:2 revealed that Zacchaeus would have most likely been viewed as a (deceitful and greedy) regional representative for a *societas publicanorum* by Luke's (Ephesian) audience, a liminal figure crossing several cultural boundaries. Matters grow more complicated when Jesus requests and receives Zacchaeus's hospitality. The exegesis proved that Jesus did enter Zacchaeus's home and that at least some part of the crowd from the city entered as well. In this public and domestic setting, Zacchaeus and Jesus respond publicly to the crowd (using the *insinuatio* technique). Regarding the literary functions of this passage, chapter 6 orbited around the themes of conflict and salvation, for their role in Jesus' encounter with Zacchaeus culminates these intertwined themes in Luke's Gospel. Zacchaeus's tenuous connections to the Romans and the role of his house both help to prepare the audience for the passion. Regarding the social-spatial implications of this passage, the juxtaposition of public scenes in both the city of Jericho and Zacchaeus's household point toward Luke's preference for urban settings and toward his habit of turning households into public venues.

A Microcosm of Previous Material: The Public Settings of Conflict and Salvation

Jesus' meeting with Zacchaeus serves as a microcosm of the public settings of conflict and salvation that precede it in the third Gospel. As the discussion on the literary form of 19:1–10 indicated, this pericope fits well with pronouncement stories that describe quests and conflicts in Luke. In 19:7 Luke states that "everyone" grumbled against Jesus, indicating the inclusive and climactic character of this conflict. However, this conflict eventually results in the salvation of Zacchaeus and his household. Jesus speaks of salvation twice in vv. 9–10, highlighting the climactic role of this theme. This story epitomizes Jesus' public conflicts in Luke and sums up the Lukan theme of salvation in the Gospel.

The conflict surrounding Jesus' encounter with Zacchaeus is climactic and representative, recalling several conflict stories in Luke. In 19:2, Luke describes Zacchaeus as a "chief tax collector" (ἀρχιτελώνης), a designation that recalls and climaxes Jesus' interactions with tax collectors previously in the Gospel.[37] Throughout the Gospel, Jesus faces conflict and hostility over his association with tax collectors (and sinners—see 5:27–30; 7:29–35; 15:1–2). In each of these episodes, the Pharisees are Jesus' primary opponents, complaining about Jesus' choice of companions. The Pharisees appear on several other occasions in the Gospel, entering into conflict with Jesus (5:21–24, 33–39; 6:1–5, 6–11; 13:31–35; 16:14–15; 17:20–21). Jesus also faces public conflict with the Pharisees in three household meal scenes (7:36–50; 11:37–54; 14:1–24; these will be explored in the household material below). Thus, the Pharisees are Jesus' typical antagonists up to 18:35–43,[38] but this pericope climaxes the opposition to Jesus by including everyone in the crowd. After Jesus invites himself to Zacchaeus's home in the middle of the city, "*all* who saw it began to grumble" (v. 7). The complaining encompasses the entire crowd (including Jesus' disciples?), and this all-inclusive conflict signifies the finality and totality of the misunderstanding and rejection of Jesus' public mission by "everyone."[39] Thus, Jesus regularly encounters conflict

---

37. Loewe, "Towards," 331.

38. Jesus also faces opposition from his hometown crowd (4:28–29), some Samaritans (9:51–56), some in the crowds (11:14–16), a synagogue leader (13:14), and even his own disciples (18:15–17).

39. O'Hanlon, "Zacchaeus," 15–16. It may be "hyperbolic" (Fitzmyer, *Luke*, 1:1224), but the literary function of the hyperbole (if it is indeed that) is to climax the theme of conflict in the Gospel.

PART THREE: IMPLICATIONS FOR LUKE'S GOSPEL AND OUR WORLD

from the Pharisees over his association with tax collectors, and Luke climaxes this conflict in 18:35–43 when Jesus faces opposition from "everyone" over his fellowship with a "*chief tax collector.*" However, this story and those preceding it do not end with conflict, but with salvation.

The end of the Zacchaeus story accentuates the theme of salvation by using both the noun form (σωτηρία, v.9) and the verb form (σώζω, v. 10) of this important Lukan concept.[40] As Loewe noted over thirty years ago, this passage does hearken back to the infancy narrative, and it does so particularly through the language of "salvation."[41] The noun forms, σωτηρία and σωτήρ, cluster in the early part of the Gospel, mostly in the infancy narrative where God the savior (1:47) sends salvation (1:69, 71, 77; 2:30; 3:6) through Jesus the savior (2:11). The noun forms do not appear again until 19:9, which recalls how God sends salvation through Jesus to the heirs of Abraham, a salvation prophesied in the infancy narrative and realized here (compare 1:55, 73; and 19:9). The noun form in 19:9 may also prepare the reader for the use of similar forms in Acts: Jesus is once again called savior (5:31; 13:23), and the message of salvation is proclaimed to people, both Jews and Gentiles (4:12; 13:26, 47; 16:17; 28:28).

In 19:10, the verb form characterizes the public ministry of Jesus (the "Son of Man") as the work of "saving the lost." The verb σώζω appears five times in the Gospel to refer to the spiritual dimension of salvation, often with eschatological overtones (7:50; 8:12; 9:24; 13:23; 18:26) and six times to describe miraculous healings (6:9; 7:50; 8:36, 48, 50; 17:19). Finally in 18:42, the blind beggar is also "saved" from his blindness. 19:10 is the last time the verb is used non-sarcastically in the Gospel,[42] and it probably refers to Zacchaeus's religious (and social) restoration from being one of the "lost." Therefore, the double reference to "salvation" in 19:9 and 10, linked literarily with the verb form in 18:42, sums up both the spiritual, bodily, and social dimensions of Jesus' public ministry of salvation. Zacchaeus repents and receives forgiveness (salvation), and the blind man cries out and receives healing (salvation). Additionally, both men are socially reintegrated: the blind beggar joins Jesus' movement, and Zacchaeus's Jewish identity is affirmed by Jesus' actions and words. Jesus offers "saving wholeness" to both spirits and bodies, with social effects in public scenarios here and throughout Luke's Gospel. However, this usage does not only sum up the two primary dimensions of Jesus' public ministry but also the two primary locations of

---

40. Marshall, *Historian & Theologian*, 92–93, 116.

41. Loewe, "Towards," 330. Luke also connects 18:35—19:10 to the infancy narrative by mentioning the two greatest patriarchs of Israel, David and Abraham. The mention of David harkens back to the angel's promises that Jesus will receive the throne of his ancestor David (1:32) and where Zechariah looks forward to a mighty savior from the "house of David" (1:69). Likewise, both Mary's private song and Zechariah's song (proclaimed in the public space of his own home) refer to Jesus fulfilling the divine promise made to Abraham (1:55, 73). Thus, in consecutive stories just before the arrival in Jerusalem, Luke has Jesus publicly, yet indirectly, lay claim to both the Abrahamic ancestry and Davidic royalty of Israel's heritage. Not only is Jewish (royal) identity attributed to Jesus (by the blind beggar) with its connotations of authority, but Jesus appears to have the authority to include people in Israel's heritage (by calling Zacchaeus a "son of Abraham"). Jesus both receives and gives identity generated by Jewish heritage. By connecting these two stories, Luke hearkens back to the infancy narrative and intensifies the public manifestations of Jesus' identity and authority.

42. Three times during the crucifixion Jesus is taunted by people who tell him to "save himself" (23:35, 37, 39).

Jesus' public ministry: the city and the house.⁴³ Jesus acts to bring salvation to Zacchaeus in both city and house, just as he healed people in both cities (e.g., 7:11-17;17:11-19) and houses (e.g., 4:38-39; 5:17-26).

The elements of quest, salvation, household, city, and conflict are all brought together in Jesus' encounter with the "sinful" woman (7:36-50) in ways very similar to the story of Zacchaeus. Jesus' encounter with the "sinful" woman in the house of Simon the Pharisee is an excellent example of a quest story according to Tannehill,⁴⁴ a quest story with conflict embedded at its core (much like the story of Zacchaeus). Tannehill highlights the importance of the ending of the story, which depicts the fulfillment of the woman's quest, yet he does not point out how Jesus' final words extend both salvation and peace to the woman (7:50), casting the theme of salvation back over the entire story through this public pronouncement (much like in the story of Zacchaeus). This entire scene takes place in Simon's home, but several non-private surprises emerge. First, the home is invaded by a "woman from the *city*." Thus, like the story of Zacchaeus, the city invades the home in a context of conflict. Furthermore, the outworking of the woman's salvation takes place in the course of Jesus' conflict with Simon. Simon (internally) objects to Jesus' contact with the woman (v. 39),⁴⁵ and her presence launches a discussion between Jesus and Simon, which ultimately results in Simon being shamed by Jesus' appeal to the woman's hospitable actions (vv. 45-47). Luke adduces conflict again at the end of the story, recalling objections to Jesus' authority to forgive sins (7:49, compare 5:21).⁴⁶ This story has several connections with Jesus' encounter with Zacchaeus: Jesus encounters a "sinful" person in a context of conflict that intertwines city and home and publicly pronounces salvation for the one who has sought him out.⁴⁷

The interrelated role of both city and house in Jesus' encounters with Zacchaeus points to other stories in Luke's Gospel that intertwine city and house, conflict and salvation. Four other passages in Luke's Gospel portray Jesus in conflict with Pharisees in a household setting which is invaded by or strongly linked to the public sphere: the healing of the paralytic in 5:17-26, Jesus' meal at the home of Levi in 5:27-39,⁴⁸ Jesus' first meal with the Pharisees in 11:37-52, and a combined healing and meal scene in 14:1-24. In each of these cases, conflict moves between the public and private spheres and often results in salvation for some character. Thus, the household setting in Luke 19:7-10 opens

---

43. The third setting that plays a role in Jesus' mission is the synagogue (4:16-28, 31-37; 6:6-11; 13:10-17). However, the synagogue is not as common as Luke's comment in 4:44 seems to imply.

44. *Narrative Unity*, 116-18.

45. This would probably lead Robbins to classify this amalgamated pronouncement story as the "objection" type ("Pronouncement Stories," 5-6).

46. Fitzmyer, *Luke*, 1:684. Fitzmyer judges vv. 48-50 to be a Lukan addition.

47. This would add one more reason in favor of the traditional interpretation that Zacchaeus resolves a new way of life rather than defending his typical, generous habits. The best precedent for Zacchaeus is the "sinful" woman who needs forgiveness, so Zacchaeus too needs forgiveness.

48. The connection between Zacchaeus and Levi has been noticed and explored by other scholars. See Kariamadam, *Zaccahaeus*, 50-53; and Hamm, "Luke 19:8," 436-37. Kariamadam develops a connection to the conflict in 5:17-26 (48-50) and mentions (without developing) a connection to 7:36-50 (53).

PART THREE: IMPLICATIONS FOR LUKE'S GOSPEL AND OUR WORLD

the way for exploring the public nature of the conflict and salvation that occurs in these preceding stories in Luke.

Preparation for the Passion: Romans and Houses

The story of Zacchaeus raises the reality of the Roman presence in Judea and sets up a contrast between Jesus' public teaching in Zacchaeus's house and the temple. The identification of Zacchaeus launches an increase in the *official* public sphere from this point on through the passion narrative. In particular, Zacchaeus's position as a tax collector reminds the reader of the presence of the Romans, who play a key role in Jesus' final week. Zacchaeus was a prominent local citizen and businessman in Jericho who would have been understood to have ties to local Jewish leadership as well as some element of the Roman political system because of his occupation. Thus, his identity in Luke's narrative gives him one foot in both the unofficial and the official public sphere and one foot in both Jewish and Roman culture. He is not a political official himself, but his position in the social and economic life of the local area grants him a level of authority and ties him to operative political systems. Zacchaeus's status changes the social-spatial valence of the narrative slightly. What was an unofficial public approach to Jericho (in the story of the healing of the blind beggar) takes on official Roman overtones with the presence of this chief "tax" collector. Zacchaeus is the first person with connections to the Roman political system mentioned by Luke since Herod in 13:31–32.[49] Zacchaeus serves as the quiet beginning of an intensification of Jesus' interaction with the official public sphere and its Roman elements, which culminates in ch. 23.

Luke also sets up a spatial comparison/contrast between Zacchaeus's house (19:9) and the temple, God's house (cf. 19:46). The two places are connected lexically by the use of οἶκος, but their typical social-spatial valence could not have been more different. The temple was a single, holy place run by a hierarchy of religious officials usually associated with political and economic power, while houses were multiple and mundane, based on kinship and solidarity.[50] Despite these stark contrasts, Luke asserts that Jesus' public preaching appropriately takes place in both venues. Whether it is the house of a man or the house of God, Jesus can be found there speaking openly to a large crowd. In 19:1–10, Jesus approaches and speaks to Zacchaeus (a local political figure marginalized from the Jewish community in Jericho), Zacchaeus gladly welcomes Jesus into his *house* and pledges to distribute his wealth justly. After this, Zacchaeus's house becomes a location for Jesus to teach a large group of people.[51] In 19:39–48, all of the local political figures mentioned—Pharisees, chief priests, scribes, leaders, those who represent the core of the Jewish nation from the temple in Jerusalem—oppose Jesus and seek to silence him and his followers. Jesus is not happily welcomed by local political hosts in Jerusalem. Rather, they resist him, and Jesus forcefully evicts merchants from the temple courts in order to

---

49. Before this there is only the centurion of 7:1–10 and the chronological anchors in 2:1–2 and 3:1–2.

50. Elliott, "Temple versus Household," 230–40.

51. Chapter 7 argued that the introductory material in 19:11 and the parable itself imply a large and diverse audience gathered in Zacchaeus's home.

Luke's Emphasis on the Public Sphere and Local Politics in the Gospel as a Whole

create a space where he can teach the people, making it a space as open to his teaching as Zacchaeus's house was.[52] Jesus' actions in the temple only earn him murderous hostility in Luke's story: leading Jewish officials, secretly but officially, plot how to eliminate him. Zacchaeus's household hospitality intensifies the tragic hostility of the temple-based leaders in Jerusalem who fail to recognize the significance of Jesus' arrival (see 19:41–44). Instead of hospitably offering a platform for Jesus to preach and distributing wealth justly, the Jewish leaders in Jerusalem create an environment in the temple where Jesus must dramatically claim pedagogical space in the temple in the face of hostility and disruptive economic practices.[53] Luke insists that both house and temple (the house of God) are proper places for Jesus' teaching ministry. Luke's contrast between the two houses points out the degeneration of the temple, shames the Jewish leadership, and forebodes the uncertain fate of the Jewish nation.

Jesus' encounter with Zacchaeus serves well as a microcosm of preceding stories of conflict and salvation in the Gospel. Conflicts over Jesus' acceptance of "sinners" are typical in Luke's Gospel, and the fact that "everyone" objects in v. 7 stresses the sadly climactic nature of the episode. The repetition of "salvation" language in this story and the healing of the blind beggar recapitulates the bodily and spiritual aspects of this theme in Luke's Gospel and ties them to the public mission of Jesus. This episode also interrelates city and household, furthering its representative capacity by linking these two places in one large public event. Finally, Jesus' interaction with Zacchaeus sounds an increase of the presence of Roman officials from this point on into the passion narrative and sets up a contrast between Jesus' public teaching in two different "houses." With the light of these literary functions, we can now turn to the social and spatial implications of 19:1–10 for the Gospel as a whole.

The Social-Spatial Implications of Luke 19:1–10 for the Gospel as a Whole

In this final section, we bring together the literary and social-spatial analyses to examine how the story of Jesus' encounter with Zacchaeus sums up the public nature of related material in Luke's Gospel. Along the way, we will also adduce comparative material from Plutarch's *Precepts* and book 4 of the *Life of Apollonius*. In the previous section on 18:35–43, the categories of the public sphere and local politics organized the survey of the social-spatial nature of Luke's miracle stories. In the case of 19:1–10, the city and the home stand out as public settings, and they recur throughout Luke's Gospel with similar functions. Jesus' actions in Jericho signal previous redactions where Luke emphasizes the city, but this episode also climaxes four important household scenes in Luke, scenes where

---

52. Note that the root of Jesus' objection is spatial. The problem lies in the fact that they were selling in the temple precincts (εἰς τὸ ἱερόν), not that they were selling at exorbitant prices.

53. This may fit into the contrasts between the temple and household in Luke-Acts noted by Elliott, "Temple versus Household," 235–40. However, despite the fact that Jesus is *welcomed* into a home and forced to *seize* teaching space in the temple, Luke insists that both locations are proper sites for ministry and proclamation by Jesus. It is not the inherent nature of the institutions as such but how they have been shaped (corrupted) by human leadership that Luke contrasts. According to Luke, Jesus reinstates the proper function of the temple in chs. 20–21. Later, the early church's redistribution of wealth (recalling Zacchaeus) is closely associated with their presence in the temple (Acts 2:44–46).

hospitality creates public conflict and salvation.[54] Therefore, the public nature of both the city and the house is a useful heuristic way to organize the social-spatial implications of 19:1–10.

Luke's Preference for the City

As seen in chapter 3, the city was one of the paradigmatic locations for public events in the ancient world, a place where crowds gather, business is negotiated, and politics is practiced. The special attention given to the city emerges from the central role of the force of place in Sack's framework. The travel narrative lacks specificity about Jesus' locations; however, this changes with the double mention of Jericho in 18:35 and 19:1. As discussed in chapter 5, Jericho was known as an agricultural, political, and military center in the ancient world and would have been a suitable place for a public event. Jesus' entry into and procession through Jericho activates the unofficial public potential of this urban center by drawing a large crowd. Jesus' encounter with Zacchaeus occurred publicly in the full view and hearing of the gathered crowd within the city. The city is the location for the first half of this pericope (19:1–6a), and Luke prefers to set many of the events of Jesus' public ministry in the spatial context of cities.[55]

Luke's preference for cities appears already in the infancy narrative: the word πόλις occurs six times in these important introductory chapters.[56] Four places feature prominently in this portion of Luke's Gospel: the temple/Jerusalem, the city of Nazareth, the home of Zechariah and Elizabeth, and the city of Bethlehem. Interestingly, no home or house is ever mentioned in Nazareth or in Bethlehem.[57] Rather, Luke always locates Mary and Jesus in the "city of Nazareth"[58] or the "city of Bethlehem" (1:26; 2:4, 11, 39, 51), casting them in more of a public, urban environment. Jesus moves from the city of Nazareth (1:26) to the home of Zechariah and Elizabeth (1:39–42) while still in the womb. During his birth, infancy, and childhood he moves from Bethlehem (2: 11, 15) to Jerusalem (2:22) to Nazareth (2:39, 51). In the first two chapters of the Gospel, Luke connotes that the public life of cities was already a part of Jesus' life in his infancy and childhood.

---

54. This is a much smaller block of material, but the meal scenes are critical because they contain a great deal of material that is unique to Luke and are a significant mode for his portrayal of Jesus. The importance of the meal scenes is illustrated in Heil's study *Meal Scenes*. The importance of meal scenes in the travel narrative is also emphasized by Moessner, *Lord of the Banquet*, 221–22.

55. Some have noticed Luke's preference for cities when searching for the geographical provenance of Luke-Acts. See Esler, *Community and Gospel*, 30; and Cadbury, *Making of Luke-Acts*, 245–49.

56. 1:26, 39; 2:3, 4, 11, 39. Note that term πόλις can show a wide variety of meaning in Luke, from a little village like Nazareth (1:26) to a metropolis like Jerusalem (19:41). The Synoptics can easily shift between πόλις and κώμη (showing little distinction between the two), but Luke prefers πόλις. See Strathmann, "πόλις," *TDNT* 6:516–35, esp. 529–30.

57. In contrast, Matthew's infancy story appears to take place in Bethlehem. No mention is made of any travel from Nazareth to Bethlehem, and Jesus and Mary are found "at home" in Bethlehem by the magi (Matt 2:11). Later, Matthew says that Jesus' family "made their home" in the city of Nazareth (2:23).

58. Luke appears to apply the term πόλις somewhat indiscriminately, applying it to places that were clearly cities, such as Jerusalem, and other places like Nazareth that were clearly villages. See Rohrbaugh, "Pre-Industrial City," 137. Or, he may have some distinction in mind about population or agricultural centers that we have not discerned. See Oakman, "Countryside," 170.

Luke's Emphasis on the Public Sphere and Local Politics in the Gospel as a Whole

Luke locates Jesus' first sermon and his first miracle in cities, Nazareth (4:16) and Capernaum (4:31) respectively. In Nazareth, Jesus not only preaches his first public sermon, but encounters his first public conflict with the people who balk at his message. On the other hand, Capernaum becomes a place of salvation where a man is exorcised and the people are amazed. In contrast to the beginning of Jesus' ministry in Luke, Mark and Matthew first place Jesus by the sea, calling disciples (Mark 1:16–20 and Matt 4:18–22). Then, Mark moves Jesus into Capernaum (1:21), not noting it was a "city in Galilee" as Luke does in 4:31. Matthew omits the exorcism in Capernaum and proceeds directly to a summary statement, portraying Jesus traveling "throughout Galilee, teaching in their synagogues" (4:23). Luke has a similar, significant summary statement at the end of chapter four where Jesus himself asserts, "I must proclaim the good news of the kingdom in the other *cities* also" (4:43). Thus, Luke does keep the tradition of Jesus preaching in synagogues,[59] but when Jesus describes his own divinely bestowed mission in Luke, it is a mission to *cities*. Luke's editing of this well-crafted "overture" to Jesus' ministry in 4:16–44 emphasizes the importance of cities and closes with Jesus' own affirmation of his mission to urban centers. This emphasis on cities in the journeys of Jesus comes up again in the summary statements of 8:1 and 13:22. In both passages, Luke states that Jesus was going through "cities and villages" teaching and preaching. 8:1 is very similar to Matt 9:35, which mentions both cities and villages, but Mark 6:6 mentions only villages. 13:22, however, is peculiar to Luke and his travel narrative, for it states that Jesus was passing through the cities and villages on his way to Jerusalem. Jesus' own statement in 4:43 combined with these summaries, confirms that Jesus' mission of bringing salvation regularly took place in the public zones of cities (and villages) in Galilee and Judea.

On several occasions, Luke either adds references to cities not found in his sources or includes unique material that mentions Jesus' urban activity. At the beginning of the cleansing of the leper (an episode of salvation, 5:12), Luke alone states that Jesus was in a city (ἐν μιᾷ τῶν πόλεων). Luke is the only evangelist to record the public raising of the widow's son in the city of Nain (another episode of salvation, 7:11). Luke uses the location of the city as a means of characterization as well. He alone states that the woman who anoints Jesus in ch. 7 was "in the city" (Luke 7:37), setting up the conflict that will follow in Simon the Pharisee's house. Similarly, the Gerasene demoniac is a man "from the city" who had resided in the tombs since being possessed by a demon (Luke 8:27, neither Mark nor Matthew mention a city). This "man from this city" is another recipient of a salvific exorcism. Luke situates the parable of the sower by stating that "many crowds from city after city" (ὄχλου πολοῦ καὶ τῶν κατὰ πόλιν, 8:4) heard him teach publicly. Mark and Matthew both set this parable by the Sea of Galilee, and they mention crowds but no cities (Mark 4:1, Matt 13:1). In Luke's version of the parable of the great banquet, the slave is first sent out to public areas—"the streets and lanes of the *city*" (εἰς τὰς πλατείας καὶ ῥύμας τῆς πόλεως, 14:21)[60] and then into the country "roads and paths" (14:23). The slave in

---

59. Interestingly, Jesus does not appear very often in synagogues in Luke's Gospel (only 4:16ff., 4:33ff., 6:6ff., 13:10ff., and only the latter two follow this summary statement). On the other hand, Jesus is quite often in cities as will be shown below.

60. These represent places where people would naturally gather in a city. Matthew himself recognizes the

PART THREE: IMPLICATIONS FOR LUKE'S GOSPEL AND OUR WORLD

Matthew's account is instructed to go out to find people, with no mention of a city (Matt 22:9).[61] Only Luke records Jesus telling a parable about a judge and a woman "in a certain city" who engage in an extended conflict (18:2). In Luke's version of the parable of the pounds, the good servants (models of good disciples) are put in charge of "cities" (19:17 and 19), rather than Matthew's more general "many things" (Matt 25:21 and 23). Only Luke specifies that Barabbas was guilty of fomenting a public insurrection "in the city" (Luke 23:19, compare Matt 27:21 and Mark 15:11). Finally, forming a link to Acts, Luke is the only Gospel that records Jesus ordering the disciples to "remain in the city" until they are empowered for their mission (24:49). Luke repeatedly adds or emphasizes the city in Jesus' mission.

The Synoptic accounts of the commissioning of the disciples are different and complexly related. Six different locations appear in these accounts: house (οἰκία and once οἶκος), city (πόλις), village (κώμη), place (τόπος), street (πλατεῖα), and road (ὁδός). However, the first two (house and city) predominate. The best way to see the relation of the material in Mark, Matthew, and Luke is to display it in a table.

Table 9.1: The Synoptic Commissioning Discourses

Mark 6:7-14	Matthew 10:1-15	Luke 9:1-6	Luke 10:1-12
6:7—Jesus sends out the Twelve (no places mentioned).	10:5—Jesus sends out the Twelve, telling them to avoid "any road[62] of the Gentiles and any Samaritan city," but to go only to the lost sheep of the "house (οἶκος)[63] of Israel."	9:2—Jesus sends out the Twelve (no places mentioned).	10:1—The Lord sends the Seventy ahead to "every city and place" he intended to go.
6:10—"Wherever" (ὅπου ἐάν) they enter a "house" they should stay.	10:11—The twelve are told to stay in "whatever city or village" they enter	9:4—The twelve are told to stay in "whatever house" they enter.	10:5—The Seventy are told to speak peace to "whatever house" they enter.

public valence of both πλατεῖα and ῥύμη, for he has Jesus condemn those who give alms and pray publicly in these locations so that others will notice them (see Matt 6:2, 5).

61. The construction ἐπὶ τὰς διεξόδους τῶν ὁδῶν in this verse probably refers to the ends of the roads at the boundaries of kingdom. It implies going out to the remotest areas to find anyone (Luz, *Matthew 21-28*, 55).

62. This phrase is probably a Semitism meaning "to/toward any Gentiles" (Hagner, *Matthew 1-13*, 270).

63. This is the only use of οἶκος in the commissioning accounts, and it is clearly metaphorical, referring to a people and not a physical structure.

Luke's Emphasis on the Public Sphere and Local Politics in the Gospel as a Whole

Mark 6:7-14	Matthew 10:1-15	Luke 9:1-6	Luke 10:1-12
			10:7—The seventy are instructed to stay in the same "house" and not to move around from "house to house."
6:11—If any "place" does not welcome them, they are to shake the dust off their feet.	10:14—The Twelve are told to shake the dust off their feet as they leave any "house or city" that has rejected them.	9:5—The Twelve are told to shake the dust off their feet as they leave any "city" that has rejected them.	10:10-11—If a "city" rejects them, the Seventy are told to go into the "street" and wipe the dust of that "city" off their feet in protest.
		9:6—The Twelve go throughout the "villages" preaching and healing.	
	10:15—Sodom and Gomorrah will fare better than "the city" that rejects them.		10:12—Sodom and Gomorrah will fare better than "the city" that rejects them.

Mark, not surprisingly, is the least public and the least developed. The apostles are only described as entering "houses" (6:10) "wherever" they go, and they are instructed about what to do if a "place" does not accept them (6:11). Matthew's account mixes several of the places together. The twelve are told to avoid Gentile roads and Samaritan cites, but to stay in "whatever city or village" of Israelites that they visit. The protest of shaking dust off of the feet can be done against either house or city, whichever might reject the messengers and their message. Thus, Matthew exhibits a very general retelling that allows a variety of spatial scenarios and lacks specificity. Luke, on the other hand, displays more spatial specificity, a specificity that fits with travel and hospitality practices in the ancient world. First, we see Luke's preference for cities at the beginning of the commissioning of the Seventy, where they are sent into every "city" and "place" (here is a touch of generality) that Jesus intended to go. Thus, Jesus intends to go to cities on his public mission, a practice in line with his own statement in 4:43. Next, for Luke, one "stays" (μένω) in houses (9:4; 10:7). That is, hospitality takes place in houses where the disciples are hosted, not in cities (compare Matt 10:11). Jesus does much the same when he is hosted by Zacchaeus in 19:6ff. However, the burden of the responsibility for rejection falls upon the city in Luke (9:5; 10:10-11), unlike Matthew who can place blame on either house or city (10:14). Furthermore, the protest against such obstinate cities in Luke takes place publicly, for Jesus instructs the seventy to go into the street (an ideal public location), wipe the dust off of their feet, and publicly announce the nearness of the kingdom (10:11). Finally, both Matthew and Luke

PART THREE: IMPLICATIONS FOR LUKE'S GOSPEL AND OUR WORLD

close by declaring that declare that Sodom and Gomorrah will fare better than those *cities* that reject Jesus' messengers.[64] Thus, Luke alone states that Jesus sent the disciples to cities (a paradigmatic public place), recognizes the central role of the house in hospitality (in a way that Matthew does not), and sets the departing, public protest of the rejected disciples both in the city and against the city.

Luke's preference for cities stands out in comparison to Mark and Matthew. The emphasis on the city as the typical location of Jesus' ministry draws upon the force of place to portray Jesus as a public figure supported by the force of social relations (added by the crowds) and meaning (added by ancient conception of the city as a public area).[65] Most of the city-passages discussed above do not mention any sort of political officials, and so they largely orient Luke's city locations in the unofficial public sphere.[66] For Luke, the city with its streets and markets and plazas and even its homes evokes the unofficial public sphere for his portrayal of Jesus. Plutarch's *Precepts* and book 4 of the *Life of Apollonius* confirm Luke's use of the city as a public arena, adding comparative insights to the way that the city functioned as part of the unofficial public sphere and local politics in Luke's milieu.

The city is the ideal and real location for Plutarch's local politics, and he employs the term πόλις over fifty times in the *Precepts*. The city is the basic political unit throughout this treatise (801a, 805b, 811c, 816f, 823a). Plutarch lived and worked in a city (811b–c) and was advising a young protégé who sought to do the same (798a–c). Most of Plutarch's anecdotes come from the golden age of the Greek city-states (Athens, Sparta, Thebes, Rhodes, etc., which he generally labels as "cities") or from late republican Rome. His repertoire of exemplary (and not so exemplary) leaders is extensive and is drawn from top levels of leadership in the same two times/places (Pericles, Pompey, Solon, Themistocles, Cicero, etc.), yet he also recognizes the importance of minor offices lower down the political ladder (808b–c, 811b–c). Finally, he sees the city not merely as a past arena for political action, but also as the current reality in which he and Menemachus can exercise virtuous and beneficial leadership (805a–b, 814e–815c, 824c–d). Luke and Plutarch both view the city as the basic unit of population and politics; however, they do differ over its "official" status. For Luke, the city is the recurring setting for the unofficial public sphere, while Plutarch emphasizes it as the basic political body. This is most likely due to the purposes of their respective works, and Luke's purpose aligns more with Philostratus's at this point.

Book 4 of the *Life* demonstrates an emphasis on cities in a different manner. This is not advice about political activity in a local urban center, but the tale of a famous wandering saint/sage (comparable to Luke's story about Jesus). Thus, it uses the tem πόλις much less often (only nine times) but tells of Apollonius encountering public settings of conflict and salvation throughout Asia Minor, Greece, and Rome. While chapter 4 of this study

---

64. Curiously, Luke concludes the commissioning of the Twelve by saying they visited "villages" on their mission. It might be said that the "city" features more prominently in the commissioning of the seventy than the commissioning of the Twelve.

65. Rohrbaugh states that despite Luke's emphasis on cities, "much of Jesus' ministry takes place outside cities" in Luke ("Pre-Industrial City," 147–48). However, he offers no evidence of this other than noting that Jesus does not enter several of what we know to be major cities in the area (Sepphoris, Samaria, etc.).

66. The two exceptions are the servants in the parable of the pounds who are given (political) authority over cities and Barabbas' revolt, which was obviously a political act.

revealed that temples were Apollonius's favorite place for preaching and lodging, much of book 4 is organized around the cities that Apollonius visits and the various public venues that he utilizes in these urban centers. In chs. 1-4, he is in Ephesus, mostly around the temple and its sacred groves. Then he moves on to Smyrna in chs. 5-9, where he gives a discourse on how the inhabitants of a city (πόλις) should behave as citizens (ch. 8). There he asserts that a city needs the proper balance of harmony and competition, where all aim to do what is best for the city. Afterwards, he returns briefly to Ephesus to save them from the spread of a deadly plague, revealing the demon at the public entrance to the city's theatre (ch. 10). After this, he goes on a tour of various tombs and shrines around the Achaean Sea (chs. 11-16) before coming to Athens. Chapter 4 discussed his public exploits in Athens: his reception during his procession to the city, his conflict with the priest before the Epidaurian festival, his exorcism of a young demon possessed man, and other scenes of conflict (chs. 17-22). He then travels to Corinth, where he saves a young man from a beguiling demon at a wedding feast (ch. 25). From there he goes to Olympia (chs. 27-28) and then Sparta, where he offers political advice (chs. 31-33). Finally, he arrives in Rome where he anticipates great conflict because of Nero's hostility to philosophy (chs. 35-39). He impresses and is welcomed by one official (Telesinus, ch. 40) but is opposed and dogged by another (Tigellinus, chs. 43-44). Near the end of his stay in Rome, he raises a young bride from the dead in the midst of her funeral procession through the city (ch. 45; recall Jesus' actions in Nain). Philostratus recognizes Apollonius's preference for temples and tells of exploits to various tombs and shrines. Yet, overall, book 4 of the *Life* is organized around the cities that Apollonius visits, and it recounts a variety of settings of public conflict and salvation that took place in these cities. Both Jesus and Apollonius take their missions to urban population centers. There they encounter opponents, whom they best in public debate, and victims, whom they save with miraculous words and deeds. Thus, both figures carry out their mission in unofficial public scenarios of conflict and salvation that are largely set in cities.

The Public Nature of Houses in Luke

Jesus does not remain in the city streets of Jericho. Instead, he moves into the home of Zacchaeus, bringing the public sphere along with him. Through the cultural practice of hospitality Jesus, and Jericho's public, gain entrance to Zacchaeus's home. The analysis of the literary functions of 19:1-10 suggested that both conflict and salvation are interrelated in the household scenes of the Gospel. Jesus' encounter with Zacchaeus is the climax of these themes and places. In this final section, we will look at four meal scenes in Luke's Gospel that intertwine city and household, hospitality and rejection, public and private, conflict and salvation: 5:27-39; 7:36-50; 11:37-54; and 14:1-24.[67] These scenes demon-

---

67. While a banquet or meal is not mentioned in 19:1-10, several factors make it quite likely that a high context audience would have assumed that a meal was provided for Jesus and his companions as part of Zacchaeus's hospitable welcome. First, meals are associated with "staying" (μένω, v. 5) in Jesus' commissioning of the seventy (10:7-8), and the other "welcome" (ὑποδέχομαι, v. 6) Jesus receives in the Gospel is most likely followed by a meal as well (10:38ff.). See the comments made by Heil, *Meal Scenes*, 153-54; and Smith, "Table Fellowship," 636. Meals were an expected part of hospitality in the ancient world (Koenig, "Hospitality," *ABD*

PART THREE: IMPLICATIONS FOR LUKE'S GOSPEL AND OUR WORLD

strate how Luke fluidly brings together the public sphere of the city with the private sphere of the household through hospitality, transforming the conflict and salvation that occurred in these household settings into public events.

The story of the calling of Levi in 5:27–32 has many similarities with Jesus' encounter with Zacchaeus: both involve a tax collector, both display Jesus' initiative, both draw criticism, and both end with a saying from Jesus.[68] Furthermore, both demonstrate a fluid interrelation of the public and private spheres. In 5:27, Jesus leaves the house in which he healed the paralytic and presumably enters a city where he meets Levi at his tollbooth (τελώνιον). This booth would have been located at one of the (few) entrances to the city or in the marketplace, locations for travel and commerce respectively.[69] A tollbooth qualifies as a public place given its location in highly trafficked areas and the large number of people who did business at and around it. Thus, Jesus' initial meeting with Levi occurs in the public sphere. While it is brief (Jesus' terse command and Levi's immediate response), it transpires in the full view and hearing of the crowd that any high-context audience would have supplied at such a location.

Much like Jesus' encounter with Zacchaeus, an initial meeting and exchange in public moves into a home where conflict and salvation follow. The scene quickly changes in 5:29 from the tollbooth to Levi's home where a great banquet is thrown in Jesus' honor. Jesus has now entered Levi's personal domicile, and while the private sphere might be expected to dominate, we find that this is a public setting in which both conflict and salvation ensue. Mark and Matthew both mention "many tax collectors and sinners" joining Jesus and Levi for this meal (Matt 9:10 and Mark 2:15). Luke picks up on this potentially public

---

3:299–301). Corley, on the other hand, denies that a meal is involved in 19:1–10 as part of her argument that Jesus never actually eats with "sinners" (like Zacchaeus) in Luke's Gospel (*Private Women*, 131–32). However, she bases her argument for the omission of a meal entirely on the use of διέρχομαι in 19:1, failing to see how Jesus' encounter with Zacchaeus interrupts his journey. The most substantial objection to Jesus having a meal with Zacchaeus is that he appears to continue on to Jerusalem immediately after uttering the parable of the pounds (19:28). This implies that Jesus either did not stay very long with Zacchaeus (unlikely given the evidence above) or that he traveled to Jerusalem by night (also unlikely). Jericho is 15–20 miles from Jerusalem, a full day's walk for a traveler on foot. The best solution to this quandary is that Luke both inserts these episodes in Jericho (19:1–10 and 11–27) into the Markan framework and compresses the time so that everything from 18:35—19:46 occurs sequentially in the narrative in one day, though it probably would take at least two days for all of these events to take place in real time (with Jesus' spending the night in Zacchaeus's home). The expectation for a meal as part of Zacchaeus's hospitality in the original audience's mind would probably trump the demands of the narrative time frame in this case.

68. This parallel is explored by Kariamadam, *Zacchaeus*, 50–53. He does note the presence of the crowd in both stories but does not pursue the household or "public" setting of each story. As will be explored below, the setting of Levi's house continues into the next pericope (5:33–39) much like the setting of Zacchaeus's home continues in 19:11–27.

69. Inscriptions regarding tax regulations in Asia stress that taxes must be paid upon arrival (using some form of εἰσάγω) or departure (using some form of ἐξάγω). See McCabe, et al., *Ephesos Inscriptions*, Ephesos 4*5 lines 9–10, 22. However, this same inscription states that taxes must be paid "wherever" a tollbooth (τελώνιον) has been established (lines 55–56). Other inscriptions mark tollbooths that were set up by fish merchants and thus probably located in the market place. See McCabe, *Ephesos Inscriptions*, Ephesos 267 lines 7–11 and Ephesos 788*5 lines 9–10. Donahue refers to places of travel and commerce as settings for tax collectors ("Tax Collectors," 45 and 54). Jeremias refers to the necessity of paying tolls at the market in Jerusalem (*Jerusalem*, 32).

Luke's Emphasis on the Public Sphere and Local Politics in the Gospel as a Whole

moment and intensifies it. For Luke, it is not just "many" at the dinner, but a "great crowd [ὄχλος πολύς] of toll collectors" (5:29). Levi has, not surprisingly, invited his toll collecting colleagues, but Luke also generalizes the crowd saying that it was made up of both toll collectors and "others" (ἄλλων), not just other "sinners." Somehow included in these "others" are the Pharisees who "grumble" about Jesus' choice of hosts (much like the crowd in 19:7). The opponents are in the house as well! They complain to the disciples and then are rebuked by Jesus (who apparently overheard them). The presence of the large crowd and the Pharisees make this scene of household hospitality into a public event, linking public and private together.

Levi's house becomes the setting for public challenge-riposte exchange. The Pharisees challenge Jesus regarding his table fellowship (5:30), and Jesus replies that his call of repentance has gone out to the "sick" (that is, those with whom he shares table in Levi's home). With this apt reply, Jesus publicly shames his opponents and affirms his association with the group gathered for this meal. The setting and the discussion continue in vv. 33-39, much like the setting and the discussion continues in Zacchaeus's home in 19:11-27 (both also contain a parable). Jesus, the crowd, and his opponents are still in Levi's home, and the Pharisees continue to challenge Jesus. This time regarding his lack of fasting, continuing on the topic of meals and food. Here again, Jesus extends salvation to his fellow diners, calling them the "wedding guests" who are feasting with the bridegroom (v. 34). Furthermore, they are the new wineskins who accept the new wine that Jesus offers, a new wine that is rejected by the Pharisees and scribes. Much like 19:1-10, Jesus' encounter with Levi in 5:27-39 begins in a public setting in the city and then quickly moves to a setting of household hospitality, which is flooded by the public sphere. The various public interactions bring forth conflict in which Jesus bests his opponents and ultimately offers salvation to his scorned host (and other guests). Luke has intertwined the public and private spheres in both stories, allowing the public sphere to predominate even when Jesus is in the home of his host.

The story of Jesus, Simon, and the "sinful" woman found in 7:36-50 was discussed above for the way that it brings together the themes of quest, conflict, and salvation. This is also the first of three occasions when Jesus is invited to dinner by a Pharisee (see also 11:37ff. and 14:1ff.). These are all examples of a "protégé dinner." Garnsey describes this type of meal, distinguishing it from the "client dinner" and the "peer-group dinner," as a meal in which a prospective member of the local hierarchy is brought in to meet important people and become accustomed to their way of life.[70] Gowler is right to note the tenser, less friendly, nature of the meals scenes in Luke, describing them as opportunities for the Pharisees to "test" this new stranger, Jesus.[71] These dinners in Luke appear to be opportunities for the Pharisees to interview Jesus, find out about him and his teaching,

---

70. Garnsey, *Food and Society*, 137. Jesus would not have been considered either a client or a peer by the Pharisees. Thus, Garnsey's protégé dinner fits these scenarios well and moves toward the local political sphere.

71. Gowler, "Hospitality," 220. This role of testing, and the unusual presence of the sinful woman make 7:36-50 less like a symposium scene (Gowler, "Hospitality," 222). He is also right to describe these scenes as opportunities for the author to portray Jesus' ἦθος ("Hospitality," 214-18). For this study, the key element of Jesus' ἦθος is his strongly public identity in Luke (something which Gowler himself mentions; see below).

PART THREE: IMPLICATIONS FOR LUKE'S GOSPEL AND OUR WORLD

and possibly persuade him to join their movement, but ultimately they become a means by which Jesus can proclaim his message in Luke's Gospel.[72] Each of these stories links the public and private together, draws in themes of conflict and salvation, and results in Jesus rebuking his hosts.

In 7:36, Jesus enters the "house" of Simon the Pharisee. However, in v. 37 Luke tells us that a "woman who was a sinner in the city" (γυνὴ ἥτις ἦν ἐν τῇ πόλει ἁμαρτωλός) appears at this scene of household hospitality and begins to bathe Jesus' feet.[73] Various interpreters note that this woman was probably a public prostitute,[74] and her presence at this meal in the home of a Pharisee is both unnatural and shocking.[75] This raises two challenging questions: How did she know that Jesus was at this particular house, and how did she gain access to the meal? The answer to the first question is simpler and reinforces the public nature of Jesus' ministry in Luke. Jesus' presence at Simon's house for this meal could have been local public knowledge (might we say "gossip") that spread through the town and was found out (ἐπιγιγνώσκω, 7:37) by this woman.[76] Another plausible alternative would be that the woman could have seen and followed Jesus to the house. The second question about access poses several problems. A category existed in symposia-related literature for an "uninvited" guest or intruder to appear at the meal.[77] Alternatively, Bailey suggests that oriental banquets were open affairs with a lot of coming and going.[78] However, both of these seem unlikely. First, most of these uninvited guests were persons of near or equal status to the host and guests (like Aristodemus in Plato's *Symposium*), not a low status person like this woman. Second, most elite Greco-Roman houses (such as those seen and imagined by Luke's audience) had small, controlled entry vestibules and dining rooms that were often removed from the entrance to provide extra privacy.[79] Thus, the guest would either have to be known to the household (uninvited but welcome) or a banquet functionary like a flute girl.[80] Neither of these characters fits this woman. Third, the Pharisees in Luke show great concern for purity and eating practices (e.g., 7:39

---

72. Smith, "Table Fellowship," 622 n. 28.

73. The textual tradition of this phrase varies the order of the words to make try to make sense of an awkward construction (Marshall, *Luke*, 308). The text as given here is probably original on the basis of its difficult nature. Luke often uses ὅστις as an equivalent for ὅς as he does here (Wallace, *Greek Grammar*, 344–45). Green (*Luke*, 309) wants to supply an ellipsis in this phrase to make it say that the woman "was known" in the city as a sinner. However, that is not necessary. The ἐν phrase here spatially specifies the label ἁμαρτωλός and refers to the location in which she carried out her "sinful" activities.

74. Corley, *Private Women*, 124; Green, *Luke*, 309; Plummer, *Luke*, 210.

75. Heil calls her an "intruder" drawing on parallels to symposia (*Meal Scenes*, 45). Malina and Neyrey call her presence here "a violation of where she should be" ("Honor and Shame," 63), but she fits very well within Luke's recurring habit of blending and public into private space.

76. This scenario is suggested by Bailey, *Poet & Peasant*, 7.

77. Marshall, *Luke*, 308; Heil, *Meal Scenes*, 45.

78. Bailey, *Poet & Peasant*, 7.

79. In the villa of the Labyrinth, the triclinium and finely decorated cubiculum are at the far end of the home from the entrance allowing for a grander and more private reception. See this and other examples in Wallace-Hadrill, *Houses and Society*, 28, 58–59, 113–14. See also the general description of the function of such rooms in Anderson, *Roman Architecture*, 291.

80. Nelson, *Leadership*, 53.

and 11:38). Thus, it is hard to believe that this outcast woman could have slipped into the house, contaminated the space, and gone unnoticed. Her placement and actions are more like a slave than an uninvited guest,[81] but she is an outsider in the home, not a part of it. What other possibilities exist to explain her ability to enter this Pharisaic home?

She could have entered with Jesus as part of his entourage. Kilgallen, followed somewhat by Corley, has suggested that the woman has already been forgiven in the past (thus the perfect tense of the verb in 7:48) through the ministry of John the Baptist and later joined Jesus' movement.[82] This is further supported by the fact that text implies that she entered with Jesus: "*Since I came in*, she has not stopped kissing my feet" (v. 45).[83] The *dramatis personae* of the scene are limited to the woman, Jesus, and Simon. However, given the spatial and religious barriers blocking this woman's entrance, and the argument that she is now "following" Jesus in some sense (after her experience of forgiveness), her presence opens the doors to a larger, more public setting for this meal. If this woman has come in with Jesus, have other "followers" come in as well? Could this be the inverse of the dinner at Levi's house? There the purity-conscious Pharisees surprisingly appear at a public meal in the house of a "sinner" who has gathered others like himself to hear Jesus. Here the "sinners" (associated with Jesus) surprisingly invade a public meal in the "pure" house of a Pharisee who has gathered others like himself to hear Jesus.

Therefore, this story demonstrates how the city (with its public nature, commonness, and impurity) embodied in a woman can enter the private home of a Pharisee who has extended hospitality to Jesus. While the scene is tightly focused on the three main characters, the bridge of hospitality (extended to Jesus) becomes a way in which a public person from the city encounters a private man and his guests in his own home.[84] Such a meal would have probably involved other local religious leaders who wanted to meet Jesus as well. Adding a bit to this, the fact that Jesus was dining at Simon's home might have been public knowledge in the city, attesting to the public nature of Jesus' ministry and the way that it could color even a private dining invitation. At the very most, the presence of this "sinful" woman signifies the presence of "sinners" and others who are now following Jesus; by their association with him, they have gained access to this private meal. At this highest degree, the bridge of hospitality extended to Jesus unexpectedly becomes a superhighway, allowing the public sphere to flood into the home. The Pharisee's home becomes a public setting of conflict that results in the shaming of Simon (vv. 45–47) and the salvation of the woman (v. 50).

In 11:37, another Pharisee invites Jesus to dinner (while he was speaking to a crowd, c.f. 11:29, 37), and he arrives in the home and joins other Pharisees and lawyers at the table. In this passage, Jesus' actions and words transform the private setting of household hospitality into a public conflict. An invitation to hospitality contained several implicit, cultural expectations for both guest and host. Among the basic obligations placed on the

---

81. Corley, *Private Women*, 125; Smith, "Table Fellowship," 632.

82. Kilgallen, "John the Baptist," 675–79; Corley, *Private Women*, 125–26, 130.

83. Plummer, *Luke*, 213.

84. Oddly, then, this becomes a case of a "public woman" at a "private meal," an ironic twist on the title of Corley's monograph.

guest are to follow cultural conventions and to respect the host.[85] However, Jesus violates both of these: he does not wash his hands as the Pharisees are accustomed to do and he goes on to attack his host and the other guests. He criticizes them and pronounces woes upon the entire group for their hypocritical and harmful behavior.[86] Hospitality is supposed to be a time when hostilities are set aside and a friendly, collegial environment predominates.[87] Instead, Luke's Jesus, through his confrontational rhetoric, transforms the scene into a public, agonistic contest for honor.[88] As Gowler says, "Jesus' response to the Pharisees' silent astonishment, of course, makes the debate public."[89] Once again, a setting of household hospitality in Luke has shifted from a private setting to a public one. In this case, Jesus is the agent of transformation in the story. He violates the basic obligations of a guest, and turns this household scene into a public honor contest with his words.

Jesus' last meal with a Pharisee takes place in 14:1–24. This passage contains several elements that tie it both to the previous two meal scenes and to Jesus' encounter with Zacchaeus, and it too exhibits the mixing of public and private spheres. 14:1 sets the scene by stating that Jesus was on his way to the house of a certain leading Pharisee. First, while it can be debated, the grammar of v. 1 implies that Jesus had already entered the house when he saw and then healed the man with dropsy.[90] Thus, Luke joins a healing with this scene of conflict and salvation during hospitality, much as he does with the blind beggar and Zacchaeus. Second, the host in this case is a certain "leader" of the Pharisees, τινος τῶν ἀρχόντων (τῶν) Φαρισαίων. The use of the term ἄρχων here climaxes Jesus' meals with the Pharisees—he now dines with their leader on the Sabbath, and he will not dine with them again.[91] The lexeme ἀρχ- in Zacchaeus's title ἀρχιτελώνης also highlights the climactic nature of that passage. In both cases, Jesus shares hospitality with "leading" men, and both terms connote a climactic force to the following story.

The healing of the man with its resulting debate (vv. 1–6) and the following material dealing specifically with banquets (7–24) form one unit.[92] The man with dropsy is in the house when Jesus heals him and the meal transpires immediately after. Again, we are not

85. Gowler, "Hospitality," 220–22.

86. See Gowler's discussion of Jesus' invectives against the Pharisees and lawyers ("Hospitality," 230–40).

87. Gowler, "Hospitality," 220; Smith, "Table Fellowship," 621.

88. Recall the basic principle that agonistic honor contests were one of the defining elements of the public sphere, while the private sphere was assumed to be more nurturing and secure. Thus, Jesus initiates a public type of speech in this private setting. See Neyrey, "What's Wrong," 78; and Malina and Neyrey, "Honor and Shame," 35–38, 49–52.

89. Gowler, "Hospitality," 229. Gowler goes on to characterize this scene and Jesus' speech as public two more times (234 and 235).

90. The form of the phrase ἐγένετο ἐν τῷ ἐλθεῖν αὐτὸν εἰς οἶκον (γίνομαι + preposition with infinitive) is a common Lukan introduction. When used with an aorist infinitive it should be translated as "when . . ." Thus, the phrase should be understood to say, "When Jesus went into the house of a leading Pharisee . . . there was a man with dropsy." This perhaps means that the man was at or near the entrance to the house. See Wallace, *Grammar*, 595. This translation is also supported by Braun, *Feasting*, 22.

91. Heil, *Meal Scenes*, 99. Both social relations (the role of the Pharisaic leader) and time (on a Sabbath) mark the climactic nature of this passage.

92. Braun, *Feasting*, 14–21; Green, *Luke*, 539–40.

told how this unusual and unexpected guest comes to be in the house, but he fills a role similar to the woman of 7:36–50. This "stranger" is probably not a part of the Pharisee's household. He is most likely another "intruder" from the public sphere, though the text does not give us any indications how or why he came there.[93] Thus, much like the woman of 7:36–50, an unexpected or uninvited person makes the house more of a public scenario and sets the stage for the discussion that takes place around the meal.[94] Then, like 11:37–52, Jesus initiates a hostile (and thus public) verbal contest between him and his fellow diners in vv. 3–5. This is followed by a direct rebuke of the guests for the way they jockeyed for the highest and most honorable seat at the banquet (vv. 7–11). Then, as the ultimate offense, Jesus dares to correct the host by instructing him about whom he should invite to a banquet: not his friends but social outcasts. As in 11:37–52, Jesus brings a public mode of conflict and contest into the private setting of household hospitality.[95]

This unit ends with the parable of a wedding banquet (much like Jesus' meals with Levi and Zacchaeus end with parables). All of the invited guests refuse to attend the banquet when the time comes (14:18). The master is infuriated and commands his slave to bring people into his home from the streets and alleys *of the city* (v. 21, "city" is not found in the parallel at Matt 22:9), most likely the dregs of the urban poor.[96] When this fails to fill up the house, the master sends the slave out into countryside to find outcasts on the limits of society and coerce them to come to the banquet,[97] for the master wants his home to be filled (γεμισθῇ) with people. This image parabolically represents the public meal scenes depicted throughout the third Gospel. Luke portrays Jesus sharing meals, teaching, and healing in houses that are filled with people, including undesirable people from the city and beyond. This unit (14:1–24) ends with the vision of a public wedding banquet in a house filled with all kinds of people. It then moves, almost seamlessly, into another public setting, for Jesus seems to turn easily to the crowd standing nearby and address them on a related topic (14:25–35), and immediately after this we find a large mixed crowd of tax collectors, sinners, and Pharisees all listening to Jesus (15:1–2).[98] There are breaks between the sections from 14:1—15:2ff, but their spatial fluidity and the large, mixed crowds that are present allow a public atmosphere to predominate throughout. The city and the house-

---

93. Plummer says he was probably not an invited guest and refers to the openness of an "eastern" house to explain his presence (much like Bailey did for the "sinful" woman). See Plummer, *Luke*, 354. Braun suggests that this man would have fallen into the category of the socially marginalized (perhaps a beggar) who were often pictured in the Greco-Roman world as loitering around elite banquets, hoping to receive something to eat. See Braun, *Feasting*, 30–31.

94. Heil, *Meal Scenes*, 99.

95. In this episode, conflict predominates. Salvation is only extended to the healed man at the beginning of the unit.

96. Braun, *Feasting*, 81–88.

97. Ibid., 88–97.

98. Is it possible that this is one continuous public setting? Did the crowds overhear the discussion in the Pharisee's house like the Pharisees seemed to eavesdrop on Jesus' meal with Levi? Green notes a topical connection that stretches from 14:1—15:2, but prefers to see a major break at 14:25 (*Luke*, 563–64). Johnson sees 14:14–35 as one continuous scene following the pattern of rejection, admonition, and call to discipleship (*Luke*, 231–32). Both recognize a connection here (Johnson's is stronger than Green's) that stretches across the public and private spheres.

PART THREE: IMPLICATIONS FOR LUKE'S GOSPEL AND OUR WORLD

hold, the public and the private are intertwined again in this section of Luke's Gospel, resulting in a strongly public portrayal of Jesus throughout this final confrontational meal with the Pharisees.

Luke's concern for the household and its importance in his Gospel is well documented.[99] Furthermore, many authors have noted how the household is a prominent place in the Gospel of Luke that serves both as an excellent location and example of Jesus' prophetic proclamation of liberation and inclusion.[100] However, while many of these scholars note the radical nature of Jesus' domestic message and praxis in Luke, they fail to note the way in which Luke transforms these household settings into *public* venues for action and proclamation. Unfortunately, by stressing the household setting (the force of place) these studies cast Luke's Jesus in the private sphere. If Jesus' message is definitively accepted or rejected at domestic banquets (Moessner), if the household embodies the generalized reciprocity that Jesus proclaims (Elliot), if inclusion happens primarily in meal fellowship (Heil), and if Luke's households are the place of new kingdom identity (Moxnes), then the private sphere seems to be the ideal location for both the person and the activity of Jesus. Sack's force of place comes implicitly to the fore in these interpretations and imbues a private coloring over Luke's portrayal of Jesus. A careful social-spatial interpretation of Jesus' encounter with Zacchaeus and the four meal scenes that precede it in Luke's Gospel gives a very different picture, but one that resonates with the work of these other scholars. All of the works noted above stress the radical nature of Jesus' message in Luke. Yet, one must note that Luke alters the very nature of the domestic places in which Jesus teaches, acts, rebukes, and forgives.

Rather than leaving Jesus in typical, private households, Luke has taken the well-known, ancient practice of hospitality and amplified it in his presentations of Jesus as a domestic guest. Hospitality was a way of welcoming the (public) stranger into the (private) household, but it has become much more than that in Luke's portrayal of Jesus. The avenue of hospitality has become a highway that allows the public sphere to flood into households. The forces of social relations, meaning, and place work together to effect these transformations. With regard to social relations, the presence of public people (the sinful woman, the man with dropsy), mixed groups (tax collectors *and* Pharisees together), and large crowds (as in Levi's and Zacchaeus's homes) turn these households into public places.[101] With regard to meaning, the nature of Jesus' harsh rhetoric, his refusal to maintain the standards of respect for host and custom, and the very content of his teachings (proposing a banquet filled with guest from the city and beyond) all make these scenarios public. Finally, the role of place comes into play as well, for Luke insists on tightly binding together public and private places: Jesus' public encounters with Levi and Zacchaeus quickly and seamlessly shift to their homes, the woman "in the city" enters Simon's house, and Jesus leaves

---

99. See, especially, Heil, *Meal Scenes*; Moessner, *Lord of the Banquet*; and Halvor Moxnes, "Kingdom," 194–202.

100. Moessner, *Lord of the Banquet*, 207–10 (who also rightly emphasizes Jesus' rejection at banquets); Elliot, "Temple Versus Household," 239–40; Heil, *Meal Scenes*, 307–11; Moxnes, "Kingdom," 200–202.

101. The force of religion may play a role as well, for Luke often combines "unclean" public persons (tax collectors and prostitutes) with "pure" persons (Pharisees).

the crowd at the end of ch. 13 to enter the home of a Pharisee (14:1–24) only to easily turn and address the crowd again (14:25ff.). The conflict and salvation that take place in these homes are not private, but public affairs. Luke does not merely present a Jesus with a radical message of liberation and inclusion that employs the household as a setting and a model. Rather, that liberation and inclusion is meant for the very nature of the house as a place as well. Luke portrays Jesus in situations where houses themselves have been transformed from controlled, private places with limited access to wide open public places where everyone is not only welcome but actually present, where all seem to have access, and where large crowds gather to hear the proclamation of the kingdom. Closed doors are opened, undesirable guests are welcomed, and all find a place in Jesus' audience.

Luke's story of Jesus encountering Zacchaeus brings together conflict, salvation, house, and city in ways that sum up several preceding episodes in Luke's Gospel. This story is both climactic ("all" grumble against a "chief" tax collector) and representative (Jesus faces conflict in public homes over his fellowship and bestows salvation). This story also prepares the audience for a contrasting description of God's "house" and the increase of Roman presence in the passion. Building on these literary relationships, this passage points toward Luke's preference for cities in his portrayal of Jesus' ministry, a social-spatial characteristic that fits well with material from both Plutarch and Philostratus. Finally and as a complement to the prominence of cities, the hospitality scene in 19:6–10 recalls other household meal scenes in the Gospel that Luke has transformed into public settings of conflict and salvation.

The Literary Functions and Social-Spatial Implications of 19:11–28

In 19:11–28, while he is still in the public space of Zacchaeus's house, Jesus continues to speak, telling a story about a king and his subjects. The social-spatial exegesis of this passage argued that Jesus teaches three groups in the audience with this single parable: the crowd, his disciples, and his opponents. The combination of these three groups summarizes their role in previous material and prepares for their appearance in the passion. Finally, this parable summarizes most of the previous eschatological teaching in the Gospel and prepares the audience for the increasingly political nature of the passion narrative. The social-spatial implications of this passage reveal two emphases found in Luke's portrayal of Jesus' teaching. First, Jesus engages in public pedagogy in Luke, for he teaches and preaches in a variety of public scenarios. Second, the political material in the parable reflects the local nature of political characters that Jesus encounters and teaches about in Luke's Gospel.

A Microcosm of Previous Material: Audiences, Parables, Eschatology, and Kingdom

Several elements in 19:11–28 encapsulate previous material in the Gospel, particularly in episodes of Jesus' teaching. The first consideration is Jesus' audience. The audience of this parable consists of the disciples, the crowd, and Jesus' opponents (as well as Zacchaeus and his household). These three groups play a significant role in the presentation of Jesus'

PART THREE: IMPLICATIONS FOR LUKE'S GOSPEL AND OUR WORLD

teaching in Luke's Gospel. Throughout the Gospel but especially in the travel narrative, Jesus teaches his followers about discipleship, calls the crowd to repentance, and pronounces judgment on his opponents.[102] The disciples are present early in Jesus' ministry, witnessing his public teaching (6:1, 17; 8:9). Later, Jesus directs his teaching specifically to them (9:1-6, 18-27, 43b-48; 10:23-24; 11:1-5; 16:1-13; 17:1-10; and 17:22-37). The crowds appear consistently in chs. 4-9 as an audience for Jesus' public teaching (5:3; 6:17; 7:24; 8:4 with a parable, and 9:11 about the kingdom). In the travel narrative, Jesus begins to warn and admonish the crowds to recognize the significance of his message (11:29; 12:54; 13:1, 22; 14:25). Jesus' opponents, often represented by the Pharisees and teachers of the law, appear in early public conflicts or exchanges with Jesus (5:17-23; 6:1-11; 7:36-50; 10:25-29). Later, the hostility increases and Jesus reprimands them more sharply (11:37-54; 14:1-24; 15:2ff; 16:14-19; 18:9-14). All of these audiences are publicly and simultaneously addressed by the parable in 19:12-27. The disciples are urged to be faithful and obedient during the master's absence (compare 12:35-48). The first and second servants serve as a model for their behavior. Jesus warns the crowds to avoid the mistaken attitude and inaction of the third servant. They must heed the calls to repentance. Jesus' opponents receive the ultimate warning in the fate of the king's enemies: if you reject the appointed king you will face destruction and death.

This story also encapsulates previous material by using a parable, one of Jesus' favorite forms of public pedagogy in Luke. Jesus speaks in parables before the travel narrative (5:35-39 and 8:4-15, perhaps also 7:41-42 and 8:16-17). The parable of the sower in 8:4-15 is marked as a public event by the presence of the crowd in v. 4.[103] Jesus goes on to speak parables in public settings throughout the travel narrative (10:25-37; 12:13-21, 35-40; 13:6-9, 18-21; 14:15-24; 15:1-32; 16:1-9, 19-31; 18:1-8, 9-14). Some of these episodes mention the presence of a crowd as an indicator of their public nature (12:13, 41; 15:1-2). In other cases, Luke juxtaposes different groups addressed by different parables to imply a large, mixed audience.[104] Therefore, by the end of the travel narrative Luke paints a picture of Jesus speaking parables to various audiences in public contexts. The parable in 19:12-27 brings together this previous material through a parable that addresses all three audiences in a single parable told in a public context.

Various interpreters discussed in chapter 7 noted the mixture (and tension) of present and future in 19:11-28. The somewhat confusing amalgamation of elements in the parable is partially due to the way it summarizes Jesus' previous eschatological teaching in Luke. The parable recalls several points but does not integrate them into an eschatological system.[105] Luke's Jesus shuns attempts to specify when and where the kingdom will arrive

---

102. Johnson, *Literary Function*, 107-8.

103. While the disciples ask Jesus what the parable means, Luke does not emphasize a private and exclusive explanation as in Matthew (13:10-23).

104. The crowds and the disciples appear side by side in 12:13, 22, and 54. The Pharisees and the crowds are set together in 14:1, 25; and 15:1. The Pharisees and the disciples are juxtaposed in 17:20 and 22.

105. While it is true that Luke portrays eschatological redemption transpiring in the present (that is in Jesus' ministry), he maintains a real, future Parousia that will culminate God's work of salvation through Jesus. See Green, *Theology*, 94-101.

(17:20, 37; Acts 1:6-7) much as he does in response to the misguided anticipations alluded to in 19:11. Also, the portrayal of servants entrusted with responsibilities during the master's absence is found earlier in the eschatological teaching of 12:35-38 and 41-48. In 12:35-38 the slave must expectantly await the master's return from a wedding banquet. If the slave is alert at the master's return, he will be served by the master himself. In vv. 41-48, the "faithful manager" is the one who actively cares for other slaves in the master's absence; he is put in charge of all of the master's possessions (v. 44).[106] The other slave knows what the master wants but does not do it, reasoning that the master will be gone a long time. He is thrown out and cut off. A closing gnomon echoes 19:26: the slave who acts according to the master's instruction will be granted even more authority (12:47). Several aspects of these two passages reappear in the parable of the king and his subjects: the character of the servant, activity during the master's absence, good servants and bad servants, and judgment based obedience/disobedience. The parable calls to mind this previous eschatological teaching and reiterates it within a similar plot.

Several other elements of Jesus' previous eschatological teaching emerge in the parable. Jesus has spoken of his own sudden return in power: he is like a thief in the night (12:39-40), he returns on an unexpected day (12:46), he will come suddenly while people are carrying on life as usual (17:27-30). This prepares for the speedy return of the nobleman in his full royal authority in the parable.[107] When the nobleman-become-king returns in the parable he rewards the servants who actively obeyed, reprimands the one who did not, and violently judges his opponents. Previously, Jesus has stated that he will reward his faithful servants at his return (12:37, 43-45; 16:10-11; 18:29-30). However, some, like the third servant, do not respond with faith and so loose their place in the kingdom. This recalls Jesus' earlier warnings to the crowds. They will be surprisingly condemned by "foreigners" at the judgment because they missed the significance of Jesus (11:29-32). They fail to interpret the present time properly (12:54-56), and some of them are turned away despite their insistence that the master knows them (13:22-29). Finally, as in the parable, Jesus has already predicted that those who reject the king and his authority will themselves be rejected. Those who decline their invitation will not share in the eschatological banquet (14:24). They will be destroyed like classic evildoers in Israel's history (17:27, 29). The characters and themes in 19:12-27 appear in previous eschatological teaching. This parable draws them all into one story, directed at the various audiences publicly addressed by Jesus before he enters Jerusalem.

Finally, Luke casts the parable of the king and his subjects as part of Jesus' teaching about the kingdom of God with the introduction in 19:11. Jesus describes his mission as one of "preaching the kingdom of God" (4:43). Luke reiterates this in a summary statement (8:1) and in the commissioning of the twelve and seventy (9:2; 10:9). Jesus opens the sermon on the plain with a reference to the kingdom of God (6:20), and he has spoken

---

106. The discussion of the "coming of the Son of Man" in-between these two passages (12:39-40) confirms their eschatological nature. Furthermore, these two passages reinforce the necessity of the master's *absence* before his (eschatological) return as in the parable of the king and his subjects.

107. While absence is necessary to make sense of the parable, a long delay is not. Jesus' and the master's return both transpire expeditiously.

to the crowds about it before (9:11). Jesus references the kingdom on several other occasions (7:28; 9:27; 11:20; 16:16; 18:16–17). Just a chapter before meeting Zacchaeus, Jesus teaches about how hard it is for the rich to enter the kingdom of God (18:24–25), but it is not impossible as Zacchaeus shows. Jesus mentions the kingdom in his eschatological teaching (13:28–29; 17:20–21) and has illustrated it using a parable as he does in 19:12–27 (13:18, 20).[108]

This parable, told in the public space of Zacchaeus's house, serves as a microcosm of previous material in the Gospel by summarizing various elements in this one story. The parable addresses Jesus' three primary audiences in Luke's Gospel: the disciples, the crowds, and his opponents (usually the Pharisees up to this point). Luke inserts this passage into the Markan framework. By doing so, he depicts Jesus using one of his most characteristic forms of public pedagogy (a parable) to speak about one of his most common topics (the kingdom). This public parable is intensified by its eschatological character, which draws elements from Jesus' previous teaching in the Gospel.

A Preparation for the Passion: Audiences, Parables, and Politics

This parable with its unique setting in Luke prepares the audience for the passion narrative in three ways.[109] First, recall that the parable of the king and his subjects addresses disciples, opponents, and the crowd who are all present in Zacchaeus's home. Similarly, while in the temple, Jesus speaks to the crowds (20:1, 9; 21:5,[110] 38), to his opponents (20:19, 20ff, 27ff.), and to his disciples (20:45). The last reference states that Jesus spoke to the disciples *"while all the people were listening,"* an excellent example of Jesus' public instruction that, while directed at one group, is overheard by a much larger audience. Thus, the parable prepares Luke's audience for Jesus' public teaching in a different house—the temple—yet in this very different house Jesus still speaks publicly to a mixed audience of crowds, disciples, and opponents just as he did in Zacchaeus's house.

Second, the Jewish leaders' animosity toward Jesus does not manifest itself as political attacks until the passion narrative, that is, after the parable in 19:12–27 recounts similar political maneuvers against a king-to-be.[111] In 19:14, the hostile citizens send an official embassy (πρεσβεία) to denounce him before the granting authority (the emperor). The "scribes and chief priests" make several political moves against Jesus in the local context of Jerusalem within the passion narrative. They attempt to trap Jesus in some treasonous teaching so that they can hand him over to the "jurisdiction and authority of the governor" (20:20ff.). Their political machinations persist as they seek for a way to put Jesus to

---

108. This mention also prepares for the mention of the kingdom in the passion, especially in 21:31 and 22:16–18 where kingdom and eschatology intersect as they do in 19:11ff.

109. Carroll notes that this parable sets the stage for the following Jerusalem section of Luke's Gospel but does not offer specifics (*Eschatology*, 97).

110. The Synoptic eschatological discourse is directed only to the disciples in both Mark (13:1) and Matthew (24:1). Furthermore, both Gospels state that Jesus spoke most of the discourse to his disciples "privately" on the Mount of Olives (Mark 13:3 and Matt 24:3). In Luke, Jesus directs the entire discourse to a large, general audience (21:5, 7) gathered in the temple (see 21:1, 5).

111. Busse, "Dechiffrierung," 439.

death (22:1-2). Next, after their own trial (22:66-71), the Sanhedrin brings Jesus to Pilate and makes political accusations against him (23:1-2; perverting the *nation*, tax evasion, and treason) in the hope of securing his execution. When Jesus is transferred to Herod, the Jewish leaders reiterate their political accusations (23:10). Finally, in a savvy (but unexplained) political move, the chief priests and leaders are able to win over the crowd and force Pilate to have Jesus crucified in order to prevent a riot (23:18-23). Luke has prepared his audience for these political maneuvers by depicting the political actions of the king's opponents in 19:12-27.

Third and finally, the form and content of 19:11-28 also anticipates the passion narrative. As noted above, the parable is one of the characteristic forms of Jesus' teaching in Luke's Gospel. Jesus publicly delivers the parable of the wicked tenants to "the people" (τὸν λαόν) very early in the passion narrative (20:9-18). The parable of the wicked tenants recounts the story of a wealthy landowner who goes to another country for a long time (20:9), similar to the (shorter) absence of the nobleman of 19:2. During his absence, he entrusts some of his resources to others, much like the slaves of 19:13. The parables end similarly with the destruction of those who reject the authority of the master (19:27 and 20:16). As noted above, 19:12-27 summarizes much of Jesus' previous eschatological teaching in Luke, and it also prepares the audience for Jesus' extended eschatological discourse in 21:5-36. The second parable in the passion narrative (and last in the Gospel) occurs within the eschatological discourse at 21:29-33. 19:12-27 made the eschatological point that the kingdom is still in the future but close enough to encourage faithful obedience among the servants of the master. A similar eschatological point is made in the parable of the fig tree (21:19-31), the kingdom is in the future but near enough that the current generation must prepare for its denouement. Thus, the parable of the king and his subjects prepares the audience for the passion narrative: Jesus speaks to his disciples, the crowds, and his opponents in parables that contain plot elements and topics similar to those found in 19:12-27. Ultimately, he faces political plots in the passion similar to those depicted in the parable of the king and his subjects.

The Social-Spatial Implications of 19:11–28 for the Gospel as a Whole

After the social-spatial and literary analyses of this parable, we can see how this pericope functions as a representative example of Luke's emphasis on the public sphere and local politics. This pericope is an excellent epitome of Jesus' public pedagogy. Jesus has often taught in public venues previously in the Gospel, so now before his passion he tells the parable of the king and his subjects to a large, mixed audience that has gathered in the publicized space of Zacchaeus's house. The narrative setting of the parable illustrates the public character of Jesus' teaching in Luke's Gospel, while the content of the parable displays local politics. Most of the action in the story transpires in the local political sphere, and the scene of evaluation and judgment in vv. 15-27 (most of the parable) occurs at a public gathering before the new king. The following discussion will examine how Luke accentuates the public sphere and local politics in Jesus' teaching while drawing com-

PART THREE: IMPLICATIONS FOR LUKE'S GOSPEL AND OUR WORLD

parisons from the other Synoptics as well as Plutarch's *Precepts* and book 4 of the *Life of Apollonius*.

The Public Pedagogy of Jesus in Luke

Luke uses the force of place to characterize Jesus' teaching as public. Jesus' inaugural sermon in the Nazareth synagogue begins Luke's portrayal of Jesus' public pedagogy.[112] Jesus stands up in front of the gathering to read and sits to deliver his sermon (4:16, 20). "All" the people speak well of him at first (4:22), though Jesus eventually provokes a violent riot in the city (4:29). Luke also portrays Jesus teaching publicly in homes (5:17-26, 29-39; 14:7-24). Luke alone casts Jesus teaching a crowd at the lakeside before calling the first disciples (Luke 5:1, compare Mark 1:16-20 and Matt 4:18-22). Luke uses the report of Jesus healing the multitudes (Luke 6:17-19, compare Mark 3:7-8 and Matt 12:15) as the setting for the sermon on the plain (not Matthew's more exclusive mountain). Luke then reminds his audience about the presence of the crowds on the plain at the end of the sermon (7:1). Finally, in the travel narrative, Luke portrays Jesus teaching publicly on the road to Jerusalem (11:29; 12:1, 13; 13:22; 14:25). In addition to the public teaching that Jesus does in houses and cities, Luke also portrays Jesus teaching in other public places: synagogues, lakesides, plains, and roads.

However, Luke frequently provides no spatial setting and instead sets the public valence of Jesus' teaching with the force of social relations. Jesus almost always teaches large, mixed crowds in Luke's Gospel. A crowd gathers to hear Jesus teach as early as 5:1 (only one chapter into Jesus' public ministry). In 5:19 and 8:3, people cannot reach Jesus while he teaches because of the crowd surrounding him. Jesus speaks to the crowds about the faith of the centurion (7:9) and the identity of John the Baptist (7:24). With Mark and Matthew, Luke reports the presence of a crowd when Jesus tells the parable of the sower (8:4). Then, Luke connects a series of public teachings in chs. 11–12. Beginning in 11:14, Jesus' rebukes the crowd that has just accused him of casting out demons by Beelzebul (shared with Matt 12:22). Following this are several references to Jesus teaching the crowd that are unique to Luke (11:27, 29; 12:1, 13, 54). Luke retains several traditions about Jesus teaching a crowd and adds several of his own in order to portray Jesus teaching publicly.

In chs. 12–18, Luke's emphasis changes. Instead of using the crowd alone to designate the public sphere,[113] Luke juxtaposes pericopes in his narrative to show that Jesus addressed audiences made of a variety of groups. This technique appears first in 10:25. Jesus has been speaking privately to his disciples after the return of the Seventy (see 10:17-22 and 23-24). Immediately after this a lawyer stands up and questions Jesus. Luke does not explain the scene and offers no transition, so the audience must conclude that the lawyer was present (with others?) during the preceding exchange with his disciples. Chapter 12 begins with references to the crowd (vv. 1 and 13), then Jesus addresses his disciples (v. 22), only to speak to the crowd again in v. 54. Peter's question in v. 41 implies a mixed

---

112. Recall that Luke considers the synagogue to be a public place.
113. Of the forty-one occurrences of ὄχλος in Luke, thirty-one appear before 13:1, only three between 13:1 and 18:34, and then seven from 18:35 to the end of the Gospel.

Luke's Emphasis on the Public Sphere and Local Politics in the Gospel as a Whole

audience: "Lord, are you telling this parable for us or for everyone?" Both the disciples and the crowds are present for Jesus' teaching. In 14:1–24, Jesus dines with the Pharisees. Then Luke then reintroduces the crowds who were traveling with Jesus in v. 25.[114] Jesus continues to speak to them about attachment to wealth (v. 33, as he did in 14:18–19) and the possibility of eternal loss (vv. 34–35, as he did in 14:24). The Pharisees and scribes surface again in 15:1–2. Thus, Luke sandwiches Jesus' public teaching to the crowds between two challenges to the Pharisaic perspective. Luke includes both the disciples and the Pharisees in Jesus' audience in ch. 16 (see vv. 1 and 14 respectively). The Pharisees' reaction in 16:14–15 demonstrates that they heard the teaching that Jesus had just directed at the disciples. Immediately after this in 17:1, Jesus speaks to the disciples again, now sandwiching the Pharisees between the disciples in a single, mixed audience. The disciples and Pharisees appear in the same audience again in 17:20 and 22. Finally, in ch. 18, Jesus speaks instructions about prayer (v. 1, probably to his disciples). Then he admonishes those who trusted in themselves (v. 9, probably his opponents). People appear bringing children to Jesus in v. 15. Then a young ruler approaches him in v. 18. Finally, Jesus shocks the entire audience in vv. 25–26. Prior to 19:11–28, Luke portrays Jesus teaching publicly by juxtaposing the disciples and the crowds (ch. 12), the Pharisees and the crowds (chs. 14–15), and the disciples and the Pharisees (chs. 16–18). In the final and summative teaching episode found in 19:11–28, Luke combines all three audiences (disciples, opponents, and crowds) in his last public parable before the passion narrative.

Much like Luke's Jesus, Philostratus portrays Apollonius addressing large audiences in a variety of public venues. At the very beginning of book 4 of the *Life*, Philostratus implies that all classes of citizens came to hear Apollonius, even the lowest craftsmen (οἱ βάνυσοι). Apollonius had a preference for speaking (and living) in temples. The pattern begins early in 4.2 where the sage addresses "the Ephesians from the platform of their temple." In 4.3, Philostratus sets Apollonius in a natural environment, a grove of trees (akin to a lakeside or plain), where he speaks "to the multitude" (πρὸς τοὺς πολλούς). Apollonius speaks to the people of Smyrna (4.5) and to supplicants in the temple of Asclepius in Pergamum (4.11). Apollonius is welcomed by students outside Athens and proceeds into the city where he bests the priest of the mysteries in a challenge-riposte exchange in the presence of a crowd of witnesses (οἱ παρόντες; see 4.18). Later in Athens, Apollonius rebukes a demon possessed man among those gathered in the temple (4.20), and he rebukes the Athenians as a whole in the theater for their behavior during the festival of Dionysius (4.21). Apollonius discoursed in Olympia from the platform of the temple (4.31). Climactically, Apollonius speaks in the temples of Rome, and people flocked from all over the city to hear his public teaching (4.41). Like Luke, Philostratus employed public places (temples, groves, cities, theatres) and varied audiences (craftsmen, citizens, worshippers, students) to portray Apollonius as a public teacher.[115]

---

114. There is no explicit change of scene (contra Green, *Luke*, 563), only the introduction of the crowd as part of the audience. The groups are juxtaposed in linked pericopes, and Luke does not alter the setting. This can be construed as one continuous scene.

115. A few examples of public speaking appear in Plutarch's *Precepts*: the orator's platform (798f), trials in the theatre (799f), speeches before the multitude (801e-f), and before the official assembly (803d-e).

PART THREE: IMPLICATIONS FOR LUKE'S GOSPEL AND OUR WORLD

Finally, Luke also presents Jesus employing public scenes *within* his public teaching, especially in the travel narrative. Jesus rebukes the Pharisees for public displays in 11:43 (par. Matt 25:6). In 12:8–12, Luke adduces a Q tradition in which Jesus exhorts his followers to acknowledge him openly (see Luke 12:8 and Matt 10:32). Luke specifies that their testimony will take place publicly (and politically) before synagogues, rulers, and authorities (Luke 12:11, compare Matt 10:18–19). In the Q material about those shut out from the house in Luke 13:25–26, only Luke has those outside protest that the owner knows them saying, "you taught in our streets" (ἐν ταῖς πλατείας ἡμῶν ἐδίδαξας), an image that reflects the public teaching of Jesus on roads in Luke. Jesus refers to the public activity of a slave who goes out into the streets of the city to bring guests into his master's house (14:21, see also Matt 22:9). After the shepherd finds the lost sheep in Luke, he does not remain in the field but returns home to rejoice with his friends and neighbors (15:6, not in Matthew's version). Similarly, the woman calls her friends and neighbors to rejoice with her (15:9, no parallel). Luke portrays two public scenes at the opening of ch. 18. The first is public legal battle of a widow pleading for justice before the local judge (18:1–8). Then we hear of two men, a tax collector and a Pharisee, going to the temple to join public prayers (18:9–14). In these instances, Jesus not only teaches publicly but does so employing a public scene in his teaching. The use of the public sphere *within* the teachings of Jesus in Luke reinforces Luke's emphasis on Jesus as a public pedagogue.

Local Politics in Jesus' Public Teaching

The parable of the king and his subjects is a story about a local/regional political official (the nobleman-king) told in the house of a local political official (Zacchaeus). Thus, it recalls Jesus' pedagogical interaction with other local officials in the Gospel and serves as an example of Jesus using local political characters and examples in his teaching.

The Pharisees are Jesus' most common opponents in the local political sphere. Luke intimates the local political status of the Pharisees when they come to Jesus with insider information about Herod's (Antipas) desire to kill him (13:31–32). While we are unsure of their motives or the source of their knowledge,[116] Luke portrays these Pharisees as leaders privy to the plans of Herod the tetrarch of Galilee (a client ruler of the Romans). As local political leaders, they have connections with the regional ruler and his circle. Jesus has several conflicts with the Pharisees in the early part of the Gospel where he confronts their objections to his words or actions (5:21–25, 30–39; 6:1–5, 6–11; 7:39–47).[117] Like 19:11–28, Jesus often uses parables (or less developed analogies) to rebuke his opponents (see 5:31–32, 34–35, 36–39; 7:41–43).[118] Jesus' confrontational pedagogy toward the Pharisees continues in the travel narrative (11:37–52; 14:7–24; 15:3–32; 16:14–31;

However, the material in Plutarch focuses on political activity and thus will appear in the next section on local politics.

116. I am inclined to see them as seeking to protect Jesus as is Fitzmyer (*Luke*, 2:1030)

117. Plutarch instructs Menemachus to cultivate the skill of sharp rejoinders to face local political conflicts (*Praec. ger. rei publ.* 803b–e).

118. As Plutarch says, political speech allows maxims (γνωμολογίαι), myths (μύθοι), and metaphors (μεταφουαί) more than legal discourse (*Praec. ger. rei publ.* 803a).

17:20–21; 18:9–14), where Jesus continues to employ parables to correct or rebuke his opponents (see 14:7–11, 12–14, 16–24; 15:3–7, 8–10, 11–32; 16:19–31; 19:9–14). When Luke tells of Jesus confronting the Pharisees, he casts Jesus as one who corrects and instructs members of the local political class.

Jesus does have a few positive encounters with figures in the local political sphere in Luke's Gospel. Jesus heals a centurion's servant and lauds his faith to those around him (7:1–10). Jesus is supported by a number of women, including Joanna, who is tied to the local political sphere by being the wife of Herod's steward. Jairus, a synagogue leader (ἄρχων τῆς συναγωγῆς), beseeches Jesus to come and heal his daughter; Jesus comes and does so (8:41–42, 49–56). Though another synagogue leader opposes Jesus (13:14–16). Finally, "a certain ruler" (τις αὐτὸν ἄρχων) approaches Jesus and asks about how to gain eternal life (18:18–27).[119] Jesus instructs the man about the commandments and calls him to discipleship. Thus, Luke portrays Jesus engaged in a variety of pedagogical activities (rebukes, parables, praise, instruction) when he encounters the officials in the local political sphere.

Finally, 19:11–28 is also a representative example of Jesus employing the local political sphere in his teachings. This begins in 4:23–28 when Jesus cites knowledge about his local activity in Capernaum and asserts that prophets are not well received in their own local context (vv. 23–24). Then Jesus cites relations between Israel and her political neighbors to underscore the local rejection of prophets (vv. 25–28). The centurion applies the power structure of local (military) politics to the authority of Jesus in 7:8, a perspective that Jesus endorses. Jesus cites a local patron's dealings with his clients to demonstrate the power of forgiveness in 7:41–43.[120] The priest and the Levite are two local leaders who appear in Jesus' parable of the good Samaritan. Then Jesus teaches about the Pharisees and their hypocrisy in 12:1–3. Luke uses the local political language of rulers (ἄρχων) and kingdoms (βασιλεία) to describe the spiritual world in 11:15–18. Kings and their military practices also appear as an analogy in 14:31–33. Jesus discusses Pilate's execution of several Galileans in 13:1–3, debating the significance of a local political event. Jesus insults Herod, calling him a fox, in 13:32, and he paints a negative picture of a local judge in 18:1–8. Thus, in Luke's Gospel Jesus employs local political topics in his public pedagogy: hometown rejection, Israel's regional politics, patron-client relationships, the structure of local political authority, and infamous local politicians. This reinforces Luke's portrayal of Jesus as one who engages the local political sphere.

In Luke 19:11–28, Jesus publicly speaks a parable to a mixed audience, a parable that employs the dynamics of local politics and a public scene to make its point. The public and local political nature of the setting and the parable are characteristic of Luke's Gospel as a whole. Throughout the Gospel Luke's audience finds Jesus speaking in public places instructing a multitude often comprised of a variety of groups (disciples, opponents, crowds). This concurs with Philostratus's portrayal of Apollonius as a public pedagogue, teaching

---

119. Luke's use of ἄρχων here and other places (11:15; 12:58; 14:1; 23:13; 24:20) reflects the language of the local political officials in Plutarch (*Praec. ger. rei publ.* 802f, 813c, 816f, 823e, etc.).

120. The patronal system depicted here (see Green, *Luke*, 311–12) was an integral part of Roman politics and the appointment of client kings (see Busse, "Dechiffrierung," 432–33).

PART THREE: IMPLICATIONS FOR LUKE'S GOSPEL AND OUR WORLD

a wide array of people in a variety of public places. The public nature of Jesus' teaching shines through *in* his teaching, for Luke has Jesus deploy a variety of public scenarios in his public pedagogy. The local political world of the parable comes through in similar ways. Jesus often corrects or instructs local political officials in Luke's Gospel. Finally, the structure and characters of local politics appear frequently in Jesus' public teaching. The public and local political qualities found in 19:11–28 are characteristic of Jesus teaching throughout Luke's Gospel.

The Literary Functions and Social-Spatial Implications of 19:29–48

After 19:28, Luke turns more strongly toward the passion narrative. Thus, while 19:29–48 does summarize the themes of acceptance and rejection in Luke's Gospel, the passage turns attention to the opposition that Jesus encounters in the passion. Similarly, while vv. 29–38 provide a climax to the development of Jesus' movement in the Gospel, vv. 39–48 set the stage for the fateful opposition from the official political sphere in the passion narrative.

A Microcosm of Previous Material: Acceptance and Rejection

Johnson has cast the story of Luke as a tale of those who accept and those who reject Jesus.[121] While the ultimate rejection of Jesus lies in the passion narrative, Luke's story of Jesus' entry culminates the dual theme of acceptance and rejection to this point in the Gospel. Johnson says of 19:37, "Luke has in the course of Jesus' ministry created the impression of growth, beginning in 8:1–3 with a small band of followers and ending here with a 'multitude of disciples.'"[122] His insight bears spinning out in more detail, for Luke portrays a gradual increase of those who accept Jesus, culminating in 19:29–38. Luke begins his portrayal of Jesus as a solo preacher with no disciples in 4:16ff. Afterwards, Jesus meets Simon (4:38–39) and calls the first three disciples to follow him (5:9–12). Next, Luke relates how Levi followed Jesus (5:27–28). This first round of disciple making culminates with the choosing of the twelve apostles from a larger group of disciples (6:12–16). The band of disciples is so large that Luke calls them a "great crowd" (ὄχλος πολύς) in 6:17. 8:1–3 gives us a small glimpse into the female members of Jesus' movement. The movement grows as Jesus sends out the twelve to extend his mission (9:1–6). Then Luke tells us of an additional seventy disciples (probably chosen out of a much larger group) who extend the scope (and size) of Jesus' mission even further. Luke does not note the increase of the movement during the travel narrative, leaving it to his audience to assume continuing growth. When Luke reaches the culmination of Jesus' movement at the entry into Jerusalem, the disciples have grown into a "multitude" (πλῆθος, 19:37).[123]

---

121. Johnson, *Literary Function*, 79–126.

122. Johnson, *Luke*, 297.

123. Luke uses πλῆθος to refer to a large group of unspecified number (e.g., Luke 1:10; 23:27). He refers to a "multitude of disciples" in Acts as well (4:32; 6:2). The use of πλῆθος at this late point in the Gospel could be parallel to the statement about "myriads" (μυριάδες) of believers among the Jews in Acts 21:20.

Luke's Emphasis on the Public Sphere and Local Politics in the Gospel as a Whole

The third Gospel is also full of episodes of rejection that Luke recalls in his account of Jesus' entry. Simeon indicates the coming conflict already in 2:34, stating that the child of Mary will be "a sign that will be opposed." Early in his ministry, Jesus encounters hostility primarily from the Pharisees: they scorn his claim to forgive as blasphemy (5:21), they complain about his eating company (5:30), and they object to his Sabbath practices (6:1-2, 6-10). This series of conflicts ends with Luke's comment that "they were filled with anger and discussed with one another what they might do to Jesus" (6:11). They continue to oppose him as evidenced in the meal scenes in Luke's Gospel (7:36-50; 11:37-54; 14:1-24). In 10:25 and 17:20, they question him, presumably to catch him in an error (cf. 11:53-54).[124] Luke says it best in the aside of 7:29-30: the Pharisees rejected John's baptism, they rejected God's purpose, and so they also reject Jesus. Luke is the only synoptic evangelist who mentions the hostility of the Pharisees as Jesus enters Jerusalem.[125] The Pharisees have repeatedly objected to Jesus' claims to authority (especially in chs. 5-6) and his teaching (especially in the travel narrative). The appearance of the Pharisees in 19:39 recalls their previous rejection of Jesus in the Gospel.

In 19:37-40, Luke contrasts the contentious Pharisees who rebuke Jesus with the joyful disciples who acclaim him king.[126] Some commentators suggest that the Pharisees' rebuke arises from political concerns.[127] However, 19:39 probably brings together the Pharisees recurring concern about Jesus' authority and religious practices. The Pharisees address Jesus as "Teacher" reflecting their assessment of his status as equal to their own local authority, and they take exception to the status that his disciples attribute to him with the title of "king." By accepting the acclamation of king, Jesus oversteps the bounds of a teacher and comes blasphemously close to claiming the royal authority of Davidic (and perhaps messianic) traditions. Thus, this final rebuke of the Pharisees recapitulates their primarily unofficial interaction with Jesus as a fellow "teacher" and presents them continuing to reject publicly his religiously outrageous actions and claims to authority.[128] Their appearance here concludes their role in the Gospel, but it is the first step toward a new level of conflict that will appear soon.

---

124. The Pharisees are not the only people who oppose Jesus. Some Samaritans turn him aside (9:53) and a synagogue leaders objects to him healing on the Sabbath (13:14).

125. Neither Mark nor Matthew have a parallel to Luke 19:39 where the Pharisees say, "Teacher, rebuke your disciples." John records the (ironic) exasperation of the Pharisees who say "Look the whole world has gone after him!" when Jesus enters Jerusalem (12:19).

126. Fitzmyer, *Luke*, 2:1251. Speckman, "Kairos," 200.

127. Marshall, *Luke*, 716; and Danker, *Jesus*, 313.

128. Nolland notes that this final appearance of the Pharisees "encapsulate[s] all that has gone before," but he does not develop this insight (*Luke*, 927).

PART THREE: IMPLICATIONS FOR LUKE'S GOSPEL AND OUR WORLD

Preparation for the Passion: Places and Opposition in 19:39–48

Hostility against Jesus as he approaches Jerusalem begins with the complaint of the Pharisees in v. 39. After Jesus responds to them (v. 40), he utters his lament for the city of Jerusalem (vv. 41–44). Jerusalem has not recognized the significance of Jesus' arrival; it has been hidden from her eyes.[129] At the sight of the city, Jesus ominously predicts his rejection and the resulting destruction of the city. This prediction anticipates the fall of Jerusalem as described in 21:20–33 and the centrality of Jerusalem near the end of the Gospel (23:7; 28; 24:18, 33, 47, 52). The cleansing of the temple follows in vv. 45–46 and sets the stage for chs. 20–21 where Jesus is constantly in the temple teaching (see 19:47 and 21:37). Jesus' cleansing of the temple also results in new opponents and a new level of opposition as "the chief priests, the scribes, and the leaders of the people" plan to murder Jesus (19:47).

The chief priests have not been mentioned since the passion prediction in 9:22, but they will be Jesus' antagonists throughout the passion (20:1, 19; 22:2, 4, 52, 66; 23:4, 10, 13).[130] The scribes appeared alongside the Pharisees in Jesus' early conflicts (5:21, 30; 6:7) and later in the travel narrative (11:53; 15:2). Luke does not provide a description of this group, but they connect the Pharisees (who have primarily opposed Jesus to this point) and the chief priests (who will primarily oppose Jesus from this point on). In the passion, they appear with the chief priests on several occasions (20:1, 19; 22:2, 66; 23:10) and on their own in 20:39 and 46. The last group mentioned in v. 47 is οἱ πρῶτοι τοῦ λαοῦ, a general term that Luke uses for unspecified leaders of groups or areas (Acts 13:50, 17:4, 25:2). Later in the passion, the third term in the list "chief priests, scribes, and . . ." will be πρεσβύτεροι (20:1, 22:66) or ἄρχοντες (23:13). These terms broadly include other official leaders in the city not captured by the first two categories. This climactic level of rejection does not emerge until Jesus comes to Jerusalem and enters the climactic space of the temple.

The Social-Spatial Implications of 19:29–48 for the Gospel as a Whole

As the social-spatial exegesis demonstrated in chapter 8, 19:29–38 focuses on Jesus and his disciples while 19:39–48 focuses on Jesus in relation to increasingly hostile Jewish leaders. The social-spatial implications of this passage reflect these two sections with more emphasis falling on the latter. First, Jesus' interaction with his disciples in vv. 29–38 climaxes the development of his movement in Luke's Gospel. Second, the interaction with old and new opponents in vv. 39–48 points to the increasing role of the official public sphere in the passion.

---

129. Thus, Jesus' arrival is *not* a fulfillment of 13:35, for the people of Jerusalem (represented by its leaders) do not welcome Jesus as the "one who comes in the name of the Lord," and therefore they do not "see" Jesus (he is hidden from their eyes).

130. Johnson, *Luke*, 300.

Jesus Develops His Movement of Disciples

Jesus and his disciples are the main characters in 19:29–38.[131] In this section, Jesus treats the disciples as his delegates, and the disciples treat Jesus as their authoritative leader. Jesus sends two disciples to fetch a colt for him with language reminiscent of the commissioning of the twelve and the seventy.[132] This reflects the development of Jesus' movement in Luke. Not just growth in numbers, but a development where Jesus trains the disciples and entrusts them with increasing authority. The disciples act as representatives of Jesus' movement early in the Gospel, for the Pharisees question Jesus about his disciples' behavior (5:33; 6:1–2). The selection of the twelve as leaders within Jesus' movement occurs in 6:12–16. Then, they observe Jesus teaching and healing for three and a half chapters before he sends them out on their first mission in 9:1–6. Thus, Jesus models what it means to "proclaim the kingdom of God and heal" before the twelve are expected to do the same (9:2). Later, a father comes to the disciples, expecting them to be able to heal as Jesus' representatives (9:40). Jesus' movement expands in the course of ch. 9, a fact underscored by all of the material devoted to discipleship (vv. 14, 23–27, 43, 46–48, 49–50, 57–62). After this growth, a larger group of seventy is sent out not to proclaim and heal but to prepare the people for Jesus' arrival (see 10:1).[133] Throughout the travel narrative, Jesus continues to teach them about the nature of discipleship (11:1–13; 12:1–12, 35–48; 16:1–13; 17:1–10; 18:1–8). Thus, Jesus gradually develops leaders and representatives within his movement of disciples from ch. 5 to ch. 18.

When we come to the parable of the king and his subjects, we see Jesus admonishing his disciples to employ the resources that he has entrusted to them wisely, for this will result in them receiving greater authority. Later in the passion narrative, Jesus' does bestow kingdom authority on them (22:28–30), and this authority partially comes to fruition in Acts (e.g., 1:12–26; 5:1–11; 15:1–21).[134] The disciples are far from perfect (cf. 18:15–17, 34), but they do recognize Jesus for who he is (5:8; 9:20) and climactically proclaim him as king when he approaches Jerusalem (19:38). Therefore, by focusing on the relationship of Jesus and his disciples in 19:29–38, Luke sums up the role of Jesus' disciples as delegates under his authority. Jesus has gathered a multitude of disciples. He trains them and employs them as an organized leader. They accord him obedience and honor, receive authority from him, and exercise that authority (or at least try to) in his absence.

---

131. The role of the disciples stands out, in part, because the "disciples" have not appeared since 18:15 with the possible exception of the "twelve" at 18:31.

132. Jesus sends (ἀποστέλλω) the two on their mission in v. 29. Similarly, Jesus "sent" the twelve in 9:2 to preach and heal. He "sends" messengers ahead in 9:52. He also "sends" the seventy ahead of him to the cities that he will visit (10:1, 3). To reinforce this connection, Luke reiterates that "those who were sent" (οἱ ἀπεσταλμένοι) found the colt just as Jesus said (v. 32). Jesus' command to "go" (ὑπάγετε) in v. 30 echoes the same command issued to the seventy in 10:3.

133. It could be said that they preach about the kingdom (10:9, 11), but such instructions are missing from Luke's introduction and the beginning of Jesus' statements in ch. 10.

134. Johnson traces this growing authority as well, starting with the parable of the king ("Kingship Parable," 157–58).

PART THREE: IMPLICATIONS FOR LUKE'S GOSPEL AND OUR WORLD

The Increase of the Official Public Sphere

Chapter 5 asserted that he healing of the blind man in Luke 18:35–43 has no official elements: no politicians, no laws, and no official bodies. The healing occurs in the *unofficial* public sphere. The description of Zacchaeus begins a subtle increase of the role of the official public sphere. Zacchaeus stood on the boundaries of the unofficial and official spheres. His title ἀρχιτελώνης incorporates the ἀρχ- stem that often refers to official leaders in Luke (e.g., 18:18), and his occupation would have put him into regular contact with local Jewish and Roman officials, though he himself was not a political official. The political sphere is at the heart of the story of the king and his subjects. The story of the nobleman-become-king displays the internal politics of a king's court but also alludes to the power of the Romans, who appointed such client rulers. The presence of the official public sphere grows even more in 19:29–48, and comes to full expression in the passion narrative. In his retelling of Jesus' entry, Luke moves from the local and more unofficial opposition of the Pharisees (19:39) to the official opposition of the chief priests, scribes and leaders (19:47–48), to Roman officials who have the power to execute Jesus (23:1). Thus, Jesus sums up previous elements of the official public sphere and prepares the audience for the role of Jewish and Roman officials in the passion.

A variety of political (and religious) officials, even emperors, appear at a limited number of critical junctures before 18:35 in Luke' Gospel, setting a political tone for the Gospel. Events recorded in the infancy narrative are temporally located by citing the reigning officials of the time. The birth of Jesus occurs in the days of the emperor Augustus and Quirinius the governor of Syria (2:1–2). The dating of the beginning of John's ministry in 3:1–2 is more extensive. These two verses identify four levels of political leadership. The first is the emperor Tiberius, then Pilate (the governor or procurator), next come the tetrarchs Herod Antipas, Philip, and Lysanius, and finally the high priests Annas and Caiaphas. Here Luke differentiates levels of political authority and ranks them hierarchically from highest to lowest. Luke also includes the high priests in this political hierarchy.[135] Luke groups these religious-political officials together with Roman figures, and they represent the most local level of officials listed here. In most of the Gospel, Jesus will interact with officials so far down the political hierarchy that they are not even mentioned in 3:1–2: Pharisees and scribes (5:17, 30, etc.), a centurion (7:1–10), some prominent women (8:3), synagogue leaders (8:41; 13:14), and an unnamed "ruler" (18:18). John encounters trouble with Herod (3:19), and Jesus is the subject of his attention (9:7–9; 13:31–32). However,

---

135. This is partially contra Bachmann, *Jerusalem*, 259–60. Bachmann divides the persons named in Luke 3:1–2 into "Politisches" (Tiberius, Pilate, Herod, Philip, and Lysanias) and "Nichtpolitisches" (Annas and Caiaphas) (see p. ix). To justify this he cites the altered grammatical construction at the identification of Annas and Caiaphas and the absence of a geographical area in 3:2a. However, the office of high priest has no natural geographical association (unlike tetrarch) and Bachmann himself notes the use of the same grammatical construction (ἐπὶ ἀρχιερέως . . .) in 1 Macc 13:42 and 14:27 in a political context. In Luke 3:1–2 and other places (e.g., 13:31; 23:1), Luke associates the Sanhedrin with political officials. Thus, the chief priests are both religious and political figures in Luke's work.

Jesus does not have any direct dealings with any of the political officials mentioned in 3:1–2 until the chief priests appear in 19:47, looking for a way to kill him.[136]

Before proceeding, we must set the parameters of the term "official."[137] This adjective refers to persons, positions, and policies associated with elected, appointed, or conquering authorities or governments. Persons who are part of the Roman administration fall into this category: emperors, senators, governors, tetrarchs, and military leaders. After this, however, the waters become murkier. I will use this term broadly, drawing on precedents in Luke-Acts. As was mentioned above, Luke associates the high priests with Roman officials, opening a window into Luke's view of who counts as an "official." For Luke, and thus also probably for his audience, the high priest is the head of the Sanhedrin and closely linked to his associates in the "sect of the Sadducees" (see Acts 5:17, 21, 27). Both Luke and Josephus support the view that the "chief priests were the traditional Jewish aristocracy, who had supreme control of national affairs from their base in Jerusalem.... They typically ruled by means of a council or senate [the Sanhedrin for Luke] headed by the serving High Priest."[138] For Luke, the chief priests are indistinguishable from the Sadducees (Acts 5:17): they are aristocrats based spatially in the temple who hold religious and political offices, with the highest office being filled by the chief priest. The Sadducees are the controlling members of the Sanhedrin, the official council of Jewish leaders (similar to a βουλή) that wielded political, judicial, ritual, and economic power in Judea.[139] They are both religious and political officials in Luke's narrative.[140] The Sanhedrin also includes rulers, elders, scribes (Acts 4:5), and the Pharisees (Acts 5:34, 23:6; see further below). Additionally, Luke recounts that the Sanhedrin had its own body of police and captains to enforce its orders (Luke 22:52; Acts 5:22, 26). While not every Sadducee or Pharisee was a member of the Sanhedrin, Luke makes it clear that these groups made up a substantive part of the highest

---

136. The chief priests are mentioned once earlier in the Gospel when Jesus predicts their hostility in 9:22.

137. Bachmann (*Jerusalem*, 172) also uses the language of "official" ("amtliche"), but he offers no explanation or justification for it and applies it only to official relationships to the temple.

138. Mason, "Chief Priests," 175

139. Saldarini, "Sanhedrin," *ABD* 5:977.

140. Bachmann's discussion of the Sanhedrin is in tension with this statement. Bachman argues against Conzelmann's description of the Pharisees as the "town council" ("Stadtrat") of Jerusalem. Bachmann returns to his thesis that Luke closely associates both Jerusalem and the Sanhedrin with the temple, which stands at the center of the Jewish world for Luke. Therefore, just as the temple has significance for all Jews (especially those in Judea), so the Sanhedrin has authority beyond the city of Jerusalem. Furthermore, just as the Sanhedrin is primarily a religious body, so its authority is primarily religious and not political according to Luke (*Jerusalem*, 216–18). Then Bachmann argues that ἄρχοντες in Luke 24:20 and Acts 3:17; 4:5; and 13:27 does not refer to political officials (*Jerusalem*, 220–27), rather these "leaders" are more closely associated with the religious significance of Abraham's descendants in "the land" (*Jerusalem*, 234–55). Bachmann does not claim that the Sanhedrin is a-political, but that Luke simply is not interested in its political functions (*Jerusalem*, 257). While Bachmann rightly objects to Conzelmann's limited view, he goes too far in claiming that the political functions of the Sanhedrin are unimportant to Luke. This is partially due to his selective focus on the role of the ἄρχοντες. My discussion will focus on the political actions taken by the chief priests and the Sanhedrin in the passion narrative and the beginning of Acts, which are critical to Luke's storyline. The Sanhedrin and the chief priests are religious *and* political officials, and Luke attends to both functions without letting one obscure the other.

PART THREE: IMPLICATIONS FOR LUKE'S GOSPEL AND OUR WORLD

official ruling body that exercised political and religious power over the Jewish people (which, of course, was ultimately subject to the Romans). Thus, any chief priest, Sadducee, Pharisee, scribe, or elder had ties to this authoritative body and can have the label "official" applied to them. Therefore, officials in Luke-Acts may be associated with the Romans (e.g., Herod, procurators, military officers) or with various regional or ethnic authorities (e.g., Sadducees, magistrates, Sergius Paulus). The presence of Pharisees, scribes, rulers, elders, police, chief priests, Sadducees, governors, tetrarchs, or their representatives (like police or military officers) brings the official public sphere into play in Luke's narrative through the force of social relations.

These parameters require two qualifications. First, various levels of politics operated in the ancient world, from the local to the imperial. The social-spatial framework of this study incorporates an awareness of these levels. Second, the presence of an "official" does not make an event completely "official" in nature. The Pharisees are an interesting example.[141] Throughout Luke's Gospel, they appear as locally known teachers with great influence among the people (not primarily as political officials).[142] This portrayal comports with their description in Josephus.[143] Luke and the audience(s) familiar with Acts know that the Pharisees are connected to a "party" that comprises part of the Sanhedrin (the highest official body among Jews). However, in the Gospel they act as local religious teachers invested with honor by the populace.[144] The presence of the Pharisees, for example, at the house where the paralyzed man is healed (Luke 5:17–19) adds official overtones to an otherwise "unofficial" setting. However, they do not act like officials who decree judgments in the Sanhedrin but as local, respected religious leaders. They disapprove of Jesus' statements, but they are bested by him in this public encounter. This event is largely unofficial with minor overtones of the official public sphere because of the Pharisees' political connections found in Acts. Thus, even the label "official" should be considered on a spectrum from public events with only the slightest hint of the official public sphere to public events that are fully official in nature.

---

141. Gowler points out that the Pharisees as a character group are given a rather complex portrayal in Luke-Acts. He states that they should not be lumped together with Jewish leaders as a whole. He says, "The separation is not complete, but it is crucial" (*Host,* 311).

142. Mason, "Chief Priests," 134.

143. Josephus portrays the Pharisees as leaders in moral, ritual, and theological matters. He says that they earned a strong following among the people, so much so that it spilled over into political influence (*Ant.* 18.15). The Sadducees, on the other hand, are explicitly said to be leaders (ἀρχή), but they must often bend to the notions of the Pharisees because of the latter's popularity. The actual historical reality of these groups and their political and religious influence is debated, but the majority opinion sees Josephus's comments here as much overstated. See Neale, *None,* 20–27. However, again, this study focuses on the portrayal of these groups and their official nature in Luke's narrative rather than the historical reality of Jesus' day.

144. Gowler comments on the continuities and discontinuities of the portrayal of the Pharisees across Luke and Acts. This would be one of the discontinuities, though Gowler does not attend to the "official" role of the Pharisees (Gowler, *Host,* 301–5). At the same time, Gowler states that it is necessary to balance a sequential reading of the text with a reading of the text as a whole, which can lead to reevaluations of previous passages (Gowler, *Host,* 239–40). After reading/hearing Acts, an audience would know of the official connections of the Pharisees when rereading/hearing passages from the Gospel.

Luke's Emphasis on the Public Sphere and Local Politics in the Gospel as a Whole

The Pharisees reappear in 19:39 to oppose Jesus after being absent from the narrative since 17:20.[145] Their presence adds a degree of official opposition to Jesus. After Jesus laments the tragedy of his rejection (19:41–44), Luke increases the level of officials in 19:47 by introducing the "chief priests, scribes, and leaders." These Jewish officials play an increasingly important role in the narrative, which Luke indicates already by stating that they "were looking for a way to kill him" (19:48). At this point in the narrative, the chief priests take over (from the Pharisees) as Jesus' primary opponents and they are often accompanied by other leaders (scribes, leaders, elders). With the introduction of the "chief priests, scribes, and leaders" in 19:47, it appears that the Sanhedrin (or the most influential part of it, compare Acts 4:5–6) has decided to oppose Jesus, planning to kill him. Jesus has now become the object of the direct attention of a regional official body in Luke's Gospel, raising the official valence of the social-spatial setting to a higher degree.

19:47–48 prepares the audience for the intersection of the unofficial and official spheres in the following chapters, for it mentions both the opposition of the Jewish leaders and the adoration of the people. The intersections begin in 20:1 where Jesus is "teaching the people in the temple," a description which keeps the scene primarily in the unofficial public sphere. However, in this setting, "the chief priests, scribes, and elders" come to question Jesus, introducing official elements into the setting. Similar overlapping occurs in 20:19, where Jesus has been teaching the people (so v. 9), but the parable he tells is perceived by the officials to be directed against them. The future actions of the Roman political leaders appears in 20:20 where some "spies" are sent (by the Jewish leaders) to trap Jesus in a politically incorrect statement for which they could then hand him over to the "jurisdiction and authority of the governor" (τῇ ἀρχῇ καὶ τῇ ἐξουσίᾳ τοῦ ἡγεμόνος). The Jewish leaders attempt to entangle Jesus in even higher levels of the official public sphere, Roman rule in Judea. However, Luke says that "they were not able to trap him *in the presence of the people*" (20:26, emphasis added, pointing out the unofficial public sphere). As the official stakes rise to the level of Roman officials, Luke continues to intersect official and unofficial groups. The chief priests and scribes continue to plot in Luke's narrative (20:27; 22:1–2), but they are temporarily frustrated by the presence of the adoring people (the unofficial public) that continues to come out in droves to hear Jesus.

At this point, Judas enters the story and agrees to hand Jesus over quietly to the Jewish authorities (22:3–6). At the scene of the arrest, Luke says that an unspecified ὄχλος comes to find Jesus on the Mount of Olives (22:47), and just a few verses later the content of this crowd is specified as "the chief priests, the officers of the temple police, and the elders" (22:52). A body of Jewish officials and their police force arrive to take Jesus into official custody. In chs. 20–21, the unofficial public ("the people") predominated over the incursions of the official public sphere ("the chief priests and scribes") and protected Jesus, but after Jesus' arrest, the balance of power, and the primary sphere of influence changes. In 22:66—23:25, official bodies dominate the people. Jesus now stands in the presence of the Sanhedrin, Pilate, or Herod, instead of in front of the people. Jesus is officially tried by the Sanhedrin, Pilate, Herod, and then sent back to Pilate. After the final trial, Pilate calls

---

145. They are mentioned by Jesus in the story about the Pharisee and the "tax" collector who went to the temple to pray in 18:10f. The Pharisees appear regularly in Luke's Gospel in chs. 5–7 and then in chs. 11–17.

an official public gathering of the Jewish leaders and people (23:13), where the people are swayed by the Jewish officials. The scene in 23:13–25 is the climax of Jesus' personal encounter with the official public sphere. Pilate (a Roman governor) decides his fate and sets the stage for the conclusion of the Gospel. The social-spatial development at the end of Luke's Gospel illustrates the range that stretches from the unofficial public sphere into the official elements that characterize the political sphere from the local to the imperial. What began as subtle hints of the official public sphere in Zacchaeus and the nobleman-king, developed further with the addition of the Pharisees, reached a new official level as the chief priests became actively involved, rose one more degree in Jesus' trials before Pilate and Herod, finally climaxed with this fully official and public scene, which concludes with a sentence of crucifixion.

The literary analysis demonstrated how 19:29–48 serves as a microcosm of previous material regarding those who accept and reject Jesus in Luke's Gospel. Those who accept him have now become a "multitude" that acclaims Jesus as king for the miracles that they have witnessed (v. 38). The disciples are given an important task by Jesus, reflecting their preparation for leadership. In 19:39–48, Luke prepares his audience for the passion narrative by increasing the level of official opposition from the Pharisees to the chief priests. A steady increase of the presence and power of the political sphere started with Jesus' entry into Jericho (with Zacchaeus), forms the basis of the parable, reappears with the Pharisees, steps up at entry into Jerusalem (with the chief priests), and culminates with Jesus' trials and sentence (by Roman officials). Jesus primarily intersects the local political sphere in most of the Gospel, but after his actions in the temple, the regional Jewish authorities successfully conspire to hand him over to imperial agents.

Conclusion

Let us summarize the main points of this chapter. The story of the healing of the blind beggar in 18:35—19:48 is the final miracle story of the Gospel, summing up both healings and exorcisms and climaxing with the healing of the blind as predicted in 4:18. It also prepares the audience for the passion narrative by setting up an illuminating comparison between Jesus' entries into Jericho and Jerusalem, illustrating Jesus' miracles, and reintroducing Jesus' Davidic significance. The location, characters, and crowd contribute to the public nature of the healing of the blind beggar and they recur in most of Luke's miracle stories, marking them as public events. Then, Jesus' interaction with οἱ προάγοντες creates some local political implications that repeatedly turn up in Jesus' interactions with his disciples in other miracle accounts.

The content and setting of Jesus' encounter with Zacchaeus climaxes previous scenes of conflict and salvation in the Gospel, and prepares the audience for the passion by introducing a Roman presence and setting up a contrast/comparison between Zacchaeus's house and the temple as God's "house." The interrelation of the city of Jericho and Zacchaeus's house indicates Luke's preference for the public space of the city and his transformation of homes into public venues for Jesus throughout the Gospel. The parable of the king and his subjects brings together the three audiences that Jesus speaks to in most of the Gospel (crowd, opponents, and disciples) and prepares for their appearance in the passion. Similarly, it recalls Jesus' teaching with a parable and prepares for the use of parables in the passion. This parable also summarizes Jesus' previous eschatological teaching and sets a political tone for the events of the passion. This passage is an excellent example of how Luke characterized Jesus' public pedagogy, and the local political flavor of the parable reflects Jesus' interaction with and use of local politics in his teaching.

Finally, Luke's account of the triumphal entry looks back over the story of acceptance and rejection, but even more so it prepares for the places and the opposition that come to the fore in the passion. The beginning of this passage represents the way that Jesus acts as a local leader in Luke, training the disciples and entrusting them with authority. Lastly, the end of the entry story signals the increase (in both degree and scale) of the political sphere in the passion narrative. Therefore, the emphasis on the public sphere and local politics that was brought to light in the exegesis of 18:35—19:48 is representative of Luke's Gospel as whole.

10

A Public and Political Christ

Contributions and Implications

Introduction

THIS STUDY OF LUKE'S GOSPEL BEGAN BY DEMONSTRATING THE NEED FOR A SOCIAL-spatial analysis of Luke 18:35—19:48. The development (and gaps) of NT scholarship on Luke and the introduction of spatial theory opened the way for a fresh examination of this unit in Luke's Gospel and for a new look at Luke's social-spatial characteristics. A broad survey of the ancient world in chapter 3 revealed the existence of a social-spatial spectrum and described new categories (e.g., the unofficial public sphere and local politics) relevant to Luke's Gospel. Chapter 4 examined socially and spatially appropriate comparative materials to set alongside Luke: Plutarch's *Precepts* and book 4 of the *Life of Apollonius*. The following four chapters engaged in careful social-spatial exegesis of the pericopes found in 18:35—19:48, demonstrating Luke's emphasis on the unofficial public sphere and local politics in each passage. The preceding chapter extrapolated from the representative literary functions and social-spatial characteristics of the material in 18:35—19:48 to show that the emphasis on the public sphere and local politics characterizes Luke's Gospel as a whole.

This final chapter will review the main contributions of this study and sketch a number of historical and contemporary implications. The first section addresses contributions to the exegesis of 18:35—19:48, the classification of ancient social-spatial zones, the nature and selection of comparative materials, and the history of NT scholarship especially with regard to Lukan studies and social-scientific analysis. Next, several historical and contemporary implications follow from Luke's emphasis on the public sphere and local politics. The social-spatial characteristics of Luke's Gospel have ramifications for our construction of the author of the third Gospel and the membership, structure, and location of his audience(s). Looking at some broader social-spatial trends and traditions of the ancient world reveals with greater sharpness Luke's response to his cultural milieu from a Christian (and sectarian) perspective. Finally, Luke's distinctive social-spatial characteristics within his milieu have implications for Christian thought, praxis, and spatiality today.

The Contributions of This Study
To the Exegesis of Luke 18:35—19:48

The social-spatial perspective of this study contributed several new insights to the exegesis of Luke 18:35–19:48. With regard to the healing of the blind beggar, the analysis demonstrated that Luke places the beggar in a culturally appropriate and public location: on a road near an entrance to a city. Luke sets up Jesus' entrance into Jericho in ways that bear illuminating parallels with his entrance into Jerusalem. The role of the crowd at the healing (and the entry) and the interchange of the terms ὄχλος (v. 35) and λαός (v. 43) establish a pattern of a fickle crowd that first adores and then turns on Jesus in the passion narrative. Finally, the προάγοντες are leaders within Jesus' movement of disciples who fail to "lead" (ἄγω) the blind man to Jesus. As Jesus enters Jericho, he encounters Zacchaeus. The investigation of Zacchaeus's status revealed that Luke's (possibly Ephesian) audience probably would have viewed this ἀρχιτελώνης as a regional representative of the despised *societas publicanorum* that still bought the rights to collect tolls and customs in the first century. The spatial focus of this study revealed that Jesus entered Zacchaeus's home through the rituals of hospitality and there publicly resolved the conflict raised among the crowd by pronouncing salvation for Zacchaeus through the rhetorical technique of *insinuatio*.

A detailed examination of the grammar and context of 19:11 showed that Jesus continued to speak in Zacchaeus's home, now using a parable to refocus the eschatological expectations of his audience. In this climactic case, Jesus addresses his disciples, his opponents, and the crowd who gathered to hear this final teaching before Jesus entered Jerusalem. The social-spatial analysis clarified the meaning of several points of the parable of the king and his subjects. First, the preliminary announcement of the nobleman's coronation must have occurred before his departure. This fits the preliminary proclamation of Jesus as "king" in 19:38 before his full accession after the ascension. Second, while a long delay is not critical to the parable, *absence* is; therefore, Luke can use the parable to exhort his audience to faithful obedience during Jesus' absence without positing a long interval before his return. This study illuminated the public nature of the king's audience in vv. 15–27 and claimed that the third servant embodies the crowd that has heard Jesus' teaching but ultimately does nothing when Jesus enters Jerusalem, neither joining in the disciples' praise nor the Pharisees' objections. The analysis of the entry into Jerusalem claimed that this pericope falls into two primary sections: Jesus in relation to his disciples (19:29–38) and Jesus in relation to his opponents (19:39–48). Luke specifically describes Jesus' approach to the city in vv. 29–37, indicating that Luke envisioned Jesus coming down the Mount of Olives and entering the temple (and city) directly by an eastern gate. Finally, Jesus' entry is largely part of the unofficial public sphere focusing on his disciples and his unofficial opponents, the Pharisees. Jesus does not encounter official resistance until after restoring the temple in order to teach there. Thus, most of the previous analogies for Jesus' entry (Solomon's coronation, Maccabean entries, governor's assizes, and Roman triumphs) are inappropriate comparisons on two counts: they are far too large in scale and they are fully official. Apollonius's entrance into Athens makes a much better comparison and illuminates the role of the disciples and the priestly hostility in Luke.

PART THREE: IMPLICATIONS FOR LUKE'S GOSPEL AND OUR WORLD

Finally, chapter 9 argued that each of these pericopes has a representative function, serving both as a microcosm of previous related material and as a preparation for the passion. The healing of the blind beggar points to the public nature of miracles throughout Luke as indicated by the locations, characters, and crowds. Jesus' encounter with Zacchaeus in both city and house embodies Luke's preference for urban settings and his transformation of homes into public spaces through hospitality. The parable of the king and his subjects exhibits Luke's habit of making Jesus' teaching public in both setting and content. Last, the entry into Jerusalem recalls Jesus authorizing his disciples as representatives of his movement and establishes the steady increase of the official public sphere that will climax with the trial and crucifixion. Chapter 9 proved that Luke emphasizes the unofficial public sphere and local politics in 18:35—19:48 and in the Gospel as a whole. Thus, Jesus is a public and political Christ in Luke's Gospel.

To the Classification of Ancient Social-Spatial Spheres

Chapter 2 developed a theoretical framework for this study, focusing on the work of Sack with insights from Soja and Hall. This framework emphasized that space draws together the forces of nature, social relations, culture, and the self to help contribute to a thick understanding of the role of place in Luke's portrayal of Jesus. This framework and recent developments in social and spatial studies indicated that the often-cited public/private dichotomy needed to be dismantled in favor of a public-private spectrum, which can attend more carefully to the nuances and varieties of culturally constructed places. From this theoretical perspective, this study engaged in a broad survey of the ancient world with some focus on classical Athens, turn of the era Rome, and Jerusalem while examining a variety of literary genres (epic, philosophy, history, drama, orations, and others). The survey closed with a detailed investigation of archaeological remains from Pompeii, Palestine, and Ephesus. All this was supported by some of the best and most recent studies of society and space in the ancient world (Cohen, Wallace-Hadrill, Wiltshire). This broad and inclusive survey affirmed that ancient social-spatial zones must be treated as a spectrum stretching from the most private of household kinship settings to the most public scale of imperial politics. A classification chart portrayed this spectrum and offered more precise categories, especially the classifications of the unofficial public sphere and the local political sphere. The fluid nature of the spectrum called for better definitions of each of the categories and greater clarity about terms such as public and private or official and unofficial. Throughout this analysis, Sack's framework served as both a useful heuristic tool and a helpful organizing guide. The classifications employed in this study and Sack's theoretical framework offer new possibilities for the social-spatial examination of other parts of the NT.

To the Selection of Comparative Material

The identification of more precise categories for the classification of space in the ancient world raised critical issues for the selection of comparative materials. First, one must consider scale. While Luke does have a Mediterranean and imperial horizon in his work, most of Luke (and Acts) falls on a much smaller scale, dealing with local matters of little importance to the empire as a whole. Second, one must consider the official or unofficial nature of ancient writings. The public sphere is not coterminous with politics (even in the ancient world), and works focused on the official public sphere are poor comparisons to Luke. The writings of Josephus have frequently and fruitfully been compared with Luke-Acts.[1] Josephus does deal with many local events in Palestine, but his perspective is primarily imperial, writing from Rome under imperial patronage. More importantly, most of his works are decidedly official in nature, dealing primarily with military and political matters, making them less apt comparisons with Luke. Similarly, Luke has often been compared with Mark and Matthew. This study highlighted how Luke's emphasis on the public sphere shaped his redaction of the Synoptic tradition, an insight that bears further investigation.

This study suggested Plutarch's *Precepts* and Philostratus's *Life* as appropriate (non-canonical) analogs for the third Gospel's social-spatial character. Plutarch focuses on the domain of the city (also favored by Luke), and while his "precepts" are political, they are also local, offering good comparisons for the local political material in Luke-Acts. Comparisons with the *Precepts* illuminated the nature of the ancient city, Jesus as a leader in his own movement, the dynamics of public speech, and Jesus in relation to (and often in conflict with) other local leaders. Book 4 of the *Life* emphasizes the unofficial public sphere in the cities of the middle to western Mediterranean world, an area known well by Luke. Comparing Luke's writing to Philostratus's portrayal of Apollonius casts light on Jesus' public teaching and healing, the variety of public locations, the place of religion in the public sphere, and the role of crowds, disciples, and opponents. These works hold more comparative insights for Luke-Acts, and scholars should search for further comparative material that fits the local and unofficial nature of Luke's Gospel.

To the History of Interpretation

This study dialogues with various levels of the history of interpretation: specific studies on place and politics in Luke-Acts, broader topics in Lukan studies, and the enterprise of social-scientific exegesis. Neyrey's articles on the spatial analysis of John, Matthew, and especially Luke-Acts were an indispensable precursor to this study. Nevertheless, the survey of ancient material and the exegesis of Luke uncovered some critical flaws in Neyrey's insightful work. Most importantly, it is necessary to move beyond the dichotomization of public and private to a fluid spectrum with more categories. The public sphere and the political sphere were not one in the ancient world; an unofficial public sphere did exist. Luke emphasizes the unofficial public sphere and even places like homes and synagogues (considered private by Neyrey) become public places in Luke-Acts. This study also offered several corrections to Kinman's study of the triumphal entry. Kinman did not take into account the epideictic (not apologetic) nature of Luke's historiography, and he selects comparative materials that are too grand and too official, resulting in his claim of an "a-triumphal" entry. More attention to the role of social space and more

---

1. For an example, see Sterling, *Historiography*.

PART THREE: IMPLICATIONS FOR LUKE'S GOSPEL AND OUR WORLD

careful distinctions between the terms, royal and political, demonstrate the unofficial nature of Jesus' entry in Luke.

The study of Luke's political perspective should take into consideration the local nature and spatial verisimilitude of Luke and Acts. First, Jesus stays primarily in the unofficial public sphere. His encounters with the political sphere are mostly local throughout the Gospel, and they are also mostly agonistic. The political analysis of Luke 4–19 should focus on Jesus' use of social power (a broad definition of politics) within his movement and among the crowds and opponents that surround him. Second, this study agrees that Luke employs geography for specific historical and theological purposes. However, Luke also aims for social-spatial verisimilitude, either consciously or unconsciously reproducing the social-spatial characteristics of his own environment. This is most necessary and most illuminating in a high-context society, for implicit social-spatial clues are critical to understanding his portrayal of Jesus.

Building on previous spatial analysis that has emerged out of social-scientific exegesis, this study sought to dialogically incorporate the close exegesis of the biblical text, a mixture of theories and models, and diverse background material. Social models offer valuable insights,[2] yet social-scientific analysis of the NT has sometimes allowed the models to dominate the text, overlooking ways that the text enriches, alters, or challenges the model.[3] Therefore, this study not only engaged in broad survey, comparison, and social theory, but also delved into particular passages to show how exegetical details fit with the operative model. This study also demonstrates an approach to models that is flexible and integrative. Sack's spatial framework was the theoretical foundation of this study, but it was also expanded by looking at other spatial theorists and complemented by the high-context/low-context theory presented by Hall. This study employed a stable theoretical framework that served as an interdisciplinary heuristic and organizing tool without becoming rigid or procrustean.[4] Finally, this study sought to investigate Luke's construction and deployment of space as it relates to possible settings for Luke and his audience (in Ephesus) and to the lived spaces of the ancient world preserved in archaeological remains.[5] The intermingling of text, theory, and *realia* produced new insights into Luke's Gospel and offers a way forward for social-scientific analysis.

In conclusion, Luke's portrayal of Jesus emphasizes the unofficial public sphere and local politics, casting him as a public and political Christ. This emphasis is confirmed by the broad survey, the close comparative material, and the careful study of Luke 18:35–48. These social-spatial characteristics of Luke serve two further functions. First, they are a window, enabling the interpreter to look back on Luke and his audience in their various

---

2. See the various essays in Neyrey, *Social World of Luke-Acts*, and the defense of the use of models and theories in Esler, *Community and Gospel*, 6–16.

3. For example, Neyrey misses that the fact that Paul's public teaching referenced in Acts 20:20 includes the "hall of Tyrannus" (Acts 19:9–10), a public space that is not political in nature ("In Public," 87–91). Elliot overemphasizes the contrast between the temple and the household, missing the fact that Jesus claims both as locations for his public teaching ("Temple," 229–30).

4. As such, it aims at an "interpretive analytics" as described by Robbins, *Tapestry*, 11–13.

5. Thus, it takes up the challenge to incorporate *realia* into NT interpretation made by White, "Visualizing," 234.

historical settings (cultural, social, and spatial). Second, they are a mirror that help the interpreter see the contemporary social-spatial settings and challenges of Christianity in a new way.[6]

Historical Implications

Using the contributions of this study as a window, one can look back on Luke, his audience, and his milieu. This can clarify our understanding of Luke and his audience in ways that contribute to future interpretations of Luke-Acts and also illuminate how Luke (and his community) responded to the social-spatial traditions and trends of his day. This section will begin by outlining some of the significant social-spatial trends of Luke's milieu and then analyze the responses to these in Luke's Gospel. Luke's setting and these responses then offer some data that help us describe the author and audience(s) of the third Gospel.

A few methodological caveats quickly emerge when moving from exegesis to historical reconstruction. First, the following implications are hypothetical inferences based on the social-spatial characteristics of Luke discerned in this study. Therefore, we must practice all the reserve appropriate to historical reconstruction.[7] Second, this study makes several (explainable but not ultimately incontestable) presumptions, such as the identification of Ephesus as a provenance for Luke and the selection of certain comparative material, that influence the data and create some circular inferences from that data. Third, one must consider whether Luke's Gospel portrays the ideal, the real, or some mixture thereof. Is Luke mostly a reflection of the social-spatial realities of his day? Or, is Luke exhorting his community to a particular social-spatial perspective? The following implications attempt to balance both, seeking to show how Luke both fit into and challenged the social-spatial characteristics of his immediate and larger environment.

The Traditions and Trends of Luke's Milieu

Luke and his audience lived in a time of change during the first century. The traditional cultures of the Mediterranean world were bowing more and more to Roman influence, and Roman power itself was becoming more and more imperial. Scholars of imperial Roman society and architecture have noted three important trends that are relevant to our understanding of Luke's social-spatial characteristics: the changing face of cities, the increasing control of homes, and the political dominance of the elite. All of these underscore the shrinking of the unofficial public sphere and offer a backdrop to perceive Luke's response to his social-spatial environment.

In the late first century, the Roman Empire was more than ever a cultural and administrative network of cities bound together by imperial power and influence. Cities in the Roman Empire of the first century were growing in both physical size and population. This was true of the empire as a whole,[8] and true of Ephesus in particular. Ephesus manifests

---

6. This language reflects the functions of biblical texts outlined by Schneiders, *Revelatory Text*, 113.

7. Johnson notes that all history is interpretive, subject to the limits of historical knowledge and our contemporary ideological influences (see Johnson, *Real Jesus*, 81–86).

8. Rostovtzeff, *Social and Economic History*, 1:134–35.

PART THREE: IMPLICATIONS FOR LUKE'S GOSPEL AND OUR WORLD

many of the empire-wide dynamics that were shaping the new imperial urban landscape. A dramatic increase in the number of donations and public buildings in Ephesus during the first and second centuries marks the wealth and growth of the city.[9] The funds for these grand projects came from the elite, especially upwardly mobile entrepreneurs who sought to join the upper echelons of society.[10] As political autonomy and activity declined, public building projects became the premier form of political expression in a local context overshadowed by Roman hegemony.[11] Archaeological and inscriptional evidence testifies to the burgeoning of public building in Ephesus and other parts of the empire as the wealthy elite (or elite-to-be) sought to increase their own prestige and the prestige of their city. These new (and old) social elite competed for public honor by sponsoring entertainment and erecting edifices for public use,[12] for at the same time that public buildings were increasing, the public itself was growing in size. Augustan Rome had approximately one million residents, and the population continued to grow into the second century, partially due to migration into the city.[13] Ephesus too was experiencing marked population growth in the first century, and immigration into the city appears to be the primary contributor.[14] Therefore, cities in the Roman Empire during the first century were expanding, growing, and stretching in dramatic ways.

However, the increase in public building projects and population does not entail an increase in the vitality of the public sphere. While public building had increased, the types and locations of public buildings shifted during the first century. Theatres or amphitheatres for gladiatorial shows became very popular.[15] In Pompeii, the amphitheatre was one of the few public buildings restored to full use after the earthquake of 62 CE.[16] The post-earthquake, pre-eruption elite of Pompeii modeled Rome and spent lavishly on baths, enlarging the Stabian Bath complex and adding the new Central Baths (both were also some distance from the city forum).[17] Wealthy cities continued to erect public temples to the emperor, but these were placed at new ceremonial sites away from the heart of daily life in the city.[18] These new public buildings move away from public places of interaction in the arenas of politics, religion, and economics. Furthermore, the old areas and buildings dedicated to these public activities were both disregarded and enclosed. Very little work was done on Pompeii's forum after the earthquake of 62, while homes, baths, and theatres

---

9. Trebilco, "Asia," 306; and Rogers, *Sacred Identity*, 141. Rogers says, "The visible leaders of the Ephesian aristocracy utterly transformed the architectural and visual character of the city through their building projects between the reign of Augustus and the time of Domitian."

10. Trebilco, "Asia," 306; Lomas, "Idea," 36.

11. Mitchell, *Anatolia*, 1 and 80–81; Edmondson, "Cities and Urban Life," 280.

12. Gleason, "Greek Cities," 235.

13. Garnsey and Saller, *Roman Empire*, 83 and 99–100.

14. White, "Urban Development," 34–38. White also notes that this probably altered the ethnic and cultural makeup of the city. This would have given impetus for the elite to guard and shape their cultural identity more carefully.

15. Gleason, "Greek Cities," 235–36; Lomas, "Idea," 31.

16. Zanker, *Pompeii*, 129.

17. Ibid., 129; Ling, *Pompeii*, 95.

18. Zanker, *Pompeii*, 131.

A Public and Political Christ

were richly restored.[19] In many other parts of the empire, fora were turned into monuments and enclosed from the rest of the city.[20] The center of general public activity shifted from the political, religious, and economic functions of the forum to structures designed for entertainment or leisure, a new set of priorities for the rising urban elite of the first century.[21] The elite fulfilled its duty to supply buildings for the public, but these new public edifices were mostly devoted to entertainment and leisure, while the old public arenas of city, places for political discourse and religious observance, became more exclusive and dominated by elite activity.[22]

Chapter 3 displayed the ideal private role that the home played among the elite in the ancient world. Recall Cicero's statements about how he took refuge in his home from public affairs (*Att.* 17) or how Vatinius violated the sacred refuge of Biblius's home (*Vat.* 22). Many elite Romans owned country villas and retreated to them from the hustle and bustle of the cities.[23] Specific evidence provided by the well-preserved ruins of Pompeii offers insight into the increasingly private nature of homes in the first century. First, in contrast to the unrepaired remains of many public edifices in Pompeii, most elite public homes were reconstructed, sometimes with even greater grandeur.[24] The layout of the homes reflects new configurations, emphasizing private space and control. The following example was cited in chapter 3.

Figure 10.1: The House of Sallust (Reggio VI.2.b)[25]

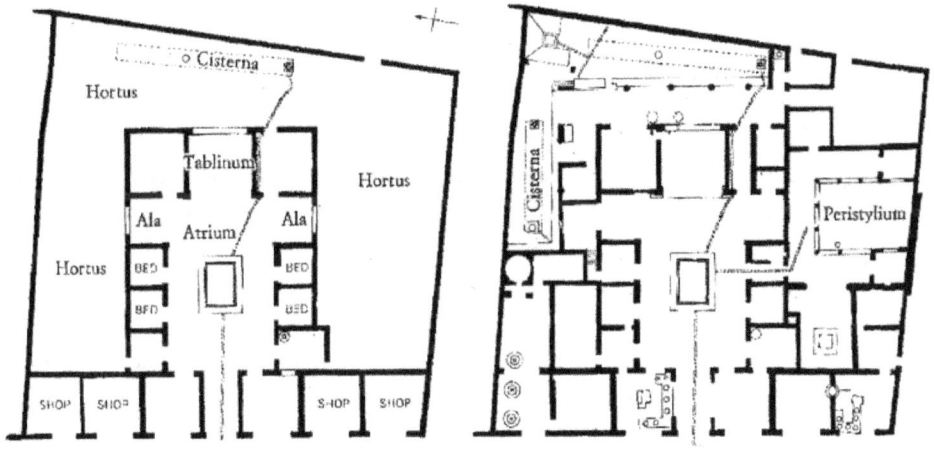

19. Ibid., 126–30. However, this is disputed on the basis of possible new finds at Pompeii. On this debate see ibid., 131–33; Ling, *Pompeii*, 91–95.

20. Lomas, "Idea," 38.

21. Zanker, *Pompeii*, 126, 130–31. Zanker says, "What really counted in the Flavian-Antonine era, and what determined the appearance of its cities was a desire to enjoy the pleasures of life, be it in sumptuous houses with marble colonnades, at shows in the arena and the theatre, or in lavishly decorated baths that developed into centers of leisure-time activity" (131).

22. Lomas, "Idea," 38.

23. Shleton, *As the Romans Did*, 74–78.

24. Zanker, *Pompeii*, 126.

25. Ibid., 166. This illustration is reproduced with the permission of Ann Laidlaw, the original artist.

PART THREE: IMPLICATIONS FOR LUKE'S GOSPEL AND OUR WORLD

The traditional atrium (with its public functions and mixed audiences) faded in size and importance in Pompeian homes and was replaced by peristyles and sumptuous dining/reception rooms surrounding the courtyard.[26] The floor plan of the house on the left (from the second century BCE) has a very basic layout around the atrium. However, the house on the right (from 79 CE) has a much more complex set of rooms with additional passageways providing less sight and more privacy. The later floor plan has added a portico along the back of the house (where the cistern formerly was) as well as a new peristyle garden on the right and a triclinium for dining just below it.[27] While the public still penetrated the private space of the home, the rebuilt home developed more selective and controlled space for private entertainment and display. Wallace-Hadrill says, "The luxurious 'private' life of the rich and powerful of the imperial period is precisely their public façade, and access to it is a privilege carefully guarded."[28] A "more inward-looking elite"[29] in Pompeii seems to be creating grand private domiciles to demonstrate their wealth and status to their fellow elite. Therefore, while private elite homes had always played a special role as safe and controlled places in the Greco-Roman world, the evidence at Pompeii manifests a trend that increases the privacy, luxury, and selectivity of elite Roman homes in the first century.[30]

The changes in public architecture and the privatization of homes both point to another important social-spatial trend in Luke's milieu: the growing dominance of the elite in social and political life. While voting in Rome was once theoretically open to all male citizens, many could not exercise this right (due to time, distance, etc.), and as the empire developed, more and more political power was concentrated in the hands of the elite connected to the emperor.[31] While politics was still a lively part of urban life, it was limited to local affairs, and many candidates came from the new upwardly mobile rich in a city.[32] Recall the *Precepts*: Plutarch and Menemachus were two local elite men seeking urban political offices and prestige in the context of Roman hegemony. Urban public buildings "provided the elite with an impressive stage on which to conduct their public activities and fashion their identity, most of all in relation to the ruling power, Rome."[33] These public buildings and the (now more exclusive) ceremonies that took place in them served to emphasize the distance between the social elite and the public and to place the elite in a (political) relationship with Rome. While leading men sought public status and political prestige, the elite were also finding ways to withdraw from philanthropic participation

---

26. Ling, *Pompeii*, 75 and Wallace-Hadrill, *Houses and Society*, 51. Ling states the new class of self-made men was attempting to recreate the country villa in an urban environment (*Pompeii*, 75).

27. For a description of the rooms in the 79 CE floor plan, see Smith, Wayte, and Marindin, eds., "Plan."

28. Wallace-Hadrill claims that this does not make homes any more "private," rightly maintaining the continuing interpenetration of public and private (*Houses and Society*, 51–52). However, in my estimation, the increased selectivity and exclusivity does make the public functions of the house more private.

29. Lomas, "Idea," 39.

30. Ibid., 166. This illustration is reproduced with the permission of Ann Laidlaw, the original artist.

31. Shelton, *As the Romans Did*, 203, 207, 232.

32. Zanker, *Pompeii*, 131; Ling, *Pompeii*, 103–4.

33. Edmondson, "Cities," 269; see also Gleason, "Greek Cities," 237.

A Public and Political Christ

in the cities. Local urban elite were expected to supply funds (called *munera*) for building and entertainment, but more and more individuals appealed to the emperor (on new legal grounds) to be exempted from such *munera*, leaving the cities with less funds and less social leverage.[34] Therefore, place and politics became tools of the elite, increasingly comprised of the newly rich. These tools established their public status and distance from the general populace and their political influence in a world dominated by Rome.

In conclusion, three social-spatial trends of the first century have come to light. First century Roman cities were growing in population and architecture. The public buildings focused on entertainment and leisure (e.g., theatres and baths) burgeoned, but classic public arenas like the forum became closed off and more exclusive. This exclusivity appears in the home as well, where new structural and decorative elements reflect an attempt to increase the privacy and grandeur of the home. The home, like the city, became a location for elite control and self-representation. The elite also came to dominate political life, seeking political offices in their local contexts while being exempted from financial donations. The unofficial public sphere was shrinking in several ways. Public space was becoming more exclusive and new public arenas focused on entertainment rather than interaction. The house was becoming more private, and the distance between the elite and non-elite was growing. We can now explore how Luke's social-spatial characteristics fit into these trends.

Luke and His Community in a Changing Social-Spatial Landscape

With regard to the author of the third Gospel, this study confirms the work of previous scholars by suggesting that Luke was familiar with and favorable toward the unofficial public sphere and local politics.[35] Luke most likely lived in and wrote for an urban environment. He finds the city to be a natural place for Jesus, and he displays an understanding of urban dynamics. However, Luke seems most comfortable with the unofficial public spaces of the city. In his portrayal, Jesus rarely enters explicitly political space in cities, and most of the public city scenes in Acts remain unofficial in nature.[36] Luke does not mention baths in either the Gospel or Acts,[37] and the only appearance of a theatre in is as scene of a shameful riot in Acts. Thus, Luke seems to move against the increasingly political and exclusive nature of many traditional public arenas in the city by avoiding them in his opus, and he does not adopt the growing predominance of baths and theatres as public space. Luke seems to preserve the city as an unofficial public arena finding possibilities for interaction in places like roads (Luke 18:35—19:48), markets (Acts 17:17), and even houses (Luke 19:6–10). Doing so resists the trends of his day and urges Christians to seek out and participate in unofficial public space in cities whenever and wherever possible. While

---

34. Edmondson, "Cities," 279.

35. See Robbins, "Social Location," 331–32.

36. When the political sphere appears in Acts, it follows after action in the unofficial public sphere: after walking through town many times, Paul is arrested in Philippi; after a riot begins, a town clerk intervenes in Ephesus; and after worshipping in the temple, Paul is taken into custody in Jerusalem.

37. Of course, Jews of the time would not have attended baths because of the practice of bathing in the nude.

certain urban dynamics operated throughout the first century, in light of developments in the latter half of the century and Luke's time of writing, perhaps it is apropos to examine Luke's community as "the second urban Christians."[38]

While Luke was probably not a part of a local political body (like Jesus), he seems to have relationships with members of the local elite who held political office (like Theophilus). He is comfortable portraying his main characters interacting with the local political sphere (and higher levels of politicians): centurions, Pharisees, Sadducees, clerks, magistrates, and governors. While many elements in the local political sphere oppose Jesus (especially the Pharisees and the synagogue leader), other members of the local political sphere respond positively to him (like the centurion) and even join his movement (like Zacchaeus).[39] Luke does partially write "up" to these social superiors in the local elite.[40] However, he stresses Jesus' acquisition of honor in the unofficial public sphere even more, and by so doing writes horizontally to others in the unofficial public sphere.[41] Jesus does not address the political sphere as an institution with his message; rather he occasionally addresses select individuals in that sphere with both rebuke and hope. Luke does not seem to suggest that his audience should reinvigorate or redemocratize the increasingly elite political sphere through their participation in it; rather he portrays Jesus actively encountering (not avoiding) members of the local political sphere with his message and calling them to join his movement.

Luke's portrayal of Jesus in household scenes of conflict and salvation flies in the face of the increasing privatization and exclusivity of elite homes in the first century. Luke moves domestic space in the opposite direction by increasing public access (the crowd floods into Zacchaeus's home) and calling for inclusivity at meals (14:12–14). Luke refuses to relinquish the household as a place of Christian activity, but he will not allow it to follow the cultural trend of privatization in his day. Also, he seeks to transform the house, not by novel means but by the deep cultural tradition of hospitality. Thus, Luke brings his own culture to work on itself as if to say, "You are not holding on to your own ideals of the home if you allow it to become overly exclusive and private." Luke portrays houses as public spaces that are open to all and should be filled with those who can receive the benefits of the kingdom, especially those most in need and on the margins of society (recall 14:21–23).

This trend and Luke's resistance to it bears crucial significance for ecclesial development in the first century, because the home is usually deemed to be one of the most

---

38. This designation is an obvious imitation of Meeks's excellent work, *First Urban Christians*. He examines first century urban dynamics (9–31) that fit better with an analysis of Paul's mission churches in the first half of the first century.

39. Stegemann and Stegemann, *Jesus Movement*, 315. They identify Zacchaeus as one of the rich members of the "retainer class" attached to the local elite, signifying that some elements of the upper stratum of Greco-Roman society (though not its highest orders) joined the Christian movement.

40. Compare Robbins, "Social Location," 321–23; Rohrbaugh, "Jesus Tradition," 1:215–16.

41. Rohrbaugh stresses the upward element of Luke's writing, but he also notes Luke's emphasis on Jesus' publicly acquired honor ("Jesus Tradition," 216–18). He does not distinguish between the official and unofficial public spheres, and does not seem to consider the possibility of Luke writing horizontally.

common locations for Christian gatherings, especially in light of Pauline evidence.[42] Even with some latitude for the possible variety of meeting places, the household had a notable impact on the identity and practice of early Christians.[43] The absence of the public space of the synagogue for Christian proclamation and teaching (a loss documented in Acts) and the decline of unofficial public structures documented above left Christians in the latter half of the first century with few options for meeting places in the unofficial public sphere.[44] Many Christian communities probably turned to higher-status members who had substantial houses that could host gatherings. The predominance of households (the force of place) in the development of early Christianity and the trend toward increasing exclusivism and privacy in households in the latter half of the first century was a catastrophic collision in Luke's view. Luke narrates against this trend, having Jesus both teach and enact the radical openness and inclusivity of private homes. Jesus brings the public, even with its "sinful" women and hostile crowds, into homes, transforming them into more public places and teaching his audience to do the same. Thus, Luke urges his community not to abandon the household meeting but to open it to the public and to continue to strive to find places to meet in the unofficial public sphere, places where they can encounter the elite, peers, opponents, and the poor of the city.

These inferences also have relevance for the nature of Luke's audience, the "second" urban Christians. The juxtaposition of the blind beggar and Zacchaeus demonstrate the social extremes included (at least ideally) in Luke's community. The healing of the blind beggar implies that this man did join Jesus' movement: he "follows" Jesus and leads the surrounding entourage in praise. Thus, even the poorest and lowest elements of society, embodied in this disabled and impoverished man, find a place in Luke's community.[45] Zacchaeus, as noted above, probably marks the highest social level participating in Luke's community, but Theophilus might represent a step higher (part of the local political elite) included in Luke's broader audience. If Luke's audience (and/or community) does contain some of the new upwardly mobile rich, then his presentation confronts them with the Christian way of profound financial sacrifice and downward mobility.[46] Finally, Luke's audience was urban as he was, and his ecclesial community had most likely grown in size and organization. This is probably reflected in the steady increase and development of Jesus' movement throughout the Gospel and into Acts. Thus, the analysis of the political actions

---

42. Stegemann and Stegemann, *Jesus Movement*, 276–77 and Meeks, *Urban Christians*, 75–55. Oakes cites the long tradition of interpreters who locate early Christian groups in homes (*Reading*, 69), but he also cites the scholarly debate over this claim, which suggests that meeting halls or apartments might have also served as meeting locations (*Reading*, 69–70).

43. Note the frequency of homes in Acts, the presence of "household codes" in NT letters, and specific passages like 1 Cor 16:19 and 1 Tim 3:14–15. See also Lampe, *From Paul*, 374–76. The functional importance of the household structure is presumed in Oakes's study, *Reading Romans in Pompeii* (see esp. ch. 3).

44. There are some alternatives as exemplified by the σχολή of Tyrannus in Acts 19:9.

45. This is contra Stegemann and Stegemann, who state that Luke's community might have included the relatively poor (πένης) but not the destitute (πτωχός), basing their conclusion on Luke 14:7ff (*Jesus Movement*, 304). Cassidy suggests the opposite (in line with my hypothesis) on the basis of Luke 14:12–14 (*Jesus*, 32–33).

46. See the discussion of Jesus' stance toward the rich in Cassidy, *Jesus*, 25–31.

of Jesus and the early church as portrayed in the Gospel and Acts may cast some like on the nature and structure of Luke's historical community.

Luke's ecclesial community might have been somewhat spatially adrift but socially more stable. While the house is an important meeting place, Luke partially deemphasizes it and otherwise insists on its transformation.[47] Luke portrays a number of other places (markets, streets, theatres, temples, riversides, etc.), but none of them are frequent or established enough to constitute a new spatial home for Luke's Christian community. However, the social structure of Luke's community appears more stable. Luke's narrative reflects clear lines of leadership in Jesus' movement: Jesus to the twelve, the adding of Matthias, the incorporation of Paul, the appointing of church elders. Furthermore, social issues like the inclusion of the Gentiles have already been settled. These do not take place without conflict, but their steady development and stability in the narrative suggest that Luke's community faced no leadership vacuum and no current social crises. Furthermore, Luke feels confident enough to warn his community to continued faithfulness (cf. the parable of the king *and his subjects*), and he narrates a steadily growing community that faces difficulties and overcomes them, often with admirable unanimity and praise to God. The narrative of Luke-Acts probably represents a social stage of consolidation and legitimation (more epideictic than apologetic) in Luke's community.[48] Thus, the social stability of Luke's community provides a balance for their temporary spatial rootlessness.

How then can one categorize Luke's response to his milieu? Previous scholars have analyzed the response of NT writings to their environment by using Wilson's typologies of sects.[49] Esler used this typology in his study of Luke's Gospel, concluding that Luke features a conversionist approach complemented by thaumaturgical and revolutionist approaches.[50] However, Robbins suggests that Luke manifests "an inner relation between thaumaturgy and conversionism that emphasizes reformist activity."[51] Wilson describes reformist sects as "aware of social organization, and concerned to improve it by use of that religious insight they regard as uniquely their own."[52] There is broad agreement that Luke manifests a wide variety of sectarian responses, but dissent regarding which one is the organizing paradigm.[53] This study reveals several social and spatial elements that fit well

---

47. Branick claims that Acts deemphasizes the house church and offers alternatives like the lecture hall of Tyrannus. Furthermore, Acts builds upon the way Luke downplays house and household in his Gospel (*House Church*, 122–23).

48. I would suggest that Luke's community did not experience as much social anxiety as suggested by Esler (*Community and Gospel*, 16-19). Luke presents a confident, well-integrated, steadily progressing narrative that probably reflects a history widely accepted by his community. If anything, the community might have been having a spatial issue over *where* to meet, but this does not seem to rises to the level of crisis in Luke or Acts.

49. See the survey and analysis in Robbins, *Tapestry*, 147–59. The sectarian responses are conversionist, revolutionist, introversionist, manipulationist, thaumaturgical, reformist, and utopian (Wilson, *Religious Sects*, 36–47).

50. Esler, *Community and Gospel*, 58–65. Esler does not even mention the reformist possibility.

51. Robbins, *Tapestry*, 158.

52. Wilson, *Religious Sects*, 46.

53. Robbins points out that it would be rare for a NT writing to manifest only one type of response (*Tapestry*, 150). Examples of the conversionist perspective were just mentioned. The healing of the blind beg-

with the reformist perspective. Socially, the reformist perspective colors even the conversionist and thaumaturgical elements in Luke-Acts. Social and political changes result from individual conversions: John the Baptist instructs tax collectors and soldiers regarding their official duties (Luke 3:10–14, no parallels), the calling of disciples in the Gospel creates a steadily developing movement in the Gospel, part of Zacchaeus's response involves professional restitution and reform, the conversion of Cornelius becomes a precedent for Christian belief and practice in Acts 15, and disciples and officials both warn Paul to avoid the riot in Acts 15:30–31. Healings and exorcisms also result in the social reintegration of outcasts especially in the Gospel (the Gerasene demoniac, the crippled woman, the ten lepers, and the blind beggar).

The spatial focus of this study reveals reformist emphases in Luke's portrayal of cities, houses, and the temple. Luke appears to have lived in and valued cities as a place for Christian activity; he emphasizes cities and their social make up in his narrative of Jesus and the early church.[54] Luke employs cities as places for unofficial public interaction where both conflict and salvation take place, thus seeking to correct the social trends of increasing elitism and decreasing public interaction. Luke also appreciates household settings, but he does not allow the house to remain private or become increasingly private, again resisting a cultural trend. Instead Luke employs the tradition of hospitality to increase the publicity and inclusivity of homes, seeking to reform negative developments in this foundational social unit. He maintains the home as a place for Christian life and reforms it by means of a cultural tradition. Jesus' attitude toward the temple is reformist in Luke. He does not condemn and dismiss the temple at the cleansing (as in Mark), but he restores it to its proper function, creating a space for his public teaching. Thus, a reformist response does seem to overarch Luke's Gospel (and Acts) with some elements of the thaumaturgical, conversionist, and utopian perspectives.

However, Wilson also emphasizes the separateness and exclusivity of reformist sects, elements that do not fit with Luke engaging social-spatial institutions and his inclusion of a variety of people.[55] Also, reformist sects are generally not of the "recruiting" or evangelistic type, while Luke advocates such activity.[56] Wilson's categories seem to prohibit the mixing of reform, conversion, and engagement with the culture. The beginnings of the Salvation Army combined some of these elements, but Wilson says that "such efforts have been unusual among sects."[57] This may either indicate a gap in Wilson's typology or

---

gar is thaumaturgical, and when Jesus and the apostles encounter the local political sphere, the conversionist response comes to the fore. Finally, Luke's portrayal of Jesus' development of his movement of disciples and their independence from and lack of threat to the Roman order may reflect a utopian response.

54. Conn, "Lucan Perspectives," 422. Conn hypothesizes that urban influences shaped the very structure of Luke's work: "Out of the social context of an urban setting, the author forged his literary design. His central concepts of Christianity's progress in the world were developed and formulated as urban progress."

A conversionist perspective appears here too, for cities must hear the gospel (Luke 4:43), and some do not accept and it and thus face condemnation (10:10–12).

55. Wilson, *Religious Sects*, 46

56. Ibid. He considers the evangelistic phase of the Quakers (his prime example of a reformist sect) as unusual and temporary (179).

57. Ibid., 63.

suggest that the ecclesial community that both produced and heard Luke-Acts had moved beyond the sectarian level to incorporate new institutional forms and responses to the world. A possible theological response to this historical and sociological problem might be offered by Matthewes in his study, *A Theology of Public Life*. Writing from an Augustinian perspective, Matthewes argues that followers of Christ see themselves as deeply embedded in God's larger act of creation. Reconciliation not only restores the self's relationship to God but also the self's relationship to itself and to God's world.[58] He sees a theological link between conversionist and reformist responses: "Conversion does not draw humans out of the world; rather it puts them more fully, and more properly, *into* it."[59] A proper view of the connectedness of human beings and creation in relation to God means that we can come to know God better through engagement with the world, and our presence and action in the public sphere is one crucial way of engaging the world.[60] Interestingly, Matthewes identifies a loss of vital public and political life in our own day, as in Luke's, though for our own specific historical reasons. Matthewes finally argues that a proper eschatological perspective helps us to see our place in the world and the world itself aright as we receive and engage God's creation in the present time.[61] Thus, Matthewes may provide a theological framework for integrating the reformist (engagement with the public sphere) and conversionist (call for personal repentance) emphases in Luke.[62]

In conclusion, Luke's emphasis on the unofficial public sphere and local politics represents a mixed and complex response to his social-spatial milieu. He embraces the city and its unofficial public places, but he is forced to work against the trend of shrinking unofficial public space in the urban settings of the latter first century. Luke retains the household as a significant setting for the ministry of Jesus, but he insists that houses be open, not privatized for elite display. Luke includes the elite and the destitute in his community, calling the former to humble themselves and raising the latter up. Luke's community may have been spatially displaced, but their social organization compensated for it. Finally, Luke holds a reformist perspective of the world, incorporating other responses and presenting a stance that may move beyond a sectarian position. This reformist view, while sociologically in tension with the conversionist perspective, may capture a deeper theological coherence expressed by the narrative of Luke and Acts.

Implications for Contemporary Christian Social-Spatial Practice

This final section will offer some thoughts and questions raised by this study for contemporary Christian reflection on and practice in society and space. To begin, the conclusions of this study wade against the tide of the most common understandings of the term "pub-

---

58. Matthewes, *Theology*, 122.
59. Ibid., 123.
60. Ibid., 86, 146.
61. Ibid., 313–15.
62. This framework might also be able to include the thaumaturgical if we consider the healing of bodies as a sign of the restoration of the creation and the utopian response if we view it as part of Luke's eschatological perspective.

A Public and Political Christ

lic" today. First, "public" can be construed as "all that occurs outside of the household."[63] What then could it mean to speak of "public" space in homes? Luke's portrayal urges a reconsideration of this dichotomy-based formulation. Second, public issues for contemporary American Christians (and many others) generally fall into a few broad categories: family-related legislation, bioethics, poverty, education, and urban development.[64] Luke's presentation of Jesus demonstrates that a wider variety of people, issues, and concerns are relevant to the public sphere and should be dealt with there. Finally, most Americans (even Christians) still lump the categories of "public" and "political" together, seeing public concerns exclusively as political matters.[65] The evidence from the ancient world showed that some in that day identified the public sphere with politics, but for most politics was only one part of the public sphere. Luke leads Christians to see that *unofficial* public spaces (however those may be culturally defined) are places where God was and is acting through Jesus Christ to proclaim the Kingdom and call disciples. Those unofficial public places in Luke 18:35—19:48 included a street, a city, a house, and a temple. Where are these unofficial public places today, and how can Christians act in them in appropriately public but not necessarily political ways?

This question raises the larger question of whether or not the social-spatial categories set forth to describe the Greco-Roman world can be stretched across space and time to have any applicability to our day and place. Sack postulates that people in premodern societies (like the ancient Greco-Roman world) lived in a world full of "thick" places—places that were thick with meaning and traceable significance. However, we moderns live in a world of specialized, "thin" places. Each individual place (home, office, church) has only one function and these places are related only in very fragmented ways.[66] Is it possible for us to have a house as "thick" as Zacchaeus's was? Could churches ever be public in ways similar to synagogues or even the temple? Part of the challenge for Christians is to make our homes and offices and churches thicker with significance in a thinned out and disconnected world.[67] The analysis of Luke's Gospel above provides one way to thicken our places, add meaning, and create a larger awareness for moral decision making: in Christian practice, one can seek to overlap and interconnect the public and private spheres as they exist in our day. We can do this using the forces of place (opening our homes), social relations (whom we host in our homes, cf. Luke 14:12-14), meaning (how we interpret and explain this distinctively Christian behavior), time (when we carry on these activities), and religion (incorporating public worship into domestic space). This overlapping can be used redemptively to offer homes and other open places to "public" people who experience alienation in a public world.[68]

---

63. Adams, *Going Public*, 23.

64. See the topics of the table of contents in Cromartie, *Public Faith*, vii–viii.

65. Adams, *Going Public*, 147–50. Adams discusses this to point out its flaws and argues for a broader understanding of the term "public."

66. Sack, *Homo Geographicus*, 7–9.

67. This "thickening" for the sake of better moral decision making is part of Sack's project (*Homo Geographicus*, 11–12).

68. The public sphere also has its destructive elements, which we must discern and eliminate as part of our spatially informed moral actions under the guidance of the Spirit.

PART THREE: IMPLICATIONS FOR LUKE'S GOSPEL AND OUR WORLD

Luke's emphasis on the unofficial public sphere encourages contemporary Christians to reimagine the spaces they do and can inhabit. Some spaces are lost to us as public arenas: roads and temples. We share other spaces with Luke, such as cities and homes, that we might see anew. Luke and his community seemed to be struggling with the diminution of unofficial public space in his day due to the rise of the urban elite and the fading of public places. Contemporary Christians struggle with a similar urban phenomenon, but one that is caused by the thinning out of specialized spaces and the increasing influence of the political (i.e., legislative) sphere. However, unlike Luke, contemporary Christians have not lost their "synagogue," the church. Yet, that space has also been subjected to thinning out and, while being public in a sense, it is no longer a space where a variety of groups meet for interaction, teaching, and sometimes conflict. Storefront churches and churches renting space in schools or community centers stretch beyond specialized spaces for worship, but they are the exceptions, and most churches still aim for the day when they can have their "own" building. Perhaps our contemporary spatial rootedness and the security we have in our self-constructed sacred places is a kind of compensation that masks our lack of social cohesion as the Body of Christ, while the opposite was true for Luke. Perhaps a reinvigoration of the social identity and social structure of Christian churches would allow for more confidence to step out into the unfamiliar places (and people) of the public sphere, places where Luke repeatedly locates Jesus.

The home is an excellent place to make bridges between Luke's portrayal of Jesus and the contemporary world. Sack says, "Virtually every culture possesses the concept [of home], and in each there is a residue of meaning that points to the home as a certain type of place in terms of the control that individuals can exercise over it."[69] Thus, the concept of home is broadly defined by the fact that its occupants have a special degree of control over that place. Luke's portrayal of Jesus challenges us in two ways with regard to our control over our homes. First, Christians need to redirect that control to create opportunities for public space to occur in homes: where one lives, how one arranges and decorates a home, whom one allows into the home, how one acts, and what one says at home. Christians must take responsibility for the authority granted to them and use it in ways that extend the kingdom of God in these public-private places. However, Luke's portrayal of Jesus also urges contemporary Christians to abdicate some of that control as well. Repeatedly in this study, the public sphere "invaded" the private sphere. These invasions came across as unexpected (with Zacchaeus), uncomfortable (with Levi), disturbing (with Simon), confrontational (in 11:37–52), and paradigm-shifting (in 14:1–24). Allowing the public sphere, with its places, people, and meanings, into our homes means relinquishing some of that control over "our" space and allowing a new "space" to emerge where God can act in our midst.[70]

This investigation emphasized the power of hospitality to create a connection between the public and private spheres. Christine Pohl writes that "hospitality requires

---

69. *Homo Geographicus*, 13.

70. Perhaps the revival in the American porch will provide an unofficial public space that lies between the house and the city. See Donlon, *Swinging in Place*, 87–88 and 165–71; and Dolan, *American Porch*, 287–311.

... settings which combine aspects of public and private life."[71] This was true in Luke's day and is true in ours. Furthermore, she emphasizes the importance of *communities* both in welcoming strangers as they cross these potentially disconcerting boundaries and in sustaining the practice of hospitality with its strains and risks.[72] Her observations are in line with Luke's presentation of Jesus. Luke creates scenarios in homes that overlap and (sometimes uncomfortably) combine aspects of public and private life in his day. Also, scenes of hospitality in Luke are never intimate meetings of host and guest in secluded dining chambers. Rather, they are vibrant and busy scenes with lots of people, both friends and enemies, meeting together in ways that further God's redemptive work in Jesus' ministry. Luke provides a canonical impetus and archetype for allowing hospitality to transform homes. However, Luke also portrays Jesus as a figure who transgresses the cultural norms of hospitality as he carries out his divine mission: he addresses his host's detractors, he fails to meet the host's expectations, he rebukes his hosts, and he requests and offers hospitality even when it is unseemly. This leads contemporary Christians to consider how one must transgress Western culture's code of hospitality so that it is more in line with the Gospel.[73] Might hospitality not involve a meal? Might it involve confrontation and conflict? Might it include unexpected and offensive guests? Might one insist on another's hospitality? Luke's portrayal of Jesus as a public figure offers two perspectives on hospitality. It is a powerful cultural practice that can bring the public and private spheres together for the proclamation (and enactment) of the kingdom, and it is a cultural practice that must be transgressed and re-envisioned in ways that serve the proclamation (and enactment) of the kingdom.

Finally, as Jesus' reputation and movement within the unofficial public sphere increased, he came into contact with local and regional political leaders. Luke's response to the political sphere is primarily conversionist—several members of the local political elite in Luke-Acts are called to repent, give with generosity, and join Jesus' mixed social movement (e.g., the rich ruler, Zacchaeus, Sergius Paulus, etc.). He does not confront the institutions of the political sphere and call them to change. However, we also saw that Luke's response also includes reformist elements and that Luke-Acts moves beyond sectarian stances. The contemporary Christian church (while sometimes sectarian in its makeup and responses) has mostly moved beyond the sect stage as well. While not addressing political structures directly, Luke confronts the members of the political elite with the message of the gospel. At the same time, Luke seeks to transform some social institutions like the city and the house in a way that is both reformist and conversionist. These formed the social-spatial basis for public and political life in the ancient world, and thus, challenging them would easily bear ramifications for politics proper as well. This combination of possibilities might explain the diverging scholarly opinions about Luke's ethical and political stance toward the culture and government of his day.[74] Thus, perhaps Luke sets a

---

71. Pohl, *Making Room*, 151.

72. Ibid., 95.

73. Pohl too notes the shortcomings of contemporary notions of hospitality as simply entertaining one's friends (ibid., 3–4).

74. For example, Conzelmann (and many others) think Luke is providing an apology for the church to the Romans (*Theology of St. Luke*, 137–44). Walasky sees Luke providing an apology for the Romans to the church

PART THREE: IMPLICATIONS FOR LUKE'S GOSPEL AND OUR WORLD

trajectory that empowers the future church to respond to the members and structures of the political sphere in a way that incorporates and transcends both the conversionist and reformist approaches.

The social-spatial characteristics of Luke 18:35—19:48 and the Gospel as a whole place Jesus firmly in the unofficial public sphere and on the edge of local politics. Luke's portrayal of Jesus both draws upon and challenges the social-spatial traditions and trends of his milieu. This dynamic relationship provides some insight into the historical situation of Luke and his community, and at the same time it provides a canonical example that can guide Christians as they negotiate and engage the social-spatial attributes of the contemporary world. The public, the political, and the private are still active categories in our day, and Luke's portrayal of Jesus offers a distinctive view that continues to engage and challenge the world around it.

---

and not vice versa (*"And So We Came"*, 10–14). Cassidy sees Luke's stance on social and economic issues as a threat to the Roman order (*Jesus, Politics*, 77–86). Esler claims that Luke includes an ancestral theme to comfort the Romans in his community (*Community and Gospel*, 201–19).

Bibliography

Aristophanes. Translated by Benjamin Bickley Rogers. 3 vols. Loeb Classical Library. Cambridge: Harvard University Press, 1924.

Aalders, Gerhard J. D. *Plutarch's Political Thought*. Translated by A. M. Manekofsky. Amsterdam: North-Holland, 1982.

Achtemeier, Paul J. "'And he followed him': Miracles and Discipleship in Mark 10:46–52." *Semeia* 11 (1978) 115–45.

Adams, Lawrence E. *Going Public: Christian Responsibility in a Divided America*. Grand Rapids: Brazos, 2002.

Aharoni, Yohanan, and Michael Avi-Yonah. *The Macmillan Bible Atlas*. 3rd. ed. New York: Macmillan, 1993.

Aletti, Jean-Noël. "Parabole des Mines et/ou Parabole du Roi: Remarques sur l'Écriture Parabole de Luc." Pages 309–32 in *Les Paraboles Évangéliques: Perspectives Nouvelles. XIIe Congrès de l'ACFEB*. Edited by J. Delorme. Lectio divina 135. Paris: Editions du Cerf, 1989.

Alexander, Loveday. "'Foolishness to the Greeks': Jews and Christians in the Public Life of the Empire." Pages 229–50 in *Philosophy and Power in the Greco-Roman World*. Edited by Gillian Clark and Tessa Rajak. Oxford: Oxford University Press, 2002.

Alexiou, Evangelos. "*Eunoia* bei Plutarch: von den *Praecepta Gerendai Reipublicae* zu den *Viten*." Pages 365–86 in *The Unity of Plutarch's Work: 'Moralia' Themes in the 'Lives,' Features of the 'Lives' in the 'Moralia.'* Edited by Anastasios G. Nikolaidis. Millenium Studies in the Culture and History of the First Millenium CE, 19. Berlin: de Gruyter, 2008.

Allison, Penelope Mary. *Pompeian Households: An Analysis of Material Culture*. Monumenta Archaeologica 20. Los Angeles: Cotsen Institute of Archaeology at UCLA, 2004.

———. "Pompeian Households: An Online-Companion." Online: http://www.stoa.org/projects/ph/index.html.

Anderson, Graham. *Philostratus: Biography and Belles Lettres in the Third Century A.D.* London: Croom Helm, 1986.

Anderson, James C., Jr. *Roman Architecture and Society*. Baltimore: Johns Hopkins University Press, 1997.

Ando, Clifford. "The Administration of the Provinces." Pages 177–92 in *A Companion to the Roman Empire*. Edited by David S. Potter. Blackwell Companions to the Ancient World. Malden, MA: Blackwell, 2006.

Arendt, Hannah. *The Human Condition*. Chicago: University of Chicago Press, 1958.

Bachmann, Michael. *Jerusalem und der Tempel: Die geographisch-theologishen Elemente in der lukanischen Sicht des jüdischen Kultzentrums*. Beiträge zur Wissenschaft vom Alten und Neuen Testament 109. Edited by Siegfried Herrmann and Karl Heinrich Rengstorf. Stuttgart: W. Kohlhammer, 1980.

Bahat, Dan. *Illustrated Atlas of Jerusalem*. Translated by Shlomo Ketko. New York: Simon & Schuster, 1990.

———. "Jesus and the Herodian Temple." Pages 300–308 in *Jesus and Archaeology*. Edited by James H. Charlesworth. Grand Rapids: Eerdmans, 2006.

Bailey, James L., and Lyle D. Vander Broek. *Literary Forms in the New Testament: A Handbook*. Louisville: Westminster John Knox, 1992.

Bailey, Kenneth E. *Poet & Peasant and Through Peasant Eyes: A Literary-Cultural Approach to the Parables in Luke*. Combined edition. Grand Rapids: Eerdmans, 1983.

Barrett, C. K. *A Critical and Exegetical Commentary on the Acts of the Apostles*. 2 vols. International Critical Commentary. Edinburgh: T. & T. Clark, 1994.

Baugh, Steven Michael. *Paul and Ephesus: The Apostle among His Contemporaries*. Ann Arbor, MI: UMI, 1991.

Bibliography

Bechard, Dean P. "The Theological Significance of Judaea in Luke-Acts." Pages 675–92 in *The Unity of Luke-Acts*. Edited by J. Verheyden. Bibliotheca Ephemeridum Theologicarum Lovaniensium 142. Leuven: Leuven University Press, 1999.

Benn, Stanley I., and Gerald F. Gaus. "The Liberal Conception of The Public and the Private." Pages 31–65 in *Public and Private in Social Life*. Edited by Stanley I. Benn and Gerald F. Gaus. London: Croom Helm, 1983.

Benn, Stanley I. "The Public and the Private: Concepts and Action." Pages 3–30 in *Public and Private in Social Life*. Edited by Stanley I. Benn and Gerald F. Gaus. London: Croom Helm, 1983.

Berquist, Jon L. "Critical Spatiality and the Construction of the Ancient World." Pages 14–29 in *"Imagining" Biblical Worlds: Studies in Spatial, Social and Historical Constructs in Honor of James W. Flanagan*. Edited by David M. Gunn and Paula M. McNutt. Journal for the Study of the Old Testament Supplement Series 359. London: Sheffield Academic, 2002.

Betz, Hans Dieter. "Hellenism." Pages 127–34 in vol. 3 of *The Anchor Bible Dictionary*. Edited by David Noel Freedman. New York: Doubleday, 1992.

Blass, F., and A. Debrunner. *A Greek Grammar of the New Testament and Other Early Christian Literature*. Translated and revised by Robert W. Funk. Chicago: University of Chicago Press, 1961.

Blois, Lukas de. "The Ideal Statesman: A Commonplace in Plutarch's Political Treatises, His *Solon*, and His *Lycurgus*." Pages 317–24 in *The Unity of Plutarch's Work: 'Moralia' Themes in the 'Lives,' Features of the 'Lives' in the 'Moralia.'* Edited by Anastasios G. Nikolaidis. Millenium Studies in the Culture and History of the First Millenium CE, 19. Berlin: de Gruyter, 2008.

Blois, Lukas de, et al., editors. *Plutarch's Statesman and His Aftermath: Political, Philosophical, and Literary Aspects*. The Statesman in Plutarch's Works 1. Leiden: Brill, 2004.

Boardman, John, Jasper Griffin, and Oswyn Murray, editors. *The Oxford Illustrated History of Greece and the Hellenistic World*. Oxford: Oxford University Press, 2001.

Bock, Darrell L. *Proclamation from Prophecy and Pattern: Lucan Old Testament Christology*. Sheffield: JSOT Press, 1987.

———. *Luke*. Baker Exegetical Commentary on the New Testament 3. 2 vols. Grand Rapids: Baker, 1994–96.

———. *Luke*. IVP New Testament Commentary Series. Downers Grove, IL: Inter-Varsity, 1994.

Boer, Roland. "Sanctuary and Womb: Henri Lefebvre and the Production of Space." Paper presented at the AAR/SBL Annual Meeting: Construction of Ancient Space Seminar. Nashville, November 19, 2002. Online: http://www.cwru.edu/affil/GAIR/papers/2000papers/Boer.htm.

Bois, Page du. "Ancient Masculinities." Pages 319–23 in *New Testament Masculinities*. Edited by Stephen D. Moore and Janice Capel Anderson. Semeia Studies 45. Atlanta: Society of Biblical Literature, 2003.

Bolchazy, Ladislaus J. *Hospitality in Early Rome*. Chicago: Ares, 1977.

Borg, Marcus J. "Luke 19:42–44 and Jesus as Prophet?" *Foundations and Facets* 8 (1992) 99–112.

Borgen, Peder. "Philo, Luke and Geography." Pages 273–85 in *Philo, John and Paul: New Perspectives on Judaism and Early Christianity*. Brown Judaic Studies. Atlanta: Scholars, 1987.

Bourdieu, Pierre. *Outline of a Theory of Practice*. Translated by Richard Nice. Cam-bridge: Cambridge University Press, 1977.

Bovon, François. *L'Évangile selon Saint Luc*. 4 vols. Commentaire du Nouveau Testament. Genève: Labor et Fides, 1991.

Bowersock, G.W. *Greek Sophists in the Roman Empire*. Oxford: Clarendon, 1969.

———. "Introduction." Pages 9–22 in *Philostratus: Life of Apollonius*. Translated by C. P. Jones. Edited by Betty Radice and Robert Baldick. Harmondsworth: Penguin, 1970.

Branick, Vincent P. *The House Church in the Writings of Paul*. Zacchaeus Studies: New Testament. Wilmington, DE: M. Glazier, 1989.

Braun, Willi. *Feasting and Social Rhetoric in Luke 14*. Society for New Testament Studies Monograph Series 85. Cambridge: Cambridge University Press, 1995.

Braund, David. *Rome and the Friendly King: The Character of the Client Kingship*. London: Croom Helm, 1984.

Brooks, James A., and Carlton L. Winbery. *Syntax of New Testament Greek*. Lanham, MD: University Press of America, 1979.

Broughton, T. R. S. "Part IV: Roman Asia." Pages 499-918 in *Africa, Syria, Greece, Asia*. Edited by Tenney Frank. Vol. 4 of *An Economic Survey of Ancient Rome*. Patterson, NJ: Pageant, 1959.
Bruce, Frederick Fyvie. *New Testament History*. New York: Doubleday, 1969.
Bruehler, Bart B. "The Public, the Political, and the Private: The Social-Spatial Characteristics of Luke 18:35—19:48 and the Gospel as a Whole." PhD diss., Emory University, 2007.
Bultmann, Rudolph. *The History of the Synoptic Tradition*. Translated by John Marsh. New York: Harper & Row, 1976.
Burger, Christoph. *Jesus als Davidssohn: eine traditiongeschichtliche Untersuchung*. Forschungen zur Religion und Literature des Alten und Neuen Testaments 98. Göttingen: Vandenhoeck & Ruprecht, 1970.
Burgos Nuñez, Miguel de. "El Relato de Zaqueo (Lc 19:1-10) Un Pacto de Justicia." *Communio* 26 (1993) 165-84.
Busse, Ulrich. *Die Wunder des Propheten Jesus: Die Rezeption, Komposition und Interpretation der Wundertradition in Evangelium des Lukas*. Forschung zur Bibel 24. Stuttgart: Katholisches Bibelwerk, 1977.
Cadbury, Henry J. *The Making of Luke-Acts*. 1927. Reprint, London: SPCK, 1968.
Camp, Claudia V. "Storied Space, or, Ben Sira 'Tells' a Temple." Pages 64-80 in *"Imagining" Biblical Worlds: Studies in Spatial, Social and Historical Constructs in Honor of James W. Flanagan*. Edited by David M. Gunn and Paula M. McNutt. Journal for the Study of the Old Testament Supplement Series 359. London: Sheffield Academic, 2002.
Cancik, Hubert. "The History of Culture, Religion, and Institutions in Ancient Historiography: Philological Observations Concerning Luke's History." *Journal of Biblical Literature* 116 (1997) 673-95.
Carrière, Jean-Claude. "Préceptes Politique." Pages 1-146 in *Plutarque Oeuvres Morales Tome XI—Duxième Partie*. Paris: Belles Lettres, 1984.
Cassidy, Richard J. *Jesus, Politics, and Society: A Study of Luke's Gospel*. Maryknoll, NY: Orbis, 1986.
Cassidy, Richard J., and Philip J. Scarper, editors. *Political Issues in Luke-Acts*. Maryknoll, NY: Orbis, 1983.
Castiglione, Dario. "Public Reason, Private Citizenship." Pages 28-50 in *Public and Private: Legal, Political and Philosophical Perspectives*. Edited by Maurizio Passerin d'Entrèves and Ursula Vogel. London: Routledge, 2000.
Catchpole, David R. "The 'Triumphal' Entry." Pages 319-34 in *Jesus and the Politics of His Day*. Edited by Ernst Bammel and C. F. D. Moule. Cambridge: Cambridge University Press, 1984.
Chance, J. Bradley. *Jerusalem, the Temple and the New Age in Luke-Acts*. Macon, GA: Mercer University Press, 1988.
Chevalier, Raymond. *Roman Roads*. Translated by N. H. Field. Berkeley: University of California Press, 1976.
Chiappari, Christopher L. "Conceptual Dichotomies and Cultural Realities: Gender, Work, and Religion in Highland Guatemala." *Anthropology of Work Review* 22.3 (2002) 14-23.
Cohen, David. *Law, Sexuality, and Society: The Enforcement of Morals in Classical Athens*. Cambridge: Cambridge University Press, 1991.
Colaiaco, James A. *Socrates against Athens: Philosophy on Trial*. New York: Routledge, 2001.
Conn, Harvie M. "Lucan Perspectives and the City." *Missiology: An International Review* 13 (1985) 409-28.
Contreras Molinà, Francisco. "El Relato de Zaqueo en el Evangelio de Lucas." *Communio* 21(1988) 3-47.
Conzelmann, Hans. "Die geographischen Vorstellung im Lukasevangelium." PhD diss., University of Tübingen, 1951.
Conzelmann, Hans. *The Theology of St. Luke*. Translated by Geoffrey Buswell. New York: Harper & Row, 1961. Translation of *Die Mitte der Zeit*. Tübingen: Mohr/Siebeck, 1953.
Corbo, V. C. *Cafarnao I: Gli Edifici della Citta*. Jerusalem: Franciscan, 1975.
Corley, Kathleen E. *Private Women, Public Meals: Social Conflict in the Synoptic Tradition*. Peabody, MA: Hendrickson, 1993.
Coulton, J. J. *The Architectural Development of the Greek Stoa*. Oxford Monographs on Classical Archaeology. Oxford: Clarendon, 1976.
Creed, John Martin. *The Gospel According to St. Luke*. 2nd ed. London: Macmillan, 1942.
Cromartie, Michael, editor. *A Public Faith: Evangelicals and Civic Engagement*. Lanham, MD: Rowman & Littlefield, 2003.
Crossley, Nick. *Making Sense of Social Movements*. Buckingham: Open University Press, 2002.

Bibliography

Cubitt, Tessa, and Helen Greenslade. "Public and Private Spheres: The End of Dichotomy." Pages 52–64 in *Gender Politics in Latin America: Debates in Theory and Practice*. Edited by Elizabeth Dore. New York: Monthly Review Press, 1997.

Culpepper, R. Alan. *Luke*. The New Interpreter's Bible 9. Nashville: Abingdon, 1994.

Denaux, Adelbert. "The Parable of the Talents/Pounds (Q 19:12–27). A Reconstruction of the Q text." Pages 429–60 in *The Sayings Source Q and the Historical Jesus*. Edited by A. Lindermann. Bibliotheca ephemeridum theologicarum lovaniensium 158. Leuven: Peeters, 2001.

———. "The Parable of the King-Judge (Lk 19,12–28 and Its Relation to the Entry Story (Lk 19, 29–44)." *Zeitschrift für die neutestamentliche Wissenschaft und die Knude der älteren Kirche* 93 (2002) 35–57.

D'Entrèves, Maurizio Passerin. "Public and Private in Hannah Arendt's Conception of Citizenship." Pages 68–89 in *Public and Private: Legal, Political and Philosophical Perspectives*. Edited by Maurizio Passerin d'Entrèves and Ursula Vogel. London: Routledge, 2000.

D'Entrèves, Maurizio Passerin, and Ursula Vogel. "Public and Private: A Complex Relation." Pages 1–16 in *Public and Private: Legal, Political and Philosophical Perspectives*. Edited by Maurizio Passerin d'Entrèves and Urusula Vogel. London: Routledge, 2000.

DeVries, LaMoine F. *Cities of the Biblical World*. Peabody, MA: Hendrickson, 1997.

Dibelius, Martin. *From Tradition to Gospel*. Translated by Bertram Lee Woolf. Cambridge: James Clarke, 1971.

Dinsmoor, William Bell. *The Architecture of Ancient Greece: An Account of Its Historic Development*. London: B. T. Batsford, 1950.

Dodd, C. H. "The Fall of Jerusalem and the 'Abomination of Desolation.'" *Journal of Roman Studies* 37 (1947) 69–83.

Dolan, Michael. *The American Porch: An Informal History of an Informal Place*. Guilford, CT: Lyons, 2002.

Donlon, Jocelyn Hazelwood. *Swinging in Place: Porch Life in Southern Culture*. Chapel Hill: University of North Carolina Press, 2001.

Donovan, Brian R. "The City and the Garden: Plato's Retreat from the Teaching of Virtue." *Educational Theory* 45 (1995) 453–64.

Dorsey, David A. *The Roads and Highways of Ancient Israel*. ASOR Library of Biblical and Near Eastern Archaeology. Baltimore: Johns Hopkins University Press, 1991.

Dowley, Tim. *The Kregel Bible Atlas*. Grand Rapids: Kregel, 2003.

Duby, Georges. "Foreword to a History of Private Life." Pages vii–ix in *A History of Private Life*, vol. 1: *From Pagan Rome to Byzantium*. Edited by Paul Veyne. Cambridge, MA: Belknap, 1987.

Duling, Dennis C. "Solomon, Exorcism, and the Son of David." *Harvard Theological Review* 68 (1975) 235–52.

Dupont, Jacques. "L'aveugle de Jéricho recouvre la vue et suit Jésus (Marc 10, 46–52)." *Revue Africaine de Théologie* 8 (1984) 165–81.

———. "Le riche publicain Zachée est aussi un fils d'Abraham." Pages 265–76 in *Der Treue Gottes trauen: Beiträge zum Werk des Lukas*. Edited by Claus Bussman and Walter Radl. Freiburg: Herder, 1991.

Dyson, Stephen L. *Community and Society in Roman Italy*. Baltimore: Johns Hopkins University Press, 1992.

Easton, Burton Scott. "The Purpose of Acts." Pages 33–120 in *Early Christianity: The Purpose of Acts and Other Papers*. Edited by Frederick C. Grant. SPCK Theology Occasional Papers 6. Reprint, Greenwich, CT: Seabury, 1954.

Eckey, Wilfried. *Das Lukas-Evangelium: Unter Berücksichtigung seiner Parallelen*. 2 vols. Neukirchen-Vluyn: Neukirchener, 2004.

Edmondson, Jonathan. "Cities and Urban Life in the Western Provinces of the Roman Empire, 30 BCE—250 CE." Pages 250–80 in *A Companion to the Roman Empire*. Edited by David S. Potter. Malden, MA: Blackwell, 2006.

Eliav, Yaron Z. *God's Mountain: The Temple Mount in Time, Place, and Memory*. Baltimore: Johns Hopkins University Press, 2005.

Elliott, John H. "Temple Versus Household in Luke-Acts: A Contrast Social Institutions." Pages 211–40 in *The Social World of Luke-Acts: Models for Interpretation*. Edited by Jerome H. Neyrey. Peabody, MA: Hendrickson, 1991.

Ellis, E. Earle. *The Gospel of Luke*. Rev. ed. New Century Bible. Grand Rapids: Eerdmans, 1974.

Elshtain, Jean Bethke. *Public Man, Private Woman: Women in Social and Political Thought*. 2nd ed. Princeton: Princeton University Press, 1993.
Engberg-Pedersen, Troels. "The Hellenistic *Öffentlichkeit*: Philosophy as a Social Force in the Greco-Roman World." Pages 15–37 in *Recruitment, Conquest, and Conflict: Strategies in Judaism, Early Christianity, and the Greco-Roman World*. Edited by Peder Borgen, Vernon K. Robbins, and David B. Gowler. Emory Studies in Early Christianity 6. Atlanta: Scholars, 1998.
Erdemgil, Selahattin. *Ephesus: Ruins and Museum*. Istanbul: NET Turistik Yayinlar, 1995.
Ernst, Josef. *Das Evangelium nach Lukas*. 5th ed. Regensburger Neues Testament. Regensburg: Freidrich Pustet, 1977.
Esler, Philip Francis. *Community and Gospel in Luke-Acts*. Society for New Testament Studies Monograph Series 57. Cambridge: Cambridge University Press, 1987.
Eulau, Heinz. *Micro-Macro Political Analysis: Accents of Inquiry*. Chicago: Aldine, 1969.
———. *Micro-Macro Dilemmas in Political Science*. Norman: University of Oklahoma Press, 1996.
Evans, C. F. *Saint Luke*. TPI New Testament Commentaries. Philadelphia: Trinity, 1990.
Faraone, Christopher Athanasious. "Talismans, Voodoo Dolls and Other Apotropaic Statues in Ancient Greece." PhD diss., Stanford University, 1988.
Finegan, Jack. *The Archaeology of the New Testament: The Life of Jesus and the Beginnings of the Early Church*. Rev. ed. Princeton: Princeton University Press, 1992.
Fisher, Loren R. "'Can This Be the Son of David?'" Pages 82–97 in *Jesus and the Historian*. Edited by F. Thomas Trotter. Philadelphia: Westminster, 1968.
Fitzmyer, Joseph A. *The Gospel According to Luke: Introduction, Translation, and Notes*. 2 vols. Anchor Bible 28, 28a. Garden City, NY: Doubleday, 1981, 1985.
Flanagan, James W. "Ancient Perceptions of Space/Perceptions of Ancient Space." *Semeia* 87 (1999) 15–43.
Foley, Helene P. "The Conceptions of Women in Athenian Drama." Pages 127–68 in *Reflections of Women in Antiquity*. Edited by Helene P. Foley. New York: Gordon and Breach, 1981.
Foucault, Michel. "Of Other Spaces." *Diacritics* 16 (1986) 22–27.
Forbis, Elizabeth P. "Women's Public Image in Italian Honorary Inscriptions." *American Journal of Philology* 111 (1990) 493–512.
Freedman, H. *Shabbath*. The Babylonian Talmud, part 2, vol. 1. Edited by I. Epstein. London: Socino, 1938.
Freyne, Sean. *Galilee, Jesus and the Gospels: Literary Approaches and Historical Investigations*. Philadelphia: Fortress, 1988.
Garnsey, Peter. *Food and Society in Classical Antiquity*. Key Themes in Ancient History. Cambridge: Cambridge University Press, 1999.
Garnsey, Peter, and Richard P. Saller. *The Roman Empire: Economy, Society, and Culture*. London: Duckworth, 1987.
Gasque, W. Ward. *A History of the Interpretation of the Acts of the Apostles*. 2nd ed. Peabody, MA: Hendrickson, 1989.
Gaston, Lloyd. *No Stone on Another: Studies in the Significance of the Fall of Jerusalem in the Synoptic Gospels*. Supplements to Novum Testamentum 23. Leiden: Brill, 1970.
George, Michele. "Domestic Architecture and Household Relations: Pompeii and Roman Ephesos." *Journal for the Study of the New Testament* 27 (2004) 7–25.
Giddens, Anthony. *Central Problems in Social Theory: Action, Structure and Contradiction in Social Analysis*. Berkeley: University of California Press, 1979.
Gillman, John. *Possessions and the Life of Faith: A Reading of Luke-Acts*. Zacchaeus Studies: New Testament. Edited by Mary Ann Getty. Collegeville, MN: Liturgical, 1991.
Gleason, Maud W. "Greek Cities under Roman Rule." Pages 228–49 in *A Companion to the Roman Empire*. Edited by David S. Potter. Blackwell Companions to the Ancient World. Malden, MA: Blackwell, 2006.
Gowler, David B. *Host, Guest, Enemy, and Friend*. Emory Studies in Early Christianity 2. New York: P. Lang, 1991.
———. "Hospitality and Characterization in Luke 11:37–54: A Socio-Narratological Approach." *Semeia* 64 (1994) 213–51.
Grahame, Mark. "Public and Private in the Roman House: The Spatial Order of the *Casa del Fauno*." Pages 137–64 in *Domestic Space in the Roman World: Pompeii and Beyond*. Edited by Ray Laurence and

Bibliography

Andrew Wallace-Hadrill. Journal of Roman Archaeology Supplementary Series 22. Providence, RI: JRA, 1997.

Green, J. R. *Theatre in Ancient Greek Society*. London: Routledge, 1996.

Green, Joel B. "The Demise of the Temple as the 'Culture Center' in Luke-Acts: An Exploration of the Rending of the Temple Veil." *Revue Biblique* 101 (1994) 495–515.

———. *The Gospel of Luke*. The New International Commentary on the New Testament. Grand Rapids: Eerdmans, 1997.

Guess, Raymond. *Public Goods, Private Goods*. Princeton Monographs in Philosophy. Princeton: Princeton University Press, 2001.

Gunn, David M., and Paula M. McNutt, editors. *"Imagining" Biblical Worlds: Studies in Spatial, Social and Historical Constructs in Honor of James W. Flanagan*. Journal for the Study of the Old Testament Supplement Series 359. London: Sheffield Academic, 2002.

Habermas, Jürgen. *The Structural Transformation of the Public Sphere: An Inquiry into a Category of Bourgeois Society*. Translated by Thomas Burger with Frederick Lawrence. Cambridge, MA: MIT Press, 1989.

Hadas, Moses, and Morton Smith. *Heroes and Gods: Spiritual Biographies in Antiquity*. Religious Perspectives 13. Edited by Ruth Nanda Anshen. New York: Harper & Row, 1965.

Haenchen, Ernst. *The Acts of the Apostles: A Commentary*. Translated by Bernard Noble et al. Philadelphia: Westminster, 1971.

Hagner, Donald A. *Matthew 1–13*. Word Biblical Commentary 33A. Waco, TX: Word, 1993.

Hahn, F. *The Titles of Jesus in Christology*. New York: World, 1969.

Hahn, Johannes Münster. "Beggars." Pages 578–80 in vol. 2 of *Brill's New Pauly: Encyclopedia of the Ancient World*. Edited by Hubert Cancik et al. Leiden: Brill, 2003.

Hall, Edward T. *Beyond Culture*. Garden City, NY: Anchor/Doubleday, 1977.

Hamel, Gildas H. *Poverty and Charity in Roman Palestine, First Three Centuries C.E.* University of California Publications: Near Eastern Studies 23. Berkeley: University of California Press, 1990.

Hamm, Dennis. "Acts 3,1–10: The Healing of the Temple Beggar as Lucan Theology." *Biblica* 67 (1986) 305–19.

———. "Sight to the Blind: Vision as Metaphor in Luke." *Biblica* 67 (1986) 457–77.

———. "Luke 19:8 Once Again: Does Zacchaeus Defend or Resolve?" *Journal of Biblical Literature* 107 (1988) 431–37.

Hands, A. R. *Charities and Social Aid in Greece and Rome*. Aspects of Greek and Roman Life. London: Thames & Hampton, 1968.

Harris, Marvin. *Cultural Materialism: The Struggle for a Science of Culture*. New York: Random House, 1979.

Harris, Murray J. *Slave of Christ: A New Testament Metaphor for Total Devotion to Christ*. New Studies in Biblical Theology 8. Downers Grove, IL: InterVarsity, 1999.

Hastings, Adrian. *Prophet and Witness in Jerusalem: A Study in the Teaching of Saint Luke*. Baltimore: Helicon, 1958.

Hénaff, Marcel. *Claude Lévi-Strauss and the Making of Structural Anthropology*. Translated by Mary Baker. Minneapolis: University of Minnesota Press, 1998.

Herrenbrück, Fritz. *Jesus und die Zöllner*. Wissenschaftliche Untersuchungen zum Neuen Testament 2, Reihe 41. Tübingen: Mohr/Siebeck, 1990.

Herzfeld, Michael. "Honour and Shame: Problems in the Comparative Analysis of Moral Systems." *Man* 15 (1980) 339–51.

———. "The Horns of the Mediterraneanist Dilemma." *American Ethnologist* 11 (1984) 439–54.

———. "Within and Without: The Category of 'Female' in the Ethnography of Modern Greece." Pages 215–33 in *Gender and Power in Rural Greece*. Edited by Jill Dubisch. Princeton: Princeton University Press, 1986.

Higgins, W. E. *Xenophon the Athenian: The Problem of the Individual and the Society of the Polis*. Albany: State University of New York Press, 1977.

Hirschfeld, Yizhar. *The Palestinian Dwelling in the Roman-Byzantine Period*. Studio Biblicum Franciscanum Collectio Minor 34. Jerusalem: Franciscan, 1995.

Horsley, G. H. R. "The Inscriptions of Ephesos and the New Testament." *Novum Testamentum* 34 (1992) 106–168.

Horsley, Richard A. *Archaeology, History, and Society in Galilee: The Social Context of Jesus and the Rabbis.* Valley Forge, PA: Trinity, 1996.

Jacobson, David M. "Three Roman Client Kings: Herod of Judea, Archelaus of Cappadocia and Juba of Mauretania." *Palestine Exploration Quarterly* 133 (2001) 22–38.

Jeremias, Joachim. *Jerusalem in the Time of Jesus: An Investigation into Economic and Social Conditions during the New Testament Period.* Translated by F. H. Cave and C. H. Cave. Philadelphia: Fortress, 1969.

Jervell, Jacob. *Luke and the People of God: A New Look at Luke-Acts.* 1972. Reprint, Eugene, OR: Wipf and Stock, 2002.

Johnson, Earl S. "Mark 10:46–52: Blind Bartimaeus." *Catholic Biblical Quarterly* 40 (1978) 191–204.

Johnson, Luke Timothy. *The Literary Function of Possessions in Luke Acts.* Society of Biblical Literature Dissertation Series 39. Edited by Howard C. Kee and Douglas A. Knight. Missoula, MT: Scholars, 1977.

———. "The Lukan Kingship Parable (Lk. 19:11–27)." *Novum Testamentum* 24 (1982) 139–59.

———. *The Gospel of Luke.* Sacra Pagina 3. Collegeville, MN: Liturgical, 1991.

———. *The Real Jesus: The Misguided Quest for the Historical Jesus and the Truth of the Traditional Gospels.* San Francisco: HarperSanFrancisco, 1999.

Johnston, R. J., Derek Gregory, and David M. Smith, editors. *The Dictionary of Human Geography.* 2nd ed. Blackwell Reference. Oxford: Blackwell, 1986.

Jones, C. P. *Plutarch and Rome.* Oxford: Clarendon, 1971.

Just, Felix N.W. "From Tobit to Bartimaeus, From Qumran to Siloam; The Social Role of Blind People and Attitudes toward the Blind in New Testament Times." PhD diss., Yale University, 1998.

Kaiser, Alan. *The Urban Dialogue: An Analysis of the Use of Space in the Roman City of Empúries, Spain.* BAR International Series 901. Oxford: Archaeopress, 2000.

Kalantzis, George. "Ephesus as a Roman, Christian, and Jewish Metropolis in the First and Second Centuries C.E." *Jian Dao* 8 (1997) 103–19.

Kariamadam, Paul. *The Zacchaeus Story (Luke 19:1–10) A Redaction-Critical Investigation.* Pontifical Institute Publications 42. Alwaye, Kerala: Pontifical Institute of Theology and Philosophy, 1985.

Kennedy, George A. *New Testament Interpretation through Rhetorical Criticism.* Studies in Religion. Edited by Charles H. Long. Chapel Hill: University of North Carolina Press, 1984.

Ketter, P. "Zur Lokalisierung der Blindenheilung bei Jericho." *Biblica* 15 (1934) 411–18.

Kilgallen, John J. "John the Baptist, The Sinful Woman, and the Pharisee." *Journal of Biblical Literature* 104 (1985) 675–79.

Kingsbury, Jack Dean. "Observations on 'the Son of Man' in the Gospel According to Luke." *Currents in Theology and Mission* 17 (1990) 283–90.

Kinman, Brent. *Jesus' Entry into Jerusalem: In the Context of Lukan Theology and the Politics of His Day.* Arbeiten zur Geschichte des antike Judentums und des Urchristentums 28. Leiden: Brill, 1995.

Kittel, G., and G. Friedrich, editors. *Theological Dictionary of the New Testament.* Translated by G. W. Bromiley. 10 vols. Grand Rapids: Eerdmans, 1964–76.

Klein, H. "Zur Frage nach dem Abgassungsort der Lukasschriften." *Evangelische Theologie* 32 (1972) 467–77.

Knoles, Thomas Gregory. "Literary Technique and Theme in Philostratus' *Life of Apollonius of Tyana.*" PhD diss., Rutgers University, 1981.

Kodell, Jerome. "Luke's Use of Laos, 'People,' Especially in the Jerusalem Narrative (Lk 19,28–24,35)." *Catholic Biblical Quarterly* 31 (1969) 327–43.

Koester, Helmut, editor. *Ephesos. Metropolis of Asia. An Interdisciplinary Approach to Its Archaeology, Religion, and Culture.* Harvard Theological Studies 41. Valley Forge, PA: Trinity, 1995.

Koh, R. *The Writings of St. Luke.* Hong Kong: Diocesan Literature Committee, 1953.

Kohn, Margaret. *Radical Space.* Ithaca, NY: Cornell University Press, 2003.

Koskenniemi, Erkki. *Apollonios von Tyana in der neutestamentlichen Exegess.* Wissenschaftliche Untersuchungen zum Neuen Testament 2, Reihe 61. Tübingen: Mohr, 1994.

Krinzinger, Friedrich, editor. *Das Hanghaus 2 von Ephesos: Studien ze Baugeschichte und Chronologie.* Archäologische Forschungen 7. Vienna: Verlag der Österreichischen Akademie der Wissenschaften, 2002.

Bibliography

Krygier, Martin. "Publicness, Privateness and 'Primitive Law.'" Pages 307–40 in *Public and Private in Social Life*. Edited by Stanley I. Benn and Gerald F. Gaus. London: Croom Helm, 1983.

La Potterie, Ignace de. "La Parabole du Prétendant à la Royauté (Lc 19, 11–28)." Pages 613–41 in *À Cause de L'Évangile: Études sur les Synoptiques et les Actes*. Edited by Jacques Dupont. Lectio Divina 123. Paris: Editions du Cerf, 1985.

Laet, Sigrfried J. de. *Portorium: étude sur l'organisation douanière chez les Romains surtout à l'épocb du Haut-Empire*. Roman History. New York: Arno, 1975.

Lake, Kirsopp. "Localities in and Near Jerusalem Mentioned in Acts." Pages 474–86 in *The Acts of the Apostles: Additional Notes to the Commentary*. Edited by Kirsopp Lake and Henry J. Cadbury. The Beginnings of Christianity 5. London: Macmillan, 1933.

Lambrecht, Jan. "Reading and Rereading Lk 18:31—22:6." Pages 585–612 in *À Cause de L'Évangile: Études sur les Synoptiques et les Actes*. Edited by Jacques Dupont. Lectio divina 123. Paris: Editions du Cerf, 1985.

Lampe, Peter. *From Paul to Valentinus: Christians at Rome in the First Two Centuries*. Translated by Michael Steinhauser. Edited by Marshall D. Johnson. Minneapolis: Fortress, 2003.

Lamphere, Louise. "The Domestic Sphere of Women and the Public World of Men: The Strengths and limitations of an Anthropological Dichotomy." Pages 86–95 in *Gender in Cross-Cultural Perspective*. Edited by C. B. Brettell and C. F. Sargent. Upper Saddle River, NJ: Pearson Prentice Hall, 2005.

Laurence, Ray. *Roman Pompeii: Space and Society*. London: Routledge, 1994.

———. "Space and Text." Pages 7–14 in *Domestic Space in the Roman World: Pompeii and Beyond*. Edited by Ray Laurence and Andrew Wallace-Hadrill. Journal of Roman Archaeology Supplementary Series 22. Edited by J. H. Humphrey. Portsmouth, RI: JRA, 1997.

Laurence, Ray, and Andrew Wallace-Hadrill, editors. *Domestic Space in the Roman World: Pompeii and Beyond*. Journal of Roman Archaeology Supplementary Series 22. Portsmouth, RI: JRA, 1997.

Lawrence, Arnold Walter. *Greek Architecture*. Rev. by R. A. Tomlinson. The Pelican History of Art. Harmondsworth, UK: Penguin, 1983.

Lefebvre, Henri. *The Production of Space*. Translated by Donald Nicholson-Smith. Oxford: Blackwell, 1991.

Levine, Lee I. *Jerusalem: Portrait of the City in the Second Temple Period (538 B.C.E–70 C.E.)*. Philadelphia: Jewish Publication Society, 2002.

Ling, Roger. *Pompeii: History, Life & Afterlife*. Stroud, Gloucestershire: Tempus, 2005.

Lloyd, G. E. R. *Polarity and Analogy: Two Types of Argumentation in Early Greek Thought*. Cambridge: Cambridge University Press, 1966.

Loewe, William P. "Towards and Interpretation of Lk 19:1–10." *Catholic Biblical Quarterly* 36 (1974) 321–31.

Loffreda, Stanislao. "Capernaum." Pages 291–95 in vol. 1 of *The New Encyclopedia of Archaeological Excavations in the Holy Land*. Edited by Ephraim Stern. New York: Simon & Schuster, 1993.

Lohmeyer, Ernst. *Gottesknecht und Davidssohn*. 2nd ed. Forschung zur Religion und Literature des Alten und Neuen Testaments. Göttingen: Vandenhoeck & Ruprecht, 1953.

Lomas, Kathryn, "The Idea of a City: Élite Ideology and the Evolution of Urban Form in Italy, 200 BC—AD 100." Pages 21–41 in *Roman Urbanism: Beyond the Consumer City*. Edited by Helen M. Parkins. London: Routledge, 1997.

Luow, Johannes P., and Eugene A. Nida. *Greek-English Lexicon of the New Testament Based on Semantic Domains*. New York: United Bible Societies, 1989.

Luz, Ulrich. *Matthew 21–28*. Translated by James E. Couch. Hermeneia. Edited by Helmut Koester. Minneapolis: Fortress, 2005.

MacDonald, Dennis Ronald. *Does the New Testament Imitate Homer*. New Haven, CT: Yale University Press, 2003.

MacMullen, Ramsay. *Enemies of the Roman Order: Treason, Unrest, and Alienation in the Empire*. Cambridge, MA: Harvard University Press, 1966.

———. *Roman Social Relations 50 B.C. to A.D. 284*. New Haven: Yale University Press, 1974.

———. "Women in Public in the Roman Empire." *Historia* 29 (1980) 208–18.

Maddox, Robert. *The Purpose of Luke-Acts*. Forschungen zur Religion und Literatur des Alten und Neuen Testaments 126. Göttingen: Vandenhoeck & Ruprecht, 1982.

Bibliography

Magie, David. *Roman Rule in Asia Minor: To the End of the Third Century after Christ*. 2 Vols. Princeton: Princeton University Press, 1950.

Malherbe, Abraham J. "'Not in a Corner': Early Christian Apologetic in Acts 26:26." *The Second Century* 5 (1985/1986) 193–210.

Malmendier, Ulrike. "Roman Shares." Pages 31–42 in *The Origins of Value: The Financial Innovations that Created Modern Capital Markets*. Edited by W. Goetzmann and G. Rouwenhorst. Oxford: Oxford University Press, 2005.

Malina, Bruce J. "Reading Theory Perspective: Reading Luke-Acts." Pages 3–23 in *The Social World of Luke-Acts: Models for Interpretation*. Edited by Jerome H. Neyrey. Peabody, MA: Hendrickson, 1991.

Malina, Bruce J., and Jerome H. Neyrey. "Conflict in Luke-Acts: Labelling and Deviance Theory." Pages 97–122 in *The Social World of Luke-Acts: Models for Interpretation*. Edited by Jerome H. Neyrey. Peabody, MA: Hendrickson, 1991.

———. "First Century Personality: Dyadic, Not Individual." Pages 67–96 in *The Social World of Luke-Acts: Models for Interpretation*. Edited by Jerome H. Neyrey. Peabody, MA: Hendrickson, 1991.

———. "Honor and Shame in Luke-Acts: Pivotal Values in the Mediterranean World." Pages 25–65 in *The Social World of Luke-Acts: Models for Interpretation*. Edited by Jerome H. Neyrey. Peabody, MA: Hendrickson, 1991.

Malina, Bruce J. and Richard L. Rohrbaugh. *Social-Science Commentary on the Synoptic Gospels*. Minneapolis: Fortress, 1992.

Marshall, Anthony J. "Symbols and Showmanship in Roman Public Life: The Fasces." *Phoenix* 38 (1984) 120–41.

Marshall, I. Howard. *The Gospel of Luke: A Commentary on the Greek Text*. New International Greek Testament Commentary. Grand Rapids: Eerdmans, 1978.

———. *Luke: Historian & Theologian*. 3rd ed. Downers Grove, IL: InterVarsity, 1988.

Marshall, John W., and Russell Martin. "Government and Public Law in Galilee, Judaea, Hellenistic cities, and the Roman Empire." Pages 409–29 in *Handbook of Early Christianity: Social Science Approaches*. Edited by Anthony J. Blasi, Jean Duhaime, and Paul-André Turcotte. Walnut Creek, CA: Altamira, 2002.

Mason, Hugh J. *Greek Terms for Roman Institutions: A Lexicon and Analysis*. Toronto: Hakkert, 1974.

Mauser, Ulrich. *Christ in the Wilderness: The Wilderness Theme in the Second Gospel and Its Basis in the Biblical Tradition*. Studies in Biblical Theology 39. London: SCM, 1963.

Maybury-Lewis, David, and Uri Almagor, editors. *The Attraction of Opposites: Thought and Society in the Dualistic Mode*. Ann Arbor: University of Michigan Press, 1989.

McCabe, Donald F., R. Neil Elliot, Allen Hilton Kang Na, and Calvin Redmond. *Ephesos Inscriptions*. 3 Vols. Princeton: Institute for Advanced Study, 1991. Online: http://epigraphy.packhum.org/inscriptions.

McKeever, Michael Colin. "Refiguring Space in the Lukan Passion Narrative." Paper presented at the AAR/SBL Annual Meeting: Construction of Ancient Space Seminar. Nashville, November 19, 2000. Online: http://www.cwru.edu/affil/GAIR/papers/2000papers/ mckeever.htm.

McNutt, Paula M. "'Fathers of the Empty Spaces' and 'Strangers Forever': Social Marginality and the Construction of Space." Pages 30–50 in *"Imagining" Biblical Worlds: Studies in Spatial, Social and Historical Constructs in Honor of James W. Flanagan*. Edited by David M. Gunn and Paula M. McNutt. Journal for the Study of the Old Testament Supplement Series 359. London: Sheffield Academic, 2002.

McRay, John. *Archaeology and the New Testament*. Grand Rapids: Baker, 1990.

McVann, Mark. "Rituals of Status Transformation in Luke-Acts: The Case of Jesus the Prophet." Pages 333–60 in *The Social World of Luke-Acts: Models for Interpretation*. Edited by Jerome H. Neyrey. Peabody, MA: Hendrickson, 1991.

Meeks, Wayne A. *The First Urban Christians: The Social World of the Apostle Paul*. New Haven, CT: Yale University Press, 1983.

Meeks, Wayne A., editor. *The Harper Collins Study Bible*. New York: HarperCollins, 1993.

Meyers, Carol. "Temple, Jerusalem." Pages 350–69 in vol. 6 of *The Anchor Bible Dictionary*. Edited by David Noel Freedman. New York: Doubleday, 1992.

Meyers, Eric M. "The Problems of Gendered Space in Syro-Palesinian Domestic Architecture: The Case of Roman Period Galilee." Pages 44–69 in *Early Christian Families in Context: An Interdisciplinary*

Bibliography

Dialogue. Edited by David L. Balch and Carolyn Osiek. Religion, Marriage, and Family Series. Grand Rapids: Eerdmans, 2003.

Meyers, Eric M., and James F. Strange. *Archaeology, the Rabbis, and Early Christianity: The Social and Historical Setting of Palestinian Judaism and Christianity*. Nashville: Abingdon, 1981.

Meynet, Roland. "Au Coeur du Texte: Analyse Rhetorique de l'Aveugle de Jéricho selon Saint Luc." *La Nouvelle Revue Théologique* 103 (1981) 696–710.

———. *L'Évangile selon Saint Luc. Analyse Rhétorique*. 2 vols. Paris: Editions du Cerf, 1988.

———. "Jésus, Fils de David dans l'Évangile de Luc." Pages 413–27 in *Figures de David à Travers la Bible*. Paris: Editions du Cerf, 1999.

Minear, Paul S. "Jesus' Audiences, According to Luke." *Novum Testamentum* 16 (1974) 81–109.

———. *To Heal and Reveal: The Prophetic Vocation According to Luke*. New York: Seabury, 1976.

Mitchell, Alan C. "Zacchaeus Revisited: Luke 19,8 as a Defense." *Biblica* 71 (1990) 153–76.

Moessner, David P. *Lord of the Banquet: The Literary and Theological Significance of the Lukan Travel Narrative*. Minneapolis: Fortress, 1989.

———. "Reading Luke's Gospel as Ancient Hellenistic Narrative: Luke's Narrative Plan of Israel's Suffering Messiah as God's Savind 'Plan' for the World." Pages 125–154 in *Reading Luke: Interpretation, Reflection, Formation*. Edited by Craig G. Bartholomew, Joel B. Green, and Anthony C. Thistleton. Grand Rapids: Zondervan, 2005.

Moessner, David P., editor. *Jesus and the Heritage of Israel: Luke's Narrative Claim on Israel's Legacy*. Vol. 1 of Luke the Interpreter of Israel. Edited by David P. Moessner and David L. Tiede. Harrisburg, PA: Trinity, 2000.

Moore, Thomas S. "'To the End of the Earth': The Geographical and Ethnic Universalism of Acts 1:8 in Light of Isaianic Influence on Luke." *Journal of the Evangelical Theological Society* 40 (1997) 389–99.

Moxnes, Halvor. *The Economy of the Kingdom: Social Conflict and Economic Relations in Luke's Gospel*. Overtures to Biblical Theology. Minneapolis: Fortress, 1988.

———, "Kingdom Takes Place: Transformations of Place and Power in the Kingdom of God in the Gospel of Luke." Pages 176–209 in *Social Scientific Models for Interpreting the Bible*. Biblical Interpretation 53. Leiden: Brill, 2001.

———. *Putting Jesus in His Place: A Radical Vision of Household and Kingdom*. Louisville: Westminster John Knox, 2003.

Nails, Debra. *Agora, Academy, and the Conduct of Philosophy*. Philosophical Studies Series 63. Edited by Keith Lehrer. Dordrecht, Neth.: Kluwer, 1995.

Neale, David A. *None but the Sinners: Religious Categories in the Gospel of Luke*. Journal for the Study of the New Testament Supplement Series 58. Sheffield: Sheffield Academic, 1991.

Nelson, Peter K. *Leadership and Discipleship: A Study of Luke 22:24–30*. Society of Biblical Literature Dissertation Series 138. Atlanta: Scholars, 1994.

Netzer, Ehud. "Jericho." Pages 723–40 in vol. 3 of *The Anchor Bible Dictionary*. Edited by David Noel Freedman. 6 vols. New York: Doubleday, 1992.

Neusner, Jacob. *The Talmud of the Land of Israel*. Chicago Studies in the History of Judaism 11: Shabbat. Chicago: University of Chicago Press, 1991.

Neyrey, Jerome H., editor. *The Social World of Luke-Acts: Models for Interpretation*. Peabody, MA: Hendrickson, 1991.

Neyrey, Jerome H. "Attitudes to the Poor in New Testament Times." Online: http://www.nd.edu/~jneyrey1/Attitudes.html.

———. "Ceremonies in Luke-Acts: The Case of Meals and Table Fellowship." Pages 361–387 in *The Social World of Luke-Acts: Models for Interpretation*. Edited by Jerome H. Neyrey. Peabody, MA: Hendrickson, 1991.

———. "Jesus, Gender, and the Gospel of Matthew." Pages 43–66 in *New Testament Masculinities*. Edited by Stephen D. Moore and Janice Capel Anderson. Semeia 45. Atlanta: Society of Biblical Literature, 2003.

———. "Spaces and Places, Whence and Whither, Homes and Rooms: 'Territoriality' in the Fourth Gospel." *Biblical Theology Bulletin* 32 (2002) 60–74.

———. "The Symbolic Universe of Luke-Acts: 'They Turn the World Upside Down.'" Pages 271–304 in *The Social World of Luke-Acts: Models for Interpretation*. Edited by Jerome H. Neyrey. Peabody, MA: Hendrickson, 1991.

———. "'Teaching You in Public and from House to House' (Acts 20:20) Unpacking a Cultural Stereotype." *Journal for the Study of the New Testament* 26 (2003) 69–102.

———. "'What's Wrong with This Picture?': John 4, Cultural Stereotypes of Women, and Public and Private Space." *Biblical Theology Bulletin* 24 (1994) 77–91.

Nikolaidis, Anastasios G., editor. *The Unity of Plutarch's Work: 'Moralia' Themes in the 'Lives,' Features of the 'Lives' in the 'Moralia.'* Millenium Studies in the Culture and History of the First Millenium CE, 19. Berlin: de Gruyter, 2008.

Nolland, John. *Luke 18:35—24:53*. Word Biblical Commentary 35c. Waco, TX: Word, 1993.

Oakes, Peter. *Reading Romans in Pompeii*. Minneapolis: Fortress, 2009.

Oakman, Douglas E. "The Countryside in Luke-Acts." Pages 151–179 in *The Social World of Luke-Acts: Models for Interpretation*. Edited by Jerome H. Neyrey. Peabody, MA: Hendrickson, 1991.

O'Hanlon, John. "The Story of Zacchaeus and the Lukan Ethic." *Journal for the Study of the New Testament* 12(1981) 2–26.

O'Neill, Shane. "Private Irony and the Public Hope of Richard Rorty's Liberalism." Pages 51–67 in *Public and Private: Legal, Political and Philosophical Perspectives*. Edited by Maurizio Passerin d'Entrèves and Ursula Vogel. London: Routledge, 2000.

Ortner, Sherry. "Is Female to Male as Nature Is to Culture?" Pages 67–88 in *Woman, Culture, and Society*. Edited by M. Rosaldo and L. Lamphere. Stanford, CA: Stanford University Press, 1974.

Osiek, Carolyn. "Archaeological and Architectural Issues and the Question of Demographic and Urban Forms." Pages 83–103 in *Handbook of Early Christianity: Social Science Approaches*. Edited by Anthony J. Blasi, Jean Duhaime, and Paul-André Turcotte. Walnut Creek, CA: Altamira, 2002.

Oster, Richard E. *A Bibliography of Ancient Ephesus*. ATLA Bibliography Series 19. Metuchen, NJ: ATLA, 1987.

O'Toole, Robert F. "The Literary Form of Luke 19:1–10." *Journal of Biblical Literature* 110 (1991) 107–16.

Parsons, Mikeal C. "The Place of Jerusalem on the Lukan Landscape: An Exercise in Symbolic Cartography." Pages 155–71 in *Literary Studies in Luke-Acts: Essays in Honor of Joseph B. Tyson*. Edited by Richard P. Thompson and Thomas E. Phillips. Macon, GA: Mercer University Press, 1998.

———. "'Short in Stature': Luke's Physical Description of Zacchaeus." *New Testament Studies* 47 (2001) 50–57.

Parsons, Mikeal C., and Richard I. Pervo. *Rethinking the Unity of Luke and Acts*. Minneapolis: Fortress, 1993.

Pateman, Carole. "Feminist Critiques of the Public/Private Dichotomy." Pages 281–303 in *Public and Private in Social Life*. Edited by Stanley I. Benn and Gerald F. Gaus. London: Croom Helm, 1983.

Patterson, Cynthia B. *The Family in Greek History*. Cambridge, MA: Harvard University Press, 1998.

Paul, André. "La guérison de l'aveugle (des aveugles) de Jéricho." *Foi et Vie* 69.3 (1970) 44–69.

Penner, Todd C. "In Praise of Christian Origins: Stephen and the Hellenists in Lukan Apologetic Historiography." PhD diss., Emory University, 2000.

Pereira, Francis. *Ephesus: Climax of Universalism in Luke-Acts. A Redaction-Critical Study of Paul's Ephesian Ministry (Acts 18:23—20:1)*. Jesuit Theological Forum Studies 1, series X. Anand, India: Gujarat Sahitya Prakash, 1983.

Perot, André. *Land of Christ: Archaeology, History, Geography*. Translated by James H. Farley. Philadelphia: Fortress, 1968.

Perring, Dominic. "Spatial Organisation and Social Change in Roman Towns." Pages 273–93 in *City and Country in the Ancient World*. Edited by John Rich and Andrew Wallace-Hadrill. London: Routledge, 1991.

Petzke, G. *Die Traditionen über Apollonius von Tyana und das Neue Testament*. Studia ad Corpus Hellenisticum Novi Testamenti. Edited by Hans Dieter Betz, G. Delling, and W. C. Van Unnik. Leiden: Brill, 1970.

Pilch, John J. "Sickness and Healing in Luke-Acts." Pages 181–209 in *The Social World of Luke-Acts: Models for Interpretation*. Edited by Jerome H. Neyrey. Peabody, MA: Hendrickson, 1991.

Plato. *The Republic*. Edited by G. R. F. Ferrari. Translated by Tom Griffith. Cambridge Texts in the History of Political Thought. Cambridge: Cambridge University Press, 2000.

Plümacher, Eckhard. *Lukas als hellenistischer Schriftsteller: Studien zur Apostelgeschichte*. Göttingen: Vandenhoeck & Ruprecht, 1972.

Bibliography

Pohl, Christine D. *Making Room: Recovering Hospitality as a Christian Tradition.* Grand Rapids: Eerdmans, 1999.

Pomeroy, Sarah B. *Xenophon Oeconomicus: A Social and Historical Commentary.* Oxford: Clarendon, 1994.

Porter, Stanley. "'In the Vicinity of Jericho': Luke 18:35 in the Light of its Synoptic Parallels." *Bulletin of Biblical Research* 2 (1992) 91–104.

Ravens, D. A. S. "Zacchaeus: The Final Part of a Lucan Triptych?" *Journal for the Study of the New Testament* 41 (1991) 19–32.

Reece, Steve. *The Stranger's Welcome: Oral Theory and the Aesthetics of the Homeric Hospitality Scene.* Michigan Monographs in Classical Antiquity. Ann Arbor: University of Michigan Press, 1993.

Reimer, Andy M. *Miracle and Magic: A Study in the Acts of the Apostles and the Life of Apollonius of Tyana.* Journal for the Study of the New Testament Supplement Series 235. London: Sheffield Academic, 2002.

Rengstorf, K. H. *Das Evangelium nach Lukas.* 14th ed. Das Neue Testament Deutch 3. Göttingen: Vendenhoeck & Ruprecht, 1969.

Richardson, Peter. "Towards a Typology of Levantine/Palestinian Houses." *Journal for the Study of the New Testament* 27 (2004) 47–68.

Riggsby, Andrew M. "'Public' and 'Private' in Roman Culture: The Case of the *Cubiculum*." *Journal of Roman Archaeology* 10 (1997) 36–56.

Riley, Henry Thomas. *The Comedies of Plautus.* 2 vols. London: G. Bell, 1912.

Robbins, Vernon K. "The Healing of Blind Bartimaeus (10:46–52) in the Marcan Theology." *Journal of Biblical Literature* 92 (1973) 224–43.

———. *Jesus the Teacher: A Socio-Rhetorical Interpretation of Mark.* Minneapolis: Fortress, 1992.

———. "Luke-Acts: A Mixed Population Seeks a Home in the Roman Empire." Pages 202–21 in *Images of Empire.* Edited by Loveday Alexander. Sheffield: JSOT Press, 1991.

———. "The Social Location of the Implied Author of Luke-Acts." Pages 305–32 in *The Social World of Luke-Acts: Models for Interpretation.* Edited by Jerome H. Neyrey. Peabody, MA: Hendrickson, 1991.

———. *The Tapestry of Early Christian Discourse: Rhetoric, Society and Ideology.* London: Routledge, 1996.

Robinson, W. C. *Der Weg des Herrn: Studien zur Geschichte und Eschatologie im Lukas-Evangelium: Ein Gespräch mit Hans Conzelmann.* Theologische Forschung. Hamburg-Bergstedt: H. Reich, 1964.

Rogers, Guy MacLean. *The Sacred Identity of Ephesos: Foundation Myths of a Roman City.* London: Routledge, 1991.

Rohrbaugh, Richard L. "Methodological Considerations in the Debate over the Social Class of Early Christians." *Journal of the American Academy of Religion* 52 (1984) 519–46.

———. "The Pre-Industrial City in Luke-Acts: Urban Social Relations." Pages 125–49 in *The Social World of Luke-Acts: Models for Interpretation.* Edited by Jerome H. Neyrey. Peabody, MA: Hendrickson, 1991.

———. "The Jesus Tradition: The Gospel Writers' Strategies of Persuasion." Pages 198–230 in vol. 1 of *The Early Christian World.* Edited by Philip F. Esler. London: Routledge, 2000.

Roller, Duane R. *The World of Juba II and Kleopatra Selene: Royal Scholarship on Rome's African Frontier.* New York: Routledge, 2003.

Roskam, Geert. "Two Roads to Politics. Plutarch on the Statesman's Entry in Political Life." Pages 325–37 in *The Unity of Plutarch's Work: 'Moralia' Themes in the 'Lives,' Features of the 'Lives' in the 'Moralia.'* Edited by Anastasios G. Nikolaidis. Millenium Studies in the Culture and History of the First Millenium CE, 19. Berlin: de Gruyter, 2008.

Rosner, Brian S. "Acts and Biblical History." Pages 65–82 in *The Book of Acts in Its Ancient Literary Setting.* Edited by Bruce W. Winter and Andrew D. Clarke. Vol. 1 of *The Book of Acts in Its First Century Setting.* Edited by Bruce W. Winter. Grand Rapids: Eerdmans, 1993.

Rostovzeff, Michael Ivanovitch. *Geschichte der Staatspacht in der römischen Kaiserzeit bis Diokletian.* Leipzig: Dieterische Verlagsbuchhandlung (T. Weicher), 1902.

———. *The Social and Economic History of the Roman Empire.* 2 vols. 2nd ed. Rev. by P .M. Fraser. Oxford: Clarendon, 1957.

Roth, S. John. *The Blind, the Lame, and the Poor: Character Types in Luke-Acts.* Journal for the Study of the New Testament Supplement Series 144. Sheffield: Sheffield Academic, 1997.

Sack, Robert David. *Conceptions of Space in Social Thought: A Geographic Perspective.* Minneapolis: University of Minnesota, 1980.

———. *Homo Geographicus: A Framework for Action, Awareness, and Moral Concern.* Baltimore: Johns Hopkins University Press, 1997.

———. *Human Territoriality.* Cambridge Studies in Historical Geography 7. Cambridge: Cambridge University Press, 1986.

Sahlins, Marshall. *Historical Metaphors and Mythical Realities: Structure in the Early History of the Sandwich Islands Kingdom.* ASAO Special Publications 1. Ann Arbor: University of Michigan Press, 1981.

Saldarini, Anthony J. "Sanhedrin." Pages 975–80 in vol. 5 of *The Anchor Bible Dictionary.* Edited by David Noel Freedman. New York: Doubleday, 1992.

Sanders, James A. "A Hermeneutic Fabric: Psalm 118 in Luke's Entrance Narrative." Pages 140–53 in *Luke and Scripture: The Function of Sacred Tradition in Luke-Acts.* Edited by Craig A. Evans and James A. Sanders. Minneapolis: Fortress, 1993.

Sawicki, Marianne. *Crossing Galilee: Architectures of Contact in the Occupied Land of Jesus.* Harrisburg, PA: Trinity, 2000.

Saxonhouse, Arlene W. "Classical Greek Conceptions of Public and Private." Pages 363–84 in *Public and Private in Social Life.* Edited by Stanley I. Benn and Gerald F. Gaus. London: Croom Helm, 1983.

Scherrer, Peter. "The City of Ephesos from the Roman Period to Late Antiquity." Pages 1–26 in *Ephesos, Metropolis of Asia: An Interdisciplinary Approach to Its Archaeology, Religion, and Culture.* Edited by Helmut Koester. Harvard Theological Studies 41. Valley Forge, PA: Trinity, 1995.

———. "The Historical Topography of Ephesus." Pages 57–93 in *Urbanism in Western Asia Minor: New Studies on Aphrodisias, Ephesos, Hierapolis, Pergamon, Perge and Xanthos.* Edited by C. Stein and J. H. Humphrey. Journal of Roman Archaeology Supplementary Series 45. Portsmouth, RI: Journal of Roman Archaeology, 2001.

Schleiermacher, Frederick. *A Critical Essay on the Gospel of St. Luke.* Translated by Connop Thirlwall. London: John Taylor, 1825.

Schneiders, Sandra M. *The Revelatory Text: Interpreting the New Testament as Sacred Scripture.* 2nd ed. Collegeville, MN: Liturgical, 1999.

Schürmann, Heinz. *Das Lukasevangelium.* 2 vols. Herders Theologische Kommentar zum Neuen Testament 3. Freiburg: Herder, 1969–94.

Scott, B. Brandon. "A Master's Praise: Luke 16, 1–8a." *Biblica* 64 (1983) 173–88.

Scott, James M. "Luke's Geographical Horizon." Pages 483–544 in *The Book of Acts in Its Graeco-Roman Setting.* Edited by David W. J. Gill and Conrad Gempf. Vol. 2 of *The Book of Acts in Its First Century Setting.* Edited by Bruce W. Winter. Grand Rapids: Eerdmans, 1994.

Segal, Arthur. "Public Plazas in the Cities of Roman Palestine and Provincial Arabia." Pages 451–488 in *Classical Studies in Honor of David Sohlberg.* Edited by Ranon Katzoff. Ramat Gan: Bar-Ilan University Press, 1996.

———. *From Function to Monument: Urban Landscapes of Roman Palestine, Syria and Provincial Arabia.* Oxbow Monograph 66. Oxford: Oxbow, 1997.

Shellard, Barbara. *New Light on Luke: Its Purpose, Sources and Literary Context.* Journal for the Study of the New Testament Supplement Series 215. London: Sheffield, 2002.

Shelton, Jo-Ann. *As the Romans Did: A Sourcebook in Roman Social History.* 2nd ed. New York: Oxford University Press, 1998.

Slotki, W. 'Erubin. The Babylonian Talmud, part 2, vol. 3. Edited by I. Epstein. London: Socino, 1938.

Smith, Dennis E. "Table Fellowship as a Literary Motif in the Gospel of Luke." *Journal of Biblical Literature* 106 (1987) 613–38.

Smith, William, William Wayte, and G. E. Marindin, editors. "The Plan of the House of Sallust." In *A Dictionary of Greek and Roman Antiquities.* London: John Murray, 1890. Online: http://www.perseus.tufts.edu/cgi-bin/image?lookup=1999.04.0063.fig10682.

Smyth, Herbert Weir. *Greek Grammar.* Revised by Gordon M. Messing. Cambridge: Harvard University Press, 1984.

Soards, Marion L. "The Historical and Cultural Setting of Luke-Acts." Pages 33–47 in *New Views on Luke and Acts.* Edited by Earl Richard. Collegeville, MN: Liturgical, 1990.

Bibliography

Soja, Edward W. *Thirdspace: Journeys to Los Angeles and Other Real-and-Imagined Places*. Cambridge, MA: Blackwell, 1996.

Speckman, McGlory T. "Beggars and Gospel in Luke-Acts: Preliminary Observations on an Emerging Model in the Light of Recent Developmental Theories." *Neotestamentica* 31 (1997) 309–37.

———. "The Kairos behind the Kairos Document." *Religion & Theology* 5 (1998) 194–221.

Sperber, Daniel. *The City in Roman Palestine*. New York: Oxford University Press, 1998.

Stegemann, Ekkehard W., and Wolfgang Stegemann. *The Jesus Movement: A Social History of Its First Century*. Translated by O. C. Dean Jr. Minneapolis: Fortress, 1999.

Steiner, Hillel. "The 'Public-Prvate' Demarcation." Pages 19–27 in *Public and Private: Legal, Political and Philosophical Perspectives*. Edited by Maurizio Passerin d'Entrèves and Ursula Vogel. London: Routledge, 2000.

Steinhauser, Michael G. "The Form of the Bartimaeus Narrative." *New Testament Studies* 32 (1986) 583–95.

Stephen, Lynn. *Women and Social Movements in Latin America: Power from Below*. Austin: University of Texas Press, 1997.

Sterling, Gregory L. *Historiography and Self-Definition: Josephos, Luke-Acts and Apologetic Historiography*. Novum Testamentum Supplements 64. Leiden: Brill, 1992.

———. "Luke-Acts and Apologetic Historiography." *SBL Seminar Papers* 28 (1989) 326–42.

Stowers, Stanley Kent. "Social Status, Public Speaking and Private Teaching: The Circumstances of Paul's Preaching Activity." *Novum Testamentum* 26 (1984) 59–82.

Strange, James F. "First Century Galilee from Archaeology and from the Texts." Pages 39–49 in *Archaeology and the Galilee: Texts and Contexts in the Graeco-Roman and Byzantine Periods*. Edited by Douglas R. Edwards and C. Thomas McCollough. South Florida Studies in the History of Judaism Number 143. Atlanta: Scholars, 1997.

Strauss, Mark L. *The Davidic Messiah in Luke-Acts: The Promise and Its Fulfillment in Lukan Christology*. Journal for the Study of the New Testament Supplement Series 110. Sheffield: Sheffield Academic, 1995.

Strelan, Rick. *Paul, Artemis, and the Jews in Ephesus*. Beihefte zur Zeitschrift für die neuetestamentliche Wissenschaft und die Kunde der älteren Kirche 80. Berlin: de Gruyter, 1996.

Strobel, Friedrich A. "Lukas der Antiochener (Bermerkungen zu Act 11,28D)." *Zeitschrift für Die Neutestamentliche Wissenschaft und die Kunde der Älteren Kirche* 49 (1958) 131–34.

Strocka, Volker Michael. *Casa del Labirinto (VI 11, 8–10)*. Häuser in Pompeji 4. Münich: Hirmer Verlag, 1991.

Swanson, Judith A. *The Public and the Private in Aristotle's Political Philosophy*. Ithaca, NY: Cornell University Press, 1992.

Talbert, Charles H. *Reading Luke: A Literary and Theological Commentary on the Third Gospel*. New York: Crossroad, 1982.

Tannehill, Robert C. *The Gospel According to Luke*. Vol. 1 of *The Narrative Unity of Luke-Acts*. Philadelphia: Fortress, 1986.

———. "The Story of Zacchaeus as Rhetoric: Luke 19:1–10." *Semeia* 64 (1994) 201–21.

Tansey, Stephen D. *Politics: The Basics*. 2nd ed. London: Routledge, 2000.

Taylor, Victor. *The Formation of the Gospel Tradition*. London: Macmillan, 1933.

Theissen, Gerd. *Sociology of Early Palestinian Christianity*. Translated by John Bowden. Philadelphia: Fortress, 1978.

Trebilco, Paul. "Asia." Pages 291–362 in *The Book of Acts in Its Graeco-Roman Setting*. Edited by David W. J. Gill and Conrad Gempf. Vol. 2 of *The Book of Acts in Its First Century Setting*. Edited by Bruce W. Winter. Grand Rapids: Eerdmans, 1993.

Tiede, David L. *Prophecy and History in Luke-Acts*. Philadelphia: Fortress, 1980.

Tilborg, Sjef van. *Reading John in Ephesus*. Supplements to Novum Testamentum 83. Leiden: Brill, 1996.

Trümper, Monika. "Material and Social Environment of Greco-Roman Households in the East: The Case of Hellenistic Delos." Pages 19–43 in *Early Christian Families in Context: An Interdisciplinary Dialogue*. Edited by David L. Balch and Carolyn Osiek. Religion, Marriage, and Family. Grand Rapids: Eerdmans, 2003.

Tsafrir, Yoram. "Jewish Pilgrimage in the Roman and Byzantine Periods." Pages 369–76 in *Akten des XII. Internationalen Kongresses für Christliche Archäolgie*. Edited by Ernst Dassmann and Josef Engemann. Jahrbuch für Antike und Christentum 20, 1. Münster: Aschendorffsche Verlagsbuchhandlung, 1995.

Tuan, Yi-Fu. *Space and Place: The Perspective of Experience*. Minneapolis: University of Minnesota, 1977.

Tyson, Joseph B. *Marcion and Luke-Acts: A Defining Struggle*. Columbia: University of South Carolina Press, 2006.

Usher, Stephen. *Dionysius of Halicarnassus: The Critical Essays*. 2 vols. Loeb Classical Library. Cambridge, MA: Harvard University Press, 1974.

Verseput, Donald J. "Jesus' Pilgrimage to Jerusalem and Encounter in the Temple: A Geographical Motif in Matthew's Gospel." *Novum Testamentum* 36 (1994) 105–21.

Veyne, Paul. "The Roman Empire." Pages 5–234 in *A History of Private Life*, vol. 1: *From Pagan Rome to Byzantium*. Edited by Paul Veyne. Cambridge, MA: Belknap, 1987.

Wagner-Hasel, Beate. "Gastfreundschaft." Pages 794–97 in *Der Neue Pauly Enzyklopäie der Antike*. Edited by Hubert Cancik and Helmuth Schneider. Stuttgart: J. B. Metzler, 1997.

Walaskay, Paul W. *'And So We Came to Rome': The Political Perspective of St. Luke*. Society for New Testament Studies Monograph Series 49. Cambridge: Cambridge University Press, 1983.

Wallace, Daniel B. *Greek Grammar beyond the Basics*. Grand Rapids: Zondervan, 1996.

Wallace-Hadrill, Andrew. "*Domus* and *Insulae* in Rome: Families and Housefuls." Pages 3–18 in *Early Christian Families in Context: An Interdisciplinary Dialogue*. Edited by David L. Balch and Carolyn Osiek. Religion, Marriage, and Family. Grand Rapids: Eerdmans, 2003.

———. "Elites and Trade in the Roman Town." Pages 241–72 in *City and Country in the Ancient World*. Edited by John Rich and Andrew Wallace-Hadrill. Leicester-Nottingham Studies in Ancient Society Volume 2. London: Routledge, 1991.

———. "Houses and Households: Sampling Pompeii and Herculaneum." Pages 191–227 in *Marriage, Divorce, and Children in Ancient Rome*. Edited by Beryl Rawson. Canberra: Humanities Research Center, 1991.

———. *Houses and Society in Pompeii and Herculaneum*. Princeton, NJ: Princeton University Press, 1994.

———. "The Social Structure of the Roman House." *Papers of the British School at Rome* 56 (1988) 43–97.

Walker, Wm. O. "Jesus and the Tax Collectors." *Journal of Biblical Literature* 97 (1978) 221–38.

Walton, Steve. "The State They Were In: Luke's View of the Roman Empire." Pages 1–41 in *Rome in the Bible and the Early Church*. Edited by Peter Oakes. Carlisle, Cumbria: Paternoster, 2002.

Weinert, Francis D. "The Parable of the Throne Claimant (Luke 19:12, 14–15a, 27) Reconsidered." *Catholic Biblical Quarterly* 39 (1977) 505–14.

Weintraub, Jeff. "The Theory and Politics of the Public/Private Distinction." Pages 1–42 in *Public and Private in Thought and Practice: Perspectives on a Grand Dichotomy*. Edited by Jeff Weintraub and Krishan Kumar. Morality and Society. Chicago: University of Chicago Press, 1997.

Weintraub, Jeff, and Krishan Kumar, editors. *Public and Private in Thought and Practice: Perspectives on a Grand Dichotomy*. Morality and Society. Chicago: University of Chicago Press, 1997.

White, L. Michael. "Urban Development and Social Change in Imperial Ephesos." Pages 27–80 in *Ephesos, Metropolis of Asia: An Interdisciplinary Approach to Its Archaeology, Religion, and Culture*. Edited by Helmut Koester. Harvard Theological Studies 41. Valley Forge, PA: Trinity, 1995.

———. "Visualizing the 'Real' World of Acts 16: Toward Construction of a Social Index." Pages 234–61 in *The Social World of the First Christians: Essays in Honor of Wayne A. Meeks*. Edited by L. Michael White and O. Larry Yarbrough. Minneapolis: Fortress, 1995.

Wilkinson, John. *Jerusalem Pilgrims before the Crusades*. Warminster, PA: Arts & Phillips, 2002.

———. "The Way from Jerusalem to Jericho." *Biblical Archaeologist* 38 (1975) 10–24.

Wilson, Bryan. *Religious Sects: A Sociological Study*. World University Library. New York: McGraw-Hill, 1970.

Wiltshire, Susan Ford. *Public and Private in Vergil's Aeneid*. Amherst: University of Massachusetts Press, 1989.

Witherington, Ben, III. *The Acts of the Apostles: A Socio-Rhetorical Commentary*. Grand Rapids: Eerdmans, 1998.

Wolfe, Alan. "Public and Private in Theory and Practice: Some Implications of an Uncertain Boundary." Pages 182–203 in *Public and Private in Thought and Practice: Perspectives on a Grand Dichotomy*.

Bibliography

Edited by Jeff and Krishan Kumar Weintraub. Morality and Society. Chicago: University of Chicago Press, 1997.

Wrede, William. *The Messianic Secret*. Translated by J. C. G. Greig. Library of Theological Translations. Cambridge: James Clark, 1971.

Yamauchi, Edwin. *The Archaeology of New Testament Cities in Western Asia Minor*. Grand Rapids: Baker, 1980.

Yoder, John Howard. *The Politics of Jesus: Vincit Agnus Noster*. 2nd ed. Grand Rapids: Eerdmans, 1994.

Zanker, Paul. *Pompeii: Public and Private Life*. Translated by Deborah Lucas Schneider. Revealing Antiquity 11. Cambridge, MA: Harvard University Press, 1998.

Ancient and Biblical Sources Index

BIBLE

Old Testament

Genesis
13:2	205
34:20	109
49:11–12	257

Exodus
2:1–10	108
2:11–15	108
3:1	108
3:16–18	108
19:3	108
19:7	108
19:20	108
19:25	108
33:7–11	108
33:19	184
34:29–35	108

Deuteronomy
21:19	109
28:1–14	206

Ruth
4:1	109

2 Samuel
15:2	109
24:14	184

1 Kings
1	282, 291
1:32–33	273
1:32–40	284
1:33–37	257
2	284
2:13–45	183
8:27	183
8:30	183
17:1–10	108
18:1	108
18	108
21:28	109

2 Kings
2:19–22	109
4:8	109
4:38–41	109
5:8–10	109
6:32—7:2	109
8:1	109
9	291
9:4–10	273
9:13	257, 273
13:14–19	109

Nehemiah
3:32	267
8:1	110

Job
27:14	172
42:10–17	206

Psalms
37:25	172
86:15	184
108:1	171
118	184, 291
118:26	257, 274

Proverbs
10:22	206

Isaiah
7:1–4	109

Ancient and Biblical Sources Index

Isaiah (cont.)
56:6–7	279
56:7	258, 279

Jeremiah
7	109, 291
7:8–9	279
7:11	258, 279
11:16	109
19:2	109
26	109
28	109
35	109

Hosea
2:19	184

Zechariah
9	261
9:9	257, 273
9:9–10	234, 257
14:3–4	258
14:4–5	241
14:21	257

Malachi
3:1–2	257

Sirach
4:1–6	172
4:3	172
15:5	110
18:33	172
21:17	110
24:2	110
25:2	172, 182
31:1–11	206
38:32b–33a	110
38:34	110
38:34b—39:3	110
39:4	110
40:28–30	172

Tobit
2:1–3	109
2:4–6	109

1 Maccabees
9:50	203
13:42	340
13:49–51	261
14:27	340

2 Maccabees
4:5	110
9:26	110
10:2	110
13:26	110

3 Maccabees
4:7	110
6:36	110
7:14	110

4 Maccabees
5:1–2	249
5:15	249

1 Esdras
5:47	110
9:38	110

New Testament

Matthew
2:11	314
2:23	314
2:23	177
4:18–22	315, 332
5:1	17
8:9	306
9:10	320
9:35	315
10:1	305
10:1–15	316–17
10:11	317
10:18–19	334
10:32	334
11:2–6	304
11:4–5	306
12:15	332
12:22	332
12:23	304
13:1	315

Matthew (cont.)

13:4	172
13:10–23	328
13:19	172
13:34–36	137
13:36	255
13:36–37	53
13:51–52	255
14:13	299, 304
14:19	307
20:29	166, 169, 175
20:29–30	174
20:30	172
20:31	175
21:1	268
21:7	273
21:8–9	174
21:9	181, 238, 273
21:10–12	268
21:17	268
22:9	316, 325, 334
24:1	330
24:3	267, 330
25:6	333
25:14–30	231
25:21	316
25:23	316
26:6	268
26:71	177
27:21	316
27:56	305

Mark

1:16–20	315, 332
1:21	303, 315
1:22	303
1:23	301
1:24	177
1:26	300–301
1:29	299
1:33	299
1:35–38	18
1:38	303
1:45	17, 53, 303
2:4	299, 304
2:15	320
3:7–8	332
4:1	315
4:10–11	53
4:4, 15	172
4:34	53
5:11	268
5:17	301
5:21	301
5:24	301
5:31	301, 307
5:33	301
6:6	315
6:7	306
6:7–14	316–17
6:10	317
6:11	317
6:30–32	137
6:31	53, 304
6:31–32	18
6:32	299, 304
6:33	304
6:34	304
6:35	299
6:39	307
7:3–4	38
7:24	302
7:33	53, 302
8:23	302
9:2	53
9:14	304
9:16	304
9:21–24	307
9:25	304
9:28	53
9:28–29	304
10:32	191, 192
10:33–34	202
10:35–45	202
10:45	202
10:46	166, 169, 170, 172, 174, 175, 202
10:46–52	165
10:47	175, 176, 177
10:47–48	202
10:48	175
10:49	175, 222
11:1	268
11:1–2	268
11:7	273
11:8–9	174, 190
11:9	191, 192, 238, 273
11:10	181, 202
11:11–12	268
11:15	279

Ancient and Biblical Sources Index

Mark (cont.)

11:15–16	279
13:1	330
13:3	53, 267, 330
14:3	268
14:17	263
14:26	267
14:67	177
15:11	316
15:40	305
16:6	177

Luke

1:1–4	5
1:8	167
1:9	263
1:21	263
1:22	263
1:24–25	49
1:26	24, 177, 314
1:27	180
1:32	180, 283, 310
1:32–33	26, 239, 298
1:39–42	314
1:40	204
1:47	310
1:50	184
1:54	184
1:55	310
1:56	214
1:58	184
1:64	187, 241
1:68	189
1:68–70	239
1:69	180, 310
1:71	310
1:72	184
1:73	310
1:77	310
1:78	184
2:1–2	51, 312, 340
2:4	177, 180, 314
2:6	167
2:11	180, 310, 314
2:14	25, 274, 277
2:15	314
2:22	314
2:25	239
2:25–32	239
2:27	263
2:30	310
2:32	259
2:34	337
2:37	263
2:38	239–40
2:39	176, 314
2:46	263
2:46–47	280
2:51	176, 314
2:52	251
3—18	189
3:1–2	51, 112, 312, 340–41
3:6	310
3:7	189
3:10–14	359
3:12	223
3:15	189, 240
3:15–17	240
3:19	340
3:19–20	5
3:22	139
3:31	180
4:1	108
4:9	263
4:14	3
4:14–15	3, 24
4:14–44	3
4:14—9:50	297
4:15	187
4:16	176, 315, 332, 336
4:16–17	144
4:16–18	169
4:16–28	311
4:16–30	168, 182, 299
4:16–44	315
4:17	144
4:18	26, 169, 186, 344
4:18–19	177, 296
4:18–21	240
4:20	332
4:21	242
4:22	332
4:22–23	144, 251
4:22–27	139, 177
4:22–29	190
4:23–28	335
4:28	177
4:28–29	308
4:29	332

Luke (cont.)

4:30	204
4:31	24, 26, 303, 315
4:31–37	177, 297, 311
4:31–41	109
4:32	303, 306
4:33	299, 301, 315
4:34	177, 306
4:35	275, 301
4:36	177, 305–6
4:37	303
4:38	204, 216, 299
4:38–39	297, 311, 336
4:38–41	51
4:38–42	143
4:39	187, 241
4:40	299, 306
4:40–41	297
4:41	276
4:42	108, 188, 308
4:43	26, 142, 159, 242, 272, 315, 317, 329, 359
4:43–44	297
4:44	112, 159, 182, 311
4:44—7:50	297
5—7	200
5:1	167, 173, 188, 332
5:1–11	307
5:1—19:27	3
5:3	328
5:8	186, 339
5:9–12	336
5:10–11	24
5:11	187
5:12	26, 48, 159, 186, 315
5:12–16	297, 299
5:15	303
5:16	53, 303
5:17	200, 299, 340
5:17–23	328
5:17–26	199–200, 297, 311, 332
5:17—19:40	141
5:17–19	342
5:18	213
5:19	200, 220, 299, 301, 304, 332
5:20–22	200
5:21	311, 337
5:21–24	239, 308
5:21–25	139, 334
5:24	225, 306
5:25	187, 241
5:26	187
5:27–28	336
5:27–30	308
5:27–32	199, 206, 320
5:27–39	311, 319, 321
5:28	24, 187
5:29	189, 321
5:29–30	51
5:29–31	223
5:29–32	200
5:29–39	332
5:30	141, 221, 337, 340
5:30–39	334
5:31	223
5:31–32	334
5:32	221
5:33	339
5:33–39	308, 321
5:34	321
5:34–35	334
5:34–36	237
5:34–37	240
5:35–39	328
5:36–39	237, 334
6:1	328
6:1–2	337, 339
6:1–5	308, 334
6:1–11	328
6:3	180
6:5	225
6:6	301, 315
6:6–10	337
6:6–11	308, 311, 334
6:8	301
6:9	310
6:11	251, 337
6:12–16	24, 336, 339
6:13–17	109
6:17	17, 188, 328, 336
6:17–19	143, 332
6:19	213
6:20	296, 329
6:24	205
6:32–34	221
6:46–49	253
7:1	204, 332
7:1–4	141
7:1–10	183, 200, 205, 241, 297, 312, 335, 340

Ancient and Biblical Sources Index

Luke (cont.)

7:2	144
7:2–10	199
7:3	200
7:6–10	251
7:8	306, 335
7:9	187, 200, 304, 332
7:10	216
7:11	26, 159, 304, 315
7:11–12	299
7:11–17	158, 297, 311
7:12	110
7:13	277
7:13–15	301
7:16	189, 240, 304, 308
7:16–18	187
7:18–23	240
7:20–21	304
7:21	296
7:21–22	169, 297
7:22	186, 306
7:24	225, 328, 332
7:28	330
7:29	205
7:29–30	337
7:29–35	308
7:32	277
7:34	221, 225
7:36	200, 204, 322
7:36–37	200
7:36–50	25, 108, 154, 183, 199–200, 308, 311, 319, 321, 325, 328, 337
7:37	200, 315, 322
7:38–40	200
7:39	221, 311, 322
7:39–47	334
7:41–42	328
7:41–43	334–35
7:45	323
7:45–47	311, 323
7:48	323
7:49	311
7:50	200, 310, 310–11, 323
8:1	159, 315, 329
8:1–3	336
8:3	332
8:4	315, 328, 332
8:4–15	328
8:4–20	137
8:5	172
8:9	53, 328
8:10	304
8:12	172, 310
8:16–17	328
8:18	233, 253
8:22–25	296
8:25	307
8:27	315
8:28	305
8:34	301
8:36	310
8:37	301
8:39	200, 301
8:40	301
8:40–42	297
8:41	340
8:41–42	335
8:42	301
8:42–48	297
8:44	187, 241
8:45	189, 301
8:47	187, 241, 301, 304
8:48	310
8:49–56	297, 335
8:50	310
8:51–56	300
8:52	277
8:55	187, 241
9:1	305, 307
9:1–2	142, 272
9:1–6	316–17, 328, 336, 339
9:11—10:24	183
9:2	272, 329, 339
9:4	214, 317
9:4–5	200
9:5	317
9:7–9	141, 143, 144, 298, 340
9:9	213
9:10	53, 299, 304, 307
9:10–11	108
9:10–17	296–97
9:11	137, 187, 328, 330
9:12	220
9:14	339
9:18–20	240
9:18–27	328
9:20	339
9:21	276
9:21–22	24
9:22	26, 225, 338

Luke (cont.)

9:23	187
9:23–27	339
9:24	310
9:27	330
9:31	241–42
9:37	26, 304
9:37–43	297
9:37–45	109
9:40	339
9:41	307
9:42	276, 307
9:44	26, 225, 241–42
9:43	304, 339
9:43–48	328
9:44–45	24
9:46–48	339
9:46–56	234
9:47	173
9:49–52	339
9:51	288
9:51–53	263
9:51–56	309
9:52	191, 204, 272, 339
9:53	337
9:55	276
9:57	48
9:57–62	339
9:61	187
10:1	24, 191, 241, 339
10:1–12	142, 316–17
10:3	272, 339
10:5–11	200
10:7	214, 317
10:7–8	319
10:8	204
10:9	329, 339
10:10	204
10:10–11	317
10:10–12	359
10:11	339
10:14	317
10:17	186
10:17–20	234
10:17–22	254, 332
10:19	305
10:21	183
10:21–24	183
10:23	53
10:23–24	240, 254, 328, 332
10:25	183, 332, 337
10:25–29	328
10:25–37	328
10:29–35	203
10:30	168
10:30–35	234
10:31	202
10:32	202, 339
10:34	273
10:38	168, 204, 216, 319
10:38–42	50
11:1	186
11:1–5	328
11:1–13	339
11:4–16	309
11:9–10	213
11:14	189, 237, 304, 332
11:15–18	335
11:16	213
11:19–20	237
11:20	26, 240, 242–43, 251, 330
11:24	213
11:27	332
11:27–29	234
11:29	188, 323, 328, 332
11:29–32	243, 253, 329
11:30	225
11:31	183
11:37	323
11:37–52	142, 200, 311, 325, 334, 362
11:37–53	50
11:37–54	25, 154, 308, 319, 321, 328, 337
11:38	323
11:42	176
11:43	252, 334
11:45	50
11:52	213
11:53	50
11:53–54	138, 251, 280, 337
12:1	332
12:1–3	335
12:1–12	339
12:6	279
12:8–12	334
12:11	334
12:13	189, 328, 332
12:13–21	206, 234, 328
12:16	205
12:22	237, 332
12:27	183

Ancient and Biblical Sources Index

Luke (cont.)

12:31	213
12:33	279
12:35–38	252, 329
12:35–40	328
12:35–48	237, 243, 328, 339
12:37	176, 329
12:39–40	329
12:40	225
12:41	237, 328, 332
12:41–48	247, 252, 329
12:43–45	329
12:46	329
12:47	329
12:50	24
12:51	240
12:54	240, 328, 332
12:54–56	234, 237, 242–43, 329
12:58	204, 335
13:1	328, 332
13:1–3	335
13:1–5	240
13:1–9	243, 252
13:2	221, 240
13:4	144, 240
13:6–9	234, 328
13:7	251
13:10	315
13:10–13	299
13:10–17	297, 311
13:11	308
13:13	187, 241
13:14	206, 301, 309, 337, 340
13:14–16	335
13:15–16	301
13:15–17	139
13:17	302, 304
13:18	330
13:18–21	328
13:20	330
13:22	109, 168, 175, 263, 315, 328, 332
13:22–29	234, 329
13:32	310, 335
13:24	213
13:25–26	334
13:28–29	330
13:31	340
13:31–32	312, 334, 340
13:31–35	308
13:32–3	324
13:33	187
13:33–34	263
13:35	338
14:1	25, 324, 335
14:1–2	299
14:1–6	297, 324
14:1–14	155
14:1–24	154, 200, 300, 308, 311, 319, 321, 324, 327–28, 333, 337, 362
14:1—15:2	325
14:3–5	325
14:7–11	325, 335
14:7–24	324, 332, 334
14:8	205
14:12–14	243, 335, 356–57, 361
14:13	169, 296
14:14	276
14:14–35	325
14:15	239–40
14:15–24	51, 234, 328
14:16–24	335
14:18	325
14:18–19	333
14:20	236
14:21	169, 315, 325, 334
14:21–23	356
14:23	315
14:24	329, 333
14:25	138, 325, 328, 332–33
14:25–35	325, 327
14:31–33	335
14:33	333
14:34–35	333
15	234
15:1	166
15:1–2	221, 308, 325, 328, 333
15:1–32	328
15:2	221, 234, 328
15:3–7	335
15:3–32	334
15:6	334
15:7	221
15:8	213
15:8–10	335
15:9	334
15:10	221
15:11–32	51, 335
15:25	167
15:26	175
15:29	175, 176

Luke (cont.)

15:30–31	359
16:1	50, 205, 333
16:1–8	51
16:1–9	247, 328
16:1–13	328, 339
16:3	170
16:10–11	329
16:14	13, 50, 333
16:14–15	308, 333
16:14–17	139
16:14–19	328
16:14–31	234, 334
16:16	242, 330
16:17	176, 276
16:19	205
16:19–31	206, 234, 328, 335
16:20	110
16:23	184
16:24	184
16:26	184
17—19	200
17:1	333
17:1–10	328, 339
17:7	175
17:11	24, 25, 167, 168, 263
17:11–19	183–84, 200, 197, 311
17:12–19	199
17:12	184, 204
17:12–13	300
17:13	184
17:19	200, 310
17:20	234, 239–40, 242–43, 275, 329, 333, 337, 343
17:20–21	237, 308, 330, 335
17:21	251
17:22	333
17:22–37	251, 328
17:24	243
17:25	24
17:26	225
17:26–30	243, 252
17:27	329
17:27–30	329
17:27–38	232
17:28	279
17:29	329
17:37	329
18:1	333
18:1–8	328, 334–35, 339
18:2	316
18:5	287
18:9	234, 333
18:9–14	275, 328, 335
18:10	263, 280, 343
18:10–14	234
18:11	222
18:13	222
18:15	192, 333, 339
18:15–17	25, 192, 309, 339
18:16–17	330
18:18	333, 340
18:18–22	206
18:18–23	201
18:18–25	199, 200
18:18–27	335
18:18–30	25, 205–206
18:22	187, 224, 279
18:23	206
18:24–25	330
18:25–26	333
18:26	200–201, 206, 310
18:28–29	253
18:28–30	25
18:29–30	329
18:31	115, 339
18:31–34	24, 25, 237, 252, 263
18:31—19:46	24, 26
18:31—22:6	26
18:34	192, 332, 339
18:35	25, 26, 166–74, 190, 201–203, 228, 314, 332, 340, 347
18:35–42	25
18:35–43	27, 158, 165–67, 185, 193, 196, 202, 295–97, 300, 305, 308–10, 313, 340
18:35—19:10	189–92, 310
18:35—19:27	7
18:35—19:46	320
18:35—19:48	3, 23–28, 35, 46–47, 53, 54, 55, 71, 91, 113, 156, 161, 180, 181, 184–86, 189, 191, 203, 261, 283, 291, 295, 344–45, 346–48, 350, 355, 361, 364
18:36	169, 174, 175, 188–89, 191, 202, 289
18:36–39	174–86
18:37	24, 175, 176, 177, 191, 202
18:38	26, 182, 271
18:38–39	26, 180, 184, 298

Luke (cont.)

18:39	180, 188, 191–92, 202, 276, 306
18:39–40	201
18:40	167, 186, 222
18:40–43	174, 186–93
18:42	201–202, 310
18:43	26, 174, 187, 188–91, 241, 289, 305, 347
19:1	26, 48, 168, 190, 201–4, 214, 228, 263, 314, 320
19:1–5	46
19:1–6	213, 314
19:1–10	25, 27, 51, 108, 109, 167, 194, 197–206, 209–10, 215, 221, 236–37, 255, 308–9, 312–14, 319–21
19:1–48	185
19:2	189–91, 201, 204, 210, 213, 225, 308–309, 331
19:3	168, 189, 200, 202, 213–14
19:3–6	201, 212–15
19:3–10	212
19:4	202, 214, 240
19:5	216
19:6	7
19:6–7	228
19:6–10	46, 327, 355
19:7	169, 190, 201–2, 206, 211, 217, 220, 225–27, 236, 239, 308–9
19:7–10	212, 215–17, 235–36, 243, 253, 311
19:7–12	242
19:8	216, 222–23
19:8–10	220, 222, 228
19:9–10	231, 236, 239, 253, 308
19:9	201–2, 206, 223, 310, 311
19:9–14	335
19:10	202, 225, 228, 234, 236, 239, 309–10
19:10—23:69	26
19:11	26, 168, 186, 187, 216, 231–37, 255, 256, 263, 312, 329, 347
19:11–12	180, 181
19:11–27	7, 27, 46, 185, 216, 243, 320
19:11–28	25, 181, 220, 227, 230, 235–36, 253, 255, 283, 327–28, 331, 333–36
19:12	26, 231, 236, 239, 244–46
19:12–14	283
19:12–27	231, 244, 250, 253, 255, 290, 298, 328–31
19:13	217, 248, 252, 254, 331
19:14	26, 180, 190, 217, 247, 251–52, 282, 330
19:14–15	231
19:15	26, 217, 244, 250, 254, 283
19:15–27	248, 331, 347
19:16–19	237
19:17	316
19:17–18	254
19:17–19	238, 245
19:19	316
19:20–23	237
19:21	253
19:24	238
19:25	250, 255
19:25–27	254
19:26	233, 253, 329
19:27	26, 231–32, 247, 252, 254, 331
19:28	24, 26, 231, 256, 263, 276, 288, 320, 336
19:29	168, 266, 272–73, 288
19:29–31	272
19:28–30	143
19:29–36	259
19:29–37	347
19:29–38	256, 263, 272, 274–75, 284, 286–87, 290–91, 336, 338–39, 347
19:29–44	238, 289
19:29–48	5, 25, 27, 191, 227, 255, 256–57, 259–60, 262, 288, 291, 336, 340, 344
19:29—24:53	189
19:31	272
19:32	272, 276
19:33	272
19:34	276
19:34–36	274
19:35	273
19:35–38	272
19:36	270, 273
19:36–37	47
19:36–38	285
19:37	143, 168, 183, 190, 192, 260, 266, 268, 274, 283, 288, 297, 336
19:37–38	192, 270
19:37–40	259, 337
19:38	26, 180, 181–82, 233, 238, 243, 251, 274, 277, 291, 298, 339, 347
19:38–39	248, 276

Luke (cont.)

19:39	26, 47, 182, 190, 191, 238, 270–71, 275–76, 280, 282, 285, 288–90, 337–38, 340, 343
19:39–40	275, 281
19:39–48	256, 263, 272, 275, 280–81, 290, 292, 312, 336, 338, 344, 347
19:40	258, 338
19:41	26, 167, 168, 263, 266, 277, 289
19:41–44	26, 202, 238–40, 247, 252–53, 257, 259, 261, 275, 281, 291, 313, 338, 343
19:41–46	24
19:42	183
19:42–43	277
19:42–44	277, 284
19:43	272, 277
19:43–44	247
19:44	277
19:45	25, 26, 183, 190, 263, 270, 277, 279, 289
19:45–46	25, 257, 275, 291
19:45–48	259
19:45—21:38	264
19:46	279–80, 285, 289, 312
19:47	26, 47, 141, 144, 279–82, 290, 338, 341, 343
19:47–48	25, 259, 262, 275, 281, 288, 297, 340, 343
19:48	144, 190, 238, 259, 285–86, 343
20	109
20—21	189–91, 280, 285, 289, 313, 343
20—22	288
20:1	24, 108, 189, 259, 330, 338, 343
20:1–2	280
20:1—21:36	25
20:9	259, 330–31, 343
20:9–18	331
20:16	232, 331
20:19	144, 252, 259, 279–80, 308, 330, 338, 343
20:20	343
20:20–26	53, 330
20:23–25	139
20:26	259, 343
20:27	280, 330, 343
20:41–43	298
20:45	259, 330
20:45–47	280
21:1	330
21:5	270, 330
21:5–36	26, 268, 331
21:7	242, 330
21:7–19	243
21:7–36	240
21:12	267
21:19–31	331
21:20–28	243
21:28	276
21:29–33	331
21:31	330
21:31–32	242
21:34–26	243
21:36	242, 276
21:36–37	268
21:37	267, 338
21:37–38	25, 259, 281, 297
21:38	190, 259, 281, 330
22:1	284, 290
22:1–2	331, 343
22:1—23:55	264
22:2	140, 144, 338
22:3–6	343
22:4	338
22:10	204, 263
22:12	220
22:16–18	330
21:20–33	338
22:28–29	272
22:28–30	253, 339
22:36	279
22:29	26, 298
22:39	267
22:47	343
22:47–53	190
22:51	296
22:52	338, 341, 343
22:60	187, 241
22:66	338
22:66–71	331
22:66—23:25	343
22:67	140, 288
23:1	340
23:1–2	140, 280, 331
23:2	53, 233, 286, 288, 291, 298
23:3	287
23:3–4	287
23:4	190, 338
23:6–7	51
23:6–12	190, 298

Ancient and Biblical Sources Index

Luke (cont.)

23:7	338
23:8	141, 297
23:8–11	248
23:9	248
23:10	331, 338
23:13	335, 338, 344
23:13–16	287
23:13–23	190–91, 238
23:13–25	252, 297, 343
23:15	190
23:18–23	331
23:19	316
23:21	248
23:22	4, 248
23:23	253
23:28	277, 338
23:35	190, 310
23:37	287, 310, 336
23:37–38	26, 233, 298
23:39	200, 310
23:39–40	200
23:39–43	199–200
23:42	26, 233
23:44–45	296
23:47–48	187
23:48	53, 190, 253, 297, 305
23:49	305
24:13–35	296
24:18	338
24:18–19	304
24:19	177
24:19–24	240
24:20	277, 335, 341
24:21	242
24:26	282
24:28	167
24:33	338
24:49	316
24:36–49	296
24:41	289
24:47	223, 338
24:50–53	296
24:52	289, 338

John

4:7–15	15
4:16–26	15
5:2	267
9:1	170
9:8	170
12:19	337
18:5	177
18:7	177
19:19	177
20:11–12	268

Acts

1:6–7	239, 329
1:6–8	234, 237, 252–53
1:6–11	243
1:11	283
1:12	269
1:12–26	339
1:13	220, 269
1:15	24
1:21–22	274
2:14	222
2:22	177
2:23	252
2:24	283
2:25	181
2:32	274
2:34	181
2:34–36	283
2:38	223
2:41	24, 252, 271
2:44–46	313
2:47	24
3:1–6	170
3:1	269, 280
3:1–10	278
3:2	174, 269
3:6	177, 178
3:7	241, 341
3:10	269
3:11	270–71, 278
3:11–12	271
3:11–26	271
3:19–21	239
3:19–23	240
3:21	251, 253
3:23	252
4:1–2	271
4:4	271
4:5	341
4:7	175
4:10	176, 178
4:12	310

Acts (cont.)

4:15	192
4:19–20	288
4:21	187
4:23–30	5
4:25	181
4:25–26	254
4:32	336
4:34	279
4:36–37	205
4:37	279
5:1	279
5:1–11	253, 339
5:10	241
5:17	252, 341
5:20	222, 278
5:21	280, 341
5:22	341
5:26	341
5:27	341
5:30–31	252
5:31	310
5:32	274
5:34	192, 341
5:35	241
6:1–7	253
6:1—8:1	23
6:2	336
6:14	177, 178
7:47–50	183
7:53	277
9:3	167
9:6	204
9:12	204
9:43	214
10:2	205, 216
10:9	167, 220
10:18	175
10:24	204
10:24–25	51
10:29	175
10:36–38	304
10:38	143, 178
10:39	274
10:38	296
11:1–18	182
11:14	216
11:28	242
12:1	190
12:3	236
12:6	188, 241
12:10	204, 241
12:13–14	220
12:19	192
12:20–23	288
12:23	241
13:7	18
13:11	241
13:15–50	18
13:21–23	181
13:23	310
13:27	252, 277, 341
13:26	310
13:34–36	181
13:44	299
13:46	252–53
13:47	310
13:48	187
13:49	187
14:1	24
14:20	204
14:27	20
15:1–21	339
15:4	20
15:6–11	182
16:4	175
16:6–7	213
16:8	176
16:13	173
16:15	18, 204
16:17	310
16:20	18
16:22	192
16:26	241
16:27	241
16:30	188
16:33	241
17:1–8	18
17:5	188
17:7	216, 287
17:17	355
17:22	222
17:31	241–42
18:5–18	18
18:7	18
18:12	18, 20
18:14–15	287
18:20	214
18:24—19:41	67
19:9	18, 357

Acts (cont.)

19:9–10	20, 350
19:10	67, 299
19:21	299
19:35–41	215
19:35—20:1	5
19:38–39	287
20:17–38	67
20:18	273
20:20	18, 19, 20, 350
20:21	20
21:2	273
21:3	233, 242
21:8	18, 204
21:20	336
21:21	24
21:24	273
21:27	278
21:33	175, 192
21:34	192, 278
21:36	278
21:40	222
22:6	167
22:8	177
22:11–13	178
22:24	192
22:30	192
23	248
23—26	248
23:6	341
23:10	192
23:20	175
23:24	273
23:29	287
23:35	192
22:39	175
24:5	177–78
24:15	242
25	248–49
25:6	192
25:13–22	249
25:17	192
25:21	192
25:22	193
25:23	192–93, 249
25:26	188
25:32	193
26:1	193
26:9	177–78
26:24–28	253
26:26	10
26:29	288
26:30–31	287
26:31–32	4
27:2	273
27:9	176
27:43	192
28:16	204
28:28	310

1 Corinthians

16:19	357

1 Timothy

3:14–15	357

~

ANCIENT SOURCES

Aeschines

Ctesiphon

78	51, 59

Appian

Civil Wars

2.15.102	88, 278

Aristotle

Economics

1343b	63

Politics

1253b	63
1254b	63
1269b	51
1274b	63
1324a—1325b	63
1337a	63

Rhetoric

1358b	17

Arrian

Discourses of Epictetus

3.4	87, 302

Ancient and Biblical Sources Index

Augustus
The Deeds of Divine Augustus
35   51

Cicero
Against Vatinius
22   81, 353

In Defense of Flaccus
28   106
57   81, 139

In Defense of Plancius
86   205

Letters to Atticus
1.18   87
17   80, 353

Letters to Friends
4.6.2   81
4.6.2   82
5.20.9   210

On Duties
2.18   215

Demosthenes
Against Leptines
9   59
57   58

Against Meidias
33–34   60

On the Crown
10   60, 132
257   58

Dio Chrysostom
In the Public Assembly at Prusa
2–3   65

Refusal of the Office of Archon
3   65

Second Tarsic Discourse
44   65

Training for Public Speaking
14   65

Trojan Discourse
15   170

Diodorus Siculus
Library of History
13.83.1   205

Dionysius of Halicarnassus
On Demosthenes
24   38

Epictetus
Diatribes
3.23.8   249

Euripides
Rhesus
710–18   171

Homer
The Odyssey
2.30–32   57
2.42–46   57
2.64–67   58
2.65   131
3.79–84   58
17.10–12   173
17.197–203   171
18.1–3   171

Horace
Letters
1.17.43–44   171, 182

Satires
1.9.58–60   83
2.1.62–74   83

Ancient and Biblical Sources Index

Josephus

Jewish Antiquities

1.2	112
11.5	267
13.15	203
13.166	113
14.91	203
14.386	246
14.394	247
15.65	113
17.193–95	203
17.194–239	261
17.200–205	246, 249
17.213–18	247
17.299	247, 252
17.237–318	245, 247, 251
17.273–74	273
17.339–41	247
18.15	342
19.343–52	248
20.220–21	270
20.38–48	113

Jewish War

1.1	112
1.61	205
1.120	203
1.167	203
1.268–96	245
1.286–89	247
1.521	247
1.569	113
1.659–60	203
2.44	271
2.261–63	274
2.287	208
2.292	208
2.537	267
2.567	203
3.55	203
4.459–75	203
4.486	203
4.602–4	113
5.67	203
14.403	247

Juvenal

Satires

3.195–202	83
3.232–36	83
3.237–61	83, 302
4.116–17	171, 182
4.116–18	173
5.8–9	173
14.134	174

Livy

History of Rome

4.4	83, 139
4.81	185, 306
6.24–25	82
34.1.5	302

Martial

Epigrams

12.19.3	174
4.53	171
5.4–5	174
12.32	171, 174
53	182

Mishnah

Shabbat

1:1	114

Ovid

The Art of Love

1.99	87, 302

Pausanius

Description of Greece

1.3.1	153
2.33.3	170

Philo

A Meeting for the Sake of Education

64	249

On Drunkenness

109	112

On the Contemplative Life
61 112

On the Embassy to Gaius
156 112, 299

On the Life of Joseph
38 59

On the Special Laws
3.169–70 111

On the Virtues
19 111

That Every Good Person is Free
143 112

Philostratus

Letters
66 149

Life of Apollonius
1.2 146
1.4 146
1.9 285
4.2 149, 150, 278, 302
4.3 150, 174, 298
4.4 151
4.5–9 151
4.10 151, 152
4.10 302
4.17 153
4.17–22 152
4.18 302
4.19 153
4.21 153
4.22 153
4.25 154
4.31 155
4.32 155
4.33 155
4.35 156
4.36 156
4.37 156
4.38 156
4.39 156
4.40 156

4.41 157
4.44 156
4.45 157, 188
8.7 159
8.26 150, 151

Lives of the Sophists
2.23 151

Plato

Gorgias
521e 62

Laws
875a–b 60

The Republic
492b–c 61, 111, 302

Theaetetus
173c–d 302

Plautus

Trinummus
339–40 171
422–24 174

Plutarch

On Curiosities
522e 249

On Listening to Lectures
45f 249

On the Face in the Moon
937d 249

Spartan Sayings
235e 171

Precepts of Statescraft
798a 136
798b 244
798c–799a 137
799b–800a 137
800d 137

Ancient and Biblical Sources Index

Precepts of Statescraft (cont.)

800f	137
801c–804b	138
801e	138
802c	138
802d	138
802f	335
802f–803a	138
803a	334
803b–c	138
803b–e	334
803b–f	193
803f	138
804c–806f	139
804d–e	139
806f	142
806f–809b	139
807b	142
807b–808d	193
808b	244
808b–d	142
809b	244
809b–811a	139
811a–c	141
811b	139
811b–813c	139
812c–d	50, 142, 307
813c	335
813d–e	54
813d	46
813e	139
813f	139
814a–c	139
814d	139
814e	140
814f	140
815a	140
815a–816a	302
816a–817f	141
815b	140
815c–d	140
815e–816a	140
816d	244
816f	335
817a	141
817c	141
817d	141
817d–e	141
818e–819b	136
819b	142
819c	244
819c–d	142
819e	139, 142, 143
819e–821a	143
820f	143
820f–821f	143
821a–e	54
821b	143
821c	143, 308
821d	143
821f–822a	143
822a–c	143
822d–823e	143
823e	335
823f–825f	136, 143

Seneca

Letters

52.11	249

On Tranquility of Mind

25.1	173

Strabo

Geography

14.1.20	150

Suetonius

Tiberius

8	247
11.3	249

Sophocles

Oedipus at Colonus

421–59	170

The Women of Trachis

335–44	64
351–52	64
371–72	64, 302

Tacitus

Annals

2.52	247
12.7	82

Dialogue on Orators
9.3   249

Talmud
Bava Batra (Babylonian)
9a   172

Eruvin (Babylonian)
32b   114

Nedarim (Babylonian)
3a   115
5b   115

Sanhedrin (Babylonian)
25b   208

Shabbat (Babylonian)
6a   114

Shabbat (Jerusalem)
1:1 XIV   114

Tosefta
Shabbat
1:1–5   114
1:2   298

Vitruvius
De Architectura
1.3.1   83, 298
1.3.2   84
5.preface.5   85
5.2   149
6.5.1   86, 220
6.5.1–2   47, 86

Xenophon
Memorabilia
1.2.30   302
2.5.1   302

Author Index

Aalders, Gerhard J. D., 136
Achtemeier, Paul J., 165
Adams, Lawrence, 361
Aletti, Jean-Noël, 231, 237, 243
Alexander, Loveday, 11–12, 20, 24
Alexiou, Evangelos, 143
Allison, Penelope Mary, 95–96, 177
Anderson, Graham, 146, 151
Anderson, James C. Jr., 104, 322
Ando, Clifford, 45
Arendt, Hannah, 22, 63–64, 89

Bachmann, Michael, 8–9, 24, 52, 259–60, 263–64, 276, 278, 281, 289, 340–41
Bahat, Dan, 269
Bailey, James L., 187
Bailey, Kenneth E., 322, 325
Barrett, C. K., 258, 270
Baugh, Steven Michael, 67–68
Bechard, Dean P., 8
Benn, Stanley I., 22, 47
Berquist, Jon L., 14
Betz, Hans Dieter, 57
Blass, F., 216
Blois, Lukas de, 136, 142
Boardman, John Jasper Griffin, 57
Bock, Darrell, 21, 108, 206, 232, 236, 238–39, 268, 272
Boer, Roland, 14
Bois, Page du, 17
Bolchazy, Ladislaus, 90
Borg, Marcus, 277
Borgen, Peder, 8, 111
Bordieu, Pierre, 66
Bovon, François, 166, 169, 180, 198–99, 205, 214, 232, 239, 296
Bowersock, G. W., 146–47
Branick, Vincent P., 358
Braun, Willi, 300, 324–25
Braund, David, 245–46
Broughton, T. R. S., 210

Bruce, Frederick Fyvie, 245, 247
Bruehler, Bart B., 55, 129
Bultmann, Rudolph, 199
Burger, Christoph, 165, 175, 180–81
Busse, Ulrich, 165–66, 232, 234, 237–38, 245, 247, 251–52, 296–97, 330, 335

Cadbury, Henry J., 4, 23, 314
Camp, Claudia V., 14
Cancik, Hubert, 7
Carrière, Jean-Claude, 136, 139–40, 142
Cassidy, Richard J., 5, 24, 179, 357, 364
Catchpole, David R., 257–58, 260–61, 271, 279, 282–283
Chance, J. Bradley, 8, 115, 183, 259
Chevalier, Raymond, 265
Chiappari, Christopher L., 44
Cohen, David, 17, 42–48, 52, 57, 60, 65–66, 79, 88, 90, 115, 130, 348
Conn, Harvie M., 359
Conzelmann, Hans, 4, 6, 8, 24, 180–81, 263, 268, 271, 280, 341, 363
Corbo, V. C., 120, 126, 128
Corley, Kathleen E., 12–13, 106, 320, 322–23
Coulton, J. J., 153
Creed, John Martin, 3
Cromartie, Michael, 361
Cubitt, Tessa, 44
Culpepper, R. Alan, 199, 232, 245, 247

Debrunner, A., 216
Denaux, Adelbert, 25, 231–38, 240, 242, 251
D'Entrèves, Maurizio Passerin, 22, 47, 63
DeVries, LaMoine F., 67–68, 203, 298
Dibelius, Martin, 199
Dinsmoor, William Bell, 151
Dodd, C. H., 21, 257
Dolan, Michael, 362
Donlon, Jocelyn Hazelwood, 362

Author Index

Donovan, Brian R., 62
Dorsey, David A., 265–66
Dowley, Tim, 267
Duling, Dennis C., 165
Dupont, Jacques, 165
Dyson, Stephen L., 105

Easton, Burton Scott, 4, 24
Edmondson, Jonathan, 352, 354–55
Elliot, John H., 312–13, 326, 350
Ellis, E. Earle, 216, 222, 231, 298
Elshtain, Jean Bethke, 22, 61, 63–64
Engberg-Pedersen, Troels, 11, 52,
Erdemgil, Selahattin, 71, 149
Ernst, Josef, 3, 24–25
Esler, Philip Francis, 5, 12–13, 79, 314, 350, 358, 364
Eulau, Heinz, 7, 27, 36, 39
Evans, C. F., 168

Faraone, Christopher Athanasious, 152
Finegan, Jack, 264–67, 269–70
Fisher, Loren R., 165, 180
Fitzmyer, Joseph A., 3, 24–25, 57, 67, 166–69, 172–73, 177, 181, 187, 190–91, 206, 211, 213–14, 216, 220, 222–23, 231, 236, 239, 242–43, 257–58, 262, 266, 268, 272, 280, 283, 291, 309, 311, 334, 337
Flanagan, James W., 14, 21
Foley, Helene P., 17, 40, 43
Foucault, Michel, 21,
Freedman, H., 114,

Garnsey, Peter, 206–7, 212, 321, 352
Gasque, W. Ward, 4
Gaston, Lloyd, 257
Gaus, Gerald F., 22
George, Michele, 73–75, 77–78, 217
Giddens, Anthony, 34, 42–43, 47–48
Gillman, John, 205
Gleason, Maud W., 46, 352, 354
Gowler, David B., 215, 321, 324, 342
Grahame, Mark, 93
Green, J. R., 61
Green, Joel B., 3, 8, 24, 170, 175, 183, 190–92, 198, 204, 206–7, 213, 215–16, 220–21, 223, 231–32, 236, 238–39, 258, 266, 272–73, 282–83, 296, 307, 322, 324–25, 328, 333, 335

Greenslade, Helen, 44

Habermas, Jürgen, 11, 22, 63
Hadas, Moses, 148
Haenchen, Ernst, 4, 24, 269
Hagner, Donald, 316
Hahn, F., 180
Hahn, Johannes Münster, 171, 174
Hall, Edward T., 32, 37, 39, 48, 53, 348, 350
Hamel, Gildas H., 172
Hamm, Dennis, 166, 169–70, 216, 222–23, 231, 269, 311
Hands, A. R., 172–73
Harris, Marvin, 41
Harris, Murray J., 247,
Hénaff, Marcell, 40
Herrenbrück, Fritz, 207–10
Herzfeld, Michael, 42, 44–47
Hirschfeld, Yizhar, 117–25, 129, 133, 217
Horsley, G. H. R., 68
Horsley, Richard A., 56

Jacobson, David M., 181, 245, 247
Jeremias, Joachim, 238, 320
Jervell, Jacob, 7
Johnson, Earl S., 165
Johnson, Luke Timothy, 3, 5, 7–8, 24–25, 46, 108, 166, 175, 179, 184, 188, 191, 201, 205–6, 220, 222, 231–34, 236–40, 242–43, 251, 257–58, 277, 279–80, 298, 325, 328, 336, 338–39, 351
Jones, C. P., 136
Just, Felix N. W., 169–70

Kaiser, Alan, 83–85, 92, 100, 132, 298
Kalantzis, George, 67
Kariamadam, Paul, 198–99, 201, 311, 320
Kennedy, George, 224
Kilgallen, John J., 323
Kingsbury, Jack Dean, 225
Kinman, Brent, 5–7, 23–24, 35, 178–79, 181, 183, 185, 208, 233, 257–58, 261–62, 273, 275–77, 279, 282–83, 287, 349
Knoles, Thomas Gregory, 146–47, 151
Kodell, Jerome, 166, 189–90
Koester, Helmut, 68,
Kohn, Margaret, 7, 21

Koskenniemi, Erkki, 146–48
Krinzinger, Friedrich, 75

La Potterie, Ignace de, 233, 237–38, 240–42
Laet, Sigfried J., 209–10
Lake, Kirsopp, 263, 266, 269, 299
Lambrecht, Jan, 24–26
Lampe, Peter, 357
Lamphere, Louise, 44
Laurence, Ray, 21, 50, 91–92, 100–101, 103–5, 122, 132, 218, 298
Lawrence, Arnold Walter, 151
Lefebvre, Henri, 14, 21
Levine, Lee I., 267–69
Ling, Roger, 352–54
Lloyd, G. E. R., 40, 43
Loewe, William P., 198, 309–10
Lohmeyer, Ernst, 180
Lomas, Kathryn, 352–54
Luow, Johannes P., 241
Luz, Ulrich, 316

MacDonald, Dennis Ronald, 57
MacMullen, Ramsay, 83, 87, 113, 206
Maddox, Robert, 4–5, 183
Magie, David, 209–10
Malherbe, Abraham J., 10–11
Malmendier, Ulrike, 207, 209–10
Malina, Bruce, 13, 139, 177, 186, 301–2, 310, 322, 324
Marindin, G. E., 354
Marshall, Anthony J., 88
Marshall, I. Howard, 6, 24–25, 175, 190–92, 198, 200, 213, 232, 236, 243, 266, 272–73, 282, 296, 298, 310, 322, 337
Marshall, John W., 45–46
Martin, Russell, 45–46
Mason, Hugh J., 210, 341–42
McCabe, Donald, 210–11, 320
McKeever, Michael Colin, 14
McNutt, Paula M., 14, 21
McRay, John, 67, 266
McVann, Mark, 13
Meeks, Wayne, 56, 83, 264, 356–67
Meyers, Carol, 278
Meyers, Eric M., 124–25
Meynet, Roland, 24–26, 166, 169, 178, 180, 201

Mitchell, Alan C., 223
Moessner, David P., 8–9, 57, 108, 188, 314, 326
Moore, Thomas S., 8
Moxnes, Halvor, 13, 15, 51, 229, 326
Murray, Oswyn, 57

Nails, Debra, 62
Neale, David A., 221
Nelson, Peter K., 322
Netzer, Ehud, 203, 298
Neusner, Jacob, 114
Neyrey, Jerome H., 12–21, 23–24, 39–40, 42–44, 46–48, 50, 111–12, 139, 154, 177, 186, 215, 299–302, 322, 324, 349–50
Nida, Eugene A., 241
Nikolaidis, Anastasios G., 136
Nolland, John, 173, 230–33, 236, 238–39, 257–58, 272–73, 279–80, 337

Oakes, Peter, 10, 56, 95, 357
Oakman, Douglas E., 314
O'Hanlon, John, 198, 220, 223, 309
Ortner, Sherry, 43–44
Oster, Richard, 168
O'Toole, Robert F., 199–200

Parsons, Mikeal C., 8, 23, 211, 213, 258
Patterson, Cynthia B., 62–63, 132
Paul, André, 165, 201
Penner, Todd C., 5, 23
Perot, André, 265
Petzke, G., 54, 147–48
Pilch, John J., 13
Plümacher, Eckhard, 57
Pohl, Christine, 1, 362–63
Porter, Stanley, 166–68

Ravens, D. A. S., 223
Reimer, Andy M., 147–48
Rengstorf, K. H., 168
Richardson, Peter, 123, 129
Riggsby, Andrew M., 94, 107
Riley, Henry Thomas, 174
Robbins, Vernon K., 14, 21, 34–35, 54, 67, 147–48, 165, 180, 202, 301, 311, 350, 355–56, 358
Rogers, Guy MacLean, 68, 76–78, 152, 214, 352

Author Index

Rohrbaugh, Richard L., 53, 77, 314, 318, 356
Roller, Duane R., 245
Roskam, Geert, 137
Rosner, Brian S., 108
Roth, S. John, 169

Sack, Robert David, 14, 21–22, 26–27, 31–36, 39, 45, 47–48, 50, 53, 55, 62, 104, 137, 193, 256, 258, 277, 281, 290, 300, 303, 305, 314, 346, 348, 350, 361–62
Sahlins, Marshall, 41, 48
Saldarini, Anthony J., 341
Saller, Richard P., 206–7, 352
Sanders, James A., 257–58, 271, 274
Sawicki, Marianne, 49, 123–25, 129
Saxonhouse, Arlene W., 49
Scherrer, Peter, 67–68
Schleiermacher, Frederick, 3
Schneiders, Sandra M., 351
Schürmann, Heinz, 3
Scott, B. Brandon, 205
Scott, James M., 8, 24
Segal, Arthur, 110
Shelton, Jo-Ann, 83, 87, 105, 156, 354
Slotki, W., 114
Smith, Dennis E., 319, 322–24
Smith, Morton, 148
Smith, William, 354
Smyth, Herbert Weir, 167, 214, 241
Soards, Marion L., 57
Soja, Edward W., 14, 21–22, 27, 31, 34, 348
Speckman, McGlory T., 166, 171, 337
Sperber, Daniel, 115–16, 129, 298
Stegemann, Ekkehard W., 356
Stegemann, Wolfgang, 206, 356–57
Steinhauser, Michael G., 165
Stephen, Lynn, 44
Sterling, Gregory L., 111, 349
Stowers, Stanley Kent, 10–11
Strange, James F., 56
Strauss, Mark L., 165, 181–82,
Swanson, Judith A., 22, 63–64

Talbert, Charles H., 199
Tannehill, Robert C., 23, 179, 188–89, 199–200, 213, 222–24, 311
Tansey, Stephen D., 7, 22, 179
Taylor, Victor, 199,
Trebilco, Paul, 67, 352
Tiede, David L., 233
Tilborg, Sjef van, 68
Trümper, Monika, 86
Tsafrir, Yoram, 267, 271
Tuan, Yi-Fu, 21, 34
Tyson, Joseph B., 211

Usher, Stephen, 38

Vander Broek, Lyle D., 187
Verseput, Donald J., 264
Veyne, Paul, 62, 82, 85, 87, 107
Vogel, Ursula, 22

Wagner-Hasel, Beate, 90
Walasky, Paul W., 4–5, 79, 363
Wallace, Daniel B., 167, 190, 216, 220, 236, 239, 251, 322
Wallace-Hadrill, Andrew, 49, 73, 86, 91, 93–96, 98, 102, 104, 107, 121–22, 133, 171, 218, 282, 322, 348, 354
Walker, Wm. O., 207
Walton, Steve, 5, 79
Wayte, William, 354
Weinert, Francis D., 232, 245
Weintraub, Jeff, 22, 47
White, L. Michael, 56, 74–75, 77, 350, 352
Wilkinson, John, 265–66
Wilson, Bryan, 358–59
Wiltshire, Susan Ford, 46, 50, 58, 80, 88–91, 106–7, 115, 134, 215–16, 300, 348

Yamauchi, Edwin, 71–72, 149
Yoder, John Howard, 5, 24, 179

Zanker, Paul, 91–92, 96–98, 104, 352–54

Subject Index

Abraham, 2, 180, 184–85, 198, 204, 225–26, 228, 231, 301, 310, 341
Aeneas, Aeneid, 46, 50, 58, 80, 88–91, 105
anthropology, 39–42, 44–47, 63
Apollonius
   miracles, 151–52, 154, 158, 174, 188
   person, 135, 146–48
   public life, 148–59, 284–86, 291, 298, 302, 313, 318, 333, 335, 346, 349
   Temple Teaching, 151, 153–54, 157, 160, 174, 278, 319, 333
architecture
   domestic. *See* homes
   Hellenistic-Roman, 22, 67–78, 86, 110, 116, 132, 151, 217–18, 351–55
   Jewish, 110, 115–28, 263
   urban. *See* forum, cities
assembly, assemblies, 17–19, 57–58, 60, 78–79, 110, 131–32, 152, 53, 155–56, 158, 187, 287–88, 301, 333
Athens, 17, 42, 54, 55, 57–58, 60, 62–66, 78, 88–90, 106, 131–32, 135, 138, 146, 148, 152–53, 155, 158–59, 284–86, 291, 318–19, 333, 347–48
atrium, 73, 94–96, 100, 103, 133, 218, 220, 354
authority
   Jesus', 155, 166, 177, 184, 186, 195–96, 225, 233, 259, 272, 286, 295–96, 299, 306–7, 310–11, 335, 337
   political, 22, 45, 76, 81, 136, 139–40, 145, 156, 179, 193, 238, 244, 286, 290, 292, 308, 318, 329, 330, 335, 340, 343
   religious, 18, 141, 288, 290, 341, 362
   royal, 1, 79, 185, 195, 242, 247, 253–54, 283, 329
   unofficial, 151–52, 204, 213, 227, 276, 312, 339, 345

banquets, 154–55, 158–59, 322–26

beggar(s), begging, 165–76, 181–86, 193–96, 201–2, 227–28, 269–71, 276, 296–300, 305–8, 357, 359
blind, blindness, 26, 169–74, 177–78, 182–83, 185, 195–96, 202, 238–39, 296, 300, 302, 310, 347
business, 19, 49, 59–60, 64–65, 78–80, 85–86, 88, 95, 97, 98, 104, 106, 124, 130, 132, 155, 201, 204, 207–12, 218, 222, 224, 227–79, 312

Capernaum, 24, 120, 126–30, 133, 177, 299, 315, 335
centurion(s), 51, 141, 144, 182–83, 187, 192, 205–6, 223, 306–7, 335, 356
church(es), 7–8, 20, 128, 178, 356
   contemporary, 2, 292, 361–64
   house, 28, 229, 358
   in Acts, 24, 205, 252–53, 313, 358
city, cities, 24, 45–47, 53, 58–62, 67–68, 71, 76–77, 83, 101, 108–11, 115–16, 131–32, 136–45, 159, 173–74, 194, 199–204, 212–13, 226–29, 248–49, 252, 260–61, 282–83, 299–304, 311, 314–27, 349, 359–63
classification system, 18–20, 47–54, 55–56, 84–85, 90, 104, 129–34, 346–48
courtyard(s), 47, 73, 84–86, 95, 114–30, 133, 218, 269, 354
crowd(s), 9, 16, 20–21, 26, 38, 46, 51, 61, 78, 81, 83, 87–88, 106, 133, 139–40, 144, 150–53, 158–60, 168–69, 174–77, 186–96, 200–202, 212–30, 234–43, 248–55, 270–71, 273–74, 278, 285–87, 289–90, 295–308, 314–15, 321, 326–33, 344–45, 347–50

disciple(s), 25–27, 46–47, 142–43, 147–48, 158–59, 185, 187, 190–93, 206, 214, 237–39, 246, 251–57, 270–77, 283–90, 305–9, 315–18, 325, 328, 330–39, 347–49, 359

405

Subject Index

entry, triumphal, 5–6, 23, 25, 135, 166–69, 178–81, 234, 237–38, 256–92, 336–37, 346–50
Ephesus/Ephesos, 20, 54, 67–79, 130–31, 148–53, 209–12, 245, 351–52
eschatology, Luke's, 233–36, 251, 258, 327–30
exegesis, social-spatial, 35, 37, 197, 230, 256, 295, 297, 308, 346

female. *See* woman, women
forces, 32–35, 39, 45, 49–51, 53, 63, 77–79, 86, 104–8, 145, 157, 160, 193–95, 226–28, 253–56, 288–91
    meaning, 31–35, 45, 47, 57–59, 62–65, 72, 77, 78, 80, 83, 87–88, 106, 110–11, 130, 138, 140, 143–45, 149–50, 154–55, 157–60, 172, 176, 186, 194–95, 212, 215, 226–28, 243, 250, 254, 258, 277, 281, 286, 290–92, 303, 305, 318, 326, 361
    nature, 32–35, 63–65, 78, 106, 114, 144–45, 159–60, 194, 254, 275, 281, 290–91
    place, 32–35, 49, 51, 58–62, 64–66, 72, 78, 80, 83, 87–88, 101, 104, 108–11, 130, 144, 149–50, 157–58, 168, 172, 176, 194–95, 202–3, 212, 215, 225–27, 243, 250, 253, 271, 285, 288, 290, 298, 305, 314, 318, 326, 332, 361. *See also* spatiality
    religion, 35, 53, 60, 77–78, 88, 106, 108, 145, 149, 151, 157, 160, 194–95, 228, 281, 286, 290–91, 349
    self, 33–35, 39, 53, 59–60, 62, 83, 87, 137, 348
    social relations, 32–36, 45, 49–53, 57–64, 78, 80, 86–88, 101, 106, 109–19, 130, 138, 141, 144–45, 149, 153–55, 157, 159–60, 174–76, 188–89, 193–95, 202, 212, 226–27, 243, 249–50, 253–55, 258, 260, 267, 271, 275, 277, 281, 284–91, 302–3, 305, 318, 326, 332, 342, 361
    time, 34–35, 73, 77, 87, 105, 152, 154, 188, 195, 202, 224, 226, 228, 235, 243, 254, 271, 284–85, 290, 302
forum, 47, 50–51, 80–81, 83–85, 87–88, 92–93, 96–98, 101, 104–6, 112, 115, 128, 131–32, 145, 173–74, 194, 278, 302, 352–53, 355

framework, theoretical, 35, 39, 48, 258, 348, 350

Galilee, 51, 119, 125–26, 168, 300, 315
geography, 4, 7, 22, 32, 45, 201, 263
    human, 14
    political, 35–37, 46
    theological, in Luke, 8–12, 21, 258–59, 271, 350
guest(s) 9, 20, 46, 49–50, 86, 90, 93, 100, 119, 121, 154, 154–55, 158–59, 214–16, 220, 300, 321–27, 334, 363

healing(s), 54, 143, 146, 165–66, 168–70, 177–78, 184–89, 192, 196, 199–200, 213, 227, 260, 270, 295–308, 311, 324–25, 339, 344, 347–49, 359
homes. *See* houses and various specific houses
honor, 5, 10, 12–13, 16–19, 28, 40–41, 44, 59–61, 64–67, 74, 76, 78, 80–81, 107, 110, 113, 138, 141, 143–45, 156, 160, 169, 174–79, 185–86, 194–95, 206, 212, 214–15, 251, 302, 306, 324, 342, 356
host(s), 46, 49, 90, 154, 158, 191, 197, 214, 300, 312, 317, 321–26, 363
hospitality, 18–19, 27–28, 46, 49–51, 90, 106–7, 134, 154, 180, 201, 204, 212, 214–17, 220–22, 224, 227–29, 309, 313, 317–27, 347–48, 356, 359, 362–63
house(s)/household(s), 1–2, 9, 15–20, 25, 28, 46–47, 49–53, 57, 59, 63, 66, 73–75, 80, 86–87, 93–107, 110–14, 117–34, 154, 167, 187, 190, 197, 200, 215–29, 234–43, 279–80, 299–304, 309–23, 316–27, 330–34, 344, 358, 355–63

Jericho, 2, 26, 27, 48, 54, 77, 158, 165–76, 180, 185, 188–92, 194, 196, 200–204, 212–17, 221, 226, 228, 246, 264–65, 270, 297–98, 302–3, 314, 319–20, 344, 347
Jerusalem, 6, 8, 12, 109, 141, 178, 230, 240, 242, 313–14, 338, 341
    architecture, 214, 264–72
    Jesus' entry, 25, 27, 35, 46, 51, 77, 143, 152–53, 166, 169, 174, 178, 181, 183, 185, 190, 192, 233–35, 237, 256–92, 297–98, 337, 344, 347–48

Subject Index

Jerusalem (cont.)
    Jesus' journey to, 24–26, 168, 173, 203, 214, 231, 239, 315, 320, 332
    Jesus' lament over, 6, 202, 238, 247–48, 252
    Jesus' ministry in, 24–26, 189, 308, 330

Jesus
    and disciples/followers, 25, 50, 142–43, 147, 175, 187–88, 191–93, 201, 252–53, 272–75, 286, 307, 317–18, 336, 339, 357
    and opponents, 189–91, 220–22, 225, 227, 236–38, 243, 251, 276–82, 285–86, 290, 309–10, 321–26, 330, 334, 337–38, 342–43
    as a local political figure, 4–6, 24, 26, 139, 145, 178–79, 193, 233, 257, 305–8, 335, 349
    as a public figure, 3–4, 8, 46, 48, 53, 72, 135, 143, 161, 165, 195–96, 201, 204, 214–15, 225–28, 271, 283, 295, 301–4, 356
    as a royal figure, 232–35, 238, 243, 246, 248, 251, 261, 273–74, 283–84, 286–92, 298
    miracles, 143–44, 153, 158, 169, 171, 173, 184, 186–87, 241, 260, 296–308
    Nazorean/Nazarene, 175–78, 180
    portrayal of by Luke, 3, 7, 9, 12–13, 28, 33, 35, 37, 54–56, 138, 144, 148, 159–60, 165–66, 212, 215, 287, 332–33, 347–48, 350–51, 361–63
    Son of David, 26, 52, 165, 169, 178, 180–86, 283, 306
    teaching/preaching, 8–9, 108, 112, 148, 158, 206, 217, 224–25, 230, 234–35, 239–41, 250–253, 255, 259, 289, 312–13, 327–334. *See also* Teaching

Jew(s), Jewish
    leaders, 141, 169, 190, 200, 203–6, 237–38, 251–52, 256, 274, 277–81, 312–13, 330–31, 340–44. *See also* Pharisees, and Priests
    people, 8, 20–21, 189, 195, 234–36, 240, 284, 342
    views of public and private, 108–29, 131–32

kings, Roman client, 181, 231–32, 244–54, 288, 335

kingdom of God, 2, 9, 142, 229, 234, 237, 239, 242–43, 329–30, 339, 362

literary Functions
    microcosm, 23, 26–27, 196, 199–200, 228, 291, 295, 296–97, 309–12, 327–30, 337–37, 344, 348
    preparatory, 26–27, 295, 297–98, 312–13, 330–32, 338, 344, 348

Luke, gospel of
    audience, 5–7, 37–39, 72, 79, 104, 169–70, 173, 176, 182, 184, 188–91, 194–95, 203–4, 208–12, 217–18, 220–21, 226–27, 230, 232–33, 252–53, 262, 298, 357–58
    author, social location, 67, 346, 351–60
    provenance, 56, 67–68, 314, 351
    verisimilitude, 117, 211, 235, 264, 269, 350

markets/marketplaces, 52–53, 59, 64, 67, 71–72, 78–79, 84, 98, 101, 104–5, 109–11, 115–16, 125, 132–33, 144, 160, 207, 214, 280, 302, 318, 320, 355
Meal(s), 9, 13, 15, 52, 109, 137–38, 154–55, 191, 216, 221, 309, 311, 314, 319–27, 356, 363. *See also* hospitality
Menander, House of, 95–96, 102–4, 121
Moralist, House of the, 98–99, 104
Moses, 9, 108–9, 113, 148, 240
movement, Jesus', 7–8, 23–24, 51, 187, 191–93, 195–96, 215, 256, 262, 272–76, 282–84, 288–92, 305–8, 336, 339, 347–50, 356–59, 363
multitude. *See* crowds

Palestine, 108, 115–28, 203, 217–18
parable
    of the king and his subjects, 25–27, 181, 185–86, 230–55, 283, 327–28, 330–31, 347
    others in Luke, 50–51, 172, 205, 234, 315–16, 325, 328–30, 332–36, 344–45
passageways/passages, 84–85, 100–101, 105, 120, 132, 159, 174, 298, 354
Paul, 10–12, 18, 20, 24, 67, 178, 248–50, 278, 287
peristyle(s), 74, 86–87, 95, 100–103, 119, 121, 123, 194, 217–18, 220, 226, 354
Pharisees, 16, 50–52, 141–42, 145, 154, 185, 190–95, 221–22, 234, 237–38, 270–71,

407

Subject Index

Pharisees (*cont.*)
  276–77, 280–82, 284–86, 289–92,
  309–12, 321–30, 333–35, 337–44
philosophy/philosophers (Ancient), 10–12,
  17, 40, 57, 60–63, 65, 111–13, 136,
  140–41, 156, 171, 249, 284–86
Pompeii, 73–75, 91–107, 121, 129–33, 214,
  217–18, 298, 348, 352–54
political
  geography, 35–37, 45–47
  sphere, 11–12, 16, 18–23, 43, 48, 56–59,
    63, 113, 131–34, 137–45, 158–60, 227,
    276–77, 287, 340–44, 349–50
politics
  definition, 1–7, 16
  imperial, 6, 23, 49, 51, 104, 131, 139,
    156–57, 277, 281, 348
  Jewish, 181, 286
  local, 24, 26–28, 51, 53–54, 56, 104,
    131, 135–45, 155–56, 158, 160–61,
    185, 191–96, 203, 207, 212, 226,
    232, 244–50, 254–55, 275, 290, 305,
    307–8, 312, 331, 334–36, 344, 348–49,
    355–57, 363–64

power(s)
  political, 245–52, 280, 284, 305, 308,
    340–41, 351, 354
  social, 4, 12, 14, 22–23, 37, 42, 139, 180,
    185, 195, 306, 350
  supernatural, 5, 153–55, 177–81, 198–99,
    237, 274, 290, 297, 306
priests, chief, 26, 47, 140–41, 144–45, 158,
  185, 248, 279–81, 286, 288, 291–92,
  312, 330–331, 338, 340–44
private
  household, 10, 16, 18–20, 59, 63, 78,
    121–27, 154, 191, 220, 226, 228–29,
    353–57, 359
  non-household, 18–20, 42, 46, 50–51, 348
  sphere, 3, 13, 17, 20, 35, 37–39, 42, 46–53,
    55–66, 72–73, 76, 78–117, 128–34,
    137–38, 143–44, 215–16, 254–55, 280,
    299–300, 302, 311, 320–28, 361–63
public and private
  dichotomy, 1, 3–4, 16–17, 22, 27, 39–48,
    53, 58, 65, 83, 84, 94, 109, 114, 116,
    124, 348

spectrum, 15, 18, 22, 27–28, 33, 35–36,
  37–40, 43, 47, 49, 53–53, 93–94, 100,
  113–16, 122, 129, 144, 248, 348, 362
public sphere, unofficial
  classification, 27–28, 52–53, 56, 83, 87,
    104, 107, 112, 116, 129, 131–33,
    137–38, 142–45, 348–49, 355–60
  and Apollonius, 146–61
  and Jesus, 141, 173–74, 194–95, 204,
    212, 215–16, 226, 229, 248, 262, 276,
    281–86, 290–92, 295, 312, 317–19,
    340, 343–44, 347–50
  contemporary, 1–4, 362–63

reputation, 13, 54, 58, 64, 66, 107, 137–38,
  143–45, 153, 213, 245, 251, 306, 308,
  363
rhetoric, rhetorical, 14–17, 40, 42, 47, 65–66,
  78–79, 86, 131, 138–39, 146, 154, 224,
  324, 347
road(s), 9, 46–48, 70–72, 74, 77, 84 92–104,
  113–16, 122–23, 132–33, 152, 159–60,
  168–69, 171–76, 183, 193–94, 202,
  214, 218, 220–21, 224, 227, 249, 256,
  264–70, 273, 298–300, 305, 315–17,
  347, 355, 362
Roman
  architecture, 91–104, 116, 121, 124–26,
    131, 217–18, 353–55
  empire, 4, 6, 14, 45–46, 54, 67–68, 113–14,
    178–79, 181–82, 190, 203, 207–8,
    227, 232, 262, 274, 341–44, 353
  officials, 4–5, 139, 141, 204, 207–10, 288,
    290, 312–13
  views of public and private, 13, 73–74,
    79–91, 104–107, 130–33, 173–74
Rome, 51, 54, 156–57, 159–60, 210, 245–47,
  254, 278, 286, 302, 318–19, 333, 352,
  354–55
royal, royalty, 26, 131, 166, 169, 177–87,
  192, 195, 203, 232–33, 244, 248–49,
  251–54, 257, 261–62, 273–77, 282–90,
  298, 337

Sallust, House of, 100, 104, 353
salvation, 14, 197–202, 206–7, 216, 222,
  224–29, 234, 236, 309–27, 356, 359
Sanhedrin, 9, 141, 192, 209, 275, 279–80, 286,
  331, 341–43

Subject Index

scale, 6, 7, 9, 12, 23, 35–37, 39, 45–47, 51, 112, 129, 136, 140, 144, 155, 230, 244, 247, 262, 282, 288, 345, 347–49
"sinner(s),"167, 190, 206, 220–25, 228, 234, 240, 309, 313, 320–25
slaves/servants, 49, 73–74, 87, 94, 132–33, 154, 199–200, 220, 230–32, 237–38, 241, 244, 246–47, 250–54, 290, 315–16, 323, 325, 328–29, 334, 347
societies
  high context, 37–39, 48, 55, 64, 81–82, 84, 88, 144, 147, 149, 153, 157–58, 160, 170, 208, 214, 216, 232, 235, 245, 248, 250, 254, 303, 320, 350
  low context, 37–38, 350
space. *See* various specific places and classifications
spatiality, 13, 14, 21, 34, 199, 346
Stallius Eros, House of, 96, 102
streets. *See* Roads
synagogues, 10–11, 14, 18, 20–21, 53–53, 112, 124, 128, 133, 144–45, 159, 177, 182, 187, 206, 299–302, 311, 315, 332, 349, 356–57, 361–62

table fellowship. *See* meals
taxes/taxation/tax collectors/tolls/toll Collectors, 26, 46, 52–53, 86, 141, 185, 197–98, 204, 206–12, 215, 221–23, 225, 227, 241, 247, 263, 309–10, 312, 320–21, 326–27, 347

temple(s)
  Jerusalem, as a center of Jewish culture, 9, 14, 52, 312–13, 341, 343–44, 359
  Jerusalem, as public space, 18, 25–26, 108–9, 170, 174, 178, 183, 185, 191, 203, 214, 222, 238, 249, 256–63, 267–72, 276–86, 288–91, 298, 314, 330, 333
  others, 46, 68, 71–72, 76, 80, 83, 88, 90–93, 97, 101, 106–7, 144, 149–60, 319, 333–34, 338, 352

vestibules, 47, 86, 322

wealth/wealthy, 28, 58, 72, 74, 83, 87, 94, 97–98, 117, 119, 121, 157, 201, 204–7, 210, 212, 217, 223, 226–27, 246, 312–13, 331, 333
woman, women
  in private, 14, 16–17, 40, 42, 63–66, 73, 79, 111, 124,
  in public, 13, 15, 43–44, 49, 106, 113, 124–25, 154, 200, 300–302, 305, 311, 315–16, 322–23, 325, 335

Zacchaeus, 2, 6–7, 25–27, 46, 51–52, 54, 177, 180, 185, 189, 197–229, 231, 234–40, 251, 296–97, 308–14, 317, 319–21, 324–27, 330–31, 340, 344, 347–48, 357, 362–63

www.ingramcontent.com/pod-product-compliance
Lightning Source LLC
Chambersburg PA
CBHW081147290426
44108CB00018B/2467